Clavis Astrologiae Eliminata:

OR A

KEY to the whole ART

OF

ASTROLOGY

New Filed and Polished.

In Three PARTS.

CONTAINING

I. *An Introduction*; By which an Ordinary Capacity may Understand the Grounds thereof, and how to set a Figure upon any Occasion: With the Schemes of the Cusps of the Coelestial Houses in Copper Plates, very useful in Horary Questions, *&c.*

II. *Select Aphorismes*; with Rules and Examples how to Resolve or Judge all Lawful Questions Astrological, from a Radical Scheme Erected: Also Elections, and other necessary Precepts of Art.

III. *The Genethliacal Part*; wherein is shewn how to Rectifie and Calculate Nativities, according to *Regiomontanus*, *Argol*, and *Kepler*; with some Varieties in the Doctrine of Directions, Revolutions, and Profections, not before published: Also Tables, and other Requisites, both for Calculation, and Demonstration.

To which are added the *Rudolphine Tables*, wherebye the Places of the Planets may be Calculated for any Time, past, present, or to come.

The SECOND EDITION, much Enlarged and Amended.
By HENRY COLEY, Student in the *Mathematicks*, and *Astrology*.

Canst thou bind the sweet Influences of the Pleiades, or loose the Bonds of Orion? J O B 38. 31.

LONDON, Printed for *Benj. Tooke*, and *The. Sawbridge*, and are to be Sold at the *Ship* in St. *Paul's Church yard*, and at the three *Flower de Luces* in *Little Brittain*, 1676.

No part of this book may be reproduced or transcribed in any form or by any means, electronic or mechanical, including photocopying or recording or by any information storage and retrieval system without written permission from the author and publisher, except in the case of brief quotations embodied in critical reviews and articles. Requests and inquiries may be mailed to: American Federation of Astrologers, Inc., 6535 S. Rural Road, Tempe, AZ 85283.

ISBN-10: 0-86690-664-9
ISBN-13: 978-0-86690-664-7

Cover Design: Jack Cipolla

Published by:
American Federation of Astrologers, Inc.
6535 S. Rural Road
Tempe, AZ 85283

www.astrologers.com

TO THE
MOST EMINENTLY ACCOMPLISH'D
IN ALL
INGENIOUS LITERATURE

ELIAS ASHMOLE

OF THE

MIDDLE TEMPLE *Esq;*

CONTROLLER GENERAL OF
HIS MAJESTIES DUTY 0F

EXCISE, &c.

HIS MOST HONOURED

MECAENAS;

HENRY COLEY,

HIS HUMBLEST ADMIRER,
WISHES ALL IMAGINATION HAPPI-
NESS, AND DEDICATES TO
HIS PATRONAGE
THESE HIS

ASTRONOMICAL,

AND

ASTROLOGICAL

ESSAYES

TO THE
MOST EMINENTLY ACCOMPLISH'D
IN ALL
INGENIOUS LITERATURE

ELIAS ASHMOLE

OF THE

MIDDLE TEMPLE *Esq;*

CONTROLLER GENERAL OF
HIS MAJESTIES DUTY OF

EXCISE, *&c.*

HIS MOST HONOURED

MECAENAS;

HENRY COLEY,

HIS HUMBLEST ADMIRER,
WISHES ALL IMAGINATION HAPPI-
NESS, AND DEDICATES TO
HIS PATRONAGE
THESE HIS

ASTRONOMICAL,

AND

ASTROLOGICAL

ESSAYES

TO THE
READER.

Upon my Respected Friend Mr. Henry Coley his Clavis Astrologiae New Fil'd & Polished.

I am now neer seventy four years of Age compleat, and after much Sickness and Indisposition of Body in my Old Age (especially these two years last part) I am now by the blessing of God upon the means used, reasonably well recovered again; and it was all along my intention if had I not been unhappily prevented and discouraged) to have freely communicated to the world (for the benefit of all honest and grateful Sons of *Urania*) what many years since I promised in my *Introduction to Christian Astrology*: But this Author (being the only Publick Person that I have hopes of) hath now with no small pains and Industry, saved me that labour, in presenting the world with this most compleat piece of *Astrology*, which (not improperly) he Intitles, *A K E Y to the whole A R T*; wherein, in my Judgment, he hath shewed himself an ARTIST, and very much obliged all the younger Students therein, who may hereafter (God willing) receive much more benefit by his Studies.

The Work (to speak my real thoughts) is well digested, his Method and Matter plain and significant; and I cannot but highly approve thereof: 'Tis judiciously Penn'd, and in every part Adorned with Variety, and many things wholly New; he hath layed a sure Foundation, and added divers necessary Demonstrations in the *Astronomical Part*, which cannot but be very satisfactory to every Ingenious Lover of Art.

He has not filled his Book with vain affected Expressions, nor impertinent *Digressions* and *Tautologies*; but he has concisely handled each particular, to his exceeding Commendation. To Conclude, I doubt not but this Author (being qualified with *Parts* and Abilities in the *Mathematicks* also) may in time become a great *Promoter of Art*, and thereby merit the Respects of all the Legitimate Sons of *Urania*; which is the real Judgment of their Old Friend,

From my House in Hersham *in the Parish of* Waltham *upon* Thames, April 10, 1676.

William Lilly,
Student in Astrology.

THE PREFACE TO THE READER.

COURTEOUS READER,

I have here adventured to present you with a Second Edition *of my* KEY *to* Astrology, *being Incouraged thereunto from the favourable Reception the* Former *found amongst the Sons of* Urania, *notwithstanding all those unhappy misfortunes it met withal both in the* Printing *and* Composing; *I have also endeavoured to gratifie your former Civilities, in rendering the work more Compleat and full in every particular, and to adorn it with many necessary and considerable Additions, which I hope will be found of singular use to every ingenious Student in this* Sublime Art. Astrology is no more but a part or member of Natural Philosophym, which teacheth by the Motions, Configurations, and Influences of the Signes, Stars, and Coelestial Planets, to Prognosticate, or Predict of the Natural effects and Mutations to come in the Elements, and these inferiour Elementary Bodies. *'Tis an Art of great Antiquity, and if we may believe Authors, it is even as antient as* Adam, *who was not unacquainted therewith, as well as all other* Natural Sciences: *That be understood the Natures of those* Coelestial Bodies *he saw glittering over his head; their harmonious Motions, secret Influences, and different Operations upon Subluminaries, according to their various Positions, Configurations and Determination can be doubted of by none, that duly considers how liberal Omnipotence seems to have been in Crowning him (whilst abiding in Innocency) with the choicest Understanding.*

What Progress was made in Astrology before the Universal Deluge *cannot certainly be Determined*: Josephus, *in his History, gives us an account, that some of the* Antient Patriarchs *were so well acquainted with the* Material Heavens, *and such Lovers of Art, that they inscribed the Principles thereof on Pillars to preserve the same to Posterity, from the overbearing fury of that* Stupendious Flood, *which probably by this Art they might partly foresee to be approaching.*

After these heaps of waters were level'd, and taught to quit their Usurpation by Keeping their antient Rendezvous, the Seas, the first people that we read devoted themselves to Syderal *Studies were the* Assyrians; *soon followed by the* Chaldeans, Aegyptians, *and* Arabians, *who all living in* Champagne *Countries, bless'd with a pure Serene Aire, and excelling in Ingenuity, seemed above other Mortals to be invited by Nature to such Divine Contemplations: whence 'tis no wonder if by their continual Studies, and repeated Experiences, they raised this Art to such a pitch of Glory, that only such that were skill'd therein were admitted to the Administration of* Sacred Rites, *or Managing Affairs of* State: *Indeed so esteemed they were, that those mighty* Monarchs *of the* East *would undertake no grand Enterprize without first consulting an* Astrologer: *Those Honours paid to* Art *soon kindled the Sparks of Emulation in the* Indians, *and* Greeks, *and tempted them to put in too as* Rivals *for the Favour of the Beautious* Urania; *it being certain, that the* Grecians *first learned this Art of the* Chaldeans, *and* Aegyptians, *as the* Latines, *and other* Europeans *have since borrowed from the* Greeks: *And thus you have a brief Account of the Original, and Growth of Astrology.*

'Tis an Art of general Use to all sorts of persons for it Directs them (in a Natural way) how they may most fortunately manage their affairs in the world; as by Elections *to choose a fit and congruous time, to begin any considerable Enterprize, by the* Directions *of the* Planets *in their* Nativities, *and Annual Revolutions, to discover the most propitious or dangerous times that are approaching to any Native: and in fine, Astrology gives them full satisfaction (if managed by an able Artist) in the Resolution of all their* Horary Doubts.

This is not all, for Astrology is eminently useful also in the Practice of Physick; *for by the Rules thereof (which have been often verified by Experience) the* Physitian *may inform himself of the Nature and quality of the Dis-*

ease, and consequently what Humour offends; also whether it may terminate in life-or-Death. 'Tis an Art which is no less useful and serviceable to the painful Husbandmen, who may be thereby taught when 'tis a good and proper Season to Manure and Till his Ground; and he may thence discover likewise the various Alterations of the Aire, and Mutation of the Weather, &c.

Lastly, By astrology in general Accidents of the World may be predicted, the changes of Empires, and Governments, the Subversion of Kingdoms and Countries; in short, a whole Volume might be written of the Utility of this Sublime Mysterious Art; the depth whereof this Age doubtless will not be able to Fathom, although I must confess there are some Famous, although I must confess there are some Famous men now living, that have waded far therein— Yet Astrology hath been (and now is) very strangely reenforced, and condemned by some which understand not the very Rudiments thereof, but use such Arguments against it as others have done before them; all which have been already sufficiently Answered by several Learned men; and in particularly that eminent Knight Sir Christopher Heydon, *who defends Astrology against the greatest Antagonists, and warrants the lawfuiness thereof, both by Scripture and Reason,* &c.

One grand reason (I suppose) that hath occasioned many ingenious persons to have but low and mean thoughts of Astrology, is this; Viz. There are (and hath been) many ignorant and illiterate Professors of both Sex) in, and about this Famous and Flourishing City *of* London, *(whose names I shall not mention) that too confidently adventure to set up with a very small stock of Knowledge of Astrology, for the sake of Gain, and profess themselves Artists, but are not able to perform anything therein according to Art; only stuff their Clients with many Impertinencies, under pretence of the Language of the Stars, thereby abusing their Querents, and consequently bring a Scandal upon this so excellent and useful a piece of Learning, and the more noble Professors thereof; which hath deterred many persons from the Study of Astrology, that otherwise (perhaps) might have proved good Proficients therein. I speak not this out of any prejudice I have to their Persons, nor in the least to advantage my own Interest, for I am a lover of Art, and those that (without abuse) do use it.*

In the next place I should give an account of the Order and Method of the Book it self, which is divided into three Parts: but least I should too much exceed the bounds of an Epistle, I shall rather refer the Reader to the Table thereof, which will sufficiently answer his Expectation in that particular. I assume no great honour to my self in the Composure of this work, but can assure the Reader I have presented him with variety of Matter, and many things wholly noval, and not hitherto handled by any other English Astrological Author; yet I dare not conclude it to be a Compleat System or BODY of Astrology, *that must be yet expected* (Nolens Volens) *from some Utopian Astrologer perhaps in the next Age.*

To Conclude; I have omitted nothing, nor spared for any paints that might conduce to the Compleating such a work: So that by this Portable Volumn, *and the help of a* Canon *of* Artificial Sines *and* Tangents *(very common to be had for a small Price) you are compleatly furnished with all necessaries, for the exact handling of a* Nativity *(which is the most considerable Part of* Astrology) *also* Horary Questions, Elections, General Accidents, *and the Effects of* Eclipses, &c.

Thus I have laboured to render every thing in this Art plain and perspicuous to the meanest Apprehension, and have not confin'd my self to too much brevity; which has occasion'd the Book to swell much bigger than was at first intended. All which I freely offer to your favourable Acceptance, desiring the Reader would be at so much paints as to Correct the Errata's *before he Reads the Book, (for notwithstanding care has not been wanting, yet some* Typographical *Faults have escaped:) In so doing, he will not only do himself a Kindness, but also oblige him who is a Friend to all that are* Mathematically *inclin'd, and a real Lover of Arts in General.*

From my House in Baldwin's Court over against
the Old Hole in the Wall in Baldwins Gardens
neer Gray's-Inn Lane, Die
Mattis, Martij 28. 1676.

Henry Coley.

The Contents of the First Part.

Chap. 1. Of the twelve Signs, and their manifold Divisions.	Page, 1.
Chap. 2. Of the Aspects of the Planets as they move through the Signs.	4.
A Table of the Dexter, and Sinister Aspects of the Planets.	5.
Chap. 3. Of the Description, and Signification of the twelve Signs.	6.
Chap. 4. Of the Names, Characters, and Antiscions, Houses, Joys, Orbs, and Latitude of the Planets.	12.
Chap. 5. Of the Natures, Descriptions, and Significations of the Planets.	15.
Chap. 6. A more Particular Description of the Planets, as they may be posited in any of the twelve Signs.	18.
Chap. 7. Of the Diseases, the Planets signifie, in general, being posited in any of the twelve Signs.	27.
A Table of the Members of the Body, every Planet Governs, being posited in any of the Signs, with its use.	34.
Chap. 8. Of the Herbs, and Plants that are appropriated to the Government of the Planets.	35.
Chap. 9. Of the Essential, and Accidental Dignities of the Planets, &c.	35.
A Table of the Essential Dignities according to Ptolomy.	36.
A Table of the Essential, and Accidental Fortitudes, and Debilities of the Planets.	38.
A Table, shewing what Planets are Friends, and what Enemies; as also their Colours.	39.
A Table of certain Countries, and Cities, under the Government of the Planets, &c.	40.
Chap. 10. Of the Terms of Art which ought to be well understood by every Student.	43.
Chap. 11. How to Add, and Substract Astronomical Fractions, and project the Part of Fortune.	45.
Chap. 12. How to use an Ephemeris; as also how to set a Scheme of Heaven, by the Tables of Houses, or the Book of Schemes.	47.
A General Table of the hourly Motion of the Planets.	50.
Chap. 13. of the twelve Houses of Heaven, and their Astrological significations.	51.
The Quarters of Heaven signified by the twelve Houses.	52.
Chap. 14. Why the Heavens are divided into twelve Houses, or Mansions, and no more?	53.
Chap. 15. Why those Houses should have such signification as Astrologers attribute unto them?	54.
Chap. 16. Of divers things to be considered, which conduce much to the better Judging of a Horary Question.	56.
Sect. 1. Of the Significators of the Querent, and Quesited in any Scheme of a Horary Question.	56.
Sect. 2. By what means, or ways things are brought to perfection.	57.
Sect. 3. To know if your Figure be fit for Judgement.	57.
Sect. 4. Of the Marks, Moles, and Scars, both of Querent, and Quesited.	58.
Sect. 5. Of varying the Houses in Judgement.	58.
Sect. 6. Of the time of receiving a Horary Question.	59.
Sect. 7. Choice Aphorismes to be considered in Judgement of a Horary Question.	59.

The Contents of the Second Part.

Of the Elements of Astrology, or Principlt1 of Judgement, by way of Preface.	65.
Certain Astrological Axioms, confirmed, and verified by Rational Experience.	65.
Certain Astrological Theorems.	66.

Six Articles to be observed, for the better Restauration of the Coelestial Science.	68.
Chap. 1. Questions, with Astrological Judgements upon the first House.	71.
Sect. 1. May the Querents Life be long, or short?	71.
Sect. 2. What part of the Querents Life may be best.	72.
Sect. 3. What Quarter of the World may be most happy?	72.
Sect. 4. Of the conditions of an absent Party.	73.
Sect. 5. To know whether the Person to be spoken with, be at home?	73.
Sect. 6. Of a Ship at Sea, her safety, or Danger.	74.
Chap. 2. Questions, and Judgement proper to the second House.	75.
Sect. 1. May the Querent ever attain Riches?	75.
Sect. 2. By what means may the Querent gain Wealth.	75.
Sect. 3. Of the time when Riches may be expected.	76.
Sect. 4. Shall the Querent receive his Money lent, or satisfaction for the Goods he has trusted.	76.
Chap. 3. Questions, and Judgements proper to the third House.	77.
Sect. 1. Of short Journeys, shall they be prosperous?	77.
Sect. 2. May the Querent, and his Brethren, Kindred, or Neighbours agree together?	77.
Sect. 3. Of the condition of an absent Brother.	78.
Sect. 4. Is the Counsel, or Advice of a Neighbour, or Friend, Real.	79.
Sect. 5. Whether Reports, or Rumours, spread abroad, be true, or false.	79.
Chap. 4. Questions, and Judgements appertaining to the fourth House.	80.
Sect. 1. Shall the Querent enjoy the Estate of his Father.	80.
Sect. 2. Shall the Querent obtain the House, Land, or other Possessions, he desires to take, or purchase.	80.
Sect. 3. May the Querent advantage himself by removal, or had he better continue in his old Habitation.	81.
Sect. 4. Of hidden Treasure, is there any in the place suspected.	81.
Sect. 5. Shall a City, Town, Castle, Fort, or Island, that is Besieged, be taken, or not?	82.
Chap. 5. Questions, and Judgements belonging to the fifth House.	83.
Sect. 1. Shall the Querent ever have Issue?	83.
Sect. 2. Is the Querent with Child? If so, of what Sex, Male, or Female? or is she impregnated with more than one, &c	83.
Sect. 3. of Ambassadors, Messengers, Gaming, &c.	84.
Chap. 6. Judgements, and Interogations proper to the sixth House, viz. of Sickness, &c.	86.
Sect. 1. Some General Rules how to Judge of Diseases.	86.
Sect. 2. Of the Nature, and Quality of the Disease in General.	87.
Sect. 3. Of the Affliction of the Moon, by Saturn, or Mars in the four Trigons, according to Hermes Trismegistus.	88.
Sect. 4. Select Aphorismes, of good use, in Astrological Judgement of Diseases.	91.
Sect. 5. Of the Fidelity, or Falsity of Servants; as also of small Cattle, &c.	93.
Chap. 7. Judgement proper to the seventh House.	94.
Sect. 1. Of Marriage, if ever Marry, &c.	94.
The cause of hindrance	94.
The time when, and of Agreement.	95.
If Marry more than once.	95.

If the Person be Marryed, or not.	95.
Is the Person, enquiring, a Virgin or not?	96.
Which may dye first, Man, or Wife.	96.
Sect. 2. Of Law Suits, War, Publique Enemies, Partnership, &c.	96.
Sect. 3. Of These, and Fugitives, or Strays, with all its Appurtinencies, &c.	98.
Chap. 8. Judgement, and Questions upon the eighth House.	102.
Sect. 1. Of the Manner, or Kind of Death the Querent may dye, viz. Natural, or Violent.	102.
Sect. 2. Is the Wives Portion considerable, or not; or will it be obtained with ease, or difficulty?	102.
Sect. 3. Shall a Person, who is fallen into trouble, either for some real Fact committed, or upon suspition, suffer Death, or Detriment for the same?	103.
Chap. 9. Judgements, and Questions appertaining to the ninth House.	103.
Sect. 1. Shall the Querent be prosperous in his Voyage to Sea, &c.	103.
Sect. 2. Shall the Querent obtain the Benefice desired.	104.
Chap. 10. Judgements, and Interrogations proper to the tenth House.	105.
Sect. 1. May the Querent attain the Place, or Office desired.	105.
Sect. 2. Shall the Querent that is in danger, lose, or be turned out of his place?	105.
Chap. 11. Judgement proper to the eleventh House, may the Querent be Fortunate in his hopes. &c.	106.
Chap. 12. Judgement proper to the twelfth House, of a Person Imprisoned, whether he may gain his Inlargement in a short time?	106.
Is the Person distempered, bewitched?	106.
Of Horse-Races, according to Haly, &c.	107.
Of the Resolutions of Divers things, made together, according to the Antients.	107.
Chap. 13. Examples of the Judgement of Questions upon each of the twelve Houses.	108.
Sect. 1. Questions exemplified from a Scheme, proper to the first House, in 6 Paragraphs.	109.
Sect. 2. Questions exemplified, proper to the second House, in 5 Parag.	111.
Sect. 3. Questions exemplified appertaining to the third House, in 4 Parag.	112.
Sect. 4. Examples from a Scheme of Questions, and their Astrological Answers, proper to the fourth House, in 5 Parag.	113.
Sect. 5. Examples appertaining to the fifth House in 4 Parag.	114.
Sect. 6. Examples belonging to the sixth House, in 2 Parag.	115.
Sect. 7. Examples to Illustrate Questions proper to the seventh House in 8 Parag.	115.
Sect. 8. Examples proper to the eighth House, in 3 Parag.	117.
Sect. 9. Questions, and their Astrological Responses, appertaining to the ninth House in 2 Parag.	118.
Sect. 10. Examples of Questions proper to the tenth House, in 2 Parag.	119.
Sect. 11. Examples upon the eleventh House, in 2 Par.	119.
Sect. 12. Examples proper to the twelfth House, in 4 Par.	120.
Chap. 14. Of the Planetary Hour, and Elections.	120.
Sect. 1. Of the Planetary Hours.	120.
A Table of the Planetary Hours, &c.	122.
Sect. 2 & 3. Of the Discription, and Use of the Table of the Planetary Hours.	124.
Sect. 4. Of the signification of those Hours.	125.
Sect. 5. Of Elections from the Nativity.	126.

Sect. 6. Brief Rules to be observed in making Elections. — 128.

Sect. 7. General Elections in buying, selling, and taking Servants, &c. — 131.

Chap. 15. Of Astral Predictions of Mundane Affairs, or the General Accidents of the World. — 131.

Chap. 16. Of the Natural signification of each Planet, that shall be Lord of the Year, in any Revolution Figure of the World. — 133.

Chap. 17. Of Eclipses, and the Natural Causes, and Reasons thereof. — 136.

Chap. 18. Of the Natural portents, and significations of Eclipses. — 137.

Chap. 19. How to Prognosticate of the Winds, and Weather, From the Conjunctions, and Aspects of the Planets. — 139.

A Table, shewing the Inclination of the Air, from the Conjunctions, and Aspects of the Planets. — 143.

Chap. 20. Ptolomy's Centiloquium Englished. — 144.

Chap. 21. Hermes Trismegistus his Centiloquium. — 150.

Chap. 22. Bethem's Centiloq of Aphorismes. — 155.

Chap. 23. Brief Rules to Compute the Stars, or Planets, Southing, Rising, or Setting, in any Latitude. — 159.

A Table of Stars, fitted for that purpose. — 160.

Its Explanation, and Use. — 160.

The Contents of the Third Part.

Chap. 1. .A Compendium of Trigonometry. — 167.

Sect. 1. Definitions, Affection, and Axioms of Spherical Triangles, &c. — 167.

A Demonstration of the Nature of Spherical Triangles, both Right Angled, and Oblique. — 168.

Sect. 2. & 3. Examples of the 28 Cases of Spherical Triangles. — 171.

Chap. 2. Containing divers useful Precepts, fit to be understood, in order to the Calculation of a Nativity. — 179.

Sect. 1. The Explanation, and Use of a Canon of Artificial Sines, and Tangents. — 179.

Sect. 2. How to find the neerest distance of a Star (or a Planet) from the next Aequinoxial, or Solstitial Point. — 180.

A Table thereof, and its Use. — 181.

Sect. 3. Exhibiting a brief Compendium of all the Propositions that are necessary in the Doctrine of Directions to be wrought by a Canon of Sines, and Tangents, &c. — 182.

2. Tables of Converting Hours, and Minutes of Time, into Degrees and Minutes of the Aequator, and the contrary. — 183.

A brief Synopsis, or rather analysis of the Method of Directing a Nativity, according to Regiomontanus, and Argol, Direct, and Converse. — 190.

Sect. 4. How to Reduce an Ephemerides, or Astronomical Tables to any other Meridian, &c. — 190.

Sect. 5. Tychoe's Table of Aequation of Time. — 192.

Of the Agreement between the Calculations by Tregonometry, and the Vulgar Tables. — 193.

Sect. 6. How to Reduce the Planets Places to any hour of the Day, or Night, &c. Also divers useful Precepts to Illustrate the Use of the Logistical Logarithmes. — 211.

Sect. 7. How to make Sexaginary Logistick Logarithmes, from the Logarithmetical Tables of Absolute Numbers. — 214.

Sect. 8. Shewing the most Compendious way of Aequating the Cusps of the Houses, in setting a Figure. — 215.

Sect. 9. Several Propositions of the use of a Table of Houses. — 216.

Sect. 10. Of the several ways of dividing the Heavens, for Erecting of a Scheme; with a Table, and its Construction for the dividing the Heavens, according to Campanus, and Gazulus. 219.

Chap. 3. Of a Nativity, and the several ways of Rectification thereof. 221.

Sect. 1. What a Nativity is. 221.

Sect. 2. How to Rectifie a Nativity several ways. 222.

Sect. 3. Examples how to verifie the Ascendant, by an Accident. 222.

Sect. 4. How to Rectifie a Nativity, by the Sun, or Moon. 224.

Sect. 5. How to Rectifie a Nativity, by the Trutine, or Scale of Hermes. 225.

Table for the ready finding the Conception, by the Nativity, and the contrary. 226.

Sect. 6. The Use of the Table of Conception. 226.

Chap. 4. How to set a Figure, the Rational way, by resolving the Oblique Spherical Triangle, with the Cadence of a Perpendicular. 227.

Chap. 5. How to set a Figure the Rational way, and Resolve the Oblique Spherical Triangle without the Cadence of a Perpendicular. 232.

New Tables of Houses for twelve several Latitudes, to be used with a Canon Calculated by the same Method. 235.

Chap. 6. How to Aequate for the odd minutes of the Circle of Position, if you work by the Ordinary Tables of Regiomontanus, &c. 237.

How to find the Declination and R. A. of a Star or Planet with Latitude by Tables. 238.

Chap. 7. Necessary Considerations before Judgment upon a Nativity, Sect. 1. 240.

Sect. 2. Of the General Signifcations of the Lord of the Ascendant in a Nativity. 240.

Sect. 3. Of the Faces of the Signes being Horoscopical in any Nativity. 242.

Chap. 8. Of the Signification of the Planets as they are Rulers of the several Houses being posited in any part of the Figure in a Nativity. 244.

Sect. 1. Of the Lord of the Ascendant his position in any of the twelve Houses. 244.

Sect. 2. Of the Lord of the Seconds position in part of the Coelestial Figure. 245.

Sect. 3. Of the position of the Lord of third House, &c. 246.

Sect. 4. Of the position of the Lord of the fourth House. 247.

Sect. 5. Of the Lord of the fifth House, his position, &c. 248.

Sect. 6. Of the position of the Lord of the sixth House, &c. 249.

Sect. 7. Of the position of the Lord of the seventh 250.

Sect. 8. Of the position of the Lord of the eighth House. 251.

Sect. 9. Of the position of the Lord of the ninth House. 252.

Sect. 10. Of the position of the Lord of the Tenth. 253.

Sect. 11. Of the position of the Lord of the eleventh. 254.

Sect. 12. Of the Lord of the twelfth's position, &c. 255.

Chap. 9. Of the General Signification of the Aspects of the Planets. 257.

Sect. 1. Of the Conjunction of the Planets, &c. 257.

Sect. 2. Of the Signification of the △ Aspect of the Planets in a Nativity. 258.

Sect. 3. Of the Oppositions of the Planets in a Nativity. 259.

Chap. 10. How to make or frame an Astrological Judgment upon the twelve Houses of a Nativity. 261.

Sect. 1. Judgement proper to the first House; viz. May the Life of the Native be long or short? 261.

§ 1. Of the Significator or Giver of Life, viz. Hyleg, &c. 262.

§ 2. Of the Giver Years, viz. Alchocodon.	262.
§ 3. Of the Lord of the Geniture, or Almuten.	263.
§ 4. Of the Complection of the Native.	263.
§ 5. Of the Manners of the Native.	264.
§ 6. Of the Wit and Understanding of the Native.	264.
§ 7. Of the stature and form of Body.	265.
§ 8. Of the Fortune or Misery of the Native in general.	265.
Sect. 2. Judgment proper to the second House of a Nativity.	266.
§ 1. Of the Signifcators of Riches or Poverty, &c.	266.
§ 2. Arguments of Wealth, and Poverty, &c.	266.
Sect. 3. Judgment upon the third House of a Nativity.	267.
§ 1. Shall the Native have Brethren or Sisters, &c.	267.
§ 2. Will the Native and his Brethren accord and agree together.	268.
Sect. 4. Judgment proper to the fourth House.	268.
§ 1. Of the Natives Patrimony or Estate left by his Father.	268.
§ 2. Of the mutual love and agreement between the Native and his Father.	268.
Sect. 5. Judgment proper to the sixth House of a Nativity.	269.
§ 1. Of the Diseases of the Native.	269.
§ 2. Of Servants, their fidelity or falsity; also of small Cattle, &c.	270.
Sect. 6. Judgment proper to the seventh House.	270.
§ 1. Shall the Native Marry, &c.	270.
§ 2. What manner of person shall the Native Marry?	271.
§ 3. Of the Natives publick Enemies.	273.
Sect. 7. Judgment proper to the fifth House of a Nativity.	273.
§ 1. Shall the Native have Children or not?	273.
§ 2. Of their Sex and Condition, &c.	273.
Sect. 8. Judgment proper to the ninth House.	274.
§ 1. Shall the Native Travel or not? to what part of the world, also of the profit that may come thereby.	274.
§ 2. Of the Natives Religion, &c.	275.
Sect. 9. Judgment proper to the tenth House of a Nativity.	275.
§ 1. Shall the native arrive to Honour or Preferment, &c.	275.
§ 2. Of the Natives Trade, Magistery, or Profession, &c.	276.
§ 3. Brief Rules to discover the kind of Trade.	276.
Sect. 10. Judgment proper to the eleventh House.	277.
§ 1. Will the Native have Friends to assist him, &c.	277.
§ 2. Aphorismes of Friendship.	278.
Sect. 11. Judgment upon the twelfth House of a Nativity.	278.
§ 1. Of the Natives private Enemies, &c.	278.
§ 2. Shall the Native suffer Imprisonment or Restraint.	279.
Sect. 12. Judgment proper to the eighth House, &c.	279.
§ 1. Shall the Natives Death be Natural or Violent?	279.
Chap. 11. A Speculum of the Nativity and the Dignities and Debilities of the Planets.	281.

Chap. 12. Contains Judgment Astrological upon the first House of the Exemplary Figure.	283.
Chap. 13. Contains Judgment upon the second House.	287.
Chap. 14. Judgment upon the Third House.	288.
Chap. 15. Judgment upon the fourth House.	289.
Chap. 16. Judgment upon the sixth House.	290.
Chap. 17. Judgment upon the seventh House.	291.
Chap. 17. Judgment upon the fifth House.	293.
Chap. 18. Judgment upon the ninth House.	294.
Chap. 19. Judgment deduced from the tenth House.	295.
Chap. 20. Judgment upon the eleventh House.	295.
Chap. 21. Judgment upon the twelfth House.	296.
Chap. 22. Judgment upon the eighth House.	296.
Chap. 23. Of Directions of Significators to their several Promittors.	298.
Sect. 1. What a Direction is, what a Significator, and what a Promissor, &c.	298.
Sect. 2. Of the Latitude of the Planets to be considered in Directions.	299.
A new Demonstration of the Latitude of the Planets in Directions, &c.	301.
Sect. 3. Observations to be noted in Directions.	304.
Sect. Of the Effects of Directions in General.	305.
Chap. 24. Of Directions in Nativities, and their Effects, According to Morine.	307.
Chap. 25. Of the Measure of Time in Directions, with useful Tables thereof, &c.	309.
Chap. 26. Examples how to find the Declination and Right Ascension of all the Planets in the Exemplary Nativity.	317.
Chap. 27. Examples of taking the Distance of each Planet from the Meridian in R.A.	321.
Chap. 28. Examples of finding the Poles Elevation above the Circles of Position of the Planets, &c.	322.
Chap. 29. Examples of Directing Significators to their Promittors.	328.
Chap. 30. How to Rectifie and Direct a Nativity according to that excellent Astronomer and Mathematician, John Kepler.	333.
Chap. 31. Of the Revolution of the Sun to his Radical place in any persons Nativity.	341.
A General Revolutional Table, and its Use Exemplified.	342.
Aphorismes of Judging a Revolutional Figure, and an Example.	347.
Chap. 32. How to Direct a Revolutional Figure, with necessary Tables and Examples of the same.	349.
Chap. 33. Of Projections, with a General and Particular Table proper thereunto, and their Construction and Use.	358.
Chap. 34. Of Transits, and their Effects.	361.
Excellent Aphorismes a/Transits.	366.
Necessary Tables of Oblique and Right Ascension, also Tables of Declination.	738, &c.

To Mr. Henry Coley.

'Tis fit (my *Friend*) thou should'st expect, I know;
What by my kindness, I am prompted to;
Some powerful Lines to tell the World, and thee,
In what Esteem thy Writings ought to be:
And were thy Subject mean, perhaps, I'de dare,
'Mongst the most forward Rhymers to appear;
But since thy glorious Theme's so bright, so high,
And Treats of nothing underneath the Sky;
My groveling *Muse*: who never could Aspire,
Sits down in silence, and resolv's t' Admire:
Nor will I fear, thoul't take this ill from me;
How can they Clash, whose *Horoscopes* agree?

T. F.

To Mr. Henry Coley upon his
Clavis Astrologia Elimata.

We much of holy *Peters Keys* do hear,

But they his (*Pick-lock*) *Sword* do mean, I fear;

Some of the *Keys* of *Death*, and *Hell* do *Boast*,

And to that *World* they send a Mighty *Hoast*;

To shew what Conqerours, in *this*, they are,

For they, like *Death*, no *Friend*, nor *Foe*, do spare;

Ev'n those that keep the *Key* of *David* too,

Make use of *Locks*, and *Bolts* (as others do)

To *shut* out whom they please; but now kind *Fate*

Hath taught to *open* Great *Olympus* Gate!

Thou giv'st a *Key*, a *Key* that will be sure

To last, as long as th' *Wards* of *Heav'n* endure:

Nor only a *Key*, but thou a *Clew* hast giv'n,

To *lead* us through the *Labirinth* of *Heav'n*;

And whilst thou mak'st *Astrology* thy *Theam*,

Thou *Prophecy'st* when others do but Dream.

Arctophylax.

An Encomiasticon upon my most obliging, and ingenious Friend Mr. Henry Coley, *and his* Clavis Astrologiae Elimata.

[1.]

Sheba the admirer of great *Solomon*'s Skill
   doth represent the State,
Of all your Readers, Sir: The Contemplation
   Of that Queens wonder, moves the Quill
     Your worth to Celebrate,
Surpassing far th' Ignoble Term of Reputation.

[2.]

Some Lines (fraught with the Dictates of your praise)
    From your own Works, may raise
    Ingenious Fancies to a strain
   Of Poetry beyond the common Vein:
    Such Poetry as can express
The strangeness of Coelestial Harmony In extasies discern'd, and can redress
The wrongs of that rare Science call'd Astronomy.

[3.]

   Art in its lustre now appears,
   The Radical Glory of the Stars
With powerful splendor doth enrich the Air:
   Behold the motions of the Spheres,
And likewise what the Astral Influences are.

[4.]

   See the Elixir of the Azure Sky
   Extract' without that vulgar *Chymistry*,
    By *Paracelsian* skill disclos'd.
Ecce, Mercurio nati, how the hand
   Of fair Urania hath expos'd
    To your discreet Command
The choicest Gem within her Golden Treasury.

[5.]

Here know your Fate, your hourly doubts unfold:
   The first by Genethlialogick Skill;
   The second by the motions of the Mind
    Which to such actings is inclin'd.

By the Syderal Aspects which Distill
Their force upon its working Faculty:
　　Here by the Rules of Art such doubts are told,
By Rules expressing Art in its Transcendency.

[6.]

　　Hence, hence Ingratitude,
That with opprobrious terms dost scandalize
The searchers into Natures Misteries,
　　And do not here intrude;
These delicate Varieties
　　For Palat's far more curious are design'd.
These Dainty's are prepar'd for a more sprightly Mind.

[7.]

　　But stay my wandring Muse,
The more thou striv'st, the less thou dost prevail:
Thy mighty Tasks their stronger force assail
　　Thy feebly guarded Apprehension;
They sterilize thy weak Invention:
　　'Tis rather necessary to peruse
And rectifie thy errours in these Lines,
　　Than to proceed in barren Rhimes.
This rare Work its own Value best displays,
Whose Merits yeild the Author everlasting praise.

It[a] approbavit Jo. Southworth
Warringtoniensis Astrophilomedicus.

To his Honoured Friend Mr. Henry Coley, *on his Accurate Treatise, Entituled* Clavis Astrologiae Elimata.

When the Divine *Idea*'s first *unfurl'd*,
Themselves, to raise this *glorious Frame* the World;
Almighty Wisdome by a *Mistique* Tye,
Spread through the *whole* a secret *Sympathy*;
Impregnating *Superiours* to dispense,
On *lower* Bodies daily *Influence*;
Which Train of Causes that in order fall,
The wiser, *Nature*, others, *Fortune*, call:
And whilst Man did in *Innocence* remain,
He knew ('tis like) each *Link* of that great *Chain*;
But when Sin *Blurr'd* his Soul, that Light was *Dump't*,
Affected *Knowledge* made him *Ignorant*;
Heavens Language then no longer he could spell,
But rudely *guest* at what he could not *tell*:
Yet though *Eclips'd*, his Mind (not quite berest,)
Had still some *scatter'd, Glimmering*, Notions left.
As *Rallying Troops* (after an Overthrow,)
By *Stratagems* seek to Attaque their Foe;
So humane-kind hopes to *Retrieve* by *Art*,
That *Skill* from which they did so fondly part:
On *Plains of Shinar* where *Enlarged* Skye,
Gluts with *vast Prospect* the admiring Eye;
The *Long-liv'd Patriarchs*, as their *Flocks* they Fed,
Observ'd the *wandering Glories* over-head;
Trac'd all their *Laws of Motion*, and from thence,
By Sage *Experience* learn'd their *Influence*;
URANIA then was *Chast*, and known to be,
A Hand-maid fit for bless'd *Theology*;
Until a *Barbarous Crew* had seiz'd upon her,
Whose Savage Rapes *deflower 'd* her blooming *Honour*;
Chaldean Figments then debauch'd her Race,
And with vile *Paint* fulli'd her *Lovely Face*;
At which, *asham'd*, more than a *Thousand Year*,

She *hid* her self, disdaining to appear;
Mean while some *Counterfeits* assum'd her Name,
Others with *Calumnies* asperst her Fame;
Ignorance call'd her *Witch*, Malice, a *Cheat*,
And every *Gypsey* did usurp her Seat;
But still with *generous* scorn she took these wrongs,
And left just *Fate* to scourge their *sawcy* Tongues;
In dark *Recess* she undiscover'd lay,
Till to her *Pallace*, COLEY found the way;
With such *Address* he woo'd the sullen *Dame*, That she was fore'd to yield unto his *Flame*; And then *Restor'd*, *Refin 'd*, abroad she *came*:
His *Industry* gave *Science* a New Birth,
And clear' d the *Entercourse* 'twixt Heaven and Earth;
Rubb'd off *Contracted Rust*, and boldly drew,
Her naked *Beauties* to the Publique View;
Framing the *matchless* KEY that does Impart,
Her Choicest *Treasures* to the Sons of Art;
Whilst *Mountain-promisers* ten Years lye In,
And scarce, as last, bring forth a *Souterkin*;
His *Pregnant Genius* has produc'd, we see,
Th' Accomplish'd *Body of ASTROLOGY*;
Th' *America* is found, here's Arts *whole store*;
And they but hope in *vain*, that look for more.
    Then *rest* dear Friend! Thy *happy Pen* lay by,
    Thou'st Writ *enough* to reach *Eternity*;
    I dare *Predict* thou shalt *Immortal* prove,
    In Smatterers *Envy*, and true Artists *Love*.

Die ☽ 17°. Apr. 1676.

Hen. Care.

To the Candid, and Impartial Reader, on my ingenious Friend Mr. Henry Coley, his Clavis Astrologiae Elimata.

As *Sol*'s appearance doth unvail the Light,
Which until then was muffled up in Night;
And by the pow'r of his resplendent Rayes,
Turns gloomy Nights into bright shining Dayes:
So pregnant COLEY here plays *Phaebius* part,
Draws back the Curtain which so shaddow'd Art;
And to the World doth fairly here display,
What until now in glimmering Twilight lay;
And by this *Enchiridion* teaches more,
Than they shall learn who Read great Volums o're:
For what so e're, in former times, was well,
Is taught, by this our Author, to excell.
What *Guido*, *Argol*, and the Antients did,
Like *Homer's Iliads* in this Nut-shell's hid;
Whilst *Tyroes* with their Folio's levy Wars,
He teaches how to Pocket up the Stars;
And in a short (yet plain, and easie) way,
Learns us to know what Heavenly Bodies say;
And when, on Mortals, they do frown, or smile,
When they shew favour, or our hopes beguile.
    An *Introduction* doth the Work begin,
Like Silken Clue, for guide of strangers in;
Which is dispos'd in such a Form we see,
Like Baits to draw in Ingenuity;
And they who farther Progress dare to make,
Their Task within the other Parts may take;
Where they, with ease, may learn to Rectifie,
And Judge their own, or Friends, Nativity;
Set *Schemes* for *Revolutions*, and *Projections*,
And by his easie Rules to make *Elections*;
When best to buy, or Court a Girl that's coy;
When see a Friend, or when (to win) to play:
In fine, our Author hath so play'd his part,
This may be term'd the *Surquedry* of *Art*;
So brief, yet full, that we conjecture may,
(Reading his Book) Posterity will say;
      Sure COLEY liv'd an Age in every Sphere,
      Or else was Guide to *Charles*'s *Wagoneer*.

                                        Richard Pitt.

The PROEME.

He that hath a desire to acquaint himself with the most sublime Study of Astrology, and would gladly be a good Proficient therein, must not think it laborious to make himself very perfect in the Fundamentals thereof; as first, To be very expert in the knowledg of the Characters of the Twelve Signs, the Seven Planets, and also the Aspects; and then he must readily know what degrees of distance in the Zodiack makes any of the said Aspects, that so he may be able to understand when he views a Figure, how the Planets in the Signs behold each other, either by a *Sextile, Trine, Square,* or *Opposite* Aspect. Again, He must endeavour to understand the meaning of the terms of Art, and so proceed gradually from one step to another, according as he is directed in this following Tract; the Rules and Directions being so plainly laid down, that any man (that is but ordinarily capacitated) may easily proceed to the several Branches thereof, and by a little Study and Practice attain to a competent knowledg therein.

In the next place, He that desires to be an expert Artist, should endeavour to be exceeding prompt and ready in the proper Natures and discriptions of the Signs and Planets, and the several significations of the twelve Houses, also how to vary their several Astrological significations, and rightly to understand the use of an Ephemeris, and setting of a Scheme: After he hath attained to these things, let him apply himself to the Judicial part; and by a serious consideration of the Position and Aspects of the several Significators in any Geniture or Question, together with a Rational Intermixture of his own Reason and Judgment with the received Rules of Art, he may thereby be able, with moderate Study and Pains, to wade through the most Abstruse and Intricate parts thereof; and all this may be acquired with much ease, provided the Students have but a Natural Inclination and propensity thereunto— For, *Ptolomy* in his *Centiloquium, Aphor.* 4. tells us, *That a Natural Inclination to any Knowledge, attains more perfection therein, than that Person which shall take great pains by Learning to obtain it.* Let the Ingenious Artist be no less mindful also of the first *Aphorisme* of *Ptolomy*; viz *A te, & Scientta, &c.* "From thy "self and Science (or Learning) For it cannot be that he who is skilful should pronounce the particular forms of things; nor can the Fancy undertake a particular, but general Notion of the sensible Matter, in such things we must use conjecture. None but those who are endued with Divine Inspiration predict Particulars."

This being premised (If I may advise) Let the Artist be curious in Recording his Experience, and diligently observe how far the general Rules of *ART* do concur with Truth: By such endeavours it may be brought to some hopeful degree of Perfection, and consequently, much refined.

By this means (I presume) the Industrious Student may avoid those Errors in Art, which many through negligence too freely run themselves into; thereby exposing this kind of Learning to the Censure of divers Persons (in other things very Learned and Ingenious) as Vain and Idle. To conclude, Let it be considered, That an *Astrologer*, as a *Poet*, is *Born*, not *Made*: And therefore 'tis not for every Person to hope to attain to be excellent therein; but such that are aptly qualified for the Study thereof, as before intimated: to such I commend the ensuing Work, wherein I hope they may find something worthy their Friendly Acceptation; which is all I require of them. But as for such Criticks, who make it their business to carp at, and undervalue (like the Fox in the Fable) what they are not able to attain to, I can silently pass by their Scomma's and Reflections, and laugh at their Folly: Let such know, *That they will find it more easie to Carp than to Copy. Astrology*, as it has in all Ages had its Champions and Promoters, and those, Men of great Judgment and Learning; so on the other side, it has not wanted its Opposers, and some of them Men of no small Fame and Reputation: Yet this is still the happiness of so harmless an Art, that the greatest Antagonists thereof were such Persons that never throughly understood it. Howbeit, most men grant, That the Stars Operate upon this Inferior World by their Qualities and Natural Vertues; and Experience testifies, That the change of the Air alters our Bodies: The Humours are also moved by Coelestial Influences; especially by the Moon in her Motion, according to whose Changes our Bodies are sensible of much Alteration.

Read then and Learn, but don't all faults object,

Since they can only Judg, that can Correct,
To whom my Book appeals, and if I find,
The Sons of Art, to favour it inclin'd;
With their propitious smiles it shall suffice,
To counterpoiz the Frowns of Enemies.

Necessary *Praecognita Astronomical,* fit to be Considered by the Learner at his Entrance into the Study of Astrology.

I.

Astrology, or the Doctrine of the Stars, is an Art which by the Motions Configurations, and significations of the Heavenly Bodies, teacheth us to Pronounce, Judg, and Predict, of future Contingencies; the Effects, Events, and Mutations, of things to come.

II.

Therefore the Stars or Coelestial Bodies in their proper Significations and Influences are the real Subject of Astrology: *for as all Arts and Sciences have a subject to which they are particularly related, as that of* Grammar, *which is* Speech, *of* Arithmatick, *which is* Number, *of* Geometry, *which is* Measure, *&c. So is that of* Astrology, *the Stars, their Natures, Qualities, and Significations, whose Affections and Dispositions shall here in this following work be declared.*

III.

These Heavenly Bodies are of two special kinds, that is to say, either Fixed or Wandering.

IV.

Fixed Stars are those which are placed in the eighth Sphere, or Starry Firmament, always keeping their Stations; or constant distance, and those most remarkable are accounted in Number 1022. *These* 1022, *are by Antient Astronomers divided into* 48 *Images, of which* 21 *are* Northern, 15 *are* Southern, *and the other* 12 *are contained in a great Circle of the Sphere which we call the* Zodiack

V.

This Circle of the Zodiack is divided into 12 *equal Parts, called Signs, and declines from the Aequinoctial* 23 *degrees* 30 *minutes, both* Northward *and* Southward (*which is also the Suns greatest Declination*) *every Sign contains a certain number of fixed Stars, and are all of them equally divided into* 30 *Parts, called Degrees, and every Degree into* 60 *Minutes, and so forwards to Thirds, Fourths, Fifts, &c.*

VI.

Wandering Stars are those which are called Planets, and they are in Number seven.

VII.

These 7 *Planets are always in some one or other of these* 12 *Signs, which by reason of their various and unconstant motion, are sometimes in one place of the* Zodiack, *and sometimes in another, thereby causing several Rayes, Radiations, or Aspects, as shall be farther shewed, and every Planet hath a particular Orb to itself.*

VIII.

The Moon, *by reason of her different motions, crosseth the* Ecliptick (*which is supposed in the midst of the Zodiack*) *in two places, called her* Nodes, *or the* Dragons Head and Tayl.

IX.

The whole Sphere of Heaven is divided by the Horizon into two Hemisphears, each Hemisphear divided by great Circles into six Parts, by Astrologers called Mansions, *or* Houses.

X.

And the Signification of these Twelve Houses *have Relation to the whole Life of Man, that is, there is nothing whatsoever, belonging or contingent to the Sons of Men in their respective and various Fortunes, both as to Body and Estate, but it is signified by one or other of the said* Houses.

XI.

There are several parts appropriated to the 12 Houses of the Heavens, whereof that appertaining to the second House, which signifies the Estate or Substance of any Person, is accounted of greatest note, and is called the Lunar Horoscope, *or* Part of Fortune.

XII.

Every one of these Houses have a particular beginning and ending; the beginning whereof is called the Cusp *of the same House, and the ending is alwayes the* Cusp *of the succeeding House or Mansion.*

XIII.

Upon the Cusps *of these Houses always one Sign or other either ascends or descends, and in some one or other of these Signs the Planets are always found.*

Now, from the Scituation or Position of the Planets in the Signs, and the Signs on the Cusps of the Houses; also the Aspects of the Planets one amongst another, according to their several Natures, and Qualities, Signification of the Houses, matter and affection of the thing propounded, Astrologers draw their Predictions, and pronounce Judgment concerning the thing desired.

XIV.

The Characters of the Planets, Signs Aspects, and Nodes (which must first be learned by the young Student) are these,

The Planets. Saturn, ♄. Jupiter, ♃. Mars, ♂. Sol, ☉. Venus, ♀. Mercury, ☿. Luna, ☽. Terra, ⊕.

The Signs. Aries, ♈. Taurus, ♉. Gemini. ♊. Cancer, ♋. Leo, ♌. Virgo, ♍. Libra, ♎. Scorpio, ♏. Sagittarius, ♐. Capricornus, ♑. Aquarius, ♒. Pisces, ♓.

The Aspects. Conjunction, ☌. Sextile, ✶. Quartile, □. Trine, △. Opposition, ☍.

The Nodes. The Dragons Head, ☊. Dragons Tail, ☋. Part of Fortune, ⊗.

Arts and Sciences Mathematical *Professed and Taught by the Author* Henry Coley, Philom. *at his House in* Baldwins-Court *over against the* Old Hole in the Wall, *in* Baldwins-Gardens, *neer* Grays-Inn-Lane.

Arithmetick. In Whole Numbers and Vulgar Fractions. In Decimals and by Logarithmes.

Geometry. The Rudiments thereof; Also the Demonstration and Practice, according to the best Authors.

Astronomy. The Use of the *Globes*, Coelestial and Terrestrial. To Project the *Sphere* in plano to any Latitude several wayes: To Calculate the Longitude and Latitude of the *Planets*, with their *Declination* and *Ascention*; also the true time, quantity, and duration of *Eclipses* of the *Luminaries* for any time past or to come.

Trigonometry. Or the Doctrine and Calculation of *Triangles*, both Plain and Spherical. With the Application of the several Cases thereof in the most useful Questions in Geometry, Astronomy, Geography, Navigation, Dyaling.

Navigation. In either of three principal kinds of *Sayling*, viz. by the Plain, Mercatores Great Circle Chart.

Dyalling. 1. Geometrically 2. Instrumentally 3. Arithmetically by Scale and Compass. The Sector, and other convenient Scales. The Logarithmes, Sines and Tangents.

Surveying. Several ready wayes to Measure, Plot, and Divide Land, &c. Also the taking of Altitudes, Profundities, Distances, &c. Together with the Mensuration of all manner of Superficies; as Board, Glass, Pavement: Also of Solids; *viz.* Timber, Stone, &c. Regular and Irregular.

Gaugeing. To find the just quantity of Liquor in any Cask, whet full or partly empty; Also the Content or Solidity Brewers Vessels; *viz. Tuns, Coppers, Backs, Collers,* &c.

Astrology. In all its parts, & according to the best Authours, with Varieties therein, not vulgarly know to every Professer.

Clavis Astrologiae Eliminata.
OR,
A KEY to the whole ART of ASTROLOGY, New Filed, and Polished.

The Introduction.

CHAP. I.

Of the Twelve Signs, and their manifold Divisions.

I. The *Zodiack* is a great Circle of the Sphere, and is divided (as all other great Circles are supposed to be) into 360 degrees, every degree is subdivided into 60 other divisions, called minutes, and every minute into 60 seconds, and so to thirds, or farther at pleasure (as was before hinted in the *Praecognita*.) Every Sign contains 30 of those degrees, and so the 12 Signs fill the whole *Zodiack*; for 12 times 30 is 360, &c. They are placed in that Circle, the first six opposite to the last six, thus;

♈ ♉ ♊ ♋ ♌ ♍
♎ ♏ ♐ ♑ ♒ ♓

[*The Reason given why they are called Signs, is because they signifie unto us the most remarkable Alterations and Mutations of the Aire in these Inferior Elements, and (to us) they are set for Signs and for Seasons, &c.*]

II. The first 6 of these Signs are said to be Northern because they decline from the Equinoxial towards the North Pole; the latter 6 are said to be Southern, because they decline from the Equinoxial towards the South Pole; and farther observe, that this Circle of the Zodiack cuts the Aequator (or Equinoxial) in the very midst in two points, which are the very beginning of *Aries* and *Libra*, usually called the Equinoxial points.

III. These 12 Signs of tme Zodiack are divided into 4 Triplicities according to the 4 Elements, *Fiery, Airy, Earthy*, and *Watry*.

Fiery		♈ ♌ ♐
Airy	Signes	♊ ♎ ♒
Earthy	are	♉ ♍ ♑
Watry		♋ ♏ ♓

Fiery signs are said to be in Nature hot and dry; *Airy* Signes hot and moist; *Earthy* cold and dry; and *Watry* cold and moist.

IIII. They are also divided into Moveable, Fixed, and Common; as,

        ♈ ♋ ♎ ♑   Moveable

        ♉ ♌ ♏ ♒   Fixed   Signes

        ♊ ♍ ♐ ♓   Common

                                    Again,

V. ♈ ♊ ♌ ♎ ♐ ♒, Signs *Fiery and Airy* are term'd *Masc.*

   ♉ ♋ ♍ ♏ ♑ ♓, Signs *Earthy and Watry* are term'd *Femi.*

   ♋ ♌ ♍ ♎ ♏ ♐, are signs of Right Ascention.

   ♑ ♒ ♓ ♈ ♉ ♊, are signs of *Oblique* Ascention.

   ♊ ♓, and the beginning of ♐ are double bodied Signes.

   ♋ ♏ ♓ are *Fruitful* Signs.

   ♊ ♌ ♍ are *Barren* Signs.

VI. The Signes are divided into four parts, answerable to the four Quarters of the year: as,

   Vernal ♈ ♉ ♊ *to the Spring Quarter, which is hot and moist, Sanguine.*

   Aestival ♋ ♌ ♍ *to the Summer Quarter, hot and dry, Cholerick.*

   Autumne ♎ ♏ ♐ *the Harvest Quarter, cold and dry, Melancholly.*

   Winter ♑ ♒ ♓ *the Winter Quarter, cold and moist, phlegmatick.*

                      The signs are also termed

                      Mute as ♋ ♏ ♓.

                      Humane as ♊ ♍ ♎ ♒.

VII. There are also the several degrees of the Signes which are teemed *Masculine* and *Feminine, Dark, Light, Smoaky, Void* &c.

                      See the Table Following.

Signes	Degrees Masculine and Feminine.	Degrees Light, Dark, Smoak, Void	Degrees Deep Pitted	Deg. Azem, Lame and Deficient.	Degrees Increas. Fortune
♈	Masc. 8.15.30. Femi. 9. 22	d 3. 1 8. d 16. 1 20. v 24. 1 29. v 30.	6.11.16. 23. 29.		19.
♉	Masc. 11.21.30 Femi. 5.17.24	d 3. 1 7. v 12. 1 15. v 20. 1 28. d 30.	9. 12. 24. 15	6.7.8. 9.10.	3.15. 27.
♊	Masc. 16.26 Femi. 5.22.30.	1 4. d. 7. 1 12. v 16. 1 22. d 27. v 30.	2.12.17. 26.30.		11.
♋	Masc. 2.10.23.5. Femi. 8.12.27.	1 12. d 14. v 18. sm 20. 1 28. v30.	12.17.23. 16.30.	9.10.11.12. 13.14.15.	1.2.3.4. 15.
♌	Masc. 5.15.30. Femi. 8.23.	d 10. sm 20. v 25. 1 30.	6.13.15. 22.23.28.	18.27. 28.	2.5.7. 19.
♍	Masc. 12.30. Femi. 8.20.	d 5. 1 8. v 10. 1 16. sm 22. v 27. d 30.	8.13.16. 21.22.		3.4. 20.
♎	Masc. 5.20.30. Femi. 15.27.	1 5. d 10. 1 18. d. 21. 1 27. v 30.	1.7. 20.30.		3.15. 21.
♏	Masc. 4.17.30 Femi. 14.25.	d 3. 18. v 14. 1 22. sm 24. v 29. d 30.	9.10.22. 25.27.	19.28.	7.18. 20.
♐	Masc. 2.12.30. Femi. 5.24.	1 9. d 12. 1 19. sm 23. 1 30.	7.12.15. 24. 27.30.	1.7.8. 18.19.	13.20.
♑	Masc. 11.30. Femi. 19.	d 7. 1 10. s 15. 1 19. d 22. v 25. d 30.	7.17.22. 24.29.	26.27. 18.29.	12.13. 14.20.
♒	Masc. 5.21.27 Femi. 15.25.30.	sm 4. 1 9. d 13. 1 21. v 25. 1 30.	1.12.17. 22.24.29.	18.19.	7. 16. 17.20.
♓	Masc. 10.23.3. Femi. 20.28.	d 6. 1 12. d 18 1 22. v 25. 1 28. d 30.	4.9.24. 27.28.		13.20.

The Explanation and use of the Table.

The first Collumn shews the 12 Signes, the second the Degrees Masculine and Feminine, the third and fourth as the Titles direct. The first 8 degrees of *Aries* are Masculine, the ninth degree is Feminine, from 9 to 15 is Masculine, from 15 to 22 is Feminine, from 22 to 30 is Masculine, and so as they stand in order, in the rest of the Signes understand the same, and proceed according to these Directions.

The third Collumn is to be read thus; the three first degrees of *Aries* are Dark, noted by d, from thence to 8 are Light; from 8 to 16 are Dark, from 16 to 20 are Light, from 20 to 24 are Void, noted by the letter v, from 24 to 19 are Light degrees, the last degree is Void, understand the same in all the rest.

The fourth Collumn shews the degrees deep or pitted, as they are there exprest.

The fifth Collumn exhibits those degrees of the Ecliptick, which are accounted Azimene, Lame or Deficient.

And the last expresses those degrees which are said to Increase Fortune.

I. The use of this Table is briefly thus, If a *Question* be proposed concerning a *Thief*, or a *Woman with Child*, what is the *Sex, Male* or *Female*. I say when the Testimonies fall equal; so that neither *Angle, Signe* or *Planet* discover it then examine the degree the *Moon* is in, and the Significator of the *Thief*, or the degree of the *Cusp* of the *House* the *Question* relates unto, and Judge from thence, if *Masculine* a *Male*, if Feminine, Female, &c.

II. If the Signe ascending in any Persons Nativity be in those degrees termed Light, the Native should be clear and fair; if those accounted dark or smoaky, his Complexion should be more obscure and cloudy, &c.

Clavis Astrologiae Elimata, The Key to Astrology New Filed

III. But if in those Degrees reputed Void, this shews that the Native (or Querent's) understanding is but mean, Judgment and Reason very shallow, and apparently defective.

IV. If the Degree Ascending be any of these termed Deep or pitted, this shews some Imperfection in the Native or Querent, in Body or Mind, or both: Understand the same if the *Moon* or Lord of the Ascendant be posited in such Degrees.

V. Those Degrees called Difficient, either Ascending or Possest by any of the Principal Significators, are said to be certain testimonies of Deformity of the Body, either Crookedness, Lameness or Blindness, *&c.*

VI. Those Degrees Increasing Fortune, if arising upon the *Cusp* of the second, or the Significators of Substance posited therein, are said to signifie much Wealth, and increase of (the Natives, or Querents) Estate. And this is the use which may be made of the afforesaid Table.

CHAP. II.

Of the Aspects of the Planets, as they move through the Twelve Signes.

I. The seven *Planets* by their motion through the *Signs* make several *Aspects* or *Angles*, the one to the other, from the *Signs* they move in; and they are called Radiations: these *Aspects* are chiefly five that is a *Conjunction*, (though improperly termed an *Aspect*), a *Sextile*, a *Quartile*, a *Trine* and *Opposition*; (there are other *Aspects* which are between these) as the *Semisextile*, the *Quintile*, &c. which are termed new *Aspects*, added by *John Kepler*. Their Names and character are these which follow.

The Old *Aspects* are five in Number. As the
Conjunction ☌, Sextile ✶, Quartile □, Trine △, and Opposition ☍.

The New *Aspects* are eight in Number, *viz.*

Semisextile—SS	Tredecile—Td.	Quincunx—Vc.
Decile—dcc.	Sesiquadrat—SSq.	Semiquadrat—S.
Quintile—Q.	Biquintile—Bq.	

II. A *Conjunction* is when two *Planets* possess one *Signe and Degree* of the *Zodiack*, and is thus Charactered ☌.

A *Sextile* Aspect is when two *Planets* are 60 *Degrees* assundar, and so possess a sixth part of the *Zodiack*, and Charactered thus, ✶. *(*viz. a *Hexagonal* Aspect.)

A Quartile Aspect is when two *Planets* are 90 *Degrees* distant, and so contain a fourth part of the *Zodiack*, and is thus Charactered, □. (viz. a *Terragonal* Aspect.)

A *Trine* Aspect is when two *Planets* are distant 120 *Degrees*, or a third part of the *Zodiack*, and is Charactered thus, △. (or a *Trigonal* Aspect.)

The ✶ Aspect is two whole Signes distant, and is accounted an Aspect of Imperfect Love.

The □ Aspect is three Signs distant, and is an Aspect of Imperfect Hatred.

The △ Aspect continues 4 Signes, and is an Aspect of perfect Love.

☍ or *Diametral*, is an Aspect of perfect hatred, and is when two Planets are in the opposite part of the Circle, or 180 degrees distant: Note also that these Aspects are two-fold, *Sinister* and *Dexter*, the *Sinister* falls according to succession of the Signes, and the *Dexter* contrary; the *Dexter* Aspects are most Powerful and Efficatious.

III.

☌ *Conjunction is good with good, bad with bad*. Are distant. 00 Degrees
SS *Semisextile is Dodectile, is indifferent good*. Are distant. 30 Degrees, or fig. 1
✶ *Sextile or Hexagon, is very good*. Are distant. 60 Degrees, or fig. 2
□ *Square, Quadrate or Quartile, is very bad*. Are distant. 90 Degrees, or fig. 3
△ *Trine, is most excellent good and friendly*. Are distant. 120 Degrees, or fig. 4
Vc *Quincunx or Quadrasextile, is bad*. Are distant. 150 Degrees, or fig. 5
☍ *Opposition or Diameter, is worst of all*. Are distant. 180 Degrees, or fig. 6

These are the Aspects which are most Considerable.

			Signe	deg.
	Decile	36 degrees or	1	6
	Quintile	72 degrees or	2	12
These Aspects	*Tredecile*	108 degrees or	3	18
are of the least	*Biquintile*	144 degrees or	4	24
force.	*Semiquadrate*	45 degrees or	1	15
	Sesquiquadrate	135 degrees or	4	13

[*The Learned* Sir Christopher Heydon *hath Admirabty demonstrated, the Foundation and power of the Aspects in a most excellent Astrological Discourse of his, printed in Octavo, 1650. And he did verily believe, that diverse Events and Effects have concurred with those New Configurations, both in Nativities and Meteorology.*]

IV. Here follows a Table of the aforesaid Old Aspects.

	☌	✶	□	△	☍	
Dexter	♈	♒	♑	♐	♎	Sinister
Sinister		♊	♋	♌		Dexter
Dexter	♉	♓	♒	♑	♏	Sinister
Sinister		♋	♌	♍		Dexter
Dexter	♊	♈	♓	♒	♐	Sinister
Sinister		♌	♍	♎		Dexter
Dexter	♋	♉	♈	♓	♑	Sinister
Sinister		♍	♎	♏		Dexter
Dexter	♌	♊	♉	♈	♒	Sinister
Sinister		♎	♏	♐		Dexter
Dexter	♍	♏	♊	♉	♓	Sinister
Sinister		♋	♐	♑		Dexter
	☍	△	□	✶	☌	

The Explanation and Use of this Table.

By this Table you may see that a *Planet* in ♈ casts a sinister ✶ sinister ♊, and a ✶ dexter to ♒ a G dexter to ♑, and □ sinister to ♋; a △ to ♐ and ♌ and an ☍ to ♎, understand the like by ♉, ♊, ♋, &c.

But if a *Planet* be in ♎ his *Aspects* are noted at the bottome of the Table, so a *Planet* in ♎ casts his ✶ dexter to ♌ and ✶ sinister to ♐ his □ to ♑ and ♋, and △ to ♒ and ♊, understand the like by ♏, ♐, ♑, &c. on the

Clavis Astrologiae Elimata, The Key to Astrology New Filed

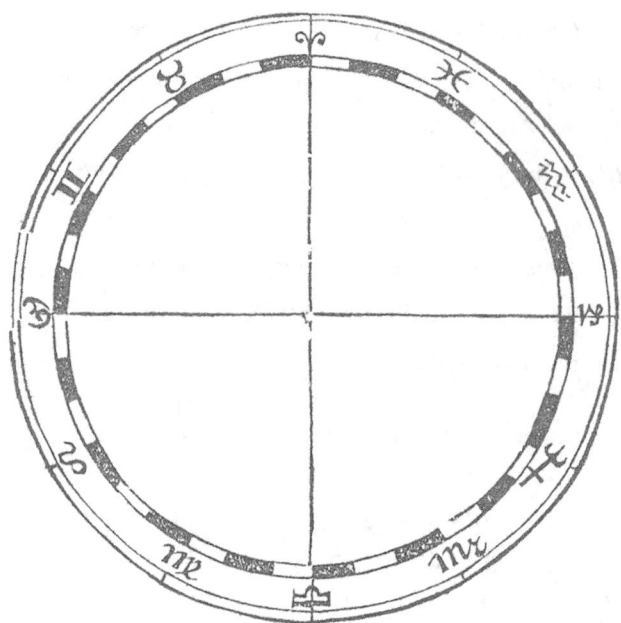

right hand Column of the Table: Where note that the *Fiery* and *Airy* Signes behold by a ✶, so do the *Earthy* and *Watry*; The △ Aspect is made from Signes of the same Triplicity: The *Fiery* Signes and *Airy* behold the *Earthy* and *Watry* by a □, and the contrary &c.

The Use that may be made of the *Aspects* or *Radiations* of the *Planets*, is very considerable, as to the Discovery of several matters past, present, and to come: for see from what Planet, the *Moon*, Lord of the Ascendant, or Significator, last separated: Also what Planets they are in Partile Aspect withal, and what Planet or Planets they apply unto; and so by consideration of the Aspect, and the Planet to whom 'tis made, and what House or Part of the Heavens it falls in, we are enabled to Judg of what. things have been past, what conditions things are in at present, and lastly, what the future may realy be expected: And note that the power of an Aspect is said to continue twelve bours before and after the time thereof.

CHAP. III.

Of the Description and Significations of the Twelve Signes of the Zodiac.

I. The Reason why these Constellations of the 12 Signes are thus called by the names of several Creatures, is partly for distinction and partly for that when the ☉ possesses those several *Signes*, he causes a various alteration ofthe seasons of the year, and makes the temperature of the Air inclinable to the Nature and Constitutions of those several Creatures from whence they receive their Denominations; of these Names are many Poetical Stories. But chiefly because those Stars in the several Signes, do represent (and appear) to the Eye in Form and Figure of such Creatures, as some are pleased to fancie.

But this by the way, I proceed to their several Descriptions, and Significations: and

I. *Of Aries*

Aries, Is an *Equinoctial, Cardinal, Easterly,* and *Diurnal Signe* of the fiery *Triplicity*, hot and dry, by *Nature, Cholerick, Masculine, Intemperate,* and *Violent*, the Day-House of *Mars* and contains 13 Stars. I. This signe describes a Person of a middle stature, lean and spare, but big bones, black eye-brows, thick shoulders, well set of a kind of a brownish or swarthy complexion, long visage, the hair curling, tending to a kind of a lightness, sometimes white or yellowish, inclinable to a sandy colour, hazle eyes, little ears and feet: the first half of the Sign gives a grosser body than the latter half.

II. *Places*. It signifies all obscure and desolate not much frequented; as the tops or coverings of houses, and all places where small Cattle use to feed: Or such parts where Thieves fly for Refuge, as Brick-Kills &c.

III. *Diseases*, Which are appropriated to this Signe, are heats in the face, Wheals and Pimples, small Pox, hare-lips, and all Diseases of the head and face; as head-ach, baldness, tooth-ach, ring-worms, Megrims, falling-sickness, Apoplexies, &c. ♈ gives a Colour, White and Red mixed therewith.

II. *Of Taurus.*

This is the second Signe in order, in the *Zodiack*, and *Southerly*, it is an *Earthy, Cold* and *Dry,* fixed *Nocturnal* Sign. *Feminine, Melancholly* and *Domestical* of the *Earthy triplicity*, the *Night-house* of ♀ and consists of 23 *Stars*.

I. It personates one of short and thick stature, a strong body, a broad face and forehead, wide nose, great mouth, a fat short neck, short arms, thick hands, thick black hair, crisping or curling, big buttocks, and short legs, slow to anger, but if once angered, not easily or suddenly reconciled again.

II. *Places*. It signifies Cellers and Out-houses, as Stables and Cow-houses, lower Rooms, Pastures, and plain grounds, Corn-fields, and all such plaees remote from houses, also such kind of places where the Furniture appertaining to Cattle and Horses are kept or laid up.

III. *Diseases*. From the Influence of this Constellation are all Infirmities of the Neck and Throat; as Wens, the Kings-Evil, sore Throats, Quinzies, Ulcers, and Imposthumes therein, also all sorts of defluctions of Rhume falling into the Neck or Throat, and whatever Diseases fall into that part of the Body. ♉ gives a Colour White and Cittron mixt.

III. *Of the Signe* ♊ *Gemini.*

This is the third Signe in Order, and is by Nature *Hot* and *Moist, Aerial, sanguine, diurnal, double bodied, Masculine of the Airy triplicity,* the *Day house of* ☿ *and consists of 18 stars.*

I. It is an *Western* Signe, and gives a person of an upright, streight and tall body, well set and composed; a good colour though not very clear, bright eyes and good sight, long arms, fleshy hands and feet, large breast, sad brown hair, an acute wit, and a person of an Ingenious fancy, a fluent tongue, and, apt discourse, yet of no great fidelity, but generally a strong active body.

II. *Places*. It signifies are all Rooms that are hung or wainscoated, Dining Rooms, Halls, Play-houses, Mountains, Hilly Places, Barns, Store-houses, Chests, and Truncks, &c.

III. *Diseases*. It signifies all that are incident to the arms and shoulders; as Corruption and Windiness in the Blood, and such Diseases are of a hot and moist Nature thence arising, sometimes a distempered fancy, &c. ♊ gives a Colour *White* and *Red* mixt together.

IV. *Of the Signe* ♋ *Cancer.*

This is the fourth Sign successively, and is naturally *Cold and moist, Phlegmatick, Feminine, fruitful, of the Watry triplicity, solstitial, Mute, the House of the Moon;* 'tis a Northerly Signe, and contains *9 Stars*.

I. Under this Signe are born persons of a little short stature; the latter 15 degrees therof give a more full body than the former 15; and the upper parts of the body are more thick and well set than the lower; little eyes, a pale and wan complexion, often times disordered teeth, a sad brown or blackish hair, with a low whineing voice; if a Woman, she will be subject to have many Children, and generally it gives a person (if a man) of a very effeminate constitution.

II. *Places*. Signified by this Constellation are usually all moist watry places, as the Sea and all great Rivers, and Navigable Waters, Brooks, Springs, Ponds, Lakes, Wells, Cisterns, Wash-houses, and Cellers, &c.

III. *Diseases*. It signifies Imperfections in the Breast and Stomack, weak digestion, Physick, Salt, Phlegm, and rotten Coughs, Cancers in the Breast and all Imposthumations in the Stomach. ♋ gives a colour *Green* and *Russet*.

V. *Of the Signe* ♌ *Leo*.

This is in Order the fifth Sign of the Zodiack, and the only House of the *Sun*, it is the second Sign of the *Fiery triplicity*, by nature *hot* and *dry*, *Masculine*, *Barren*, *Diurnal*, and a commanding *Eastern Sign*, which *consists of 27 Stars*.

I. Under this Constellation are born persons generally of a full large body, courageous, and stout hearted, a body of something above a middle stature, a great head with large goggle eyes; broad shoulders, a dark flaxen hair curling, the latter part gives a lighter hair than the first part, in fine, it gives a big voice, a resolute Spirit, and an aspiring brain, a person of a generous free hearted and courteous disposition, sanguine complexion, and an active body.

II. *Places*. All desart places, as Woods, Forrests, Rocks, both steep and cragged, Castles, Forts, Parks, and all inaceessable places; also Kings Pallaces, and in Houses; such places where fire is, or hath been kept, as Chimneys, Stoves, Furnaces and Ovens, &c.

III. *Diseases*. Signified by this Signe are Infirmities of the Back, pains in Ribs, as Pluisies, and Convulsions, and all Diseases of the heart, violent burning Feavors, the Plague, the Pestilence, yellow Jaundies, and sore Eyes. ♌ gives a Colour *Red* and *Green*.

VI. *Of* ♍ *Virgo*.

I. The sixth Sign is ♍, and it is an *Earthy cold Barren, Melancholly, Feminine, Nocturnal, Southern Signe; the House and Exaltation of* ☿, *consisting of 24 Stars*.

I. It personates a decent well composed body, of a mean stature, slender, the members inclinable to brevity, a discreet witty ingenious person, but not very beautiful, a sad brown, or for the most part black thick hair, the visage somewhat round, the voice small and shrill; in short, it gives a Native witty, and excellently well spoken, studious, and much inclinable to all manner of Learning.

II. *Places*. It signifies all Studies where Books are laid up, and Clossets, where Maps and Writings are kept; it denotes Corn-fields, Store-houses, Dary-houses, Malt-houses, and places where Hay, Barly, Pease, or Wheat-ricks are made, &c.

III. *Diseases*. It excites in the body, all Infirmities of the Belly, Wind collick, Worms, Croaking of the Guts, obstructions in the Bowels, and all Infirmities in the Stones, &c. ♍ gives a Colour *Black*, and *Speckled* mixed together.

VII. *Of* ♎ *Libra*.

The seventh Signe in order is ♎, a Signe *Hot and Moist, of the Airy triplicity, sanguine, Masculine, moveable, Cardinal, Equinoxial, Western Signe, the Day-house of* ♀, *consisting of 8 Stars*.

I. The shape of the body represented by this Signe, is a most delicate comely streight body, of a round and beautiful Visage, and well favoured, the hair for the most part tending to flaxen, or yellowish, but sometimes (and that rarely) a sad brown or black, not curling but long and smooth, a grey eye, more slender in body than gross, and in age subject to pimples and spots in the face, with a very high colour; and lastly, an indifferent tall stature, a courteous impartial creature, both just and upright in all actions.

II. *Places.* Signified by this Signe are these; In Houses it signifies all upper Rooms, as Chambers and Garrets, Balconies and Turetts; in the fields it denotes Grounds neer Windmills, all Out-houses, Barnes, and such places where Wood is cut, Saw-pits, all places where Hawking and Hunting is used, also all Sandy and Gravelly places.

III. *Diseases.* All Infirmities of the Reins, Kidneys, and Bladder, as Stone and Gravel, Heats and Imposthumes, or Ulcers in the Reins or Loins, weakness in the Back, and Corruption of Bloud. ♎ gives a colour *Black* or *dark Tawny*.

VIII. *Of* ♏ *Scorpio.*

Which is the eighth Signe in order, is a *Constellation fixed Nocturnal, Cold* and *Phlegmatick, Feminine,* and a *northern Signe,* of the *Watry Triplicity, the House and Joy of* ♂, *and consists of 12 Stars.*

I. It personates a strong able corpulent body, but a mean stature, yet big limbed, strong and active, wilful malitious, false and deceitful, of a sad brown hair, crisping or curling, a dark sallow complexion, an hairy body, short neckt, broad fac'd, and oftentimes bow-legg'd, quick in bodily motion, and a person of reserved thoughts.

II. *Places.* It signifies all Muddy, Moorish grounds and stinking Lakes, Ditches, and Quagmires, Gardens, Vineyards and Orchards, all Sinks in Houses, Wash-houses, ruinous houses, neer Waters, all places where creeping and venemous Creatures frequent, and such places where usually Rubbish and Jakes are laid.

III. *Diseases.* The Ghonorrhea, or Running of the Reins, Ruptures and Fistulas, Infirmities in the Bladder, as Gravel and Stone, Defects in the Matrix, Piles and Ulcers, and all Diseases belonging to the Privities. ♏ gives a Colour *Brown*.

IX. *Of* ♐ *Sagitarius.*

Which is successively the ninth Signe, and is bicorporeal or double bodied, *Fiery, Masculine, Chollerick and diurnal, by Nature hot and dry, and of the Fiery Triplicity, he House and Joy of* ♃, *consisting of 31 Stars.*

I. It indows the Native with a streight well proportioned body, somewhat tall, of a loving cheerful countenance, high colour, Oval visage, a Ruddy sanguine Complexion and brown hair, subject to baldness, a strong able body, and generally good Horsemen; great shooters and stout hearted.

II. *Places.* It signifies are usually Stables, or places where all sorts of Horses are kept, and other great Cattle; it denotes high places, as Hills, and the upper Rooms in Houses, as also such places where fire is, and hath been frequently kept.

III. *Diseases.* It signifies all Infirmities of what kind soever that belongs to the thighs and buttocks, as Ruptures and Fistula's in those parts, falls from Horses, over heating of the blood, Pestilential Feavers, hurts, by Fire, and all intemperateness in Sports, Pastimes and Recreations. ♐ gives a Colour *Yellow* or *Green*.

Of ♑ *Capricorn.*

This Signe is the tenth in order, and is by Nature *Cold and Dry, Nocturnal, Melancholly, Earthy, Feminine, Solstitial, Moveable, Cardinal, and a Southern Signe, consisting of 28 Stars, the House of* ♄, *and Exaltation of* ♂.

I. The persons born under (or signified) by this Signe are usually very slender weakly men, of a mean stature, and dry constitution, the face lean and thin, blackish hair, and thin beard, (if any at all) a long neck, narrow chin; and in fine, but a disproportioned body, chollerick, sad, but yet witty, and subtile.

II. *Places.* It denotes are for the most part such where Cattle are put, as Cow-houses, Sheep-pens, Wood-houses, Tools or Implements of Husbandry, barren thorny fallow Fields, Dunghills, lower Rooms, and obscure dark places neer the Earth, such as Caves, Dungeons, and Prisons, &c.

III. *Diseases.* It signifies are such especially as are incident to the Knees, the Leprosie, Itch and Scabs, Strains, Fractures, and Dislocations, and such like. ♑ gives a Colour *Black* and *Russet*, or a *Swarthy Brown*.

XI. Of ♒ Aquary.

The eleventh Signe in order is by nature *Hot and Moist, Masculine, sanguine, diurnal, fixed Rational, Humane*; *of the Airy Triplicity, the Day-house of* ♄, being a Constellation of 24 Stars.

I. It denotes a person of a well set, and strong able body, not very tall, yet decently enough composed, a clear skin, a sanguine complexion; a bright hair, and many times a dark flaxen; in short, it gives a well shaped body, yet more lovely than curious or beautiful, a fleshy face, inclinable to an Oval form, and sometimes a pale and whitely countenance.

II. *Places.* It denotes stone Quarries, and Mines, Hilly grounds, and places lately dug up, and upper part of houses, as Roofs, Eaves, or Windows, Vineyards, and such like neer adjoyning, Conduit or Springheads.

III. *Diseases.* All such as afflict the Leggs and Ancles, as Cramps, Gouts and Mellancholy winds, gathered in the blood or veins, and so disturb and afflicts those parts. ♒ gives a *Sky color* or *Blew*.

XII. Of ♓ Pisces.

This is the last Signe in the Zodiack, and is *Cold and Moist, Phlegmatick, a Nocturnal, Bicorporeal Northern Signe, of the Watry Trilicity*, and by some termed an idle sickly Signe; the House of ♃, and Exaltation of ♀, and consists of 24 Stars.

I. It gives a person that is but short, and none of the handsomest, yet a good face, and of a clear complexion, thick shoulders, brown hair, a fleshy body, not going very streight, and sometimes crooked, or an inclination thereunto, and with an incurvetting of the head.

II. *Places.* All Fish-ponds, and Water-springs, Moats and Water-mills, Places where Caves and Hermitages have been, and in houses the Well, Cistern, Pump, and any place that's appointed to keep water in.

III. *Diseases.* All that are incident to the feet, as the Gout, and Lameness, Aches, Boyles and Ulcers, Chilblaines, Salt, Fhlegm, cold and moist diseases, and also all Diseases that proeed from the blood putrified. ♓ gives a *Bright white glittering Colour*.

XIII. *Of the Qualities and Natural Dispositions of Persons signified by the 12 Signes.*

I. Although the Signe Ascending doth principally describe the person of the Native or Querent, yet it hath been observed, that such which have been born under *Aries* are generally very Active and Ingenious Persons; those under *Taurus* more dull, yet Laborious, under *Gemini* more Wits, curious Fancies, apt for Inventions; under *Cancer* very unconstant mutable persons; under Leo more serious and reserved, with a becoming Gravity; under *Virgo* Solid Ingenious Persons, and general Lovers of Learning, if their *Mercury* be but well posited and free from affliction; under *Libra* generally good Natur'd persons, somewhat conceited and subtil, not addicted to quarrel, but for the most part very Affable, Courteous, and Obliging; those under *Scorpio*, although they may be Ingenious, yet they are generally very Confident Rash Persons, full of Revenge and Malice, too subject to Boast and Lye; Active and Courteous for a time, where they are obliged, but rarely continue Faithful to their Friends, *cum multis aliis*; those under *Sagitary* generally Noble, Free-hearted Creatures, and such as cannot well resent an Injury offered: yet (for the most part) they are persons of an Obliging deportment, and true lovers of their friends; under *Capricorn* are usually born serious persons, but yet too subject to Mutability, and to give way to their own unbounded desires and Inclinations; under *Aquarius* are born generally, persons free from Envy. Affable and Courteous to most they deal with, and such as love to do good to others, haters of Strife and Debate, and too soon put up Injuries heaped upon them; under *Pisces* are borne genaral Spirited Persons, such as delight to do good, and abhor Ignoble Actions in all.

These Generals may sometimes be Contradicted by other more prevalent Causes and to be reconciled only by the Judicious and expert Artist.

II. These be the particular Descriptions of the 12 Signes, but if many Planets be happen to be placed in the Ascendant where any of these Signes arise, in any persons Nativity; their Significations must be mixt according to their various shapes, at the discretion of the Industrious Student.

III. The form and stature of any person, is to be judged from the Signe Ascending (in any Nativity or Question) the Lord, thereof, and Planet posited in the Ascendant; the fixed Stars are not to be neglected in this Judgment, and in especial manner the *Luminaries*; see what Signes they are in, and how they behold the Ascendant, and by a due consideration and commixture of their several significations; you cannot fail to give an exact and compleat discription in any Figure; and this the Artist should endeavour and labour to be very expert in.

The Quarters of the Heaven which the Signes Signifie, according to their Triplicities, are thus, viz.

I.
♈	East.	♌	E and by N.	♐	E and by South.
♎	West.	♊	W and by S.	♒	W and by North.
♋	North.	♏	N and by E.	♓	N and by West.
♑	South.	♉	S and by E.	♍	S and by West.

But others are of Opinion they ought to be considered according to their Declination from the Aequinoctial, thus; viz.

♈	East.	♌	N W and by N.	♐	S W and by S.
♎	West.	♊	N E and by N.	♒	S E and by S.
♋	North.	♏	S W and by N.	♓	S E and by E.
♑	South.	♉	N E and by E.	♍	N W and by W.

Let every man make use of that he findes most truth in: The Rule that I generally follow, and rarely fails, is to account *Fiery* Signes *East*; *Aiery* Signes *West*; *Earthy* Signes *South*; and *Watry* Signes *North*.

Note. that the Northern Signes give a more Cheerful Countenance than the Southern.

Humane Signes shew Persons of Humane Conditions; Signes representing Beasts, usually give men of action; those of the Fiery Triplicity, shew naturally Chollerick persons, and very high spirited; which is the more aggravated if ♂ or ☉, or Lord of the Ascendant be posited in such Signes.

[*And here observe by the way that the Signe Ascending doth principatly shew the discription of the Native or Querent, consideration being had to the Signe that the Lord thereof is posited in: Now whereas there is a description Assigned to the Planets also (which, I suppose, is chiefly grounded upon the Signes that are allotted for their Houses) yet the Planets themselves considered as Lords of the Ascendant in any Nativity or Question, shall in particular denote the persons Qualities and Conditions, either good or evil, according to the Nature of that Planet which is significator; for Hermes, Aphor. 79, speaks to the very same purpose, where he says. The Ascendant signifies the Body, and the Lord thereof the mind.*]

Although these things admit not of any real Demonstration; yet they are confirmed by long Experience, and we find the Stars by their Influence gently Incline though not Compel or Force the Will. But . . .

The Wife for every Chance doth fit his Mind.
And by his Art makes coming Evils Kind.

CHAP. IV.

Of the Seven Planets, their Names, Characters, Antiscions, Joyes, Orbs, and Latitudes.

I. Astrologers do principally consider (besides the Signes) seven wandering Stars, vulgarly called planets, whose Names and Characters are here again repeated, *viz.* ♄ *Saturn,* ♃ *Jupiter,* ♂ *Mars,* ☉ *Sol,* ♀ *Venus,* ☿ *Mercury,* ☽ *Luna*; as also the *Moons* two *Nodes*, called the *Dragon's Head* ☊, and *Dragon's Tail*, ☋. To which may be added the *Part of Fortune*, thus Charactered ⊕.

These Characters both of Signes, Planets, and Aspects, the young Artist must make himself very expert and ready in (as in the *Praecognita* was Intimated) for by their various Motions and Configurations through the 12 Signes, is deduced the whole Art of Science, and a Judgment drawn according to Rules, as shall in its proper place be plainly declared, even to the meanest Apprehension.

These seven Planets are for brevity sake Charactered as before shewed; and they are also called by other Poetical Names; as *Saturn* ♄ is also called *Chronos, Phoenon,* and *Falcifer*.

♃ *Jupiter* sometimes called *Phaeton* and *Zeus*.

♂ *Mars, Aries, Pyrois, Mavors, Gradivus*.

☉ the *Sun, Titon, Ilios, Phoebus, Apollo, Paeon, Osyrus, Diespiter*.

♀ *Venus, Cytheria, Aphrodite, Erycina*.

☿ *Mercury, Hermes, Stilbone, Cyllenius, Archas*.

☽ *Luna*, or the Moon, *Lucina, Cynthia, Diana, Phoebe, Proserpina, Noctiluea, Latona*.

Note that ♄ and ♂ are generally called Infortunes, ♃ and ♀ Fortunes, ☉, ☿, *and* ☽ Indifferent.

Of the Antiscions, Contrantiscions of the Planets in Signes.

II. The Antiscions of the Planets in Signes are no more but Signes equally distant (and beholding each other) from the first points of ♋ and ♑ the two Tropicks; as suppose a Planet in the first degree of ♊, he is as far disitant from the first point of ♋, as when he is in 29 degrees of that Tropick, accounting from the first degrees of both Tropicks: so if ☉ be in the tenth degree of ♉, he is as far distant from the first degrees of ♋, as when he is in the 20th degree of ♌; therefore let a Planet be in the tenth degree of ♉, he casts his Antiscion to the 20th degree of ♌; that is, he gives virtue to any Planet that shall be there placed, or casts any Aspect unto that point; and the Learned do hold an Antiscion to be equivalent to a ✶ or △ Aspect, especially if they were Fortunate Planets; and a Contrantiscion to be of the nature of a □ or ☍.

By this Figure may be seen that the Beginning of ♊ is a whole Signe distant from the beginning of ♋, and so is the last degree of ♋ (or beginning of ♌ as far distant from that Tropick as the former: hence a Planet in ♈ casts his Antiscion to ♍, a Planet in ♓ sends his Antiscion to ♎, & *contra*; so a Planet in ♉ sends his Antiscion to ♌ and Cotrantiscion to ♒, as the Lines in the Scheme better direct than many words.

A Table of the Antiscion in Signes.

	♋	♊
	♌	♉
The Antiscion of	♍	♈	The Planets in Signes.
	♎	♓
	♏	♒
	♐	♑

A scheme of the Antiscions, and Contrantiscions.

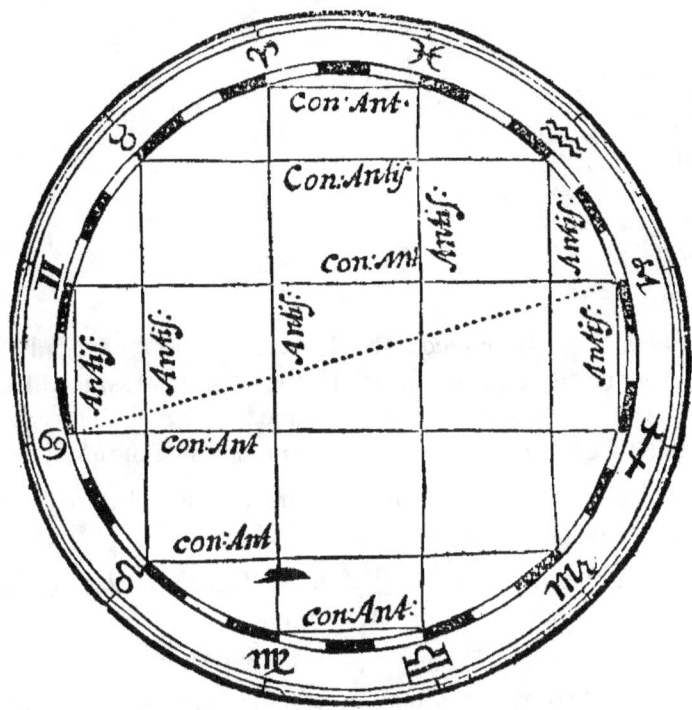

By this Table you may see a Planet in ♋ sends his Antiscion to ♊, and Contratiscion to ♑ the opposite Signe, and so to the rest. And to obtain the Planets Antiscion in degrees and minutes of those Signes where their Antiscions fall, substract the degrees and minutes of a Planets Longitude from 30 degrees, and the Remainder is the exact place of the Antiscion: as for example, suppose ♃ in 29d. 21m. of ♈, his Antiscion falls in 0d. 19m. of ♍, and his Contrantiscion in 0d. 19m of the opposite Signe ♓, understand the same in others—the business being so plain and obvious, needs no farther Illustration.

III. *Of the Houses and Joyes of the Planets.*

A Table of the Planets Houses.

♒	*Saturns* Day-House				☍	
♓	♃ His Night-house			△		
♈	♂ his Day-House		□			
♉	♀ her Night-house	✶				
♊	☿ his Day-house					
♋	☽ Moon	☿	♀	♂	♃	♄
♌	☉ Sun	☿	♀	♂	♃	♄
♍	☿ his Night-house					
♎	♀ her Day-house	✶				
♏	♂ his Night-house		□			
♐	♃ his Day-house			△		
♑	*Saturns* Night-house				☍	

The Joyes of the Planets in the Signs are these.

♄ Joyeth in ♒
♃ Joyeth in ♐
♂ Joyeth in ♏
☉ Joyeth in ♌
♀ Joyeth in ♉
☿ Joyeth in ♍
☽ Joyes in ♋

By this Table you see the ☉ hath only ♌ allotted to his House, and the ☽ hath only ♋ for her house, they being Signes of the same nature with these planets; (*viz.* the Luminaries) Assigned Rulers thereof; the ☉ is *hot* and *dry*, so is the Signe ♌; the, ☽ is *cold* and *moist*, of the same nature and quality is the Signe ♋ &c. and note further, that when the ☉ is in ♌ we have the hottest weather on this side of the Aequator.

1. ♄ hath ♒ and ♑ for his Houses, as being agreeable in nature, and note that his Houses are in ☍ to the Houses of the Luminaries; for ♄ is Cold, and an Enemy to Heat.

2. ♃'s two Houses fall next, *viz.* ♓ and ♐, and are in △ to the Houses of the Luminaries; and hence ♃ is accounted temperate, a helper to mankind, and the greater Fortune.

3. ♂'s two Houses follow next, *viz.* ♈ and ♏, and are in □ to the Houses of the ☉ and ☽; and ♂ is therefore Accounted Unfortunate, though not so bad as ♄, that directly opposes the Houses of the Luminaries: hence ♂ is termed the lesser Infortune.

4. ♀ is a Planet of a temperate Constitution, and the lesser Fortune; her houses are next alotted, *viz.* ♎ and ♉, which are in ✶ to the Houses of the ☉ and ☽ (an Aspect of Love and Amity) and since a ✶ is not so Amicable an Aspect as a △ (by which ♃'s Houses behold the Houses of the Luminaries) therefore ♀ is termed the lesser Fortune, as ♃ the greater.

5. ☿'s two Houses follow in the next place, *viz.* ♍ and ♊, and do immediately precede and follow the Houses of the Luminaries: he is never one Signe distant from the ☉ in motion; and since naturally he inclineth neither to good or bad, it is therefore termed Convertible in nature, and participates with the Planet he is joyned with.

Note that every Planet hath that part of the Zodiack assigned unto him, for a Mansion, or House which in respect of the Nature they have the most Agreement with, by an Intrinsical Nature of the Elements, as also their great Correspondency according to their Influence; For every Planet hath vertue and power in the Signes of the Zodiack, and they do agree as well in the Elements, as their Influences; and therefore these parts of the Zodiack assigned to each Planet are fitly called their Houses.

IV. *Of the Orbs of the Planets Aspects.*

An Aspect of a Planet is either platique or partile, a partile Aspect is when two Planets behold each other directly to the same degree and minute; as suppose ☉ 10d. 20m. in ♈, and ♃ 10d. 20m. in ♊, this is a partile ✶ Aspect; now a platique Aspect is when two Planets behold eaoh other within the moiety of their Orbs.

A Table of the Planets Orbs			The Planets Mean Motion.	
	d. m.			d. m. sec.
♄		10. 0. *some say* 9d.	before	♄ 0. 2. 1.
♃	Orbs	12. 0. *others say* 9.	and	♃ 0. 4. 59.
♂	are	7. 30. *most hold* 7.	after	♂ 0. 31. 27.
☉		17. 0. *some say* 15.	any	☉ 0. 59. 08.
♀		8. 0. *others say* 7.	aspect.	♀ 0. 59. 08.

| ☿ | 7. 30. *all agree* 7. | ☿ 0. 59. 08. |
| ☽ | 12. 30. *others say* 12. | ☽ 13. 10. 36. |

By the Table of the Planets Orbs, you may perceive right against each Planet what degrees are allotted him; as against ♃ 12 degrees, and against ♂ 7 degrees 30 min. So that if two Planets do not behold each other to the very degree and minute of the Signes they are in partile; yet if they are within the moiety of their Orbs, they are said to be in platique Aspect.

So if the ☉ be in 10 degrees 20 min. of ♈, and ♃ in 15 degrees 15 min. of ♊, they are said to be in platique ✶; and if they are 14 degrees distance from a partile Aspect, they are still within the moiety of the Orbs, for half the Orb of the ☉ is 8 degrees 30 min. and half of the orbs of ♃ 6, which is 14 degrees 30 min.

V. *A Table of the Planets Latitudes.*

			North Lat. d. m. sec.		South Lat. d. m. sec.
	Saturne		2. 48. 0.		2. 49. 0.
The	Jupiter		1. 38. 0.		1. 40. 0.
Greatest	Mars	is	4. 31. 0.	is	6. 47. 0.
Latitude	Venus		9. 2. 0.		9. 2. 0.
of	Mercury		3. 33. 0.		3. 35. 0.
	Luna		5. 9. 17.		5. 0. 12.

Note that the ☉ *moves always in the Ecliptick, and hath no Latitude.*

CHAP. V.

Of the Natures, Descriptions, and several Significations of the seven Planets in General.

The Young Artist in the next place ought to be well acquainted with the Natures and several Significations of the Planets.

I. *Of* ♄ *Saturne.*

I. *Saturne* is said to be by Nature Cold and dry, Author of Melancholly, Masculine, Diurnal, the greater Infortune and slow in motion, neer 30 years finishing his Course.

II. He Signifies a Person about a middle stature, of a black swarthy Complexion, sometimes pale and muddy, little Eyes, thin Beard, and many times none at all, thick shoulders, oft times crooked; a lean Face, thick Lips, black or sad brown Hair; he hath a shoveling gate, and delights to be alone; he is Wilful, Covetous, Malicious, aiming altogether at his own ends: this must be understood when he is ill dignified.

But if well dignified, he gives Men of Grave and Sober Spirits, Sound Judgments, sharp Fancies, good Students; and men that heap together the Goods of this life.

III. *The Qualities and Professions* of men in general, Old Men, Grand-fathers, and Fathers, Beggars, Husbandmen, Day-labourers, Monks, Jesuites, Sextons of Churches, &c. Curriers, Dressers of Leather, Diggers of the Earth: also Brick-layers, Tinners, Plummers, Maltsters, and Colliers: Dyers of Black cloth, all Dealers in black or sad Commodities, as Black-smiths, &c. ♄ Generally Denotes Aged People, Lands, Houses, and all Country Affairs, &c.

II. Of ♃ Jupiter.

I. He is a Planet Masculine and Diurnal, and by Nature temperately Hot and Moist, the greater Fortune, Author of Moderation, Temperance, Justice and Sobriety, he finisheth his Course in about 12 years.

II. *Jupiter* Denotes one of an upright and streight Stature, of a brown ruddy Complexion, an Oval Visage, Hair between red and dark sandy brown, inclinable to have much Beard, large Belly, great Thighs, great well-proportioned Legs, long Feet; and if well dignified, a sober well-spoken, and fair-conditioned Person, abhorring Covetousness, and cares not for worldly Wealth.

III. *Qualities and Professions of Men*; Judges, Lawyers, young Scholars, all sorts of Clergy-men, also Clothiers, Woollen-drapers, and such like: If *Jupiter* be well disposed he incites men to honest Principles, stirs them up to good Duties, Pious, Magnanimous, Modest, Wise, Diligent, Liberal; but being ill plac'd, gives Prodigal, stout persons, unfaithful, weak in Judgment, and altogether careless of themselves and Relations. ♃ Generally denotes Youth.

III. Of ♂ Mars.

I. *Mars* is a Masculine Nocturnal Planet, by Nature Hot and Dry, the lesser Infortune, the Author of Strife, Debate, Quarrels, and Contentions; he is about 2 years finishing his Course in the *Zodiack*.

II. *Mars* describes a person of a middle Stature, strong and well set, a ruddy Complexion; his Hair red or sandy flaxen, crisping or curling, hazel eyes, quick, sharp and piercing; a furious Aspect, proud and presumptuous, Variant, full of words, boasting and lying; in fine, a very strong body and active, rather big boned than Fat.

III. *The Qualities and Professions* are for the most part Souldiers, or such as use Weapons or Edge tools, also Apothecaries, Watch-makers, Barbers, Dyers, Tanners, Chyrurgions, Butchers, Gunners, Smiths, Marshals, Bayliffs, &c. Inclining rather unto Chollar than Mirth or Melancholly: being well placed, makes Valiant men, Generous, Hasty, careless of Riches, and much addicted to Warlike Actions: But if ill placed, he incites men to Tyranycal Actions, to Thieving and Murders, and all kind of Sedition. ♂ in Questions is a general Significator of Chollerick deboist Rustics, (except he be very well seated) he also signifies War, Strife, and, Debate, and all manner of Cruelty.

IV. Of the ☉ Sun.

I. The most glorious body of all the Planets, he is Masculine, Diurnal, and by Nature Hot and Dry (as every man may easily experience). He finisheth his Course in one year for by the *Suns* motion is all time measured out into Days, Months, and Years.

II. The Sun represents a person of a goodly fair Stature, the body and face both full and fleshy, of a Saffron ruddy Complexion, the Hair yellow and somewhat thin, a full goggle and hazle Eye, sharp and piercing, quick fighted, much Beard, and soon bald; and in fine, a generous and high minded Creature, aiming at no base or mean things.

III. *Qualities and Professions*, the *Sun* predominates, over Chief Rulers, Governours, Commanders, whether Emperours, Kings or Princes, and men in power and bearing Rule, &c. It signifies also Gold-smiths, Copper-smiths, Minters, and Coyners of Money; all Pewterers and Braziers, &c. To conclude, the Solar person is Magnanimous, Valiant, Provident, Long liv'd, Wise and Famous, and desirous of Honour. ☉ is a general Significator of men in Love Questions; he also signifies Honour, Greatness, Noble Persons of all Degrees, &c.

V. Of ♀ Venus.

I. *Venus* is a Feminine Nocturnal Planet, and by Nature Cold and Moist, the lesser Fortune and finishes her Course (to our appearance) in about a years time; she is the Author of Pleasure, Mirth, and Jollitry.

II. *Venus* represents a person of a short Stature, or rather about a middle size, pretty well set, plump and fat, of a whitely Complexion, and sometimes a little blush Colour, a round face, light brown Hair and smooth, an Eye much Rolling, with Chearful looks.

III. *Qualities and Professions*, one that delights to go spruce and neat, and to frequent merry meetings, an affable courteous person, and a delighter in Curiosities, all men and women that deal in divers sorts of Apparel or Linnen, and things delightful to wear; Lapidaries, Silkmen, Mercers, Linnen-drapers, Upholsters, Picture-drawers, or such as sell Perfumes and such like.

Venus well plac'd, makes men pleasant, fair spoken, given to pleasures, sociable and merciful, &c. But if ill affected, inclines men to be Effeminate, Timerous, Lustful, followers of Wenches, very sluggish, and addicted to Idleness, and an ill habit of body. ♀ generaily denotes Women of Questions—Youth, Pleasures, Pastimes, all kinds of Delights, Mirth, sweet Odours, &c.

VI. Of ☿ *Mercury*.

I. Mercury is said to be a Planet convertible in Nature, and participates of the Planet he is joyned with, and therefore cannot be said to be either Masculine or Feminine; he is by Nature Cold and Dry, and finishes his Course (to our appearance) in about one Year, and is the Author of all subtil tricks, Thefts and Perjuries.

II. *Mercury* personates one of a tall and spare body, a long face and nose, of a yellowish whitely Complexion, a little beard, but much hair on his head, inclining to blackness; and this Planet above all other much alters according to the Planet he is joyned with, (as before mentioned).

III. *Qualities and Professions*, he signifies all men of Learning, as Clerks, Merchants, Scholars, Secretaries, &c. Sometimes Embassadors, Commissioners, and Poets, Orators, Printers, Stationers, Userers, Cheaters (if ill dignified) and all such as live by their Wits; ☿ is much conformable to the Company he is with, be it either Mirth or Sorrow: If he be well posited, he gives a Sharp Wit, makes men Studious, and capable of any Learning; but if ill seated, inclines a person to Subtilty, Craftiness, Maliciousness, and all lying fraudulous Actions; he is also the Patron of Philosophers, Astrologers and Mathematicians. In Question ☿ generally signifies Youth.

VII. Of ☽ *Luna*.

I. This Planet is a Feminine Nocturnal Planet, and by Nature Cold and Moist, finisheth her Course in about 28 days she is a general Significator in all Questions.

II. She Personates one of a large and fair Stature, brown Hair, of a whitely Complexion, a full and fleshy body, louring look, and many times some blemish or defect in or neer the Eyes, short Arms, fleshy Hands, slow of Speech, Fat, and Phlegmatick, a Mutable, peevish Creature, seldome contented, and delights not much in Idleness nor Action.

III. *Qualities and Professions.* She signifieth the highest sort of Women, whether Queen, Governess, or Mistriss of the House; also Men whose Imployments lie upon the Waters; all Dealers in Fish, Vintners, Tapsters, Midwives, Nurses, and all sorts of common people; to which may be added Travellers, Fugitives, and Stray's amongst Cattle; all persons of an unconstant and wavering Disposition. *These Descriptions being perfectly learn'd and understood, the Artist cannot be to seek in making an Artificial Description of any Significator in all Questions.* Note that ☽ is said to be a General Significatrix of all Sick people.

Brief Observations in drawing a Description from the Planet that is Lord of the Ascendant.

1. If no Planet Aspect the Lord of the Ascendant, then judge by him, not considering the Signe he is in.

2. But if he be Retrograde, or in his fall or detriment, judge by the Signe he is in.

3. If the Lord of the Ascendant behold the Ascendant, judge by the Signe Ascending.

4. Lastly, if two Planets Aspect the Ascendant, take him that beholds it most partile, or he that is in his own House, before a Planet in his exaltation.

[*These Observations are to be considered as well in the Conditions and Qualities of a Person as in the Description and Corporature of the Body.*]

CHAP. VI.

Of the particular Descriptions, and several Dispositions the Planets give being Significators, and posited in any of the twelve Signes of the Zodiack.

SECT. I.

Of Saturne *in the Twelve Signes.*

I. *Saturne* in *Aries* gives a *Ruddy Complexion* but somewhat *obscure*, a *spare, raw-bon'd* person, full fac'd, big voice, a dark hair, not much beard; but addicted to boasting and commending himself for his Valour, and Couragious undertakings, when there is but small cause; in fine, a contentious quarrelsome person in general, and consequently very ill-natured.

II. *Saturne* in *Taurus* gives no comely person, but a heavy, lumpish, obscure kind of *Physiogonomy*, a dark hair, a ruff skin; a mean Stature, no handsom Conformity of the Members, for Qualities and Conditions a person as rugged in his Carriage and Deportment, as the Description; inclinable to vitious and sordid Actions, unless the Fortunes by their propitious Rayes friendly Interpose—

III. *Saturne* in *Gemini* gives a person of a reasonable tall Stature, a dark sanguine Complexion, an Oval Visage, a well proportioned Body, and the Hair sad brown or black—an Ingenious person, but generally Infortunate in most of his Actions; his Conditions somewhat unpolish'd, and perverse, and therefore warily to be dealt with.

IV. *Saturne* in *Cancer* personates one of a Crazie, or Sickly Constitution of Body, an indifferent Stature, rather inclining to Brevity than otherwise; a sad Hair meagre Countenance or thin Face, the whole Body disproportioned, sometimes Crooked, and the Conditions the same; subject to Jealousie and Malicious Actions, as well as divers other Vitious Inclinations; which may be sometimes aleviated by the Friendly Rayes of Forunate Planets, which must be left to the direction of the judicious Artist to Determine—

V. *Saturne* in *Leo* gives a person of a moderate large Stature, broad Shoulders, a lightish brown Hair, a Surly Austere Aspect, big bon'd, not very Fleshy, sometimes the Eyes fall in, and such persons usually stoop in their going; but for their Qualities and Conditions they are tollerably good, and carry a shew of Generosity or Nobleness in their Actions; somewhat passionate, and seeking Revenge, but not Courageous or Valiant when put to the Test—

VI. *Saturne* in *Virgo* represents a person of a tall spare Body, a swarthy Complexion, dark brown, or black hair, and much of it (upon some Members), a long Head, and solid Countenance, but generally an Unfortunate person, much inclined to Melancholly, and retaining Anger long; a Projector of many Curiosities to little purpose, Studious, very subtile and reserved, and sometimes (without other Configurations of the Planets contradict) too much addicted to pilfering, and indirect Dealing.

VII. *Saturne* in *Libra* describes a person above a middle Stature, a reasonable Comly, a sad brown Hair, an Oval face, a large Nose and Forehead, a moderate clear Complexion, yet not beautiful; for Conditions usually such persons are not willingto entertain low or mean thoughts of themselves, somewhat prodigal in Expence, and consequently rarely leave Estate considerable behind them for their Children to enjoy; they are easily moved to Controversie and Debate, and often come off Victors.

VIII. *Saturne* in *Scorpio* represents a person of a mean Stature, a squat thick well truss'd Body, broad Shoulders, agreeable thereunto, black or dark hair, and usually short and thick; for Conditions they should be most unsavoury, and offensive, a very Quarrelsome Contentious person, that delights to create Mischief, and promote all violent and dangerous actions, though to his own Detriment and Infelicity.

IX. *Saturne* in *Sagitarie* usually gives a large Body, a brown Hair, (and much of it upon some parts thereof) the

Members very comfortable and decent, the Complection not much a miss; for Conditions, a person sufficiently obliging, not Covetous, but moderately Frugal, rarely Profuse, but somewhat Chollerick, and by no means can bear an Affront, yet willing to do good to all, and sometimes (being induced thereto) too apt to comply and rashly, (without due consideration) make such promises that cannot conveniently be performed without prejudice—a real lover of his Friend, and merciful to a very Enemy.

X. *Saturne* in *Capricorn* personates a Lean Raw-bon'd Person, sad or black Hair, a rough Skin, a middle Stature rather inciined to Brevity than Tallness, an obscure duskish Complexion, little Eyes, long Visage, and an ill posture in going; for the Qualities of the mind, *Saturne* so posited and Significator, usually gives a Discontented, Melancholly, Peevish Person, Covetous of the goods of this Life, not addicted to use many words, a lover of the Earth, and all things of Profit produced from thence, fearful, subject to retain Anger (when 'tis supposed to be forgotten) yet such a one that rarely wants a reasonable portion of Gravity.

XI. *Saturne* in *Aquarius* gives a reasonable full bodied Person, a large Head and Face, the body rather inclinable to Corpulency than otherwise, a middle Stature, a sad brown Hair, and moderate clear Complexion, a sober graceful Deportment, very Affable and Courteous to all, of an excellent searching Fancy, and generally a very happy proficient in what he labours after, whether in Sciences or Curious Mysterious Arts, yet apt to conceit well of his own Parts and Abilities—and therefore subject to no ill-becoming Pride; but naturally a person of a very Pregnant Genius.

XII. *Saturne* in *Pisces* personates (or represents) a middle Statur'd person, of a Pale Complexion, sad Hair, tending to blackness, a large Head, and a full Eye, sometimes the teeth distorted, no very comly person, yet Active, and, too much inclined to Dissimulation, Contentious, Malitious, and prone to many ill Actions (which are abated as the person grows in years) not Loquatious, but very deliberate; in fine, it denotes an uncertain fickle person in most of his or her Actions, one that is able to present a reasonable good outside, but will prove notwithstanding in the end Fraudulent and Deceitful, and therefore warily to be Confided in.

SECT. II.

Of Jupiter *in the Twelve Signes.*

I. *Jupiter* in *Aries* Represents a middle Statur'd Person, of a Ruddy Complexion, a light brown or flaxen Hair, a quick and piercing Eye, a high Nose, and sometimes Pimples in the Face, an Oval Visage, the Body rather Lean, than Corpulent or Fat; but generally a person of a very Noble and Free Disposition, one that loves a good Credible outside, and to demean himself with much Generosity amongst his Friends and Associates, and consequently, a very obliging Person.

II. *Jupiter* in *Taurus* gives a person of a mean Stature, well set, a swarthy dull Complexion, a sad brown rugged Hair, somewhat Curling or Frizled, a notable well compacted Body, but not decent, the Disposition should be reasonable good, the Judgment sound, and a person of no contemptible Deportment, a lover of the Female Sex, and generally good Natur'd, and free to such Objects that deserve a charitable Compassion.

III. *Jupiter* in *Gemini* Represents a Curious, Decent, Well-composed plump Body, a sanguine Complexion (not very clear) a person above a middle Stature, rather tall than otherwise, a brown Hair, a full becoming Eye, a Graceful Deportment, a very Affable, Courteous Behaviour, a gentle, mild, obliging person, an Admirer of the Female Sex (especially those of the most refined Wits and Beauty) a general lover of Learning; yet if Jupiter be neer *Violent fixed Stars*, it renders the person Rash and Unstable in his Actions, and consequentiy Enemical to himself, and unacceptable to others.

IV. *Jupiter* in *Cancer* gives a person of a middle Stature, a pale, unwholesome, sickly kind of Complection, Fleshy, or inclined to Corpulency, a dark brown Hair, or Oval Face, and the whole body Disproportioned in the Members thereof in general; a busie Loquatious person, too apt to Intermeddle with other mens Affairs, conceited and high, thinks no mean thoughts of his own Abilities, a great Favourer of Women, Fortunate by Water, and delights to be thereon, and yet a person of the very ordinary Courage or Valour, unless his Significator be well beheld of *Mars*.

V. *Jupiter* in *Leo* represents a Strong, Well-proportioned Body, tall of Stature, a light brown, or yellowish Hair Curling, a Ruddy Complexion, a full Eye, and a person sufficiently Comly; for Disposition very Noble minded, Couragious, Magnanimous, Lofty, delighting in Valiant Warlike Actions and Achievments, he proves a Terrour to his Enemies, and a person that scorns to truckle to an Adversarie, but will Encounter with much Grandeur and Honour.

VI. *Jupiter* in *Virgo* gives a person of a reasonable full Stature, a sad brown Hair tending to blackness, a ruddy Complection, but not Fair or Clear, a well-built person, and one we term handsome, having a due Proportion and Conformity in all the Members; for Disposition, somewhat Chollerick, and ambitious of Honour, inclinable to Boasting, Studious, yet Covetous; and through Rashness subject to Losses and considerable Detriment in Estate: in fine, not easily wrought upon by any person.

VII. *Jupiter* in *Libra* personates a Compleat body, an Inviting Countenance, a most clear Complexion, a full Eye, an Upright Stature, rather tall than otherwise, not Gross, but Slender, an Oval Face, a light brown Hair, sometimes flaxen, subject to Pimples in the Face; a very mild Disposition, and winning behaviour, a great delighter in Noble Exercises, and Recreations, obliging to all Persons, and consequently gains much honour, and esteem thereby.

VIII. *Jupiter* in *Scorpio*, represents a middle statur'd Person, a well compact Body, a sad Hair, a full fleshy Face, a muddy dull Complexion; but for his disposition, a lofty proud ambitious Person; one that desires and endeavours to bear rule over his equals, resolute, and ill-natur'd, covetous, and guilty of too much subtilty in all his actions and therefore ought warily to be dealt withal by any that shall be concerned with such a Person.

IX. *Jupiter* in *Sagitarius,* gives an upright tall stature of Body, a Chestnut coloured Hair, an Oval Face, Ruddy Complexion, much Beard, a good Eye, a Person every way decently enough composed; for disposition a very courteous fair condition'd Person, of a most noble graceful deportment and behaviour, just in his actions, and injurious to none, generally a great lover of Horses; and in fine, a most accomplish'd Person, deserving commendation, and more than ordinary respect from all Persons he converses, or doth associate him self withal.

X. *Jupiter* in *Capricorn,* gives a mean Stature of Body, a pale Complexion, thin Face, a little Head, not much Beard, a small timber'd weakly Person generally, yet ingenious, sad Hair sometimes the Beard lighter of Colour, from the Hair of the Head; for qualities and conditions not very commendable, low spirited, peevish, not very active, nor fortunate in the World, unless some other testimonies assist; in fine, a very helpless, indigent, harmless Person.

XI. *Jupiter* in *Aquarius,* Personates a middle statur'd, brown-hair'd Person, indifferently well set, a cleer Complection, rather a corpulent Body than otherwise, and well compacted; for disposition a cheerful affable Creature, hurtful to none, but obliging to all, delights in decency and moderate recreation, very just and merciful, even to those that are enemies; in short, a very good humour'd laborious industrious Person, rarely guuilty of any extravagancy, but generally of a very commendable disposition and deportment.

XII. *Jupiter* in *Pisces,* personates a mean statur'd Person, of an obscure Complection, a fleshy Body and a lightish brown Hair, a harmless Creature, yet studious in profound matters, and indowed with very excellent natural parts and acquirements, fortunate upon the Water, and one that gains love from those he hath conversation withal, sometimes proves a reasonable good Fellow, and delights in good Company, if the *Moon* dart her Quadrat, or opposite Aspeets.

Note, that Jupiter, *usually signifies good Teeth, (as Saturn doth the contrary) and sometimes produces some notable and aparent mark in the fore-Teeth. Jupiter in an Airey sign, gives broad fore-Teeth, in a Fiery sign, crooked, or distorted, in an Earthy sign, foul Teeth, but in a Watry sign, the Teeth decay suddenly, and wax black and rotten, and this the more certain if* Jupiter *be in any bad Aspect of* Saturn *or* Mars *or in* Conjunction *with the Dragons Tail.*

Jupiter *significator and posited in a Watry sign, the Person is fat and comly, in an Aiery sign, more strong and corpulent, with a decent comliness and proportion of Body, in an Earthy sign, a well composed Body, not fat, nor lean, but a mediocrity, provided he have not much Latitude, and in no Aspect with other Planets, but if in a Fiery sign, the Body is rather square, than Corpulent, if* ♃ *be significator and posited in a Watry sign, the Person has some Impediment in his speeeh, or speaks with great deliberation; this the more certain, if in* Quartile, *or* Opposition *to* Mercury; *by this you may be able to judge of the rest of the Planets, &c.*

SECT. III.

Of Mars *in the twelve Signs.*

I. *Mars* in *Aries*, represents a middle statur'd Person, of a Swarthy Complexion, well set, big Bon'd, a light Hair, sorretimes Red and curling, an austeer Countenance; if *Mars* be Occidental, the Complexion is more ruddy, and the Body more smooth, if Oriental, the Person is more tall of stature, and the Complexion not so swarthy, as aforesaid, but it renders the Native more comly and valiant; For disposition *Mars in Aries* ever shews a bold undaunted confident Person, cholerique, subject to Rebellion and various Contests, lofty, desirous to bear rule over others, and scorns to subject himself to any Person; a true Lover of War, and oftentimes gains preferment, and great advancement thereby.

II. *Mars* in *Taurus*, gives a middle statur'd Person; well set, rather short than tall, pretty corpulent, of no cleer Complexion, sad or black rugged Hair, a broad Face, wide Mouth, generally a well truss'd Body, sometimes ruddy, and marked in the Face; it represents a gluttonous Person, one that gives himself much liberty in all manner of vitious Actions, *viz*. Gameing, Drinking, Wenching, *&c*. and in fine, a very treacherous, debauched, ill-natured, unfortunate Person, unless the fortunes interpose their friendly Rays (but if *Mars* be neer the Pleiades this discription is aggravated).

III. *Mars* in *Gemini*, personates a reasonable tall stature, a black Hair, or sad brown; the beginning of the sign gives it more light; if it falls near *Aldebaran* the Complexion is tending to Sanguine, the Body well proportioned, and the Members conformable, but a very unlettered Person in most of his actions, yet ingenious in many things, though unfortunate in all; and generally lives in some mean condition, shifting here and there, exercising his wits for a livelyhood.

IV. *Mars* in *Cancer*, gives a short Person of no good Complexion, a brown Hair, and much of it, a disproportioned Body, sometimes Crooked, and the conditions for the most part as crooked, a dull sottish Person, guilty of few or no commendable actions, unfortunate, imployed most in some servile or mean imployment, and is rarely capable of better; such is this Persons stupidity naturally, unless other testimonies assist.

V. *Mars* in *Leo*, gives a strong able bodyed Person of a sun-burn'd Complexion, tall, and of a dark flaxen Hair, large Limbs, and great Eyes, a hasty cholerique Person, whose passion too often oversways his reason, delights in War-like Exercises; as shooting, riding, fighting &c. but a noble, generous free spirited Person naturally, especially to such as observe him, and endeavor to oblige him.

VI. *Mars* in *Virgo*, gives a middle statur'd, well proportioned Body, a black, or dark brown Hair; the Complexion, Swarthy, and sometimes a scar, or blemish in the Face, a hasty revengeful Person, too subject to passion, and to retain an injury, or affront, a long time in memory, very humoursome and difficult to be pleased, conceited, but generally unfortunate in all, or most of his Actions.

VII. *Mars* in *Libra*, gives a decent well proportioned Body, somewhat tall, a light, brown Hair, an Oval Face, and Sanguine Complexion, a brisk cheerful Aspect, a lover of the Female-sex, conceited of his own abilities, and parts, inclinable to boast, delights in noble Recreations, loves decentness in his Apparel, and is generally beloved of Women, to his predjudice.

VIII. *Mars* in *Scorpio*, gives a well set middle statur'd Person, black Hair curling, a broad Face, a corpulent Body, a swarthy muddy Complexion; for disposition, a very ill humoured Person, passionate, quarrelsome, unsociable, rash, revengeful, and ungrateful; but, notwithstanding his ill nature, he has some good qualities also intermixt; such a Person has a quick and ready apprehension, and becomes excellent in any faculty or mistery, his active Fancy leads him into the Inspection of.

IX. *Mars* in *Sagitarus*, gives a tall Person, with a well proportioned Body, neatly compacted together, a sanguine Complexion, a brown Hair, an Oval Visage, a quick Eye, a Person of a large Heart, and of a cholerique hasty disposition, yet a cheerful, merry, jovial companion, active, couragious, loquatious, delights in decency, and to hear himself applauded by others; and in fine, of no contemptible humour, or temper.

X. *Mars* in *Capricorn*, gives a mean stature, a lean Body, an ill Complexion, and black lank Hair, a thin Face, little Head, but an ingenious Person, and, of a reasonable good disposition, a penetrating Fancy, and generally very fortunate and happy in most of his undertakings.

XI. *Mars* in *Aquarius*, describes One of a well composed Body, reasonable, corpulent, a reddish or Sandy-coloured Hair, a moderate clear Complexion, middle-statur'd, but of a turbulent spirit, too much addicted to Controversie, many times to the detriment of Body and Estate, if other testimonies do not concur.

XII. *Mars* in *Pisces*, gives a mean statur'd Person, rather short, and fleshy, than otherwise, no handsome Body, nor good Complexion, a light brown Hair, or fair flaxen, a sottish kind of a debauched Person, very dull and stupid, yet a lover of Women, a meer dissembler, an idle Companion, not a friend to himself or any other.

[*Note, that if Mars be in* Conjunction, Quartile, *or* Opposition *of* Saturn, *or with* ☋ *and they in Angles, then the Native is more fierce and violent; in Fiery Signs, he is cholerique and hasty, and many times hath a falling in the Cheeks; in other Signs the Face is more full and fleshy; Mars in Earthly Signs, renders the Native, of a sullen dogged temper, not courteous or affable; in Airey Signs, more free and obliging; in Watry Signs, somewhat stupid and sottish, unless he be well beheld of Jupiter, Sol, or Luna: their friendly Aspects doth something meliorate the aforesaid significations, which must (or at least should) be warily considered by the ingenious Artist in his Judgement; as also the nature of those fixed Stars that are joyned to the Particular significator.*]

SECT. IV.

Of the Sun being posited in any of the twelve Signs.

I. *Sol* posited in *Aries* (which is accounted his exaltation) discribes a Person of a reasonable stature of Body, yet strong and well composed, a good Complexion, though not very clear, a light Hair, flaxen, or yellowish, a noble spirited Soul, very couragious and valiant, delights in all War-like Actions, gains victory, and honour thereby, appears a terrour to his Enemies, and thereby makes himself famous in his Generation, sometimes even beyond his Capacity of Birth.

II. The *Sun* in *Taurus* represents a short well set Person, with brown Hair, not very comly, but an obscure duskish Complexion, a wide Mouth, a great Nose, a broad Face, a good confident bold Person, sufficiently strong, and not a little proud thereof, delighting much in opposition of others, and generally becomes Conqueror.

III. The *Sun* in *Gemimi*, represents a well proportioned Body, of a sanguine Complexion, above a middle stature, and a brown Hair, a good disposition'd Person, affable, and courteous to all, not very fortunate in any affairs, subject to the checks and controlement of others, and patiently passes over slight abuses, which none but a very mild tempered Person would be content to do.

IV. The *Sun* in *Cancer*, personates, or represents a mean statur'd Person of an ill Complexion, some deformity in Face, a very unhealthy Aspect, a brown Hair, and an ill proportioned Body, but a very harmless, innocent Creature, cheerful, and a lover of the Female-sex, also an admirer of sports and Pastimes; Musick, Dancing, and such kind of inviting Recreations, but cares not to labour or take pains, unto which he appears indisposed and averse.

V. The *Sun* in *Leo*, gives a strong well proportioned portly Person, of a very sanguine Complexion, a light brown, or yellowish Hair, a full Face, and a large Eye, sometimes a mark or scarr in the Face, a very just Person, faithful to his Friend, punctual in the performance of his promise, yet delights to take his pleasure, is ambitious of honour, whether in War, or btherwise; and usually promotes all things in order thereunto.

VI. The *Sun* in *Virgo*, gives a Person somewhat above a middle stature, a well proportioned Body, not corpulent, but rather slender, a moderate good Complexion, the Hair sad brown and much of it; for disposition, an ingenious cheerful Person, rejoycing in all civil Recreations, and to please his Fancy, both with the delights of the Ear, as well as those for the Pallat, (viz. *Musick and good Meat and Drink are his frequent Companions, if not otherwise obstructed*).

VII. The *Sun* in *Libra*, gives an upright, strait Body, an Oval Face, a ruddy cheerful Complexion, light Hair, and a full Eye, sometimes Pimples in the face; but (if Authors may be credited, and there is both reason and experience to confirm it) the Sun in *Libra*, signifies a very unfortunate Person in all, or most of his Actions, especially in War-like affairs; for therein he is sure to come off with dishonour, if he escapes other dangers, unless his significator be befriended, by some potent Planet, &c.

VIII. The *Sun* in *Scorpio*, gives a notable square Bodied Person, a full Face, a cloudy Complexion, like to Sunburn'd, a brown Hair, and a very plump fleshy Body in general; for disposition, an ingenious Person, but of a rugged nature, ambitious of honour, one that would not willingly admit of an equal; fortunate upon the Seas, and sometimes in the Practice of Physick, &c.

IX. The *Sun* in *Sagitarius*, gives a tall well proportioned comly Person, with an Oval Visage, a curious sanguine Complexion, and a light brown Hair; for qualities and disposition, a very lofty proud spirited Person, aiming at great things, and too severe in the exercise of power; yet some honourable exploits are performed by him, which adds much to his commendation, and renders him a very noble humoured Person.

X. *Sol* in *Capricorn*, usually represents a mean statur'd Person, of a sickly Complexion, Brown Hair, not curling, an Oval Face, a spare thin Body, not decently composed, but rather a disproportion in the Members thereof; for disposition, very just in his Actions, thereby gaining love and friendship; sometimes passionate, a favourer of the Female sex; and in general, a reasonable, good humoured Person to those he hath Conversation withal.

XI. The *Sun* in *Aquarius*, discribes a Person of a middle stature, a corpulent Body, decently composed, a round full Face, a light brown Hair, and generally a clear Complexion; the disposition moderately good, but subject to Ostentation, and desirous to bear rule, but free from malicious Actions against any Person.

XII. The *Sun* in *Pisces*, gives a Person rather short, than tall of stature, a round Face, and an indifferent good Complexion, a light brown Hair, sometimes flaxen, a reasonable plump, or corpulent Body, a general Lover of the Female-sex, and his own delights and pleasures; addicted to Gaming, and Feasting, many times to his own detriment; yet a Person very harmless to others, injures none but himself by too much extravagant expense and prodigality, so far as his substance will extend.

SECT. V.

Of Venus *being posited in any of the twelve Signs of the Zodiack.*

I. *Venus* in *Aries*, describes a middle statur'd Person, rather slender, than gross-bodied, a light Hair and usually some marks, or scars in the Face, a reasonable good Aspect, or Phisogmony; but generally a very unfortunate Person, neither lucky to himself, or any other he has concerns withal; the reason may be, because Venus receives her detriment in Aries.

II. *Venus* in *Taurus*, gives a comly Person, of mean stature, a ruddy Complexion, but not clear, a sad brown Hair, a plump Body, yet not gross, but decently enough composed, a mild temper'd Person, of a winning disposition; reasonable fortunate in most of his Actions; injurious to none, but rather obliging to all, thereby gaining a general respect from all, or most Persons he converses withal.

III. *Venus* in *Gemini*, usually gives a Person above a midale stature, reasonable tall, a slender well composed strait Body, a brown Hair, and a moderate clear Complexion; for disposition, a good humour'd loving Person, very liberal to such as appear fit Objects of Charity; and is easily wrought upon to do good, being a lover of all just Actions, and rarely guilty of any thing which is dishonourable, or unworthy—*Ergo* a Person of a clear and unstained reputation in the World. [*This general judgment may in some things be contradicted, if* Saturn *or* Mars *direct, a malignant Beam to* Venus, *which is left to the consideration of the Artist to moderate.*]

III. *Venus* in *Cancer*, generally represents a short statur'd Person, a round Face, a sickly pale Complexion, light coloured Hair, and a reasonable corpulent fleshy Body; for disposition, an idle sloathful Person, too much addicted to Good-fellowship, and Recreations of the worser sort, yet puts the best side outward, seems to be in reality when he is not; in fine, it shews a very mutable inconstant Person, in most of his Actions.

V. *Venus* in *Leo*, gives a reasonable tall Person, and the Members well compacted, a clear Complexion, round Face, a full Eye, sometimes Freckles in the Face, a light brown or flaxen Hair, and many times of a sandy red; for disposition, not to be disliked, such a Person should be moderately passionate, soon angry, and quickly over; of a generous free disposition, a little addicted to Pride, but not extream; often indisposed in Body, but not much prejudic'd thereby; in fine, a sociable good humour'd Person in the general.

VI. *Venus* in *Virgo*, gives a tall well proportioned Body, an Oval Face, a sad coloured, or black Hair, an obscure duskish Complexion, an ingenious Person, a good Oratour, but somewhat unfortunate, in most of his affairs; a subtile active Person, of an aspiring Fancy, but rarely attains his desire.

VII. *Venus* in *Libra*, gives an upright tall Person, a decent composed Body, and a conformity in all the Members thereof, a sanguine Complexion, a brown Hair, (sometimes Freckles in the Face) and Dimples in the Cheeks; for disposition, a Person of curious obliging deportment, and generally well beloved of most he has any dealings, or converse withal.

VIII. *Venus* in *Scorpio*, personates a well set Body, reasonable Corpulent, a broad Face, a duskish Complexion, and sad brown, or black Hair; but for disposition a very debauched Person, too subject to contention, and envy; guilty of many vitious unworthy Actions, not fit to be named; and this the rather, if Venus happen to be in any ill Aspect with *Saturn* or *Mars*.

IX. *Venus* in *Sagitarius*, gives a Person rather tall than otherwise, of a moderate clear Complexion, tending to sanguine, a brown Hair (not sad), an oval visage, and a very proportionable Body in the general; for disposition, very generous spirited, one that aims at no mean base things; a connnendable deportment, something proud, a little passionate; yet in the main, of a very curious temper, no way to be disliked, delighting in many harmless Recreations; and in fine, a very obliging fortunate Person.

X. *Venus* in *Capricorn*, represents a mean statur'd Body, rather inclining to brevity, than otherwise; of a pale sickly Complexion, thin fac'd, a dark Hair, tending to black; for disposition, none of the best, he should be a general lover of Women, (or if a Woman, a delighter in the Courtships, and daliance of Men,) one that loves his Belly well, and to take his pleasure, but not fortunate; too subject to change his station, and suffer sudden Catastroph's in his affairs.

XI. *Venus* in *Aquarius*, personates a handsome decent composed Body, reasonable Corpulent, a clear Complexion, and a brown Hair generally, sometimes (but rarely) of a flaxen Colour; but for quality and disposition, exceeding good and commendable; a very affable Courteous Person, inclinable to few, or no vitious Actions, one that loves civil Recreation, a peaceable quiet Person, obliging to all, reasonable fortunate in his affairs, and well respected by his Friends, and acquaintance in general.

XII. *Venus* in *Pisces*, personates a middle statur'd Body, of a moderate good Complexion between pale and ruddy, a round Face, a brown Hair (sometimes flaxen) with a Dimple in the Chin, a fleshy plump Person; for disposition, a good humour'd Creature, just in his Actions, very mild and peaceable; ingenious, but somewhat mutable in his resolutions, yet moderately fortunate in the World.

SECT. VI.

Of Mercury in the twelve Signs.

I. *Mercury* in *Aries,* gives a Body of a mean stature, spare and thin, an oval Face, a light brown Hair, and subject to curling; no clear Complexion'd Person, very ill conditioned in the general, and too much addicted to debate, lying, stealing, and such like unworthy and dishonourable Actions.

II. *Mercury* in *Taurus,* gives a Person neither tall, nor very short of stature, but a well set corpulent Body, of a swarthy Sun-burn'd Complexion, a sad brown Hair, short and thick; for conditions, a very sloathful idle Person, one that loves his cafe, and his Belly well, and to take pleasure amongst Women and otherwise to his own detriment and misfortune.

III. *Mercury* in *Gemini,* gives a reasonable tall Person, an upright strait Body, every way well composed, a brown Hair, and a moderate good Complexion; for disposition, a very ingenious pregnant Person, a good Oratour, and sometimes becomes a very cunning Lawyer, or a Person dealing in Books, *&c.* In short, *Mercury* in *Gemini,* gives a person that well understands his own interest, and is rarely overcome by the most subtilest Politian, nor deluded by the most craftiest Knave that he may have ocoasion to encounter withal; but generally outwits the most cunning Sophisters, especially if *Mercury* be no way afflicted.

IV. *Mercury* in *Cancer,* personates a low, or short stature of Body, of an ill Complexion, a sad Hair, a thin Face, sometimes a sharp Nose, and little Eyes; and for disposition, a mere dissembler, a sottish kind of Pot-Companion, light-finger'd, *&c.* In short, an ill natur'd Person, unless the *Moon* and *Jupiter* be in good Aspect to *Mercury.*

V. *Mercury* in *Leo,* gives a Person of a pretty large stature of Body, but no clear Complexion, rather swarthy or Sunburn'd, of a brown Hair, a round face, a full Eye, and a broad, or high Nose; for disposition, a hasty cholerick proud conceited Person, ambitious of honour, a boaster, and too often subject to contention.

VI. *Mercury* in *Virgo,* discribes a tall slender well proportioned Person, of a dark brown (or black hair,) yet no clear Complexion, rather obscure, a long Visage, and an austeer Aspect; for disposition, and qualities of the mind, a most ingenious Person, of a profound wit, a notable searching Fancy, (a fit Person to make a Princes Secretary,) capable of attaining divers Languages, besides other rare accomplishments; and this in some notable degreee provided Mercury be free from affliction [*but here understand that every Person that has Mercury their significator so posited, must not expect such qualifications, the capacity of Birth, Parents, and Education, must also be considered, by every Judicious Artist in their Judgement.*]

VII. *Mercury* in *Libra,* describes a decent composed Body, rather tall, than otherwise, a light brown smooth Hair, a ruddy, or sanguine Complexion, the Body reasonable Corpulent; for disposition, a very just and virtuous person, prudent, a lover and promoter of Learning. In short, a Person most happily qualified, with both natural and acquired parts and embellishments.

VIII. *Mercury* in *Scorpio,* gives a Person of a mean stature, well set, broad Shoulders, a swarthy Complexion, sad brown Hair, frizled, or curling, no decent composed Body; the conditions scarce to be born withal, such a Person is very subtile, a lover of the Female sex, inclinable to Company keeping, and Acts of Good-fellowship, (as we usually term it,) yet ingenious and studious, for the promotion of his own interests.

XI. *Mercury* in *Sagitarius,* Personates a tall stature, a well shap'd Body, not corpulent, but rather big bon'd, and spare, or a moderate quantity of flesh, an Oval Face, brown Hair, a ruddy Complexion, and a large Nose; for qualities and conditions, passionate, but, soon over; too rash in his Actions (which many times occasions his own detrirnent), but moderately good conditioned in the general, and delights in Noble things, yet rarely attains his ends.

X. *Mercury* in *Capricorn,* signifies a Person of mean stature, a thin Face, a brown Hair, and a duskish muddy complexion, sometimes Bow-leg'd, or some defect in those Members; and for disposition, a peevish discontented Person, unfortunate (without other testimonies concur;) and in fine, an impotent dejected Person.

XI. *Mercury* in *Aquarius*, denotes a Person of an indifferent stature of Body, reasonable corpulent and fleshy, a good clear complexion, a brown Hair, a full Face; for disposition, an ingenious obliging Person, inclinable to the study of Arts and Sciences, of a pregnant wit, and apt to find out many curious Inventions.

XII. *Mercury* in *Pisces*, gives a Person of a low stature, a brown Hair, a thin Face, of a pale or sickly Complexion, generally very hairy upon the Body; for disposition, a repining froppish Person, yet a lover of Women, and addicted to Drinking; and consequently the greatest Enemy to himself.

SECT. VII.

Of the various dispositions, and descriptions of Persons, the Moon usually gives, being posited in any of the twelve Signs of the Zodiack.

I. The *Moon* in *Aries*, discribes a Person of an indifferent stature of Body, a round Face, light brown, or flaxen Hair, reasonable corpulent, or fleshy, and a moderate good Complexion; for disposition, a mutable Person, rash and passionate, ambitious of honour, an aspiring Fancy, but rarely fortunate, or (at least) continues not long in suoh a condition.

II. The *Moon* in *Taurus*, gives a well composed Body, of a middle stature, (rather inclinable to brevity) corpulent strong Body, of no clear Complection, a sad brown, or black Hair; but a Person of gentle disposition, and obliging temper, a sober carriage and deportment, just in all his Actions, and consequently gains respect from all (or most) Persons he converses withal; as also most easily attains preferment in the World, suitable to his degree and quality of Birth.

III. The *Moon* in *Gemini*, personates a well composed Body, and tall, a sad brown Hair; a moderate good Complexion, not sanguine, nor pale, but between both; the Members well proportioned, and the Body very upright and comly; but the qualities and disposition not commendable, but rather offensive; an ingenious subtile Person, notably crafty, yet generally unfortunate, unless other testimonies assist.

IV. The *Moon* in *Cancer*, represents a middle statur'd Person, well proportioned, and fleshy, a round, full Face, a sad brown Hair, a pale duskish Complexion; for disposition it signifies a flexable Person, jocular, and pleasant, often addicted to Good fellowship, very harmless and generally well beloved; fortunate in most affairs, yet mutable and uncertain in his resolves, but free from passion, or rash Actions.

V. The *Moon* in *Leo*, denotes a Person somewhat above middle stature, a well proportion'd Body, strong and big bon'd, a sanguine Complexion, a light brown Hair, a full Face, a large Eye; for disposition, a lofty proud aspiring Person, very ambitious of honour, desires to bear rule over others, but abhors Servitude, or subjection, and rarely proves a fortunate Person.

VI. The *Moon* in *Virgo*, signifies a Person sometimes above middle stature, of a sad brown or black Hair, an Oval Face, but no clear (yet something of a ruddy) Complexion; for disposition, an ingenious Person, melancholy, very reserved, covetous, unfortunate, and guilty of few commendable Actions.

VII. The *Moon* in *Libra*, signifies a well composed Body, compleately compacted, moderate tall of stature, a curious smooth light brown Hair, and sanguine Complexion, mixed with white; the disposition no less pleasant, a very jocund Person, a lover of Mirth and Recreation, as also very well respected of the Female-sex in general. If a Woman, admired, or at least courted by divers Lovers; yet subject to misfortune, unless *Venus* be well placed and in good Aspect to the *Sun*, *Moon*, or *Jupiter*.

VIII. The *Moon* in *Scorpio*, represents an ill shap'd Person, thick and short, fleshy, and of a very obscure Complexion, a sad brown, or black Hair; and in short a very ill disposition'd Creature, and rarely qualified with any good humours, a sottish, malicious, treacherous Person naturally, unless Aleviated with good Education, or the *Moon* be in some good Aspect of the Fortunes: If a Female, she rarely lives free from severe censure, and not without desert, except (as I said before) the *Moon* be befriended by some benevolent Configuration of other good planets.

IX. The *Moon* in *Sagitarius*, gives a handsome well proportioned Body, an Oval Face, a bright brown Hair, and sanguine Complexion, a generous free spirited Person, passionate for a short time, ambitious, aiming at great things, and generally of a good obliging temper, and consequently gains respect of such Persons he associated himself withal.

X. The *Moon* in *Capricorn*, signifies a Person of a low stature, and of an ill Complexion, a spare thin Body and Face, sad, or black Hair; sometimes a defect, or weakness in the Knees, and at best no strong Bodied Person; one of small activity or Ingenuity; inclinable notwithstanding (naturally) to Debauchery, and scandalous Actions, which renders him a Person, but of low esteem; yet if the *Moon* receives the friendly Rays of *Jupiter*, the *Sun*, or *Venus* from good places of the Figure, the disposition is thereby much corrected.

XI. The *Moon* in *Aquanius*, gives a Person of a middle stature (not tall, nor short, but between both,) and clear sanguine Complexion; an ingenious Person, of a very affable courteous disposition inoffensive to all, loves Curiosities, and moderate Recreation; apt for invention, which conseqnently shews an active Fancy, a pregnant Brain, and is rarely guilty of any unworthy Action.

XII. The *Moon* in *Pisces*, discribes a Person of a mean, or low stature of Body, and the Complexion rather pale, than otherwise, the Hair a bright brown, the Body plump, or fat, a Person not much delighting in action, (unless those of the worst kind,) and unfortunate in most undertakings, neither good for himself, or others; the disposition may be somewhat meliorated, provided the *Moon* be posited in a good place of the Figure, and in Aspect with good and adjuvant Planets, which must also be considered in all the Planets in their particular significations (especially of the disposition and qualities of the mind) throughout the twelve Signs, which by an ingenious pregnant Artist may most easily be effected.

CHAP. VIII.

Of the Diseases the Planets naturally signifie, being posited in any of the twelve Signs of the Zodiack.

SECT. I.

Of the Diseases of Saturn.

Saturn *in general is Significator of the Tooth-ach, Leprosie, Rhumes, Consumptions, Black Jaundies, Palsie, Trembling, Vain fears, Gouts of all sorts, Hemorrhoides, Fractures, Dislocations, Ruptures. Deafness, pains in the Bones, Iliack passion, Chin-cough, pains in the Bladder, Madness, and all long and tedious Diseases, that proceed from Melancholy, Fear, or Grief, also corruption of Blood from the same cause, and forgetfulness; therefore if* Saturn *be Lord of the sixth House, and posited:*

I. In *Aries*, he signifies Distillations of Rhume, melancholly Vapours in the Head, cold there, obstructions, or stoppage in the stomach, pains in the Teeth, Deafness, or noise in the Ears.

II. In *Taurus*, he signifies swellings about the Neck, and Throat, the Kings-Evil, sometimes the Scurvy, often hoarsness, with a melancholy dulness, and indisposition of the whole Body; and all tedious Distempers, incident to the Neck and Throat.

III. In *Gemini*, he signifies pains, or any infirmities that are incident to the Arms, and Shoulder; also Melancholy Consumptions, or Black Jaundies, and divers other Diseases, proceeding from the Blood.

IV. In *Cancer*, *Saturn* being Significator, denotes Ptisicks, and ulceration of the Lungs, Colds, and Coughs, Putrifaction, Obstructions, and bruises in the Breast, or Stomach; Agues, Scurvey's, Cancers, and such-like Distempers.

V. In *Leo*, the Heart is afflicted with some violent grief, or Poyson; a decay, or Consumption in the Reins, and inward parts; ill and noysome. Vapours oppress the Heart; pains or weakness in the Back.

VI. In *Virgo*, stoppage of the Urine, Obstructions in the Bowels, bound in the Body, a weakness in the Thighs, and extream parts; the Person is also afflicted with Melancholy, and Griping in the Guts, sometimes the Stone.

VII. In *Libra*, the Blood is corrupted, the Back and Kidneys are distempered, the Strangury suspected, the Body is Consumptive; pains in the Knees and Thighs, sometimes the Sciatica, or Gout.

VIII. In *Scorpio*, shews swellings, or other Distempers, in the secret parts, Melancholy, the Piles, the Palsie, some obstructions of the Nerves, the Gout in the Leggs, and Feet.

IX. In *Sagitarius*, weakness in the Hyps, and Thighs, or Sciatica, old Aches, and bruises in those parts, sometimes it signifies the Gout.

X. In *Capricorn*, he signifies the Gout in the lower parts of the Body, occasioned from cold, and melancholy; also pains in the Head, and obstructions therein; sometimes an Ague, or a Distemper equivolent.

XI. In *Aquarius*, *Saturn* signifies Distempers in the Head, and Teeth, and defects in the Ears, pains in the Joints, bruises, or swellings in the Leggs, and sometimes a sore throat.

XII. Lastly in *Pisces*, Saturn signifies defluctions of Rhume, the Kings-Evils, or a Consumption; all Distempers of the Feet and Toes, as the Gout therein, or some other Maladies, occasioned by cold, taken in those Members.

SECT. II.

Of the Diseases of Jupiter.

Jupiter in general, *signifies all Infirmities of the Liver and Veins, Inflamations of the Lungs, Plurisies, Imposthumes, about the Breast, and Ribs, Squinzies, Catarrhs, windiness, and corruption in the Blood; Surfeits, Scurvy, and all obstructions, both of Liver, and Stomach. Now if* Jupiter *be lord of the sixth House, or posited therein, in any Figure of a Decmbiture.*

I. In the Sign *Aries*, he signifies the Distemper lies in the Head, sometimes, an Imposthume there, a Squinsey, or swelling in the Throat; the Disease arises chiefly from ill Blood in the Veins of the Head, which disturbs the Patients rest, and produces strange Dreams and imaginations.

II. In *Taurus*, the Distemper lies in the Throat, perhaps from swelling there, Wind offends the Blood, Obstructions, or griping in the Bowels; a Goutish humour afflicts the Arms, and Hands.

III. In *Gemini*, (being an Aiery Sign) you may suspect a Plurisie upon very good grounds, and some Distemper of the Reins; sweating, or bresthing, a Vein, is in this case very proper.

IV. In *Cancer*, gives great suspition of a Dropsie, the Stomach is offended, and therefore a bad Appetite follows; a waterish humour corrupts the Blood, and produces sometimes the Scurvey, it aptly denotes a Surfeit also.

V. In *Leo*, the Patient is invaded with a Feavour, the Blood is over-heated, a Bastard Plurisie may well be feared, the Heart is ill affected, now bleeding, and sweating may not be unseasonable.

VI. In *Virgo*, he signifies Consumptions, Obstructions, of the Lungs, the Blood corrupted with Melancholy, a cold and dry Liver; the Patient is much afflicted in the Bowels, too subject to a Flux; and in the Female-sex, it portends Fits of the Mother, or some Disease equivalent.

VII. In *Libra*, the Patient hath too much Blood, whence arises Obstructions and corrupt humours, also Diseases occasioned from thence, as Feavours, and Surfeits, sometimes the Piles, and Tumours, near the secret Parts, with Inflamations in other parts of the Body; bleeding in this case is very proper.

VIII. In *Scorpio*, the Strangury, the Piles, some Distemper occasioned by cold, taken in the Feet; the Blood is offended with waterish humours, whence the Dropsis may be much feared.

IX. In *Sagitarius*, some cholerick Distemper arising from Putrafaction of the Blood; and in all probability a Feavour, pains, or swellings about the Knees, or parts Adjacent.

X. In *Capricorn*, the Patients Blood is afflicted with Melancholy, whence arises divers pains in the Body, and sometimes some stoppage, or Obstructions in the Throat; in this case let some means be used to cleanse the Blood.

XI. In *Aquarius*, the Blood abounds, whence the humours are corrupted, and many Diseasses, and running pains afflict the Body.

XII. In *Pisces*, the Blood is too thin, and waterish, whence sometimes prooeeds a Dropsie, or other Distemper of that kind.

SECT. III.

Of the Diseases of Mars.

Mars *generally signifies Diseases occasioned by corruption of Blood, through Choler, as the Pestilence, Burning Feavours, Tertian, and Quotidian Agues, Megrim, Carbuncles, and Plague-foes, Burnings, Scaldings, Ringworms, Blisters, Frenzy, Yellow Jaundies, Bloody-flux, Fistulas, Shingles, Calenturs, St. Anthonies Fire, and Diseases of the Instruments of Generation, the Stone in the Reins, and Bladder, Small Pox, and Meazles, all Diseases of Choler, and hurts by Iron, Anger, and Passion, Doglike hunger, Diabets, &c.*

If *Mars* be Significator of the Disease, and posited:

I. In *Aries*, he signifies the Patient is almost distracted, and much tormented with violent pain in the Head, occasioned through some hot and dry Distemper of the Brain, Rhumes in the Eyes, Imposthumes in the Head, want of rest, and sometimes the Patient in this case is afflicted with violent pains and gripings in the Bowels.

II. In *Taurus*, he signifies some extream pain, or Tumour in the Neck, Throat, or Wind-pipe, sometimes breakings out there, or the Kings-Evil suspected, a weakness in the Back, or Stone in the Reins.

III. In *Gemini, Mars* signifies the blood is corrupted, and over-heated, and frequently produces the Itch and breaking out in most parts of the Body, sometimes a Surfeit, or Pestilential Feavour, also pains in the Arms, and Shoulders, and Distempers in the secret parts; as the Strangury, and such like.

IV. In *Cancer*, he signifies violent pains in the Breast, and Stomach, occasioned by cholerick sharp humours, settled, or gathered there, whence the Patient is thirsty by reason of the heat thereof; and many times afflicted with a dry Cough, also some cholerick Tumour in the Thighs, because *Mars* in *Cancer* governs the Breast and Thighs.

V. In *Leo, Mars* signifies affliction at the Heart, the Body abounds with cholerick humours; and therefore a violent Feavour may be expected, or the Stone in the Kidneys, and pain in the Knees; the Patient in this case is very passionate and restless.

VI. In *Virgo*, he shews cholerick humours, and Obstructions in the Bowels, and the Body much bound; but sometimes the Patient in this case is afflicted with the Cholick, and sometimes with Bloody-flux, and not improperly the Worms in Children, besides *Mars* in *Virgo*, doth afflict the Legs, by some violent humour, which falls into those Members.

VII. In *Libra*, he afflicts the Reins, and Kidneys, either by Stone, or Gravel lodged in those parts, and consequently pains in the Bladder, the Urine is hot; the French-pox, or Gonorrhea, in this case, may well be suspected.

VIII. In *Scorpio*, he signifies great suspition of some Venerial Distemper, or some great pain, or Ulcer in the secret parts, sometimes the Stone, or the Dropsie, Smallpox, Surfeit, pains in the Head, Rheums in the Eyes; in Women, an overflowing of their Monthly Courses, or other detriment from Venerial Acts.

IX. In *Sagitarius*, *Mars* signifies many times a Sciatica, or some pain, or Ulcer in the Hyps and Thighs, proceeding from cholerick humours, lodged, or settled in these parts, sometimes an extream heat or dryness in the Mouth or Throat; *because* Mars *in Sagitarius governs both* Taurus *and* Sagitarius, *as is expressed in the Table* [Ed. after this chapter], *wherein may be seen that every Planet makes his* Aries, *or governs the Head, being posited in his own House.*

X. In *Capricorn*, he signifies lameness in the Knees, Arms, or Hands, or violent pains in those Members, occasioned from cholerick humours, sometimes the Running Gout.

XI. In *Aquarius*, the Blood is putrified, or overheated; pains, or swellings in the Leggs; a Plurisie, or Feavour, and sometimes a Surfeit.

XII. In *Pisces*, lameness, or violent pains in the Feet, proceeding from corrupt humours, settled, or fallen down into those Members; and sometimes *Mars* in *Pisces* Significator of a Distemper, shews the Heart is afflicted, and the Patient subject to fainting-fits, most frequent in the Female-sex.

SECT. IV.

Of the Diseases appropriated to the Sun.

Those that are attributed to the Sun in general, are all Diseases of the Heart, and such as proceed from red Choler, Pimples, or Burles in the Face, all kind of breakings out, weakness in the Eyes, Swoundings, Burning Feavours, &c.

Now if the *Sun* be Significator of the Disease, and posited:

I. In *Aries*, it portends sore Eyes; pain, or swelling in the Hyps, the Megrim, the Patient is disturbed in his Head, and takes no rest; a Feavour may be suspected, or some other hot Distemper, proceeding from Choler.

II. In *Taurus*, the Sun shews some Cholerick Tumour in the Knees; a Quinsey, or sore Throat, may in this case be feared, probably breakings out, Kernels, or swellings in that part of the Body.

III. In *Gemini*, he inflames the Blood, and shews Pestilential Feavours, or breakings out in several parts of the Body, sometimes the Scurvey, with pains, or weakness in the Leggs, occasioned by corrupted Blood.

IV. In *Cancer*, the *Sun* therein produces the Meazles, or Small-pox, a disordered Stomach, a hoarse Voice, and sometimes a Dropsie, or swelling in the Feet.

V. In *Leo*, he signifies violent pains in the Head, even to Madness, and Raging; the Stone in the Reins, pains in the Back, sometimes the Plague, or spotted-Feavour, Swounding, and Fainting-fits.

VI. In *Virgo*, some Cholerick humour offends the Bowels, the Bloody-flux may be feared, Obstructions in the Stomach, a sore throat, or, swelling in or near the Neck.

VII. In *Libra*, inflamation, and corruption of Blood, with violent pains in the Arrns, and Shoulders, slight Feavours, Stone, or Gravel in the Reins, sometimes the Distemper is Venerial; (but very rarely) Choler too much abounds, and thereby disorders the whole Body.

VIII. In *Scorpio*, he signifies Distempers in the Secret parts, sharpness of Urine, sometimes a Clap, great Obstructions at the Stomach; and in Women, their Courses too much abound, or overflow.

IX. In *Sagitarius*, the Thighs are afflicted by some hot and Choldrick humour, sometimes a Fistula near the Hyp, a Feavour, the Heart is much oppressed, and the Patient subject to Swounding.

X. In *Capricorn*, he only signifies weakness, or lameness, in or about the Knees; the Bowels are disordered with pain therein, and the Patient seldome escapes, upon such a position, without a Feavour.

XI. In *Aquarius*, the Blood is inflamed, and 'tis strange if the Patient suffer not breakings out in his (or her) Leggs; the Reins are disordered, and wasting, and many times afflicted with Gravel, or the Stone; and consequently a difficulty follows to make Wa:ter.

XII. In *Pisces*, not much different from the former; the Secret parts are much afflicted with violent pain, sometimes the Strangury, or Disury much torments the Patient.

SECT. V.

Of the Diseases signified by Venus.

Venus *in general, aptly denotes all Diseases of the womb, Suffocation, Precipitation, Dislocation, and all such Diseases incident to the Instruments of Generation, viz. Gonorrhea, French-pox, Womens Courses, Fits of the Mother; and all those which proceed from Love, or Lust, let them be of what kind soever.*

Therefore, if *Venus* be the proper Significator of the Distemper, and posited:

I. In *Aries*, signifies the Disease is in the Head, proceeding from some cold cause, aboundance of moist humours flow from thence, the Patient is very heavy and dull, subject to a Lethargie; also there is upon such a position cause to suspect a Venerial Distemper, or that the Reins are afflicted; sometimes the Patient hath taken cold in the Feet, and thereby the Head is offended.

II. In *Taurus*, she signifies pains in the Head, and Secret parts, swellings in the Neck, by reason of those moist humours that Distill from the Head, occasioned by cold, taken originally.

III. In *Gemini*, she shews the Blood is corrupted with moist humours, a Dropsie may be expected to follow, or the Kings-Evil, by reason the extream parts are afflicted by a Flux of Rheum that flows from the Head: [*Venus is by Nature cold and moist, not much different from the Moon in quality, and must aptly therefore signifie cold and moist Distempers; but in this Sign doth also disorder the Blood, Aiery Signs properly signifying the the same.*]

IV. In *Cancer*, she shews the Stomach is much offended with cold, raw, undigested humours, many times a Surfeit, with a strong inclination to Vomit (which doth also disturb other parts of the Body.)

V. In *Leo*, the Distemper prooeeds from some ill affection of the Heart, Obstructions at stomach, Love Passions, and sometimes swellings, or pain in the Leggs; yet the Distemper will not prove of dangerous consequence to the Patient, [*except the proper Significators be afflicted by some Malignant Aspect of either of the Infortunes, which must be well considered, and left to the Judgement of the eperienced (and expert) Artist.*

VI. In *Virgo*, shews some Distemper in the Bowels, a Flux, or the Worms, occasioned by either raw slymy humours ingendered in the Guts, or by cold taken in the Feet.

VII. In *Libra*, a Gonorrhea may well be feared, or some Distemper in the Reins, sometimes a Surfeit, by too plentiful Eating, or Drinking, pain in the Belly, and Head, the Blood disordered, and Wind doth much afflict the Body.

VIII. In *Scorpio*, some Venerial Distemper, in all probability the French pox, at least some great affliction, or pain in the Privy parts, taken from a polluted Person; sometimes the Dropsie, Scurvey, or Kings-Evil.

IX. In *Sagitarius*, the Sciatica, or Hyp-Gout, or swelling in the Thighs, corruption of Blood, Surfeits, cold and moist humours too much abound.

X. In *Capricorn*, she sometimes denotes the Gout in the Knees, or Thighs; pains or swellings in those parts, arising from cold humours, settled there.

XI. In *Aquarius*, always pains, or swellings in the Leggs, or Knees, occasioned from some cold cause, and such a position doth also shew the Heart is afflicted.

XII. In *Pisces*, shews Distempers, or Lameness in the Feet, and swellings in the Leggs occasioned from cold taken in the Feet, it also signifies a Flux, or the Body is too much tormented with Wind, and cold, raw, undigested humours.

SECT. VI.

Of the Diseases attributed to Mercury.

Mercury *in general is the proper Significator of Catarrhs, Illiack, passion, Stammering, Lisping, Hoarseness, Coughs, Snuffling in the Nose, Imperfection in the Tongue, and all Diseases of the Brain, as Vertigo's, Appoplexies, Madness; also those of the Lungs, as Asthma, Ptisicks; and in fine, all Diseases that belong to the Brain, Tongue, and Memory.*

Now if *Mercury* be Significator of the Disease, and posited:

I. In *Aries*, he shews the Distemper lies in the Head, and Brain, the Patient is subject to a Vertigo, or Wind in the Head, sometimes Distempers of the Womb, and Vapours arising thence; if Mars afflict *Mercury*, the Distemper is so much the worse, and it often causes the Patient to be Light-headed, and sometimes almost Distracted, if a speedy Remedy be not procured.

II. In *Taurus*, he signifies defects in the Throat, stoppage, hoarseness, or wheesing therein; sometimes hard swellings in the Neck, with pain therein, as also in the Feet, arising from cold taken in those Members, which may produce Lameness, &c.

III. In *Gemini*, *Mercury* signifies sometimes pains of the Gout, windiness in the Blood; the Head, and Arms are much afflicted.

IV. In *Cancer*, he signifies distempered cold Stomach, the Patient is tormented with gripings there, proceeding from Wind, and Cold, sometimes the Patient upon this position has a Cough, or Distillation of Rheum, also Lameness in the Leggs, proceeding from a cold cause.

V. In *Leo*, he shews Tremblings, or some melanoholy Distemper at Heart, and violent pains in the Back by fits, occasioned by an extream Cold taken in the Feet.

VI. In *Virgo*, he signifies much Wind in the Bowels, Obstructions, pains in the Head, a short Breath, and sometimes the Wind-Cholick, always pains in the Belly, proceeding from some cold cause.

VII. In *Libra*, *Mercury* shews stoppage of Urine, Obstructions, the Blood is much disordered, weakness in the Reins, the Breast and Lungs afflicted, Phlegm too much abounds.

VIII. In *Scorpio*, he shews pains, or some Distemper in the Secret parts, sometimes an affliction of the Bowels, from a cold cause, as also running pains in the Arms, and Shoulders, because *Mercury* in *Scorpio* governs *Virgo* and *Gemini*.

IX. In *Sagitarius*, Distempers in the Reins; weakness in the Back, stoppage at Stomach, Coughs, and sometimes pains or swellings in theThighs, or Hype.

X. In *Capricorn*, *Mercury* sometimes signifies stoppage of Urine, pain, or Goutish humours, in, or about the Knees; the Heart is also afflicted from some melancholy cause, pain in the Back, proceeding from Cold.

XI. In *Aquarius,* he shews Wind in the Blood, with running pains in many parts of the Body, Fluxes, and Wind, with such kind of Distempers in the Bowels.

XI. In *Pisces*, he shews pains in the Head, with weakness in the Legs, and Feet; Gonorrhea, or Distemper in the Veins may be suspected.

SECT. VII.

Of the Diseases signified by the Moon.

The Moon *generally signifies the Cholick, Belly-ach Dropsie, Fluxes, the Terms in Women, all cold Rheumatick Diseases, Surfeits, Rheum in the Eyes, Worms, rotten Coughs, Convulsions, Falling-sickness, Kings Evil, Imposthumes, Small pox, Measles, Lethargies, and all Diseases of crude humours, and Phlegm.*

If she happen to be Significator of the Distemper, and posited:

I. In *Aries*, she signifies Convulsions, the Falling-sickness, Diffuxions of Rheum from the Head, Lethargy, a defect, of weakness in the Eyes, and pain in the Knees.

II. In *Taurus*, the *Moon* gives pains in the Legs, and Feet, with swellings, stoppage, or soreness in the Throat from some cold cause.

III. In *Gemini*, she shews the Distemper to be the Running gout in the Leggs, Arms, Hands, and Feet, sometimes a Surfeit, or great Obstructions afflicts the Patient.

IV. In *Cancer*, the Stomach is much afflicted, sometimes a Surfeit, or Small-pox may be feared; it also signifies Convulsions, Falling-sickness, Timpany, or Dropsie.

V. In *Leo*, the Heart is afflicted, also a sore Throat, Quinsie, or Kings-Evil, may very much be suspected, upon such a position.

VI. In *Virgo*, the *Moon* signifies great pain, and disorders in the Bowels, proceeding from melancholy Blood settled, Obstructions, and weakness in the Arms, and Shoulders.

VII. In *Libra*, the Reins are distempered, Obstructions at Stomach, weakness in the Back: the Whites in Women, sometimes a Surfeit, in this case, afflicts the Native, or a Pleurisie.

VIII. In *Scorpio*, she signifies Distempers in the Secrets, the Small-pox, Poyson, the Dropsie, the Heart is afflicted, sometimes Swounding, all which is much more aggravated if the *Moon* be in any bad Aspect to *Mars*; this ought to be well considered by the skilful and industrious Artist.

IX. In *Sagitarius*, she signifies in particular, either lameness, or weakness in the Thighs, the Wind-Cholick, Distempers in the Bowels, &c. but in all cases, consider what Aspects the *Moon* is in with any other Planet, and accordingly moderate your Judgement.

X. In *Capricorn*, if the *Moon* be posited therein, and Significatrix of the Distemper, she signifies the Stone in the Reins, (or pain there,) the Gout in the Knees, a weak Back; and the Whites in Women, proceeding from some melancholy cause, or great discontent.

XI. In *Aquarius*, she signifies Fits of the Mother, swellings, or pains in the Legs, the Secret parts, Diabets, and cold waterish humours hath infected the Blood.

XII. In *Pisces*, she shews cold taken in the Feet, and the Body much disordered thereby, swelling in the Leggs and Thighs, Dropsies; and in fine, the Body doth too much abound with moist, humours.

Here follows a Table, shewing what Members of the Body every Planet governs, being posited in any of the twelve Signs of the Zodiack, useful in the Judgement of Diseases.

The Table.

	♄	♃	♂	☉	♀	☿	☽
♈	♋♊	♌♉	♈♍	♐	♓♎	♒♏	♑
♉	♌♋	♍♊	♉♎	♑	♈♏	♓♐	♒
♊	♍♌	♎♋	♊♏	♒	♉♐	♈♑	♓
♋	♎♍	♏♌	♋♐	♓	♊♑	♉♒	♈
♌	♏♎	♐♍	♌♑	♈	♋♒	♊♓	♉
♍	♐♏	♑♎	♍♒	♉	♌♓	♋♈	♊
♎	♑♐	♒♏	♎♓	♊	♍♈	♌♉	♋
♏	♒♑	♓♐	♏♈	♋	♎♉	♍♊	♌
♐	♓♒	♈♑	♐♉	♌	♏♊	♎♋	♍
♑	♈♓	♉♒	♑♊	♍	♐♋	♏♌	♎
♒	♉♈	♊♓	♒♋	♎	♑♌	♐♍	♏
♓	♊♉	♋♈	♓♌	♏	♒♍	♑♎	♐

The use of this Table.

Suppose a Person fell sick at a certain time, when Mars his Significator was in *Leo*; then I enter this Table with *Mars* at top, and I search the Sign *Leo* in the first Collumn to the Left-hand; against which in the common Angle I find *Leo* and *Capricorn*; this tells me the Patient is much afflicted at his Heart, with pains in the Back, also weakness in the Knees, & the extream parts of the Body; in short, those parts of the Body are afflicted in one kind or other that are represented by these Signs that fall under the Planet in the Table, as also that Sign the Planet is posited in; understand the same in the rest, this will be easily understood by an industrious Scrutator in this Art. The Foundation of this Table is grounded upon this Rule, that every Planet governs the Head, if posited in his own House, in the second Sign to his own House, the Neck, and Throat; in the third Sign from thence, the Arms and Shoulders; which is very apparently expressed in the Table itself, and needs no farther illustration.

And thus I have shewed what Diseases are signified by the seven Planets, as they may be posited through any of the twelve Signs; and for your better instruction in finding out the nature of a Disease from the Figure of the Persons decumbiture, observe farther these three particulars, viz.

First consider in your Figure, the sixth, seventh, and twelfth Houses (which principally signifie Diseases) as also the Lords (or Rulers) thereof.

Secondly consider also the nature of the Signs upon the Cusps thereof; for Fiery Signs signifie Diseases proceeding from Choler, Earthy Signs shew the Disease arises from Melancholy, Airy Signs demonstrates the, Disease occurs from Wind, and corruption of Blood; Lastly, watry Signs denote such Diseases that proceed from Salt, and watry Phlegm.

Thirdly observe the nature of the Planets themselves, as also those Planets with whom they are in Aspect, or cast Aspects unto, do but seriously mind their several significations as well as Configurations, which being judiciously mixed, will clearly discover the humour offending, and conuquently the nature of the Disease.

CHAP. VIII.

*Of the Herbs and Plants that are appropriated
to the Government of the seven Planets.*

I. To *Saturn's* Government is assigned, Fumitory, Shepherds purse, Night-shade, Poppy, Mandrake, Henbane, Hellebore, both white and black, Beardsfoot, Hemlook, Burdock, Fern, Night-shade Moss, Angelica Parsnip, Clowns Wound-wort, Comfrey, Plantain Yarrow, Tamarisk, Polipody, Beets, Barley, Stinking Gladon, Blackthorn, Melancholy-Thistle.

II. To *Jupiter* is attributed, Bettony, Centory, Marjoram, Violets, Borage, Bugloss, the Gilly-flower Mint, Lungwort, Wheat, Pyony, Self-heals, Liquorrish, Wall-wort, the Dazie, Fumitory, Elecompane, Colts-foot, Cinkfoil, Dandelion, Endive, Succory, Blood-wort, Hyssop, Liver-wort, Sage, Scurvey-gras, Bill-berries, Bar-Berries, Mul-berries, Cherries.

III. To *Mars*, all manner of Thistles, Onions, Leeks, and Garlick, the Nettle, Mustard-seed, Pepper, and Ginger, Carduus Benedictus, Worm wood, Brook-lime, Madder, Hops, Broom, the Bramble, Radish, Crow-foot, Haw-Thorn, Furs-bush, Rheubarb, Horse-radish, Spear-wort, Dane-wort, Birth-wort, Colloquintida.

IV. To *Sol*, Saffron, the Mary-gold, Rosemary, Celandine, Eye-bright, Angelica, St. John's-wort Buglos, Cloves and Mace, Nutmegs, Wood-sorrel, Borage, Bawm, Camomile, Century, Butter-bur, Pimpernel, Raisons, Ivy, Lavender.

V. To *Venus* is attributed, Cowslips, Dazies, Feather-few, Bur-dock, Maiden-hair, Penny-royal, Mallows, Chickweed, Elder, Spinage, Melilot, Daffadil, Lillies of all sorts, Groundsel, Mug-wort, Ladies-mantle, Gromwel, Blites, Bugle, Ale-hoof, Devils-bit, Stinking Arrach, Arch-Angel, Clary, Cocks-head, Stone-Parsley, Sanders, Roses, Sow-Thistle, Wild Tansie, Marsh-mallows, Clary, Primrose, Periwinkles.

VI. To *Mercury*, Hore-hound, Pellitory of the Wall, Dill, Fennel, Smallage, Savory, Honey-suckles, Columbine, Carroways, Liquorish, Sweet marjoram, Parsley, Sampire, Trefoyle, Carrots, the Hazel-Nut tree, Oats, Valerian.

VII. To the *Moon*, Cole-wort, and Cabages, Flower-de-luce, Water-Lillies, Poppies, Orpine, Purslane, Privet, Toad-stool, Water Arimony, Water-Plantain, Moonwort, Mouse-ear, Wall flowers, Fluellin, Water-flags, Graves, or Ducks meat, Water-Agrimony-water, Betony, Willow-Tree, House-leek, Turnips, White Roses, Saxifrage, both White, and Burnet.

As to the time of gathering these Herbs, it shoud be when the Planet that governs the Herb is essentially dignified, if possible; however let the Planet be Angular, either in the Ascendant, or tenth House, and in some good Aspect of the Moon: let them be taken in their prime, being full of juice, and green, and from such places they flourish, and thrive most in, forbear to gather them when they are decaying, or have lost the most part of their strength, and lustre; and being so gathered, they will be the more effectual in their operation, being applied by a skilful hand.

CHAP. IX.

Of the Essenrial, and Accidental Dignities of the Planets, &c.

I. To be well acquainted, how a Planet is dignified, or debilitated in any part of the Heavens, is absolutely necessary for any Student in this Art; for without this knowlege no part of *Astrologie* can be weli understood; know therefore that a planet is said to be essentially dignified when he is posited in his own House, Exaltation, Triplieity, Term, or Face, a Table whereof with its explaination immediately follows, by which may be Collected the essential fortitudes, and debilities of the Planets in any Figure, and thereby their strength, or weakness, is found, and accordingly judge: Farther, there is a greater probability that what they signifie may be effected and come to pass when they (being Significators in any Scheme) are essentially strong, then when they are weak and much debilitated: the Table follows; which being but well understood, comprehends the whole Art, and ought to be perfectly learned by heart, by every Person that intends to make any Progress in this kind of Learning.

A Table of the Essential Dignities of the Planets according to *Ptolomy*.

Signs	Houses of the Planets	Exaltation	Triplicity of the Planets D Noc.	The Terms or Bounds of the Planets					The Faces of the Planets			Detriment	Fall
♈	♂ D	☉ 19	☉ ♃	♃ 6	♀ 14	☿ 21	♂ 26	♄ 30	♂ 10	☉ 20	♀ 30	♀	♄
♉	♀ N	☽ 3	♀ ☽	♀ 8	☿ 15	♃ 22	♄ 26	♂ 30	☿ 10	☽ 20	♄ 30	♂	
♊	☿ D	☊ 3	♄ ☿	☿ 7	♃ 14	♀ 21	♄ 25	♂ 30	♃ 10	♂ 20	☉ 30	♃	
♋	☽ ND	♃ 15	♂ ♂	♂ 6	♃ 13	☿ 20	♀ 27	♄ 30	♀ 10	☿ 20	☽ 30	♄	♂
♌	☉ ND		☉ ♃	♄ 6	☿ 13	♀ 19	♃ 25	♂ 30	♄ 10	♃ 20	♂ 30	♄	
♍	☿ N	☿ 15	♀ ☽	☿ 7	♀ 13	♃ 18	♄ 24	♂ 30	☉ 10	♀ 20	☿ 30	♃	♀
♎	♀ D	♄ 21	♄ ☿	♄ 6	♀ 11	♃ 19	☿ 24	♂ 30	☽ 10	♄ 20	♃ 30	♂	☉
♏	♂ N		♂ ♂	♂ 6	♃ 14	♀ 21	☿ 27	♄ 30	♂ 10	☉ 20	♀ 30	♀	☽
♐	♃ D	☋ 3	☉ ♃	♃ 8	♀ 14	☿ 10	♄ 25	♂ 30	☿ 10	☽ 20	♄ 30	☿	
♑	♄ N	♂ 28	♀ ☽	♀ 6	☿ 12	♃ 19	♂ 25	♄ 30	♃ 10	♂ 20	30	☽	♃
♒	♄ D		♄ ☿	♄ 6	☿ 12	♀ 20	♃ 25	♂ 30	♀ 10	☿ 20	☽ 30	☉	
♓	♃ N	♀ 27	♂ ♂	♀ 8	♃ 14	☿ 20	♂ 26	♂ 30	♄ 10	♃ 20	♂ 30	☿	♀

The use of the former Table.

I. Every Planet hath two signs for his Houses, Except ☉ and ☽, they but one a piece; ♄ hath ♑ and ♒; ♃ ♐ and ♓, ♂, ♈ & ♏, ☉, ♌, ☽, ♋, &c. One of these Houses is called Diurnal, noted in the second Column by the Letter D; the other is Nocturnal, noted by the Letter N. In these Signs the Planets have their exaltations which the third Column points out, as the ☉ in 19 ♈, ☽ in 3 ♉, ☊ in ♊ three degrees, &c.

II. These twelve Signs are divided into four Triplicities. The fourth Column tells you which Planet, or Planets, both Night and Day govern each Triplicity; as over against ♈, ♌, ♐, you find ☉ & ♃, *viz.* ☉ governeth by Day in that Triplicity and ♃ by Night. Over against ♉, ♍, and ♑, you find ♀, and ☽, *viz.* that is ♀ hath dominion by Day, and ☽ by Night, in that Triplicity. Over against ♊, ♎, ♒, you find ♄ and ☿, which rule as aforesaid. Over against ♋, ♏, ♓ you find ♂, who according to *Ptolomy*, and *Naibod*, ruleth over that Triplicity, both Day and Night.

III. Over against ♈, in the 5, 6, 7, 8, 9, Columns, you find ♃, 6, ♀, 14, which tells you, The first 6 degrees of ♈ are the terms of ♃, the terms of ♀ &c.

IV. Over against ♈, in the 10, 11, and 12, Columns, you find ♂ 10, ☉ 20, ♀ 30, *viz.* the first 10 degrees of ♈, are the Face of ♂; from 10 to 20 the Face of ☉; from 20 to 30 the Face of ♀, &c.

V. In the 13 Column, over against ♈ you find ♀ detriment, *viz.* ♀ being in ♈, is in a Sign opposite to one of her Houses, and so is said to be in her detriment.

VI. In the 14 Column, over against ♈ you find ♄, over his Head, Fall, that is ♄ when he is in ♈ opposite to ♎

his exaltation, and so is infortunate, &c.

VII. A Planet dignified as abovesaid, is said to be in his Essential Dignities; Accidental Dignities are, when Planets are casually in an Angle, or succeedent House, direct; free from Combustion.

VIII. A Planet in his House, or exaltation, being Significator of any Person, denotes him to be in a happy and prosperous condition, not wanting for the Goods of this life, and comparatively, as a Man in his own Castle secure from dangers.

IX. But a Planet Debilitated as being in detriment, or fall, and afflicted; denotes the Querent to be in a very low and mean condition, much dejected, and disconsolate, &c.

X. The ☉ is the principal Planet of the seven, and is accounted King amongst the rest, and has therefore the Sign *Aries* appropriated to him for his exaltation, as being the principal point of the whole Zodiack, and the Superiour Planets have Assigned unto them the other Cardinal points, as ♎ to ♄, ♋ to ♃, ♑ to ♂.

XI. The exaltations are taken proportional to the Planets vertues and power, and therefore the ☉ being the most glorious Planet hath Assigned him ♈, the grand point of the Zodiack, wherein 'tis supposed he was created, ♄ being the next ♎ the other Aequinoctial point, and ♃ and ♂ the two Trophicks, and thus are the four Cardinal points disposed.

XII. As the three Superiours have the three Cardinal points ♎, ♋, and ♑ allotted them, for exaltation, and the ☉ the principal point ♈. So the Inferiour Planets have Assigned to them those Signs next following, or adjacent to the Cardinal and Aequinoctial points, as to ☿, ♍, to ♀, ♓, and to the ☽, ♉. *Something as to the reason for their Houses was before hinted in the fourth Chapter.*

II. A Table of the Essential and Accidental Fortutudes and Debilities of the seven Planets, and Part of Fortune.

Essential Dignities.	Essential Debilities.
In House or Reception by House 5	In Detriment 5
In exaltatation or in reception thereby 4	In Fall 4
In Triplicity 3	Peregrine 5
In Term 2	
In Face or Decanet 1	

Accidental Fortitudes	Accidental Debilities
In the MC or Ascendant 5	In the 12th. House 5
In the 7th, 4, and 11, Houses 4	In the 8th. and 6th.
In the 2d. and 4th. Houses 3	Retrograde 5
In the 9th. House 2	Slow in Motion 2
In the 3d. House 1	♄ ♃ ♂ Occidental 2
Direct. 4	♀ and ☿ Oriental 2
Swift in motion 2	☽ decreasing in light 2
♄ ♃ ♂ Oriental 2	Combustion of the ☉ 5
♀ ☿ or ☽ Occidental 2	Under the ☉ Beams 4
Free from combustion 5	Besieged of ♄ and ♂ 6
In Cazimi or in the heart of ☉ 5	Partile ☌ with ☋ 4
Besieged by ♃ or ♀ 5	Partile ☌ with ♄ or ♂ 5
Partile ☌ with ☊ 4	Partile ☍ of ♄ or ♂ 4
Partile ☌ with ♃ or ♀ 5	Patile ☐ of ♄ or ♂ 3
Partile △ of ♃ or ♀ 4	In ☌ with caput Algol in 21d of ♉ or within 5d 5
Partile ✶ to ♃ or ♀ 3	In the terms of ♄ or ♂ 1
☌ with cor ♌ in 25d of ♌ 6	
☌ with spica ♍ 19d ♎ 5	
In the terms of ♃ or ♀ 1	

III. A Table of the Fortitudes and Debilities of the Part of Fortune

Dignities	Debilities
The Part of Fortune in	The Part of Fortune in
♉ or ♓ 5	♂ ♑ ♒ 5
♎ ♐ ♌ ♋ 4	♈ neither gets nor loses. 0
♊ 3	the 12 House 5
♍ 2	the 8 House 4
the Ascen. or MC 5	the 6 House 4
the 7 4 or 11 House 4	☍ with ♄ or ♂ 5
the 2 or 5 House 3	☌ with ☋ 3
the ninth House 2	☌ of ♄ or ♂ 4
the third House 1	☐ of ♄ or ♂ 3
☌ with ♃ or ♀ 5	Terms of ♄ or ♂ 2
△ with ♃ or ♀ 4	☌ with Caput Algol in 21d of ♉ 4
✶ with ♃ or ♀ 3	Combust. 5
☌ with ☊ 2	
☌ with Regulus 25d ♌ 6	
☌ with Spica ♍ 19d ♎ 5	
not combust. 5	

These Tables are plain and obvious; for having from them Collected the Fortitudes and Debilities of the Planets, or Part of Fortune in any Figure, Subtract the lesser from the greater, thereby you gain the strength or weakness of the Planets therein; and accordingly judge, which shall be exemplified in its proper place.

IV. A Table of the Friends, Enemies and Colours of the Planets.

Planets.	Friends.	Enemies.	Colours.
Saturn	♃, ☉, ☿, ☽.	♂, ♀.	Black.
Jupiter	♄, ☉, ♀, ☿, ☽.	♂.	Purple, mixt with Red.
Mars	♀.	♄, ♃, ☉, ☿, ☽.	Red, Yellow or Fiery.
Sol	♃, ♂, ♀, ☿, ☽.	♄.	Purple, and Yellow.
Venus	♃, ☉, ♂, ☿, ☽.	♄.	Skie Colour, or Blew.
Mercury	♄, ♃, ☉, ♀, ☽.	♂.	Various according to the Sign he is in.
Luna	♃, ☉, ♀, ☿.	♄, ♂.	A mixt Colour, spotted with White.

By this Table it appears, that ♃, ☉, ☿, ☽, are friends to ♄, but ♂, & ♀, Enemies, understand the same of the rest: But observe also that Friends by reason of agreement in Nature, Quality, Substance, and Power, are ♂ and ☉, ♃ and ♀, and ☽. Enemies by ☍ of Houses, are ♄ and the ☉, ♄ and the ☽, ♃ and ☿, ♂ and ♀. Enemies by exaltation are, ♄ and ☉, ♃ and ♂, ☿ and ♀.

A Table of Certain Countries and Cities under the seven Planets, and twelve Signs.

♈ and ♂	♉ and ♀	♊ and ☿	♋ and ☽
England	Russia	Sardinia	Scotland
France	Polonia great	Lumbardy p.	Granado
Germany	Swedeland the North p.	England p.	Burgundy part.
Silesia the higher	the North p.	Flanders	Holland
Polonia p.	Lorraigne	Brabant, the Dukedom of	Zeland Prusia
Burgundy	Campania	Wertenburgh	Numidia
Denmark	Holuetia	Hircania	Africa
Basternia	Rhetia. Poland	Armenia	Bithinia
Syria	Franconia	Maritania	Calchie
Palestine	Parthia	Cyrienia	Carthage
Of Cities	Persia	Marmarica	
Naples	Ireland	Aegypt the lower	Of Cities.
Capua	Cyclades		Constantinople. Tunis
Ancona	The Islands	Of Cities.	Venice
Ferrara	Cyprus the Sea	LONDON	Genoa
Florence	Towns of Asia the less	Carduba in Spain.	Lucas Pisa
Verona		Viterbium	Millaine
Bergamio	Of Cities	Cecenam	Vincentia
Padua	Bononia Sona	Turnye	Berne
Utrecht	Mantua Tarentum Pan-orme in Sicyly	Vercellas	Yorke
Lindaw	Perusium	Rhegium	St. Andrews in Scotland
Marcelles	Caput Histrie	Lovane	Lubeck
Epidaure	Brixi, Zurich	Bruges in Flanders	Magdeburg
Crackow	Lucerne	Mentz	Wittenburg
Augustam	Nants	Kitzing	Gorlick
Caragosa	Herbibolis	Hasford	
Wenieza	Carolstade	Bamberge	
	Posnania	Villacum	
	Liepsig	Norimberg though some say under ♐	
	Gnesna		
	Novograde		

♌ and ☉	♍ and ☿	♎ and ♀	♏ and ♂
Gallia	Achaia	Austria	Norway
Togata	Greece. Creet	Alsatia	Bavaria uper
The Alps	Croatia	Livonia	Metagony
Italy	Carinshia	Sabaudia	Comogena
Sicyly	Arthesina the Dukedom	Delphinat	Cappadocia
Apalia	of Athens	Bastrina	Idumea
Bohemia	Mesopotamia	Thusia, Seres	Mauritania
Turky part.	Babylon	Caspia	Fes
Aemilia	Assyria	Thebaida	Gethulia
Sabina	Mesopotamia	Oefim	Catalonia
Phenicia	Babylon	Trogloditica	
Chaldea	Assyria	Sundgavia	Of Cities.
Orchinia	Gallia		Algiers
	Comata part	Of Cities.	Valentia in Spain
Of Cities.	Rhone part	Lisbone	Trabezond
Damasco	Silesia lower	Cajetam	Urbine
Syracusa		Laudam	Pestorium
Rome	Of Cities.	Suessam	Aquilegia
Ravenna	Hierusalem	Placentia	Camerinum
Cremona	Corinth	Felkirch	Tarvisum
Confluente	Rhodes	Friburge	Forum
Prague	Papia	Argentine	Julium
Liniz	Signia	Spiers	Messana
Crimisium	Brundusium	Franckford at Mene.	Vienna
	Aretium	Halam suenorum.	Alchstade
	Novaria	Wimpina	Monacum
	Tholosa	Heilbran	Gaunt
	Lyons. Paris	Frifinge	Frankford upon Odor.
	Basill	Mospachium.	
	Heidleburg	Landshut	
	Erphord	Vienna in Austria	
	Wrutislaiv	Anwerpe	

Clavis Astrologiae Elimata, The Key to Astrology New Filed

♐ and ♃	♑ and ♄	♒ and ♄	♓ and ♃
Spain	Macedonia	Amazonia	Cilicia
Dalmatia	Illyria	Sarmatia	Calabriana
Sclavonia	Thracia	Tartary the great	Portugal
Hungary	Rosina	Valachia	Galitia
Moravis	Albania	Muscovia	Normandy
Misnia	Bulgaria	Swedeland South part	Phasunia
Celtica	Greece part	Westphalia	Nasomonia in Libia
Thirronia	Masovia	Mosell	Garamentes
Arabia the happy	Lituania	Piemont.	Lypia
Of Cities	Saxony	Bavaria part	Pamphilia
Toledo	Hassia	Aethiopia	Aegypt the higher
Voleteras	Thuringia	Oxiana	Of Cities.
Mutina	Marchia	Sogdiana	Alexandria
Narbon	Stiria	Media	Hispalis
Avinion	Orchades	Arabia desert and stony	Compostella
Colonia	India	Of Cities.	Parentium
Agrippina	Ariana	Hamboroagh	Rhems
Studgard	Gedrosia	Breme	Worms
Rotenburg	Of Cities.	Mountserate	Ratispone.
Ludenburg	Oxford	Pisarum	
Buda	Mechlin	Trent	
Gascovis	Juliacum	Salizburgh	
	Berga	Ingolstade.	
	Gaunt, some say Vilna		
	Brandenburg		
	Austusta		
	Vindelicorum		
	Constane		
	Derthona		
	Faventia		

CHAP. X.

Of the Terms of Art which ought to be well understood by every Student in this Art.

I. *Application* of Planets are considered three ways, the first is when a Planet swift in motion applies to a Planet that is more slow, as ☿ in 15 d. of ♊, and ♂ in 20 d. here ☿ applies to a ☌ of ♂, they being both direct in motion, and is called a direct application. Secondly, when they are both Retrograde, as ☿ in 15 d. ♊ and ♂ in 14 d. here ☿ being the lighter Planet meets with the Body of ♂ by Retrogradation, this is an ill application. Thirdly, when one Planet is direct in motion, and the other Retrograde, as suppose ☿ Retrograde in 15 d. of ♊ and ♄ direct in 12 degrees of the same Sign; here ☿ being a light Planet applies to the ☌ of ♄ by his Retrograde motion. This is no good application; but yet not so bad as the second. By which you may observe, a superiour Planet (as ♄, ♃ or ♂) cannot apply to an inferiour (☉, ♀, ☿, ☽) except he moves contrary to the succession of the Signs, which is called a Retrograde motion.

II. *Retrograde*, understand is for a Planet to move backwards in the Zodiac, (*i.e.*) out of ♉ into ♈, &c. and is noted in the *Ephemeris* thus R.

III. *Separation*, is when two planets have lately been in Aspect or ☌ together, and are separated or going from it, as suppose the ☉ in 10 d. of ♈, and the ☽ in 15 d. here the ☽ is separated from a partile ☌ of ☉, yet she is said to be in ☌ platick; because she is still within the moiety of their Orbs; what their Orbs are, is already shewn.

IV. *Reception* of Planets are, when they are in each others dignities; whether House, Exaltation, Triplicity, Term, or Face, as the ☉ in ♋, and the ☽ in ♌, here they are in reception by House.

V. *Translation* of a Planet is thus, when a light Planet separates from a ponderous Planet, and immediately applies to another superior Planet; then this is said to be a Translation of light and nature, as ☿ a light Planet being in 15 d. ♊ and ♄ in 12 d. and ♃ in 20 d. of the same Sign, here ☿ separates from the Body of ♄ and applies to a ☌ of ♃, and so Translates the light and nature of ♄ to ♃.

VI. *Prohibition* is only thus, when one Planet is applying to the ☌ or Aspect of another, and before they come to it another Planet meets with the ☌ or Aspect of the former, and so prohibits it; so ♄ in 12 d. ♊, and ♃ in 8 d. and ☿ in 3 d. of that Sign, here ♃ is going to ☌ d of ♄, but ☿ being a lighter Planet, and swifter in motion; meets with the ☌ of ♄ first, and so prohibits ♃.

VII. *Frustration* is to be understood thus, when a light Planet applies to the Aspect of another more ponderous, and before he is come to that Aspect, the ponderous Planet meets with the Body or Aspect of some other, as suppose ♄ were in 15 degrees of ♊, and ♃ in 14 d. of ♌, and ♂ in 10 d. of ♌, here ♂ applies to ☌ of ♃, but before he comes to it, ♃ meets with a ✶ of ♄ first, and so frustrates ♂.

VIII. *Refranation* is only thus, one Planet applies to the Body or Aspect of an other, and before he comes to that Aspect, he becomes Retrograde; as suppose ♃ in 14 d. ♌ and ♂ in 10 d. ♌, here ♂ applies to a ☌ of ♃, and before he comes to 14 d. ♌, he becomes Retrograde, and so refrains by his Retrograde motion to meet with ♃ that continues still direct.

IX. *Combustion*, a Planet is said to be Combust when he is not 8 d. 30 m. distant, either before, or after, from the Body of the *Sun*, and note that that Planet is more afflicted by Combustion to whom the Sun applies by his Body; than that Planet from whom he is separated, as suppose ☿ be in 15 d. ♊ and the ☉ in 20 d. and ♃ in 25 d. ♊, here ☿ and ♃ are comburred by the ☉, and ♃ receives the greatest affliction because the ☉ applies unto his Body but separates from ☿.

X. *Peregrination*, a planet is accounted Peregrine, when he is posited in a Sign, wherein he hath no essential dignities at all; neither House, Exaltation, Triplicity, Term, or Face; as ♄ in the 6, 10, or 26 degrees of ♈, is there said to be a stranger, or Peregrine, having no dignities there, understand the like of others.

XI. *Void of Course* is only thus, one Planet separates from the Body or Aspect of another, and applies to no other Planet, whilst he is in that Sign.

XII. *Cazimi* is, when a Planet is in the heart of the ☉ which is, when he is within 16 minutes of his Body, in respect of Longitude and Latitude.

XIII. *Sun Beams*, a Planet is accounted as under the Beams of the ☉ till he is separated (or elongated) 17 d. from his Body.

XIV. *Besieging*, a Planet is besieged when he is between the Bodies of ♄ and ♂, so ♃ in 10 d. of ♊, ♄ in 4 d. and ♂ in 14 d, here ♃ is besieged of ♄ and ♂.

XV. *Oriental*, is when a Planet riseth before the ☉, or may be seen before Sun-rising.

XVI. *Occidental*, is when a Planet sets after the ☉, or may be seen after ☉ set.

XVII. *Increasing in Light*, is when a Planet is departing from the ☉, or the ☉ from him; so the ☽ at her greatest distance from the ☉ appears with the greatest light.

XVIII. *Swift of Course*, a Planet is said to be Swift, when he moves more than his mean motion, in 24 hours; and he is accounted slow of Course if he moves less than his mean motion in the same time.

XIX. The *Longitude* of a Star or Planet, is the degree of the Ecliptick he is in, being numbered from the first point of *Aries*.

XX. *Latitude* of a Planet or Star, is the distance either North or South from the Ecliptick.

XXI. Declination of a Planet is his distance North or South from the Equator, or Equinoctial.

XXII. Right Ascension is the number of degrees and minutes of the Equinoctial (accounted from the beginning of *Aries*) which cometh to the Meridian with the Sun, Moon, Star, or any portion of the Ecliptick.

XXIII. Oblique Ascension, is the degree of the Equinoctial that comes to or riseth with the degree of Longitude of any Star in the Horizon: or it is the degree of the Equinoctial that comes to the Horizon with any Star or Planet in an Oblique Sphere.

XXIV. Oblique Descension, is the degree of the Equinoctial that sets in the Horizon, with the degree of Longitude of any Star or Planet, in an Oblique Sphere, *viz.* the Equator makes an Oblique Angle with the Horizon.

XXV. Ascentional Difference, is the difference between the rlght and oblique Ascention of any Planet or Star reckoned in the Equator.

XXVI. By the Pole of Position, must be understood the Elevation of the Pole of the World above the Circle of Position of any Star or Planet.

XXVII. Circles of Position, are certain Horizons (upon which a Star or Planet doth rise) passing by both the intersections of the Horizon with the Meridian, and are as well above the earth as underneath; so there may be divers Circles of Position imagined or supposed to be between the Horizon and Meridian of any place, upon some one of which the Stars and Planets continually rise and set, and in the Art of Directions, the Poles Elevation must be found above the Cirole of Position of any Star or Planet you are to direct, before you can proceed; and how to perform this, an easie and familiar way (by the help of a Cannon of Artificial Signes and Tangents) shall be shewed in the third part of this Book.

CHAP. XI.

How to add and Subtract Astronomical Fractions, and Project the Part of Fortune; Take these familiar and easie Examples, which will sufficiently illustrate the matter to any Ingenious Tyro, *viz.*

I. Admit I would add together these signs, degrees, minutes, and seconds in the Margent, I proceed thus.

fig.	deg.	m.	sec.
10.	17.	32.	17.
02.	11.	05.	19.
04.	12.	09.	17.
17.	10.	46.	53.

First, add the units of the seconds together, and that makes 23. Set down the 3. and carry the two 10ths. to the 10ths of the second, and they make 5. set that down also, and it makes 53 seconds.

Secondly, add the units of the minutes together, and they make 16. set down 6. right under, and carry your 10. to the three 10ths. and that makes 4, which is 46. I place under the minutes as you see.

Thirdly, add the unit of the degrees together, and that makes 10. which I carry to the 10ths, and set down a Cipher 1 tenth added to the other 3. makes 4 tenths. I set down 1, and carry 3 tenths or 30 d. to the signs, (because 30d. makes a sign) then I proceed and say 1 and 4 is 5 and 2 is 7, which I set right under the unites of the signs; to which I add the 1 tenth of the signs under the tenths place, and it makes 17 signs, so the total is 17 signs, 10 degrees, 46 minutes, and 53 seconds; and because 17 signs is more than the Circle, I cast away 12, and there rests 5 signs, 10 degrees, 46 minutes, 53 seconds, *Et sic in aliis.*

II. *An Example of Subtraction.*

	Sig.	deg.	mi.	sec.
Let there be	7.	10.	42.	06.
Out of which subtract	2.	22.	17.	25.
There Remains	4.	18.	24.	41.

I begin with the 25 seconds, and say 25 from 6. I cannot; but 25 from 66 rests 41 seconds, which I set down right under; then I proceed to the minutes, and say 17 m. and then 1 that I borrowed is 18, from 42 rests 24 m. which I also set down right under the minutes; then to the degrees; 22 d. from 10 I cannot, but borrow 1 from the Signs that is 30 and say 22 from 40 rest 18 d. which I set down right under the degrees; then to the signs; 1 that I borrowed and 2 is 3 from 7 signs, and there remains 4 signs, which I also set down, and there rematns 4 signs, 18 degrees, 24 minutes, 41 seconds. After this manner work in any other summs, for without the young Artist have so much Arithmetical skill, he cannot erect a Scheme either by a Table of Houses, or by the Table of Right and Oblique Ascension of *Regiomontanus*.

III. *How to Compute the part of Fortune or the Lunar Horoscope*

The Rule.

♈	0
♉	1
♊	2
♋	3
♌	4
♍	5
♎	6
♏	7
♐	8
♑	9
♒	10
♓	11

1. Account the Signs as they are numbered in the margent, as from the beginning of ♈ to the beginning of ♉, one whole Sign from the beginning of ♉ to the beginning of ♊, 2 whole signs &c. and by this Rule from the beginning of ♓, to the beginning of ♈ will be 12 whole Signs.

2. Substract the Sign, degree and minute of the Suns place in your purposed Scheme, & from the sign degree, and minute, of the Moons place, by adding 12 Signs, if otherwise, subtraction cannot be made.

3. To the Remainder add the sign, degree and minute of the Ascendant of your figure, (numbering the signs as in the Table) and that sum so added shall be the place of *Sors* or the part of fortune desired.

4. Or if you substract the Longitude of the Moon from the Longitude (or place) of the Sun, in Signs, degrees and minutes, the remainder will be the complement of those signs, degrees, and minutes, of distance obtained by the second hereof, to the whole Circle or twelve Signs, these subducted out of the Ascendant leaves the true place of the Part of Fortune as before, which will be more obvious to a mean capacity, being exemplified thus,

I. Suppose the place of the Moon in some persons Geniture were ♍, or five whole signs 14 degrees 54 minutes, and the Suns place in ♏ or 7 signs, 5 degrees, 20 minutes, the Ascendant of the figure being ♒ or 10 whole signs, 10 degrees and 10 minutes, by the aforesaid precepts, I operate thus, first the old way and then otherwise, *viz.*

I. From the aforesaid place of the ☽ and 12 Signs added, *viz.* I subduct the Longitude of the ☉.

And there remains the complement of the Circle of the distanoe of the Luminaries. To which I add the Ascendant of the Figure. The sum is 20. 19. 44. from whence abate 12 Signs, and the remainder is the true place of the Part of Fortune. That is 19d. 44. in the Sign ♐.

Sig.	deg.	min.
17.	14.	54.
07.	05.	20.
10.	09.	34.
10.	10.	10.
20.	19.	44.
8.	19.	44.

II. Otherwise thus by the fourth precept.

From the place of the ☉ I substract the place of the ☽. Remains the Complement of the former distance to twelve signs (or the true distance of the Luminaries) whioh deducted out of the Ascendant. Leaves the place of ⊕ as before.

Sig.	deg.	min.
07.	05.	20.
05.	14.	54.
1.	30.	26.
10.	10.	10.
8.	10.	44.

III. Whence note, that so farr as the as the ☉ is distant from the Moon in signs, degrees, and minutes, so far distant is the true place of the ⊕ from the point Ascending, which may serve as a Rule to prove the truth of the work, and is performed thus; having found out the Place of the ⊕, substract that from the Ascendant, and the remainder is the Luminaries distance, as in the last example. But for a further confirmation of the work observe that the ⊕ be taken upon a new Moon, it falls in the Ascendant, if upon the first quarter in the fourth house, if at the Full Moon in the 7th; and lastly, if upon the last quarter in the tenth house, hence after the Change or New Moon till the first quarter, you may easily estimate where the part of Fortune should fall, *viz.* between the Ascendant and fourth house, from the first quarter to the full, between the fourth and seventh house, *&c.* which needs no farther Illustration.

IV. The use that may be made of it is briefly thus, if the ⊕ in any Figure be placed in a good house, or quarter of the Heavens, and well beheld bya fortunate Planet or Planets then the Estate or Condition of the Native or querent, should be the more considerable, he is well provided and stands firm, otherwise judge the contrary.

CHAP. XII.

How to understand an Ephemeris, *as also to erect (or set)
a Scheme of the Heavens by the Tables of the Houses, for any Latitude, &c.*

SECT. 1.

Of the use of an Ephemeris.

It will be needless to make any large explanation hereof, since every Author that publishes Ephemerides performs that work sufficiently, But for the sake of such persons as only peruse a single *Ephemeris*, (which they may and do renew annually) yet perhaps ignorant of their use; I have inserted these directions for their Information.

I. An *Ephemeris* is nothing else but a Dyary or day book, containing the daily motion of the Luminaries, and the rest of the Planets, with the Retrocession of the Dragons head, (or North Node of the Moon) throughout the whole year, calculated to the Noontide of every day in each month.

II. The left hand page contains 10 Columns, the first the days of the month; the second, the days of the week; the third Column contains the motion of ♄; the fourth the motion of ♃; the fifth of ♂; the sixth of the ☉; the seventh of ♀; the eighth of ☿; and the ninth of the ☽; the last column you have usually the ☊, the ☋ is always the opposite sign and degree, to the Dragon's Head ☊.

But in some Ephemerides, you shall find the ☉ placed in the third Column, and the ☽ in the fourth, and so on; which difference may soon be understood by any young Artist that knows the their places the former way.

III. The Latitudes of the Planets you will find noted by these Letters M.S.D.A. which are to be understood thus, M.A. shews the Planet hath Meridional or South Latitude Ascending; but if you find the Latitude noted with S.A. that signifies the Planet hath North, or Sepentrional Latitude Ascending. So that A denotes Latitude Ascending and D Descending, M South, and, S. North.

IV. And at the foot of every page you shall find the Planets Latitude for every tenth day set just under every respective column belonging to each planet. But the Moons latitude is usually joyned in a Column next to the Column of her Longitude, and in some Ephemerides the Latitude of each Planet also. Note, that the Letter R. signifies Retrograde, D. Direct.

V. But in the right hand page of an Ephemeris you have usually 8 Columns (or sometimes 9) the first is the days of the month, and the other six Columns are the Moons Aspect to the Planets; And in the last great Column you shall find the Planets mutual Aspects amongst themselves, and are so noted at top of each Column, with Figures joyned to every Aspect, to signifie the time of the day or night those Aspects happen; always observing that you must begin the day at noon, for so all Astronomers account, and begin and end their day. The very Titles of each page are almost sufficient direction to any person that doth but understand the Characters of the Signs and Planets, and therefore I shall waive all farther discourse of this particular.

SECT. II.

How to set a Scheme by the Tables which you have frequently adjoyned to an Ephemeris.

I. Seek the place of the ☉ in your Ephemeris for the time proposed; and having the ☉ place, if the odd minutes be above 30, add 1 degree more to his place; if less then 30 minutes neglect them, and enter the Tables of Houses with the whole degrees of the ☉ place in the Column of the tenth house, and right against it, in the first great Column to your left hand you shall find certain hours and minutes (and sometimes seconds) to be added to the hours and minutes afternoon of your given time, and if those numbers so added exceed 24 hours, cast away 24, and seek the remainder in tbe first great Column, intituled, Time from Noon, and just against that number in a right line you shall find the signs and degrees to be placed upon the Cusps of 6 of the houses, &c. (viz.) the 10th. 11th. 12. 1st. 2d. and 3d. And upon the Cusps of the other six houses are to be placed their opposite signs and degrees. As the brief Synopsis directs, viz.

	Houses		Opposites.		Signes		Opposites	
	10				4		♈		♎
	11				5		♉		♏
	12				6		♊		♐
	1				7		♋		♑
	2				8		♌		♒
	3				9		♍		♓

Thus you see that the 10th house is opposite to the 4th, the 11th to the 5th, the 12. to the 6th, &c. The first six signs are Opposite to the latter six, as ♈ to ♎, ♉ to ♏, ♊ to ♐ &c.

II. Having drawn your Figure in form of the following Example, and found the several signs and degrees of the cusps thereof (for those lines that divide the several Houses are called Cusps) you are in the next place to take the Planets places out of your Ephemeris, and insert them in the signs of figure respectively; as also the ☊ and ☋ (which are always opposite) and likewise the part of Fortune in his proper place (having found it as before directed.

III. But since the Planets places are calculated and set down in the Ephemeris, for every day at noon; if the time given be not just at Noon their places will require a Reduction to the hour of the day given; which to perform you must first gain the Planets Diurnal motion, by substracting their places, the Noon before from the Noon after your time given, and then say by the Golden Rule, If 24 hours gives so many degrees and minutes for the Planets Diurnal motion, what shall the hours of your time from Noon give, and so if you multiply and divide, the Quotient will be the result to be added to the Planets places the Noon before.

IV. But there needs none of this exactness in a Horary question, for a mentall reduction of the Planets places will be sufticient, in any ordinary matterot this kind, for it is but allowing about a degree in the Moons place for every 2 hours afternoon, and 5 minutes for every 2 hours in the Suns place, and the rest accordingly; considering their Diurnal motions, or whether they are swift or slow, as you may easily discover by considering their places in the Ephemeris, but to make all plain I shall present the Reader with this forgoing Example.

Let it be required to set a Figure by the Tables of Houses, for the 18th day of October, 1667. at two hours afternoon.

V. I look into the Ephemeris and find the Suns place to be in 5d. 0m. of ♏. In the next place I repair to the Table of Houses, and seek Sol in *Scorpio* at top, and having found it, I guide my eye down in the Column (which is always noted at top 10th House (or Dom X) and figured thus, 1. 2, 3, 4, &c.) till I come to the degree of the Suns place at 5. and right against 5 I find in the first great column (entituled, Time from Noon) 14h 10m, 48 seconds, to which I add my two hours, P. M. or *Post Meridian*, and that makes 16h. 10m. 48 seconds, which I seek in the said great column, and find it not exactly, but accept of the next less, viz. 16h. 8m. against which under the 2 column that belongs to the 10 house I find 4 and ♐ at top; for the Cusp of the 10 house, and for the Cusp of the 11 house 17 degrees 38 minutes of ♐ in the Column of the 12 house I find ♑ 3 deg. 25 m. and the rest of the Oriental houses, viz. 1, 2, and 3, as in the foregoing Figure; and having the 6 Oriental houses, I place the opposite signs and degrees upon the opposite houses as before directed. *The Figure follows.*

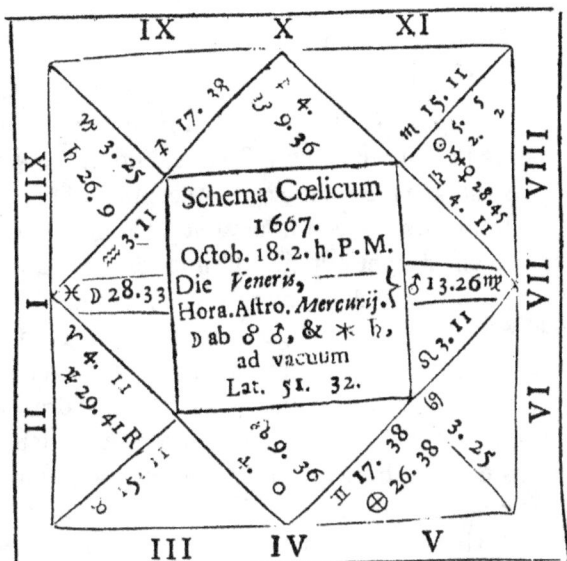

VI. After the Cusps of the Houses are filled with the Signs as as before directed, then you are to place the Planets in their proper places as you see them in the Figure, which you may perform thus, *viz*. the 18 day of *October*, 1667. just at noon, I find the Planets places thus in the *Ephemeris*.

October 18 at Noon		The Planets Diurnal	
deg. min.		deg. min.	
♄ 26. 9 ♑	Now if I substract their	♄ 0. 3	
♃ 29 42 ♈ R	places the 18 day at	♃ 0. 7 R	
♂ 13 23 ♍	noon, from their places	♂ 0.38	
☉ 5 0 ♏	the 19 day, I shall gain	☉ 1.0	
♀ 28 40 ♎	their Diurnal motion,	♀ 1. 15	
☿ 1 56 ♏	which will be thus, *viz*.	☿ 1.36	
☽ 27 31 ♓		☽ 12.27	
☊ 9 36 ♊		☊ 0.3 R	

VII. Having proceeded thus far, you may reduce their places to the hour of the day given, (*viz*. 2 hours afternoon) by the rule of proportion; Reasoning thus, if 24 hours of time gives (in any Planet) so many degrees or minutes of motion, what shall your proposed time after Noon give? but this exactness needs not in Questlons as I hinted before; a mental Reduction may serve very well; but I shall in the third part hereof show how to reduce their places exactly by the Logistical Logarithms, as also shew how to Aequate the Cusps of the houses with many useful conclusions of the same nature. In the Close of this Chap. I have also inserted a Table which shews you the hourly mot ion of the Planets by bare inspection, entring with the Diurnal motion of a Planet in its proper Column twice it need be) thus it a Planet moves 36m in 24 h. his hourly motion is 1m. 30 seconds; or if the ☽ moves 14 degrees in 24 hours, her hourly motion by the Table is 35m. this is so plain it needs no farther explanation, and will readily serve for the Reduction of the Planets. Note that G. signifies degrees, M. Minutes, and S, Seconds.

VIII. If your Planet be more degrees in any Sign then is upon the Cusp of the House, you are to set him farther into the house over the Cusp, but if less, place him without the house; as ♄ being 26 deg. 9m. in ♑, and but 3 degrees 25 minutes upon the Cusp of the 12th, I therefore place him over the Cusp in the house, and the ☉ being 5 deg. 5m of ♏ and 15 of ♏ upon the Cusp of the 9th. I therefore place him out of the house. in the 8th, as you may see in the figure; and thereby you may learn truly to place the Planets in any Scheme.

Clavis Astrologiae Elimata, The Key to Astrology New Filed

IX. If you desire to set the same Figure by the Schemes in this Book which are drawn to every other degree of the *Mid-heaven* or Tenth house, (and may be of good use in the Horary Questions;) Proceed thus, suppose the aforesaid Example, *October* the 18, 1667, 2 hours after noon.

First, turn to the Tables entituled *A Table of the Right Ascension of the Sun in time*; seek *October* at top amongst the months, and the day (18) in the first Column to the left hand, and in the Angle of meeting right under the month of *October* find 14 hours 12 minutes (which is the right Ascension of the Sun that day in time) unto which I add two hours afternoon, and it amounts to sixteen hours twelve minutes, which I seek at top amongst the Schemes (which are noted to every seven or eight minutes of time) or the nearest less which I find to be sixteen hours eight minutes, in which Scheme I find ♐ 4 deg. upon the Cusp of the 10 house, and 3 deg ♒ upon the Ascendant, and the rest of the Houses as in the precedent figure, now if my two numbers had exceeded 24 h. I must have cast away 24 h. and entred the Schemes with the remainder, this is exceeding easie and needs no farther Explanation, thus having your *Figure* before you, you may (if you please) draw another by it on a Paper, and so place in the Planets out of the *Ephemeris* as before directed, or having the Planets places in your mind, and the Scheme for your time before you 'tis easie to frame a Judgment upon any horary question without setting the Scheme it self, which I leave to the pleasure of the Practitioner, besides there are many other good uses to be made of these Schemes ready formed which I may touch upon in some other place of this book, But I proceed.

A general Table of the hourly motion of the Planets, useful in Reduction of their Places to any hour of the day.

Diurn, Mot. G M S	One hours motion. G M S M S T S T F	Diurn. Mot. G M S	One hours motion. G M S M S T S T F	Diurn. Mot. G M S	One hours motion. G M S M S T S T F
1	0 2 30	22	0 55 0	43	1 47 30
2	0 5 0	23	0 57 30	44	1 50 0
3	0 7 30	24	1 0 0	45	1 52 30
4	0 10 0	25	1 2 30	46	1 55 0
5	0 12 30	26	1 5 0	47	1 57 30
6	0 15 0	27	1 7 30	48	2 0 0
7	0 17 30	28	1 10 0	49	2 2 30
8	0 20 0	29	1 12 0	50	2 5 0
9	0 22 30	30	1 15 0	51	2 7 30
10	0 25 0	31	1 17 30	52	2 10 0
11	0 27 30	32	1 20 0	53	2 12 30
12	0 30 0	33	1 22 30	54	2 15 0
13	0 32 30	34	1 25 0	55	2 17 30
14	0 35 0	35	1 27 30	56	2 20 0
15	0 37 30	36	1 30 0	57	2 22 30
16	0 40 0	37	1 32 30	58	2 25 0
17	0 42 30	38	1 35 0	59	2 27 30
18	0 45 0	39	1 37 30	60	2 30 0
19	0 47 30	40	1 40 0	61	2 32 30
20	0 50 0	41	1 42 30	62	2 35 0
21	0 52 30	42	1 45 0	63	2 37 30

CHAP. XIII.

Of the twelve houses of Heaven, and their Astrological Signification

I. Having in the last Chapter shewed how to erect a *Scheme* of the Heavens, by a Table of Houses fitted or Calculated for the Latitude of the place desired, I am now to declare their *Astrological Significations*, but first observe how the Heavens are suppceed to be divided in setting of Schemes.

II. The whole *Sphere* or *Globe* of Heaven is first divided into four equal parts by two great Circles, *viz.* the Horizon and the Meridian, and every one of those quarters are subdivided into three other parts by great Circles which pass by the intersection of the Horizon and Meridian, called Circles of Position, and thus the Heavens are divided into twelve equal parts in the Equinoctial by those Circles, which also divide the Ecliptick unequally, and are, the very cusps of the houses themselves which may be very well represented to the fancy by the *Celestial Globe*, which is called the *Rational Way of Regiomontanus*; there be other divisions of the Heavens which I shall take occasion to shew in the third part hereof, and therefore now proceed to the various *astrological* signification of the Heavens being thus divided, and by *Astrologers* called *Houses* or *Mansions*, with the reasons thereof.

III. The first house or East Angle called the Ascendant in Questions, because the ☉ Ascends there, but *Horoscope in Nativities* in respect of the house of Birth, it signifies the Life, Complection, Disposition, Will, Manners, and Understanding of the Native or Querent; and finally all enterprizes, it signifies the head and face of man, the Consignificators of this house are, ♈ and ♄, for as this is the first house, so ♈ is the first Sign, and ♄ the first Planet, the same method must be understood in all the rest of the houses, in Eclipses and great Conjunctions, or in Solar Ingresses, the Ascendant signifies the common people, or general state of the Kingdom or place where tbe Scheme was set, if the Ascendant be vitiated the native or querent is marked in the face by some Mole or Scar, it is a Masculine house, and of colours signifies White.

IV. The second House signifies Riches, gain and traffick: gold, silver, and all moveable goods without life; it also denotes loss and gain by traffick, it is a house succedent as following the East Angle or Ascendant. It signifies a mans Assistant, in private Duels the Querents second, in Eclipses or great Conjunctions, the Wealth or Poverty of the Nation or Kingdom in general, therein is included the subjects or common people, so in the ☉ ingress into ♈ it signifies the Countries or Commonwealths Magazine or Ammunition, it also represents their Allies and Supports, or whatsoever is assistant to them; it is a Feminine house and of colours signifies green.

V. The third house signifies brethren, sisters, kindred small voyages, short journies, interpretation of dreams, Rumors, &c. advice given, it is a Cadent house. And also signifies Epistles written, or Letters, Messengers, &c. It is Masculine, and of colours denotes yellow or Sorrel colour.

VI. The fourth house signifies fathers, houses, lands, immovable goods, orchards, tillage, minerals, hidden treasures, all things under the earth, prisons and obscure desolate places, the grave, and good report after this life, and finally the period of all things undertaken; 'tis called the North Angle. It also signifies Towns, Cities or Castles, besieged or not besieged, all Ancient Houses, Gardens, Orchards, Pastures, Fields, with the nature and quality thereof. The Lord of the fourth house signties the Governour of a Town, the Cusp of the House the Town or Castle, 'tis Feminine, and of colours it signifies Red, because *Cancer* and *Sol* are consignificators thereof.

VII. The fifth house signifies Children, all younger kindred, joy, pleasure, gifts, delights and bravery, the riches of the father, all profit of the fourth house, playing, gameing, drinking and revelling, *&c.* and is a succedent house.

It also signifies the State or condition of Women with Child, and the Sex, it denotes Messengers or Agents for Republick Embassadours, the Ammunition or Provision of a Town besieged, 'tis a Masculine house ♀ and ♋ consignificators, and of Colours it represents black and white or Hony colour.

VIII. The sixth House signifies Servants, Sickness, all Cattle that are unfit for Labour, as Sheep, Dogs, Hogs, Fowls, Wild beasts, Hunters, Goalers, Prisons, false Accusations, &c. it is a Cadent house. It also signifies uncles, and Ants, or the Fathers Brothers and Sisters, Farmers, Tenants, Warriners, Shepherds and Hogherds, all such as appertain to Cattle, or deal in Birds; 'tis a Feminine house, and of colours signifies black.

IX. The seventh house signifies marriage, wives, lawsuits, contention, controversies and quarrels, common persons; and all the men we deal with, &c. This is called the West Angle. In Law suits it signifies the Defendant, in War the Enemy, or persons that make opposition; also Thieves and Thefts, in a figure of Decumbiture the Doctor, in Astrology the Artist, in the Scheme of the Suns Ingress into *Aries*, it signifies the publick enemies of the place, and shews whether there may succeed peace or war; it is a house Masculine, and of colours signifies dark, sad colour or black.

X. The eighth house signifies death, sadness, riches not thought of, as legacies, dowries, the estate of those we deal publickly withal, all known or publick enemies; and all the benefit of the seventh house, and is a succedent house. In Law Suits it signifies the Defendants Estate, as also his Assistants, in Duels the Adversaries second; its a Feminine House, and of colours signifies green and black.

XI. The ninth house signifies religion, pilgrimage, dreams, long journeys or voyages, ceremonies, sacrifices, faith, Clergy-men, Navigations, Arts and Sciences, the Law, the kindred of the wife, &c. it is termed a Cadent or falling house. Itt also signifies Learning in general, and all Church-livings, 'tis a Masculine house, and of colours represents green and white.

XII. The tenth house signifies honour, dignities, preferment, offices, trade or calling, Magistrates, Kings, Princes, Governours, Renown, Advancement, Captains and conductors in War, all help, aid or succor, the mother; and all the benefits of the ninth house, the father of the wife or husband, as being the fourth from the seventh, 'tis the South Angle or Mid-heaven. It denotes all persons in power, also Lawyers, but more particularly Kingdoms and Countries, whether Dukedoms, or Empires; it's Feminine, and of colours signifies red and white.

XIII. The eleventh house signifies friends and acquaintance, hope, the things we desire, companions, the counsel of friends, their falseness or fidelity, all the profit of the tenth, &c. it is a succedent house. It also signifies both praise and dispraise of any person, as to Kings this house signifies their Associates, Councellours, Allies, their Treasure, Ammunition, Soldiery, &c. It represents Assistants to any person in power; 'tis a Masculine house, and of colours signifies yellow.

XIV. The twelfth house signifies secret or private enemies, prisons, captivity, bondage, evil spirits, torments, treasons, slavery, villany, all great Cattle fit for labour, as Oxen, Horses, &c. this is a Cadent falling house. It signifies sorrow and tribulation of all sorts; 'tis a Feminine house, and, of colours signifies Green.

The Quarters of Heaven signified by the Twelve houses are as folllloweth, viz.

The First House is East	The Seventh House is West
The Second House is N E by E	The Eighth House is S W by S
The Third House is N N E	The Ninth House is S S W
The Fourth House is North	The Tenth House is South
The Fifth House is N W by N	The Eleventh House is S E by S
The Sixth House is W N W	The Twelfth House is E S E

These significations are neatly comprized by a Modern Author, in the following Verses.

1	2	3	4	5	6
Vita	Lucrum,	Fratres,	Genitor,	Nati,	Valitudo
7	8	9	10	11	12
Uxor,	More,	Pietas,	Regnum,	Benefactaq,	Carcer.

First House shews life, the second wealth doth give;
 The third how brethren, fourth how Parents live:
Issue the fifth, the sixth diseases bring;
 The seventh wedlock, and the eighth death's sting;
The ninth Religion, the tenth honour shews;
 Friendship th' eleventh, and the twelfth our woes!

CHAP. XIV.

Why the Heavens are divided into twelve Parts, called Houses, and no more or less.

Morinus, *a great Philosopher, Physician, and Astrologer, (as well as a general Scholar) doth in his Cabal of the 12 houses very Learnedly shew the reason of the division of the 12 houses, as also why the several houses should have the aforesaid significations, which although others have shewed some reasons or the same before, yet were they thought by this learned person invalid, because that reason which was produed to defend one house, the very same really destroyed all the rest, and gave occasion to the Antagonists of this most noble Science to deride, laugh and hiss at the significations of the twelve hosues, and consedquently at the whole Art; Now because this may be some satisfaction to the young Artist, I shall in this place briefly repeat those Reasons of his, which are both Learned and Rational, and will yeild not a little contentment (I presume) both to Artists and others, in this very matter, whereon the whole Science of Astrology hath its foundation and principally depends.*

I. That the heavens are divided into four Cardinal points as before hinted at, is no way feigned, but natural and agreeable to sence, reason, and demonstration, as without doubt none will deny that understands any thing of the Globe or Circles of the Sphear, for the Heavens are divided into four equal divisions by the Horizon and Meridian.

II. That every one of those parts are divided into two other parts in heaven of the same nature, *viz.* those with whom it makes an Equilater Triangle in the Equinoxial (which is the principle Circle of the worlds first motion) or which it beholds by a Partile *Trine* in the Aequator. The *Trine* aspect is demonstrated by the learned Sir *Christopher Heydon*, to be an Aspect of perfect love: As being in exact proportion with one of the three perfect Concords or Harmonies in Musick, *viz.* the *Diapente*, and two Stars so beholding one another, do proportionably use, ocoupy or take up the whole center of the World in the same moinent, and are said to Aspect each other by a Partile *Trine*; and therein the perfection of the first *Trine* (*viz.* the Eternal Trinity of Infinite love) is so strong and lively shewn by a similitude of nature, that it is called a perfect Aspect of friendship.

III. Hence these parts of the Aequator that behold one another by a partile *Trine* Aspect, do make up a triplicity of the same generical nature, *viz.* the East Angle beholds the 9th and 5th house; the South Angle the 6th and 2d; the West Angle the 3d and 11th; and the North Angle beholds the 12th and 8th house, all by a Partile *Trine* Aspect in the Aequator, as shall immedlately be farther explained.

IV. Every one of the former Cardinal points do challenge to it self a Triplicity of its own nature, and by these 4 triplicities, heaven is divided into 12 parts, called houses: and this division is accounted most absolute, and truly perfect, as containing 2 *Sextiles*, 2 *Squares*, 2 *Trines*, and also the Oppositions which are all the Coelestial Aspects, from whence (not omitting the ☌) all variations to the general Influences happen, and those Aspects do perfectly agree with all the parts of the number 12, which are, 1, 2, 3, 4, 5, 6, where 1 is referred to the ☌, 2 (the 6th part of 12) to the *Sextile* Aspect, 3 (the 4th part thereof) to the *Quartile*, 4 (the 3d part thereof) to the *Trine*, and 6 (the middle part of one half) to the ☍ and as in the Circle there are no more Aspects considerable, so in the Number 12 no more parts, for all things were made by God in Number, Weight and Measure. Therefore the division of the 12 houses, ought not to be accounted feigned or as wanting a natural foundation.

CHAP. XV.

Why the twelve Houses should have such significations as are usually attributed unto them by Astrologers.

The Premises being considered and well weighed in the ballance of reason; it makes way for a second consideration, that the life of man consists of 4 parts or ages, *viz.* Childhood, Youth, Manhood, and Old Age; and that in man are 4 different things observable, unto which all the other be reduced, as it were to their first beginnings, (*viz.* Life, Action, Marriage and Passion, and these agree with the Rise or Beginning, Vigour, Declination, and End or death; as these 4 are insinuated generally to agree with all the effects of nature, for man is said to rise into the world, when he first receives life in the world; and to be strong in action, when he acteth or reduceth his strength and vigour into action, and to decline as soon as a plentiful dissipation of this innate heat, and radical moisture beginneth, as at Marriage; and from Manhood (the best time of Marriage) he declineth to old age, and at length dies, when he sustains the last passion of his life; therefore Mans life, Action, Marriage and Passion, belongs to the same Coelestial principles as doth the Birth, Vigour, Declination, and Death of all other things in the World, *viz.* life to the *East Angle* or Ascendant, action to the Mid-heaven, Marriage to the *West Angle*, and Passion to the *Angle* of the *Earth*.

Whence arise 4 Triplicities of the same Generical Nature, and 12 houses as before mentioned.

The first Triplicity is of the *East Angle* (or first house attributed to Childhood) called the Triplicity of life, and being; the other houses of the Triplicity are the 9th and 5th and both behold the first, by a Partile Trine Aspect in the Equator, where is made this rational division of the houses.

Man liveth in a threefold respect; in *himself*, in God, and in his *posterity*; but the first is given man; *viz.* Life, that he might worship God and beget his own likeness, which is said to be the Compleat intention in the production of man.

I. Now as touching the life of man in its self, (because it is the first of all other things in the order of Nature, and without it the rest could not be) it justly challenged the principal house of this Triplicity, *viz.* The East Angle.

II. Life is God, (the second in order,) exists in the house of Religion, *viz.* the 9th subsequent to the 1st house in this Triplicity, according to the motion of the Aequator.

III. And lastly, life in the Posterity, bestowed on the house of Children which is the 5th, wherefore this whole Triplicity 1st, 9th, and 5th houses concern life, and are in Trine.

The 2d. is the Triplicity of the Angle of the *Mid-heaven* which is termed the 10th house, and appertaineth unto Youth; this is called the Triplcty of *Action*, and of gain in the World, or worldly goods flowing from thence; because that everything working *Physically*, worketh for some *Physical* good, for as the motion of the Aequator is from the East Angle to the Mid-heaven, so is their Progress made from Childhood unto Youth; and from Being or Life, to Action; the two other houses of this Triplicity are the 6th and 2d.

I. The first (in order of dignity) is *Immaterial*: as are Arts, Magistracy, dignities and honours, unto which a man is Raised; to which may be added Majesty and Power. Therefore is allotted for this the principal House of this Triplicity, *viz.* the Angle of the Midheaven.

II. The second is *Material* and *Animated*, as are subjects, servants, and all other living creatures and is placed in the 6th house according to the motion of the Aequator in this Triplicity.

III. The last is *Material Inanimated*, as are Gold, silver, household stuffe, and even all other immovable goods gotten by our own labour, which are attributed to the second house, under the name of Riches; therefore this whole Triplicity is of action and gain thence arising.

The third is the Triplicity of the *West Angle*, called the 7th house, and belonging to Man-hood, this is called the

Triplicity of Marriage or Love, for as by the motion of the Aequator; the progress is made from the Angle of the *Midheaven*, to the *West Angle*; even so there is a progression from Youth to Manhood, and from famous deeds to Marriages and friendships of men which thence is purchased, the two other houses of this Triplicity are the 3d, and 11th. But a man is joyned to another in a threefold respect.

I. The first Conjunction (in order of dignity) is that of the body which we call Matrimony, and therefore the principle house of this Triplicity, *viz*. the West Angle is thereunto dedicated.

II. The second is that of Blood, which constitutes brethren and kindred; in the 3d house according to the motion of the Aequator in this Triplicity.

III. The last is that of simple benevolence or favour, whence do arise friends, in the 11th house; therefore this whole Triplicity is of Marriage and Love.

The 4th triplicity is of the *Dark Angle* or 4th house, (in the middle of night or bottom of heaven) and the Den or Cave of the Planets, attributed to old Age; and termed the Triplicity of passion, affliction and death, whereunto every man is subject; the 2 other houses of this Triplicity is the 12th and 8th.

I. But the first affliction in order of nature, is a sorrowful expectation of the natural death of his Parents, or rather (to speak Cabalistically) it is the stain of Original Sin which our Parents imprints in us, and through which we are from our very birth made obnoxious to every misery, and finally to death it self; therefore the Parents, and their condition, during the life of the Native, as also death and heritages, left by them to the Native, do possess the principle house of this Triplicity, *viz*. the Angle of the 4th house.

II. The second affliction consists in the hatreds, deceits, machinations, treacherousness and injuries of enemies, especially secret ones; so likewise in prisons, servitude, poverty, and all other miseries a man suffereth in his whole life time, now for that all these are enemies to life; and therefore are they contained under the only considerwtions of an enemy; in the 12th house, which is truly called the valley of miseries, and imnediately follows in this triplicity according to the motion of the Aequator.

III. The last affliction inhabiting the eighth house is death of man himself, which is an end of this temporal, and a beginning of an eternal life; wherefore according to the 2d motion or the motion of the Planets which is from West to East, there is an entrance made out of the eighth into the ninth house, which is the house of life in God; where man is given to understamd, that he is to pass by the second motion of the soul, which is attributed to the mind or reason (as the first or rapt motion is to the body, or sensitive appetite) from a temporary death unto life in God, which is Eternal. Therefore in these Triplicities, that which is first in the order of nature or dignity; possesses always the more noble houses, *viz*. the four *Angles*, that which is second in order, the *succedent Houses according* to the motion of the *Aequator*, that which is last, *Cadent*, according to the motion of the Ecliptick and *Planets*.

Now what man is he that will suppose this division of the 12 Coelestial houses by Triplicities, appearing in this so excellent a Consent, and in such a wonderful order, to be a wife fained or casual? Or whether by chance, such consents are wont to be in things so abstruse and intermixed? Or if altogether Fictitious, whether therefore wanting altogether a natural foundation, which before I plainly proved to be false, and now made that most orderly consent of the Houses themselves manifest.

Therefore is this division Natural, and ordained by great Wisdom, as comprehending (at least Genetically) all worldly things that can possibly be enquire of, or conoerning man, for as much as the knowledge of contraries is the same; and that an affirmative or negative may be sought of anything belonging to any house.

Morinus *is more copious upon this subject, but this being sufficient for my present purpose, I omit the rest, and refer those that would be farther satisfied as to the Rationality of Astrology to the Author himself,* viz. *his Astrologia Gallica.*

CHAP. XVI.

Of divers things to be considered, which conduce much to the better Judging of a Horary Question.

SECT. I.

Of the Significators; viz. *the Querent (he or she) that propounds the Question, as also the Quesited;* viz. *the Person or Matter enquired after, &c.*

I. The Person that propounds the Question (of what degree or quality soever) is always signified by the first House, and his Lord in particular; as suppose in a Question *Pisces* ascend upon the Cusp of the first House, then *Jupiter* is Lord of the Ascendant, and shall be admitted the Significator of the Querent. But the Sign ascending doth chiefly signifie the Corporature, and form or shape of Body; and the Lord of the Ascendant, the *Moon* and Planets in the Ascendant, or any other Planets beholding them, shall denote the Conditions and Qualities of the Querent; but their several significations must be mixed together by the judgment and discretion of the Artist, as hath already been shewn.

II. The Quesited, or matter sought after is known by that House which signifies the thing in Question, and the Lord thereof; as if the Question be what part of the Life will be most fortunate; or concerning an absent party, or the safety of a person at Sea, you must judge by the first House.

III. If concerning the Substance, Riches, Goods or Moneys of any person, or the Wages due; judge from the second House.

IV. If about Journeys, or concerning Brethren, Sisters, or Kindred; judge from the third House, and his Lord, and see how he beholds the Lord of the Ascendant.

V. If concerning a Father, or Treasure hid, or a thing miss-laid, or of Inheritances, Houses, Lands, *&c,* consider the fourth House.

VI. If concerning a Child or Children, or of a Woman with Child, whether Male or Female, time of delivery, safe or dangerous; or of Messengers, Agents, Gameing, Playes; or of Taverns, Alehouses, Recreations, Sports or Pastime; then consider the fifth House.

VII. When about Sickness, the Cause and Cure thereof, of recovery or irrecovery therefrom; of the Unkle or Aunt, of Servants, their Fidelity or Knavery; of small Cattle, if good to deal with them or not; then consider the sixth house.

VIII. If, concerning Law, Controversies or Contentions, Enemies, Partnerships, Fugitives, Thefts, and all matters concerning or relating to Love or Marriage; then regard the seventh House and his Lord, and see how he is disposed.

IX. When concerning the Wives Dowry or Portion, or the Husbands Estate, or of Wills, Deeds, Legacies, *&c.* of the manner or time of Death, or whether Man or Wife shall die first; then consult the eighth House, *&c.*

X. If concerning long Journeys or Voyages, or a Ship at Sea; of Arts or Sciences, Law, Religion, and their Professours, of Dreams or Visions; then have regard to the ninth House, and consider the position of the Lord thereof, his strength or weakness, *&c.*

XI. If concerning Emperours, Kings, Princes, Dukes, Lords, Colonels, *&c.* Magistrates, or of any Preferment or Honour, of the Mother, or any thing relating to her, of a Profession or Trade, of Lodgers, *&c.* then consider the tenth House.

XII. If concerning the Fidelity or Falseness of Friends and Acquaintance, of things hoped for or expected; then take notice of the eleventh House.

XIII. Lastly, when concerning Captivity and Imprisonment, private Enemies, great Cattle, Horse-races, Arrests or private Plottings and Designs; then consult the twelfth House and his Lord.

XIV. So that let the Question be what it will, give the Ascendant and his Lord for the Querent. Then consider the matter in Question and see to what House it properly belongs, (which you may easily do by the foregoing directions) then having pitch'd upon the House that signifies your business, consider the Sign and Lord thereof; see in what Sign and House he is posited, how Dignified or Debilitated; how he beholds the Lord of the Ascendant, whether by good or bad Aspect; consider also what Planet beholds your Significator, who is Friend unto him, or what Planet afflicts him; then consider the House he is Lord of, and from thence you may judge, from such a person your Querent shall receive help or prejudice, if the Planet that beholds your Significator be an Infortune, and Lord of a bad House; then you may assure your self, he signifies mischief to the Querent, from such a kind of person as that Planet represents; joyn the *Moon* as Configurator with the Querent in all questions; and having well considered the several Aspects, Separations and Applications of the Significator, and also of the *Moon*, you may from thence be able rationally to determine wheiher the business enquired after shall be brought to perfection, yea or no; and accordingly moderate your judgment, and thereby informe the Querent, as shall be plainly exemplified in the Second Part.

[*Note that a Planet is said to be a Fortune when he govens good Houses or places of the Figure, and is essentially strong, beholding the Significator of the Person or Estate of the Querent by good Aspect, or applying thereunto; but if Lord of bad Houses, and emit ill rays to the Ascendant or Principal Significator, or posited in abject places of the Scheme look upon such a Planet or Planets as Accidental Infortunes.*]

SECT. II.

By what means are things brought to Perfection, in the business of a Horary Question.
It is observable that things are brought to pass five wayes, viz.

I. When the Planet that denotes the Querent, and that Planet that signifies the thing inquired after, are applying by a ✶ or △ Aspect, or it they are going to a Conjunction: this argues the business shall be effected.

II. When the Significator of the matter inquired after shall apply to the Lord of the Ascendant, and be in his essential Dignities, this signifies the business shall be perfected unexpectedly.

III. If the Significators apply friendly from Houses they delight in, or from Signs they joy in, the business or matter sought after comes to a happy conclusion.

IV. If the Significators do not behold each other, yet if a fortunate Planet collect or translate their beams of light, the matter will be brought to pass.

V. Lastly, when the promising Planets dwell in Houses proper and convenient, though there be no Aspect, the matter may be brought to perfection.

[*By dwelling in Houses understand that it is when the Planet which is significator, is Accidentally posited in the Ascendant, or some other House of promising Signification to the Querent.*]

SECT. III.

To know if your Figure be Radical or Fit to be Judged.

I. Consider if the Lord of the Ascendant and Lord of the hour be both of one Nature, or Triplicity, then you may adventure a Judgment.

II. If few degrees, *viz.* the very beginning or the latter end of a Signe ascend, 'tis not safe to give Judgment, for the Querent hath been tampering with others.

III. See that the seventh House and his Lord be not impeded, or the *Moon* in the very end of the Signe, or in the combust way, if so, the Ancients forbid to give Judgment.

IV. But when the Sign Ascending, and his Lord represent the Querent, or a Planet in the Ascendant signifies him truly, you may safely venture to give your Judgment.

V. And lastly, a Question well and seriously propounded, cannot fail of a satisfactory Resolution; for a foolish and indiscreet Querent may cause an able Artist to err in his Judgment, and so cause a scandal to be cast upon the Art and Artist, when they are innocent and unblameable.

SECT. IV.

Of the Marks, Moles and Skarrs both of the Querent and Quesited.

I. Consider the Ascendant, *[viz.* the Sign that arises thereon] as also what Sign the Lord thereof is posited in, then what parts of the body are represented by those Signs, and you may conclude there are Moles, Marks or Skarrs upon those parts of the Body.

II. See also what Sign descends upon the Cusp of the 6th, and what Sign the Lord of the 6th is posited in, upon those two parts (or members of the body) represented by those Signs, you shall discover two other Marks or Moles, &c.

III. Take notice also what Sign the *Moon* is in, and upon that member that Sign represents in Mans Body, you may say there is another Mark; and this the rather, if those Signs signifying Marks, be afflicted by the Presence or Aspect of an Infortune; for *Hermes* in his 87th *Aphorism* sayes, *There will be some Impediment about that Part of the Body represented by the Sign which was afflicted at Birth.*

IV. If the Signs be Masculine, it declares the Mark to be on the right side; if Feminine, on the left side of the Body.

V. If the beginning of a Sign Ascend, or the Lord thereof be in few degrees of a sign, the mark is on the upper part of the Member, but if the middle of the Sign Ascend, or the latter end thereof, moderate your Judgment accordingly, and say the mark is posited upon the middle, or the lower part of the Member so signified: if ♄ be in the Sign and so signifie the Mark, it is a black duskish coloured one, somewhat osbscure; but if ♂ be in the Sign, a red one, and if he be in a fiery Sign, it denotes a Cut, Scar, or Spots of Gunpowder, or other Blemish in that part of the Body, if ♃ signifie the Mark, it is generally a Blewish or Purple Mole: if ☉, 'tis a Chestnut or Olive Colour: if ♀ signifie the Mark, 'tis Honey Colour; if ☿, a whitish or pale Leaden Colour: the ☽ usually gives a white Mark or Mole; but you are also to consider the colour of the Planet she is in Aspect with; and thus varying the Houses, the Rules hold true upon the Body of the Quesited also.

SECT. V.

Of Varying the Houses in your Judgment according to any Question Propounded.

I. This is General that the first House, the Sign Ascending and his Lord, together with the *Moon*, denotes the Querent, the second House his Substance or Riches, the third his Brethren, Kindred, and Neighbours, and the rest as has been already shewed in *chap.* 13.

II. The 12th House signifies his private Enemies, the Ascendant their Substance, and the 2d their short Journeys, and Kindred, &c. For the Ascendant is the second House from the 12th. &c.

III. The 7th House alwayes signifies publick Enemies, or a Wife, or Husband of the Querent: Then the 8th is their 2d and denotes their Riches, the 9th their Brethren, being the third from the 7th House, and so vary all the rest of the Houses of the Figure.

IV. The 4th House signifies the Querents Father, then the 5th (being the 2d from the 4th) denotes his Substance, and the 6th his Brothers and Sisters, and therefore the Querents Unkles and Aunts, the 7th the Grandfathers, &c. *Ptolomy*, Aphor. 89. sayes, *Require what concerns the Grandfather from the 7th House, but the Unckle from the 6th.*

Thus all the Houses may be most easily varied according to their several Significations, and these things are of singular use in Astrology for the Artist to be expert in.

Hence it comes to pass that an Artist oftentimes gives a Judgment to Admiration, and the great Credit of himself and the Art. In fine, this may be esteemed as the whole Mystery or Key of Astrology. Note also what House each Planet is posited in from his own; which will not a little assist in Astrological Judgments.

SECT. VI.

Of the Time of receiving a Horary Question.

My Honoured Friend, Mr. *William Lilly* tells us, *That there hath been large Disputations amongst the Arabians, concerning the Time an Artist should take for the Basis or Ground of the Question.*

I. Whether that point of time the Querent first comes into the house of the Artist, and salutes him, ought to be taken, and to set the Scheme for that moment, and so give Judgment: Or the time the Querent first breaks his mind to the Artist, or propounds his desire: some have consented to the former, but the latter seems the most Rational, and therefore wholly to be imbraced. Hence then I conclude, that very instant of time that an Artist understands the desire of any Querent, he ought to take for the true and radical time, whereon Astrologically to build his Judgment. The same if a Letter be sent from any Querent to an Artist; let him not accept of the time it comes to his hands, but of that moment he breaks it open, and first understands the desire of the Querent therein.

II. Some have thought it not convenient, that the Artist should judge his own Questions: 'tis true, any man will be apt to give a favourable Judgment in his own case, and upon that consideration it's not altogetner so proper for him to resolve his own doubts, as another: But if an Artist be much perplexed in mind, concerning the success or proceeding of any of his concerns, that he is principally interested in, let him take the moment of time he is most desirous of a Resolution, and proceed to judge his own Question, not minding it to be his own; and if he be able to lay aside all Love and Partiality to his own Cause, he may as freely and successfully Resolve his own Doubt, as any other. And this Opinian is confirmed by that great Luminary of Astrology, Mr. *William Lilly*, whose Experience has been very considerable in all varieties relating to Art.

III. To which I may add, that if the Querent have but his own Radical Figure of Birth, he may (with the aforesaid Caution) draw the judgment of his Question from thence more safely, as upon a surer Foundation: for if the Nativity be but known, an Horary Question is but of small validity, especially in general Questions, such as these, *viz.* Shall I be Rich, or attain to Honour or Preferment in the World? Shall I ever Travel, and see remote Parts: But if that cannot be procured, a Question is acceptable it being as it were a second Birth, *viz.* The Birth or motion of the Mind.

SECT. VII.

Choice Aphorisms to be considered in the Judgment of Horary Questions.

I. In a Question truly Radical, there is an Agreement between the face of Heaven and the Question propounded: for a Radical Figure resembles either the Nativity or Revolution.

II. No person moves a Question at any time with earnest desire of satisfaction, but the Ascendant of the Figure will be either the same, or of the same Triplicity with the Signe ascending at Birth.

III. Judge not upon light Motions of the Querent, for a Question fit to be Judged, ought to be premeditated, and seriously pondered bytbe Querent, therefore Judge not unless the Querent be of a Capacity rightly to state the Question.

IV. Figures of Horary Questions prove true or false according to the intent of the Querent.

V. Astrologers ought to be Impartial men; for Love and Hatred, causeth Errour in their Judgment.

VI. Seldome comes a good end of a Question when the *Moon* is Impeded; you may Judge the same if the Fortunes do not behold her with a Benevoient Aspect.

VII. If you find the Lord of the Ascendant opposite thereunto, or in *Quartile* to the Ascendant, or the *Moon* detrimented, it argues the Querent is careless in his Question.

VIII. Take notice from what Planet the *Moon* last separated, and that shews what hath already past in any Business, if you consider the House he is Lord of, and whether it were a good or bad Planet or Aspect, you may thence Judge of the good or ill proceedings; and also the Nature of the Matter in Question.

IX. The Application of the *Moon* to a Fortune either by Body or Aspect, and from good Houses, gives great hopes of the Matter in Question; but if to an Infortune, she makes also an ill Application; it denotes very bad success, and an unhappy conclusion.

X. Be not very forward to give Judgment when the seventh House and his Lord are afflicted, for those signifie the Artist himself; and it they are impeded in any Question, it bids the Artist beware his Judgment be not clouded, and he come off with disgrace.

XI. The *Moon* cannot be more afflicted than to be in ☌ of the ☉, and the business of any Question lies very obscure when the Planet that is Significator is under the Earth, or under the Beams of the ☉.

XII. If the Nativity or Revolution may be had it will help much in the Judgment of any Question, by considering the strength or weakness of the Lord of the Ascendant in your present Figure, &c.

XIII. Observe what Planet is Lord of the Ascendant, and accordingly as he is placed and beheld, as also considering his Nature, you may thence farther Rationally Judge of the thoughts, as well as of the disposition of the Querent.

XIV. The Position of the Infortunates unfortunate or ☋ in the tenth, foreshews no credit to the Artist by the Question.

XV. An Infortune unfortunate, and beholding that Planet which is Significator in any Question, brings powerful Mischief and Detriment to the Matter in Question, and this according to Natural Causes.

XVI. There is great hopes in any Question where the Fortunes (♃ or ♀) are Significators: but if ♄ and ♂ be Significators, there is great danger; for ♂ usually spoils matters by too much haste; and ♄ by too much delays, and sloath.

XVII. ♄ and ♂ Significators, and in Angles Essentially dignified, usually performs what is promised by them in any Question, neither ought an Artist to confide too much in what is promised by the Fortunes, unless they are in their Essential Dignities, and well placed.

XVIII. The *Part of Fortune* well seated in a good House of the Figure, promises Gain to the Querent by Persons or Matters signified by that House and the Lord thereof; but if Debilitated expect the contrary.

XIX. Beware of such Men and Things signified by that House and his Lord, where you find the ☋ placed, for many times the Querent receives loss and danger, as well as Scandals, and Slanders by Persons, or Matters relating to that House.

XX. Be not too forward to give a positive Judgment upon any Question, although your Significators be in Conjunction, before you have seriously considered the Signe they are in, whether it be a Signe of their own Nature or not, and whether they are said to delight therein; if so, it argues what they promise to be easily and speedily performed, otherwise the contrary.

XXI. Lastly, the Nature of the fixed Stars, that are joyned to your Significators, ought in especial manner to be warily considered in your Judgment, for if those Stars that are neer the Ecliptick, are of the same Nature, they mightily help. On the contrary, they do as much retard and hinder a Business in Question, if they are Stars of a contrary Nature to your Significators: I say, the consideration of the fixed Stars (that are within the Beams or Rayes of the Significators) being omitted, in my Opinion may be (in part) the occasion that *Artists* too often fail in their Judgment, and make good the Saying—

Ars vera est sed pauci Artifices, reperiuntur.

Here Ends the INTRODUCTION.

Clavis Astrologiae Eliminata;
OR
A KEY
To the whole Art of
ASTROLOGY
NEW
FIL'D and POLISHED.

The Second Part

CONTAINING

Brief Rules and Examples how to Resolve or Judge All Lawful Questions Astrologically, Contingent unto mankind, from a Radical Scheme of Heaven erected: Together with Elections, and several other useful precepts of Art.

By *Henry Coley*, Philomat.

Judge nothing or elect any thing positively, the sign Scorpio being in the Ascendant, or when the Angles are of such signs as ascend obliquely, or if Mars *be therein; for a wrong Judgement will be given, and the event will prove contrary to the Judgment, for* Scorpio *is a sign of Falsity*. Her.Aph.9.

As seven stream'd Nile *to whose kind over-flow,*
The Egyptian Plains their yearly plenty owe;
Takes its first rise from some small unknown Fountain
That Bubbles at the foot of some steep Mountain:
So whilst ARTS *spreading Branches mount a height,*
And with their Lustre Dazle our dull sight:
The Root whereon they all depend and grow,
Lyes Couch'd in such brief principles below,
He that peruseth these with piercing eye,
Views the Cabal *of true* Astrology:
But if some Thick *Scull'd* Fopp *presumes to peep,*
And thinks they'r Non-sence cause they are so deep,
Let him set down, and Plod on what h'as read,
And learn with's Nayls to scratch a wiser head.
    —Operum Fastigia Admirantur, Latent plerumq; Fundamenta.

OF THE
ELEMEMTS
OF
ASTROLOGY,
OR
Principles of JUDGEMENT,
By Way of
PREFACE.

Every Natural Science (as *Aristotle* himself witnesseth) owes its birth and Original discovery either to the senses or to experience: which last is threefold, *viz.* Intellectual, Sensible, and Mixt, or Rational, acquired not only by Sense, nor alone by Reason, but by the Concourse of both. Now since *Astrology* is a Natural Science, and ordained for Practice in like manner as the Art of *Physick*; therefore as the one is, so the other ought to be Founded upon Experiments, and who ever would deliver the Doctrine of *Astrology* Scientifically (saith the Famous *Morinus*) must heedfully observe what *Rational Experience* affords concerning it: For as the Science of Astronomy springs from the Apparencies of the *Planets Motions*, beheld from the Earth in the Heavens, so *Astrology* is built on the effects and *Influences* of the same Bodies observed from the *Nativities* of Persons born here below: And as one that should deny the Scituation of the Stars, or their places as they are set down in the Tables by *Skilful Astronomers*, must be sent to those Instruments whereby their places are measured for satisfaction, so he that shall deny the *Principles of Astrology* is to be referred to the *Radical Figures* of Natives, and their lives and accidents correspondent thereunto for his conviction: For as we come to know not by any Reason, but only sense and sensible experience that *Fire* is *Hot*, and the Attractive vertue of the *Loadstone* upon Iron; so that the *Sun* doth effect one thing when in *Aries*, another thing in *Taurus*, one thing when in Trine of *Mars* and a different when in his Opposition: As also one thing in the first House of a *Figure*, and another in the *twelfth*, is a truth which only *Rational Experience* teacheth us, for though these effects of the *Coelestial Bodies* have in those Bodies their Causes and Principles which are their formal vertues, yet because these vertues appear not to us, but only by their Effects, and that such *Effects* are to us the first means of discovering such hidden vertues: Therefore, we ought to esteem them as the first principles and grounds of *Teaching* and *Learning Astrology*.

Here follow certain Astrological Axioms confirmed, and verified by Rational Experience, and therefore very considerable useful in Astrological Judgments.

I. The same *Planet* hath one effect, when in one house of a Figure, and another Specifick or particular effect, when in another House, which is also true of the fixed *Stars* and Signs of the Zodiack.

II. In the same House of a Figure, the *Sun* by himself hath one effect, the *Moon* another, *Saturn* another, &c. which is also true of the Fixed Stars, and the twelve Signs.

III. The same *Planet* hath one effect when in *conjunction,* of another *Planet,* or posited in one house of a Figure, and a different effect when in *Opposition, Trine, or Square*, to the said or any other *Planet*, or being posited in any other house.

IV. The *Square* or *Opposition* of *Saturn*, or *Mars*, hath one effect, the *Square* or *Opposition* of *Jupiter* and *Venus* another.

V. The same *Planet* hath one effect when Lord of the *first House*, and another special, or *Specifick* effect, when Lord of the second House, another when Lord of the third, &c.

VI. The same point of *Heaven* if it be the place of the *Sun* in any *Genesis* retains a *Solar* force and influence in respect of that native, so long as he lives; so doth *Saturns* place retain a *Saturnine* vertue; understand the same in the Position of the rest of the *Planets* in any *Geniture* whatever.

In like manner the same point of Heaven that is the *Horoscope* of any Nativity, shall more or less continue to have an influence over the *Natives* Life. That point which is the *Midheaven* over the *Actions* and Profession, and the same of the rest of the houses in their particular significations, as also of the *Aspects* of the *Planets*; *There is no rational person (I mean of an Artist) will I presume question the verity of this* Axiome, *if they consider that 'tis dayly confirmed by the progression of* Directions *of the* Hylegiacal *significators, to their several promittors in divers persons* Genitures, *who are sensibie of their secret operations, as also the* Transists *of the* Planets *by their own, and each others* Places *at Birth; which have their various Influences upon Mortals during Life.*

VII. The same Point of Heaven which to one Native is the Place of the ☉, to another may be the place of ♄, ♃, ♂, ♀, ☿, or the ☽.

VIII. Every Agent acting by it self, acts only according to its own proper Force and Nature.

IX. Every Patient suffers according to its proper Nature, or whatever is received, according to the Capacity of the Receiver.

X. The same remaining, the same always hath the same effect, in or upon the same Subject.

Hence arises the Cause that Twins, not born at the same Moment, have not the same Accidents happen alike to both, though they are both of the same Sex, and were both begotten by the same Parent. The same Reason may be given also why an Ordinary Person or Rustick and a Noble-Man, being born at the same Moment and Place, should not have the same Fate; nor the Accidents of their Lives Correspond, although the Constitution of the Heavens in both Genitures be precisely the same.

[Note that by this word Axiome *is to be understood a Maxime or general Ground in any Art, or it is a Proposition or short Sentence generally allowed to be true; As in saying The whole is greater than its part*]

From these Experienced Axioms, the following Theorems *Comprehending (at least Generally) the whole* Art *of* ASTROLOGY, *do necessarily follow.*

Astrological Theorems.

I. The several *Houses* of a *Coelestial Figure* differ amongst themselves in Vertue or Propriety: *For the same* Planet *hath one effect in the first House of a* Figure, *and another different Effect or Influencial Virtue being posited in the second House, and another if in the third House, &c. and so of the rest of the Twelve Houses.* Axiom. I.

And this must be understood in respect of the Mansions, *or Houses of Heaven, as they are usually divided, (or at least supposed to be so) Hence then, If a* Planet *hath diversity of Effects, at the same Instant in the Heavens, in respect of the whole Globe of the Earth, it must necessarily follow, that the Houses (or unequal parts of Heaven) have a diverse Nature, Vertue or Propriety; According to this first Theorem, which was to be Demonstrated.*

II. The several *Planets* differ from each other in Nature and Vertue, at least Influentially. *Axiome 2.*

III. The several *Signes* in the Zodiack differ from each other in Nature and Vertue either Elementally or Influentially or both. *Axiome 3.*

IV. The several *Aspects* of every *Planet* differ either in *Vertue,* or quantity of *Virtue. Axiome 3.*

V. All the *Fixed Stars* have not the same *Nature* and *Vertue: For the Virgins Spike hath one effect in the Ascendant, and* Cor Scorpij *another, &c. therefore a diversity of Vertue.* Axiome 2.

VI. The Vertues of the Coelestial Bodies are mixt together in the Patient or Subject, as Man, &c. Axiom 2.

VII. A *Planet* in, or rather with the same Signe, hath always the same *Specifick* effect, as well Elementally as Influentially: *For every Signe of the Zodiack have a different Vertue amongst themselves*, Theor. 3. *And therefore the same Planet in diverse Signes hath not the same Power and Vertue*. Axiome 9.

IX. Two *Planets* do not severally effect the same thing, in the same Signe of the Zodiack: *For every Planet differs between themselves in Vertue. According to* Axiome 2. *And therefore two Planets in the same Signe have not the same Vertue*, Axiom 9.

X. The same *Planet* in the same House of a Figure hath the same Effect.

XI. *No Planet* doth the same thing, from or in several Houses of a Figure.

XII. Two *Planets* have not severally the same effect in several Houses of a *Figure: According to the aforesaid* Axioms.

XIII. No *Planet* hath the same effect alone, as he hath when joyned to another *Planet*, by Body or Aspect. *Axiome* 2.

XIV. The same *Planet* hath the same Effect when ever joyned in the same manner to the same *Planet* or Cuspe of a House. *Axiome 9.*

XV. And hence no *Planet* produces the same Effects, being joyned to one *Planet* or Cusp as it doth to another. *Theor, 1, 2.*

XVI. No *Planet* hath the same Effect when differently joyned to the same *Planet* or *Cuspe* of a House. *Theor. 4.*

XVII. Two *Planets* have not severally the same Effect in their Operation or Influence, by the same kind of Aspects. *Theor. 2. Axiome 4, 9.*

XVIII. The Vertue of the Houses of a *Coelestial* Figure is not of it self able to produce Effects, but doth determine the Vertue of the *Coelestial Bodies* to such kind of Effects as are agreeable to the Vertue or Propriety of every House. *Theor. 1.*

XIX. The Influence of every *Planet* in the causing or producing Effects, is of it self General, and Universal. *Axiome 1, 2, &c.*

XX. The Influence of every *Planet* in particular is in it self but one and the same, and not changed by their Motion through the Signs, *by the aforesaid Axioms*.

XXI. No *Planet* Restrains the Influences of another *Planet* that it shall not flow forth and act upon Subliminary things, though it may restrain its Elemental force. *Theor. 13.*

XXII. Every *Planet* can have some Effect on every kind of Body Naturally pnoduced. *Theor. 13. & 21.*

XXIII. No *Planet* can do all things on every kind of Body, or Effect upon Corporal things, as *Plagues, Dearths*, Constitutions of the *Aire, Wars*, &c. *Theor. 13, & 15.*

XXIV. The Vertue (at least Influential) of two *Planets* cannot be the same on anything that is born. *Axiome 9.* and *Theor. 15.*

XXV. The same *Planet* with the same Influential Vertue, may at once cause divers effects in relation to the same *Numerical* Native or Individual Person or Thing. *Axiome 1, 3, 4.*

XXVI. No *Planet* hath the same effect by its influential Vertue in Subjects *Specifically*, or even only *Numerically* different. *Axiome 18.*

XXVII. Two *Planets* severally, do not (at least Influentially) produce by themselves the same effect by the same Patient. *Axiome 7, & 9. Theor. 2. & 15.*

XXVIII. Lastly, a *Planet* out of his own House shall have one effect by reason of the House of the Figure wherein he is posited, and another by reason of his Dominion in another House of the Figure. *Axiome 4, & 9. & Theor. 1.*

Note that by the word Theorm *is understood a Speculation, or an undoubted Rule or Principle in any Science or Art, and is that which respects Contemplation more than Practice.*

It was (not many years since) the desire of a Learned Plilosopher and Astrologian (who was the Author of these Astrological Axioms *and* theorems*) That for the better* Restauration *of the Coelestial Science, Astrologers (that have any respect to the Art they Study and Profess) should observe well these six following Articles, which being short and least they should be lost, (for their sakes that never saw them) I have (not improperly) Transferr'd hither, that they may be revived again*: Viz.

First, To Collect from the *Histories* of several *Nations* of the World the most Eminent and Notable Changes that have therein happened in respect of *Sects, Empires, Kingdoms, Wars, Famine, Deluges*, &c. with the exact times of their Changes and the true postures of the Constellations and Planets proceding the same.

Secondly, To observe, the Changes of the *Aire*, in respect of *Heat, Cold, Moisture*, and *Drought*; as also the *Winds* throughout the whole *Latitude* of the *Earth*: and then the different Places of Longitude in their *Nature*: and *Qualities* at the same and at several times erecting *Coelestial Figures* most congruous for that purpose, and to mark well how from thence *Plants, Bruits* and *Men* are affected, and all these Observations to compare one with another.

Thirdly, to erect the several *Nativities* of such as Dyed not long after they were borne, of those that be *Sickly*, or any wayes *Hurt, Blind, Lame,* or any wayes *Ulcerated, Wounded Burn'd, Mutilated* &c. diligently observing the parts so affected, the which may most conveniently be done in a Spacious City (such as *London* and *Paris* are) where are many Hospitals and poor people almost innumerable, many Chyrurgeons, and every day various Casualties.

Fourthly, By help of the Physitians to find out (if possible) the *Beginnings, Species, Accidents* and *Solutions* of all Acute and dayly Diseases that every where abound, Erecting *Coelestial Schemes* to those *Beginnings:* and that especially in great Cities where these exorbitant practices (in particular at *Paris* where this Author lived) of frequent Blood-letting does much disturb *Natures Motions* and *Crisis* in *Diseases*, and very often crude and frustrate the Astrological Predictions of the Ancients concerning them.

Fifthly, What the Antient Astrologers have delivered upon every Subject, the same to collect and observe in several by diligent reading thereof, and to correct the Figures of their Experiments in respect of the Errors of the Old *Astronomy*.

Sixthly, To Argue and Determine by *Physical* and *Astronomical* Reasons concerning the *Systeme* of the world, now so much Controverted, betwixt the *Copernicans* and *Tychonists*, for so much as in this thing (although both *Mensurable and Visible*), *Geometry* and the sight are both destructive: Neither can the quickest sighted man living conclude anything thence for certain with what *Telescope* soever, because the same *Phoenomena* are deduced from both the *Systems*: For albeit the thing it self be senslble, yet does it elude and pass the sense of Man: The truth whereof so much concerns *Astrology*, that *Tycho* and *Keplar* thought fit rather to destroy her, than that their own new Systems should not be established. Afterwards out of the confused Sayings of Ancient *Astrologers*, and the Observations of past and present things, with the proper and Corrected Schemes of Heaven, by accurate Speculation and dividing rightly, to attain unto the first Causes of Effects, which are the first Principles of this Science; few in number both in this and other Sciences, yet so valid, that from thence (they being firmly established) the whole Science of *Astrology* and her innumerable Conclusions, may easily be drawn to a Method. Whence I dare boldly affirm, that *Astrology* which is partly a *Physical*, partly a *Mathematical* Science), may be more certainly and more evidently Demonstrated; yea and in a more excellent Method than either Natural *Phylosophy* or *Physick* have hitherto been by any man whatsoever.

Thus far this Learned Author (as sufficient for my present Design) and I presume enough to satisfie any Reasonable man, that *Astrology* is Demonstrable, and not onely Lawful and True, but Divinely Excellent and necessary for a Christian; and that none but the Ignorant and Malicious will condemn or oppose the same.

Desicile est Judicare, per ca qua scripta sunt; longe difficllius Artemipsamtradere: difficilimum autem artem ipsam invenire. Carden Segm. 1. Aph. 25.

Hence Fiery *Zelots* you I dare to tell,
Astrology's from *Heaven*, not from *Hell*.
'Tis no Black *Art*, no Damned *Necromancy*,
No *Witchcraft* neitber, as some please to fancy:
    'For *Shallow-brains* think all that's hard or high,
    'Unlawful, or Impossibility.

[*Having premised these things, in the next place I proceed to shew the Astrological Rules and Aphorisms of judging the most usual and necessary Horary Questions in a plain and easie Method, wherein I shall use as much Conciseness and Perspicuity as the Subject will conveniently bear.*]

Clavis Astrologie Eliminata.

OR

A Key to Astrology new Filed and Polished.

The Second Part.

CHAP. I.

Questions with Judgments (or Astrological Responses) thereunto, Appertaiing to the Ascendant or First House.

SECT. I.

May the Querents Life be Long or Short?

This question (above all others) may be supposed by some persons too Nice and Curious to be Determined by the Rules of Astrology, since the Lives (and Actions) of all Humane Creatures are only at the Dispose of the Almighty: To which I Answer, 'Tis an undoubted Truth, that although our days are Number'd, and no man knows the day of his Disiolution; howbeit, from certain Rules of ART, (which for many Years have been confirmed by Experience) and a due consideration of Natural Causes a man may be able thereby to give a probable Conjecture (as the Physician upon his sick Patient) whether a person may live many Years or few: And if we may Credit History many Persons have been foretold neer the times of their Expiration; as Julius Caesar *was advised by* Spurina *to beware the Ides of* March, *(upon which he was slain in the Senate House.* Picus Mirandulanus *by* Bellantius, *that it should happen in the thirty-third year of his Age, and so was* Vetillius, *an Emperour of* Rome, *and* Aechilus *the philosopher, who perished by the stroke of a Shell Crab or Tortoise let fall upon his naked head by an Eagle as he walked in the Fields: divers other Examples might be produced which we find upon Record; and who can deny but an Artist by the same Rules (God not Contradicting secondary Causes) may predict the same, especially from a serious Consideration of the Scheme of the Nativity, (which is a surer Foundation to build a Judgment upon, than a Figure of a Horary Question, which ouught rather to be consulted for Particular Actions than Generals.) But without farther digression I proceed to Astrological Judgment upon the aforesaid Question, and divers others appertaining to, or dependant upon this, and the rest of the twelve Coelestial Mansions.

I. First observe the *Ascendant* and Lord thereof, also the *Moon*; if neither of these are Afflicted by the Malevolent Aspects of the Infortunes, not Combust of the Sun, but essentially fortified and free from the Malignant Rayes of the Lords of the Fourth, Sixth, Eighth or Twelfth Houses, you may then judge a long life, or at least that the Native may live to years of Maturity; But the time of Limitation is best discovered by the Direction the *Hylegiacal* points of the *Radix,* to the Body or ill Aspect of that Planet who is *Anareta* or Killing Planet, which shall be shewed in its proper place.

II. If you find the aforesaid Significators, *viz.* the Ascendant and Lord thereof, or the Luminaries afflicted, and posited in abject places of the Figure, you may then upon good grounds of *Art* judge but a short life, and this the more certain, if the *Moon* or Lord of the Ascendant be in the Eighth or in Conjunction with the Lord of the eighth House.

III. If good and fortunate Planets happen to be in the Ascendant, or behold the Lord thereof by any benevolent Aspect; also the Planets being generally well fortified and in good places of the Heavens, this shews not only long life, but it adds happiness thereunto; the Querent is then subject to few troubles or vexations in the whole course of life: But if the Infortunes vitiate the Ascendant, or afflict the Lord thereof, or the Luminaries, 'tis a great Argument in *Art* that the Querent will be much perplext with sorrow and discontent, and consequently live very uncomfortably in the General, unless by the force of good Direction and Transitts, the evil is accidentally abated for a time; and if the *Dragons Tail* happen to fall in the Ascendant, the Querent, (whether Man or Woman) is rarely free from Scandal and Reproaches, and oftentimes not without desert, (as I have often prov'd by experience.)

SECT. II.

What part of the Querents Life may be best?

I. Consider the place of the Fortunate Stars and Planets, and if they be in the Ascendant twelfth or eleventh House, judge the Infancy of the Querent should be most Fortunate; if in the tenth, ninth, or eighth Houses, judge his Youth; if in the seventh, sixth, or fifth Houses, his middle Age, or declining years; if in the fourth, third or second House, his latter Age will be most happy.

II. You may allow (the Significators being weak) for every House five Years, if they happen to be accidentally fortified six years: but being very strong, and Essentially dignified for every House from the Ascendant (accounting towards the tenth) you may allow seven years, and thereby praedict the time or, most happy years, and by the same Rule, considering the position of the Infortunes or afflicting Planets, you may judge also of the most probable Infortunate or unhappy years.

III. Here I have intimated that the position of the Planets only ought to be considered, but some observe another Rule, and judge of the Houses, consideration being had to the Lords thereof, whether Fortunate or Unfortunate; thus the Lord of the fifth or sixth Houses being strong, and posited in the tenth or eleventh, they will rather judge those years signified by the fifth or sixth, than those by the tenth or eleventh Houses, let every Artist follow that way he finds best corresponds with Truth, in my Judgment the first is to be preferred rather, but the Directions of the Nativity above all.

SECT. III.

What Quarter of the World may be most Happy and Fortunate?

I. At the end of the third Chapter of the Introduction you have the Quarters of the Heavens signified by the twelve Signes, and in the close of the 13th Chapter thereof, is exppess'd the Parts or Points of the Heavens signified by the twelve Houses.

II. Consider then the position of ♃, ♀, the ☽, or ⊕, (some will have it where they have most essential Dignities which in my opinion is not so rational) having considered the parts of Heaven where the Fortunes are posited, direct the person that way, according to the former Rules, but withal let Reason guide your judgment, and by the Conjunction of Reason and Art together you may sometimes deserve Admiration.

III. Consider the Nature of the Question. If for Health then let the Position of the Lord of the Ascendant and the *Moon* be observed; if for Riches, the Lord of the second House and *Part of Fortune*; if for Honour the Lord of the tenth House and the *Sun, &c*, always remembering to consider those Planets that are friendly to the Lord of the Ascendant, Lord of the second House, and the *Moon*.

SECT. IV.

Of the Condition of an Absent Party.

The Rules of the Ancients are briely thus:

I. If the Party be related to the Querent, take that house for the quesited that signifies him or her as if a Brother or Sister; the third House and its Lord, if a Husband or Wife; the seventh house and Lord thereof, and so varie the Houses according as the Relation requires; but if the party enquired after be not related, then let the Ascendant and the *Moon* signifie the absent party. (I must confess I should rather take the Lord of the seventh, or eleventh House if the party enquired after be an Acqaintance; but if the Question be asked in a general way, what is the condition of an absent party, and the Querent altogether a stranger to the Quesited, then the Ascendant and his Lord and the *Moon* may be accepted for proper Significators.)

II. If the *Moon* or Lord of the Ascendant be posiited in the eighth House, or in ☌ or ☍ with the Lord thereof, from or in bad places of the Figure, it is an Argument the absent party is dead; if the parties Significator be afflicted by the Lord of the sixth House, you may conclude he is sick. My Honoured Friend Mr. *William Lilly* affirms he hath ever found in his Practice the party alive notwithstandmng it were contrary, if he found the Lord of the Ascendant in the ninth, tenth, or eleventh Houses, *Vide Christian Astrolog.* pag. 151. ult.

III. If you find the Lord of theAscendant and the *Moon* well dignified, and in Aspect with good Planets, and Lords of good Planets, you may then judge the person to be in a safe condition, and amongst such persons that are both friendly and obliging unto the Quesited.

IV. The most probable time when you may expect to hear of the obsent party is when his or her Significator meets with some good Aspect of the Lord of the Ascendant, sometlmes when the Lord of the Ascendant and the Lord of the eleventh House comes to a ✶ or □ Aspect, or note the degrees the *Moon* wants of a ✶ or △ of the Lord of the Ascendant, and for every degree of distance from Angles and fixed Signes allow, years or months; if from succedent Houses and common Signe, say months or weeks; if from moveable Sign, weeks or days, as shall be farther shewed in the Judgments of some other of the Houses.

SECT. V.

To know whether a person to be spoken with be at home or not?

I. If the person be not Related, but only an Acquaintance, then consider the position of the Lord of the seventh House, in a Figure set for the time.

II. If he be posited in any of the four Angles the person is undoubtedly at home: *This Rule rarely fails, and hath encouraged many young Students to make a farther progress in the study of this Art for the Verity they have often found herein.*

III. If the Lord of the seventh House be found in any of the succedent Houses, the party is not far from home, but probably at some Neighbours House, and may soon be spoak with, but if he be in a cadent House judge the contrary.

IV. If the Lord of the Ascendant and the Significator of the person you would meet withal be applying to a ✶ or △ Aspect, it's an Argument you may meet with the party as you goe, or at least have some intelligence accidentally where you may find him. [*Always remember to take a Proper Significator if you seek a Relation.*]

SECT. VI.

Of a Ship at Sea, her Safety or Danger.

I. The Ascendant and the *Moon* Signifies the Ship it self and whatsoever Burthen it carries; but the Persons therein are denoted, or properly signified by the Lord of the Ascendant, and those Planets that are in ☌ with him.

II. If the Significators of the Ship and persons therein are found strong and powerful in your Figure, and no way afflicted by the Infortunes, you may conclude the Ship and all therein are in a good and safe condition, and free from danger at that instant: But if you find the Significators, lately separated from evil Planets, or their malignant Rayes, you may judge they have lately been in danger; or if you find their Significators in bad Houses, or beheld by evil Aspects of the Lords of bad Houses, or much afflicted by the Malevolents, you may then conclude the ship is lost, or in very eminent danger.

III. Upon the setting out of a Ship, if the Angles be Fortunate, by the position of Fortunate Planets therein, as also the *Moon,* and the unfortunate Planets Cadent and Debilitated, the Ship then will go safely to the place intended, and the contrary: But if the Midheaven be unfortunate, and *Mars* the afflicting Planet, then the Ship will be in either Burnt, or be in great danger thereof; if *Mars* be in a humane Signe, it may be by Conflict of an Enemy, but if *Saturne* afflict, the Ship suffers by violent Winds and Tempests, Leaks, *&c.* and the Damage will be the greater according to the strength of the Infortunes.

IV. The Significators Angular and moveable, increasing in Light and Motion, is a Signification of much gain, a profitable Voyage, and quick Return, and Contrariwise: But of this I may hint something more in the Discourse of Elections to which it doth properly belong.

The Parts of a Ship are Attributed to the twelve Signes of the Zodiack, as followeth, acording to *Haly.*

♈ The Breast of the Ship.

♉ That part under the Breast toward the Water.

♊ The Stern or Rudder.

♋ The Floor or Bottom.

♌ The Top above Water.

♍ The Belly of the Ship.

♎ That part which lies between Wind & Weather.

♏ That part where the Seamen abide or perform their Office.

♐ The Mariners themselves.

♑ The ends of the Ship.

♒ The Captain or Master.

♓ The Oars.

CHAP. II.

Questions and Judgments proper to the Second House.

SECT. I.

May the Querent ever attain Riches?

I. Here you are to consider the Cusp of the Second House, and Lord thereof; the *Part of Fortune,* and those Planets posited in the House of Substance, or such as behold the Significators thereof by any Friendly or Benevolent Aspect.

II. If you find these Significators well fortified, and free from the Cross Aspects or Bodies of the Infortunes, the Querent will then certainly live happily, and enjoy a considerable portion of Riches, and this the rather if ♃, ♀, ⊕ or ☊ be posited in the second House Essentially strong. [*This must always be understood according to the Degree or Quality of the Persons Birth.*]

III. On the contrary, if you find the Significators of Riches posited in abject places of the Heavens, or much afflicted, or debilitated, and not assisted by the benevolent Rayes of the Fortunes, you may then judge the Querent will rarely gain Wealth, but rather suffer by Poverty, or live in a very mean and poor Condition, in the General [*unless something of Assistance happen accidentally upon the effects of good Directions or Transits in the Persons Nativity (if it may be had) which ought chiefly eobe consulted in such general Questions.*]

IV. The Lord of the Ascendant or the *Moon* joyned to the Lord of the second, or posited in the second House, or the Lord of the second in the Ascendant promises Riches by the Querents own proper industry.

V. If ♄, ♂ or ☋, be in the second House the Querent is poor, or in a declining condition; but if the Significators of Riches are well posited as aforesaid, and be swift in motion, and Angular, the Querent thrives on a sudden, beyond expectation.

SECT. II.

By what means may the Querent gain wealth?

I. If you find the Significators of Substance strong and well placed in the Ascendant, this shews the Querent should acquire gain by his own proper Industry; if in the second House, by buying and Selling, and an Industrious improvement of his Estate thereby.

II. If the Significators are posited in the third, or be friendly beheld by the Lord thereof, then the Querent may gain by the means of Brethren, Kindred, Neighbours and Friends, *&c.* and thus you may judge of the rest of the Houses, or Lords thereof, according to their Natural and proper Significations, already exprest in the Introductory part.

III. I shall conclude this Section with words of the famous Mr. *Lilly,* in his *Christ. Astrolog.* pag. 172. who sayes, That the most assured Testimony in Astrology upon a Question propounded, whether the person shall be Rich, and so continue, is this; If the Lord of the first and second, and ♃ be joyned together, either in the first, second, fourth, seventh, tenth or eleventh Houses; but if they be not in ☌, yet if they apply to a ✶ or △ Aspect, to each other with mutual Reception, this is a strong Argument the Querent will thrive and get an Estate, though with intervening difficulties; he adds farther, that if the Application be by □ or ☍, the party yet grows rich, or rather abounds than wants, though what he gains be with much labour and toyl.

SECT. III.

Of the time when Riches may be expected.

I. The best and most surest way to determine this is after you have found the principal Significators, to direct them to their proper Promittors, as is usual in a Nativity, and use the same measure of time if the Question be General; but if that be thought Laborious, then only account the degrees of distance between the Significators and their Aspects and judge according as the Significators shall happen to be placed in Angles, Succedent or Cadent Houses, or in Fixed, Moveable or Common Signes.

II. If they are in Angles and Fixed Signes, let their degrees of distance signifie years or months; if in suceedent Houses and Common Signes, say months or weeks; if in Moveable Signs, weeks or dayes; and so moderate your judgment by discretion for the time, according as your Reason shall dictate, and your Scheme promises: but I rather advise to consult the Nativity (if it be possible) in all general Questions.

III. The way I would offer (as very rational) for Limitation of time when Accidents may happen in matters usually propounded as Horary Questions, is this, Take the difference of the oblique Ascention of the Ascendant of the Figure of the *Suns* ingress into *Aries* for the same year, and that which follows, or precedes; which will be about eighty five, or eighty six degrees, and that shall be the measure of time for a whole year: so that four dayes and some odd hours will answer to one degree, by which you may measure out the time of any Accident to fall out within the Compass of the said year, as l shall farther illustrate when I come to shew the Method of Directing Solar Revolutions in Nativities. However, Let every Artist make use of what way he finds most agreeable with verity, for nothing can be a better confirmation in these Cases, than Experience, which always proves the best Director.

SECT. IV.

Shall the Querent recover his Moneys Lent, or Satisfaction for the Goods he has Trusted?

This Question being so necessary (and in regard some persons have occasion too often to propose it) I thought convenient to Insert, before the Conclusion of this Chapter.

I. The Lord of the Ascendant and the *Moon* are in all Questions the Significators of the Querent, and the seventh House, and Lord thereof (if the person be not Related) signifies him or her enquired after (as has been sufficiently shewed in the Introductory part hereof) But as to the Judgment of the Question proceed thus;

II. If the Lord of the Ascendant, or the *Moon* be in ☌ with the Lord of the Eighth (which always signifies the Substance of the person enquired after) or if either of them be in ☌ or Benevolent Aspect with a Planet in the Eighth House, provided that Planet be a Fortunate Planet, then the Querent may expect the recovery of his Money or Goods sought after, according to the Judgment of *Guido Bonatus*.

III. If either of the aforesaid Significators shall happen to be joyned to the Fortunate Planets only in a good place of the Figure, especially if they have Dignities in the Ascendant, then the matters in Question will soon be ended, and this is the more certain, and hopeful, if there be but favourable reception between the Significators.

Note that this Judgment is the more certain when the Business in question happens amongst persons of a mean degree, as one Tradesman with another, or one Citizen or Country man with another; Kings and Princes must be exempted, and all Persons of Quality, &c. as Guido *well notes in his Judgment upon this Subject.*

IV. To conclude this *Section*, Do but observe whether the proper Significators behold each other Friendly, from good places of the Heavens, and are free from any malignant Aspect of the Infortunes, then expect a speedy and successful issue of the Matter in Question; if not, you may conclude the Contrary, as Reason it self will direct.

CHAP. III.

Questions and Judgment proper to the Third House.

SECT. I.

Of short Journeys, shall they be prosperous to the Qudrent or not?

I. If *Jupiter, Venus*, or the *Dragons Head* be posited in the third House, or the Lord of the Third free from affliction of the Infortunes, or well beheld of the Lords of the *Ascendant* and the *Moon*, these are Arguments of a pleasant and successful Journey, and the Contrary, *&c.*

II. If the Lord of the Third House Friendly behold the Ascendant by a ✶ or △ Aspect, or if the *Moon* be in the Third in ✶ to the Ascendant, or the Lord of the Third in the Ascendant, and behold the Cusp thereof Friendly, or if the Lord of the Ascendant be swift in Motion in any of the Dignities of the Lord of the Third, or in good Aspect unto him, this portends a happy and prosperous Journey to the Querent.

III. If *Saturne* afflict the Lord of the Ascendant, the Third House, or the *Moon*, this shews a tedious Journey, the Querent is discontent therein, or probably looses his way, or meets with many unhappy Crosses and Vexations before his Return.

IV. If *Saturne* happen to be in *Scorpio* in the Third the Querent meets with Thieves and Robbers; and if *Mars* be posited in a Fiery or Humane Signe, the Querent receives Wounds, and unkind Greetings besides: *Therefore 'tis good for all Persons that have Occasion to Travel, to Consult with the Astrologer first, and thereby choose such a time that they may Travel with safety, or forbear, and so avoid the Danger impending.*

SECT. II.

May the Querent and his Brethren, Kindred or Neighbours, &c. agree together.

I. If *Jupiter* or *Venus* have great Dignities in the Ascendant, or are posited therein, and in no Aspect to *Saturne* or *Mars*, the Querent is then very peaceable, and will not willingly contend or quarrel with any person, much less with a Relation; But if *Saturne* or *Mars* are ill posited in the Ascendant, or afflict the Lord thereof, or the *Moon*, it is very probable the Querent may then prove of a hasty ruggy Temper and Disposition, and consequently too Subject to Controversie and Contention, whether he be provoked or not; Understand the same of the Relation, whether Brother or Sister, Respect had to the Third House.

II. If you find the Lord of the the third House, and the Lord of the Ascendant behold each other by some Amicable Aspect, or if they are in Reception, or the *Moon* be in ✶ or △ to ♃ or ♀ in the House of Brethren, this shews the Querent and his Neighbours and Kindred shall assuredly agree and love each other.

III. When a Fortunate Planet is in the third House, and beholds the Ascendant or his Lord by a Friendly Aspect, or if ♃, ♀, or the ☽ be in the Ascendant, and behold the Cusp of the Third, or the Lord thereof by any benevolent Aspect, this portends the Querent and his Relations are generally good dispositioned persons, and very rarely differ, but rather have together in much Unity and Love.

IV. But if *Saturne* or *Mars* happen to be posited in the Ascendant, the Querent is then doubtless to blame, and is the occasion of the Discontent; if they are in the Third House, then the Querents Brethren or Neighbours prove Contentious Quarrelsome Persons, and in all probability must be the occasion of Difference by their cross perverseness: where note that those persons whose Significators make no application, are the most obstinate and daring, and those, whose Significators apply by any good Aspect are most willing to stoop to a Compliance, and mutual Agreement.

V. If there happen a malicious Aspect between the Lord of the Ascendant or the *Moon*, and Lord of the third

House, or any Planet posited therein; you may then conclude there is very small hopes of Agreement and Concordency between the Querent and his Relations, but rather he contrary; and farther observe, that if *Saturne* or the *Dragons Tayl* be posited in the third House, the Querents Kindred or Neighbours prove Covetous or Clownish Ill-bred People; If *Mars* be there, they are Treacherous, Ill-natur'd, Thievish, Pilfering Persons; and this the rather, if they are not Essentially Dignified, according to the Judgment and experience of the famous Mr. *Lilly*.

SECT. III.

Is an Absent Brother, &c. Fortunate or Miserable, or in what Condition may he be?

I. Consider the position of the Lord of the Third House (which is the proper Significator of the Person enquired after) see where or in what House he is posited, and consider with what Planets he is in Aspect withal: If he be in ☌, □ or ☍, of ♄ or ♂, or with ☋, or joyned to the Lord of the sixth, eighth, or twelfth Houses, either by body, or beheld by evil Aspect, then the condition of the absent party is both miserable and deplorable; But on the contrary, if his Significator be posited in a good place of the Figure, and there ✶ or △ of ♃ and ♀ free from the evil beams of the Infortunes, then you may (upon good grounds in Art) conclude the Absent Brother to be in a very happy and prosperous Condition.

II. If the Lord of the third house be posited in the fourth House (which is the second from the first) and free from affliction there, then the absent Brother is in some hopeful way of increasing his Estate, or augmenting his Fortune.

III. If in the fifth House with the Lord of the fifth, or in reception with the Fortunes, the absent Brother is in a good condition, and likes the persons he converses withal, and this the more certain if the Lord of the fifth be strong: But if the Lord of the third be in the fifth House unfortunate or afflicted, judge the contrary.

IV. If the Significator of the Absent Brother be in the sixth House, or in Conjunction with the Lord of the sixth, or the Lord of the sixth in the third House, the Quesited is not in health, but much indisposed in Body; and if the Lord of the third be also in ☌ or otherwise afflicted by the Lord of the eighth House, it portends the Distemper may end in death; and this is the more certain if you take the Lord of the eighth from the third—But if you find the Lord of the third in the seventh, he is in the place he first went unto, and you may judge of his condition there according as his Significator is seated in that part of the Figure.

V. If the Lord of the third be posited in the eighth House, 'tis no good signe (especially if it be the eighth from the third) if he happen to be afflicted there either by Combustion, or the malignant Aspects of *Saturne or Mars*, then the person is in a sad condition and despairs of life; and without other Testimonies fall in to assiist, he may in all probability dye; and this the rather if he labour then under any unhappy Direction of the Ascendant, *Sun* or *Moon* to dangerous Promittors in his Nativity.

VI. If the Significator be posited in the ninth House, the absent party is then removed much farther, and has a mind to see more variety in his Travel, and may probably at last retire himself to a solitary place, *viz.* a *Nunnery* or some or some place equivolent where he will resolve to spend his time in matters of Religion, or amongst Religious persons, *&c.*

VII. If the Significator be posited in the Tenth House in reception or good Aspect of the Fortunes, then you may conclude he has attained some hopeful preferment, or some Imployment, Office or Command where he is; but if afflicted therein by ill Aspects of the Fortunes or Combust of the Sun, judge the contrary, he is either dead, or in some unhappy condition: So saies *Guido Bonatus*, part 2d, page 240. and from him our late *English* Authors.

VIII. The same Author goes on, *Si vero suer it in undesima junctus fortunis a bono Aspects*, &c. If he be in the eleventh House joyned to the Fortunes by any good or favourable Aspect, or in ☌ with the Lord of the eleventh, the Absent Brother is then very safe, and in a good Condition at the house of some Friend; But being posited in the eleventh, and afflicted there by the Infortunes or otherwise, then judge the Quesited is troubled and much discontented, and doth not at all delight in his present condition.

IX. If in the twelfth House in Reception or good Aspect of the Fortunes, and they free from affliction, the absent party then deals in great Cattle, as Oxen or Horses, &c. and may probably gain thereby: But if unfortunate in the twelfth, either by the evil Aspects of the Infortunes, or Lord of the eighth, or Combust, then the absent party is much discontented, and dispairs of returning to his own Countrey again and not without cause, for in all probability he may be prevented by death.

X. If the Significator be in the Ascendant (which is the eleventh from the third) the Absent Brother is then in a good condition, and likes well the place where he is (especially if he be fortunate there) and is well beloved by the Persons he is with; But if posited in the second, there is some danger of Restraint, that the person cannot get his liberty, 'tis probable he may be imprisoned (for the second House is the twelfth from the first) yet if his Significator be Retrograde he will endeavour to make his Escape the first opportunity: And thus you may judge varying the Houses of the Condition of any other absent person let the Relation stand how it will.

SECT. IV.

Is the Councel or Advice of a Neighbour or Friend Real or not?

I. The Judgment of Authors in this case is to consider whether there be a fortunate Planet posited in the tenth House, *viz. Jupiter* or *Venus* or the *Dragons Head*, or the *Moon* in good aspect to the Lord of the Ascendant, then judge the advice of your Friend or Neighbour is good, and no ill design intended thereby.

II. But if you find *Saturne, Mars*, or the *Dragons Tayl*, in the Mid-heaven, judge the contrary, your pretended friends and Councellours are Treacherous, and come rather to ensnare you, and eclipse your Honour, than in reality to assist and befriend you: judge the same if the Sign Ascending be moveable, or the Lord of the Ascendant, and the *Moon* be in moveable or double bodyed Signes.

SECT. V.

Whether Reports or Rumours spread abroad be True or False?

I. If you find the *Moon* in the Ascendant or the tenth, eleventh, or third Houses separated from some good Aspect of a Fortunate Planet, (or indeed any Planet) provided she apply to ☌, ✶ or △ of the Lord of the Ascendant, then you may conclude the report is true.

II. If the *Moon* be void of Course at the time of the Question or Report, 'tis false and will be suddenly contradicted: if the *Moon* be □ or ☍ of ☿ and neither of them behold the Ascendant well, judge the same.

III. If the Lord of the Ascendant or the *Moon* be Angular, and in fixed Signes, or in Friendly Aspect with the *Sun, Jupiter*, or *Venus*, there is then great probability the Report is true.

IV. But if you find the *Moon*, or Lord of the Ascendant in bad Aspect with the Infortunes, and posited in Cadent Houses; or if *Mercury* be in *Conjunction* with the *Dragons Tayl*, or in *Opposition, Quartile*, or *Conjunction* of *Saturne* or *Mars*, then you may assure your self the Report is altogether false, and will come to nothing.

CHAP. IV.

Questions and Judgments appertaining to the Fourth House.

SECT. I.

Shall the Querent enjoy the Estate of his Father?

I. The Ascendant and his Lord with the *Moon* always signifies the Querent in all Questions (as I have already intimated) and in this Question the fourth House and his Lord signifies the Quesited (*viz.* the Father) the fifth House (which is the second from the fourth) his Estate or Substance.

II. If you find the Lord of the fifth in Reception or good Aspect with the Lord of the Ascendant, or rather the Lord of the second, this is one good Argument the Querent may enjoy his Fathers Estate.

III. If the Fortunate Planets happen to be posited in the fifth House, and from thence behold the Lord of the Ascendant or second House by any Friendly Aspect; or if the Lord of the fifth be in the second, or Lord of the second in the fifth, these are promising Arguments, and if the *Part of Fortune* be disposed of by the Lord of the fifth, in the Ascendant or second House, it doth much confirm the judgment, and in point of Art shews that in all probability the Querent may enjoy his desire.

IV. But if you find the Lord of the fifth House much afflicted, and in no good Aspect of the former Significators, or an Infortune in the fourth or fifth Houses, these are testimonies of small hopes of good to the Querent: In short, in this Question consider the Lord of the fifth and second Houses, and see how they behold each other, as also the Lord of the fourth and Ascendant, consider whether these Significators be in friendly Aspect or not, or how they are beheld by other planets, and accordingly moderate your Judgment, and you cannot err in giving the Querent a Rational Answer to his Query, both as to the Respect or Concordancy that is between the Querent and his Father, as also whether he may enjoy the Estate (if any) that he hopes for.

SECT. II.

Shall the Querent obtain the House, Land, or other Possessions he desires to Take or Purchase?

I. If the Lord of the Ascendant or the *Moon* (which signifies the Querent) shall be in ☌ or otherwise in good Aspect and Reception with the Lord of the fourth House or Planet therein (which signifies the House or Land sought after) or if the Lord of the fourth be posited in the Ascendant, these are very promising Testimonies that the Querent may be so happy as to attain his end in this matter.

II. If the Lord of the seventh which (according to *Haley*) signifies the Seller be in good Aspect, or apply to the Lord of the Ascendant, this is an Argument that the Owner of the House is willing to Bargain with the Querent; if there be Reception or Translation of Light between the Significators, judge the same—or if they apply to a ☌, or the *Moon* transfer the light of one Significator to the other, this shews a great probability that the business may be effected either by themselves or assistance of others, and in fine shews a very hopeful issue of the Matter in Question.

III. But if there be no Reception, or Translation of Light, nor the Significators in any hopeful Aspect, judge the contrary; and if you find an Infortune in the seventh, be careful how you deal with the Owner of the House, least you be over-reached, or Knavishly dealt with; if the fourth House be afflicted, the House or Land is faulty, and there is no probability of a good end; but if Fortunate Planets are posited therein, judge the contrary, as Reason with Art will direct you, both in this and all other Questions.

IV. As to the *Quality* of the Ground or Land that you would Buy or Purchase, if a *Fiery* Signe be upon the Cusp of the fourth House, you may then conclude the Land is Hilly, Dry, Hungry, or Stoney Ground—if an *Airy* Signe, say the ground is good in the general, and probably mixt and not all of one Quality; if an *Earthy* Signe be upon the Cusp of the fourth, it is good plain Pasture, and will prove well—if a *Watry* Signe be thereon, judge the ground is moist, probably some Springs therein, or a River running through or neer it, and yet good; but if it be the Signe *Scorpio* upon the Cusp of the fourth House, 'tis ten to one but the Ground is Boggy and Unwholsome, and annoyed with standing Water, or subject to be overflowed—Some Authors say, if a Fortunate Planet be direct in the tenth House, there is plenty of Timber upon the Ground; if that Planet be Ocddental, it conforms the Judgment: But let every man take a strict view in this Case before he adventure to lay out his Money.

Note that in Buying or Hireing of a Ship, (which falls under the same Head with this Section) that the Ascendant and Lord thereof, with the Moon, signifies the Buyer; and the seventh House, and Lord thereof, the Seller: (as in Houses and Lands, &c.) The fourth House and his Lord must signifie the Ship, the tenth House and his Lord and Planets posited therein the Tackling and Masts thereof, consider the several Significators, and judge in all respects as in Buying or Purchasing of Houses or Land, and you cannot err, consideration being had to the Parts of the Ship, signified by the Signes, which were express'd in the Judgment of the first House.

SECT. III.

May the Querent Advantage himself by Removal, or had he better continue in his Old Habitation?

I. If you find Fortunate Planets in the Ascendant or fourth house, then give the Querent Incouragement to stay in the House where he is, or if the Lord of the Ascendant and the Lord of the fourth be ✶, △, or ☌, or in good Aspect with the Fortunate Planets, advise him to stay rather than remove.

II. But on the contrary, if you find the Ascendant or fourth House vitiated or afflicted by the presence of the Infortunes, then the Querent had better remove than remain in the House where he is, and if you observe what Houses the afflicting Planets are Lords of, you may from thence discover the occasion of the injury the Querent suffers—Consider also the Separation and Application of the *Moon*, which will help much in this Judgment.

III. Observe that the seventh House and his Lord signifies the Place or House to which you would remove; the fourth House and his Lord the present Habitation of the Querent; and Authors say, the tenth House and his Lord, denote the benefit or prejudice that may arise by Removing.—Now by a due consideration of the Aspects and Configurations of the Significators, as also how the Fortunes or Infortunes behold them, you muy accordingly judge and direct the Querent, what in all probability he had best resolve upon; and therefore there needs no farther Discourse upon this Query.

SECT. IV.

Of Hidden Tresure, Is there any in the Place Suspected or Not? &c.

I. If the Fortunate Planets be in the North Angle strong and free from the Hostile Rayes of the Infortunes, or if the ⊕, or the ☋ be therein, or the Lord of the fourth in the fourth House, these are Arguments that there may be Treasure concealed in the place suspected, and it is of the Nature of that Planet which is the Significator thereof as if the ☉ be Signiflcator, say 'tis Gold, if the ☽, Silver, &c.

II. But if you find the fourth House afflicted by the presence or ill Aspects of the Infortunes (if they happen not to be Significators) it is then more than probable that there is no Treasure hidden, and therefore invain to make search after it. Yet if the *Moon* or Lord of the fourth House did last separate from ♃ or ♀, you may then conclude that Treasure has been hidden there, but now removed or taken away: And farther note, that if the aforesaid Significators did separate ill, that there was never any thing of that kind hidden in that place.

III. If you find good Testimonies that there may be Treasure hidden, and desire to know whether it be attainable or not, then Consider whether the Lord of the Ascendant or *Moon* be in the fourth House, or in good Aspect to the Lord thereof, or Fortunate Planets therein; if so, you may tell the Querent there is a probability he may by diligent search attain his desire; but on the contrary, if Infortunes be in the fourth House, and the Lord of the Ascendant and Luminaries afflicted, then there is very small hopes of Profit, and the Querent had better waive all endeavours after the same.

IV. If the Question were concerning any thing that is Hid or Mislaid (whether in jest or otherwise) then consider (after you have set your Scheme) whether the Lord of the second House, (which signifies the thing miss-laid, if it be the Querents own Goods) be in the Ascendant, or in ♂ with the Lord thereof, or in either of his Houses, then the thing Miss-laid is in the House, and in that part thereof which the Querent himself delights chiefly to be in; if in the tenth House, say it is in the Shop, if the Querent be a Trades-man; if a Gentleman, say 'tis in the Hall, or Dineing-room; if a Countryman, say in the first Room after the Entry: if the Significator be in the seventh House, then you may conclude it to be in that Room where the Querents Wife most frequents, or Women use; if in the fourth, in some decayed part of the House, or where Ancient people Lodge; if in *Fiery* Signs, say near the Chiminey; if in *Earthy* Signs, in some lower Room, or rather the floor thereof; if in *Watry* Signs, search neer some Watry place, *viz.* the *Cistern, Pump, Wash house, Buttery, Dairy, &c.* but if the Significator of the thing missing be found in *Airy* Signs, 'tis hid in some upper Room, or in some high place from the Floor. If you would observe the Quarters of Heaven that the Signs shew, the better to find the part of that House where the thing is laid; then consult the *Introductory Part*. There needs no more discourse upon this Question, in regard it tends more to *Pastime*, and *Sport*, than any serious matter; yet the truth of these rules have been often verified to admiration.

SECT. V.

Shall a City, Town, Castle, Fort, or Island, that is besieged, be taken, or not?

I. In this Question, the Ascendant, and Lord thereof, signifies the Querent, or Persons Besieging; and the seventh House, the Lord thereof, the Enemy; the fourth House, the Town, City, or Strong-hold; and the Lord of the fourth the Governour thereof; the tenth House, and Lord thereof, shall represent the Commander of the Besiegers; and the fifth House the Ammunition, Assistance, and Provision of the Besieged Persons. [*But others are of opinion, that we ought to give the Ascendant to him that propounds the Question, and his Lord, to the Army, or Persons that beleaguer the place of which the Question is propounded: the seventh House shall signifie the City, Town, or Fort, Besieged, and his Lord the Governour thereof, or Persons Besieged therein; to this latter Haly agrees, but the former Rules are generally accepted.*]

II. If fortunate Planets be posited in the Ascendant, or in favourable Aspect to the Lord thereof, and the fourth House, and Lord thereof afflicted; this argues the Strong-hold will be taken, and the contrary.

III. If ♄, or ♂, or the *Dragons Tayl* be posited in the fourth House, and ♃, or ♀, be in no friendly Aspect to the Cusp, or Lord thereof; there is then great danger that the Fort will not be able to hold out long, or that some treacherous Action will be suddenly committed, and the Governour himself out of all hope of securing it. [*Note, that a Planet in his exaltation is accounted more potent than a Planet in his House; and a Superiour Planet is to be preferr'd before an Inferiour one, in all Questions, (especially those of this Nature) moreover Mars (who is the proper Patron of Warr) if he be powerful and in his own Dignities, and in good Aspect to a particular Significator, to him you may pronounce Victory.*]

IV. If the Lord of the seventh House be strong and powerful, or fortunate Planets posited therein, or in good Aspect to the Lord thereof; you may then conclude the Enemy to be in good heart, and will boldly rencounter, and oppose when they are attempted: And if the Lord of the fourth House be strong in the fourth, the Fort, or *Strong-hold* will not be taken, judge the same if the Lord of the seventh be well posited in the fourth House; but if the Lord of the fourth be in such a House as beholds not the fourth, and the Lord of the seventh out of the North Angle, there is danger it may be taken.

V. If the Significators be posited in fixed Signs, the Siege may continue long, in moveable Signs, the contrary: to conclude, in questions of this nature, do but consider the strength of the Significators, see how they are befriended, or afflicted, and accordingly judge of the event; for 'tis impossible to lay down Rules for every thing which may happen: such is the great variety that may be drawn from some *Schemes*, both in this, and other questions; the consideration whereof must be left to the Prudence, and Discretion of every *Artist*.

[*Some Authors rank this Section amongst those appertaining to the seventh House, which, in my opinion, doth not improperly belong to the fourth.*]

CHAP. V.

Questions, and Judgement, properly belonging to the fifth House.

SECT. I.

Shall the Querent ever have Issue, or is she capable of bearing Children?

I. See whether the Lord of the Ascendant, and the *Moon* behold the Lord of the fifth; or if any Planet transferr the light of the Lord of the Ascendant, to the Lord of the fifth: or if the aforesaid Significators be posited (any of them) in fruitful Signs, these are Testimonies in Art, that the Querent may have Issue.

II. Judge the same, if you find the Lord of the Ascendant, or the *Moon* in the fifth House, or the Lor d of the fifth in the Ascendant, or ♃, or ♀ in the fifth; or casting a benovolent Aspect thereunto, or unto the Lord of the fifth House; these are good Arguments that the Querent may have Children.

III. But if ♄, ♂, or ☋, be in the fifth House, or afflict the same, or any of the principal Significators; or if ♀ be combust, or the Sign of the fifth a steril Sign; or the Significators in barren Signs: these are notable Arguments that the Querent will very rarely have Children.

SECT. II.

Is the Querent with Child? If so, of what Sex, Male, or Female; or is she impregnated with more than One, &c.

I. If the Lord of the Ascendant, or the *Moon* be posited in fruitful Signs, and behold the Cusp of the fifth House, or Lord thereof, by a ✶, or △ Aspect; or ♃, or ♀ be Angular, and free from the affliction of ♄, or ♂; or if the *Moon*, or Lord of the fifth House be Located therein: these are signal Testimonies that the Woman enquiring, is undoubtedly with Child.

II. But if you find the aforesaid Significators afflicted by the Hostile beams of ♄, or ♂, or either of them in the fifth (which is the House of Children) or ☋ there; or if ♀, ♃, or the *Moon*, be afflicted by the ☌, □, or ☍ of ♄, or ♂: you may, upon good grounds in Art, judge that the Querent is not impregnated.

III. If by the foregoing Rules you come to discover that the Querent is with Child, and you would also know whether it be a Boy, or a Girl; you are then to consider the aforesaid Significators, whether they be in Mascullne, or Feminine *Signs*; and by an exact Collection of the Major Testimonies, you may pronounce Judgement: if they be found Masculine, say a *Boy*; if most Feminine, Testimonies judge the Querent is with Child of a *Girl* [*which are Masculine, and Feminine Planets and Signs, and already shewed in the Introductory part; and therefore need not here be repeated again.*]

IV. If you find the Lord of the Ascendant, or the *Moon* in double-bodied Signs; or the Ascendant it self, or Cusp of the fifth House double bodied, or Bicorporeal; or if ♃, ♀, or ☋ shall be in the fifth, posited in fruitful Signs. These are good Testimonies that in all probability the Querent is impregnated with Twins, or more Children

Clavis Astrologiae Elimita, The Key to Astrology New Filed

than one; Judge the same if ♃, or ♀ cast their △, or ✶ Aspects to the Cusp of the Ascendant, or fifth House; and those double bodied, or common Signs: but if fixed Signs be upon those Houses, or moveable, if the ☉, or ☽ be, therein, you may conclude a single Conception.

V. *If the Question were how long it will be before a Woman may be wiith Child?* Finding Testimonies that the Querent may have Children, consider then the position of the Lord of the fifth House; if in the Ascendant, tell the Querent it will be the first Year; if in the second House, the second Year; if in the tenth House, the third Year; if in the seventh House, the fourth Year; if in the fourth House, say the fifth Year; but withal observe what Sign the Lord of the fifth House is posited in, and whether he be swift, or slow in motion; for a Planet direct and swift in motion, in a movable Sign, doth generally hasten the matter, or time; double-bodied Signs do not put forward so soon, and fixed Signs usually prolong the time in such cases.

VI. *If you would make a Conjecture how long the Woman has Conceived*, Mr. *Lilly* gives these Rules, that the *Astrologian* should consider the *Moon*, Lord of the fifth, and Lord of the hour; and observe which of those are neerest from the separation of any Planet; if the separation was frdm a △ Aspect, say she is in the fifth, or third Month of her Conception; if 'twere a ✶ Aspect, say the seconnd, or sixth Month of Conception; if the separation was a □ Aspect, judge she is in the fourth Month; but if the separation was from an ☍, say seven Months; if from a ☌, you may conclude only one Month; a little experience may confirm, or contradict these Rules.

VII. *If it were enquired how many Children the Querent may have?* Then let the *Artist* observe diligently the several Significators of Issue, how many of them he finds in fruitful and common Signs, also how many are posited in barren Signs; then for every Planet in a fruitful Sign, allow one; and for every Planet in a common, or double-bodied Sign, two Testimonies; and in fine, Substract all the Testimonies of Barrenness, from those of Issue, or promising Children; and the Remainer (if any be) shews the Numbet of Children desired; according to the judgement of some Authors.

VIII. *As to the time when the Birth will be*, Authors advise to direct the part of Children to the Cusp of the fifth House, or to his Lord, or to ♃, or his benevolent Aspects, by allowing a day to every degree of Distance, will point neerly out the time of her delivery; but first observe how long she may Naturally go, and then consider the premises. [*The part of Children is taken by Day, and Night, From ♂ to ♃, and projected from the Ascendant.*] Observe also when the Significator of the Question moves out of one Sign, into another, and thereby changes his form, that is a proper time wherein the Birth may be expected; otherwise consider how far distant the Lord of the fifth House is from the Cusp thereof; and for every Sign distant, allow one Month; by this Rule, together with other Testimonies, an *Artist* may come very near the matter, in such a dubious Case as this. [*Thus much shall suffice, concening the Birth of Children.*]

SECT. III.

Of Embassadours, Messengers, Gameing, &c.

I. Always the Lord of the fifth House shall signifie the *Embassadour*, or *Messenger*, the *Moon* must be accepted a Co-significator; and the Planet, or Planets, to whom the *Moon*, or Lord of the fifth applies, shall shew the cause of the Embassage, or Message; the sixth House, and the Lord thereof shall signifie his Assistants, orAttendants &c. If it be a common Messenger, that is sent with a Letter between Persons of ordinary Degree, still the fifth House signifies the Messenger, or Letter sent; but the seventh House, and Lord thereof, the Person to whom it is sent; the third, and ninth Houses, and their Lords, what may happen in the Journey; and the fourth House, and Lord thereof, the final end, or conclusion of the matter; or the good, or ill success of the Answer.

II. Now by a due observation how these several Significators behold each other, or separate, or apply, to, or from each other other by friendly, or Hostile Aspects, (that is by ✶, or △, or by □, or ☍) and observing from what parts of the Figure those Aspects are made (if any be) you may thence deduce a rational Judgment what the event may be of the proceedings of the *Embassadour*, and his *Embassage*, or of the *Messenger* (which is a minor *Embassadour*) and his *Message* &c.

III. As if you find the Lord of the fifth in good Aspect with the *Moon*, the Lord of the Ascendant, or Cusp thereof; you may then conclude the Messenger (let him be of what quality soever) will perform his business faithfully, with all diligence, and industry, for. the Person, or Persons, that imploy'd him; but if the aforesaid Significators behold each other by □, or ☌, judge the contrary.

IV. When the Lord of the fifth doth separate from the Lord of the seventh House, 'tis an Argument the Messenger is returning; and if he applies by good Aspect to the Lord of the Ascendant, there is great hopes he has effected the buiness, and returns to the Persons content that sent him; herein observe what House that Planet is Lord of, from whom the Lord of the fifth separates; and from the consideration thereof you may easily judge of the Account the Messenger brings: If he separates from Fortunes you may hope well, if from Infortunes, judge the contrary, all is not well as to the content of the Querent, or Person that sent the Messenger.

V. If you find a friendly reception, either by House, or exaltation between the Significator of the Messenger, and the Significator of the Person to whom he was sent; then you may in reason judge the Messenger is friendly entertained; and if it so happen also that there be a Translation of Light, or Vertue between the Lord of the seventh, and Lord of the Ascendant; or if any good Aspect be between them, this is sure Testimony the Querent will obtain his desire, as to the Message, and all things succeed according to his expectation, to his great content and satisfaction: But if contrary Testimonies fall out, judge the contrary.

VI. *If the Question were, shall I gain or Lose by Play?*

If you find a reception between the Lord of the fifth House (which always signifies the Game) and the Lord of the Ascendant (which always signifies the Querent) or if they are in friendly Aspect, judge the Querent is fairly promised much encouragement by his sport, and may happily gain profit thereby; and this is the more certain, if ♀ (who naturally signifies sports, Pastime, and all sorts of delights and pleasures) shall behold the Lord of the second, or Ascendant, by any friendly Aspect; or if there be a Translation of Light, or Vertue, between the *Moon*, the Lord of the fifth, or Lord of the eighth House, (which signifies the Adversarys substance) and Lord of the Ascendant, or second House; if none of these happen, there is but small encouragement for the Querent to adventure, least he comes of with loss—from the consideration of the premises, observing well the Position, & Constitution of the Significators, a contrary judgement is as easily deduced; and therefore there needs no more to be said to this particular, unless to advise the Querent that he rather consider the strength of the Lord of the fifth House in his Geniture (if it may be had) and to see how he is beheld, or what Planets Transits the fifth House, or the good Aspects of the Lord thereof at the time of the Question. Again, consider the Significator of Gameing also in the Revolution for that Year; and by a strict Inspection into these things (would the Querent be so curious) he might from thence expect greater satisfaction, at least proceed upon a more certain and firm Foundation, if the business be rightly managed by an able Artist.

VII. *If the Question were, shall a Petition delivered to some great Person be granted?*

Here the Petition is signified by the fifth House, the Lord thereof, and the *Moon*; and you are to take the tenth House, and Lord thereof, and the *Sun* for the great Person you present it unto. Now if you find Reception, or good Aspect between the Lord of the tenth House, and Lord of the fifth, you may then conclude the Petition may be heard: the same judgement may be given, if the Lord of the tenth be in good Aspect to the *Moon*, especially if he be a fortunate Planet; the same also if it happen to be ♄, or ♂ in their own Essential dignities, and they in good Aspect and reception with the Significator of the Querent, or his Petition.

VIII. If the Lord of the Ascendant, and Ascendant, or the *Moon* be no way afflicted by the Infortunes, there is great hopes the Petitioner may go on without obstruction, or opposition, with much cheerfulness, and boldness; and if the *Moon* apply to the ✶, or △ of ♃, or ♀, this intimates the Contents of the Petition will be well received, and approved of, to the great satisfaction of the Petitioner; judge the same if the Lord of the fifth be in good Aspect to the *Sun*: but if the Lord of the Ascendant be in □, or ☌ with the Lord of the fourth, eighth, tenth, or twelfth Houses: or if the *Moon*, or Lord of the fifth House be afflicted, then you may easily judge an ill Issue, that the Petition will be disliked, and by no means granted, but rather a check, or slight Answer returned.

CHAP. VI.

*Judgments and Interogations proper to the Sixth House;
which hath Signification of Diseases, &c.*

SECT. I.

Some General Rules how to Judge of Diseases.

I. Observe that the Ascendant and Lord thereof, together with the *Almuten* of the Figure always signifies the Person of the Sick, but the sixth House, and Lord thereof, also the Planets that shall be posited therein, together with the ☽ and the Sign she is in, these shall signifie the Disease, not omitting to consider in your Judgment, the Ascendant and Gubernator thereof: The seventh House and Lord thereof alwayes represents the Physician, but the tenth House and *Almuten* thereof, together with those Planets that may happen to be posited therein, shall signifie the Physick or Medicine which is applyed to the sick Party. Now if the seventh House or Lord thereof be afflicted, 'tis an ill *Omen*, and shews that the Doctor shall not be so fortunate as to cure the Patient; and if you find the Lord of the tenth House afflicted, or the Infortunes posited therein, then you may conclude the Physick which is Administered to be very improper for the Distemper, and doth rather aggravate it, than help, or give ease to the sick party.

II. If a *Urine* be brought either with or without the consent of the sick party; the Ascendant shall represent him; but if the *Urine* be brought, and the Question be propounded without the consent of the Patient, then the Ascendant shall represent the Querent, and the sick persons Significator shall be taken according as his or her Relation to the Querent stands. [*How that may be performed has been already shewed in the varying of the Houses, &c.*]

III. What Diseases every Planet signifies naturally of itself and through the twelve Signes, I have exprest in the seventh Chapter of the Introduction, and the Diseases appropriated to the twelve Signes, you may read in the third chapter thereof.

IV. *The several parts of Mans Body that are appropriated to the seven Planets are these*, viz. ♄ is said to Govern or bear Rule over the Bones, the Teeth, the Spleen, the right Ear, and the Rententive faculty throughout the Body, *Jupiter* Rules the Liver, Lungs, Ribs, Sides, Blood, Veins, the Natural Virtue in Man, and the Digestive Faculty. *Mars* bears Rule in Mans Body over the Gall, the Tast, the Stones, the Face, and in short, the Apprehension too. The *Sun* is said to bear Rule over the Sight, (and the right eye in particular) the Heart, the Back, the Arteries. To *Venus* is assumed all the Instruments of the Generation, as the Testicles, the Yard, the Womb, Womens Breasts, the Milk and Seed, also the Throat, the Reins and Kidneys. To *Mercury*'s Government is attributed the Rational part of man, the Brain, the Imagination, the Tongue, the Hands, the Feet, the Spirits. To the *Moon* is Assigned the whole Bulk or Body of the Brain, the Stomach, the Bowels, the Bladder, the right Eye of a Woman, the left of a Man, and some say the Tast also.

V. *The seven Planets Rule or Govern the Spirits also, both Vital, Animal and Natural*. The Vital remain in the Heart, and are appropdated to the *Sun*; the Animal are seated in the Brain, and Ruled by *Mercury* and the *Moon*; *Mercury* hath power over the Operative part, and the *Moon* over the Brain it self: *Jupiter* and *Venus* Rule the Natural Part, which is said to be scituated in the Liver: So the *Sun* Governs the Attractive Power, *Jupiter* the Digestive, *Mercury* the Imaginative or Apprehensive Power, the *Moon* the Expulsive, and *Saturne* the Retentive Faculty, as before I intimated: So in the Signes, the Attractive Faculty is Ruled by the *Fiery* Triplicity, the Digestive by the *Airy*, the Retentive by the *Earthy*, and the Expulsive by the *Watry* Triplicity.

VI. *Having promised these things, I proceed to the General Rules of Judging a Figure of the Decumbiture*; viz. *Enquire whether the Sick Party may Recover or not?*

If the *Moon* and Significator of the Disease are no way afflicted, but apply to the good Aspects of Fortunate

Planets, or are in Reception with them; this shews that there is great hopes of Recovery; or if you find Fortunate Planets in the Mid-heaven, or Ascendant in the Figure of the Decumbiture, and posited in either of these Angles free from affliction, Judge the same, that Nature being assisted will conquer the Disease.

VII. If *Jupiter* or *Venus*, or the *Sun* or *Moon* be posited in the Ascendant, and none of them Rulers of the eighth House, nor afflicted by the Lord thereof, these are Testimonies of a speedy Recovery: you may also hope well if the ☽ be in ☌ of ♃ in a good place of the Figure.

VIII. *Saturne* being Significator of the Disease, or a fixed Sign upon the Cusp of the sixth, shews that the Disease may continue long, or not easily removed, if the latter degrees of a Sign possess the Cusp of the sixth House, or *Jupiter* or *Mars* signifie the Disease, judge. the contrary, that the Disease will not continue long, but end one way or other: the same if moveable or common Signes possess the Cusp of the sixth, or if *Venus*, *Mercury*, or the *Moon* shall be Significators, then the Disease is either very short or suddenly alters. [*And by these Rules alone an Artist may Judge whether the Disease will be Chronique or Acute.*]

IX. But if you find the Lord of the eighth, strong and Angular, and the *Moon* weak and Cadent, having Dignities in the Ascendant, or if the Lord of the Ascendant or the *Moon* are afflicted by the Infortunes, or Combust of the *Sun*, these are dangerous Testimonies, and threaten Death, unless there be Reception, or some Friendly Aspect of the Fortunes interposing: Moreover, if the Lord of the eighth House be in his Essential Dignities in the Ascendant at the time of the Decumbiture, or in ☌ with the Lord thereof, 'tis a mortal Signe, and the Patient rarely Escapes.

SECT. II.

Of the Nature and Quality of the Disease in General.

I. By what has been already written 'tis no hard matter for an Artist to discover the Nature of the Disease that afflicts the Patient, provided the real Decumbiture may be procured.

II. If ♄ be Significator and the afflicting Planet, he generally produces lingering or tedious Distempers, as Consumptions, Coughs, Quartain Agues, &c. as you may read more at large, *chap. 7 of the Introduction*. If he be posited in a Fiery Sign, he threatens a long and dangerous Feavor; If he be in a Watry Signe, the Disease arises from some gross and vitious Humour, or it proceeds from some Cold or moist Distemper, which may prove *Chronique*, sometimes accompanyed with a Flux.

III. *Saturne* in Earthy Signes produces lingering and tedious Melancholy Distempers, as Consumptions, &c. But in Airy Signs, the Gout, and pains proceeding from Goutish Humours lodged in several parts of the Body.

IV. *Saturne* in moveable Signs usually produces a Flux of Humours in most parts of the Body, as the Dropsie, &c. and this more certain if the *Moon* be joyned unto him. In common Signes he gives Compound or mixt Distempers; which, with great deliberation alter from one Disease into another: In fixed Signes he produces Feavours, Gouts, Leprosies, and other unwelcome tedious Diseases.

V. If *Jupiter* be Significator of the Disease, the Liver is disordered, the Digestion not good, the Blood too hot, according to the Signs he is posited in. If in a Fiery sign, the Disease is such a Feaver as arises from the Blood not Corrupted or Putrified, and continues not long. If in Earthy Signs, the Collick or Scurvey; In Airy Signes, Diseases that arise from Corruption of Blood, as Surfeits, &c. If in Watry Signes, the Scurvey, Dropsie, Itch, &c.

VI. If *Mars* be Significator of the Disease, you may conclude it to be a violent Feavour, arising from Corrupt and Putrified Blood; If in a Fiery Signe, 'tis a Burning Feavour, or the Plague. *Mars* in an Earthy Signe sometimes gives the Bloody Flux or Jaundice; in an Aiery Sign, Quotdian Feavours, Frenzy, Madness, &c. If in a Watry Sign, judge the Small-pox, Measles, the Dropsie or Scurvey.

VII. If the *Sun* be much afflicted at the Decumbiture by the Hostile Beams of *Saturne*, the Disease arises chiefly from Melancholy; If of *Mars*, judge Cholar is the cause; The first may produce a consumption, and the last the Yellow-jaundice, or some Distemper equivolent.

VIII. If Venus signifie the Disease, judge the Distemper arises from Intemperance or Debauchery; If she be ill Aspected to *Saturne*, there is danger of Poyson; If *Jupiter* afflict, 'tis a Surfeit; if *Mars*, 'tis some Venerial Distemper; if the *Sun*, judge a Feaver; if *Mercury*, judge a disturbed fancy, either for Love or some other cause; if the *Moon*, 'tis a Palsie.

IX. If *Mercury* be Significator, and afflicted, the Distemper lies in the Brain, and the Patient is then Mad or Phrensical, and this the more certain if *Mars* or the *Sun* be in ill Aspect to *Mercury*: if *Saturn* afflict *Mercury*, the Party is Melancholy; if *Venus* behold *Mercury*, you may be sure the sick Party is disturbed in his fancy concerning some Woman, probably he is Love sick; if the *Moon* be in ☍ or □ of ☿, judge the Convulsion-fits, or Falling-Sickness; or a Distemper of that Nature offends the Patient.

X. If the *Moon* be in ♈, and principal Significator in the eighth House, the Head is afflicted, probably the Megrim; if posited in any of the other Signes, judge as you are directed in Chap. VIII.

[*And thus the Nature of the Disease may easily be discovered, always observing, that the Planet describes the Disease, and the Sign he is posited in, the part of the Body that is offended, not omitting the House he is in, which shews the true and natural cause thereof, as Authors, who have written Astrologically upon this Subject do copiously demonstrate*]

XI. *If you were to discover whether the Distemper lay in the Body or the Mind*, Consider that if the *Sun*, *Moon*, or Ascendant be much afflicted, or very weak, and their Lords or Dispositors no way impeded, then you may conclude the Body is distempured, and the Mind free; But on the contrary, if the Ascendant and the Luminaries be free from all manner of affliction, and their Dispositors debilitated or much impeded, then you may Rationally conclude that the Distemper lies in the mind, and the Body is free.

XII. If. *Saturne* be the Planet concern'd in this matter, say that Grief, Care and Troubles of the World, and extream Melancholy and Discontent is the Principal cause; if *Jupiter*, 'tis a hundred to one but Religion, or Religious Persons have occasioned the Patients Injury and affliction; if *Mars*, say 'tis some unhappy Quarrel, or rash Act the Patient may then grow Frantick or Mad; if *Sol*, the Party is Ambitious, Proud, Vvain-glorious and Aspiring, and the cause of this affliction proceeds from thence; if *Venus* be concerned, 'tis Love-passion that disturbs the Patient, or something equivolent, perhaps the unkindness of, or affront from some Female Creature, or Mistress; if *Mercury*, the Person hath Over-studied himself, and so disturbed his Brain that way, or else some foolish Imaginations do possess him, and that is the cause; if the *Moon*, say some Ordinary Person has affronted him, or some Woman or Neighbour proves very unkind, or else some publick concern offends him; and thus joyning Reason to Art, you may Conjecture to Admiration.

SECT. III.

Of the Affliction of the Moon *by* Saturne *or* Mars *in the four* Trigons,
being the Diagnosticks *of* Hermes.

First, Of the Moons Affliction in the Fiery Triplicity.

I. If at the Decumbiture of the Sick, you find the *Moon* in ♈ afflicted by the ☌, □, or ☍ of ♄, then the Disease proceeds from a Cold Cause, with heaviness of Head, weakness of the Eyes, Distillation of Rhume in the Breast, stoppage of the Throat or Wind-pipe, with Phlegm, an outward Chillness or Shivering with Cold, Loathing in the Stomach, Swounding, and irregular and faint Sweatings, &c.

In this Case Blood-letting is improper, but such things which heat, mollifie, and loosen the Belly, may fitly be applyed: If the Moon *apply not by good Aspect to either of the Fortunate Planets, the Person is in great danger of Death.*

II. If the *Moon* be in ♈, and afflicted by the ☌, □, or ☍ of ♂, then the Disease proceeds from some Distemper in the Brain, thence continual Feavours, the Patient is Restless, the Mouth hot and dry, the sick Party is extream

Thirsty, an Inflamation in the Liver, a high Pulse, and in this case there is much danger of a Frenzy or Madness to ensue.

Blood-letting, and such Medicines as Refrigerate, or Cool and Nourish are very helpful and convenient: But if the Moon *separate from* Mars, *and apply to the ill Aspects of* Saturne, *the sick Party is then in great danger of Death: but if shee apply to the Benevolent Aspects of either of the Fortunes, the Sick may Recover.*

III. If you find the ☽ in ♌ at the Decumbiture afflicted as aforesaid by ♄, this signifies a violent Feavour, and abundance of Corrupted Blood, heat and driness in the Stomach, with great heat and burning both within and without.

Now things that gently moisten, heat, and mitigate are good to be applyed: when the ☽ *meets an* ☍ *of* ♄, *if the Fortunes interpose not their Friendly Rayes, the Patient may expire.*

IV. If the ☽ be in ♌, and afflicted by the ill beams of ♂, at the sick Parties first lying down, then the Patient abounds too much with Blood, causing violent Feavours, a weak Pulse, Frenzy or Madness sometimes follow, loss of Appetite, a general Indisposition or heaviness over the whole Body, the heart is much afflicted, and a Consumption may be feared,

Such Medicines that are Astringent and Refrigerative or Cooling, are now very proper to be applyed: The ill Aspect of ♂ *and the* ☽ *in this Signe is more dangerous than in any of the rest of the twelve, insomuch, that unless there be other Testimonies of Assistance fall in, the Patient may end his dayes the ninth day.*

V. The ☽ in ♐ afflicted by ♄, signifies that the Patient is afflicted with a defluxion of sharp and thin Humours, with pain in the Joynts and Arteries, some danger of a Feavour approaching, by extremity of Heat and Cold, sometimes by Violent Exercise, and Cold taken thereupon.

If ♂ *behold the* ☽ *at the same time, then the sick Person has a most violent Feavour invades his Body; Now such Medicaments which gently heat and mitigate, moisten and assuage, may be properly Administered: when the* ☽ *is in* ✶ *or* △ *to* ♃ *or* ♀, *provided neither of them have Dignities in the sixth, eighth, or twelfth Houses.*

VI. The ☽ in ♐ afflicted by ♂ shews a violent Distemper occasioned from a Surfeit, Gluttony, Drunkenness, or over-much Repletion, whence a high Feavour proceeding from Choler, with a Flux of the Belly.

In this Case Cooling Remedies may help; the Sickness may continue long, but not kill, unless other dangerous Testimonies concur.

Secondly, the Moons *Affliction in the Earthy Triplicity.*

VII. The ☽ in ♉ afflicted by ♄ shews that the Disease arises from Luxury or Wantonness, Surfeits, or too much Repletion, causing Feavours proceeding from Obstructions of the Arteries, and Distempers of the Inward parts neer the Heart, Liver, Lungs, or from Choler, with Inflammation of the whole Body, and Exulceration of the Lungs.

Here Phlebotomey, and such Medicines that purge and dissolve gross Humours, are convenient to be applyed: now if the ☽ *Receive not the Adjuvant Rayes of the Fortunate Planets, the Case is dangerous.*

VIII. If the ☽ be in ♉ afflicted by ♂, the sick Party is tormented with continual Feavours, and the whole Body obstructed, Inflammations in the Neck and Throat, probably a Quinsie, pain in the Bones, and hinder part of the Head, a desire to Drink cool Liquors, and inordinate Watchings.

Now Phlebotomy, and such things which mittigate and extenuate, are helpful and convenient; But if the violence of ♂ *his Influence be not suppressed or repelled by the Fortunes, the Sick rarely lives to the ninth day; and if the* ☽ *be conjoyned, or in good Aspect with either of the Fortunes, the sick Party may recover, or be in a fair probability thereof the sixth day.*

IX. The ☽ in ♍ afflicted by ♄, the Cause of the Distemper arises from Crudities, and all ill Digestion of the Stomach, the Bowels and Intestines are obstructed with Phlegm, Head ach, pain under the Ribs, Inordinate Feavours.

Now such things which mollifie and dissolve are convenient to be applyed; if the ☽ be not assisted by the benevolent Rayes of the Fortunes, the Patient will be in great danger the fourteenth day; but if they are adjuvant to the ☽, the Sick Recovers, though after some long time.

X. If at the Decumbiture the ☽ be in ♍ afflicted by ♂, the Distemper arises from Fretting, Ulceration of the Intestines, with a Bloody Flux, small Feavours, the Stomach loathing of Meat, an inclination to Vomit.

Things that obstruct and repel sharp Humours may help; But unless othner Testimonies concur, the sick Party may expire in thirty dayes.

XI. The ☽ in ♑ afflicted by ♄, the Disease proceeds from some cold Cause, thin Distillations, a pain or heaviness at the Breast, the Lungs are opprest, a violent Cough or Cold, and difficulty of Breathing: sometimes a Noise in the Head or Head-ach afflicts the Patient.

Now Medicines that heat and moisten are very prevalent and helpful.

XII. The ☽ in ♑ afflicted by ♂, shews an ill Digestion, a bad Stomach, Choler abounds, the Disease is very dangerous, a Tumifying of the Nerves, the Joynts are offended with Ulcerations, as also a Flux of the Belly, sometimes the Party is inclinable to the Yellow-Jaundice, the Blood all over Corrupted, and the Disease almost Incurable.

Medicines Astringent and Obstructive are necessary to be used; the greatest danger is when the ☽ meets with the ☍ of ♂.

Thirdly, of the Moons Affljction in the Airy Tripticity.

XIII. If the ☽ be in ♊ afflicted by ♄, this shews that the Original of the Disease proceeds from the Disturbance of the mind, or it is too much opprest with Care or Business, or by much weariness in Travel, or over-watching, pain all over the Body, especially in the Joynts and Arteries, Sweating, the Spleen is disturbed, a small Feavour, and the sick Party is inclinable to a Consumption.

If the Fortunes Assist not, and the ☽ be (also) in bad Aspect to ♂, the Cafe is very dangerous, and the sick Party rarely Recovers.

If the ☽ be ♊ afflicted by ♂, the sick Party is then assaulted with a dangerous and violent Feavour, great Obstructions, sickness at Heart, with a very irregular and high Pulse.

Phlebotomy is seasonable now: But if the ☽ be in no good Aspect to the Fortunate Planets, and apply to any bad Aspect of ♄, the Patients life is in great danger.

XV. If the ☽ be in ♎ afflicted by ♄, shews that the Disease arises from Ebriety, Gluttony, Surfeiting (sometimes too much Venery) loss of Appetite, Feavers, Coughs and Hoarseness, with a Distillation of Rheum, the Pulse Remiss.

In this Case, things that Qualifie and heat are not improper: If the ☽ at the same time be Combust of the ☉, and in no good Aspect of ♃ or ♀, there is great Danger; but greater if ♂ afflict her and be Lord of the eighth House.

XVI. If at the Decumbiture the ☽ be found in ♎ afficted by ♂, the Disease arises from too great a quantity of Blood, thereby causing Intense Feavers, with an Inflamation of the whole Body, and high Pulses.

Now Blood letting may help, and such Medicines as provoke Sleep; but unless the Friendly Aspects of the Fortunes Interpose, the Patient will be in great danger when the ☽ meets with the body of ♂.

XVII. The ☽ in ♒ afflicted by ♄ at the Decumbiture, declares the Disease arises from much Labour and Toyl, Weariness. Watching, and a want of necessary refreshment, sometimes a sore Throat follows.

The Patient in this case is usually taken with Remission & Intention till the ☽ is past the ☍ of her own place; then if she meets with the Benevolent Aspects of the Fortunes, there is great hopes of a Recovery. Judge the same in the rest.

VIII. The ☽ in ♒ afflicted by ♂, shews that the Disease proceeds from a sharp and violent Cause, and the Patient is much afflicted with hot and violent Passions.

If ♃ or ♀ do but behold the ☽ by any good Aspect when she comes to the □ or ☍ of her own place, the sick Party Recovers in twenty dayes.

Fourthly, Of the Moons *Affliction in the watry Triplicity.*

XIX. The ☽ in ♋ at the first lying down of the sick, afflicted by ♄ shews that the Party has taken some violent Cold, and being Complicated with Melancholy, and vitious Matter, causeth Distillations upon the Lungs, and too much Moisture, with Catarrhs, Obstructions, Hoarseness, Feavers.

Now those Medicines that Heat and Mittigate are prevalent, and helpful.

XX. The ☽ in ♋ afflicted by ♂, shews a Surfeit, too much Blood, mueh Sweat, Phlegm offends the Stomach.

Now Vomiting may be helpful, and such Medicines as are Cooling, observe the motion of the ☽, (by whom the Crisis is made) and accordingly judge what the end may be, and how the Distemper alters.

XXI. The ☽ in ♏ afflicted by ♄, shews the Distemper is Exulceration or Bubo' s in or neer the secret parts, the Piles in Ano, or some obstructions in the Urine, sometimes the Stone in the Bladder, swellings in the Legs, Dropsical Humours or Flux, if a Man, a Gonorrhea, if a Woman, an overflowing of the Menstrua's, *&c.*

XXII. But if the ☽ be in ♏ and afflicted by ♂, the Disease proceeds from Imposthumations or Ulcerations in or about the Secrets, the Hemorrhoids, the Pox, the Small-pox, or Measles, (if a Child,) sometimes the Pestilence, or Leprosie.

Now such Medicines as Heat and Comfort are very fit to be applyed.

XXIII. The ☽ in ♓ afflicted by ♄, shews the Distemper arises from Rheum and cold Distillations, the sick Party is troubled with a continued Feaver, paints under the Breast, extention of the *Precordiacks* and Heart-strings, a sore Throat, rotten Coughs, with much Watry Humours offending the Stomach.

In this Case, such Medicaments that heat and mitigate are very helpful.

XXIV. The ☽ in ♓ afflicted by ♂, shews the Body abounds with gross Humours caused by Ebriety and Gluttony, or too much Repletion, a Frenzy or Madness sometimes follows, the Sick is most opprest in the night time, it also denotes violent Thirst and sharp Feavers, with an extream Loosness or griping pain in the Belly, and sometimes a continual Defluxion of Rheum from the Head, and great symptoms of a Dropsie.

Note that if the ☽ be afflicted of ☿, you may judge the same as of ♄, with some small mitigation: or if the ☽ be afflicted by the ☉, judge the same as of ♂, with a very little alteration; and thus you may judge of the Disease, and whether it will end in Life or Death, by the position of the ☽, at the Decumbiture, or upon demand of the Question: According to the Rules of Hermes Trismegistus.

SECT. IV.

Some Select Aphorisms of great use in the Astrological Judgment of Diseases.

I. In every Disease have a great regard to the place of the ☽, she being a general Significatrix in all Questions.

II. The sick Person is in great danger of Death when at the time of the Question, or the Decumbiture, the *Luminaries* are found under the Earth; and the more dangerous if they are afflicted there.

III. If the ☉ and ☽, or Lord of the Figure, or Lord of the Ascendant be free from affliction and have no affinity with the Lord of the eighth House, then there is no doubt but the Sick will Recover, if only two of these Significators be so afflicted, the sick Party will do very well, otherwise he dies.

IV. When the Signiflcator of the Sick is weak, or debilitated, and the Lord of the eighth strong, and afflicting him, then there is great danger the Patient may die of his Distemper, Nature being weak and the Disease very prevalent.

V. If the Lord of the Ascendant be posited in the eighth House of a Figure of the Decumbiture, or Question for the sick Party, and received by the Lord of the eighth in some Essential Dignity though there be no mutual reception between them, yet the Patient Recovers beyond expectation.

VI. The Physician hath great cause to fear his Patient when the ☽ and Lord of the Ascendant do both apply by ill Aspect to a Planet under the Earth; the contrary may be expected if they apply to some good Planet by a friendly Aspect above the Earth.

VII. If the Lord of the sixth House be in the Ascendant, or the Lord of the Ascendant in the sixth, it protracts the Disease, and is an argument of much affliction therein; so doth the □ or ☍ of the Lord of the Ascendant, and Lord of the sixth House.

VIII. The Ascendant and the ☽ being afflicted, and the Lord of the one, and the Dispositer of the other free, the Disease is in the Body, and not in the mind or Spirits.

IX. Moveable Signs easily cause the Disease to vary; Fixed Signs shew it will be long and permanent, and not without difficulty removed; Common Signs shew much variation, or a kind of ebbing and flowing of the Disease.

X. In the beginning of Diseases, the ill position of the ☽ is much to be feared, mix her Signification, with the good or ill position of the Lord of the Ascendant, and thereby Judge of the good or ill that shall attend the sick Party.

XI. If the Nativity of the sick Person may be obtained, observe if the ☽ at the time of the first Decumbiture or Question asked, be then in a place where an Infortune was in the Radix, or in □ or ☍ thereof, if so, the Cure will be performed with more difficulty, and much danger of a good end thereof.

XII. If at the Decumbiture the ☽ be in the sixth, fourth, seventh, eighth, or twelfth Houses of the Nativity, and both in Radix or Decurnbiture there happen to be an Infortune joyned to the ☽ in some of those places of the Figure, there is great danger of Death, unless the Fortunate Planets interpose their friendly Rayes.

XIII. When the Ascendant at the Decwnbiture is opposite to that of the Radix, and the Lord thereof in the fourth, sixth, eighth, twelfth or seventh Houses, (the Ascendant of the *Suns* Revolution not being the same) the sick party rarely Recovers.

XIV. The ☉ in the Ascendant at a Decumbiture usually brings health speedily; if in the sixth House, the sickness doth immediately chang or alter, if the Lord of the eighth be combust, the Sick Recovers.

XV. Fear not the Death of a Patient if ♃ be in any good Aspect with the ☉, though the Lord of the Ascendant apply to the Lord of the eighth.

XVI. When a Disease first invades a Patient, observe what time the ☽ separates from Combustion, for the sickness usually increases till the ☽ meets with an opposition of the ☉.

XVII. The Significator of the sick Party being Occidental in a Decumbiture, shews *Chronique* Distempers, but being Oriental, the contrary; or a change from one Disease to another: in Acute Distempers, consider the Separation and Application of the ☽, and accordingly judge of the Increase or Decrease of the Disease—observe the same Method in *Chronique* Diseases by the Separation and Application of the ☉, to and from the good or bad Aspects of the Fortunes or Infontunes.

XVIII. Lastly, take notice that the ☽ is most afflicted by the beams of ♂ when she is increased in light, (or got remote from the ☉) and much more oppressed by the Malevolent Rayes of ♄ when she is in her Wain, or decreasing in light: when the ☽ is thus afflicted in a Decumbiture the case is dangerous: If ♂ be in a Masculine Signe, Oriental, and above the Earth, he is then powerful to influence Mischief upon a Native or sick Person, judge the contrary by ♄.

Thus much shall suffice for the Astrological Judgment of Diseases: Those that would see more variety, may read several Authors upon the same, now easie to be had: Amongst the rest I recommend them to an ingenious Tract, Intituled, Synopsis Medicine, *wherein this Subject is most accurately performed. But* Medicina â Medico, Medela ab Altissimo.

SECT. V.

Of the Fidelity and Falsity of Servants, as also of small Cattle, &c.

I. If you find the Lord of the sixth House in good Aspect to the Lord of the Ascendant or the ☽; or if the Lord of the sixth House be in the Dignities of the Fortunes, or well beheld by them, or in good Aspect to the Lord of the second House, or Cusp thereof, these are Argurnents that the Querents Servant, or Servants are just and honest.

II. On the contrary, if you find the Lord of the sixth House (which signifies Servants) or any Planet therein, in bad Aspect to the Lord of the Ascendant or second House, or in evil configuration with ♄ or ♂, or the ☋ in the sixth House, these are Testimonies of unjust or dishonest Servants, and such persons that are not to be trusted unto. *Probatum est.*

III. *If the Question were, shall a Servant get from his Master &c.* In this case you are advised by Authors, to consider whether the Lord of the Ascendant be in partile Conjunction with the Lord of the tenth House (which signifies the Master) or with the ☉ (who is a general Significator of Masters, Commanders or Rulers.) If so, there is a probabillty, the Servant may get free in some short time: If the Significators are separated, though but some few minutes, he is as good as at liberty already; but if the Significators are applying and want some degrees of a perfect ☌ or Aspect, judge the Master and Servant must not suddenly part.

IV. If the Lord of the Ascendant, or the ☽ be in the Ascendant, or any of the other Angles, or joyn'd to a Planet in any of the four Angles that is direct in motion, there is but small hopes of being delivered from his Servitude; but if the Planet the Significator is joyned with, or the Significator of the Servant be Retrograde, 'tis an Argument the Servant may obtain his Liberty with some delay and difficulty; but if his Significator be Angular, and afflicted by the Bodies or Oppositions of the Infortunes, or Combust of the ☉, this argues no Freedom, but he must *nolens volens* continue with his Master, &c.

V. *Let the Demand be, Shall the Querent be fortunate in dealing in small Cattle, such as Sheep Hoggs, Goats, Coneys, &c. to which may be added Birds of all sorts?* If you find the lord of the sixth House strong, free from affliction, and in good Aspect to the Lord of the second House, the Cusp thereof, ⊕, or posited in the second House, or if the Lord of the sixth be in the Dignities of ♃ or ♀, and they behold the Lord of the second by any good Aspect, or posited therein, all these are notable Argument the Querent should be very fortunate in dealing in small Cattle, and that they should thrive with him, and consequently he should be a gainer considerably by them.

VI. But on the contrary, if the Lord of the sixth House be Infortunate, or the ☋ in the sixth House with ♄ or ♂, or if the Lord of the sixth behold the ☽ or Lord of the second House by any ill Aspect, or if you find the Significator of small Cattle Combust, Retrograde or Cadent, all these are Testimonies of Infortunacy, and shew that the Querent can expect no advantage by dealing in any such Creatures. *Therefore it concerns all such persons that deal either in small Cattle, or any sort of Birds, whether* Pidgions *or* Singing-birds, *to consult their own Nativities (if they can be procured) and to examin the postion, of the Lord of the sixth House, or what Planets are posited therein, &c. Or take the Advice of some able Artist in that particular, that they may be the better directed in their Adventures—and Elections for Merchandizing in such kind of Living Goods. And thus I conclude the Judgments appertaining to the sixth House.*

CHAP. VII.

Judgment upon Questions proper to the Seventh House, which includes Marriage, Contracts, Law-Suits, Controversies, Fugitives, Thefts, &c. This House is called (by some Astrologers) the Great Angle of Business, in regard it admits of many Branches, and more variety than any of the rest: something, of every Principle or Head thereunto belonging, I shall Insist upon, and briefly Exhibit, according to the Rest, and most Appoved Authors now Extant.

SECT I.

Of Marriage.

I. If the Question be propounded thus, in a general way, *Shall I ever Marry?* Then you are to observe the Lord of the Ascendant, together with the ☽ or ♀, (who are General Significators,) if you find the Lord of the Ascendant, or Planet posited therein, in ☌, ✶, or △, with the Lord of the seventh, or the ☽, or Lord of the Ascendant in the seventh House; or if the Lord of the Ascendant be in Reception with the Lord of the seventh, or the Lord of the seventh and ♀ in the Ascendant, these are Arguments the Querent may Marry.

II. If you find the Significators in Fruitful Signes, or in the Dignities of ♀, this promises very fair, that such a business may be effected, and the more probable if the Lord of the Ascendant be in some good Aspect to ♀ also, and she free from affliction posited in an angle, or some good place of the Figure.

III. If you find none of these Testimonies, but the Lord of the Ascendant, the ☉, ☽, and ♀, or the major part of these Significators in Barren Signes, or if they behold each other by cross Aspects, and no Reception between any of them being dejectedly placed in obscure places of the Figure, in this case you may pronounce Judgment *Negatively*, that the *Querent* will not Marry, having no Inclination thereunto, but rather an Antipathy against the same.

IV. Were the Question stated thus, *Shall I obtain the Person that I desire to be my Wife?* Here the seventh House and Lord thereof signifies the Person enquired after, and sometimes neither of them, but that Planet (though Lord of another House) with whom the Lord of the Ascendant or the ☽ is in friendly aspect withal; and the Ascendant, Lord thereof, and the ☽ doth ever more signifie the Querent, to which add ♀ for a Man, and the ☉ in a Womans Question: Now if you find in your Figure that the Lord of the Ascendant or the ☽ be joyned by Body or Aspect (especially of the ✶ or △.) This is a strong Testimony (in Art) the Querebt may obtain his Desire, and with ease too, provided the Significators are in Reception; but if the Aspect be by □ or ☍ without Reception, 'tis probable it may be effected, but with no small difficulty; Interest then exceeds true and real Affections, and no great felicity follows (nor indeed can reasonably be expected) of such Marriages.

V. If the Lord of the Ascendant be posited in the seventh House, or the Lord of the seventh in the Ascendant; or if any Planet Translate or Collect the light of the Significators, this gives great hopes of a good Issue, and that it should be effected by the endeavours of a third person signified by that Planet that Collects the light of the Significators: Or, if you find ♀ or the Luminaries, and Lords of the Ascendant and seventh Houses *Angular* and in good Aspects to each other, these are very promising and hopeful Testimonies the Marriage will be Consummated, and that to the Querents great content and satisfaction.

VI. If the Significators be in Cadent Houses, or not beholding each other, nor any Reception or Translation of light be between them, you may confidently affirm there is very small hopes the Business in Question should be brought to perfection, and therefore the Querent may forbear any farther progress therein.

Now the next thing to be sought after is to discover the Cause why two persons may not be United in Marriage.

VII. If you find the Lord of the seventh House in no Aspect to the Lord of the Ascendant, or the ☽, but in ✶ or △ to some other Planet: you may then conclude that the Party or Mistress enquired after, hath an Affection rather for such a Person signified by that Planet, than for the Ouerent: or if the Lord of the Ascendant or the ☽ apply to some friendly Aspect of the Lord of the seventh House, and before they come to a perfect Aspect ♄ or ♂ interpose their malicious beams and so frustrate the good hopes that might have followed the aforesaid approaching good Aspects of the Significators: If such a thing happens you may conclude the intended Match shall be broken off by such a person that is signified by the Frustrating Planet; now if you consider what House he is Lord of, you may not only describe his person (as well as the Wife sought after if occasion be by the Rules before given) but also discover what Relation (if any) he is either to the Ouerent or Quesited; or if no Relation, the cause of the Separation of these two Lovers.

VIII. As if the Planet frustrating be Lord of the *second* or *eighth* Houses; then conclude 'tis *Money* of one side or the other that is the occasion: If the Lord of the third from the Ascendant or seventh, say some Brother, Sister, Neighbor, or some such Relation; if not, the going some Journey may spoil the business, *&c*. And so order your Judgment according to the proper signification of the Impeding Planet, let him be Lord of any House in the Figure; whose signification need not in this place be any farther mentioned, that being already done at large in the Introductory part hereof.

IX. *As to the Time when the Querent may Marry, finding the Significators applying, judge thus,* viz.

Consider the Degrees of Distance that the Significators want of a *Partile Aspect*, and measure out the Weeks, Months, Dayes and Years, as you are directed *Chap. 2, Sect. 3*. but be not too positive unless you find notable Testimonies in *Art* to incourage you, and the Significators be found swift in motion.

As to the true time of Marriage, the Direction of a Significator to an apt and proper Promittor *in the Nativity (if it may be procured) doth best discover that; but if it canot be had, use such wayes as are shewed in the aforementioned place of this Book.*

X. *The Agreement after Marriage is Astrologically discovered thus; viz.* Observe whether the Principal Significators in the *Figure* of the *Question* did behold each other by ✶ or △, or if there were mutual Reception between them, these are Testimonies of a very good Agreement; the same if the ☽ behold the Lord of the seventh House well, or ♀ be in ✶ or △ to the Lord of the Ascendant: But if in the *Figure* you find the Significators in evil Aspect to the *Infortunes*, judge no agreement, or if ♄, ♂ or ☋ be Infortunate, in the seventh House, the Woman proves Contentious and Ill-natur'd; if they are found in the Ascendant, the Man will be the cause of Strife and Contention.

XI. *If it be Demanded whether the Querent may Marry more than once?* Then consider whether you find many Planets in the seventh House in good Aspect to the Lord of the Ascendant or the Luminaries, this is a good Argument that the Native shall Marry more than once; judge the same if the Significators of Marriage be in Bi-corporeal Signes: But if you find the Significators fixed, or a Sign representing one Body possessing the Cusp of the seventh, or the Lord of the Ascendant, or the ☽ in no Aspect to any other Planet, or but one at most, then you may conclude only one Wife.

[*What is said of Mens Marriages understand the same of Womens also, they being Querents, &c.*

Judge of the Portion of the Wife from the strength and position of the Lord of the eighth House, or Planets posited therein.

XII. *If you desire to know whether the Querent be Marryed or not (as some to try the skill of an Artist are Pleased to conceal, and ask when they shall Marry?) proceed thus; viz.* Take notice in your *Figure* whether there be any Application between the Lord of the Ascendant, the ☽ and the Lord of the seventh House, or between the ☉ and ♀, these are Arguments that the person is or hath been Marryed, and 'tis the "more certain if the Lord of the Ascendant be in good Aspect to ♀ and they both posited in fruitful Signes: If you find the Significator so posited, and in bad Aspect to ♂ from the fifth or the ☋ therein this gives suspition, (if it be a *Female Creature*) that she has been debauched and probably had a *Basterd* if other Testimonies concur.

Clavis Astrologiae Elimita, The Key to Astrology New Filed

XIII. *If out of Curiosity you should desire to discouer whether a Female Creature Propounding a Question be a Virgin or not? Examin the Business thus; viz.* If you find her proper Significators posited in fixed Signes, free from the ill beams of ♂, and no Infortunes in the Ascendant or fifth House but her Significator (*viz.* the Lord of the Ascendant, ♀, or the ☽) in good Aspect to the ☉ or ♃, judge she is Chast, and no way corrupted; but if you find contrary Testimonies, you may conclude her otherwise, that she has been tempted, and consented too to her own dishonour, a thing very frequent in this Age. After the same manner you may discover whether a *Marryed Woman* be concerned with any other person besides her *Husband* or not; but I shall not insist farther upon this particular, least some Innocent Women should receive prejudice from the hasty judgments of their Jealous Husbands or others—not well experienced in this Art.

XIII. *Sometimes an Artist is requested to give his Judgment, which of the two, Man or Wife may Dye first?* The Old Rule for this is to consider which of their Significators are strongest, or go first to *Combustion* of the ☉, or are afflicted by the Lord of the eighth House, and accordingly pronounce Judgment which may first expire, but this must be done with great Caution, and an Artist ought not to be too positive in such matters. The most certain way is to consult the *Directions* in the *Nativity, viz.* when the *Hyleg* or giver of life is brought to some dangerous *Direction* of the Lord of the eighth, or the *Anareta*; but of this more in the third part hereof. In short, observe whose Significator suffers *Combustion* first, and what Signe it falls in if in fixed Signes, it will be some considerable time; if in a *Moveable* or *Tropical Signe*, it points out but a short time, if in a *Common* Sign, something longer; *And thus I conclude the Rules of Judgment for Marriage, these being the most considerable Questions that are usually propounded concerning the same, some other varieties shalt be inserted concerning* Marriage *in the third (or Genethlical) Part of this Book.*

SECT. II

Of Law Suits, Warr, Public Enemies, Partnerships, &c.

I. *Of Law-Suits, let the Question be, Who shall overcome in a Tryal at Law, the Querent or the Adversary?* The *Querent* is always signified by the Ascendant and his Lord, and the *Adversary* by the Opposite House, *viz.* the seventh and Lord thereof, the *Judge* by the tenth House and his Lord, the *Jury* by the ☽, and the end of the Business alwayes by the fourth House and Lord thereof, having knowledge of every Significator, the Question is easily answered thus; Consider the Figure well before you pronounce Judgment, and see which of the Significators are strongest and best fortified, and accordingly judge: for if you find the Lord of the Ascendant, more powerful than the Lord of the seventh House, then (in all probability) the *Querent* overcomes, and Casts his *Adversary*; But if the seventh House and Lord thereof be best fortified, then the *Querents Adversary* becomes *Victor*, and gains the day.

II. If both Significators be well beheld by Fortunate *Planets*, this Argues the Difference may be composed by Friends; and if both the Significators be strong and Angular, it declares the *Querent* and this *Adversary* will stand upon high Terms on both sides; but if you find that they Apply to a ✶ or △ Aspect, or there be a Reception between the Significators, it's then a strong Argumrent they may Compose and agree the Business themselves; where note that that *Planet* which applyes, signifies the Party that shall first move to Reconcile the Difference: and by what is said in this Case, the same may be understood in *Duels*; or what Issue may be expected between any person and his publick, open and profess'd Enemy, let the Querent be of what Degree or Quality soever.

III. If you find many Planets in the Ascendant or second House, judge the *Querent* hath good assistance and many Friends; if the Lord of the tenth House be in good Aspect to his Significator, say the *Judge* will be kind to him; if the ☽ be in the eleventh House or Lady thereof, and in ✶ or △ to the Lord of the Ascendant or Cusp thereof, then the *Jury* proves kind and favourable; if the Lord of the second House be more potent than the Lord of the eighth, the *Querent* has the best Purse, and the Contrary, *&c.*

IV. If the Significators behold each other by a *Square* or *Opposite Aspect* without *Reception*, and the Significator of the Querent be in a *fixed Signe*, judge they will proceed in Law with Courage one against the other; If a *moveable* Signe Ascend, it shortens the business, and it will not be tedious; if a *Common* Signe arise, and the Lord of the Ascendant in a *Common* Signe, the Querent delays the Suit, and removes it often out of one Court into another.

V. If you find the Lord of the *tenth House* if good Aspect or *Reception* with the Lord of the second, you may conclude the *Judge* Will accept of a *Bribe* or *Present* from the *Querent*; But if his Significator friendly behold or receive the Lord of the Ascenuant, judge he has more kindness for his Person, and with easie *Importunity* he will be heard effectually; and if the Lord of the tenth House be an Inferiour Planet, and the Lord of the Ascendant a Superiour, the *Judge* will be very inclinble to act for the Querent without great Solicitation or Petitioning: But if the Lord of the tenth Receive both Significators, or behold them well, 'tis then probable he may Compose the Difference without a Tryal: Judge the same from any other *Planet* so qualified, and consider what House he is Lord of, and you thereby discover what Relation he is either to the Querent or Quesited.

VI. *If the Question were concerning Buying or Selling any Comodity whatever, what the event may be;* viz. *will it be Advantagious to the Buyer or Seller? This is a milder kind of Contest, and falls under the same head with Law-suits.* If you find the Lord of the Ascendant in the seventh House, the *Querent* has a mind or Inclination to deal with his *Chapman*, and the Contrary; and if you find the Lord of the Ascendant or the ☽ in Reception or good Aspect with the Lord of the seventh House the *Querent* may buy if he please: and in this Case the *Buyer* and *Seller* usually agree in their Contract, and are very friendly to each other.

VII. If you find the Ascendant or Lord thereof vitiated by the presence of the ☋ or ♄ or ♂ therein, the Bargain goes on very irregularly, and in this Case the *Buyer* usually proves *Knavish*, and indeavours to cheat or deceive the *Seller*: Judge the same of the Person that Sells the Comidity; if the seventh House or his Lord be afflicted in the same manner.

VIII. *If you desire to know the Agreement of two Partners*; Consider whether both the Significators *(viz.* the Lord of the Ascendant, the Lord of the seventh) behold one another by any friendly Aspect, or see if they are in Reception by House or Exaltation; if so, judge a good Agreement between them; if they behold by any Bad Aspect, judge the Contrary.

IX. If you find ♄, or ♂, or the ☋ in the second House, judge that. the *Querent* suffers in his Estate; if you find them in the eighth House, the evil falls upon the *Quesited's* Estate; if the Fortunes be in the Ascendant, the *Querent* himself is *Treacherous* and *Knavish*; if in the seventh, his *Partner* is to blame, and very Ill conditioned: But if you find none of these Positions, and the ☽ apply to *Fortunate Planets,* then the Partners go on well in their way of Trade; and if the ☽ separate from the *Fortunes,* and apply to the *Infortunes,* then although things may be carried on seemingly fair at the beginning, yet the end will be Contentious; or if the ☽ be both separate, and apply to & from *Infortunes*, neither their beginning nor end can be expected to be Good; but much strife and debate will arise, and consequently a very bad Agreement.

X. *If the Question were, Shall the Querent return safe from War?* In this Question you are to consider whether the *Ascendant* be assisted by the presence of the *Fortunate Planets*, or the Lord thereof free from the Afflictions of the *Infortunes*, or the Lord of the eighth House; if so, this is good encouragement for the Querent to adventure: If ♂ be also strong in his Ascendant, he will be very prosperous and secure, and (probably) come off with Honour and much safety; judge the Contrary if contrary Testimonies appear in the Figure.

XI. If you find ♄ or ♂ in the Ascendant, and the Lord of the Ascendant weak, or otherwise afflicted, 'tis not good for the *Querent* to go to War; if the Ascendant be free, and an Infortune in the eighth or fourth Houses, the end looks dangerous, the Querent may be taken, kill'd, or dangerously wounded, and therefore unless the Heavens favour the *Querent* (if it may be avoided) let him forebear.

XII. *If the Question were, Shall a Man of War that is setting out to Sea be Forftunate, in taking Purchase, or shall he return home safe, and with Honour?* If the Lord of the seventh House be applying to any Bad Aspect of the Lord of the Ascendant or the ☽ neer a ☌, □, or ☍ of the Lord of the seventh or ninth Houses, or to any *Planet* or *Planets* posited therein; these are certain Arguments of meeting an Enemy: And if many *Planets* are in the

West Angle, and the Lord of the Ascendant applyes to any of them whilst he is in the Signe he possesses: It also shews that this *Man of Warr* shall meet with many Enemies, or Prizes: the same if the Cusp of the seventh be double bodyed, or the Lord thereof be posited in a double bodyed Sign, or in ☌ with several *Planets*. Now by a due consideranion of the position, strength and Aspects of the several Significators, a Judgment may be deduced what the success of this *Ship* may be, by the Rules laid down in some of the precedent Subsections.

SECT. III.

Of Theft, and Fugitives, or Strayes, &c.

It will be expected that some Rules should be given concerning Theft, which properly belongs to the Judgment of this House; But how seldome doth any Artist gain Credit in his Responses to such Questions, notwithstanding he describes the Thief never so exactly, because the Corporature and Complexion of one person, may very much resemble another; and no man ever yet could force back Stolen goods by the help of Astrology only; yet the Thief may be well described by the Rules thereof; and the Querent may have so much satisfaction as to know whether there be any probability of procuring (or by any means a discovery made) of the Goods lost; and in order thereunto I shall briefly shew what Rules are to be observed in such Cases.

I. *How to know the Significator of the Thief is very material*: Haly tells us the Ascendant and Lord thereof signifies the Querent both in this and all manner of Questions whatsoever; the second House, and Lord thereof shall Represent the Goods lost, and the *seventh House* and Lord thereof shall signifie the *Thief*; (if there be no *Peregrine Planet* in an Angle or the second House) the fourth House, (*viz.* the Cusp thereof) shews the place where the goods are. If a *Peregrine Planet* be in the Ascendant, take him for the Significator of the *Thief*, and the rather if he happen to be Lord of the seventh House; if no *Planet* be in the Ascendant, yet if you find a *Planet* in any other Angle *Peregrine* or afflicting the Lord of the second House or ⊗, accept of him to be Significator of the Thief; many *Peregrine Planets* in Angles shew more Thieves than one: However, have special Regard to the Lord of the seventh House, and those *Planets* he is in Aspect with, especially if he afflict the Significator of Substance, and you cannot easily Err.

II. *In the next place, it must be considered whether the Goods, &c. be really stolen or not, or casually mislaid and forgotten.* If a *Peregrine Planet* be found in the Ascendant, or the Lord of the Ascendant *Peregrine* (that is out of all his Essential Dignities) 'tis an Argument the things missing are stolen; If the Lord of the seventh House or a *Peregrine Planet* therein, (afflict or) behold the Lord of the Ascendant or the ☽ by ☌, □, or ☍, or rather the Lord of the second House or Cusp thereof, or the ⊗, or Dispositor thereof, then judg the thing (be it what it will) is really stolen. Judge the same if neither the Lord of the Ascendant, Lord of the second House, the Dispositor of the ⊗ or the ☽ do separate from other Planets, but other Planets separate from them. If you find none of these Arguments judge the contrary.

III. If the Lord of the second House and the ☽ be in the seventh House, or in the Sign thereof, and the Lord of the seventh behold them, by ✶ or △ Aspect (though Platickly) then the goods taken away, though very probably in jest; But if the Lord of the seventh House be in ☌, □, or ☍ of any of them, they are taken away fraudulently, and will not be recovered without difficulty and much Solicitation; and it is very probable the Thief hath too fair opportunities to act such exploits; observe also whether the ☽ gives virtue to ♄ or ♂, or to the Lord of the Eighth, or any other Planet in a Cadent House; and by some of these Rules you may discover whether the thing missing be stolen or not.

IV. If the Figure of the Question set for that moment of time when the Querent propounds it to the Artist, be not satisfactory, or truly *Radical*, then consult a Scheme of Heaven for the time when the Goods lost were first missed, and let that be the *Basis* or Foundation to ground judgment upon, or rather the exact time when the fact was done, (if it could be known) and then the Ascendant and Lord thereof shall signifie the Thief, and the seventh House and the Lord of the seventh House and the Lord of the seventh the person that lost the Goods.

V. *If the Artist would discover whether the Querent be theThief*, Then consider whether the Lord of the fourth, or Lord of the Term of the ☽ be joyned to the Lord of the Ascendant, or if you find the Lord of the seventh in the Ascendant, you may suspect the Querent to be the Thief; and this the more certain if that Planet do well describe the Querent. This is usualy for guilty persons to repair to an *Artist* to discover the Thief, out of design to acquit themselves of Suspition, and some again out of Policy will Rob themselves, which may be discovered by the same Rule.

VI. If the Lord of the seventh be *Peregrine* in the Ascendant, and that Planet Lord of the second House, 'tis to be feared the Querent consented to the Theft, or was willing it should be so; If the Lord of the seventh be in the Ascendant, and the great Dignities in the third also, then some of his own Relations, *(viz.* a Brother or Sister) may be suspected, &c. But this kind of Judgment is something dubious, and therefore let the Artist make use of it sparingly and with great Caution; and in all Questions of *Theft* deliver not Judgment to many pesons together, nor to none but such that understand how to make a due application thereof, to avoid future Trouble and Contention, which too frequently follows Thievish Questions.

VII. *To Discover the Age and Sex of the Thief*; Observe these Rules, If the Significator of the Thief be a Masculine Planet, and posited in a Masculine House and Sign, 'tis a *Man*; If a Feminine Planet, and posited in a Feminine House and Signe, say a Female; consider also the Cusp of the tenth and seventh Houses, and Lords thereof, and Planets that have exaltation in those Signes, or other Essential Dignities, see which are Masculine, and which are Feminine, and judge by the Major Testimonies. If the Significator of the Thief be Oriental, say he is young; if Occidental, more in years; ♄ generally signifies Aged persons, unless in the very beginning of a Signe; ♀ and ☿ Represent Youth, ♃, ♂, and the ☉, denote Middle Age, from thirty to forty; the ☽ must be considered according to her Age, which is divided into four Quarters; Youth is represented by the ☽ in her first Quarter, the second points out about 25 or 30; the third Quarter ends at 40 or 45; and the ☽ in her last Quarter shews from 45 to 50, and upwards; consider the Quarter of Heaven a Planet which is Significator is posited in, as if in the East Angle or between the Ascendant and Mid heaven, say Youth; If in the Mid-heaven, or between the tenth and West Angle, say Middle-age; If between the seventh House and the fourth, in the declining part of Age, *viz.* between forty and fifty; If the Significator be found between the fourth House and Ascendant, say Old-age; Consider also the Significators Distance from the ☉, (as in that of the ☽) and accordingly moderate your Judgment.

VIII. *If you would discover by Art whether the Thief be a Stranger, or one familiarly Acquainted with the Querent, proceed thus*; If you find the Significator of the *Thief* in the Ascendant, or joyned to the Lord of the Ascendant, 'tis a person in the same House, or very neer him; If the ☉ and ☽ behold each other, or the Lord of the Ascendant, 'tis a person known to the Querent; or if the *Luminaries* behold the Ascendant, or are posited in the Dignities of the Lord thereof, judge the same; If you find none of these Testimonies, judge the contrary.

IX. The Lord of the seventh in the second accuses one of the Family; and if the Significator of the *Thief* be Femiinirie, 'tis then probable the Querents Wife did the Fact, or some other Female well known to the Querent—Judge of the Relation of the Thief by the position of the Significator in the Figure, which is easily done, if the *Artist* be but ready in varying the Houses, as has been shewed.

X. If you find the *Thief* to be one of the Family, ♄ shews a Stranger accidentally Sojourning therein; ♂, a Relation, *viz.* a Son, Brother, or Kinsman; the ☉ alwayes signifies a Father, or Master of the House, ♀ a woman, or the Wife; the ☽ the Mother or Mistress; ☿ some young person intimately acquainted in the Family; and sometimes ♂ and ☿ signifie *Common Thieves, Notorious Villains*, unless they be Lords of such Houses which signifie the Querents Relations; If you find the Lord of the seventh (which generally doth represent the *Thief*) in the Ninth from his own House, judge the *Thief* is a Stranger; but if the Lord of the Ascendant be in the third or fourth Houses, some Servant of the House is guilty.

XI. *Whether the Suspected Party be Thief?* If the ☽ or Lord of the Ascendant behold the Lord of the seventh, by any bad Aspect, or be in ☌ with the Significator of the Thief, the person suspected is guilty; The same if the Lord of the Ascendant being posited in an Angle beholds a *Planet* in a Cadent House; or if you find the ☽ in ☌ with a Planet in Angle.

Clavis Astrologiae Elimita, The Key to Astrology New Filed

XII. If the *Luminaries* behold the Significator of the Thief, the Querent knows him that play'd the Thief; or if the Lord of the Ascendant be in ☌, or Reception or lately separated from an Infortune, the Suspected person is assuredly guilty of the Fact; But if the Lord of the seventh, or *Peregrine Planet* in an Angle, be in no Aspect either to the *Luminaries*, or Lord of the Ascendant, judge the Contrary.

XIII. *Marks and Tokens to know the* Thief *by are these; viz.* Consider the Signe of the seventh House, and the position of the Lord thereof, also the place of the ☽ (especially if she be unfortunate or afflicted) and judge the *Thief* has a Mark, Mole, or Scar upon that part or Member of the Body Represented by that Signe: If the Significator of the *Thief* apply to the ☌, □, or ☍, of ♄ or ♂ out of Angles, some Mischief or shameful punishment will assuredly befal him; as if ♄ or ♂ be Lords of the twelfth, (especially) from the seventh, it signifies Imprisonment; If they are Lords of the eighth, judge Death; If of the tenth House, he is obnoxious to the severe sentence of a *Judge*; if of the fourth House, an ill end will follow.

XIV. *The Colour of the Cloaths of the Thief*, is known from the Colours of the *Planet* that is the Significator of him or her, together with the property of the Sign and House of the Significator is posited in; as also the Planet he is in Aspect with.

[*What Colours are appropriated to each Planet, you may see in the Table of the* Introduction, *and the Colours of each House are inserted in the 13th* Chapter *thereof.*]

XV. *To know the* Thiefs *House*, See in what Sign and Quarter of Heaven his Significator is posited in; If in the Ascendant, say *East;* If in the Mid-heaven, judge *South*; If in the seventh House, say the *West* part of the Town; and if in the fourth, he, lives *North*; What Quarters or Points the Signes signifie, as also the Houses, you may Read in the First Part; and by a due Commixture of the *House* and *Signe* the Significator is posited in you may easily judge which way theThief lives, or is gone.

XVI. Let the ☉ in particular signifie the House of the *Thief*, and the ☽ the Door thereof, (or rather the Signe where the ☽ is) by a due Consideration of which you may judge of the Scituation thereof, whether it faces the *East, West, North, or South*; If the ☽ be in a Fixed Signe, there is but one Door to the House; If she be in a Moveable Sign, you go up steps to the Door, and probably there is more than one way into the House; if ♄ behold the ☽, the Door is Old and Decayed, and wants Repairing; If ♂ be in Aspect to the ☽, especially in □ or ☍, some part of it has been burn'd; If the Infortunes be in ⚹ or △ to the ☽, or the Sign she is in, then the Door is made strong (though Old) with Iron.

XVII. *Is the Thief in the Town, or Fled?* &c. If you find his Significator just leaving one Signe, and entering into aanother, he is likewise leaving the Town; If you find him entering into his own Essential Dignities, he is going to some Friends or Acquaintance, or where he is well known; but if he enter a Signe wherein he is *Peregrine*, then judge he is going amongst strangers, and desires to obscond himself; Judge the same if he separate from the Combustion of the ☉, and apply to any *Planet* in a Cadent House; But if none of these Arguments appear, and you find the Lord of the seventh House Angular, especially if he be conjoyned therein with the Lord of the second House, you my then conclude the Thief to be in Town; and if he be in a Fixed Signe also, he doth not intend to remove, but continue where he is. *Now if you have a Curiosity to know whether the* Thief be Marryed or not? Consider the position of the Lord of the Ascendant; If you find him in an Angle, judge he is Marryed; if in a succeedent House, he is not yet, but doth endevour it; if in a Cadent Houae, say he is not Marryed, nor is there any probability thereof.

[*I must confess I have not yet Experienced this Rule; there may be Truth in it, which I shall. not contend for.*]

XVIII. Shall the Goods or Things Lost be Recovered again or not?

[*This is a very Considerable Query, and for the Resolution thereof take these Brief Rules and Directions.*]

If you find any Aspect (but in particular those of a ⚹ and △ between the Lord of the Ascendant, and the Lord of the second House, or the Dispositer of the ⊕; or if the Lord of the eighth House be in Reception or friendly Aspect with the Lord of the second House, these are Arguments of Recovery; the same if the Lord of the eighth, or Lord of the second Houses are posited in the Ascendant, or apply to any good Aspect of the Lord thereof.

XIX. The ☽ in the second House in ✶ or △ to the Lord thereof, or in the seventh or tenth Houses in good Aspect to the Lord of the Ascendant, or Planet in the second House, or to the Disposer of the ⊕, these are promising Arguments of Recovery; to which may be added the *Luminaries* beholding each other Friendly, or the Lord of the second in the eleventh or fourth Houses; but if none of these Testimonies be found in the Figure, and both the *Luminaries* are under the Earth, and the second House, Lord thereof, or ⊕ afflicted by ♄, ♂, or the ☋, judge there will be no Recovery of the things lost; the same if you find the Infortunes in the second House, and their Disposer in the eighth, or Combust of the ☉, or any way Impeded, as aforesaid.

As to the time of Discovery or Restauration of the Goods Lost (if you find any hopes thereof in your Figure) you are to observe the Application of the Significators, and convert their Distance into *Time*, as hath been already shewed; or observe when the *Luminaries* (either of them) come to any good Aspect of the Lord of the Ascendant, second, seventh or eighth Houses, and accordingly measure out the time according to Art.

XX. *Of Fugitives or Strayes, shall they be Found or Return?* The Lord of the seventh House, the ☽, and ☿ shall properly signifie the *Fugitives* Person; and if you find the Lord of the seventh or the ☽ apply to any good Aspect of the Lord of the Ascendant or the ☉, or if there be any promising Aspects between the Significators at the time of the Question, there is then great hopes that the *Fugitive* Person will be suddenly discovered and found out; and it also shews a willingness to Returne; and this the more certain, if the Lord of the seventh be Retrograde.

XXI. But if you find the Significators in no Aspect or in □ or ☍ of each other, judge the Contrary, *viz.* an unwillingness to return, and small probability that the Querent should find him—If you would discover the Inclination and Condition of the *Fugitive*, consider his Significators position in the Figure; see what Signe and House he is in, and how Aspected, and joyning your Reason to Art, you maybe able to make a neer *Conjecture* of the *Fugitives* progress and *Intention*.

XXII. To Estimate the Distance between the Querent and the *Runaway*, account for every degree of the distance between their Significators three miles, if they are in Fixed Signes; If in Common Signes, one mile; If in moveable Signes, so many half miles; but these Distances must be limitted with great Caution, consideration must also be had to the distance of the ☽ and the Planet that represents the Fugitive or Stray, whether *Man* or *Beast*; some allow for every degree of Distance only one mile, or 1058 paces being in Fixed Signes; But in Moveable Signes so many Poles or Rods; in Common Signes, 105 paces to a degree; Let every Artist use his own Judgment and Experience in this matter.

XXIII. If any great Cattle, such as Horses, Oxen, Cows, &c. are strayed away, take the Lord of the twelfth House for their Significator; if they are small Cattle, as Sheep, Hoggs, Doggs, &c. then look to the Lord of the sixth House, and by a due observation of the aforesaid Rules, and regard had to the proper and Respective Significators, you may forme a Judgment in any Case relating to these kind of Interrogations.

XXIV. If you find the ☽ Translate the Light of the Significator of the *Fugitive* or Stray to the Ascendant, or if she be in good Aspect to ♃ or ♀, and either of them in the Aseendant, or in good Aspect thereunto, or to the Lord thereof, these are Signal Testimonies in Art of Recovery.

XXV. If any Planet separate from the House of the ☽, or from the Lord of the second, the Beast Strayed is secured, and taken away, and in all probability Sold, or otherwise disposed of; But if the ☽ or proper Sinificator of the Beast or Stray, &c. shall be in the eighth House from his own Ascendant, or apply to any bad Aspect of the Lord thereof, there is then great danger that the *Beast, Fugitive* or Stray is Dead; If the Significator of the Beast, or the Lord of the House of the ☽ shall be located in the eighth House applying or in □ or ☍ to ♄ or ♂ in the North Angle judge the same.

XXVI. If the Significators of the Beasts strayed be in the Mid heaven, or ninth House, or in the sixth or twelfth Houses, it shews the Beasts should be in custody, either secured by some Officer, or else in the Pound. If the ☽ be unfortunate in the twelfth House, judge the same. If ♄ be in the twelfth House also, or afflict the ☽, the Cattle may continue long there to their prejudice; if ♂ afflict the ☽ therein, they may either Dye there, or be killed or starved.

[*And thus much shall serve for the Judgment of the seventh House; I could have been more Copious in every particular Branch thereof, but my design was rather to Contract the most Material and Useful Rules and Aphorisms appertaining to the said House, that they need not be burthensome to the Memoryes of* Tyro's *and other Students in this Coelestial Science.*]

CHAP. VIII.

Judgment and Questions proper to the Eighth House, &c.

SECT. I.

Of the Manner or Kind of Death the Querent may Dye, viz. *Natural or Violent?*

I. This Query is Answered from the consideration of the eighth House and Planets posited therein, or beholding them; when the Lord of the Ascendant or the ☽ shall be in good Aspect with the Lord of the eighth, or Planet therein, it shews the Querent will dye a Natural Death; the same if the Fortunes be in the eighth, or have Dignities therein, or behold the ☽ by any good Aspect.

II. If one of the Fortunate Planets be in the eighth House, and the other in the Ascendant, or if the Lord of eighth, the ☽, or Lord of the Ascendant be not in violent Signes, or neer violent fixed Stars, this Argues the Querent will not be subject to a violent death.

III. But if the *Luminaries* are in violent Signes, not beholding each other, or if they do behold each other by □ or ☍ from Angles, or are afflicted by the Infortunes, it threatens a violent death; and if ♄ or ♂ happen to have Dignities in the eighth, it confirms the Judgment, and there is then the more danger of the same.

Or if ♄ or ♂ be in ☌ in an Angle, or in ☍ from Angles, and in violent Signes, or the ☽ in the seventh House afflicted by ♄ or ♂, or if she be in the twelfth, and so afflicted, it denotes a violent death, unless other Testimonies fall in to mitigate their Influence. Now the kinds of violent Deaths are thus found; If ♄ or ♂ be in the tenth House in Fiery Signes, afflicting the ☽ or Lord of the Ascendant, and they neer violent Fixed Stars, shews Death by some violent fall from a high place. ♄ in ♋ afflicting as aforesaid, shews Drowning; and ♂, afflicting Planet, in a Fiery Signe, shews death by Iron, Fire, Sword, Gunshot, *&c.* But of these things more in the Third Part.

IV. ♄ being Lord of the eighth House, (and the death found to be Natural) signifies some tedious Ague, Dropsie or Consumption. ♂ threatens Death by Wounds, or some Fiery Hot Distemper, as Feavers; the ☉, by some obstructions of the Vital Spirits or Pluresie; ☿ by Phrenzy, Madness, Ptisick, Lethergie, *&c.* The ☽ by Diseases arising from Phlegm, cold and moist Humours, and sometimes Drowning. See more of this Subject in the Judgment of the sixth House.

SECT. II.

Is the wives Portion Considerable or not; or will it be obtained with Ease or Difficulty.

I. As the Ascendant Signifies the Querent, and the second House his Substance; so the Wife is Signified by the seventh House, and her Estate by the eighth House and Lord thereof, as has been already shewed. Now if you find the Lord of the eighth strong, and the eighth House free from the pretense of the Infortunes, and both well behld by ♃ and ♀, this argues the Portion is Considerable; The same if you find ♃, ♀, the ☊, or ⊕ in the eighth House, no way afflicted: From the consideration of the premises, it doth not only appear that the Wives Dowry is valuable, but the Querent will obtain it with ease; understand the same if a Woman propounds the Question concerning the Estate of her Husband, *&c.* Now if you find none of these Testimonies, you may judge the Contrary, that the Wives Portion is mean and inconsiderable, if any.

II. If the Significators be found weak and infortunate, either Combust, Retrograde or Slow in Motion, and afflicted by the Infortunes, this argues not only a very Inconsiderable Fortune with a *Wife*, but great Vexation and Trouble in obtaining what there is, or a very uncomfortable enjoyment thereof.

III. If the Lord of the Ascendant be in □ or ☍ of the Lord of the eighth House, or if ♄ or ♂ be *Peregrine* therein, or the ☋ there, 'tis in vain for the Querent to hope for any good; for either the Portion is small and invaluable, or the Querent will be strangely Cheated thereof, or suffer much prejudice concerning the same, insomuch that he had better desist than make any progress as to the obtaining thereof.

[*What is said of Dowryes, may be understood likewise of Legacies, or the Wills of Deceased Persons also, signified by this House.*]

SECT. III.

Shall a Person that is brought into Trouble, either for some Real Fact Committed, or upon Suspition thereof, suffer Detriment or Death for the Same?

I. If in the Figure of the Question propounded you find the ☽ or Lord of the Ascendant applying by any bad Aspect to the Lord of the fourth, eighth, tenth, or twelfth Houses, there is great danger the Person may suffer for the Fact that he is Apprehended for.

II. If the ☽ or Lord of the Ascendant apply to the ☌, □, or ☍ of ♄ or ♂ in bad places of the Heavens, and the Fortunate Planets no way Assist by their Friendly Beams, you may then conclude the *Querent* is guilty of the Crime he is Charged withal, and the Case seems very dangerous on his side.

III. But if the Lord of the Ascendant or the ☽ be with ♃ or ♀, or in ✶ or △, or Reception of either of them, then the Querent speeds well, and comes off with Honour, without the least prejudice; and this the more certain if either of the Fortunes happen to have Dignities in the tenth, eleventh, or fourth Houses, and are posited in the Ascendant, or Mid-heaven.

IV. If the Lord of the Ascendant be free from affliction, and another Planet who has any Essential Dignity therein be in bad Aspect to the Infortunes, then the Querent goes off clear, and some of his Confederates are brought into Trouble.

V. In fine, If the Significators of the Querent be Essentially strong, and free from the Malicious Rayes of ♄ and ♂, and located in some good place of the Figure, then the Querent is safe, and comes off without the least Damage; notwithstanding, all Fears and Jealousies of Danger that otherwise might affright and perplex him.

CHAP. IX.

Judgments and Questions Appertaining to the Ninth House, &c.

SECT. I.

Shall the Querent be Prosperous in his Voyage to Sea.

I. In this Question you must have Recourse to the ninth House, and his Lord, to the Planets posited therein, or beholding the said Significators, as also the ☽ and the Lord of the Ascendant, which are also Significators to be taken notice of in this Question; if you find any of the Significators impeded, or much afflicted, you may then suspect much Hazzard in the Voyage; if ♄ be the Planet afflicting, it signifies the Querent is threatened with some tedious Disease, or loss of Goods; if ♂ afflict, or the ☋, it portends prejudice by Thieves or Pyrates, and oftentimes Couzening and Cheating among themselves, &c.

II. But if you find the Significators strong, and no way prejudiced but free, and the Lord of the Ascendant in Friendly Aspect of the Lord of the ninth, or if there be Reception between them, and the Fortunes happen to lend their Assistance, you may then conclude the Querent may make a Happy, Prosperous and successful Voyage; and by considering the Sign of the ninth, whether Fixed or Moveable, and the Significators, whether swift or slow in Motion, you may judge of the length of the Voyage.

III. Moreover, the Ascendant and the Lord thereof must be much Regarded in this Case; for if the ninth and tenth Houses be well fortified, and excellently Fortunate as can be desired, yet if the Lord of the Ascendant be afflicted by the Lord of the eighth House, or otherwise, the Querent may end his dayes in the Voyage, and never Return again; or if he be afflicted by the Lord of the sixth, or in the sixth House by ♄ or ♂, he may be sick in his Voyage, or Wounded; if the Lord of the twelfth afflict, Imprisonment or Restraint is to be feared; if the Lord of the fourth, the Grave may swallow him up; therefore 'tis very considerable to observe the Ascendant and the Lord thereof, as well as the ninth and tenth Houses in all such Questions.

IV. This Question is frequently propounded by *Seamen*, what part of the World they had best Direct their Course unto, for Profit and good Success? In this Case, observe in what part of the *Scheme* you find the ⊕ and the Dispositer thereof, or ♃ or ♀ free from affliction, or any of the *Planets* that are powerful in the *Figure*, I say, observe the Quarter of Heaven, where any of these Promising Planets are posited, and direct the Querent that way; But see that they are not posited in an obscure dejected place of the Heavens; if so, take that Planet that is next in Power, always rejecting the Consideration of the places of ♄ or ♂, unless they are strong and in their Essential Dignities in good Aspect to the Fortunes or Lord of the Ascendant

Verbum sat Sapiente

SECT. II.

If a Question be propounded concerning the obtaining of a Benefice.

I. You are in this case to see what Aspect there is between the Lord of the Ascendant, the ☽ and the Lord of the ninth House, or Planets therein; & if you find they behold each other by good Aspect, or if the ☽ be in the ninth, or the Lord of the Ascendant there, or if there be a friendly reception between the Significators, these are good Arguments, that the Querent may obtain his desire; the same if the Lord of the Ascendant, or the ☽ be in ✶ or △ to ♃ or ☉, but if the Aspect be by □ or ☍; yet if there be Reception or Translation of Light, it argues the Business shall be accomplished, although with some Trouble and Pains.

II. If you find the Infortunes in the Ninth House or the Ascendant, or otherwise afflicting those Houses, or their Lords, and if so be you can find none of the aforesaid Testimonies in the Figure, you may then conclude there is small hopes, and the Querent will then very rarely obtain his desire, nay there is no probability of any such thing to be procured.

The like you may understand from the position of the aforesaid Significators, if the Question be proposed concerning the attaining to any Science, or Knowledge in some Art or Mystery, &c.

CHAP. X.

Judgments and Interrogations proper to the tenth House.

SECT. I.

May the Querent attain the Office or Place of Dignity Desired.

I. Here you are to consider how the Lord of the tenth House, & the ☉ do either of them Aspect the Lord of the Ascendant, & the ☽: if they are in friendly Reception by House or Exaltation, or in ✶ or △ of each other; if so, these are assured Testimonies that the Querent may by using means obtain the place desired; the same if you find the Lord of the Ascendant or the ☽ posited in the tenth House, or the Lord of the tenth, or the ☉ in the Ascendant; and if they happen Friendly to behold each other also at the same time; why, then you need not question but your desire will take effect.

II. But on the contrary, if nothing of this kind can be found in your Figure, neither the good Aspect of the Significators, translation of Light, Reception, or dwelling in Houses, this is an evident Testimony that the Querent shall not have the Place desired, notwithstanding he be never so fairly promised.

[*Note that the Advantage that may arise from the Office or Dignity desired must be considered from the strength and position of the Lord of the eleventh House.*]

SECT. II.

But if the Querent be in an Imployment, and fears he may be turned out.

I. Then you are to look to the Significators, and see if there be any good Aspect between them (as before noted) or if there be Reception, & judge accordingly, that the Querent stands sure, and needs not fear a remove from his present Imployment; and this the rather if the Lord of the Ascendant, or the ☽ be in good Aspect of ♃ or ♀ in the tenth House.

II. But if you find the Significator of the Querent in any bad Aspect with those Planets which are in friendly Reception, or behold the ☉ or Lord of the tenth House by ✶ or △, you may then inform the Querent he is in danger of being outed of his place, through the means of such persons signified by those Planets that afflict the Querents Significator.

III. As to success in Trade from this House also (considering what hath been said) a man may judge of the event thereof, whether there be a probability of gaining or loosing thereby, or if he may thrive by his present Imployment or Profession, and consequently what kind of Profession or Trade will be most suitable for his Genius, which I shall touch more largely upon in the Third Part.

IV. If the Significators of Trade be posited in fiery Signes, you may then conclude any Profession of that Nature will best agree with the Querent; if in Earthly, Airy, or Watry Signes, judge accordingly, considering the qualities and professions which the Planets naturally signifie, as is before directed in this Book, an ingenious Artist will not be able to seek how to order his Judgment in Questions of this Nature; therefore I shall enlarge no farther in this place, and the rather, in regard I shall have occasion to write more of this Subject before I conclude the Book.

CHAP. XI.

Judgment proper to the Eleventh House.

May the Querent be Fortunate in his Hopes, &c.

1. The Lord of the eleventh, and the eleventh House signifie the thing in Question, and if the ☽ or Lord of the Ascendant be in ✶ or △ to the Lord of the 11*th* House, or any good Planet be posited therein, or if there be a Reception, or dwelling in Houses, or translation of light between the Significators, these are good Arguments the Querent shall obtain what he hopes for.

II. But if you find Cross Aspects between the Significators, or if they be Combust, Cadent, or Retrograde, or ♄ or ♂ sends forth their malicious Rayes to the Significators, Judge the contrary.

This is to be understood when the thing hoped for is not Nominated; but if you understand by the Querent what it is he hopes for, then consider also the Planet and House that signifies the thing hoped for; as if the thing were Money, why then take notice of the second House, and the Lord-thereof, see how the Lord of the eleventh beholds that Planet, and accordingly judge.

III. What is said of Hopes, may be fitly applyed to the Querents Friends, (not related) whether they will prove real or not, if you find the Significators in good Aspect of the ☽, or the Lord of the Ascendant, or Planets therein, you may judge the Friends of the Querent are Faithful, Just, and true unto him; but if you find contrary Aspects, you have reason to Judge the contrary: 'tis not safe to impose Truth or Confidence in them.

CHAP. XII.

Judgments proper to the Twelfth House.

A Person being Imprisoned, desires to know when he may be released, either within a short time or the Contrary.

I. A Fixed Signe Ascending, and the Lord thereof Angular, especially ♄ argues a tedious Imprisonment, the same if the Lord of the Ascendant, or the ☽ be in the fourth, sixth, eighth or twelfth Houses, and there afflicted, or otherwise unfortunate, being Combust or Retrograde, to which may be added, that if the Lord of the hour in which he was apprehended be ♄ or ♂, and they not well placed in the Figure, the Querent then undergoes a long and tedious Restraint and Captivity.

II. But if the Lord of the Ascendant or the ☽ be swift in motion, or if they shall be stronger than the Lord of the twelfth, or dispose of him, and in moveable Signes, and well beheld of or ♃ or ♀, these are Testimonies of a speedy Releasment.

III. If you find the Lord of the Ascendant in any bad Aspect of the Lord of the twelfth, or Planet therein, you may thence conclude the Querent hath private Enemies, and he suffers prejudice by them; or if any other Planet being Lord of some other House afflict the ☽, or Lord of the Ascendant, the Querent hath private Enemies.

IV. But if the Significators of the Querent be in good Aspect of the Fortunes, and free from all bad Aspects of the Infortunes, or any other Planet, he may then conclude, he hath no private Enemies, And by considering the position of the former Significators, you rnay Judge if the Querent shall be infortunate in great Cattle, &c.

V. *If a Question be demanded whether a Distempered Person be Bewitched or not*, &c. See if you find the Lord of the Ascendant in the twelfth House, in ☌, □, or ☍ with the Lord thereof, or if the Lord of the sixth be in the twelfth House, or Lord of the twelfth in the sixth in any bad Aspect to the ☽ or Lord of the Ascendant, these are

Arguments in Art the Party is Bewitched, or under the power of some evil Person; the same if one Planet be Lord of the Ascendant and twelfth Houses then the Disease is more than Natural.

VI. If the Infortunes be posited in the twelfth House, weak and debilitated, or the Lord of the twelfth in the Ascendant, or the ☽ in the twelfth in ☌, ☐ or ☍ of the Lord of the twelfth House, these are great Arguments that the Disease is not only Occult, but more than Natural. Now if you consider what House the Lord of the Ascendant and the Planet afflicting, are posited in, you may from thence give a neer Conjecture whence, or from what person the Mischief proceeds.

I am sensible this is a Matter much disputed by some in these days, that will not allow of any such thing; others very Ingenious and Learned, maintain the contrary; I am inclined to believe there is such a thing as Witchcraft, *if the Reports and Relations of several Persons of good Credit may be confided in, who have been eye-witnesses of some poor Creatures that have been Tortured to Admiration and strong Fitts, which must undoubtedly be more than Natural: But I shall not take upon me to Determine any thing positively in thiis dubious matter, let every one enjoy his own Opinion.*

Of Horse-Races, according to Haly *in his Book* de Judic. Astrorum, *fol.* 142. When it shall be demanded which of the two Beasts that are to Run a Race shall Win, and that the *Querents* Horse, or another about which he shall be solicitous shall be one of them that shall Run; Then regard the Lord of the Hour in which the Question is propounded, and if thou findest him in the *Horoscope*, the *Querents* Horse, or the Horse about which he asks the Question shall win; but if the Lord of the Hour shall be in the Mid-heaven, say that he shall be the second from the first, and if he be in the eleventh or third House, say the same: But if he be in the seventh House, say he will be between the first and the last; and if in the fourth House, say he will be the last of all; if the Lord of the Hour shall be in his Fall, the Rider shall be fearful, (judge the same if it be the Lord of the Ascendant so qualified) and not only fearful, but in danger of falling from his Horse; and if the Infortunate Planets shall cast any Aspect unto him (chiefly from bad places of the Figure) he will go neer to break some of his Limbs, and the hurt will be in that Member represented by that Signe in which the Significator is posited: But if the Aspect of the Infortune be an ☍, the Rider will be in danger of Death; and the Danger will be the more aggravated if the Lord of that Sign Ruling the Member be unfortunate, and the ☽ unfortunate also: But if the Querent have not his Beast in the Race, and inquire which Horse shall win the Race, behold the Lord of the Hour, and if you find him in the Ascendant, Mid-heaven, or eleventh Houses, say that Horse shall winn the Race, that is of that colour of that Planet as shall be posited in any of the aforesaid places; and if the Significator of the Winning Horse shall be in his *Exaltation House, Triplicity, Terms or Face,* he shall be the more Remarkably known and discovered; for if he be in his *Exaltation,* &c. it denotes the Horse to be more than ordinary Noted and Famed: But if the Significator shall not be in any of the aforesaid places, the Horse is then a stranger and unknown, and if in this we find him in his fall, the Horse is unlucky, ill favoured, and of evil qualities and conditions; but if he be in his *Exaltation* or *House,* he will be singularly famous in himself; if in his Triplicity, he is noted all over the Countrey, but not very excellent in himself; if in his Terme or Decanate, he is known, &c. If the Age of the Horse be enquired of, consider the Significators position, whether he be Oriental, then he is young; if Occidental, he is old; if he be in the North Angle, he is very old.

The Resolution of Questions made of Divers things together at one time.
According to *Guido Bonatus.*

I. Many people will usually come to the Astrologer indiscreetly, asking many things of him, and think it as light and easie a thing to answer, as it is to ask; and that the Astrologer may as well answer all Questions together as one when it is otherwise: wherefore when you have not the Ascendant Contracted to the Question, take the more general thing for the Querent, which is the ☽, and the other Planets shall signifie the things quesited or sought after; and then consider the number of Questions; for if they are six, or less, judge of them according to the ☌ the ☽ makes with the other six Planets; and you may know the Nature of the Question, by the nature of the Planet to whom the ☽ is first joyned after the Question proposed, and observe the disposition of the Planet, and accordingly judge of the effect of that thing; for if he be strong, and well placed, free from Impediments, judge the effect of it will be good, if ill posited, judge the contrary.

II. Then see to what Planet the ☽ is next joyned after her separation from that Planet, and according to his disposition judge of the second thing; then observe the next Application from that separation, and judge accordingly for the six Questions, and give the same judgment of an Aspect as of a Corporal Conjunction.

III. And if your questions exceed six, then afterwards judge by the Lords of the Triplicities of the Houses in which the Planets are when the ☽ is joyned to them by Body or Aspect.

IV. As for Example, if the ☽ be joyned to ♂ in her first ☌ which she makes after the question, and ♂ be in ♍, then when thou hast compleated the first six questions, according to the number and nature of the first six Planets, then judge of the seventh question according to the Ruler of the first Triplicity of ♍, which is ♀.

V. And also judge of the eighth according to the Lord of the first Triplicity of ♋, which is ♂; and thus to the twelve questions; and if the questions be more, judge by the three Lords of the Triplicities, as by the first and second; and if the questions exceed this number, then judge by the Lords of the Angles; and if they exceed still, then judge by the Lords of the Triplicities of the Angles.

VI. But if the question be concerning any thing, whether it be true or false; or concerning two or three things, which is better to take than the other; or whether News or Rumors be true or false, judge as is usually directed in the ninth, tenth and eleventh Houses.

VII. For if any one ask concerning many things, which is best for him, or most profitable; or concerning Rumors, whether they be true or false; or of any thing else he would obtain, behold the Lord of the Ascendant and the ☽ and see which of them is strongest, and by him opperate; and if the stronger of them be in an Angle, free from Impediment, and in Reception, the thing first named will be best and most true, and fittest for the Querent, and best obtained: But if the Lord of the first, or the ☽ be impeded, there will be some mention of the thing, but afterwards it will come to nothing; yet if the Lord of the first or the ☽ behold the first, and be received in a succedent House, or free from Impediments, the Querent shall obtain the thing quesited; and if they be impeded, it will be lost after 'tis obtained; and ·if he be in a Cadent House, free from other Impediments and received, the Querent shall obtain the thing quesited; or it is true if it be concerning any News or Rumors: But if the Lord of the Ascendant or ☽ be Impedited in a Cadent House, whatever the Question is it will come to nothing.

VIII. If several persons come together, & propound Questions to the Artist, let him take the Ascendant for the first person that propounds, and the second House shall be the Ascendant of the second person, and the third House the Ascendant of the third person, &c. and so vary all the rest accordingly; but the surest way is for every person to go to an Artist single without other Company that would be Querents also.

Here ends the Rules how to judge the several Questions appertaining to the Twelve Houses of Heaven. Brief Examples follow.

CHAP. XIII.

Examples of Judging the Questions upon each of the Twelve Houses.

[*That these Rules may be the better understood, and put into Practice, I shall give Examples of some Questions upon each of the Twelve Houses, the letter to illustrate the foregoing Rules from the former Exemplary Figure, which I here again insert,* viz.]

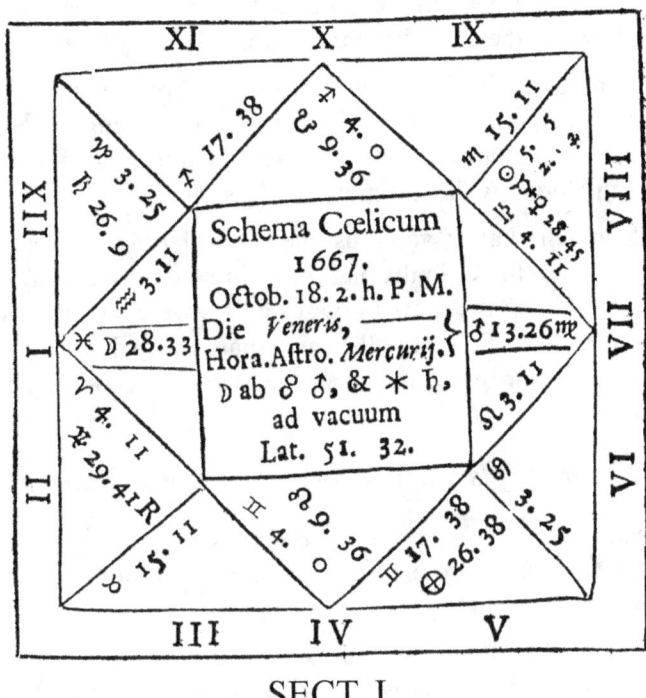

SECT. I.

Questions proper to the First House.

[Paragr. I.] *Is the Querent Long-Liv'd?*

Here I find ♄ Lord of the Ascendant (which signifies Querent) in ♑ his own House, in the twelfth, in □ of ♀, Lady of the eighth (or House of Death) and the ☽ lately in ☍ of ♂ from Angles, ☿ is also Lord of the fourth, Combust of the ☉ light of the time in the eighth (*viz.*) the House of Death. Hence I conclude, that according to Natural causes, the Querent is not long lived, but subject to Diseases, because the ☽ is lady of the sixth, and afflicted by ♂, as before noted, and consequently his Life but of a short date. But this Judgment is in part mittigated by reason ♄ and ♀ are in Reception by Exaltation, and Triplicity, (♄ is Exalted in ♎ in the eighth, and ♀ hath Triplicity in ♑ in the twelfth) and the ☽ locally in the Ascendant, and in ✶ to ♄, who is in his own Dignities in the Figure, *&c.*

[Paragr. II.] *If the Question were, Is the Party at Home I Would speak withal?*

Here, in this case (if the person hath no Relation to the Querent) I take the Lord of the seventh, *viz.* the ☉ to be his Significator, and finding him not to be in an Angle, I conclude the party is not at home, but neer home, beeause the ☉ is in a succedent House, *viz.* the eighth, neer the Southwest quarter (or more westerly from the South) in ☌ of ☿ representing the person he is in company withal, and probably the Querent may be directed to him by some female servant, because the ☽, Lady of the sixth, was lately in ☍ of ♂, who is posited in the seventh House, and she in the Ascendant in ✶ of ♄, the Querents Significator. If the party enquired after have any Relation to the Querent, Judge the like from the Lord of that House that signifies the Relation.

[Paragr. III.] *If the Question were, Is the Absent Party Dead or Alive, or in what Condition may he be in at present?*

If the Party be not Related to the Querent, then the Ascendant & his Lord, with the ☽, signifies the Absent Party, and finding ♄ Lord of the Ascendant in his own Dignities, and in ✶ to the ☽, I may hope well that the quesited is at present in health; but by reason ♄ is in □ to ♀, Lady of the eighth, and posited in an abject House of the

Clavis Astrologiae Elimita, The Key to Astrology New Filed

Figure, I may thence conclude he hath been in some danger of death, or that he hath lately undergone some sharp conflict with a Disease, because the ☽, Lady of the sixth, was lately in ☍ to ♂.

The ☽ a general Significatrix, and being lately afflicted by ♂, Lord of the ninth and second Houses, may also intimate that the Quesited hath undergone some trouble in mind concerning some Religious circumstances, or by reason of some long Journey, or probably he hath suffered for the want of Moneys, and thereby Imprisonment, because ♄ is in the twelfth House, which intimates no less.

If it were a Husband or a Wife enquired after, you must then consider the ☉, Lord of the seventh, and ♂, who is posited therein, and by reason I find the ☉ in the eighth, within the Orbs of a □ Aspect with ♄, I might judge the absent party to be in an ill condition; the same I might say if it were an absent Brother, Sister, or Kinsman, &c. Because ♀ is Lady of the third, and afflicted in the same manner, by the □ of ♄ from bad Houses, and their affliction should partly proceed from, or by the means of the Querent, who is signified by ♄, and he a General Infortune.

[Paragr. IV.] *Is a Ship at Sea, in Safety or Danger?*

This Question hath some dependance upon the ninth House, by reason a Ship relates to Voyages; but since the Question is concerning her safety, it therefore properly belongs to the first House, and the parties therein, by the Lord thereof.

Now the Ascendant, and the ☽ being Significators of the Ship, and Lord therefore, & ♄ of those persons in her. I view the position, and finding ♄ so strong in his own Dignities, and in ✶ to the ☽, therefore the Ship at present, I may conclude is safe and free from danger, with those persons that are therein.

But considering also, that ♄ hath & still is in □ to ♀, Lady of the eighth, & the ☽ lately separated from the ☍, of ♂ intimates that they have lately been I great perplexities, & (in all probability) not only in danger of Death, or bieng Cast away, but also of Pyrates, and received prejudice or loss that way; this Judgment is the more to be credited by reason ♄ is also Lord of the twelfth, and in the twelfth, having great Dignities in the eighth, and ♂ Lord of the ninth, Angular, and lately beholding the ☽ by a Malevolent Aspect, as before noted.

[Paragr. V.] *If the Question were, Shall good or ill succeed the thing that hath suddenly happened to the Querent.*

Note that reports first dispersed, the ☽ being then in the first, ten degrees of ♏, are either false or forged on purpose. In the Figure I find ♂ Lord of the House of the ☉, ♃ of the House the ☽ is in, intercepted in ♓ in the Ascnendant, and ♄ Lord of the Ascendant in his own Dignities, here ♄ is strongest, and in ✶ to the ☽, which intimates the Querent needs not much fear danger, but yet he will not be altogther freed from some kind of prejudice that shall arise by this sudden accident. Because ♄ is also Lord of the twelfth, and in □ to ♃ Lord of the tenth from Cardinal Signes, and the Disposter of the ☽ in the Ascendant, which advises the Querent to beware of a Magistrate, or Man in Power, or some Scandal that may arise (for the ☋ is in the tenth) occasioned by some secret Enemy, and the Querents own Head-strong Actions.

[Paragr. VI.] *Lastly, If it were desired to know what Marks, Moles or Scars the Querent hath about his Body.*

I consider the Signe Ascending, which is the beginning of ♒, a Signe that represents the Leggs, therefore the Querent should have a black Mole upon the upper part of the right leg, because ♒ is a Masculine Signe, and ♄ Lord thereof, a Masculine Planet, and the mark is apparently to be seen, because ♄ is above the Earth.

The Querent should have another upon, or neer one of his Knees, because ♄ is in ♑; also another upon one of his feet, but not so apparent, because the ☽ in ♓ is not yet ascneded above the Horizon, and this should be upon the left foot, because ♓ is a Feminine Signe, the ☽ is a Feminine Planet; you may also discover another upon the Breast, for ♋ descends upon the Cusp of the sixth, the ☽ is vertually in the second House, though located in the first; therefore I conclude the Querent to have some kind of pale Mark or Mole neer the left side of the Neck or Throat, for a Planet in the Ascendant discovers one upon the Head or Face; a Planet in the second, a mark upon the Neck or Throat, &c.

Note that the twelve Houses have for their Consignificators, the twelve Signes, and seven Planets, beginnning with ♈ and ♄, for the first House; and ♉ and ♃ the second; ♊ and ♂ for the third, and so on to the rest, beginning again with ♄ for Consignificator of the eighth House, &c.

SECT. II.

Questions proper to the Second House.

[Paragr. I.] *If the Question were, Shall the Querent be Rich, or ever attain to any Competent Fortune in this World?*

I. Consider ♂ is Lord of the second, and posited in ♍, the House of ☿ intercepted in the seventh, and ♃ located in the second in ♈ Retrograde, but in ✶ to ⊕ in the fifth House in ♊ who is beheld by a △ of ☿, Dispositer thereof, and the ☽ vertually in the second House, the House of Substance; all which (according to the Rules of Astrology) promise a very Competent Fortune to the Querent, according to his Degree or Capacity.

[Paragr. II.] *If it be Enquired by what Means it shall be Obtained?*

Finding the Lord of the second in the seventh, disposed of by ☿, who is also the Dispositer of the ⊕ in the fifth, I conclude the Querent may be a Gainer by Gameing, or by following such things that are signified from the fifth House, as being a Player, or by keeping an Ale-huose, or Tavern and the like, or by the means of a Wife, the reason is the Lord of the second is in the seventh, & in Reception with his Dispositer, (the premises withal considered) and ♀ being so strong in the eighth, the House of the Wives Substance confirms the same. In fine, the Querent may arrive to a competent Fortune by the exercise of his Wit, which is here declared to be pregnant and acute enough, and therefore he may imploy it to his advantage in the procuring of a Wife, and thereby raise his Fortune, &c.

[Parag. III.] *If it be enquired, Shall the Estate I now possess be Durable, or Continue?*

Herein I consider the Cusp of the second House is ♈, a movable Signe, and ♃ Retrograde therein, and the Lord of the 2d. in ♍ having no Dignities there. And lastly, ☿ the Dispositer of the ⊗ is combust of the ☉, to which I may add ♀, the Significatrix of a Wives Substance, she being in □ to ♄; All which are Arguments of its no long continuance; but that the Estate gain'd by the Querent will soon be squandred away; and this the rather, because ♃ in the second is in □ to ♄, Lord of the Ascendant, which intimates (in an Astrological sense) the Querent will be Extravagant, and addicted to illicit Courses, and thereby deminish, and at length totally wast what Substance he had before heaped together: he ought also to beware of trusting, for loss is threatned by Debts likewise, becasue the Lady of the eighth beholds the Lord of the Ascendant, ♄, by a □ from Cardinal Signes, and from bad Houses of the Figure, the being in ☍ to ♃ from the same Signes also, doth very much confirm the Judgment, and notably Coutionate the Querent to double diligence in his endeavours to mittigate the evil threatned.

[Paragr. IV.] *If it be enquired, the time when the increase of Fortune may happen, or the Contrary,* viz. *Loss or Damage.*

Authors advise in the case to take the degrees of distance, that the Lord of the Ascendant, or the ☽ wants of a perfect ✶ or △ Aspect of the promising Planet, and thereby to proportion out the time; observing also that fixed Signs prolong the expectation; double bodyed Signs shew a medium (that is neither very long nor short) moveable Signes give great hast, or speed in the matter; and this must be conjectur'd at by discretion, wehther to give dayes, weeks, months, or years, for the degrees of distance, according as there is a probability of the thing

Clavis Astrologiae Elimita, The Key to Astrology New Filed

propounded; but this being but an uncertain way, may serve upon frivial occasions; yet where the business is of consequence, the time is best pointed out by the direction of the several Significators, to their Promittors, which shall be shewed in the third part, and to be performed only where the Question is in General; but for a particular sum that a man expects to receive, the other way is exact enough.

In this Figure, when the Ascendant or the ☽ meets the Body of ♃ by direction is the most hopeful time of gain, and the Ascendant directed to the ☍ of ♂, Lord of the Second, shews prejudice both to Body and Estate.

[Paragr. V.] *If the Question were, Shall I receive or procure the Money I have Lent, or that is due from a certain Person?*

In this case, consider he ☉, who is Lord of the seventh, signifies the Person, and the Lady of the eighth (*viz.*) ♀, his Substance. Now, that the party is in a Capacity to pay, is clear, because ♀, Lady of the eighth, is in ♎, her own Dignity; but being in □ to ♄, Lord of the Ascendant signifies no great willingness he has to part with his Money, and the rather because the ☉ is within his Orbes of a □ of ♄ also; but by reason there is reception between ♄ and ♀, there is a probability the Querent (with mcuh ado) may at length procure some Moneys, though perhaps not all the Debt; for ♀ is in ☍ to ♃ from the eighth and second, the two Houses representing both parties Substance.

Now if you did expect Moneys from some Noble-man, then consider the Lord of the tenth, ♃, who is in the Querents second, he is also Lord of the eleventh, and denotes the Noble-man's substance, and disposes of the ☽, but in □ to ♄, which intimates the Querent may have his Money, but with some trouble, or at least some displeasure or check from the Noble-man: if you do expect Moneys from any Relation, then consider the Planets and Houses that are their Significators, and accordingly order your Judgments.

SECT. III.

Questions Answered Appertaining to the Third House.

[Paragr. I.] *If the Question were, Shall the Querent and his Brethren, Sisters or Neighbours, &c. Agree together, and love each other?*

Finding ♀, Lady of the 3*d*, in □ to ♄, Lord of the Ascendant, this argues but small Love; nay, it is an Argument of almost perfect hatred between the Querent & those Relations; here both their Significators are in their own Dignities, strong and potent (though accidentally posited in bad Houses of Heaven) which intimates the Querent and his Relations are very high, and care not one for the other, but stand upon their Reputation, the one (as it were scorning to stoop or submit to the other, yet the Querent will (and doth) expet the most observance.

[Paragr. II.] *If the Question be concerning an Inland Journey, whether it may be Prosperous or not?*

♀, Lady of the third House, 'tis true, is strong in her own Essential Dignities, and therefore denotes a prosperous Journey, but being in □ to ♄, & ☍ to ♃, it declares rather that the Querent shall receive prejudice thereby, both to his Purse, and Person, and probably light amongst Thieves, who may endanger his Life: In short, the person of the Querent is by the Figure threatned with eminent danger, in case he takes his Journey, and therefore he ought to be disswaded from it.

[Paragr. III.] *If the Question be, Is the Report true or false, that is thus noised about?*

I then consider the Lord of the Ascendant, ♋ and the ☽ and her Disposiler; now the Lord of the Ascendant being in □ to ♀ and ♃, the Disposiler of the ☽, (as well as Lord of the tenth) and the ☽ lately separated from an ☍ of ♂, this argues there is but small probability that the News is true, and this the rather, because the Angles of the tenth, and fourth Hosues are not fixed, but Common-Bi-corporeal, or double bodyed Signes.

[Paragr. IV.] *So, If it were a Question propounded concerning the Advice of a Friend, whether it be for Good or Evil?*

Finding then in the tenth House, and the Lord of the tenth, ♃ Retrograde, and in □ to ♄, Lord of the Ascendant, I thence conclude the Counsel or Advice of this pretended Friend is not given with an honest intent, but that he meant thereby to injure the Querent, and therefore let him by no means take this deceitful Admonition.

SECT. IV.

Questions and their Answers belonging to the Fourth House.

[Paragr. I.] *If the Question were, Shall the Querent Purchase the House or Land he is about,* &c.

Here ☿ is Lord of the fourth House, Combust of the ☉ in the eighth, & both within their Orbs of a □ Aspect, with ♄ Lord of the Ascendant, the ☉ denotes the Seller, ♄ the Land, and being in □ to ♄, the Buyers Significator; this argues both it will be purchased with great toyl, expense & pains, and that the Seller is indifferent whether he deals with the Querent or not. Now although ☿ be Combust, and may denote some incombrance upon the House or Land, yet by reason 'tis a frequent thing for ☿ to be neer the ☉, (since he cannot be far Elongated from him) I look upon that affliction the less considerable: ☿ being Dispositer of ⊕ and the ☊ in the fourth, doth somewhat abate the evil, and argues the Land to be good, the ☽ and ♄ beholding the Cusp of the fourth by benevolent Aspects (as by a ✶ and △ within Orbes) declare a willingness in the Querent to it, and that with much ado, he may at last obtain his desire, though the Seller be a person of a contrary nature.

[Paragr. II.] *If the Question were, Is it good to remove unto some other House or stay where I am?*

Finding ☊ in the fourth House, and the Lord of the fourth *viz.* ☿, and the ☉ in △ to ♓, the Intercepted Sign in the Ascendant, I should upon this consideration advise the Querent to stay where he is, and the rather because the Lord of the Ascendant and the ☽ do very well behold the Cusp of the 4*th* House, (as before hinted) and therefore it argues the Querent will reap more Advantage to continue where he is, than to remove to another place; besides, to encourage him to stay, the ☽ applyes to a void of Course.

[Paragr. III.] *If the Query were, Shall I enjoy my Fathers Estate?*

I consider my Scheme, and in the first place finding ☿ the Significator of the Father, (within Orbs) in □ to ♄, Lord of the Ascendant, Argues but small Love between the Father, and the Querent his Son, but finding ♂ Lord of the second, and ☿ of the fifth (the Fathers House of Substance) in strong Reception by House, and applying to a ✶ Aspect, this is an Argument the Querent may enjoy what he desires, and that the Estate is considerable, because ⊕ is in the fifth House, *&c.*

[Paragr. IV.] *If the Question be, Is there Treasure Hidden in such a place, and whether it is Attainable or not?*

The ☊ being posited in the fourth House, and the ☽ in ✶ unto the Cusp thereof, argues that there is Treasure hid, and reason ☿ is Lord of the fourth House, he in particular denotes the Quality thereof; it must be therefore, Medals, Books, or Pictures, *&c.* And finding ☿ afflicted by the ☌ of the ☉, & □ of ♄, intimates that the Querent shall very hardly find it, or that there is but small hopes of attaining the Treasure so hidden, and therefore in vain for the Querent to make any attempt.

[Paragr. V.] *If the Question be concerning any thing that is hidden or miss-laid, Whether it may be found in the House?*

Then consider ♂ being Lord of the second House, and in an Angle, denotes it to be in the House, the ☽ being

Angular, the same; and by reason ♂ is in the seventh House, and the ☽ in the Ascendant, it declares the thing to be hid in the Room in which the Querent and his Wife most frequent, where you ought to make diligent search for the finding thereof.

[*Consult the fourth of* Sect. 4. *and you may help your self to raise a more Copious Judgment.*]

SECT. V.

Questions and their Answers proper to the Fifth House.

[Paragr. I.] *Let the Question be, Shall the Querent have Children?*

The Cusp of the fifth House is a Barren Sign, ♂ in □ thereunto, ☿ Lord of the fifth in □ to ♄, (the other Infortune) and in ☌ of the ☉, these are Arguments of no Issue; to which I may add the ☍ of ♃ and ♀; But finding the ☽ in ♓, a fruitful Signe, and applying to a ✶ Aspect of the fifth House, ☿ is also in ♏, a fruitful Signe, and in ☌ of ♀, who is in ♎ her own Dignities, these Arguments are the most prevalent; *ergo*, the Querent may have Children, which Judgment is augmented by the position of the ⊕ in the House of Children, & in all probability they may be most Males, for the Lord of the Ascendant is a Masculine Planet, and the ☽ is just entering a Masculine Sign, also the Lord of the fifth is in ☌ of the ☉ a Masculine Planet (as well as with ♀ a Feminine) but in fine, the Querent may have Children, and those of both Sex, yet not many of either. The best way is to collect the Testimonies *pro* and *con*, and judge by the Major.

[Paragr. II.] *Let the Question be, Is the Querent with Child or not?*

The ☽ hastens to a ✶ of the Cusp of the fifth House, the ⊕ in the fifth, and the Lord thereof in ☌ of ♀, to which I may add ♃, the natural Significator of Children, being in ✶ to the ⊕ in the fifth, are Arguments the Querent hath Conceived; but considering also the □ of ♀ & ♄, and the ☍ of ♃ and ♀ from Cardinal Signes, with the □ of ♂ to the Cusp of the fifth, and the Lord of the fifth being in A with the ☉ a barren Planet; hence I may conclude 'tis but a false Conception, and the Birth will prove Abortive, and come to no Maturity.

[Paragr. III.] *Let the Question be, Concerning the success of a Messenger being sent of an Errand, whether he will perform the Message faithfully, and effectually or not?*

☿ is the Significator of the Messenger, and the ☉ the person to whom he is sent; I find ☿ in □ to ♄, Lord of the Ascendant, which is an Argument the Messenger doth not intend with Honesty to discharge his Trust; yet he is in ☌ with ♀, and applying to a partile ☌ of the ☉, Lord of the seventh House, which intimates he is safely arrived to the person to whom he is sent, and great probability there is that he hath delivered his Message; and when the ☽ comes to a good Aspect of ☿, or ☿ of ♄, the Querent may expect an account of his proceedings.

[Paragr. IV.] *Let the Question be, Shall the Querent gain by Play?*

The Lord of the fifth is in □ to ♄ (as yet) but applyes to his ✶ Aspect, and is in ☌ of ♀ the lesser Fortune, & the ⊕ in the fifth House, to which I may farther add, that ☿ doth dispose of the Lord of the second, *viz.* ♂, and there is Reception by House, between them, all which are Arguments that the Querent shall be (for the most part) fortunate in gameing, yet seeing ♂ is in □ to the Cusp of the fifth House, and ☿ Combust of the ☉, and in □ to ♄: This therefore signifies that the Querent shall not be much inrich'd thereby, but must expect to see an end of what comes that way; and also (sometimes) loss and detriment therein, as those that are generally most fortunate in that kind, can no way escape.

SECT. VI.

Questions and Judgment belonging to the Sixth House.

[Paragr. I.] *If the Question be concerning a Sick Person, viz. what part of the Body is afflicted or whether he may Recover?*

In the Scheme I find the ☽: Lady of the sixth House in ♓ in the Ascendant, and she lately afflicted by the ☍ of ♂, who is posited in an Angle in ♍; Now ♂ being the afflicting Planet, Rules (according to the Table for that purpose) the Leggs & Belly, & in those parts lies the parties Grief; the Diseases thereof are the Plague of the Guts, *Hypocondriack*, Melancholy, & all kind of Obstructions therein; & those of the Leggs must needs be, Cramps, Swellings, Aches or Blood settled, *&c*. In fine, the Disease proceeds from a cold and moist Cause.

Moreover, that the Party will very hardly escape death is plain, because the Lady of the eighth is in □ to ♄, Lord of the Ascendant, so is ☿ Lord of the fourth, and ♃, who hath Dignities in the Ascendant, is in ☍ to the Lady of the eighth also, all which are Testimonies of a dangerous Consequence, and the worse, because these Aspects are from Cardinal Signes.

All the hopes that may be gather'd is, the ☽ being in ✶ to ♄ out of the Ascendant, ♄ having Exaltation in the 8*th* House, and being in Reception with the Lady thereof, and in his own Dignitier, these things being considered, Nature may at last overcome; but the ☋ in the tenth, and ♃ in □ to ♄, doth aggravate the evil, and denotes Improper Physick is Administered to the Sick Person.

[Paragr. II.] *If the Question were, Shall the Querent be Fortunate in his Servants— as also Small Cattle, &c.*

Considering the ☽, Lady of the sixth House, is in the Ascendant, and in friendly ✶ to ♄, Lord thereof, 'tis an Argument the Querent may have faithful Servants, and be Fortunate in small Cattle; yet the Querent is advised not to impose too much Confidence in them, because the ☽ was lately in ☍ to ♂, Lord of the second, and ♃ who is posited Retrograde in the second, hath great Dignities in the sixth, & is in □ to ♄ Lord of the Ascendant from Cardinal Signes, hence the Querent ought to have a strick eye over them, and then he needs not much question their Fidelity; but in general, the Figure speaks well for them to be honest and love their Master, and this according to the Rules of Astrology, which ought to be carefully observed by every Artist that values his Credit.

SECT. VII.

Questions and Astrological Answers belonging to the Seventh House.

[Paragr. I.] *Let the Question be (in a general way) Shall the Querent Marry?*

[*Note that if the Question be demanded for a Woman, simply take Signification from ♀; but determinately from the seventh House.*]

In the Figure I find the ☽ (a general Significatrix of Marriage in mens question) to be in a prolifical Sign, and in friendly ✶ to ♄, Lord of the Ascendant. This is one Argument of Marriage, but the □ of ♀ (another general Significatrix in Questions and Nativities) to ♄, speaks the contrary, and this Judgment is confirmed the rather, because ♄ is in □ to the Lord of the seventh, *viz.* the ☉ and ♂ in the seventh, in ♍ a barren Signe, and ♌ upon the Cusp thereof, another barren Signe, from hence I may conclude that notwithstanding the Native or Querent may have a strong inclination at sometime of his life to Marriage, yet he will rarely Marry, (if at all) for the former Reasons; or if he happens to Marry, he will find much trouble in the prosecution thereof, for ♄ and ☉ are Planets of contrary Natures, and by Astrologers accounted Enemies one to the other, and here they behold each other very ill.

Again, from what hath been said, may be drawn this Result, that if the Querent Marryes, 'twill be a Person so different from his own Nature, that there will be no mutual Love and concord between them, but on the contrary, much hate and Discord, which is not merely seconded by the position of ♂ in the seventh, and ♀ in □ to ♄ before noted.

The Querents Wife (if he should Marry) you must describe by the ☉ and ☿, and so mixt your judgment according to the Rules given at the beginning of this Book, and the time when is best discovered by directions.

[Paragr. II.] *Let the Question be, Is her Portion Considerable, and whether obtained with ease or Difficulty?*

To this I answer, ♀, Lady of the *8th* House, in △ to the ⊕ and in her own Dignities posited in the eighth, declare a very considerable Portion, but that it will be difficult for the Querent (or Native) to obtain is not to be doubted, because ♀ is in □ to ♄ from Cardinal Signes, and bad Houses of the Figure, as also in ☍ to ♃.

[Paragr. III.] *If it be demanded whether the Querrent (or Native) may overcome his Publick Enemies, or in a Suit of Law, &c. which may have the Day? Or if Return safe from the Warr?*

Finding ♄ so strong in his own Dignities, and the ☽ in the Ascendant, and in ✶ unto him, and finding the ☉ Lord of the Seventh in ♏, having no Dignities in that place, I may in reason conclude the Querent is strongest, and shall therefore overcome his Adversaries; yet this is also to be noted, that the ☉ is in ✶ to his Disposer and in ☌ of ♀, and ☿, who is Lord of the tenth and eleventh, from the *7th* House, which argues the Quesited may have great hopes, and find many Friends, and ♃ Lord of the tenth being in □ to ♄ may intimate some unwelcome news from the Judge, or some great lawyer concerned with the Querent; yet notwithstanding all this, the Querent (in all probability) will come off Victor (though perhaps with some expence more than ordinary) for the former Reasons before alledged, or they may at length compound, because the ☉ applyes to a ✶ of ♄, not ♄ to the ☉. Judge the same in Warr Affairs; that notwithstanding all danger, the Querent returns home safe from the Warr, &c.

[Paragr. IV.] *Let the Question be, Shall I have the Desired Party?*

Now here is a person in particular Nominated, & in the Figure, signified by the ☉, and at the time of the Question she seems to deny, for the ☉ is in □ to ♄, but within short time the Querent may have his desire; for the ☉ not long after comes to a ✶ of ♄, and then the business may be concluded, and brought to a final end, and the rather, because the ☽ (a general Significatrix) is in ✶ to the Querents Significator, the ☽ did also separate from a △ of the ☉, and applyed to an ☍ of ♂, the Disposer of the ☉, and in the next place translates their light and vertue to ♄ by a ✶ Aspect, and meets with the Aspect of no other Planet during the time she continues in that Sign, and therefore the quesited will comply, as well as her Significator doth apply to ♄, the Significator of the party enquiring.

[Paragr. V.] *Let the Question be, which way is the Fugitive or Stray gone, or whether or not will he be found, or Return again?*

☿ and the ☽ with the ☉, Lord of the seventh Denotes the Fugitive or Stray, and by reason I find ☉ and ☿ in ☌, and as yet within Orbs of a □ Aspect of ♄, Lord of the Ascendant, I conclude at present he hath no mind to return; but by reason the ☽ is in ✶ to ♄, & ☿ applying to the ✶ of ♄ also, it argues the party will be heard of again, and probably return when the ☉ and ☿ come to a ✶ of ♄. The Quarter he is in, is Southerly, or rather South-west.

[Paragr. VI.] *If the Question were, There are Goods lost, Shall they be recovered, or what kind of Person (or Persons) did the Fact?*

Some would take ♂, being Peregrine in an Angle, to be the Significator of the Thief, but by reason he is in Reception with the Disposer of the ⊕, and doth not as yet behold thee by a □ Aspect, and because he is Lord of the Querents second, I shall not accept him as Significator, and the rather, because he afflicts not the House of Substance.

But I shall accept the ☉ to be Significator of the Thief, who is Lord of the seventh, & within the Orbs of an ☍ of ♃ in the second, and thereby afflicts the Significator of the Querents Substance; therefore the ☉ is true Significator, and the rather, because he also Combures ☿ the Dispositer of the ⊗; what kind of person the ☉ denotes, you may see in the Rules before given, at the beginning of this Book. Say the Thief is about a middle age.

Now there is but small probability that the goods lost will be recovered again, by reason ♀, Lady of the Thiefs 2d, is in the eighth, in ☍ to ♃ in the Querents second, and in □ to ♄ Lord of the Ascendant, to which may be added the ☉ is in □ to ♄, and to the Cusp of the Ascendant; And the ☉ and ♀ are both in △ to the ⊕, which intimates the Thief will keep the Goods, and loves them too well to restore them again.

Lastly, finding the ☉ Lord of the seventh in ☌ with ♀, Lady of the eighth, the ☽ under the earth, the ☉ in □ to the Ascendant, and ♂ in ☍ to the Ascendant, argues no Discovery or Restitution. If it were Cattle loft, either great or small, finding the ☽ Lady of the sixth in ✶ to ♄, Lord of the twelfth House in the twelfth; ♄ being also in □ to ♃ in the second, gives very small hopes of recovery.

[Paragr. VII.] *If the Question were, Shall two Partners Agree together?*

To this I answer, finding the Lord of the Ascendant, ♄, and the Lord of the seventh (*viz.* ☉) in bad Aspect *viz.* a □, and being Planets of contrary natures, I should hence conclude they would agree like Fire and Water, and by no means advise them to joyn together in Partnership.

[See more of these Judgments in the seventh Chapter hereof, where you are directed at large to judge the various Questions belonging to this House.]

[Paragr. VIII.] *If the Questions were, (in the time of War) whether such a Town or Strong-hold should be taken?*

In this case finding ♄ who in particular signifies the Besiegers to be strong, and his own Dignities argues they are strong; and in good heart, Courageous and Resolute, &c.

☿ is the Significator of the Governour of the place Besieged, as also of his strength, *viz.* men, Ammunition, Provision, &c. as being Lord of the fourth & fifth Houses.

Now considering ☿ is in the eighth combust of the ☉, and applying to the ✶ of ♄, but this is an argument that the Governour at last will rather yield up the Fort then stand it out, finding they are uable to hold it out against so strong a Force. But not presently for ☿ is now in □ to ♄, and the ☊ is in the fourth, abd the ⊕ in the fifth, which declares they are in a good condition within, and do perhaps expect more supplies, by reason ☿ is in reception with ♂, but considering ♂ is the Lord of the second, and dispositer of ♃ Lord of the tenth, and in reception so strongly by house with ☿ the Significator of the Governour, (or chief Commander) this intimates that he would willingly accept of a Bribe, and is possest with many fears in the case, and in the conclusion, rather resigns up upon conditions then longer to stand in opposition, now when ☿ and the ☉ come to a ✶ of ♄ is the time most probable, that this should be effected.

[By this brief Example, and the Rules given Sect. 5. of Chap 4. the young Artist may easily enlarge his Judgment upon any such Query which may be propounded.]

SECT. VIII.

Questions and Judgment proper to the Eighth House.

[Paragr. I.] *Of the Time of Death.*

To enquire after the time of a parties Death, I take to be a very nice Question; but if the Nativity be known, and the Directions run down according to Art, (as it shall be shown in its proper place) the Native may then see as in a glass, the most dangerous Direction that threatens to cut assunder the Thread of Life; but I pass by any farther Discourse of this Subject, in this place.

[Paragr. II.] *If it be demanded, what manner of Death the Querent may dye?*

Here finding ♀ Lady of the eighth House, and in the eighth strong and Potent, and neer *Spica Virginis*, a Benevolent fixed Star, argues a natural gentle death, and this the rather, because ♀ is in ☌ of ☿ Lord of the fourth, but ♀, Lady of the House of Death, being in ☐ to ♄, Lord of the Ascendant from Cardinal Signs, denotes an unwillingness in the Querent to leave this world, and to interchange this life for a better.

This House denotes the Portion of the Wife, of which I have already spoken.

[Paragr. III.] *If the Question were, shall the Man or Wife Dye first?*

To this I answer, that finding ♄ the strongest Planet, I should judge the Querent longest live'd, be it who it will, Man or Wife, the Lord of the seventh House, *viz.* the ☉, comes first to a ☌ of the Lady of the eighth, before ♄ to her ☐, which confirms the Judgment; thus an Artist may give a probable conjecture upon such a Question: but the surest way is to view both their Nativities, & from thence deduce a Judgment, which is the most rational; if they cannot be procured, let there be the more pains taken in the Question, and order it as if it were a Nativity: but to say the truth, I do not much approve of such kind of nice Questions; and an Artist ought to be exceeding wary in giving Judgment thereupon.

SECT. IX.

Questions and their Astrological Responses belonging to the Ninth House.

[Paragr. I.] *If a Person be going to Sea, and desires to know whether his Voyage will be Prosperous or Dangerous?*

I find ♏ upon the Cusp of the ninth House, and ♂ Lord thereof in ♍ angular, and in strong Reception with ☿ Lord of the fourth & fifth, who is the Dispositer of the ⊗, and ♂ Dispositer of ♃ in the second House, these are Arguments that the Querent may advantage himself by the Voyage, and need fear no danger that can happen therein because the ninth House, & Lord thereof are no way afflicted; and although ♂ be not in his own Essential Dignities yet he is accidentally reasonably well posited, which confirms the Judgment; yet the Querent is not hereby promised an extraordinary profit by the Voyage; but however, he may expect to reap advantage, rather than loss or damage, which is some encouragement.

[Paragr. II.] *If it be demanded, whether a Clergy-man may obtain the Benefice desired?*

Considering there is no Aspect between the Lord of the Ascendant, and the Lord of the ninth House, this declares but small probability thereof; and finding the ☽ lately separated from an ☍ of the Lord of the ninth, and ♃ (a General Significator in these matters) being in ☐ to ♄, Lord of the Ascendant, this gives small encouragement to seek after it, but 'tis but in vain, and for these Reasons he can expect but a small Revenue thereby, and therefore, not worth his trouble farther to seek after it.

The same Judgment might be given, if a man desires to know whether he may profit by any Art or Science intended; For what advantage will any Artist judge can follow, when the ☋ is in the tenth House, (the second from the ninth) and the Lord thereof Retrograde, and in Square to Saturne from Cardinal Signes.

SECT. X.

Questions and Astrological Answers belonging to the Tenth House.

[Paragr. I.] *Let the Question be, shall the Querent obtain the Place or Office he seeks after?*

The ☉ is a General Significator of Honour and Dignity, and he is here in □ to ♄, ♃ Lord of the tenth House is Retrograde in the second, and in □ to ♄ from Cardinal Signes; to which may be added the ☋ in the tenth, from these Considerations, 'tis plain (in Astrology) that the Querent shall hardly obtain the place desired; if he do, 'twill be with much difficulty, and expence of Money; and when procured, not so beneficial to the Querent as 'tis probable he expects.

'Tis true, the ☉ doth apply to the ✶ of ♄, which Argues it may perchance come to pass; but finding ♃ the particular Significator of the Place in □ to ♄, as aforesaid, it intimates there is but small hopes of continuing therein, without he bribes those concerned in it, which will not countervail; for the ☋ in the tenth House, declares the place not worth acceptation *gratis*, and therefore disswade the Querent from farther progress therein, rather than spend his time to so little purpose.

[Paragr. II.] *If the Question was, Shall the Querent benefit himself by his Trade or Profession he follows?*

Finding the ☋ in the tenth House, argues the the Querent shall have but bad Trading, generally, yet 'tis probable he may get moneys thereby, but he shall not be inrich'd with it; for ♃, Lord of the tenth House, being Retrograde in the second, and in □ to ♄, denotes that what he gains with one hand, he will spend with the other, *ergo*, not fit to manage a Trade, but think of some other imployment; in short, his Trade will no way prove Fortunate to the Querent. The same you may understand by taking of Lodgers (as is much used in *London*) you ought to be cautious in this particular, for you shall generally lose more than gain by entertaining such persons in your House, that come upon such a position of Heaven.

SECT. XI.

Questions and their Answers proper to the Eleventh House.

[Paragr. I.] *Let the Question be, May the Querent obtain what he hopes for?*

If the thing hoped for be not nominated, but propounded in a general way, why then I here consider ♃ is Lord of the eleventh House, and in □ to ♄ Lord of the Ascendant from Cardinal Signes (which I before hinted) and this gives a denyal of the Querents hopes, or that he shall not obtain the thing hoped for, but with much difficulty, and the greater loss thereby, than the thing it self can make requital or restitution, if obtained.

Now if the thing hoped for be nominated, I consider its Significator, and accordingly judge as I find him Aspect the Ascendant or his Lord: as suppose a man hopes to receive Money in a General way; now considering ♂ is Lord of the second House, and in ☍ to the Ascendant, and not beholding ♄ Lord thereof, and ♃ a Planet in the second in □ to ♄, this argues the Querents hopes will not take effect, or that he shall not receive the Moneys he hopes for.

[Paragr. II.] *Let the Question be Shall my Friends prove true and faithful, according to their promises and pretences?*

The Querents Friends are signified by ♃, he being in □ to ♄ Lord of the Ascendant, (which always denotes the Querent) this is but a bad Signe of their Fidelity; nay it intimates they will prove deceitful and persidious, careing not for the Querent but for their own ends, and the Querent will rather receive loss and prejudice by them; for ♃ beholds ♄ ill out of the second House.

SECT. XII.

Questions and their Answers appertaining to the Twelfth House.

[Paragr. I.) *If the Question was, Hath the Querent private Enemies?*

Finding ♄ in the twelfth House in his own Dignities, I might Judge, if the Querent be not an Enemy to himself, he needs not fear another; but by reason I find ♀ in □ to ♄ from the eighth House (*viz.*) both obscure places of the Figure, I may thence conclude the Querent hath private Enemies; and such that are of no rnean account; but ♄ being strong, and the most ponderous Planet, the Querent need not fear what prejudice they can do unto him.

Note that if a Question be propounded concerning private Enemies, absolutely or in general, judge from the twelfth House, but if it be determinately, or a person nominated, then judge from the seventh House.

[Paragr. II.] *If the Question was, Is there any probability a Prisoner may be released, &c.*

♄ the Querents Signnificator being Lord of the Ascendant, and twelfth House, and posited in the twelfth, there in □ to ♀ & ♃, declares a long Imprisonment; and this the rather, because a fixed Sign Ascends, and ☿ Lord of the hour is in □ to ♄, the principal Significator of the Querent.

[Paragr. III.] *If it was Propounded thus, shall the Querent be fortunate in great Cattle?*

I consider the position of ♄ in the twelfth House, strong and potent, but in □ to both the Fortunes from Cardinal Signs, ♄ being Lord of the Ascendant also, which is the second from twelfth, and denotes the profit that may arise from all things signified by the twelfth House; so that what the Querent gains this way, he may put in his eye and see never the worse. According to the usual Proverb.

[Paragr. IV.] *If the Question was, Is the Party Suspected, Bewitched or not?*

Finding ♄ Lord of the Ascendant and twelfth Houses and posited in the twelfth in □ to ♀ Lady of the eighth, and the ☽ Lady of the sixth in ✶ to ♄, argues the Querent is under an ill tongue, or bewitched. *This is a matter in these dayes much controverted by Learned Persons, and therefore I shall insist no farther upon the Subject.*

And thus I have briefly run over several Questions belonging to the twelve Houses, which, with the Rules before given, are sufficient to instruct any Ingenious Tyro in the Judicial part of Astrology.

CHAP. XIV.

Of the Planetary Hours and Elections.

SECT. I.

Of the Planetary Hours.

I. Observe that every Artificial day, (that is from *Sun* rising to *Sun* setting) is divided into twelve equal parts, called Planetary or unequal Astrological hours, for they are unequal in respect of the lengthning and shortning of the dayes: Thus if the day be sixteen hours long, a Planetary hour must be a twelfth part thereof, that is, one hour twenty minutes, or eighty minutes long, (which is twenty minutes more than a common hour) and then the night is eight hours long, which must also be divided into twelve equal parts, and the Planetary hour for the night will be but forty minutes; for this you must note, that so many minutes as a Planetary hour of the day is longer than the common hour, so many minutes is the Planetary hour of the night shorter than the common hour (or sixty minutes) hence then a Planetary hour in the Summer, that is from the *Suns* ingress into ♈, to his entrance into ♎, is in the day longer than sixty minutes, and in the night shorter by the same quantity; but when the ☉ is just in those Equinoctial Points, the dayes and nights are of equal length, *viz.* twelve hours, and consequently the Planetary hour of the same length with the common hour.

II. But from about the twelfth of *September*, to the tenth of *March*, the Planetary hours will be less than sixty minutes in the day, and greater than sixty minutes in the night, by the same space of time: this is easily understood, and therefore needs no farther discourse thereupon, but I shall present you with the Table it self, which is fitted for the middle part of *England, viz. Lat. 52.* and may without sensible errour serve in most parts thereof.

I am sensible that there are some Artists which have but very mean thoughts of these Planetary Hours, and others again have relinquished their former Opinion; I shall not go about to New Model Astrology, nor fight or undervalue Antiquity, but leave every person to their freedome, both in this, and divers other things in Art imbraced by the Ancients, and transmitted by them to Posterity, knowing that the Judgments and Opinions of Men are as various as their Faces: All I shall say, Let every person make use of those Rules he affects and finds verity in, and omit those he cannot easily digest, or takes a prejudice against.

III. Here followeth a Table of the length of the Planetary hours, for the Day and Night throughout the Year.

	Hours before Noon.						Hours after Noon.					
☉ Pl.	1	2	3	4	5	6	7	8	9	10	11	12
♈ ♍	h. m.	h. m.	h. m.	h. m.	h. m.	h. m.	h. m.	h. m.	h. m.	h. m.	h. m.	h. m.
0 30	7 0	8 0	9 0	10 0	11 0	12	1 0	2 0	3 0	4 0	5 0	6 0
6 24	6 50	7 54	8 54	9 56	10 58	12	2	4	6	8	10	13
12 18	39	43	48	52	56	12	4	8	13	17	21	25
18 12	28	35	41	47	54	12	6	13	19	25	32	38
24 6	18	27	39	43	52	12	8	17	25	33	42	50
♉ ♌												
0 30	6 1	7 18	8 29	9 39	10 50	12	1 11	1 20	3 32	4 42	5 43	7 3
6 24	5 58	16	23	35	48	12	13	25	38	50	6 6	15
12 18	48	3	17	31	46	12	14	29	43	57	12	26
18 12	35	5 55	12	28	44	12	16	32	49	5 5	22	37
24 6	30	48	6	23	43	12	18	36	54	12	30	48
♊ ♋												
0 30	5 23	6 42	8 2	9 21	10 40	12	1 20	1 39	3 59	5 18	6 38	7 57
6 20	16	37	7 58	18	39	12	21	42	4 3	23	44	8 5
12 11	19	32	54	16	38	12	22	44	6	28	50	12
18 12	6	29	52	14	37	12	23	56	9	31	54	17
24 6	3	27	50	13	36	12	24	47	10	33	57	20
♎ ♓												
0 30	7 0	8 0	9 0	10 0	11 0	12	1 0	2 0	3 6	4 0	5 0	6 0
6 24	11	9	7	4	2	12	58	1 56	2 54	3 51	4 49	5 47
12 18	21	17	13	8	4	12	56	50	48	40	39	35
18 12	30	24	19	13	6	12	54	47	41	35	28	21
24 6	42	33	25	17	8	12	52	43	34	37	18	10
♏ ♒												
0 30	7 53	8 42	9 32	10 22	11 10	12	0 50	1 39	2 29	3 18	4 8	5 57
6 24	8 23	50	38	25	12	12	45	35	23	10	3 58	45
12 18	12	57	43	29	14	12	46	31	17	3	4 8	38
18 12	21	9 5	49	3	16	12	44	28	11	2 55	39	21
24 6	30	12	50	36	18	12	43	34	6	48	30	13
♐ ♑												
0 30	8 38	9 18	59	10 39	11 20	12	1 41	1 21	2 2	2 41	3 23	4 3
6 24	44	22	10 4	41	21	12	39	18	1 57	36	15	55
12 18	8 50	28	6	45	22	12	38	16	54	32	10	48
18 12	54	31	9	46	23	12	37	14	51	28	5	43
24 6	58	32	10	46	24	12	36	13	49	22	3	40

	Hours before Midnight.						Hours after Midnight.					
☉ Ri.	1	2	3	4	5	6	7	8	9	10	11	12
h. m.	h. m.	h. m.	h. m.	h. m.	h. m.	h. m.	h. m.	h. m.	h. m.	h. m.	h. m.	h. m.
6 0	7 0	8 0	9 0	10 0	11 0	12	1 0	1 0	3 0	4 0	5 0	6 0
5 47	11	9	7	4	2	12	58	1 56	2 54	1 51	4 41	1 47
35	21	17	13	8	4	12	56	52	48	43	39	35
22	30	25	19	13	6	12	54	47	41	35	28	22
10	42	33	25	17	8	12	52	43	35	27	18	10
4 57	7 53	8 42	9 32	10 11	11 10	12	0 50	1 39	1 29	3 18	4 8	4 57
45	8 3	50	38	25	12	12	48	35	23	10	3 58	40
34	12	57	43	29	14	12	46	31	27	3	48	30
23	21	9 5	49	32	16	12	44	28	12	2 55	39	23
12	30	12	54	36	18	12	42	24	6	48	30	13
4 2	8 38	9 18	9 59	10 39	11 20	12	0 41	1 21	2 2	2 41	3 3	4 3
3 55	44	23	10 2	41	21	12	39	18	1 57	36	15	3 55
48	50	28	6	44	22	12	38	16	54	32	10	48
43	54	31	9	45	23	12	37	15	51	28	5	43
40	57	33	10	47	24	12	37	14	50	27	3	40
6 0	7 0	8 0	9 0	10 0	14 0	12	1 0	2 0	3 0	4 0	5 0	6 0
13	6 47	7 51	8 54	9 56	10 58	12	2	4	7	9	11	13
25	31	43	48	52	56	12	4	8	13	17	21	25
38	28	35	41	47	54	12	6	13	19	25	32	38
50	18	27	35	43	52	12	8	17	25	33	42	50
7 3	6 8	7 18	8 29	9 39	10 50	12	1 11	2 21	3 32	4 43	5 53	7 3
15	5 58	10	23	35	48	12	13	25	38	50	6 3	15
26	48	3	17	31	46	12	14	29	44	57	12	26
37	39	6 55	12	28	44	12	16	32	49	5 5	21	37
48	30	48	6	24	42	12	18	36	54	12	30	48
7 57	5 42	6 42	8 2	9 21	10 41	12	1 20	2 39	3 59	5 18	6 38	7 57
8 5	16	37	7 58	18	39	12	21	42	4 2	23	44	8 5
12	10	32	54	16	38	12	22	44	6	28	50	12
17	6	29	52	14	37	12	23	46	9	31	54	17
20	3	27	50	13	36	12	24	47	10	33	57	20

Clavis Astrologiae Elimita, The Key to Astrology New Filed

IV. A Table shewing what Planets Rule every hour of the Day and Night.												
The hours of the Day.												
	1	2	3	4	5	6	7	8	9	10	11	12
Sunday	☉	♀	☿	☽	♄	♃	♂	☉	♀	☿	☽	♄
Munday	☽	♄	♃	♂	☉	♀	☿	☽	♄	♃	♂	☉
Tuesday	♂	☉	♀	☿	☽	♄	♃	♂	☉	♀	☿	☽
Wednesday	☿	☽	♄	♃	♂	☉	♀	☿	☽	♄	♃	♂
Thursday	♃	♂	☉	♀	☿	☽	♄	♃	♂	☉	♀	☿
Friday	♀	☿	☽	♄	♃	♂	☉	♀	☿	☽	♄	♃
Saturday	♄	♃	♂	☉	♀	☿	☽	♄	♃	♂	☉	♀
Hours of the Night.												
	1	2	3	4	5	6	7	8	9	10	11	12
Sunday	♃	♂	☉	♀	☿	☽	♄	♃	♂	☉	♀	☿
Munday	♀	☿	☽	♄	♃	♂	☉	♀	☿	☽	♄	♃
Tuesday	♄	♃	♂	☉	♀	☿	☽	♄	♃	♂	☉	♀
Wednesday	☉	♀	☿	☽	♄	♃	♂	☉	♀	☿	☽	♄
Thursday	☽	♄	♃	♂	☉	♀	☿	☽	♄	♃	♂	☉
Friday	♂	☉	♀	☿	☽	♄	♃	♂	☉	♀	☿	☽
Saturday	☿	☽	♄	♄	♂	☉	♀	☿	☽	♄	♃	♂

Note that to every day in the Week there is appropriated a several Planet; as ☉ to *Sunday*, ☽ to *Munday* ♂ to *Tuesday*, &c. and therefore each Planet governs the first hour; As, by this Table you may perceive that the *Sun* governs the first hour after *Sun-rising* on *Sunday*, *Venus* the second, *Mercury* the third, the *Moon* governs the fourth Planetary hour, and so on, *Jupiter* governs the first Planetary hour of the Night, (that is, after *Sun-set*) *Mars* the second, the *Sun* the third, as you may discern in the same Column. Understand the like by the rest.

SECT. II.

The Description and Use of the Table of the Planetary Hours.

In the first Column is placed the *Suns* place to every six degrees through the twelve Signs and noted at top [☉ Pla.] then [♈ ♍] after that you shall find 0, 30, 6, 24, 12, 18, &c. which intimates that the *Sun* rises at the same time when he is in six degrees of ♈, as he doth when he is in the 24th of ♍. The twelve Planetary hours are noted at top, 1, 2, 3, 4, 5, 6, &c. before Noon, and after Noon.

II. In the second Column under I, you have the quantity of the first Planetary hour from *Sun-rising*, as against six degrees of the *Suns* place in ♉, or the 24th of ♌, I find that the first Planetary hour continues from *Sun-rising* until 58 minutes after five, the second until ten minutes after seven, the third continues till twenty three minutes after eight, the fourth until 35 minutes after nine before Noon, and so on: understand the like in the rest.

III. The right hand Page of the Table, shews in the first Column, the hour and minute of the *Sun's-rising*, and the last Column in the left hand page his setting, and all the other Columns in the right hand page shew the length of the Planetary huors after *Sun-set*, both before Midnight and after Midnight, until *Sun-rising* again: thus much may serve for the Description, I proceed to its Use.

SECT. III.

The Use of the Table.

I. On the 15*th* day of *April* 1668, being *Wednesday*, at nine hours 15 minutes in the morning, I would know what Planet Rules, I enter the Table, and against the sixth deg. of ♉ (the *Suns* place at that time) I guide my eye along, until I come to my hour proposed, the first Column shews five hours, and 58 minutes, the second 7 hours and 10 minutes, the third Planetary hour is until 8 hours 23 minutes, and the fourth Planetary hour until 35 mintues past 9, which is the hour required; then to know what Planet Reigns, I turn to the other little Table, entitituled, *A Table shewing what Planets Rule every Hour*, &c. and finding *Wednesday* in the first great Column, and right under the fourth Planetary hour of the day, (noted at top of the Table) I find ♃, which tellsl me that ♃ Rules that Planetary hour, which ends at thirty five minutes past nine in the morning.

II. But if it were required to find what Planet Rules at thirty minutes past three the same day; I guide my eye along in the great Table, as before directed, until I come to my hour desired, and I find three hours thirty eight minutes under the ninth Planetary hour, then I repair to my small Table, and right against *Wednesday*, and just under the ninth hour in the collaterate Column I find ☽, which informs me that the ☽ Governs that hour, *viz.* from twenty five minutes past two, until thirty eight minutes after three, which includes my proposed time. *Et fic in aliis*.

III. Again, If it were required to know what Planet Rules at twenty minutes past eight at night for the same day, I turn to the right hand page, and right against 6 d. ♉ (in the first Column of the left hand page aforesaid) I guide my eye, and under the first hour I find eight hours three minutes, under the second house, eight hours fifty minutes, under the third hour, nine hours thirty eight mintues: which includes my time given; and because it is the third Planetary hour of the Night, (or after *Sun-set*) I turn to my smaller Table, and to that part thereof, which are the hours of the Night, and right against *Wednesday*, under the third hour of the night, I find ☿, which tells me that ☿ Governs that hour, *viz.* from fifty minutes past eight, unto thirty eight minutes past nine at night.

IV. But if you have occasion to enter with any of the intermediate degrees not mentioned in the Table, you may easily make proportion, (if you desire to be so curious) but the differences (between the hours and minutes of the Planetary hours for each six degrees of the *Sun's* place) being but small, there need snot so much exactness.

SECT. IV.

Here it will be necessary, briefly to shew the Signification of each Planetary Hour, and what use may be made of them, &c.

I. In the hour of ♄ take no Voyage to Sea, neither take any long Journey by land; for crosses will assuredly attend, and small success may be expected; take no Physick: entertain no Servant, for they will prove idle, careless Persons: Not good to put on a new Garment, or cut your Hair; but this hour is good to buy, or take Leases of Houses, or Lands; good to buy any kind of Grain, or to dig in the Earth, or Plow; not good to borrow Money in this hour, or to fall sick in; for it threatens a long Disease, and sometimes terminates in death.

II. In the hour of ♃ 'tis good to apply to Ecclesiastical Persons, and all great Men, to obtain their favour; the same from all grave Senators, Judges, Lawyers, *&c.* In this hour 'tis good to take a Journey; or to go out of the House with success; good to sow all kind of Seeds, or to plant all kind of Seeds, or to Plant; not good to be let blood; he that falls sick in this hour will soon recover; good also to lend, or borrow Moneys; not good to enter a Ship; not good to buy Beasts: to conclude, this hour is good to Contract Matrimony in, *&c.*

III. In the hour of ♂ begin no worthy Action, or Enterprize, for it is a very unfortunate hour in all things, and therefore as much as may be to be avoided, it is ill to take a Journey, for you shall be in danger of Thieves; very ill to take a Voyage to Sea, and generally in all things.

IV. The hour of the Sun, is not to be chosen, as being generally infortunate, unless in makeing Application to great Persons, not good to begin a building, or put on new Garments, not good to enter into a mans own house, for discontent and brawling may then be expected to follow, this hour is good for a man to receive preferment in, not good to Court the Female Sex, or lay down moneys upon any account, 'tis also very dangerous for any person to fall siek in.

V. In the hour of ♀ 'tis good to court Women, or to begin a Joμrney, but not a voyage, good to enter upon any Play, Sport or pastime; not good to be let blood in, good to go out of a mans House with success, but not so good to return again in, good to take Physick in, but if a man falls sick in that hour, the disease proceeds from some Venereal distemper, this hour is generally good to undertake any business relating to the Womens concerns, or any delightful Actions, not good to begin a new Garment, but singular good for Marriage, and contracting in Matrimony, &c.

VI. The hour of ☿ is very good to Merchandize in, *viz.* Buy or sell, or to write Letters, or to send Messengers, to take Physick in, to send Children to School, to begin a Journey, to lend or borrow Moneys in, to put forth Apprentices, to begin any Building, but not good to Contract Marriage, or to Buy Houses or Lands, or to Re-enter your House being abroad, lest discontent or Brawling arise; nor good to take or hire a Servant, or to Redeem a Prisoner, but good to Plant or Graft in, and finally to make Suit to great Persons.

VII. The hour of the ☽ is not accounted good to Buy Cattle in, especially of the smaller Sort, nor to take Physick in, or begin any Building, not good to lend Money in, or to make new Cloaths; 'tis good to Court the Female Sex in, or send Children to School, and in some cases to take a Journey, or to pursue an Enemy, and to conclude, you may make choice of this hour to leave your Native Country in, (if desired to Travil) but choose another hour when you return, and are to reenter your own Countrey again.

[*These Significators of the Planetary Hours are very Ancient, approved of by the* Arabians, *and confirmed by* Haly *and later Authors, and may be of good use, though they are not of that Efficacy as well-grounded Elections, from an apt posture of the Heavens, which doth sympathize with the Natuvity (if it be known) of which I shall treat in the next Section.*]

SECT. V.

Of Elections.

In the next place, (for variety sake) I shall present you with some General Rules how to make an Election, But 'tis not my purpose here to handle that Subject at large, for he that hath made any considerable progress in Astrology cannot be to seek (upon any occasion) how to Elect a fit and Congruous time for this purpose.

I. An Election is no more than an apt time chosen, for the obtaining of some desired good promised, as also how to avoid, or escape any kind of danger or evil threatened at the time of the persons Birth, or Nativity, and generally by Elections, men may choose such times to begin their business, that the end thereof may prove prosperous and happy, especially in such things that lie in their own power to prosecute as taking of Journeys, &c. But if it be to speak with great Persons, 'tis true, they may make choice of a fortunate time to make their Addresses, could they have an opportunity at that day and hour, conveniently to meet with the Person, but this will be a matter of difficulty, and very rare to be brought to pass, by reason a man must not rush into the presence of a King or Person of Quality at any particular point of time, unless he be so happy as by the means of some Friend to get leave to come into his presence, and to present his Petition, or Request, of what kind soever it be.

II. To make a proper and fit Election, requires much care and diligence, if it be for a matter of Consequence, and not slightly to be passed over, but well considered, and managed with prudence and discretion.

Thus an Election ought to be made, if you desire the end should crown your Actions, and they differ from *Horary Questions* only in this, *viz.* Questions end, and determine in the knowledge of the business enquired after, and are not so certain, by reason the Question is often proposed by persons unconcerned, or not rightly stated; therefore an Artist should remember that notable *Aphorisms* of *Hermes, Not to Determine any thing be-*

fore he knows the Intention of the Querent. &c. For in so doing, he many times judges amiss, and the Querent receives little or no satisfaction, (for many know not what to ask, neither can they express what they would have) how then can it be otherwise, since the blind lead the blind? And every Artist knows 'tis no easie matter rightly to apprehend the intention of the Querent.

III. Elections differ from Questions thus, They are ordained and appointed for Action, and in respect of their ends they tend to, have dependance chiefly upon matters or things to be done hereafter: but Questions end, in the knowledge of business sought or enquired after. Elections, as to their ends, having relation principally upon our future Actions; and *Ptolomy* saith, the Election either of day or hour shall then be advantagious to a person, when 'tis constituted from his Nativity, otherwise though it be well made, it shall not profit. *Ptolomy. Centiloque, Aph. 6.*

IV. From what hath been said, may be gathered that there are two kind of Elections, the first from the Nativity, and the second (in a more general way, the Nativity not being known) from a Question; but the first is only to be imbraced, and the second wholly to be rejected as Erronious and Illegitimate, because an Election so made, although it may be singular good as to the present position of Heaven, yet the Lord of the Ascendant in this Election may happen to be the Lord of the eighth, or twelfth in the Radix (or Nativity) of the said person, and probably upon some such promising position of Heaven a person may begin some great Enterprize, and yet in the end receive great damage in Body or Estate, or both; and another may upon a very bad face of Heaven, begin a Business (or Action) of great concernment, and yet happen to be exceeding Fortunate and happy therein, which may to some seem strange: now the reason is this, in their *Nativities*, the Infortunate Planets, *viz.* ♄ and ♂ in the one may be Significators of Life, Riches, Honours and Preferments, &c. and in the other Persons Nativity, the Fortunate Planets, ♃ and ♀, may be Significators of evil to the Native, as being Rulers of bad Houses, and beholding the Ascendant or Lord thereof, and the *Luminaries*, by some Malevolent Aspects, and by consequence be evilly disposed and affected to the Native, and the contrary may happen in another Mans Nativity.

V. Thus, 'tis clear to the eye of Reason, in my opinion, that except the Nativity be known, 'tis but a vain and foolish thing for any person to constitute an Election; and this hath been long since much pleaded for, by Antient and Authentick Authors, who have laid down many good Arguments, and convincing Reasons for the same: yet some Artists (and those no mean persons in their own conceits) have favoured a contrary Opinion, which in time they may renounce, and acknowledg their Errour in this as well as other things in Art. And hence may be discovered, what necessity there is that the *Nativities* of Persons should be known, and therefore Parents should be more careful in Recording them, or *Clerks* of *Parishes* rather to register the time of Birth, than the day of Christening, which sometimes is a fortnight or three weeks after the Birth-day, &c. For I know many persons, that whereas they would give Six-pence for their Age (as they call it) out of the Church Book, would rather give six Shillings, yea oftentimes six Crowns for the estimate time of their Births, which may be Registered with the same pains.

VI. It was the Opinion of a Modern Author that hath written of this Subject, That we ought to consult the Revolution Figure of the World, *(viz.* of the *Sun's* ingress into ♈) and make that the Radix or ground of our Elections; observing how that Planet which signifies our Business is dignified or affected therein, and so to judge, (this was I suppose because he would not have the Nativity consulted) I must confess I cannot apprehend it to be rational, and the rather, because that Figure is not very easily attained; for amongst the best *Astronomers* of our times, there is much Discrepancy, as to the true time of the *Sun's* ingress; neither do I think that Figure much to concern any particular person, but the people in general of the place for which it was set: however, I shall submit to better Judgments, and in the interim, imbrace and follow those wayes that seem most rational, and carry the most probability of truth in them.

This being premised, in the next place, I shall exhibit such necessary short Rules, as may be useful in the making apt and fit Elections, upon the most urgent occasions that shall Occur to any person.

SECT. VI.

Brief Rules to be Observed in making Elections upon any Occasion.

I. Let this be considered, that from an unfortunate Geniture there can no good Election be constituted; for if the Radical Ascendant, or his Lord be much afflicted, how can good be expected to succeed unto the Body of any Person, notwithstanding the Election be made never so happily and convenient for the thing or matter desired; so if the Lord of the fifth in the Radix, or the fifth House it self be much vitiated, or infortunate, the Election (though never so carefully made) will prove but of small advantage to the Native in point of Fortune in Gaming, and the like of any other thing belonging unto the twelve Coelestial Houses, that concern the Body or Estate of Man; for an accidental good can in no way extinguish, abate or contradict an Essential Evil in the Radix or Nativity of any Person.

II. The Nativity being the Basis or Ground work whereon to build a Rational Election, it will be necessary, or at least convenient, withal to consider the position of Heaven at the *Sun's* Revolution to his Radical point, and see how hew that concurs with the Radix, for if there be a sympathy between those two Figures, the years Actions in general will prove the more Fortunate, and all things will go on more pleasantly with the Native; but if there be an Antipathy between them, the Years Actions, and the Natives affairs, generally go on Cross and Unfortunate much to his discontent, and (perhaps) ends with loss and detriment.

III. Observe if there be any good Direction in force, as also the Diurnal transits of the Planets upon the most remarkable places of the Radical Genesis, *viz.* how they behold the grand Angles thereof, the *Luminaries* or Lord of the Ascendant; consider whether their transits be good or bad, and also how they behold their own Radical places; this will much enlighten your Judgment, and (in a Natural way) help you to conjecture at the success of your dayly concerns, and consequently the whole years Actions.

IV. Let not the Ascendant, Mid-heaven, or place of the ☽ in the Radix be evilly beheld at the time of your Election, neither let those places be the Cusps of the sixth, eighth, or twelfth Houses therein, but rather (if it be possible) let them be the Cusps of such Houses as concern your Business sought after; and let the proper Significators be well beheld by the Fortunes, (except the Fortunes were Lords of bad Houses in the Radix, and so unfortunate.)

V. Be exceeding careful that you begin no Enterprize when the ☽ separates from the ☌ or ☍ of the ☉, and applyes to the Body or Aspect of an Infortune, and especially if that Infortune was Ruler of a bad House, *viz.* the eighth or twelfth in the Nativity; neither let the ☽ be posited in the Ascendnt for she is therein accounted very Infortunate, and some say the ☉ is not good therein neither, unless he be in a Sign of his own Nature, *viz.* ♌, ♐, or ♈. See also that the Luminaries be not joyned (say they) to a Retrograde Planet: But the Planets are not much (if any thing) afflicted by Retrogradation, since they are not really so, but appear only to be so as we behold them from the Earth.

VI. Let not the ☽ be afflicted by any of the Planets that were Infortunate to the Native in his *Genesis* when you begin a work of Consequence: But whatever you do, be sure to fortifie the ☽ in any Election, although she were Governess of a bad House in the Radix; because the ☽ is a general Significatrix in all things relating to the concerns of Mankind and is said to bring down the Influence of the other Planets upon us.

VII. If it be possible that you can, let the ☽ be posited in that House which signifies the thing you make your Election for, especially if that House were Fortunate at Birth; and generally in all Elections have an eye to the ☽ and Ascendant see that they be free, and let not the Infortunes be placed in Angles, or behold the Ascendant or his Lord, except they were Lords or Rulers of good Houses in the Radix, and so Significators of good to the Native; and here note by the way, that ♃ and ♀, though they are general Fortunes, yet they may sometimes accidentally (as being Rulers of bad Houses) prove Infortunes, and ♄ and ♂, though Infortunes, to many men are Fortunes, being Rulers of good Houses and Fortunate in their Nativities: this is worth your Observation, and in particular to be minded in the Doctrine of Elections.

VIII. If you would Elect a time for any thing that requires speed, choose a moveable Sign to Ascend; but if you would Elect a fit time for any thing that requires durability, then choose a fixed Sign to Ascend, provided (still) that they belong to no bad Houses in the Radix.

IX. The fixed Stars ought to be considered in all Elections, (as well as Questions) that is, those Principal Stars neer the Ecliptick, having small latitude; for those Stars that are of benevolent Nature being joyned wjth the particular Significators, do much help in any Election, and the success doth usually happen to be the more prosperous.

X. In all Elections let the Ascendant of the Nativity (if it be possible) ascend, with this provisor, that there be no bad Planet therein, or otherwise Angular (except the Lord of the Ascendant) and 'tis alwayes good in such cases to have the Fortunate Planets in Angles also, if it may be.

XI. As often as the ☽ comes to that Age, she was at any persons birth, that day proves more Fortunate to that party, it being (said to be) conformable in Nature to his person, and an Election then made, will prove very effectual and Fortunate unto him, if so be it may at that time conveniently be made.

XII. It is good the ☽ should be strong and potent in all Elections, and in good Aspect of those Planets that were Fortunate, and Lords of good Houses in the Radical Genesis, and free from the malignant Beams of such as were therein unfortunate, neither should the Lord of the Geniture be in a Cadent House, if he happen to be an Infortune place him in a succedent House, and by all means fortifie the Ascendant and Mid-heaven in the Radix, (if it may be done) and it is not amiss, if you make the tenth or eleventh House in the Radix Ascendant in the Election if they were Fortunate and free, and no afflicting Planet therein.

XIII. Let the Lord of the Ascendant at the beginning of any Enterprize (*viz.* the Lord of the Ascendant in the *Nativity*) be placed in a good and fortunate place of the *Figure* of the Election, let him be a Fortune or Infortune; for the *Ancients* affirm, that ♄ or ♂ according to their Radical Significations, determine good to those persons in whose Nativies they govern good and Fortunate Houses; therefore in all Elections, let the Lord of the Radical Ascendant be in an Angle or succedent House.

XIV. In all things relating to the second House (viz. *Money matters*) be sure to fortifie ♃, let him be free from Combustion, and let the Lord of the second House in the *Nativity* be also free from affliction, and placed in a good place of the Figure, in some benevolent Aspect of the Fortunes, or those Planets that were Co-significators of Substance at birth, *viz.* posited in the second House, or in good aspect to the Lord thereof.

XV. For Friendship between Brethren, Kindred and Neighbours, *&c.* you are to fortifie the Radical third House, and Lord thereof; and if it be possible, let the Lord of the third apply to the Ascendant or his Lord by some good Aspect; or if there be Reception between them, 'tis the more hopeful: If you are to make Application to an Elder Brother, Authors advise to let ♄ behold the Ascendant or third House, or their Lords by some Benevolent Aspect.

But in taking a short Journey, fortifie the Ascendant and Lord thereof, as also the ☽ and her Dispositer, together with the ⊕, the third House and Lord thereof: the same should be considered concerning that House and Lord thereof, which relates to the Business you go about.

XVI. In all Business relating to the fourth House, ♄ should be fortified as much as may be, especially if the Business relate to Houses, Lands, *&c.* you are also to strengthen the fourth House, and Lord thereof in the Radix, not neglecting the ☽, by choosing such a time when Fortunate Planets are in Friendly Aspect to these Significators.

XVII. In all things appertaining to the fifth House, that House and the Lord thereof ought to be fortified, and made as strong as may be: as for Example in *Play* or *Gameing*, he that would choose a fit time to Win, must place the Signe of the Radical fifth House upon the second, let it be the Cusp thereof in the Figure of Election, and beheld by the good Aspect of ♃ or ♀ therein, and look that the Ascendant at that time be free from affliction, and debilitate the seventh House and Lord thereof as much as may be, and this is an apt and fit Election for a man to Win at Play; and if the ☽ be in good Aspect to ☿, or in ✶ or △ to the Cusp of the second, or Lord thereof at the same time, 'tis so much the better.

XVIII. In making an Election for any thing appertaining to the sixth House, as taking a *Servant*, or entering into a Course of *Physick*, special regard ought to be taken in making a Convenient Election for the same. If the Distemper be such that in General afflicts the whole Body, Authors direct, that in the Election for the same, you let the Ascendant be ♎, or some other humane Signe. But if the Patient be afflicted only with some particular Distemper that afflicts only some Member or part of the Body, then let the Sign that Represents that Member or part of the Body be placed upon the Ascendant, and both the Ascendant and his Lord free from affliction; the same is to be observed by the *Planet* that bears Rule over that part of the Body that is afflicted; and then the Remedy may be safely applyed. But in taking a Servant, let the Lord of the sixth House be in good Aspect with the Lord of the Ascendant, and the second House in the Radix, and the ☽ free from Affliction.

XIX. In making Elections for any affair signified by the seventh House; as for Example in *Marriage*, see that you fortifie the Ascendant, as also the Lord of the Ascendant and the ☽, with their Dispositers, the Ascendant ought to be a fixed Signe, and the ☽ therein in ✶ or △ to the ☉; but by any means let not ♏ Ascend: and 'tis observed that if a Fortune shall be in the tenth House in the hour of Marriage, it signifies the Woman shall Conceive the first night she lies with her Husband. In contracting Marriage for Gain, let the Ascendant for that Moment be fortified, also the Lord thereof and the ☽, with their Dispositers, and let there be arising a Moveable or Common Signe, and the ☽ in any Common Signe except ♊; and let the Lord of the House of the ☽ be in ♌, and the Significators all free (if it be possible) and in good places of the *Figure*; and if there be Reception between some of the Significators, 'tis so much the better; but be sure you fortifie the *first, second, fourth, tenth and eleventh Houses*, or as many of them as may be, with the Lords of those Houses, and the ⊕, who should in this case be beheld by the ✶ or △ of ♃ or ♀, and all the Principal Significators free from affliction.

XX. If the Premises be but well observed, the Portion or Dowry of the Wife may come with Ease, and prove Considerable: But in making *Wills* and *Testaments*, or settling of Estates that they may continue, let the ☽ be slow in Motion, and increasing in Light; and in this case 'tis so much the better if the ☽ and Lord of the Ascendant behold ♄ by some Benevolent Aspect.

XXI. In taking a long Journey, beware there be no Infortune in the ninth House of the Radix, and be sure the Lord of the ninth House be free from Affliction. Let him be fortified as much as may be, and the success will be so much the better: understand the same if you design to learn some curious Art or Mystery.

XXII. In the beginning or setting up of any *Profession* or *Calling*, fortify the Ascendant of that Figure for the time you intend to begin, and let it be the Cusp of the tenth in the Radix; see that the Lord thereof be strong, (or at lease free from affliction of the Infortunes) and consider the position of the ☽ also, that she be well seated, and then you may expect a hopeful event.

XXIII. But in entering into *Contracts*, or Leagues of *Friendship* by which Gain or Profit is expected, let the ☽ be in the Ascendant, or in a Sign of the same Triplicity; and if it be possible, in some Essential Dignity, or in some good Aspect of her Disposiiter; and be not unmindful to see that the Lord of the *Eleventh House* in the Radix be free from affliction, and posited in some good place of the Figure.

XXIV. Lastly, if you would Elect a good time to Buy a *Horse*, or other serviceable *Beast*, fortify the Ascendant, his Lord and the ☽, who should apply to some good Aspect of a Fortunate *Planet* that is free from affliction: Consider also the Position of the Lord of the twelfth House in the Radix; see he be in no bad Aspect to ♄ or ♂.

XXV. In Elections for Horse races be sure you Aptate the Lord of the twelfth House, and if it be possible, make him more Powerful than the Lord of the sixth House; place a Signe of the Superiour Planets upon the Horoscope (especially ♐) and let the ☽ and Lord thereof be strong and powerful, swift in Motion, and in good Aspect of each other from good places of the Figure; and debilitate the Lords of the sixth and seventh Houses as much as may be.

[*These Rules being carefully observed, an Artist cannot easily commit an Errour in framing his Election, unless the general Fate of the person for whom he Elects unhappily Contradict.*]

[*Many more of these kind of Rules might be given, but these are most considerable; and by what hath been already delivered hereof, a Man may be enabled to make a substantial Election upon any occasion; and therefore*

I shall forbear any farther Discourse of this Subject, knowing that a multitude of Rules do but rather dull the Active Fancy, than increase knowledge.

SECT. VII.

General Elections for buying and selling, and taking of Servants, from the position of the Moon in the several Signs of the Zodiack.

I. He that would sell any Commodity to profit thereby, let him chuse a time when the ☽ is in ♉, ♋, ♍, or ♓ separating from the ☉, ♃, ♀, or ☿, For if the ☽ do separate from good Planets and apply to bad, it is good for the seller, but ill for the buyer: and here you should note from your Nativity, which are good and which bad Planets, (if it may be procured.)

II. But if you would buy cheap (as most desire to do) let the ☽ be posited in any of the aforesaid signes, separating from evil Planets and applying to good, this is ill for the seller, but good for the buyer: For Separation and Application are as contrary as Buying and Selling.

III. If thou wilt take a Servant, let the ☽ be in ♊, ♍, or ♉.

IV. If the ☽ be in ♌ when thou takest him, he will prove proud and high minded, and fails not to make a singular Trencher-man, (as the proverb is) or hath a good stomach.

V. If the ☽ be in ♑ or ♒ he will run a way from thee, but return again and make no long stay before he departs again, (and this perhaps with the consent of his Master.)

VI. If the ☽ be in ♓ when thou takest a Servant, he will assuredly prove Unfaithful and Dishonest.

VII. Therefore when thou takest a Servant thou mayst venture to let the ☽ be in ♌, ♍, ♉, or the latter part ♐ because it is reputed good to take a Servant when the ☽ is in fixed Signes, &c.

VIII. If thou takest a Man Servant let the ☽ be in ♊, ♍, ♎, ♐, or ♒.

IX. Lastly if thou takest a Woman Servant, let the ☽ be in ♉, ♋, or ♓.

[*I have Inserted these short Elections of the Moon that they may be put to the Test, but I dare not affirm they are infallible.*]

CHAP. XV.

Of Astral Predictions of Mundane Affairs; or the General Accidents of the World.

In the Judging of General Accidents, a due Method ought to be Observed, viz. to Demonstrate the Radix, *or* Foundation *upon which an Astrological Judgment ought to be given in* Praedicting *of any Mutation that shall happen in this Sublunary World, and how many Figures ought to be Erected for the Performance thereof.*

I. There hath been much Controversie and Dispute amongst the *Ancients* (who were *Masters* in this *Art*) concerning the Time the *Astrological Philosopher* ought to take for the *Basis* or *Foundation* of his Judgment in Annul Affairs; Some would ground their Judgment of Mutations that should happen, upon the *Conjunctions* of the *Planets;* others, from the *Ascendant* or first beginning of the *Kingdome, Nation,* or *Common-wealth;* and others, from *Ecclipses,* &c. But *Ptolomy,* who was *Princeps Astrologorum,* the Chief, and Prince of Astrologers in his time, gives us this Rule; *Ex Solis Existentia in Arieta deprehenditer, vernalem qualitatem Cognoscemus:* By the Sun his entrance into *Aries,* we are to judge the Events and Success of the Accidents of the Spring-Quarter (that is by the Position of the Heavens for that moment of time when he makes his first Ingress into that *Aequinoctial* Point) and not without good reason, since the *Sun* is *Anima Mundi,* the Soul the Life of the World, which is clearly manifested by the encreasing Quality of Humidity, the Earth and all things thereon do plentifully abound with at that time: The dayes do then begin to encrease, and the nights deminish, and all things begin to flourish and appear in their greatest Lustre and Splendour.

II. Nor is *Ptolomy* singular in his Opinion, That the Affairs of a Kingdome or Nation are to be known from the *Scheme* of the *Suns* Ingress into ♈, and the other Cardinal Points for that Year, (Respect being had also to the Preventional, and Postvential *Lunations* and Eclipses of the *Luminaries* that may happen in the same:) But the most Learned and Judicious of our *Modern Astrologers* do also approve of this Method as Rational. *Ptolomy's* words at large *in Lib. 2, Quadr. Chap.* 10 are to this effect; *It seems to me most convenient and Natural in the Judgment of Annual Events to assume four Beginnings, Regard being had to the New and Full* Moon *next Preventional, especially if therat either of the Luminaries are Eclipsed, and so give Judgment of the State of the Spring Quarter from the beginning of* Aries; *of* Summer *from* Cancer; *of* Autumn *from* Libra; *of* Winter. *from* Capricorn: his Reason is, *Nam ipsas quidem universales constitutiones temporum & modos, &c. For these General Constitutions, and the manners of them are caused by the* Sun, *whence even many that are unskilful in* Art *do come to the knowledge of Future Events.*

III. *Origanus* he proceeds yet farther, and sayes; *Non tantum qua Coeli forma affluant*, &c. *We must observe (if we mean to Prognosticate to gain Honour or Credit thereby) not only in what form of Heaven the* Luminaries *move unto, but also in what manner they leave the Cardinal Points in their several* Conjunctions *and* Oppositions: That is, to Erect three Figures for every Quarter, one for the ☌ or ☍ of the ☉ and ☽, proceeding the Ingress; the second for the time of the Ingress it self; and the third for the ☌ or ☍ suceeding or following the same.

IV. But *Haly*, and *Guido Bonatus* were of another Opinion, and would have the Judgment of the Year deduced af.ter this manner, *viz.* If at the *Sun's* Ingress into ♈ the Ascendant shall be a *Fixed* Signe; then that *Figure* shall serve for the Judgment of the whole Year; and that Planet which is *Almuten* of the Figure, shall be Lord of the whole Year; but if the Ascendant be a Common Signe, that *Revolutional Figure* shall continue but half a year, and end at the *Sun's* entrance into ♎, for which moment another Scheme shall be Erected for the other half year, and the Planet that is then found to bear the most Rule, shall be Lord of the latter half Year. But if the Ascendant be a Moveable Signe at the *Sun's* Ingress into ♈, then that *Revolution Figure* shall be of force but till the ☉ enters ♋, and New Schemes are to be Erected for the other three Quarters of the Year, and their several *Almutens* Elected, with this provisor, that the Lord of the first Quarter shall participate, or be Co-partner with the Lord of the second, and the Lord of the second with the Lord of the third, &c.

V. But the Doctrine of *Ptolomy* is generally accepted to be the most Rational: and has not wanted the Approbation of the latest and best Masters in the Art of Astrology, (as before was intimated) which Method take as followeth; *viz.* Erect for every Year, Figures for the *Sun's* Ingress into the four Cardinal Points, ♈, ♋, ♎ and ♑; as also the *Lunations* preceding, and succeeding the *Sun's* Ingress into the same Signs: then collect the Essential Dignities and Debilities of the Planets, *viz.* examin what *Planet* hath the most Testimonies of Strength in the Ascendant, Mid-heaven, and the Places of the *Luminaries*, in each of the three aforesaid Figures, and that Planet so qualified shall be chief Ruler, or *Almuten* for that Revolution, or Lord of the Year; and 'tis the most Rational way to Elect him so; the thing is so plain, and obvious that he that hath made but a slender progress in this Study, may easily perform the work, without an Example, if the Table of the *Essential Dignities* of the *Planets*, and its use be but consulted.

VI. What may be judged from a Figure of the Annual Revolution of the ☉ we are plainly informed by *Guido Bonatus*, an expert *Italian, Astrologer* and *Contemporary* with *Fryer Bacon*, where he sayes, *Per Revolutionem Annorum Mundi scitur quod in illo Anno sit futurtum, de Bono aut Malo utrum tranquillus aut guerra*, &c. We know by the Revolutional Figures of the years of the World, what accidents will happen each year, whether Good or Ill, Peace or War, Plenty or Scarcity; the Condition of Kings, Princes, Nobles, the Religious, and all other sorts and degrees of Men and quality of things whatsoever, according to the property of Man therein, of the Dearness and Cheapness of divers Commodities, and what increase may be expected from the Fruits of the Earth, &c.

VII. In General Accidents from ♄ Judgment is drawn of Antiquities, of Sects, Schisms, Heresies, Renovation of Ancient Customs of things already begun, Depopulation and Destruction of Kingdoms and Countreys; he hath in particular, Influence upon Monks, Fryers Jesuits, all Jewish Ceremonies or Superstition, Ruine of Antient Buildings and Foundations, all sordid inhumane Debauchery, Shipwracks, Captivities, Death, Famine, &c.

VIII. ♃ signifies such matters and things which principally concern Religion, the more Pure and Orthodox Principles thereof as relating to Church Discipline, or the Worship of God. He also particularly Represents the Nobility and Gentry of any Nation or Kingdome, as also the Clergy and Lawyers, the most grave and solid Practitioners thereof.

IX. From ♂ Judgment is drawn concerning all Martial and Military affairs, Wars, Commotions, Insurrections, Massacres, Persecutions and Murthers, Fireing of Houses, Cities and Towns; Theft, Rapine, and all manner of Tyranny, Oppression and Villany.

X. The ☉ Generally signifies new Monarchies, Empires, Kingdoms which should continue in great Glory, Splendor and Renown; also Kings, Princes and Magistrates in General.

XI. From ♀ Judgment is declared concerning all manner of Delights and Pleasure, Adulteries, Fornications, Women, both Noble and Ignoble, Gameing, Sports and Pastimes; but a General Tranquility, and Plenty of all things, &c.

XII. ☿ signifies all manner of Arts and Sciences; Also Merchants, Treasurers, Secretaries, Clerks, and Scribes in general; Philosophers, Astronomers, Mathematicians, Accomptants: ☿ also signifies the Discovery of all secret devices, and shews the Investigation or Discovery of all Ingenious Inventions.

XIII. From the ☽ Judgment is drawn concerning the Condition or State of the Common people; But the ☽ being but the Earths Attendant, and a Secondary *Planet* cannot signifie such grand Alterations in the world, as the Primary and Superiour Planets do, especially when they happen to be conjoyn'd, &c. These are the several Significations of the Planets themselves in particular, or considered alone; But Astrologers well know their power and Influences are *Intended* and *Remitted* by their Configurations and Mixtures, and by their Positions in Signes and Houses; for in some Signes of the Zodiack their Influences are Augmented, and in others their Operations are Deminished and depressed, notwithstanding their various Aspects; which *Kepler* defines thus; *An Aspect is an Angle formed at the Earth of the Beams of two Planets or Stars, at a certain proportionate distance one from another, and have great power to stir up Influence.*

CHAP. XVI.

Shewing the Natural Signification of each Planet (strong or weak) that shall be Lord or Gubernator of the Year in any Revolutional Figure of the world.

I. Observe what Planet is Lord of the Year, and if you find him well Dignified, it denotes a Plentiful Year, Temperate and Heathful for the People, Successful and Prosperous, and generally good in all the Significations of that *Planet, Signe* and *House*; but if you find him weak and unfortunate, judge the contrary; especially if the ☽ concur in Signification, for she is the General Significator of the People.

II. Whatever portents shall be signified by the *Lord of the Year* will more especially be manifested in those *Regions* or *Countreys* subject to the Signe of his position; (as also of the Signe that *Planet* is in, which is in Aspect with the Lord of the *Revolution*) and the Nature thereof is taken from the Consideration of the House of the Figure, wherein he is posited; If in the Ascendant, judge the effects or portents signified may operate upon the Lives and persons of those people; if in the second House, say it will be their Estates and Substance; if in the third House, in their Journeys and Relations signified by that House; if in the fourth House, judge the operation may be on their Houses, Lands, and Inheritances, &c.

III. Again, observe if the Lord of the Year be beheld by any Laudable Aspect of his Dispositer, and free from Impediment, this denotes good in its proper Signification; But if he be not well Aspected by his Dispositer, judge the Contrary; *viz.* that Trouble and Anxiety may succeed; but if he be well beheld and not strong, or strong and not beheld by his Dispositer, judge between both, *Consideratis Considerandis.*

[Note that Annual Revolutions are rather Signes of what Accidents shall or may happen in each Respective Countrey, for which the Revolutional Figure is made, than Causes of Natural Events, and must be considered with other Over ruling Configurations and Phoenomena's; for a Revolutional Figure of the Sun's Ingress into any point of the Zodiack is not sufficient for the Judgment of the Year without the Consideration of Eclipses, great Conjunctions, Comets, Blazing-Stars, &c. But the Stars of Heaven are the most Excellent Characters of the Divinity, Power, Wisdome and Glory of the Creator, in that they are Written and Engraved by God himself.]

IV. ♄, Lord of the Year, and well disposed in the Figure, inclines the people of the Country to Build and Erect new Fabricks; the Husbandman shall much increase his Store, and be very successful in all his Labours; the People shall be Honoured and Esteemed, and Love one another: But if ♄ be weak and afflicted, he portends much Cold, and many grievious Infirmities, Damages, and Afflictions to Mankind; also the death of Ancient People in General. *If ♄ be not Aspected of ♂, expect an extream cold Season for the most part in most Northern Countreys.*

V. ♃, Lord or Ruler of the Year, well posited in the Figure, shews much Prosperity to the Nobility and Gentry, and to all sorts of Men of Religious Orders, or of the Ecclesiastical Function; also Lawyers, and all sorts of Men and things signified by ♃: People in general shall live prosperously, with great Content and Respect to and from their Superiours; and this the more certain if ♃ happen also to be in Reception with their Significator: But if ♃ be Infortunate [*Significat malos status Nobilium Hominum, &c.*] judge the contrary; or if ♃ be in ☌ or bad Aspect of ♄, this portends much Sadness to Mankind; if ♂ afflict ♃, judge much Prejudice, Loss and Damage shall happen to persons of Dignity and Renown; or such as are imployed in places of great Trust, &c. *If ♃ be in no Aspect with any other Planet, it portends a very temperate Aire, and wholesome North-wind, to the great Comfort of all living Creatures, as well as the Seed in the Earth; for the Salubrious breathing North-winds, which are stir'd up bythe power and influence of ♃ makes the Aire both sound and healthful, and consequently very wholsome both for Man and Beast.*

VI. If ♂ be Lord of the Year, and powerful and free from affliction, this portends much Felicity and Prosperity to all Martial Persons in General; Souldiers will now be very successful, and perform many notable Exploits, and overcome their Enemies, and gain good Esteem and Honour thereby; but if ♂ be found weak, and ill posited in the Figure, then judge the contrary in all particulars. *Cardan* sayes, if ♂ be Lord ofthe Year, Great Heat follows, *Burning of Houses, Lightning Warrs,* &c. *If ♂ be in ♏, it portends much Rain and Hail, unless he be joyned with other Planets; if so, moderate your Judgment accordingly, consideration being had to their Natures.*

VII. If the ☉ be Lord of the Year, and posited in some good place of the Figure strong, this denotes that the *King* and his *Nobles* shall not only be happy and Fortunate that Year, but shall be much esteemed and Honoured by the People, who shall be in a good condition, very prosperous and successful in all their Affairs in the General; Corn, Cattle, and other Provisions shall be plenty; also Gold and all Solar things: But if the ☉ be posited in an abject place of the Figure, and in □ or ☍ of ♄ or ♂, judge just contrary; *viz.* much prejudice and Detiment to the aforesaid Persons, with scarcity of Provisions, &c.

The ☉ alters the Seasons and Quarters of the Year as to change of Air, according as he happenst to be in Configuration with other Planets; as if ♄ be with the ☉ in Aspect to ♂, this increases the Cold in Winter, and abates the heat in Summer, especially if they are in Cold Signes, or neer Fixed Stars of that Nature. This is according to the Judgment both of Ancient and Modern Authors, and confirmed by Experience.

VIII. If ♀ bear Rule, and have the chief Dominion of the Year, and well disposed, *Haly* sayes, that the year shall prove Fortunate and successful, the people shall thrive and prosper, and delight themselves in Sport and Recreations; they shall rejoyce and be merry, Feast and Contract many Marriages, Women shall deiight in the society of their Husbands, and easily conceive and bear Children; so that the Year in General should be accompanyed with much pleasure and felicity; but if ♀ be not well qualified, judge the contrary.

♀ bearing Rule in any Quarter or Revolution, usually increases Humidity in Winter, and abates Siccity in Summer or Autumn; and this the more certain if her position be in a moist or watry Signe, viz. ♏, ♋, or ♓; or if she be in a moist Asterisme, and in Aspect to no Planet of a contrary Nature or Quality, as ♂ in particular.

IX. If ☿ be *Dominus totius Anni*, or chief Ruler of the Year, and well seated in the Figure, free from Impediments, *Haly, Part* 8. *Chap.* 6. tells us, it denotes much Profit and good success to all persons addicted to Learning and Science; as *Mathematicians, Philosophers, Poets*; also to Merchants, and Tradesmen, Artisicers, &c. Men should be much addicted to the searching after New and Curious Inventions this Year, and be prosperous therein; but if you find ☿ afflicted, the contrary may be expected, without there be other Testimonies of good concur.

☿ usually prerluces much diversity, and varies the Quality of the Air, and corrupts the Winds according to the Nature or Quality of the Signe he is posited in; generally he produces great Winds, &c.

X. If the ☽ be Lady of the Year, and well disposed, this promises Felicity to great Persons of the Female Sex, and to the Common People in general; for now Men enjoy their Healths well, and deal justly one with another; 'tis a very calm and tranquil time, but if you find the ☽ chief Governess of the Year, and ill disposed, judge the contrary in all respects.

And note that the Quality of the Air is frequently altered every month, when the ☽ meets with the body of the ☉, as the Quarters of the Year vary by the motion of the ☉ through the twelve Signes, especially at his Ingress into the four Cardinal Points the ☽ is accounted warm and moist in her first Quarter, in her second Quarter warm and dry; in her third, cold and dry; and in the fourth cold and moist; in fine, if the ☽ have Dominion as aforesaid, she produces by her gentle Influence, plenty of seasonable Showers, which do much refresh the Earth.

If you find the Lord of the Year strong in the Ascendant, let him be supposed to be ♄, then considering the Nature of ♄, and what the Ascendant properly signifies (which you may read at large together with the significations of every House Chap. 13. *of the* Introduction) *and accordingly form a judgment, as in this Case the Ascendant in a Figure of the world (denotes or) represents, the Common People, and general state of the Kingdome or Countrey, ♄ being posited therein strong and well Aspected by the ☽, shews much felicity to the Common People, and respect from their Superiors (for ♄ is a superiour Planet) if ♄ be afflicted there, judge then great affliction and trouble to the People of the Nature of ♄, and so moderate your Judgment according to his affliction, and position in any of the Houses; and the like for any other Planet may easily be performed by any person of an apt Genius that has made but some reasonable progress in this Study, which I shall leave to the Industry and Ingenuity of every expert Artist; for 'twas not my intent to form a large Discourse of this Subject: That is already done by many Famous Authors, only I thought good for variety sake to add something hereof, that the young Artist might see upon what Foundation General Judgments of Mundane Affairs depends, and conclude that from those General Rules already laid down may be deduced a sufficient Judgment of the state of any Year, if it be considered that good Planets do Augment the signification of every House, but evil Planets contradict and produce contrary significations; observe likewise the strength and debility of the Planets in general, as also their Aspects to the Lord of the Year or Ascendant, and so help your self in your Judgment, and forget not that every Planet doth proauce by vertue of his Influence either good or evil, according to each Planets proper Nature; to which the consideration of the Signes, wherein the Planets are posited must also be added. For ♈ is Violent, ♋ Sudden, ♎ Moderate, ♑ Slow, ♉ is Heavy, ♊ Nimble, ♌ is Valiant, ♍ is Barbarous, ♏ False and Trecherous, ♐ Manly, ♒ Sober and Moderate, ♓ Cowardly. Great Actions have the superiour Planets for their Significations, Petty matters are from the inferiours: ♄ in ♈ shews high matters transacted with fear and care; but in ♉ with great Labour to no purpose; in ♊ with much speech to no effect, &c. There is in Astrology a certain Arcana equivolent to Prophecy, and so by God distributed to Man, that one man cannot easily communicate it to another: And it is the Opinion and Advice of my Honoured Friend, Mr.* William Lilly; *That an Artist ought rather to judge by the strength of his Reason guided by Art, from the Consideration of the Aspects and mixtures of the Planets, than from ill concocted Aphorismes laid down by some Authors, which if not applyed with great Judgment, the Artist seldome speaks Trutih; and therefore Ptolomy writ judiciously when he in his first Aphorisme of his* Centiloquium *begins with* Ate & Scientia, &c.

He that would be excellent in these General Judgments, should be conversant in Histories, and thence observe either the great Happiness or Calamity that has formerly happened to a People in any Kingdome and Countrey; and then observe what Planet was in those times most dignified or debilitated, what Comet or Blazing Star preceded, and the Sign it appeared in, also what greater or minor Conjunctions were then in force, as also Eclipses, &c.

A General Calamity and Misery never afflicts any People, but you shall find ♄ much concerned, Peace and Plenty are from the Influence of ♃ in a Natural way; Commotions from ♄, the ☽ and ♂; Warrs from ♂ and the ☉: Consider what Fixed Stars of the first or second Magnitude, &c. *are neer the place of any greater or lesser Conjunction or Comet,* Stella Crinata, *or unusual Apparition; or whether the Declination be North or South, also their Colour, and what little Fixed Stars are neer them; also the Constellation or Constellations; for in these things there ought to be, not only iood Consideration taken, but also much Circumspection used.*

CHAP. XVII.

Of Eclipses and the Natural Causes and Reasons, Thereof.

Before I write any thing of the Natural Signification or Portents of Eclipses, accordine to the Doctrine that hath been transmitted to us by the Ancients, it will be convenient to shew the Natural Cause of an Eclipse, and what Use may be made thereof.

I. The ☽ is a Dark and Opacous Body, receiving light of the ☉ by Reflection, as may appear by her Increasing and Decreasing, as she is neerer or farther off from her Conjunction of the ☉.

II. At the Ecliptical Conjunction of the *Luminaries* (or *New Moon*) the Dark Body of the ☽ passeth directly between the ☉ and us, and doth hide or Eclipse him from our light: But at an Ecliptical Opposition (or *Full Moon*) the ☉, the ☽ and the Earth are in one Direct and Diametrical Line, the Dark Globe of the Earth being between the ☉ and ☽, doth deprive the ☽ of the ☉'s Light, whereby she becometh Darkned, having no Light of her own.

III. The Line or way wherein the ☽ maketh her continual Periodical Revolutions, doth cross the Ecliptick, whereon the ☉ doth always move at an Angle of about five degrees; and the distance of these Lines is the ☽'s Latitude; the places in the Ecliptick Line where these Lines Cross each other, are called the *Dragons Head,* and *Dragons Tayl,* and these places of the ☽'s *Nodes*, *viz*. the ☊ and ☋, are not alwayes in one place of the Ecliptick, but move once through the same, contrary to the sequel or succession of the Signes in eighteen years and two hundred twenty one dayes.

IV. If the ☽ at the *Full* be distant from the ☊ or ☋ more than 15 degrees there can be no Eclipse of the ☽; and when at the time of the *Change,* the ☽ is more than 19 degr. distant from the ☊ according to the succession of the Signes, or from the ☋ more than 19 degrees, contrary to the suceession of the Signes there can be no Eclipse of the ☉; neither can there be any Eclipse of the ☉ when the ☽ at the Change is above seven degrees from the ☋, according to the succession of the Signes, or more than seven degrees from the ☊, contrary to the sequel of the Signes.

V. Eclipses of the ☉ are various both in Quantity and Quality, being beheld from several parts of the Earth, the Inhabitants of some parts of the Earth beholding the ☉ partilly, Eclipsed on the North side his Body, and some on ihe South side, and others at the same instant beholding him not at all Eclipsed: The Reason whereof is the ☉ in his Eclipses is not indeed obscured, but only hid from our sight by the Interposition of the ☽, whose various parallaxes cause this diversity in the *Sun's* Eclipse.

VI. The Eclipse of the ☽ appeareth in like manner and quantity to all those above whose Horizon she is at the time thereof, for when she is deprived of the light of the ☉ she becometh really darkned.

VII. For the more Methodical Estimation of the Quantities of Eclipses, their Diameters are supposedly divided into twelve equal parts, called *Digits*, because their Diameters appear to sight about a foot in length, so that when the ☽ hideth half the ☉'s Diameter, he is said to be six *Digits* Eclipsed, &c.

VIII. Amongst the Coelestial *Phoenomena* the Doctrine of Eclipses takes precedency, because from their Observations the primary Foundation of the whole Body of *Astronomy* is Confirmed and Demonstrated.

IX. And thus the *Solar Eclipses* do manifest the ☽ to be lower, and less than the ☉: The *Lunar Eclipses* do manifest that the Earth is not founded infinitely below us, but that the Heavens (under us) are distant from the Earth as far upwards (in respect of those that be our *Antipodes*) as here they are; and consequently that the Earth is not *Cubical, Pyramidal*, nor *Cylindroidol*, &c. but on every side perfectly Round or Terminated by a Globular Figure; because not only the shadow of the Earth (in the ☽'s body) is alwayes and on every Part observed to be Round, but also for that such as live *Eastward* number more hours from their *Meridian* for the beginning or ending of an *Eclipse*, than such as live *Westward*, proportionably to their Distance.

X. *Lunar Eclipses* demonstrate the shaddow of the Earth to be *Conical*, terminating in a sharp point: and in the same places of the *Moons Transits* to be sometimes thicker, at other tlines more slender, notwithstanding a certain Rule and Respect had to the ☉'s motion; and consequently that the ☉ is moved (or rather so seems to be) in an *Eccentrical Orb*.

XI. By Eclipses also the ☽ we know that the Earth is moved (or placed) in the middle of the *Zodiack*, because she is Eclipsed in the Opposite places thereof.

XII. The *Lunar Eclipses* best discover to us the Longitude of places upon the Earth, and assure us that the Earth and Water make but one Globe.

XIII. The *Oriental* or *Occidental Eclipses* of the *Moon* inform us that one half of the World is always visible, and that dayly one half of the *Zodiack* rises above the Horizon.

XIV. The true and certain place of the ☽ cannot be had by any Instrument whatsoever, because of her *Parallaxes* Nature, or rather the God of Nature, hath supplyed this defect by her Eclipses; for the ☽ posited in *mediis tenebris*, is then understood to be opposite to the ☉, by these defects therefore the motions and mutations of the ☽ are found out, and rationally demonstrated.

XV. By *Lunar Eclipses* we gather that the ☉ is far greater than the Earth, and the ☽ lesser; so by *Solar Eclipses* are demonstrated the distance of the Luminaries from the Earth to be different, and therefore to be moved in *Eccentricks* or *Epycycles;* hereby a Rule is found out for Measuring the distances of the ☉ and ☽ from the Earth, and the magnitudes of their several Bodies.

XVI. And lastly by *Eclipses* of the Luminaries, the God of Nature fore-warns this Sinful World of the *Revolutions* of Kingdoms and States, the Death and Detriment of *Princes,* Governours, and *Great Men;* of *Heresies, Sects,* and *Seditions* in the Church; Alterations of *Laws* and Customs, of Drought and Inundations of Rivers, Wars, Famine, Plague, and Pestilence; in fine, the Vicissitude of all Sublunary things.

CHAP. XVIII.

Of the Natural Portents and Significations of Eclipses.

I. Erect your *Coelestial Scheme* to the middle time of your Eclipse, and observe what Planet is Lord thereof, according to *Ptolomy*'s Rule, *viz*. Take the place of the *Luminary* Eclipsed, and the Angle succeeding it, which must always be the *Ascendant* or *Mid-heaven* in a visible Eclipse, that is to say, the Ascendant, if the *Eclipse* happen in the Oriental Quarter, *before Noon,* or the Mid-heaven if after Noon.

II. But it is the Judgment or *Origanus, Chap, 2, Part 3. de Effectibus*, and some others of the latest and best *Astrologers* that we ought to take that *Planet* to be Lord of the Eclipse, who hath most Dignities in the *Ascendant, Mid heaven,* and place of the *Eclipse:* If one *Planet* hath not the same Dominion in both places, or in the aforesaid three, then accept of that *Planet* who is Lord of the place *Deficient*, with this Caution, that the Planet who hath most Dignities in the aforesaid place of the *Eclipse,* shall be Co-partner, or joyned with him in Dominion. If many *Planets* claim an equal share, yet that Planet who is Angular, Oriental or Direct, *&c.* shall be preferred before the other.

III. *Of the Quality of the Events, According to* Ptolomy, *& the easie & Familiar Method of the Famous Mr.* Lilly, *viz.* When ♄ is Lord of an *Eclipse*, He is generally the Cause of Corruptions by reason of Cold, more properly he declares continued Diseases in the Bodies of men, as a general decay of Nature, Wasting, or a Consumption which hath its Original from some deflux or Rhume; he denotes disturbance of the Radical Humours, Fluxes, Quartane Agues, Banishments, Poverty, Misery, Lamentation, vain Fears, Mortality of old Men especially, a scarcity of such Cattle as are useful for Mankind, afflicting those Cattle which escape Death with Diseases, *&c.*

In the Aire ♄ stirs up most violent Colds, with tedious Frosty Weather, Cloudy and Pestilent, Misty and Foggy, much Snow, more destructive than Profitable: In Rivers and the Sea he stirs up strang Tempests, sudden Shipwracks, dangerous and difficult Voyages, Scarcity of Fish and Water Fowl, Overflowings of the Sea-banks, Inundations and Corruptions of Rivers.

Upon the Earth a scarcity of Corn and Fruit, and most Provisions are Dear, Grass and Hay is destroyed by Floods and Immoderate Rain, Hail, Storms, and furious Tempests, whence Famine may be feared; Aged Persons are now more Afflicted and dye, than in former years, also much Controversie, Malice and Envy between men and men, and consequently many tedious Law-suits follow, especially amongst the most Rural sort; and there are the Natural portent of ♄ when he bears Rule in an Eclipse.

IV. When ♃ bears Rule, or has the chiefest Dominion in an Eclipse, he produces the increase of all things in general; As to Men, he signifies encrease of Riches and Goods, and all things necessary; Glory, Fertility, Tranquility, Peace and Plenty: every person signified by ♃ enjoyes Health of Body, and Peace of Mind; many times they receive Favour or Gifts from great Persons; now Magistrates, and Rulers or Governours have Honour and Fame confirmed upon them, and consequently flourish and live in great Estimation. All Creatures fit for the use of Man do now increase, and such *Animals* that are prejudicial to Mankind are destroyed: ♃ declares a wholesome temperature of the Air, moderate and seasonable Showers, nourishing the Fruits of the Earth by his gentle and sweet Influence: Merchants and Saylers do now receive little or no Damage, but make prosperous Voyages: Ecclesiastical Persons, and Men appertaining to the Law or Religious Orders, do now encrease, and divers of them are advanced to great preferment: now the Laws are well executed, and many Upright and Just Judges are very Active for the Publick Good: new Customs or Privileges, new Corporations, new Honours, *&c.* are now most happily conferr'd upon the People in General: And there are the Portents and Significations of ♃ when he bears Rule in an Eclipse.

V. If the Planet ♂ be Lord of the Eclipse, he usually by his Influence stirs up amongst men Warrs, Tumults, Intestine Hatred, Dissentions, and much Violence, Imprisonments, Banishments, sudden Death, the Wrath and Displeasure of Men of the highest degree: Tertian Feavers, and divers Diseases proceeding from the Corruption of Blood: many Roberies and Man slaughters, Law-suits, Duels, Burning of Houses, *&c.* In the Air he (produces or) stirs up Thunder and Lightning; unwholesome or Infectious Winds, and notable Droughts. In the Seas expect Terrible Shipwracks, and Tempestuous violent Storms: he dries up Rivers, and signifies Dearth or Scarcity of Corne: in fine, ♂ being Naturally a Planet of a Malignant Influence, and being chief Ruler at the time of an Eclipse of either of the Luminaries, nothing but Mischief can rationally be expected to follow, unless at that time some other Planet of a more Gentle Influence happen by his Friendly Rayes in part to Aleviate his Malice.

VI. ♀ is accounted a Planet of gentle Influence, and hath signification equivolent to that of ♃: To Mankind she produces kind effects, Fortunate Marriages, many Children, increase of Honour, much Joy, Health of Body; Peace and Plenty, a wholsome Air, and a very fruitful Season, and all things contrary to what has been exprest may be the Effects of ♂, though not so powerfully; for ♀ is an Inferiour Planet.

VII. ☿ is a *Planet* Convertible in Nature, and Operates in his Influence according to the Nature or Quality of that Planet he is joyned with by Body or Aspect; but generally in Humane Affairs he signifies much Subtility, and a quick dispatch of what matters may be in Controversie upon the Stage of the World: he signifies Robbers upon the Highwayes, and Pyrates at Sea; and as to Diseases of Mankind, they should be Coughs, Consumptions, Quotidian, Feavers, &c. In the Aire, High Winds, Thunder and Lightning, with sudden Tempests, much prejudicial to the Fruits of the Earth: If he be Lord of an Eclipse, and joyned by Body or Aspect to any other Planet, mixt the Portent of that Planet more especially, which must be left to the Judgment of every Industrious Son of Art; for 'tis impossible to give such exact Rules that shall hold good in every position of the Heavens.

VIII. If at an Eclipse of the ☉ ♂ be chief Gubernator thereof, and posited in an Airy or Fiery Signe, and also Lord of the Year, this portends Fireing or Burning of Houses. If ♄ be Lord of the year and place of Heaven wherein the defect falls free from affliction, and posited in Earthy or Watry Signes, ♂ at the same time being ill affected, Authors say it signifies Inundations or Earthquakes.

IX. Eclipses of the *Luminaries* in the Firy Triplicity, threatens the Distruction of Sheep and Oxen, &c. also the Banishment, Imprisonment, or Deposition of some Great Person, with Discord and Hatred between the Common People and some great Ruler or Governour: many Repinings, Grudgings, and Dissentions; Motions of Armies, much Warr and Slaughter of Men, Burnings of Houses, Depopulations, Rapes, Thefts, Sharp Feavers, Pestilent Diseases, Abortive Births, scarcity of Fruit and Corn; and these things will (or may) happen principally in those Countries or Regions that are subject to the Signe Eclipsed *Junctinus de Eclipsibus*.

X. But if either of the Luminaries happen to be Eclipsed in the Earthy Triplicity, this portends a scarcity of Corn and Fruit; if in the Airy Triplicity, it betokens Famine, Pestilent Diseases, with Stormy Tempestious Winds, very prejudicial to Mankind: If it happen in the Watry Triplicity, this portends the Death of the most Inferiour Common sort of People; also Warrs, &c. Destruction of Fish and Fowl, and all such Creatures that live in or neer the Water.

XI. *Ptolomy* tells us that an Eclipse of either of the Luminaries falling in any of the Angles of a Nativity or *Annual Revolution* portends much Detriment to the Native; the same if it happen in the Radical place of the ! or @: and *Hermes* says there shall be many Troubles happen in the World when both the *Luminaries* shall be Eclipsed in one month; and especially in such places where there is a particular Signification of them.

Note that so many hours as the ☉ is Eclipsed, so many years will the Effects thereof continue; but if it be a Lunar Eclipse, judge so many Months: As to the time when the Effects begin to operate, observe at the middle of the Eclipse how far the Luminary Eclipsed is distant in time from its Rising, and how long it continues above the Horizon, Reduce this time into Minutes, and say by the Golden Rule, *if the whole continuance of the* Luminary *above the Horizon give one year, or 365 dayes, what shall the time from the Rising to the middle of the Eclipse give? and by Operation you will discover the time when the Effects begin to operate: But with* Origanus, *I believe they begin at the very day of the* Eclipse. &c. vide Origanus Part 3. de Effectibus, Chap. 2.

And thus much shall serve for the Judgment of Eclipses: Those that would see more in English *of this Subject, I refer them to Mr.* Lylly's Annus Tenebrosus, *Printed at* London, 1652. *wherein the whole Doctrine is compleatly handled.*

CHAP. XIX.

[Part I.] *How to Predict or Prognosticate of the Winds and Weather from the Conjunctions and Aspects of the Planets.*

I. To Predict the Winds is difficult, and depends upon many Causes, and they are as Various as Inconstant; yet they are appropriated to each proper Planet, as to ♄ and the ☉ the East Wind, to ♃ the North, to ♂ and the ☽ the West Wind, to $ the South; ☿ is indifferent, to all the rest of the Planets, according as he shall be in Conjunction or Aspect to any of them; for if he be Conjoyned or in Aspect to ♄, he produces Cloudy or Rainy Weather, with Lofty Winds: If to ♃, some Rain and warm Winds; and if with the ☽ or ♀, moist Winds. If ☿ be Stationary or Retrograde, or leaving one Signe and entering another, or changing his Latitude, then usually follow great Winds; ♄ upon his change of Signe alters the Weather for many dayes together; and this the rather, if he have North Latitude: the *Apogaeon* and *Peregaeon* ought also to be considered, as also the Signes the *Planets* are posited in; for Fiery Signes in this Business of the Winds, some say they are appropriated to the *North West* Wind, Airy Signes to the *North East,* Watry Signes to the *South West,* and the Earthy to the *South East* Winds.

II. If either ♄, ♃, ♂ the ☉ or ♀ Rise or Set with any of these Fixed Stars, *viz. Arcturus, Hercules, Auriga's Right Shoulder, Orions Girdle, Praesepe, the Two Asses,* or the *Triangle, &c.* all these produce Winds, and many times Violent Tempests; and the rather if any of the Planets be either Retrograde or Stationary: And ☿ also produces Winds if he riseth or setteth with the *Pleiades*, The *Rams Head*, the *Thigh of Pegasus*, with *Auriga, Hydra's Heart,* the *Vulture,* the *Dolphin,* either of the *Dogg,* or with *Regulus, Praesepe,* the *Eagle:* If ☿ Ascend or Descend the Horizon with any of these Stars, oftentime Winds and Cloudy Weather follows; but if he rise or set with those Stars of the Nature of ♃, then expect warm Winds, and clear Dayes.

III. It is and hath often been observed by some curious persons, that there is never any great Mutation of the Aire (even in our Island of *England*) without the Conjunction or Aspect of either of the Superiour Planets, *viz.* ♄, ♃ or ♂; the reason is, they are slow in motion, great Conjunctions of the Planets that are of contrary Natures too generally cause much Rain, violent Winds, with *Snow* or *Rail,* according to the Season of the Year: the Wandering Stars in their swift motions generate Heat and Drought; the same if Direct and Oriental: but if slow in Motion, Retrograde or Occidental, then they produce Rain, except ♂: If the Planets are Stationary, usually Winds follow; if ☿ be in Configuration with other Planets, expect an unsettled Aire, and if there be many Conjunctions or Aspects of the Planets concurring at one and the same time, it seldome fails but a great Alteration or Mutability of the Weather follows, but in regard the *Mutual Aspects* of the *Planets* ought to be considered in this Matter, and are approved of as the surest and best Rule to follow in things of this Nature, which depend upon so many uncertain Causes: In the next place I shall exhibit the Judgments or Predictions of the Weather from their Conjunctions and Aspects one with another, according to the Method of *Maginus*, improved.

IV. But in the first place the Artist ought to consider whether either *Planet* were Retrograde at the time of Conjunction or Aspect, or otherwise qualified as aforesaid: where note that the Planets have the greatest power in the alteration of the Aire at their Conjunction, which continues the longest in force; the Opposition is the next, and then the Quadrat or square Aspect, the ✶ or △ is accounted the weakest, and seldome observed in this case of the Weather, unless in the superiour Planets, ♄ and ♂; or else ♀, ☿ or the ☽, separatirig from ♃, and applying to ♄ or ♂; if so, you may expect an alteration of the Aire is neerly approaching, and at sometimes of the year produce a Turbulent Season.

[Part II.] *Predictions of the Weather from the Conjunctions and Aspects of the Planets, &c.*

I. Saturne in *Conjunction or Aspect with* ♃ ought to be considered according to the Nature of the Signes; as in Fiery Signes they produce Heat and Drought; in moist Signes, Rain, Hail and Winds, and considerable mutation of the Aire both before and after, if other Causes contradict not: but more particularly in the Spring they cause a disturbed or moist Aire; in Summer, Thunder and Hail; in Autumn, Rain and Winds; in Winter, Frost or Snow, generally a troubled Aire, and Storms that continue.

II. If ♄ be in ☌, □, or ☍ of ♂, and he slow in motion, then usually Hail or Rain follows, and sometimes accompanied with Lightning and very Tempestuous Weather; in moist Signes, Dark and Cloudy Weather, the Aire is Corrupted and Hurtful; but this is increased or diminished according as ♂ or ♄ meets with Fixed Stars; more particularly in the *Spring*, Rain and Thunder; in *Summer*, Hail or Thunder; in *Autumn*, Wind or Rain; and in *Winter*, Cold Remiss Weather, and sometimes Snow follows.

III. If ♄ happen to be so Conjoyned with the ☉, then in the *Spring*, expect Cold Showers, in *Summer* Thunder and Storms of Hail, in *Autumn* Cold and Rain, in *Winter* sometimes Frost, but usually Moist, Dark, Cloudy or Snowy Weather. Generally these Planets being in Conjunction or Aspect as aforesaid produce Cold Rainy Weather, and sometimes Hail, both before and after, especially if they are Conjoyned in Watry Signes, 'tis an *Apertio Portarum* or opening of the Gates of Heaven, and rarely passes without notable Alteration of the Aire.

III. If ♄ be Conjoyned, or in □ or ☍ of ♀, then in the Spring follows Cold Rain, in the Summer Hasty Showers, in Autumn Cold Stormy Weather, and in Winter usually follows Snow, Sleet or Rain, generally Cold Showers or Hail follows (especially if these Planets are in Signes accounted of a Watry Nature) but in short, they do produce very uncertain Weather for the most part, at any season, yet not violent.

IV. ♄ in ☌, □, or ☍ of ☿, in the Spring, this betoken Rain and Cold winds, or Cloudy weather, in the Summer some few showers and brisk Gales of wind; in Autumn dark obscure weather; and in Winter it portends some times violent storms of wind driving Snow; in short, if these Planets meet in moist Signes, judge moist weather, in dry Signes the contrary, in earthy, cold unwholsome cloudy weather, and in Airy Signes lofty winds if other Aspects contradict not.

V. If ♄ be in ☌, □, or ☍ of the ☽, in the Spring portend a moist and troubled Aire; the same in Summer, with an abatement of Heat and sometimes Hail; In Autumn cloudy weather, and a little Frost; In Winter cold and cloudy, which is Aggravated if at the same time ♄ behold ☿ by □ or ☍; generally ♄ and the ☽ so conjoyned in moist Signes produce cold and cloudy weather; in ♐ or ♑, in particular or in Airy Signes the cold is augmented, and sometimes Hail follows especially about the full ☽; but at the new ☽ dry weather, if in dry Signes, sometimes Frost or dark obscure and cloudy, at other times more pleasant, with an intermixture of gentle showers, where note that when the ☽ is joyned to ♄ the Tydes are also increased.

VI. ♃ in ☌, □, or ☍ of ♂, in the Spring and Autumn produce Winds of a violent Nature, in Summer an increase of Heat, with Thunder also; in Winter the Cold is deminished, and the Aire becomes Temperate and calm: The Natural Portents in general of these Planets so conjoyned, are Thunder, Lightning and Rain, if in moist Signes; but if in Fiery Signes, there usually follows Thunder, Rain, Corruscations, and sultry heat; if these Planets rise with any Stars of a tempestuous nature, they make a very considerable alteration in the Aire, sometimes Hail in Winter, or strang turbulent weather.

VII. If ♃ be in ☌, □, or ☍ of the ☉, this produces winds in the Spring and Autumn; in Summer Thunder and Lightning; in Winter an abatement or Remission of Cold, and a temperate and pleasant Aire: This Congress of the ☉ and ♃ generally produce wholsome gales of wind, and pleasant, fair and temperate weather if it happen in Airy Signes; if in moist or watry Signes, then pleasant sprinkling showers follow; in fiery Signes, an auginentation of heat and fair pleasant weather; but if in earthy Signes, not so delightful.

VIII. If ♃ be so joyned by Body or Aspect to ♀, then expect pleasing Gales, with grateful pleasant weather, wholsome both for Man and Beast, in any Quarter of the year, according to the Season: these Planets generally produce very temperate, tranquile, calm weather in most Signes, no way to be disliked by any.

IX. If ♃ be in ☌, □, or ☍ of ☿, 'tis generally observed that they stirr up winds and Tempests, and seldome Rain herewith; if in fiery Signes, they portend dry weather, and warm winds; in airy Signes much more pleasant weather with gentle Gales; in short, ☿ produces winds more or less, let him be with any Planet, or at any season or Quarter of the Year.

X. ♃ and the ☽ being in ☌, □, or ☍, doth the most part produce very propitious, favourable and serene weather, with gentle Gales of Wind, and in some Signes of a moist nature, an increase of spreading white Clouds, and in every season of the year you may expect upon such configurations very calm and temperate weather in general.

XI. If ♂ and the ☉ be in ☌, □, or ☍, they usually produce or occasion (in a natural way) Thunder, Lightning, Rain, Hail, and with violence too, if it be in the Summer, and they in any Signe of the Fiery Triplicity: It also increases heat and drought; in Airy Signes not only diseases are ingendred, but a dark Sky and dripping Clouds follow, sometimes in the Spring and Summer they ingender Whirlwinds and dry weather, and in Autumn more temperate, in Winter they abate the Cold, but in no quarter produce serene wholsome Aire for the benefit of mankind.

XII. If ♂ be in ☌, □, or ☍ of ♀, in the Spring and Autumn they generate Rain, and even in Summer they produce many Showers; in Winter warm weather for the Season, but it often varies, if these Planets be in watry Signes, they produce much Rain by their *Apertio Portarum* or opening of the Gates of Heaven, yet the weather in general in this case is moderately good and favourable.

XIII. ♂ in ☌, □, or ☍ of ☿, generate in the Spring & Winter Snow; in Summer Tempestuous weather, violent Storms, Thunder, Lightning and Hail; in Autuim, winds and sudden showers of Rain or Hail: in fiery Signes they signifie an increase of heat and drought in excess; in watry Signes Rain, in Airy Signes warm winds, but often turbulent and dangerous.

XIV. If ♂ be in ☌, □, or ☍ of the ☽, they produce flowers in the Spring or Autumn; in the Summer Haile, Thunder and Lightning, but not often: in Winter a remission of Cold and some Rain, but not much; in general they portend Rain in watry Signes, drought in Fiery, and in Airy Signes warm weather, spreading the Heavens with red and yellow Clouds in many places thereof (sometimes a Rainbow) prognosticating Rain to follow.

XV. The ☉ and ♀ in ☌ do for the most part bring moist weather, especially in Signes of the watry Triplicity, and in particular in Spring and Autumn gentle showers; in Summer they are sometimes accompanyed with Thunder, if other things in Nature concur; but in Winter usually this ☌ produces Foggy moist weather, and this the rather, if they are also in Aspect to ♄.

XVI. If the ☉ and ☿ be in ☌, they generally produce brisk gales of wind in Airy Signes, and this is the more certain if ☿ be leaving his Signe; Rain in watry Signes, or drifting moist weather; in Fiery Signes 'tis dry, with warm winds which are very unwholsome, ♀ and ☿ always attend the ☉, and are never elongated far from him, and do not occasion much alteration of the Aire in any Signes.

XVII. If the ☉ be in ☌, □, or ☍ of the ☽, in moist Signes, they produce Rain and reddish Clouds with great drops of water; in Fiery Signes fair weather, and the Air is changed according to the season of the year, and present temperature of the time; the ☽ causeth the greatest flux of the Sea at her ☌ or ☍ of the ☉, the same in all watry humours, which is augmented if she be neer the *Pleiades*, or *Hyades* at the same time, together with other causes which ought to be considered with these Judgments.

XVIII. If ♀ be in ☌ of ☿, in watry Signes usually they generate showers, and for the most part at any season of the year, they afford us moist winds: If at the same time the Luminaries are in ☌, □, or ☍, or neer it, then expect plenty of Rain, if other more prevalent causes hinder not.

XIX. If ♀ be in ☌, □, or ☍ of the ☽, they generally presage mild and gentle showers, or dropping moist weather, more or less according to the season augmenting the Tydes, if joyned to Stars of violent or Tempestuous Natures; In the Spring they produce a cloudy moist season; in Summer a remission of Heat and Drought; in Autumn cloudy and dark Aire; and in the Winter cold, sometimes Snow or Sleet a little before or after, but not violent, or of any long continuance, unless produced from other Causes more prevalent.

XX. If the ☽ be in ☌, □, or ☍ of ♀, they prognosticate Clouds, Wind and Rain, with variety of weather at any season; if they be in watry Signes, then expect moisture, in Airy Signes they presage wind, in Fiery Signes dry weather, in Earthy Signes a cold and dull Season, foggy and Cloudy, but of a very short continuance, except other Planets happen at the same time to make any notable configuration.

And now I shall Present a good old Table of the Weather, which is as it were the Epitomy of what has been said of the Weather, and so conclude this Subject.

Those that would Read more of this Subject, may peruse a small Piece written by one Cock, *and sold at the* Raven *in* Duck Lane.

A Table containing a General Judgment of the Inclination of the Aire by the Conjunctions and Aspects of the Planets, &c.					
Spring Summer Autumn Winter	♄ ♃	Wind & Rain Rain & Thund Wind & Rain Turbulent Air	♃ ♂	Turbulent Air Thund & heat winds but warm Temperate W.	♂ ☉	Dry & Windy Wea Thunder & Lightn Dry and Windy Remiss of Cold
Spring Summer Autumn Winter	♄ ♂	Rain & Thund Thund & Hail Rain & Temp. Remiss of Cold	♃ ☉	Windy Weath. Thund & Ligh Wind yet warm Remiss of cold	♂ ♀	Much Rain Small Rain Rainy Weather Rain or Snow
Spring Summer Autumn Winter	♄ ☉	Cold Rain Hail rain Thun Cold Rain Snow or Rain	♃ ♀	Springing Wea Pleasant Wea Clear Air Warm Season	♂ ☿	Wind and Rain Thunder and Hail Wind and Hail Snow or Rain
Spring Summer Autumn Winter	♄ ♀	Cold Rain Sudden Rain Cold Rain Snow or Rain	♃ ☿	Great Winds Wind & thund Wind & moist Wind & Rain	♂ ☽	Sometimes Hail Thunder Storms Intemperate Variable
Spring Summer Autumn Winter	♄ ☿	Wind & Rain Windy Winds & clouds Winds & Snow	♃ ☽	According to the Sign commonly white clouds & fair W	☉ ☿	In Airy Signs South winds, in watry rain, Ever Rain if *Mercury* be Retrograde
Spring Summer Autumn Winter	♄ ☽	Clouds & moist Cool Rain Cloudy Clouds & snow	☉ ♀	Moist Weather Thunder, &c. Small Rain Rain & Mists	☉ ☽	According to the time and the Planet that is predominate
Spring Summer Autumn Winter	♀ ☿	Sweet Showers Rain or clouds Variable somtimes floods	♀ ☽	Clouds, moist Remiss Heat Cloudy Weath Winds & Snow	☿ ☽	Variable Weather according to the nature of the Signe

The Use of the Table.

Observe what Aspects of the Planets are upon the day you would know the Inclination of the Aire (more especially if it be a ☌, □, or ☍ of any of the Planets) then seek the Characters of those Planets in the Table, and in the same part against the season of the year you have your desire: you are also to consider the Quality of the Signe wherein the Planets are for ♈, ♌, and ♐ are hot and dry, ♉, ♍, and ♑ are cold and dry; ♊, ♎, and ♒ are hot and moist, ♋, ♏, and ♓ cold and moist: Respect is also to be had to the *Apertio Portarium* or the opening of the Gates, which is when there is a ☌ or Aspect of those Planets whose Houses are opposite, or when the ☽ separates from one Planet and applyeth to another whose Houses are opposite; for upon these you may certainly expect change of Weather, according to the same.

CHAP. XX.

Centiloquium Ptolomei.

Or Ptolomy's Centiloquium Englished.

I. *Ate & Scientia;* from thy self and Learning: for it cannot be, that he who is skilful should pronounce the particular forms of things; nor can the fancy undertake a particular, but general notion of the sensible matter; in such things we must use conjecture. None but those endued with Divine Inspiration predict particulars.

II. When he that consults shall better consider of it; he shall find there will be small difference between the thing propounded, and the form thereof. The meaning of *Ptolomy* is no more than this; *viz.* the sympathy any one shall observe that propounds his Question, betwixt the matter intended, and the position of the Heavens at the time of its Proposition.

III. He that is inclinable to any Art, without doubt in his Nativity had some Star of the same Nature very well fortified.

IV. A natural inclination to any Knowledge, attains more perfection therein, than one that shall take hard pains by learning to obtain it.

V. He that is skilful may divert many effects of the Stars when he knows their Natures, and will prepare himself before their event or coming.

VI. The Election either of day or hour shall then advantage when it is constituted from the Nativity; otherwise, though the Election be well made, it will not profit.

VII. None can discern the mixture of the Stars, unless he first know their natural differences and mixtures one amongst another.

VIII. A judicious man helps forwards the Coelestial operations, even as the discreet Husband-man assists Nature in his Ploughing and preparing the ground.

IX. In generation and corruption earthly formes are subordinate to the Coelestials; wherefore they that frame Images, do then make use of them, by observing when the Planets do enter into those Constellations or Formes, &c.

X. In Election of dayes and hours, make use of the two Malevolent Planets ♄ and ♂; for even so doth the expert Physitian use poison moderately for cure of man.

XI. Make no election either of day or hour, before you know the quality of the thing intended.

XII. Love and Hatred cause error in Judgment; for affection magnifies even trifles, and envy as much depresseth weighty things.

XIII. When the position of Heaven shall signifie any thing to come to pass, make use in the business as assistants of the Malevolent Planets, though in the question they were not friendly.

XIV. The Astrologer plunges himself into many Errors, when the Cusp of the seventh House, and Lord thereof are unfortunate or afflicted.

XV. The Ascendants of a Kingdoms Enemies, are those Signes which decline from the Ascendant of the Kingdom: the Ascendant of the Kingdoms Friends are the Signes of the Angles, and of the Signes succeeding those Angles; the same is considerable in the rising or beginnings of Sects and Schisms.

XVI. When benevolent Planets have dominion in the eighth House, & are ill dignified, he that is then born shall receive damage from honest men; but if those Planets be well affected, the contrary shall happen.

XVII. Being demanded of the length of an old mans life, be not rash to give your Judgment before you have considered or measured according to his Nativity, how long he may live according to Nature.

XVIII. When the ☉ and ☽ are in one of the self same degree and minute at the time of any ones Birth, and a benevolent Planet is Lord of the Ascendant, the Native at that time born, shall be fortunate in all his Actions; the same shall happen if the two Lights be in opposition, the one in the Ascendant, the other in the seventh House, so qualified as before: but if an infortune be placed in the Ascendant, you may well judge the contrary.

XIX. A Purging Medicine shall not operate so effectually, when the ☽ is ☌ with ♃.

XX. Draw not Blood from that Member, whilst the ☽ is in a Sign Representing the same. The meaning whereof is this, that if you find at any time the ☽ in ♊ (which signifies the Arms) to be unfortunately afflicted of ♄ or ♂ in ♐, ♍, or ♓, it's not then, saies he, so good to let blood at that time, as when she hath made her progress out of that Signe: many expert Physitians now living know the truth hereof.

XXI. When the ☽ is in ♏ or ♓, and the Lord of the Ascendant in Aspect to a Planet under the Earth, it's good to give purging Medicines: but if the Lord of the Ascendant apply to a Planet above the Earth, it's probable the sick shall vomit up his potion.

XXII. Neither cut out, or first put on a new Garment, whilst the ☽ is in the sign ♌; if she then be unfortunate, it's so much the worse: this Aphorisme smells of the Superstition of the *Arabians*, and pertains to Elections. Mr. *Lilly* saith, once casually, without inspection to the position of the ☽, he put on a new Suit, the ☽ being in ♌, and ill digified, and tore many holes in the Suit going a Nutting, within a fortnight after; nor did that Suit ever do him any service: yet we must not be superstitious, but modest in our Elections, only use them as natural helps.

XXIII. The Aspect of the ☽, or her ☌ with the Planets, inclines the Native to be moveable in his disposition; if the Planets be strong, they shew him to be active, or full of spirit; but if they be ill fortified, they incline to sluggishness.

XXIV. An Eclipse of the ☉ or ☽ in the Angles of a Nativity or yearly Revolution, is obnoxious; but we take the time thereof from the distance which is between the degree Ascending and place Eclipsed: and as in a Solar Eclipse we give or allow for each hour one year; so for every hour in a Lunar Eclipse, we admit one moneth for the effects continuance.

XXV. Direct the *Medium Coeli* of a Nativity by the Table of right Ascentions, but the Ascendant by the oblique Ascentions under the elevation of the Pole where the Native was born, &c.

XXVI. The matter of any question is obscured, when the Planet signifying it, is either under the Earth, or joyned to the ☉ in an obscure House: but is manifested, when a Planet is brought out of his depression into his altitude, and posited in his proper Sphere or Element.

XXVII. *Venus* demonstrates that member to be neatly formed or shaped, in which she is posited at time of Birth; the like do the other Planets.

XXVIII. In Elections, if you cannot fortifie the ☽ by her joyning to, or aspecting of two Planets, see that she be neer some fixed Stars of that nature your Planet ought to have been of, &c.

XXIX, The fixed Stars do design immeasurable and admirable preferments, which notwithstanding determine in unusual Calamities, unless the Planets concur in judgment, or be in ☌ with them.

XXX. Consider well the time of the Coronation or Creating the first King of any Kingdome; for if the Ascendant of his or their Coronation concur with the Ascendant of the Kings Son, he shall then be successor to his Father.

XXXI. When the Principal Significator of a Kingdom shall come to his Climacterial year, either then the King of that Kingdome shall dye, or some of the most eminent Heroes of that Nation: this was verified in the death of a Valiant Worthy Person, and true Lover of his Countrey, that Deceased some years since in *England*.

XXXII. An amicable Aspect of the Stars doth conduce much to the Frieridship of two persons; but if you will know the quality or the thing wherein they shall agree, you must observe that from both their Nativities.

XXXIII. From the Benevolent or Malevolent positure of the ☉ and ☽, and each others ascending sign at time of birth is discerned the love or hatred betwixt any two: those Signes which we call obedient, do encrease unity and Friendship.

XXXIV. That Planet who hath most dignities in the degree wherein the ☽ changes, if he be Cardinal, *viz.* in an Angle, he doth demonstrate the principal actions of that month: this is of most force in the change of weather, &c.

XXXV. When the ☉ by transit shall come to the degree of the Zodiack, wherein any principal Significator, *viz.* Planet is, he makes that Planet more active in such things as concern change of Air or Weather.

XXXVI. In the new Construction of any City, make use of the Adjuvant fixed Stars; in building Houses take the Planets: Those Cities that in the time of their foundation have ♂ culminating, their Princes usually dye by the Sword.

XXXVII. Who hath the Sign of ♍ or ♓ in their Horoscope shall attain preferment by their own industry and worth; but they who have ♈ or ♎ their Ascendants, shall wilfully or innocently be the cause of their own deaths.

XXXVIII. When ☿ shall be well fortified or placed in either of the Houses of ♄ in any ones Nativity, the Native hath a divining Soul, and is capable of prying far into matters; if he be placed in the House of ♂, especially in ♈, he inclines to eloquence.

XXXIX. If the eleventh House be unfortunate, at what time a King is Crowned, it's an Argument his domestick Servants shall thrive little by him, or will that King grow Rich; but if the second House of the Figure be afflicted, it shews his Subjects shall be impoverished under his Government.

XL. When the Sign ascending is besieged or infortunated by the malignant Planets, he who is then born will delight in course actions, and in his sense of smelling shall take pleasure in filthy odours.

XLI. When thou settest forth upon any Journey, beware that the eighth House and Lord thereof be not unfortunate; when you return, in the same manner have regard to the second House and his Lord.

XLII. A Disease or sickness first beginning, whilst the ☽ is in a sign wherein a Malevolent was in the Nativity, or in □ or ☍ thereunto, will prove very grevious; and if at that time she is in ill aspect of an Infortune, it will be very dangerous; but if at the first Decumbiture she do possess the degree where a Fortune was, there's little danger.

XLIII. The Infortunate Planets do impedite those matters which they performed according to natural existence, as, Matrimony: but what things are acted according to Nature, and not unto Laws or Customes; or those affairs which neither are performed naturally, or according to Laws; such things receive destruction from the fortunes.

I must truly acknowledge, neither *Pontanus* or *Trapezuntius*, have given any light to this Aphorisme; I have followed *Haly*: it's as followeth in *Pontanus*.

Contrary Configurations of the times do intend or remit the obnoxious figures of a Nation. *Utrum horum mavis accipe.*

XLIV. When the Figure Erected at the beginning of any sickness is contrary to that of the Nativity, if no propitious thing be then in force, the sick party is like to be in great Peril.

XLV. Whosoever hath not the Predominant Planets of his Nativity in humane Signes, will be little sociable, and not very humane.

XLVI. Excellent prosperity is designed in Men's Geniture from the fixed Stars, and from the Angles of the preceding Lunations, and from the degree of the ⊕, when the degree ascending at the Birth chances to be the same.

XLVII. When in any ones Nativity a Malignant Planet is placed where a Fortune was in anothers Geniture, he who hath the fortune so placed, shall receive prejudice from him that had the Infortune so posited.

XLVIII. When the *Medium Coeli* of a King's Nativity is the Horoscope of a Subject, or the principal Dominators are in benevolent Configuration, they shall continue inseparable: judge the like when a Servants sixth House is the Ascendant of his Master: it may be thought the late Duke of *Buckingham* had such a one.

XLIX. When the Ascendant of a Subject shall culminate in his Princes Nativity, his Lord shall so entrust him, that he will be ruled by him. This must be understood of such of the Nobility or Gentry that have offices or commands in Princes Services.

L. [*N. B.*] Forget not in general Judgments the one hundred and nineteen Conjunctions: in well considering these, you shall understand what will be done in the world both of Generation and Corruption. What the Conjunctions are, and how to understand them, you may have recourse to Mr. *Lilly's Prophetical Merlin*, fol. 51.

LI. In what Sign the ☽ is at the time of Birth, make that Sign the Ascendant in Conception; and in what Sign she is found at the Conception, make that or its opposite the Sign Ascending at the Birth.

LII. The Lords of the Geniture of men of tall Stature are in their sublimities, and their Horoscopes in the beginning of Signes: but the Lords of their Nativities who are of short stature, are found in their Falls: Together with this, enquire whether the Signes be of Right or Oblique Ascention.

LIII. The Lords of the Geniture of lean men have no latitude, but of fat men they have: if the latitude be South, the Native will be nimble; if North, more sluggish.

LIV. When the Principal Lords in Buildings are joyned unto a Planet under the earth, they hinder the erection of Building.

LV. The malitious influence of ♂ against Ships is lessened when he is neither placed in the tenth or eleventh House of Heaven; in either of those places, he destroys the Ship, Thieves surprizing and possessing her by force; but the ship will be Fired if the Ascendant be afflicted by any fixed Star of the mixture of ♂.

LVI. When the ☽ is in her first quarter, that is, from the time she is receded from the ☉'s Conjunction, the moistures of Bodies do flow, until her second quarter, at other times they decrease.

LVII. Change your Physitian when you shall see the seventh House and his Lord afflicted in any Sickness.

LVIII. Consider the place of the ☌, in which part of Heaven it falls to be from the Ascendant of the year; for when the Profection shall arise unto that part of Heaven, then shall the event appear.

LIX. Pronounce not rashly that the absent person shall dye, before thou considerest whether he be not drunken; or say that he hath received a Wound, before you have enquired whether he were not let blood; or do you judge that he shall find Treasure, before you have searched out, whether perchance he took nothing to pledge of late, seeing the Figures of all these demands are alike.

LX. In consideration of the sick, behold the Critical dayes, and the peragration of the ☽ by the angles of a figure of sixteen sides; for where you shall find those angles well affected, it will fall out well to the sick party: On the contrary, it will fall out ill if you find them afflicted. *How to set a Figure of sixteen sides, see* Mr. *Lilly's* Introduction, *Page 294.*

LXI. The ☽ signifieth those things which appertain unto the Body, as what have resemblance unto her in regard to her motion.

LXII. When you shall make the minute of a ☌ your *Basis* or *Radix,* you may give judgment of the change of Weather in that moneth; for your judgment shall be framed according to the principal Dominator of the Angle of every Figure, for that Planet overcomes in the Nature of the Aire; assuming together with these things the quality of the present time, *viz.* the season of the year.

LXIII. When ♄ and ♃ make their ☌, see which of them is most elevated, and pronounce judgment according unto his nature: do the like upon all the Conjunctions of the other Planets.

LXIV. When thou hath considered the Lord of the Question, see what Essential Dignity he hath in the Querents annual Revolution, or in the Ascendant of the new ☽ preceding, give judgment accordingly.

LXV. *In minima Conjunctione, differentia media conjunctionis, & in media maxima conjunctionis differentia.*

LXVI. Use not profection alone, but also the and agreement of the Interficient and benevolent Planets and their Aspects. *This Aphorism hath relation unto Nativities, and is for discovery of the true time of the Native's Death.*

LXVII. The years of the Native are diminished and made much shorter, by reason of the imbicility of the giver of Life.

LXVIII. A malevolent Planet when he is Matutine, signifies a fall; when Vespertine, a Disease.

LXIX. There will be a blemesh in the Native's sight when the ☽ is in ☍ to the ☉, and is neer to Nebulous or Cloudy fixed Stars; or when the ☽ is in the seventh House, and both ♄ and ♂ in the Horoscope: but if together with this the ☉ be angular, the Native will quite lose his sight.

LXX. ☿ is not in ☌ with the ☽ in their Nativities, who divine by a kind of fury of things to come, or is either of them in the Ascendant of those who are *Daemoniack*, in such a kind of a Figure in the night time ♄ shall possess that angle, but in the day time ♂, especially in ♋, ♍ or ♓.

LXXI. In mens Nativities, when both the ☉ and ☽ shall be in Masculine Signs, their actions shall appear according to the Nature thereof: but in the Nativities of Women, these very Actions are augmented. Judge the same thing of ♂ and ♀, or being matutine, they incline to be more manly; but Vespertine they are effeminate.

LXXII. Require such things as concern the Native's Education from the Lords of the Triplicity of the Ascendant: what may concern life, must be derived from the Lords of the triangularity of the conditional Luminary.

LXXIII. Where the ☉ is found to be with *Caput Algol*, if then he is neither aspected by a benevolent Planet, or that a benign Planet doth govern the eighth House, and the Disposer of the temporal Light shall be in ☍ to ♂, or afflict him with a □ Aspect, he that then is borne shall be beheaded: But if the Light shall culminate, or be in the tenth House, his Body shall be wounded: if this Copulation be in ♊ or ♓, his hands and feet shall be cut off.

LXXIV. Who hath ♂ in the Ascendant of his Nativity will not fail to have a Scar in his Face.

LXXV. When the ☉ is joyned unto the Lord of the Ascendant in ♌, or that ♂ hath no prerogative in the Ascendant, or no benevolent Planet is placed in the eighth House, he that is born under such a constellation shall be burned, *viz.* shall dye by fire.

LXXVI. When ♄ possesseth the tenth House, *viz.* is posited therein, and the temporal Light of the time is in his ☍, and an earthly Signe is in the fourth, he who is then born shall perish by the ruine or fall of houses or buildings: if the Signe of the fourth be a watry Signe, he will dye in the water or by water, *viz.* he will be drowned: if the Signe of the fourth be humane, he will dye by the hands of Man, *viz.* will either be hanged or strangled, &c. but if a benevolent Planet is posited in the eighth, he will be neer to death by such accidents or casualities as aforesaid, but shall evade and not dye thereby.

LXXVII. Make use of, or direct the Profection of the Ascendant for such things as concern the body; direct the ⊕ for external or outward things; the ☽ for such things as concern both the body and the mind; the M.C. for the actions, Magistery or Professions, &c.

LXXVIII. A planet doth many times exercise his influence in that part of the heaven wherein he hath no Essential Dignity, bringing unto the Native unlooked for Wealth. This hath relation unto the Antiscions of the Planets.

LXXIX. When ♂ is in the eleventh House of Heaven, he that hath him so posited, shall not have dominion over his Master or Lord.

LXXX. When ♀ is joyned unto ♄, and he hath any dominion in the seventh House, he that is then born will be *sordidi coitus*.

LXXXI. The times of the events of things are discovered seven manner of wayes: first, from the intervall or distance of the two Lords or Rulers: secondly, from the distance of their Configuration each unto other: thirdly, by their access each unto other: fourthly, from the interval betwixt themselves, or the one of them, from the place signifying the thing desired or looked after: fifthly, from the setting of that Star which gives assistance or impediment: sixthly, from the mutation of the Principal significant Planet: seventhly, from the access of a Planet unto his own proper place.

LXXXII. When the figures of the new and full ☽ are equal, behold the Ascendant, which if that be also equal, then defer your judgment for that time.

LXXXIII. The time of craving any thing at the Kings hands, doth shew the affection betwixt the King and the Petitioner; *viz.* the time when the Petitioner receives the Dignity granted him, shall shew the quality of action depending upon the preferment, *&c.*

LXXXIV. When ♂ is the Lord of the Ascendant at the time of taking Possession, and doth also govern the second House, or is in ☌ with the Lord of the second, he brings much damage or loss.

LXXXV. When the Lord of the Ascendant is in configuration with the Lord of the second, the Prince or Lord shall willingly consume much Treasure. *This hath relation to the two preceding Aphorisms.*

LXXXVI. The ☉ is the Fountain of Vital Power, the ☽ of Natural.

LXXXVII. Monthly Conversions consist of twenty eight dayes, two hours, and about eighteen minutes; but some there are who judge them from the peragration of the ☉ when he is equated partitely unto the degree and minute he was in at the beginning of the month.

LXXXVIII. When we direct the Profection of the ⊗ for the whole year of a Revolution, we take it from the ☉ to the ☽, and project it only from the Ascendant.

LXXXIX. Require what concerns the Grand-father from the seventh House, but the Unckle from the sixth House.

XC. When the Lord of the Aacendant doth behold the Ascendant, the thing which lies undiscovered is of the nature of the Ascendant: if he behold not the Ascendant, its quality shall be according to the nature of the place where the Lord of the Ascendant is; the Lord of the hour demonstrates the colours, but the place of the ☽ the times: if that place of the ☽ be above the earth, the thing or matter is new; if under the Earth, old: the ⊕ shews its quantity, whether it be long or short; the Lords of the Terms of the fourth and tenth Houses, and of the ☽, shew its Substance.

XCI. It's an ill Sign when the Lord of the sick party is combust, especially if the ⊕ be afflicted.

XCII. ♄ being Oriental, doth not so much oppress the sick body, nor doth ♂ when he is Occidental.

XCIII. In Questions do not pronounce judgment before you consider the next subsequent new ☽; for the first beginnings are varied in every ☌, wherefore mix both together, and you shall not err.

XCIV. The Place of Heaven wherein the principal and most powerful Significator is posited, doth declare such things as are in the thoughts of the Querent to be demanded.

XCV. Those Images which do arise with the several *Decanates*, they declare the Inclination of the Native to that Profession he handles. What these are, see *Scaliger* upon *Manilius* or *Johannes Angelus*.

XCVI. The Significations of an Eclipse shall be most apparent when the Eclipse is neer unto an Angle: consider also the nature of the Stars in Configuration to one another, as well of the Erratical Planets, as of the fixed Stars; so also the Images co-arising with the Signe Ascending, and pronounce Jugment accordingly. By *Image* he means *Asterismes*, of which see *Maginus, Origanus,* and *Argol*.

XCVII. The matter or thing in question which is demanded, will be performed in a short time, when either the Lord of the new or full ☽ is Cardinal.

XCVIII. Blazing Stars, and shootings of the Stars in the Aire (or prodigious Apparitions therein) have a second Signification in mundane affairs; *viz.* Eclipses are in the Heavens, but apparitions in the Air, therefore events portended by Eclipses are first preferred.

XCIX. Fiery Apparitions shew want of Rain, or a dry Aire, which if they are carried or moved unto one part of Heaven, they declare Wind to come from that Quarter of Heaven: but if those Apparitions are carried diversely, or into sundry parts, they shew scarcity of Rain or Waters, the Elements often troubled, and the incursions of Armies.

C. Comets, whose Distance is eleven Signes from the ☉, if they appear in Angles, the King of some Kingdom, or one of the Principal men of the Kingdome will dye; but if they appear in a succeedent House, his Treasures are like to do well, yet shall the King or Kingdome change their Governour: if they appear in a cadent or obscure House, Disease, and sudden Deaths will succeed: if they move from the West toward the East, a forreign Enemy shall invade several Kingdoms and Countries: if the Comet move not the Enemy shall be Provincial.

CHAP. XXI.

Hermes Trismegistus, his *Centiloquium* in *English.*

I. The *Sun* and *Moon*, next unto God, are the Life of all living things: Yet many Nativities have no *Hylech*; yet because the *Sun* and *Moon* friendly behold their Ascendant, or be therein free from affliction, their lives shall be longer continued.

II. All Diurnal Nativities are strengthened by the *Sun*, when well beheld by the Fortunes Nocturnal of the *Moon*, when she is so fortified. If this happen not, yet if good Planets be found in Angles, the Nativity shall be good.

III. When ♂, Lord of the Ascendant shall be posited in the tenth, it confers on the Native dignity and power; which will be accompanyed with injury and cruelty; and may therefore be said, a misfortune, rather than happiness.

IV. ♃ in good Aspect with the infortunes, changes their malevolency into good. ♀ cannot effect any such thing, unless assisted by ♃; therefore in procuring good, and prohibiting ill, ♃ is found much better than ♀.

V. The Artist cannot make a commixion of the Significations of the Stars, before he know their Friendships and Enmities, which is threefold. First, according to their Nature. Secondly, according to their Houses. Thirdly, according to their Aspects.

VI. ♀ is opposite to ☿. He comprehends Languages and Discipline; she delights and pleasures, ♃ the like to ♂; this coveteth Mercy and Justice; that, Impiety and Cruelty.

VII. Make the ☉, or any of the Superiours to signifie Princes and great Persons, Scribes and Rusticks, the inferiour Planets, chiefly the ☽.

VIII. The Signification of the Conjunction, is not lessened by an Aspect; but the Aspect is by the Conjunction; as having lesser force, than it.

IX. Give not Judgment, neither Elect any thing, while ♏ is ascending, neither when the Angles are oblique or crooked, or if ♂ be in the Ascendant; the event will prove cross, and the matter comes to no good end; for ♏ is a Sign of falsity.

X. Good Planets, afflicted of the Infortunes from the sixth, or twelfth Houses, signifie ill.

XI. Rumours spread, when the ☽ is in the first face of ♏, are false, and knavishly forged.

XII. The Judgments of Astrologers are not many times true, by reason of the Error of their instruments, or Querents Ignorance; or when the ☉ is neer the Mid-heaven, or when the Arguments of promise and denyal of the thing are equal in the Figure.

XIII. While the ☽ shall be South descending in ♏ or ♓, begin not then to build; for a Fabrick then erected quickly comes to ruine.

XIV. ☿ being strong and in proper place of the Heavens, well configufated of other Stars or Planets in Nativities, denotes convenient dignity to the Native thereby; but ☿ of himself is a Planet weak.

XV. Whosoever contendeth with another & overcomes when the Significators are in Signes bi-corporeal, gets a great victory; if overcome, looseth much; for then the good or evil is doubled.

XVI. Give not judgment before thou knowest the intention of the Querent; for many ask they know not what, nor can they express what they intend.

XVII. When thou shalt be interrogated for a Father, behold the fourth House; for a Brother, the third; of a Son, the fifth; of a wife, the seventh: But if for a sick person, behold the Ascendant only.

XVIII. When the ☽ shall come to the Quadrate of the Fortunes or Infortunes, and the testimonies of the helps or hinderances of the matter doubtful; it is to be doubted that the strength of the bad Planets will more impede, than the others can assist.

XIX. In the beginning of Journeys, and returns therefrom, let not the ☽ be in the Ascendant, fourth, or ninth Houses, although she be not afflicted. In the entring of a City, place her neither in the Ascendant, second, or fourth Houses.

XX. There are three wayes of discovering the Accidents proper to Men; *viz.* from the Geniture of the Native, Birth of his first Child, or by a Question propounded, with which the mind was solicitous and affected.

XXI. Every beginning when the ☽ shall be joyned to a Retrograde Planet, will soon be destroyed, and if she shall be otherwise impeded, the mischief will happen the sooner.

XXII. Make ♄ and ☉ Significators of Kings and Princes, with the Planet, and Planets of the tenth; but their helpers take from the eleventh, and the assistants of vulgar Persons from the second House.

XXIII. When a King or Prince sets forth to journey, be sure to reject that time when ♋ Ascends.

XXIV. ♊ and ♐ obey the head and tayl of the Dragon, more than any other Signes: therefore do they work more mischief in those Signs, than they do in any other.

XXV. When either ♉ or ♎ ascend in Womens Nativities, and ♂ therein, the Native will be immodest, and unchaste; the same if ♑ shall ascend.

XXVI. The virtues of the Planets are received by the ☉, when he is posited either in the Ascendant or Mid-heaven, in ☌ of them. The ☽ in the night-time receives them also, if in the aforesaid places, she be joyned to them.

XXVII. ♃ dissolves ♄'s malice; and $ dissolves ♂'s.

XXVIII. When a Question is propounded of a Woman, take ♀ as her natural Significatrix: but more particularly the seventh House. But if a Question be asked of an Ememy, respect the twelfth House; but, then more particularly, the seventh also.

XXIX. When any one goeth to War, especially a King, let the Ascendant be one of the Houses of the Superiour Planets, or of the ☉. And let the Lord of the Ascendant, and the ☉ be potent in the Figure; but the Lord of the seventh weak and unfortunate.

XXX. The ☽ increasing in Light and Motion, and in ☌ of ♄ or ♃, is generally good in all things: but if she be diminished in Light, 'tis ill; understand the contrary wholly, when she is in ☌ of ♀ and ♂.

XXXI. Let not ♃ be under the ☉'s beams, or otherwise impeded, when you either pawn or lend things; which if he shall be so, and not received of the Planet impediting, there will be little or no hopes of redemption.

XXXII. Fortunate Planets going to Conjunction or Aspect of one of the Infortunes, in any figure, diminish their evil influence. If the Figure be good, the greater good they do; if ill, the lesser. But the Malevolents in □ or ☍ of the Benevolents diminish and abate of their Virtues, the other Aspe.ccts hinder not.

XXXIII. ♄ passing out of one Sign into another, causes strange Apparations in the Heavens, which the *Arabians* term *Assub*; or certain other signs of a Fiery Nature.

XXXIV. The ☌ of ♃ and ☉ produceth temperate Air, chiefly, when celebrated in aereal signs. From the ☌ of ♄ & ☉, comes cold; and from ☌ of the ☉ & ♂, in the Spring season, proceeds a cloudy dark Air, it happening in double bodied Signes, whence diseases very frequently follow.

XXXV. In Summer, when the ☉ enters the terms of ♂, Heat is caused; in Winter, Drought, and scarcity of Rain and Waters.

XXXVI. In the Nativities and Questions of Men, make *Hyleg*, and *Alchocoden*, and their directions; chiefly, in Questions concerning Kings and great Persons, by which their accidents are chiefly known, let them be good, or evil.

XXXVII. If the Ascendant be Fortunate, and the Lord thereof unfortunate, it indicates a sound and healthful body, but an afflicted mind. But if the contrary happen, judge the contrary.

XXXVIII. Always note the Configurations of the Stars, not by their Signs, but Orbs.

XXXIX. Let the ☽ be increasing in Light, and free from the Aspects of the Infortunes, when you would cure sore Eyes.

XL. The ⊕ with ill Planets in the fourth, ninth, or tenth Houses, denote death to the Sick.

XLI. When the Significator of either good or evil shall be stationary, and Angular, it shall be more durable. But it shall be the more mutable and variable, if the Significator shall be cadent from Angles, and Retrograde.

XLII. The Lord of the second House hath the same strength in hurting, as the Lord of the eighth; the Lord of the sixth, the same with the Lord of the twelfth.

XLIII. ♂ Occidental in ♋ not beheld of ♄, ♃, ♀, or ☉, makes a good Phlebotomist. But if ♂ shall be in ♑, it makes a destroyer of Men, and one that delights to shed blood.

XLIV. The best artist in the world may chance to err, when he mistakes a true Significator for a false one.

XLV. When ♄ shall be elevated above ♀, and in □ of her, it makes the Native shameless, and a perfect Woman-hater. But if ♀ be elevated above ♄, he shall be a great Friend unto Women.

XLVI. If in any Nativity ☿ shall be in the Ascendant, Oriental, and swift; the Native will be eloquent, and learned in the Liberal Sciences: the same happeneth, if he shall be in ♐ in his proper terms.

XLVII. The first of the Angles is the Ascendant: the second, the M.C. the third, the seventh House; the fourth Imum Coeli. But of the rest of the places, the eleventh is first, then the second; after that, the fifth; then the ninth, and third, but the sixth, eighth, and twelfth, are accounted the worst.

XLVIII. ♂'s influence is never abated, unless by the interposure of a benevolent Planet.

XLIX. Let your Significator agree with his, whom you intend to supplicate.

L. The Ascendant, or a Planet found in the last degree, the signification must be taken from the following Signe; but if in 29 deg. in the same Signe, the strength of a Planet is considered three wayes, *viz.* in the degree where he is found, and next preceding and succeeding.

LI. We should consider of future contingents from the Conjunctions of the Planets, but things past or present from their separations.

LII. When ♃ shall be in ♋ removed from the Ascendant, and no way impeded of any other Star, the Native will be rational, and very expert in Science; but delighting to lead a recluse life, and shall not have the due applause of his Learning.

LIII. In the world many evils will happen, when in one month there shall happen an Eclipse of both Luminaries; chiefly in those places subject to the Sign in which they happen.

LIV. When the ☽ shall be in the Combust way, or peregrine, in the beginning of a Journey, the person will either fall sick in his journey, or shall be otherwise grievously troubled and molested.

LV. It behoves the Astrologer to consider the time in Directions of the Planets; but in the fixed Stars it is not so needful.

LVI. The Fathers Estate shall pass to the Son, if ♄ shall be fortunate, and in friendly Aspect of the Lord of the Ascendant: but this more freely, if ♄ shall be Lord of the fourth.

LVII. Fortunate Planets being in Signs wherein they have no dignity, their benignity is translated another way.

LVIII. ♂ Almuten of a Nativity, and not joyned to good Planets, signifieth the Native to suffer by envy and hatred.

LIX. The fortunate Stars confer great felicity, when they shall be received of each other in their proper Houses; and when the evil Planets are so received, they refrain from doing much mischief.

LX. The Native will be sickly and weak, when ♄ is elevated above ♂; but if ♂ shall be elevated above ♄, he shall be fat and lusty.

LXI. In Men's Nativities, if the part of Marriage shall fall in Signs obedient; and in Women's in Signs imperant, the Woman shall Rule the Man, and the Man shall obey: *Sin autem contra, dic contra*.

LXII. If the Lords of the Triplicity of the ☌ of the Lights shall friendly respect each other, the first to the second, the second to the third, it shews eminent prosperity, and a freedom from sorrows.

LXIII. ☿ in ♓, in deep or pitted degrees, makes the Native foolish and slow of speech; and if ♃, shall be in the Houses of ♂, in pitted degrees, he will be sorded and needy, and receive hurt from Souldiers; but if in the Houses of ♄, chiefly ♑, and in such degrees, he will be morose, rigid, and odious to all men.

LXIV. ☿ in reception of ♂ by Houses, or if he shall be in Aspect of him falling from Angle, the Native will be a lover of Hunting, and to play at Dice and Tables: but if they shall not be cadent, he shall prove an excellent Souldier.

LXV. Planets under the ☉'s beams, or within twelve degrees thereof, are unfortunate, unless in the same degree with him, but when passed 12 degrees from him (*existentes Orientales*) they are fortunate.

LXVI. The ☊ with the Infortunes, denotes terrible mischiefs, for he increases their Malice; but with the Fortunes he works good, and augments their benignity. But the significations of the Dragons tayl are to be noted the contrary way.

LXVII. ☿ in the sixth house of a Nativity, the native shall change from one Religion to another, & will have his Felicity in part impeded by reason of his inconstancy.

LXVIII. The first signe hath pre-eminence in signification, when there be two signs have to do with the thing.

LXIX. Accept the beginning of every thing from the Moon, but the end from her dispositor.

LXX. If ♃ in the Revolution of the world shall be in his house, exaltation, or oriental in any angle, and otherwise freed from evil, he signifies plenty, (*my Author says* penury, *if time and ill handling haue not abused him*) of all things.

LXXI. When the ☽ and the Lord of the Ascendant shall be impeded by the Lord of the 8th, the sick person hath cause to fear.

LXXII. 'Tis ill to begin any Law-suits or other Controversies when the ☽ is ill dignified: the Plaintiff witlmt doubt will be overcome.

LXXIII. All Rebellious breaking out at the beginning of the year, are not easily suppressed.

LXXIV. The ☽ in ruminating signes joyn'd to retrograde Planets, it is not then good to purge; the potion will work upward to the Patients injury.

LXXV. Oriental Planets signifying either good or evil, perform their work speedily; Occidental, more slowly.

LXXVI. The middle stay of a solar Eclipse is by the of the ☌ of the lights.

LXXVII. There will many Wars and difficulties happen, when in a Revolutional Figure of the World, ♄ and ♃ shall be in their Exaltations.

LXXVIII. Be wary and circumspect in your Judgment, when a Fortune is with a malevolent; nor be you over-confident that the malice of the infortune shall be averted.

LXXIX. There are twelve Signes, one of which is constantly ascending: the Ascendant signifies the body, and the Lord thereof the mind. Let not that Signe ascend for your purpose, whose Lord is impeded.

LXXX. Planets in fixed Signs shew the matter durable; in Bi-corporeal Signes, doubtful; in moveable, convertible to good or evil.

LXXXI. In matters of secrecy, let not the ☽ be combust, but going from combustion.

LXXXII. When the ☽ is in a fixed Sign, neither cut out, or put on any new Garments, chiefly in ♌, for 'tis extream dangerous: 'tis the same if she be in ☌ or ☍ of the ☉, or impedited of the Infortunes.

LXXXIII. The ☽ hath great power in all Questions, except when ♌, ♑, or ♐ ascend: for either of those Signes abate of her Significations; chiefly ♌ or ♒.

LXXXIV. ♄ is under the Sun beams until he be 15 degrees distant from him. Understand the same of ♃.

LXXV. Refuse the ☽ in ♋ or ♍ for Marriages, unless it be in marrying of Widdows.

LXXXVI. An Infortune in his own House or Exaltation, and Oriental, is better than a Fortune Retrograde, or impedited.

LXXXVII. There will be some impediment about that part of the body represented by that Sign which was afflicted at Birth.

LXXXVIII. Immense prosperity is portended, when the Lords of the Triplicity of the Luminaries shall have vertue in an angle or succedent House, and be in their proper places, remote from the Aspects of the Infortunes; and if the Lord of the Ascendant shall be well seated also, the happiness shall be the more and the greater.

LXXXIX. The Aspects of the ✶ or △ have the same quality: but the ✶ is less forcible than the △, either in good or evil.

XC. ♄ performs evil slowly, but ♂ swift; and therefore ♂ is reputed to hurt more than ♄.

XCI. When the three superiour Planets shall be conjoyned in Regal Signes, it is termed a great Conjunction; and when the ☉ beholds them, they make most Potent and Flourishing Kingdoms.

XCII. Those doubts are soon resolved, that are propounded when the ☽ and the Planet to whom she applies are in Signes, having voice, and in the first or third Houses, or in opposition of them.

XCIII. The Infortunes in the eighth House have their malice increased; but the Benevolents being there, portend neither good nor evil.

XCIV. There will neither good or evil be performed, but when the good or bad Planets in a Nativity or Revolution shall aspect the ☽ by a Quadrate.

XCV. If ☿ be afflicted in the sixth House, the Native shall die in Prison: if ♄ shall be in the twelfth, and ♀ in the eighth, he shall end his dayes by precipitation.

XCVI. When the ☉ in the day-time, and the ☽ in the night, in the beginning of any Sickness, is impedited, the person is to be feared.

XCVII. The Significations of the Stars are always varyed, as they vary in their Configurations and Latitudes.

XCVIII. The ☽ in the fourth, seventh, ninth or twelfth Houses shews the true cause of the Question propounded:

the same is known by her separation from ☿. And if the Ascendant and ☽ shall be in double-bodied Signes, the cause of the question is confirmed.

XCIX. An Infortune in his House or Exaltation denotes the matter by him signified to come to a good end, but with delays: but if he shall be impeded in the Ascendant, though in his House or Exaltation, the matter will be obstructed, and come to an ill end..

C. The event of every Enterprise that is doubtful, is terminated by these Significators, *viz.* by the fourth House and his Lord, and the Planet strong in the same; also by the light of the time and the Lord thereof; and by the Planet, and his Disposiʇer to whom the said Light of the Time is Conjoyned.

The End of Hermes *his* 100 *Aphorismes.*

CHAP. XXII.

Bethem's Centiloquium *Englished.*

I. We will begin this Book, according to Custome used in the judgment of the Stars.

II. Thou mayest know, when a Planet is Retrograde, he is as a man infirm, stupified, and sollicitous.

III. If Cadent, he is as a man dead, and Hath no motion.

IV. If Combust, as a man in Prison, without hope of Liberty.

V. If Stationary to Retrogradation, as a healthful man receding from health; yet there is hope of Recovery remaining.

VI. If Stationary to Direction, as a sick man amending.

VII. If Besieged, as a man fearful, between two Enemies: (*i.e.*) when between the two Infortunes.

VIII. A Planet between ♃ and ♀, is as a man pleasant and free from Want and Trouble.

IX. If Aspected of the Infortunes from the fourth House, as a Man on whom Death is approaching.

X. A Planet in Aspect of his Enemy, as a man fearing to be Trapann'd or Betrayed.

XI. A Planet in Conjunction of an Infortune, is as one fighting with his Enemy.

XII. A Planet in Conjunction of a Fortune, is as one in his Friends Embraces.

XIII. A Planet in anothers House, who rules the same Trigon, is as a man in the House of his friend.

XIV. Cadent from House or Exaltation, he is as one absent from hie abode.

XV. A Planet in his House of Exaltation, is as one in his Castle or Strong-hold.

XVI. If there Retrograde, he is as a sick man at home.

XVII. If Combust in his own House, he is as a man confined thereto by his King.

XVIII. If in his own Dignity and Cadent, as a man vexed and fearful.

XIX. Fortunate Planets Retrograde, are unfortunate: if Cadent from Angles, or their Houses, *&c.* as one hoping for good but misses it.

XX. A Fortune Retrogr. with an infortune, strengthens the Infortunes nature, but abates the worth of his own.

XXI. An Infortune in his own House Direct, & there joyned to a Fortune, his malignancy shall turn to good.

XXII. A Planet in the last degree of a Sign, is as one falling from his Estate.

XXIII. A Planet in the first degrees of a Signe, he is but weak in Signification.

XXIV. From the first degree to the fifteenth, a Planet is rising; but from the 15*th* to 25*th*, he is compleat in strength.

XXV. A Planet in the last five degrees of a Sign, is as a man leaving his House.

XXVI. An Earthy Planet in the Ascendant strong, argues good in any thing, *i.e.* A Planet ruling the Earthy Triplicity.

XXVII. A Planet not in his own House, as a man knocking at anothers door; and his signification is to be slighted, he having no power in that place.

XXVIII. When Planets are with the *Sun*, their significations and power are abated & much lessened thereby.

XXIX. When Planets are in the last degrees of a Signe, Retrograde, their Judgments are transmitted, their Light lessened, and their Strength and Glory abated.

XXX. A Planet seven degrees distant from the *Sun* in his own House, Retrograde, is as a man in his Castle in the power of his Enemy, striving to abandon Slavery.

XXXI. A Planet in the House of his Enemy, is as a man in such a Condition, *viz.* a real Prisoner.

XXXII. A Planet in his own House, free from affliction, declares the perfection of the Question, or thing interrogated.

XXXIII. The *Moon* separating from a Planet, shews what is past.

XXXIV. But applying to one, denotes what is to come.

XXXV. If she be separating from *Saturn* in any Question, she shews Sorrow, Discord, Trouble.

XXXVI. If from *Jupiter*, Mirth, Pleasure, Wealth, and good Fortune, *&c.*

XXXVII. If from *Mars*, Contention, Strife, Bloodshed, Bonds, False-witness, *&c.*

XXXVIII. If from the *Sun*, she signifies Sicknesses, Cares, Fears, Imprisonnent, *&c.*

XXXIX. If from *Venus*, then judge, Lust, Sport, Laughter, Dancing, Singing, *&c.*

XL. If from *Mercury*, judge according as ☿ is posited.

XLI. The *Moon* applying to a Planet, shews things to come, according as her Application is with them.

XLII. The *Moon* fortunate in the morning, the Querents business prospers the better all the day long. One born then, will be fortunate, *&c.*

XLIII. But if she be Unfortunate in the morning, it shews Corruption in the Question, *&c.* He that is born then dies quickly, or will be sickly.

XLIV. The *Moon* in *Conjunction* of *Saturn*, usually proves an ill day for every work, *&c.*

XLV. The *Moon* in *Conjunction* of *Jupiter*, is observed to be a good day for all things in general.

XLVI. The *Moon* in *Conjunction* of *Mars*, is unfortunate for every purpose, as has been experienced.

XLVII. The *Moon* in *Conjunction* of the *Sun*, is fit for private business. He that then falls sick, dyes.

XLVIII. The *Moon* in *Conjunction* of *Venus*, 'tis a good day, chiefly in Love matters.

XVIX. The *Moon* in *Conjunction* of *Mercury*, 'tis a good day, chiefly for Contracts and Writings.

L. The *Moon* in *Opposition* of *Saturn*, a bad day in all things, especially to Saturnine people.

LI. The *Moon* in ☍ of *Jupiter*, bad in all things, (*Vix Credo.*) for *Oppositions* rarely produce good effects.

LII. The *Moon* in *Opposition* of *Mars*, begin nothing of weight that day, for no good end can be expected.

LIII. The *Moon* in *Opposition* of the *Sun,* good in no manner of Work or business, therefore to be avoided.

LIV. The ☽ in ☍ of ♀, a laudable day in all things. (*Vix Credo*) The contrary often happens, especially to women.

LV. The *Moon* in ☍ of *Mercury,* a good day for every work. *Not for Contracts, I'm sure*. Let them be excepted.

LVI. The *Moon* in □ of ♄, is a bad day. Chiefly in meeting with Kings, and great Persons. Let not Noble and Eminent Men take Journeys; for they will prove ill. The sick man will hardly escape, that is taken sick at such a time.

LVII. The *Moon* in □ of ♃, is a good day in access to great men, to attain Friends, but in △ to ♃ is much better.

LVIII. The *Moon* in *Quartile* of *Mars*, is unfortunate in all things; chiefly in contending with great men; in Marriage; the sick man dyes, or bleeds, that then fall sick.

LIX. The *Moon* in *Quartile* of the *Sun*, is good to manage the affairs of great Persons; but the *Trine* Aspect must be preferred before it.

LX. The *Moon* in *Quartile* of *Venus*, is good in all things, chiefly in Love matters. *These Aphorisms must be warily understood.*

LXI. The *Moon* in □ of *Mercury*, is a good day to Merchandise, Study, or Converse with Kings, &c.

LXII. The *Moon* in ✶ of ♄, is good to convese with Ancient People, or to begin any work of a Saturnine Nature.

LXIII. The *Moon* in ✶ of *Jupiter*, good to settle things, and to do Justice, to Marry, &c.

LXIV. The *Moon* in *Sextile* of *Mars*, is good to fight an Enemy, to reduce or divide an Army.

LXV. The *Moon* in *Sextile* to the *Sun*, is a good day to manage the affairs of great Persons.

LXVI. The *Moon* in *Sextile* of *Venus*, is excellent in all things, chiefly in Love-matters.

LXVII. The *Moon* in *Sextile* of *Mercury*, is a singular good day for Contracts, Agreements, Marchandizing.

LXVIII. The *Moon* in *Trine* of *Saturn*, is a good day to talk with Magistrates; to Build, Till, &c.

LXIX. The *Moon* in *Trine* of *Jupiter*, is a good day in all things; but principally to meet Kings, Judges, Lawyers, &c.

LXX. The ☽ in △ of ♂, is a good day to begin War, & end Controversies; to Hunt, or converse with Martialists.

LXXI. The ☽ in △ of the ☉, is a good day to meet Kings, Princes & Nobles, or Court or to Petition their Favor, &c.

LXXII. The *Moon* in *Trine* of *Venus*, is good for every thing, chiefly in Marriage-matters, and all Love affairs.

LXXIII. The *Moon* in *Trine* of *Mercury,* good to converse with Lawyers, Scribes, Secretaries, &c.

LXXIV. *Saturn* in the Ascendant hurts the Question; and when Retrograde there he destroys it.

LXXV. *Saturn* in the tenth House, he destroys the most hopeful things, let it be in a Nativity or Question.

LXXVI. *Saturne* in the seventh, oft changes the business and brings Mischief to it by some means or other.

LXXVII. *Saturn* in the 4*th*, shews an unhappy end of every business, though carryed on with much care & pains.

LXXVIII. What *Saturn* bindeth, *Jupiter* dissolveth.

LXXIX. The Like doth *Venus,* in what *Mars* bindeth.

LXXX. The *Moon* separating *from Jupiter* or *Venus,* undoes what's bound by *Mercury,* in any Nativity, Question, or Election.

LXXXI. The three Superiour Planets in *Opposition* of the *Sun,* Corrupt and hinder the Question.

LXXXII. *Saturn* in *Quartile* of the *Sun,* shews a good progress, but a bad end of a thing.

LXXXIII. *Saturn* in *Quartile* or *Opposition* of *Jupiter,* dissolves Oppression and Violence threatened.

LXXXIV. *Saturne* in *Conjunction, Quartile* or *Opposition* of *Mars*, prohibits Mirth, impedes or destroyes the Question though never so hopeful.

LXXXV. *Saturne* in *Conjunction* or *Opposition* of *Venus* in the tenth, the Question then propounded aims at Dishonesty.

LXXXVI. *Saturn* in *Conjunction, Quartile,* or *Opposition* of *Mercury*, destroys the Question, makes things that are impertinent and idle, more idle and impertinent.

LXXXVII. *Jupiter* in *Conjumction, Quartile* or *Opposition* of *Saturn*, hinders his evil portended, and turns it to good.

LXXXVIII. *Jupiter* in *Conjunction, Quartile* or *Opposition* of *Mars*, hinders the force of Generation and Corruption.

LXXXIX. If he be in *Conjunction, Quartile* or *Opposition* of *Venus*, shews the aptness of the Question, & its good end.

XC. Or if he be in *Conjunction, Quartile* or *Opposition* of *Mercury*, the business enquired after comes to a good end, with an addition to what the Querent expects.

XCI. The Infortunes in the Ascendant or second House, strong, shews the Querents Fortune to be transmitted from evil to good. Understand the same both in Nativities and Questions.

XCII. But if in those Houses unfortunate, it is then changed from good to evil, which must be left to the Astrologers Judgment to determine.

XCIII. 'Tis the same when they arc posited in any of the other Angles. An ingenious Artist knows how to apply these.

XCIV. The Lord of the Ascendant in *via Combusta*, the Question is corrupted. The Combust way is from 15 d. of ♎, to 15 d. of ♏.

XCV. An Infortune in the tenth or fourth from the Ascendant of the Question, obscures the matter or thing quesited; and the Querent shall tremble (saies *Bethem*) to think of the evil attending it.

XCVI. An Infortune in the Ascendant or second, Fortunate, portends the business to answer the Querents desire; but shews him to reap small gaain thereby.

XCVII. If in the same Houses Infortunate, it denotes the matter or thing enquired after will come to nought.

XCVIII. Few degrees Horoscopical, and the Lord of the Ascendant in the ninth or sixth descending, the Question never obtains the thing he expects: The Fortunes Cadent, and Infortunes Angular, the same.

XCIX. A Planet signifying any matter, evilly disposed at the time of the Querent's first moving the same, Denotes a Vexatious, and Unhappy End to the thing required: if well disposed, judge the contrary.

C. When the Significator of a thing is in Reception, a good Aspect of an Infortune in an Angle, the Querents business may then be accomplished; but he usually takes away what he gives hopes of at the last. The knowledge of Reception is, when a Planet shall be in the House or Exaltation of another, and that other in his; and both there free from the beams of the Infortunes.

Here Ends the Hundred Aphorismes of Bethem.

[*In these 300 Aphorisms is contained concisely the whole Mistery of Astrology; and though they have been already formerly Printed in Almanacks; yet, that the Artist might be furnished with them altogether at one view in* English, *I thought it very necessary to insert them here, which I hope will not be ill taken by any, but rather friendly accepted, especially by the true Sons of* Urania.]

CHAP. XXIII.

Brief Rules how to Compute the Stars of Planets Southing, Rising, and Setting in any Latitude.

I. *For their Southing*] To the estimate time of the Planets Southing (which you may neerly find by a Table of Houses) compute his true Longitude and Latitude, then by the Rules for that purpose, (either by Trigonometry or by Tables) find the RA of that point, so also the ☉'s R. A for the same time, lastly subtract the ☉s R. A from the R.A of the Planet or star, (by adding the circle where there is occasion) and the remainder converted into time is the time of the Planets southing; if the remainder is under 12 hours the time is after noon, if more than 12, substract 12 from thence, and the residue is the time after midnight or in the morning; or instead of substracting the ☉'s R A, add the complement thereof to 360 d. to the R A of the Star, and the sum converted into time is the true time of Southing aforesaid.

II. *For their Rising*] (I.) To the estimate time of the Planets rising, get his Oblique Ascension (as shall be taught in this Book) and also the ☉s R A for the same time. (2.) From the Obliq. Asc, of the star or planet increased by a circle (if need require) subtract the ☉s R A. Lastly, if the remainder exceed 90 d. substract 90 d. from it, if it be less than 90 d. add thereunto 270 d. this sum or remainder thus made couverted into time, is the true Astronomical time of the Planets or Stars rising required.

III. *To find the time of a Planets Setting*] Having the estimate time, and the true longitude and latitude of the Planet for that time; find the Oblique Ascension of the opposite point, with opposite latitude, (always under the latitude of your place) and having the ☉s Right Ascension for that time also, proceed in all respects as you did in computing his Rising, &c.

Note that by reason of parallax and refraction, the ☽ always appears to our sight to rise later and set sooner than really she doth, and contrarily, all the planets and stars do seem to rise sooner and set later, by the quantity of 2 m. of an hours.

To conclude, let the young Artist take notice, that having the fixed Stars longitude truly rectified for the year, he may proceed to find their Risings, Southings and Settings, as is before shewed in the Planets; for there is no need of the estimate time first known in them, by reason their annual progression in longitude is inconsiderable, (viz.) about 50 or 52 Seconds; but in the ☽ and the rest of the Planets the estimate time is absolutely necassary, because of their swift diurnal motion (most of them) that thereby their true places may be found to that time, and consequently their Ascensions and Discensions, &c.

Examples are needless here, because this will be Exemplified in effect, in the Examples of Directions of a Nativity at large, in the Third Part of this Book. Howbeit, to make these Rules the more plain to the Learner, I shall illustrate the master in the Rising, Southing and Setting of Certain Fixed Stars, as followeth.

A most useful Table, by which may be known the Rising, Southing, and Setting, (and consequently the Hour of the Night;) the Amplitude, the Meridian Altitude, and Magnitude of 32 of the more principal Fixed Stars, to be used with the Table of the Sun's *Right Ascension in time.*

Names of Starrs.	Rise. H. M.	South. H. M.	Sets H. M.	Mer Alt.	Amplitud	Magnit
The bright Star of the Whales Tayl	20 18	0 27	4 34	18	34	2
The Girdle of *Andromeda*	14 50	0 51	10 52	72	69	2
The former Hora of *Ariet*.	17 58	1 35	9 12	55	30	0
The South Foot of *Andromeda*.	Rise not	1 43	Sets not	88	0	2
The Head of *Medusa*.	Rise not	2 46	Sets not	77	0	3
The bright Star in *Perseus* Side.	Rise not	2 59	Sets not	86	0	2
The Bright Star of the 7 Stars.	19 15	3 27	11 41	61	40	5
The Bull's Eye, or *Aldebaran*.	20 53	4 17	11 43	53	26	1
The Goat.	Rise not	4 52	Sets not	83	0	0
The Left Foot of *Orion*.	23 45	4 58	10 13	29	14	1
The North Home of *Taurus*.	20 8	5 5	14 2	66	51	0
The Former Shoulder of *Orion*.	22 36	5 7	11 38	44	10	2
The Middle Star in *Orion*'s Girdle.	23 28	5 19	11 12	36	2	2
The Right Shoulder of *Auriga*.	Rise not	5 35	Sets not	83	0	0
The Greater Dogg-Star.	1 59	6 30	12 1	21	27	1
Castor.	21 29	7 13	16 57	70	62	2
The Lesser Dogg-Star.	0 50	7 22	13 54	44	10	2
Pollux.	22 23	7 25	16 26	66	52	2
The Lyons Heart.	4 37	9 50	17 4	51	23	1
The Lyons Tayl.	6 2	11 32	19 2	54	28	1
The Virgins Girdle.	7 10	12 38	19 6	43	9	0
The Virgins Spike.	9 57	13 7	18 18	28	15	1
Arcturus.	2 21	14 0	22 0	59	36	1
The South Ballance.	6 51	14 32	19 14	23	24	2
The North Ballance.	9 41	14 59	20 17	30	13	2
The Scorpions Heart *Antares*.	12 44	16 9	19 34	12	45	1
The Head of *Hercules*.	9 39	16 59	0 19	53	25	0
The Bright Star of the Harp.	Rise not	18 24	Sets not	76	0	1
The Swans Tayl.	Rise not	20 30	Sets not	82	0	2
Fomahant *Aquarius*.	20 8	22 39	1 10	6	59	1
The First Star in *Pegasus* Wing.	15 36	22 48	6 0	51	22	2
The Head of *Andromeda*.	15 4	23 51	8 39	65	48	2

The Explanation an Use of the Table of Rising, Southing, and Setting of 32 Eminent Fixed Stars.

I. In the first Column you have the Names of 22 more Principal Fixed Stars.

In the second Column you have the Oblique Ascention of those Stars.

In the third Column you have their Right Ascention, and in the fourth Column their Oblique Discention, all in Hours and Minutes: Now if you substract the ☉'s Right Ascention in time, (a Table where of is placed at the bginning of the Schemes) from the Stars oblique Ascension, the reaminder will be the time of their Risings: Substract also the ☉'s Right Ascension for the day given from the Right Ascension of the Stars, and the remainder will be the time of their Southing: And if you substract the ☉'s Right Ascension from the Stars Oblique Descentions, the Remainder is the time of their Setting.

II. The fifth Column contains the Meridian Altitude of those Stars. The Sixth contains their Amplitudes; *viz.* the degrees of the Horizon whereon they Rise and Set from the East and West: Those Stars whose Meridian Altitudes are more than the Equinoctial Hight: [*which here is about 38 degrees; the Complement of the Latitude of 52 degrees, being neer the midst of England, and therefore may indifferently serve for any part of the same without sensible Errour.*] their Amplitude is toward the North, and those Stars whose Meridian Altitudes are less than the AEquinoctial Height, their Amplitude is towards the South part of the Horizon. The last Column shews their Magnitude, compared with the Globe of the Earth; A Star of the first Magnitude is greater than the Earth 68 tiems; a Star of the second Magnitude exceedeth the Earth 28 times; and a Star of the third Magnitude is greater than the Earth 11 times.

III. *Examples of the Use of the Table.* Suppose that upon the 15*th* day of *July* 1675 I desire to know when the *Scorpions Heart* Riseth, Southeth, and Setteth. (I.) O. veragainst the 15 day of *July* (in the Table of the ☉'s Right Ascension appertaining to the Schems) I find 8 hours and 19 minutes, which subtracted from the oblique Ascension of the *Scorpions Heart* 12h. 44m. there remains 4h. 25m. being the time of that Star's Rising; The Right Ascension of the same Star is 16h. and 9m.; from which substract 8h. 19m. the ☉'s right Ascension, and the remainder 7h. 50m. is the time of the Stars coming to the Meridian or SouthPoint; the oblique Descention of that Star (under the Title Set) is 19h. 34m. from which subtract 8h. 19m., and the remainde 11h. and 15m. is the time of that Star's Setting. His Meridian Altitude is 12d. being less than the Aequinoctial height; therefore his Amplitude 15 degrees in the Table must be toward the South.

When the Ascention or Descention of the Stars are less than the ☉'s right Ascention, you are to add 24 h. thereunto that Substraction may be made.

IV. When the Remainder is less than 12 h. (as in the Example) it shews the time after Noon; but when the Remainder is more than 12 hours, cast away 12 hours, and the Residue is the time after midnight, or in the Morning. The same work may be performed for the Planets, *&c.*

Usus Optimus Magister.

Here ENDS the Second PART.

Clavis Astrologiae Elimata:
OR A
KEY to the whole ART
OF
ASTROLOGY
New Fil'd and Polished.

The Third PART.

CONTAINING.

The Genethliacal Part of Astrology.

Exactly
Performing, and briefly Comprehending the whole
Doctrine of *Directions*; and *Judgment* of *Nativities*.

Wherein is shewed (by an exact Method) the manner of their Rectification several wayes: together, with their precize Calculation onely by Proportions in *Trigonometry*.

Also, how to set a Scheme Artificially the *Rational* way, and whatsoever is Requisite in Directing Significtors to their several Promittors; with some varieties therein, not hitherto published; and divers useful Tables Added in this Second Impression.

With Annual Revolutions and the manner of their Directions, *&c*. Togehter how to Judge the General Fate of the Native: and Consequently point out the most Prosperous or Dangerous times that may probably happen in the whole Course of Mans Life.

By Henry Coley Philomat.

Great is the Dignity *of* Souls, *that every man from his first Rising and Appearing under the Stars in his* Nativity, *hath an Angel Delegated to him for his Custody or Safety.* St. *Hierom* on *Mat.* 18. 10.

From hence, you Carping Momus, *hence begon,*
To your deserved Center, Acheron*:*
Keep Court with Pluto *by the* Stygian Lake*;*
'Tis not for you of Heaven to partake,
Whose sordid Minds tend to your Mother Earth,
A Badge of your Extraction and first Birth;
Whose Viperous Tongues abuse the Sons of Art,
When Knowledge to the Blear-ey'd world the' impart,
Let all such know that 'tis not my Intent,
To teach fine Language to the Eloquent,
Or to the Learned Skill; nor to conduct
More able Guides in Art: but to Instruct
The More Unskilful, and Young Artists Guide
To Paths of Knowledge, which they never try'd:
   For only such who have not known the way
   To this Most Sublime Skill, I make this KEY.

THE PREFACE TO THE READER.

THIS most Excellent and useful Part of Astrology, *admits of many varietie, and hath divers Intricate turnings therein, therefore it ought the more to be facilitated, and explained; which is the chiefest end aimed at in the following Discourse for the encouragement of such Ingenious Persons that are lovers of this kind of Learning.*

The Calculation of Nativities is a Subject that hath been of good esteem with many learned Persons, in former Ages: and there are divers able Men now living, that for the usefulness thereof, and the truth they have found by Experience therein, have as high thoughts of the same; Although *in some* Nativities *the Accidents and Directions have not (perhaps) so nearly agreed and concurred together as was expected. This may be for want of a due* Correction, *and it is no easie matter for an Artist to verifie the* Ascendant *of a* Nativity: *For if a* Nativity *be carefully Rectified; and directed exactly, the* Accidents *that Occur to the Native, Rarely fail to* Correspond *with the* Directions, *and many times take place so punctually, even to admiration, to confirm the truth of this, we have had many* eminent Examples, *both Antient and Modern which sufficiently manifest the excellency of this* Doctrine.

And Note that the usual Omission of the odd Minutes adhering to the Pole of Position (notwithstanding the uncertainty of the Planets places*) may instead of helping, make the errour the greater. The* Transits and Revolutions *ought also to be considered herein, which are truly called the Harbingers of a Direction; and the learned Sir* Christopher Heydon *affirms,* That events proper to Men, may be both Anticipated and continued before, or beyond a Direction. *Def. Astro. p.* 412. *unto which I may add, that a Rational measure of time ought to be chosen, which is of great Concernment in the matter of Directions; of which I shall speak farther in its proper place,*

The Doctrine of Directions *is Copiously handled by several Learned Men, especially Forreign Authors, amongst the which the Learned* Argolus *is accounted the Best, who hath taken great pains to Calculate Tables* (viz. *his* Primum Mobile) *which compleatly performs the work; Neither are those of* Regiomontanus *much inferiour to the former, and unto these famous Men the World is exceedingly beholding; who before were much at a loss, and went a tedious obscure way about to perform this work.*

But here I have endeavoured to perform this same with all the plainness and perspecuity that may be; (and no less exact and easie than by the former Authors) only by the help of a Canon of Artificial Sines and Tangents *frequently to be had at a small price; (By which the Doctrine of spherical Triangles is with much ease performed) to which I must refer the Ingenious Artist (and I suppose there are few lovers of Art, but are already furnished with them) Those Tables being the Foundation of all Astronomical Tables of Directions; and by them alone, are the other Calculated from the Globe, or Sphere. I shall not only give the proportions and operations, but also the Figures of the Sphere, wherein the several Triangles lye, presupposing the Artist already grounded therein.*

If I might advise, I would have those that desire to be curious in this Doctrine, *to* Calculate *the Planets places* (de novo) *from the latest and best* Astronomical Tables, *and so lay the Foundation of their work as sure as may be; for I think it not safe to trust to some* Ephemerides *which want of that* Exactness *as may be expected, and is required herein; and therefore to supply all those that are not yet provided, I have hereunto added the* Rudolphine Tables *to perform the work, which Tables have hitherto had as good esteem in the World as any Tables of that kind.*

This is the Subject that was chiefly intended in this work; I hope my endeavours in this kind may be a motive to stir up some more able, to publish their experience in this Learning for the honour of Art; what I have done I should rather have seen performed by some other, but herein I hope I shall prejudice no Person, since what is written, was intended for the general good of all, The first Rudiments and Principles, to initiate Tyro's and this Doctrine of Directions by Trigonometry, for those that have made some progress in things of this Nature, both which I have contracted into this small Volumn that it might be a low prized, portable Companion to the Sons of Art. And farther I may inform the Reader that in this second Impression I have made considerable Additions, and Alterations as will most plainly appear to any Person that has perused the former Book; as also added apt Demonstrations to inform the Fancy, that Students may understand the ground and reasons of their operations (which too many are yet ignorant of) in all which I have laboured to express the Rules (and operations) with as much plainness as the Subject will bear, so that I hope 'twill prove very intelligible to the meanest Capacity whose Genius prompts and leads him to this kind of Contemplation. Thus wishing my self ready at hand to resolve what doubts may be objected, I remain a Friend to all Lovers of Urania.

H. C.

CHAP. I.

A Compendium of Trigonometry.

SECT. I.

Definitions, Affections, and Axiomes of Spherical Triangles, &c.

I. A Spherical Triangle is a Figure consisting of three Arches of the greatest Circles upon the superficies of a Globe, or Sphere; every one being less than a Semicircle.

II. A great Circle is that which divideth the Sphere, or Globe, into two equal parts; The *Horizon, Meridian, Ecliptick,* and *Aequinoctial,* &c. are all great Circles; and there must be three Arches of these Circles (or any other which bisect the Globe into two equal parts) to make a spherical Triangle, and every one of these Arches severally must be less than a Semicircle.

III. A spherical Angle is that which is contained by two Arches of the greatest Circles upon the Superficies of the Globe, intersecting one another; and Angles made by the Intersection of two little Circles, or of a little Circle with a great one, there is no notice taken of in the Doctrine of Trigonometry.

IV. A spherical Angle is measured by the Arch of a great Circle discribed from the Angular point between the sides or the Angles, those sides being continued to Quadrants, and is either right, or oblique Angled.

V. A right Angled spherical Triangle, is that which hath one right Angle at least, and an oblique spherical Triangle is either Obtuse, or Acute; the Acute Angled Triangle hath all its Angles Acute; the Obtuse Angled spherical Trianble hath all its Angles either Obtuse, or Acute, and Obtuse, *viz.* mixt.

VI. The Sides of a spherical Triangle may be turned into Angles, and the Angles into Sides, the Complements of the greatest Side, or greatest Angle being taken in each Conversion.

VII. In right Angled spherical Triangles, there are but five of the six parts (*viz.* the three Sides, and three Angles) which crime into Question, *viz.* the three Sides, and two Acute Angles; because the third being a right Angle, or 90 deg. is always known: of these five parts, any two being given, the rest may be found as shall be shewed.

VIII. In right Angled spherical Triangles there are sixteen Problems, or Cases; six for finding the Legs, or Sides, four for the Hypotenusa, and six for the Angles. And in Oblique Triangles there are only twelve Cases, in all twenty eight, as shall be exemplified; The sixteen cases of right Angled spherical Triangles, and ten of the Oblique Angular Triangles may be resolved by these two following Axiomes.

[Axiome I.] *In all spherical right Angled Triangles, having the same Acute Angle at the Base, the Sines of the Hypothenusas are proportional to the Sines of their Perpendiculars.*

[Axiome II.] *In all spherical (Right or) Rectanguled Triangles, having the same Acute Angle at the Base, the Sines of the Bases and Tangents of the Perpendiculars are proportional.*

IX. Now that all the Cases of a right Angled spherical Triangle may be resolved by these two *Axiomes*, the several parts of the spherical Triangle must sometimes be continued to Quadrants (as may be seen in the Type, or Diagram) that thereby the Angles may be turned into Sides, the Hypotenusa's into Bases and Perpendiculars, and the contrary.

X. Hence the proportions as to the parts of the given Triangle, instead of Sines do sometimes fall in Co-sines, and instead of Tangents sometimes in Co-tangents.

XI. Now those Conversions which for the most part change their proportion, are usually noted with their Complements, that is, both the *Acute Angles,* and the *Hypotenusa*; but the Sides which contain the right Angle are not so noted. *As for Example in the Diagram in the right Angled spherical Triangle A B C: the Angle C is ac-*

counted a Complement, G H the Complement to H Q, being the measure thereof; so likewise the Acute Angle A is accounted a Complement, and is measured by the Arch D E, the Complement of E R to a Quadrant; and the Hypotenusa, C A is a Complement of the Arch C E.

XII. The right Angle is not reckoned amongst the Circular parts, and therefore the two sides which do contain it are supposed to be joyned together; now each of these five Circular parts may by supposition be made the middle part, and then the two Circular parts which are next to that middle part are called Conjunct Extreams; and the two other that lye remote from the middle part assumed, are called the Extreams Disjunct. As for Example in the Triangle A B C. If Complement A C be made the middle part, then Compl. A and Compl. C are the Conjoyned Extreams; and the Sides A B, and B C are the Disjoyned Extreams; and so of the rest as they are plainly laid down as followeth according to the Catholique proposition of the *Lord Nepair. Note that signifies a Sine,* t *or* T *a Tangent,* R *Radius,* + *more, or Addition,* - *less, or Substraction,* = *equal to* cs, *or* sc; *Sine Complement, or Cosine;* cT, *or* tc *Tangent Comp. or Co tangent.*

XIII. Middle Part I. Extream Conjunct.   Analogismes

Aequality.

1   S. AB+Rx=CT.A.+t BC. As   ct. A:Rx::S. AB:t BC.
2   CS.A+Rx=CT.A.C.+t.AB.   As   ct AC:Rx::Sc. A:t AB.
3   CS.AC+Rx=CT. A.+CTC.   As   ct A:Rx::Sc. Ac:ctC.
4   CS.C+Rx=CT. AC+TBC.   As   ct AC:Rx::Sc C: t BC.
5   S. BC+Rx=CT. C+T. AB.   As   ct. C:Rx::S.B.C:t AB.

Middle Part II. Extreme Disjunct.   Analogismes

Aequality.

1   S AB+Rx=SAC+S.C.   As   s ACRx:: S. AB:t.C.
2   CSA +Rx= SC.+cs BC.   As   s. C:Rx::cs A: cs BC.
3   CSAC+Rx= cs AB+cs BC.   As   cs. AB:R::cs AC: cs BC
4   CS. C+Rx= SA+cs AB.   As   S. A.:Rx::cs C: cs AB.
5   CS. BC+Rx=SA+S. AC   As   S.A: Rx::S BC: S AB.

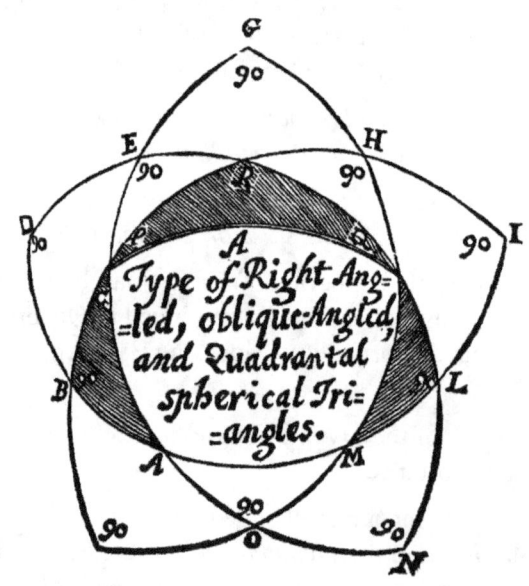

XIV. Having thus distinguished the Five Circular parts of the Triangle, with the Aequality and proportions or Analogismes thereof grounded upon the *Lord Nepairs* universal Proposition which is this, *viz*. [*The Sine of the middle Part and Radius are Reciprocally proportionable with the Tangents of the Extreams Conjunct, and the Cosines of the Extreams Disjunct*] That is as the Radius to the Tangent of one Extream Conjunct, so is the Tangent of the other Extreams Conjunct to the Sine of the middle Part. And as the Radius to the Cosine of one Extream Disjuncts, so is the Cosine of the other Extream Disjunct to the Sine of the middle Part, &c. I shall next explain the aforesaid AEqualities of the Parts of a right Angled spherical Triangle, and then proceed to Examples.

XV. In a right Angled spherical Triangle there is usually two things given, besides the right Angle to find out any of the other Parts thereof; This may be easily performed from the former Work, or Table, if you have but the middle Part which is readily obtained thus, *viz*. If the three things given and required lye together, and are not separated neither by Side or Angle (excepting the right Angle) then the middlemost part is the middle part desired.

XVI. But if any of the three parts (that is the two parts given) besides the right Angle,) and the part required) be disjoyned by a Side or Angle, then that very remote or separated part is the middle part sought: with which enter the Table appertaining to the 13*th*. hereof, and if you require an Extream Conjunct use the first of those Tables (marking your Triangle with the same Letters as in the following Examples) but if you require an Extream Disjunct, then make use of the second of those Tables, and you have therein both the AEquality of the Parts of your Triangle, and the proportion to work by with your Canon of Sines and Tangents, as for Example.

XVII. Suppose in the right Angled spherical Triangle, A, B, C. you have given the Side or Leg, A, B. and the Angle, A,. to find the Side, C, B. now in regard the Parts given & that required lye all together, & are not separated, or disjoyned (but by the right Angle, B. which is accounted no separation) I conclude the Side, A, B, to be the middle part, and C, B, the Side required a Conjunct, or adjacent Extream, I therefore enter the first Table with A, B, under the middle Part, and I find it thus, S A B +Rx = ct A+ t B C, *That is the Sine of the middle Part A, B, added to Radius is equal to the Co-tangent of the Angle A, added to the Tangent of the Side B, C, the Side required*. Therefore if from the Sine of the Side, A, B, and Radius added, I subtract the Co-tangent of the Angle A, the remainder is the Tangent of the Side B, C, sought; *Et sio de certeris*. &c.

XVIII. Or if you desire to put that Equation into proportion, observe this Rule, B, C, is required, therefore I put that part, *viz*. The Co-tangent of A. (which is joyned on the same side of the AEquation in the *first place*, and either the Sine A, B, or Radius, (which stand on the other side of the AEquation) in the second and third places, and the part required in the fourth place, thus, As the *ct* A:R::*s*,AB:t, BC, as in the Table under the Title Analogismes, understand the same in the rest; and thus the 16 Cases of right Angled spherical Triangles may most easily be resolved, as also ten of the Oblique by the help of a Perpendicular, which ought to be let fall thus.

XIX. In every Oblique spherical Triangle if a Perpendicular be let fall it reduces the said Oblique Triangle into two right Angled Triangles; which Perpendicular ought to be so let fall as two of the given things must remain in one of the right Angled Triangles; if the Perpendicular fall within the Triangle it must fall from the Obtuse Angle, if it fall without it must fall from one of the Acute Angles upon one of the sides of the Obtuse Angle continued.

XX. Note, that if the middle Part, or either of the Extreams Conjunct be noted with its Complement in the Circular parts of the Triangle instead of the Sine, or Tangent you are to use the Cosine or Co-tangent; and if either of the Extreams Disjunct be noted by its Complement in the Circular parts of the Triangle instead of the Cosine use the Sine of such an Extream Disjunct, according as you find them express'd in the foregoing Table.

[*Axiome* III.] In all spherical Triangles the Sines of their Sides are in Direct proportion to the Sines of their opposite Angles, and the contrary.

[*Axiome* IV.] As the Sine of half the Sum of the Sides to the Sine of half their difference, so is the Co-tangent of half the contained Angle to the Tangent of half the difference of the other Angles.

Again. As the Cosine of half the Sum of the Sides to the Cosine of half their difference, so is the Co-tangent of half the contained Angle, to the Tangent of half the Sum of the other Angles.

[*Axiome* V.] As the Sine of half the Sum of two Angles to the Sine of half their difference, so is the Tangent of half the Interjacent Side, to the Tangent of half the difference of the other Sides.

Again. As the Cosine of half the Sum of the Angles, to the Cosine of half their difference; so is the Tangent of half the Interjacent Side, to the Tangent of half the Sum of the other Sides.

[*Axiome* VI.] As the Rectangle of the Sines of the containing Sides, to the square of the Radius; so is the Rectangle of the Sines of half the Sum of the three Sides, and of the difference of the Base therefrom, to the square of the Cosine of half the Angle sought. Examples of all the Cases of Right Angled and Oblique spherical Triangles follow.

Here followeth Examples of the twenty eight Cases of spherical Triangles.

SECT. II.

A synopsis of the Solution of the sixteen Cases of a Right Angled spherical Triangles.

Given		Requir'd	Theoremes.	Operat.	Case
Ang.	A C	Side AC	To the Cotangent 68°. 15'. Ang. C. Add Cotangent 23°. 3'. Ang. A. Their Sum—R is the cs of 23°. 26'. AC	960092 <u>1036169</u> 996261	I
Ang.	A C	Side CB	From the Co.s. of 23°. 30'. Ang. A. + Rx Subtract the Sine of 68°. 15'. Ang. C. There remains the cs of C B, 9°. 7'.	1996239 <u>996792</u> 999447	II
Side Ang.	AC A	Ang. C	From the Co.s. of AC 23°. 26'. + R. Subtract Co. T of A. 23°. 30'. The remainder is the Co.T. of C. 68.15	1996261 <u>1036169</u> 90009	III
Ang. Side	A AC	Side CB	To the s. of 23°. 26'. The Side A C. Add the s. of 23°. 30'. The Ang. A. Their sum—Rx is the s. of CB, 9°. 8'.	959953 <u>960069</u> 920022	IV
Ang. Side	A AC	Side AB	From the cs of 23°. 30'. Ang. A. + R. Substract the CT. of 23°. 36'. AC. There remains the Ta. of 21°. 41'. AB	1996239 <u>1036308</u> 959931	V
Ang. Side	A CB	Ang. C.	From the cs. Of 23°, 30'. Ang. A + R. Substract the cs of CB 9°. 7'. There remains the s of 68°. 15'. Ang. C	1996239 <u>999447</u> 996799	VI
Ang. Side	A CB	Side AC	From the s. of 9°. 7'. BC+R. Substract the s. of 23°. 30'. Ang. A. There remains s. 23°. 25'. AC.	1919987 <u>960069</u> 959918	VII
Ang. Side	A CB	Side AB	To the CT. of 23°. 30'. Ang. A. Add the Ta. Of CB. 9°. 7'. Their Sum—R is the s 21°. 40'. AB.	103616 <u>920540</u> 956709	VIII
			Note, That if you take the Arithmetic Complement of the Number to be Substracted, and add it to the other Number abating Radius, the Work wil be the same.		

Given	Requir'd	Theoremes.	Operat.	Case
Ang. A Side AB	Ang. C.	To the s. of 23°. 30'. Ang. A Add the cs. of 21°. 40'. Side AB The Sum is the cs of the Ang. C. 68.15	960069 996812 956881	IX
Ang. A Side AB	Side AC	From the cs. Of 23°. 30'. Ang. A + R Substract Ta. 21°. 41'. AB Remains the Co. T. of 23°. 27'. AC.	1996239 959945 1036294	X
Ang. A Side AB	Side CB	From the s. of AB. 21°. 41'. + Rx Substract the c. Ta. of 23°. 30'. Ang. A. There remains the Ta. 9°. 7'. Side CB	1956758 1036169 920389	XI
Side AC Side CB	Ang. A	From the s. of 9°. 7'. + Rx Side CB Substract the s. of 23°. 26'. Side AC There remains the s. 23°. 30'. Ang. A	1919988 959953 960035	XII
Side AC Side CB	Ang. C	To the Cotangent of AC 23°. 26'. Add the Tangent of CB 9°. 7'. The Sum - R is the cs of 68°. 15'. Ang. c	1036308 920540 956848	XIII.
Side AC Side CB	Side AB	From the cs. Of AC. 23°. 26'. + Radius Substract the cs. of CB. 9°. 7'. Remains the cs. of Ab. 21°. 41'.	1996261 999447 996814	XIV
Side AB Side BC	Ang. C	From the s. of CB, 9°. 7'. and Rx Substract the Tang. of AB. 21°. 41'. Remains the c T. of C. 68°. 15'.	1919987 959945 960042	XV
Side AB Side CB	Side AC	To the Co. s. of 21°. 41'. AB. Add the cs. of 9°. 7'. CB. The Sum less Rx cs. 23°. 27'. Side AC	996812 999447 996259	XVI
		Note, that the Sine of an Arch greater then 90 deg. or a Quadrant is the Cosine of the Excess above a Quadrant, and the Cosines of the same parts exceeding a Quadrant are the Sines of the Excess; understand the same in Tangents also this will be of use in Quadrantal Triangles.		

SECT III.

The Calculation of the several Cases of Oblique spherical Triangles.

Given	Requir'	Theoremes.	Operat.
P Q R Q R P Q Case 1	By Ax. 3 P R Q obtuse	To the Arith. Comp. of the s. RS, 38°. 28'. Add the s. of Ang. P, 37°, 3'. And the s. of the Side PQ, 69°. 47'. Their Sum—R is the Sine of PRQ 114°. 39	020617 977996 <u>997238</u> 995851
P R Q P Q R P Q Case 2	P R less then a Q t	To the s. of the Ang. R 114°. 38'. Comp Add the s. of P Q, 69°. 47'. (Arith And the S. of Q, 45°.0'. The Sum—Rx is the s of PR. 46°. 53'.	004144 997238 <u>984948</u> 906330
R P Q P Q P R Case 3	P R Q P Q R	1. To the Arith. Comp. of the s. of the ½ Sum of PQ, and PR, *viz.* 58°. 20'. Add the s of their ½ Diff. 11°. 27'. And the Tang. Comp. of ½ the Ang. P18.31 And the Sum is the Tang. of ½ the Diff. of the Ang: R & Q, 34°. 51'. (abating Rad.)	007001 929779 <u>1047506</u> 98286
By Ax. 4		2. To the Arith. Comp. of the cs.of the Sum of the Sides PQ & PR, 58°. 20'. Add the cs. of ½ the Diff. Of the Sides 11.27 And the cT. of ½ the Ang. P. 18°. 31'. The Sum will be the c TA. of ½ the Sum of the Angles, R & Q, 79°. 49'.	027986 <u>99127</u> 1047406 1074619

Having by the Operation found ½ Sum, and ½ difference of the Angles, if you add the ½ difference to that ½ Sum, you have the greater Angle PRQ. But if from the ½ Sum you Substract the ½ difference there remains the lesser Angle. PQR required.

And observe if the Sum of the two containing Sides exceed 180d. then Substract each side from 180d. or a Semicircle, and proceed with those Remainders, as with the Sides given in the aforesaid Example the Operation produces the Complements to 180 d. of the Angles enquired.

The Calculation of the several Cases of Ob. Sph. Triangles.			
Given	Requir'd	Theoremes.	Operat.
R P Q P R Q P R Case 4	P Q R Q	1. To the Arith. Compt. of the s of the ½ sum of the ang. P & R. 82° 9' Add the s. of ½ the D. of those A. 55° 46' Also the Ta. of ½ P R 40° 55' And the sum is the Ta. of ½ the Diff. of the sides PQ & RQ 35°. 52'.—Rad.	000409 991738 993787 985937
By Ax. 5.	74d. 21m	2. To the Ar. Compt. of the sc. of ½ the sum of the Ang. P&R 82°. 9'. Add the sc. of ½ the D. of the A. 55° 46' Also the Ta. of ½ P R 40° 55'. And the sum will be the Tan. of ½ the sum of the Sides PQ & RQ—Rad.	086461 975017 993789 1055267

Thus by the operation having obtained the ½ sum, and ½ Difference of the Sides, add them together you have the greater Side; but the ½ Difference Subtracted, leaves the lesser Side required.

And you are to Note, that if the Sum of the Angles exceed 180 deg., then Substract each Angle from 180 deg. and proceed in Operaiton with the Remainder, which will produce the Complement of each side to a Semi-circle. [This Case may also be resolved by the Cadence of a Perpendicular, as by the proportions for finding the Cusps of the Houses, (which is afterwards Inserted,) doth appear.]

Given	Requir'd	Theoremes.	Operat.
P R R Q Case 5	P Q Less than a Quadr.	1. To the Ar. Com. Of the s. PR 46° 53' Add The s. of the Ang. Q 45° 05' Add The s. of the Side RQ 38° 28' Their sum is the s. of the Ang. P 37° 3'	013670 984948 979383 987001
	By Axiom 3 & 5	2. To the Ar. Com. ½ of the Diff. of the angles P and R 3° 58' Add the s. of the ½ sum of the A. 41° 1' And the Ta. of ½ the Diff. of the Sides PR and RQ 4° 12' abating Rad. And the sum is the Ta. of ½ PQ 34° 52' This 34° 52' being doubled makes 69° 44'. The Side PQ required.	16001 981709 886090 984303

| The Calculation of the several Cases of Ob. Sph. Triangles. ||||
Given	Requir'd	Theoremes.	Operat.
R P Q P Q R R Q Case 6.	P R Q Obtuse	1. To the Com. Ar. S. of An. P 37° 3' Add the s. of RQ—38° 28' And the s. of PQR 45° 00' Their sum is the s. of the side PR 46° 53'	022004 997383 984915 986335
	By Axiom 3 & 4	2. To the Ar. Com. of the s. of the ½ sum of the sides PR & QR 4°. 12'. Add the s of ½ the sum of the sides 42° 40' And the Ta ½ D. of the A. P&Q 3° 58' Their sum is the ct. of ½ the An. R 57° 19'. abating Radius, the thing required.	113527 983106 884100 980733
		This 57° 19' doubled, *viz.* 114° 38' is the Angle R required.	
P Q R P Q P R Case 7	R P Q Acute By Axiom 3 & 4	1. To the Arith. Comp. S. PR 81° 50' Add the s. of P Q R 45° 0' Add the s. of PQ 110° 13' Co. to 180° Their sum is the s. of PQR 137° 55'	000443 984948 997230 982629
		2. To the s. of the ½ the D. of the sides PQ, & PR, 14° 11' Comp. Arith Add the s. of ½ the sum of the sides 96° 1' And the Ta. of ½ the Diff. of the Ang. R and A 46° 27' Their sum is the ct. of ½ RPQ required, *viz.* 13° 11' which doubled, makes 26° 22' the Angle P required.	061079 999760 1002199 1063038

[*Note that the Letter D. stand for Difference, the Letter A. for Angles, and Co. for Complement.*]

| The Calculation of the several Cases of Ob. Sph. Triangles. ||||
Given	Requir'd	Theoremes.	Operat.

P Q R
R P Q
R Q
 	
Case 8
	P Q
	Less
	than a
	Quadr.
	
	By Axiom
	3 & 5
		1. To the Ar. Of Com. of s. RPQ 37° 3'
		Add The s. of R Q 38°. 28'.
		Add The s. of P Q R 45°. 0'.
		The sum is the s. of P R 46°. 53'.
		
		2. To the s. of ½ the Diff. of the Ang.
		   P & Q 3°. 58'. Compt. Arith.
		Add the s. of ½ the sum of the Angles, 41°. 01'
		And the Tang. of ½ the Diff of the Sides P R,
		   and R Q 4° 12'.
		Their sum Rx is the Tang. of ½ P Q 34°. 52'.
		   required, which doubled, produces 69°. 44'.
		   PQ the side sought.
			023003
			979383
			984948
			986338
			
			116005
			
			981709
			
			886590
			984304

P R Q P R R Q Case 9 PQ By the Catholick Proposition and a supposed Perpend. for this Case & the next following.		1. To the sc. of P R Q 137° 55' &c. Add the Ta. of R Q 38°. 28'. Their sum abating Rad. Is the Tangent of a fourth Ark 30° 31'. *Note that if the Angles given contained between the two Sides given be less than a Quadrant, then Substract this fourth Ark from the greater side, but if it be greater than 90 degrees as here, then Subtact it from the Complement of the greater side of 180 degrees, the Remainder called a Reserved Arch. Here 67 degrees 39 minutes.*	987050 990009 977059

		2. The Comp. Arith. of the fourth
		   Arch *viz.* 30 deg. 31 min.
		Add the cs. of this Reserved Ark 67° 39'
		And the cs. of the lesser side 38°. 28'.
		The sum is the cs. of the Compt. to 180° of
		   the side Required P Q 69°. 47'. abating Rad.
		   Viz. 110°. 13'.
			006476
			
			958008
			989174
			
			953858

The Calculation of the several Cases of Ob. Sph. Triangles.			
Given	Requir'd	Theoremes.	Operat.
P R Q R P Q P R Case 10	P Q R	1. To the cs. of P R the side Interjacent 46°. 53'. Add the Tangent of R P Q the lesser Angle 37°. 3'. The Sum is Ta: of the fourth Arch (abating Rad.) 27°.17'.	983473 <u>987790</u> 971263
Here Note, that if the Side Interjacent between the two given Angles be more than 90 degrees, *then deduct this fourth Ark, from the greater Angle; if less, from the Compt. of the Angle to* 180 degrees, *the Remainder call the Reserved Arch to be used in the next Operation, and here, it found* 38 degrees 4 minutes.			
		2. To the Arith Compt. of the fourth Arch 27°. 17'. Add the cs. of the Reserved Arch 38°. 4'. And the cs. of R P Q the lesser Angle, 27°. 3' The Sum is the cs. of P Q R 45° 0', the Angle Required.	005123 989614 <u>990206</u> 984943
Observe that in the ninth and tenth Cases, the true state or affection of the Required Angle or Side may be determined by the Reserved Arch: For if the Contained Angle, or Interjacent Side be less than 90 degrees, or a Quadrant and the Reserved, or Residual Arch more, or when the contained Angle or Interjacent Side is greater than a Quadrant, and the Reserved Arch less, the Side or Angle Required is greater than a Quadrant or 90 degrees: But in all other Cases less.			

The Calculation of the several Cases of Ob. Sph. Triangles.		
Given	Requir'd	
P Q P R R Q Case 11.	P R Q By Axiome 6.	For ease and speed in this Operation, Add the three Sides given together, and from their halfe Sum substract the Side Opposite to the Angle required. Having so done, to the Arithmetical Complement of the Artificial Sines of the containing Sides, add the Artificial or Logarithme Sine of halfe the Sun and Remainder, and halfe the Sum of these four Sines shall be the Sine Complement of halfe the Angle required: as for Example,
	P R. R Q P Q Sum ½ Sum Remain.	81°. 50'. (The Containing) s. co. ar. 000442 8°. 28'. (Sides Given) s. co. ar. 020616 110° 13' The ½ Sum is 115°. 15' s. 995639 Remainder 5° 2' s <u>894317</u> 230.31 Their Sum 1911014 115.15 5.2 The ½ Sum 955507 Which is the Co-sine of 68 deg. 57 min. And being doubled, makes P R Q 137 deg. 54 min. Required.

Clavis Astrologiae Elimita, The Key to Astrology New Filed

The Calculation of the several Cases of Ob. Sph. Triangles.		
Given	Requir'd	
P R Q P Q R R P Q Case 12.	R Q By Axiome 6.	*This Case is performed by the sixth Axiome, if the Angles be converted into Sides, and the Sides into Angles by taking the Complement of the greatest Angle to 180 deg. or in Semi-circle.* EXAMPLE. *The greatest Angle P R Q is supposed to be* 137 deg. 55 min. *whose Complement to 180 deg. is 42 min., and thus the Angles of this Triangle are Reduced into Sides; as may be seen by the Type or Figure of Spherical Triangles; and now I proceed as before,* viz.

Compt. P R Q ≈ 42° 5'
P Q R ≈ 45° 0'
R P Q ≈ 26° 23'
 	
Sum. ≈ 113.28
 	
½ Sum. 56.44
 	
Remainder 30.21
	The Adjacent Sin. co. ar 017378
	Angles given Sin. co. ar 015051
	½ Sum Sin. 56.44 992227
	Remaind. 20. 21 Sin. 970353
	
	                   Sum 1995009
	
	    Whose ½ Sum is 997504
	
	Which is the Sine Compt. of 10 deg. 15 min.
	this doubled is 28 deg. 30 min. the side
	Q R Required.	

Here ends the 28. Cases of Spherical Triangles.

CHAP. II.

Containing divers useful Precepts fit to be understood by the Industrious Student in order to the Calculation of a Nativity, &c.

SECT. I.

The Explanation and use of a Canon of Artificial Sines and Tangents which every Artist ought to be furnished with.

Because I shall have occasion to make use of those Tables in the following Work, it will be necessary to shew their use, which is briefly thus, viz.

I. Having an Ark, or Angle, of any degree, being given, to find the Artificial *Sine*, or *Tangent* thereof.

When the Number of Degrees are less than 45, you will find the Degrees in the head of the Canon, and the Minutes in the first Column on the left hand signed by the Letter *M* (usually) and just over against those Minutes, and right under the Title [*Sine*] you shall have the Logarithme, or artificial *Sine*; and under the Title [*Tangent*] you shall find the artificial *Tangent* of the Ark, or Angle desired. Thus the Sine of 6d. 12m. is [9033421] and the Tangent of the same Arch is [9035969] and so find any other Arch under 45d. after the same manner.

But if your Arch exceed 45d. seek it at the bottom of the same Table, and the Minutes in the first Column to the right hand, marked usually with a *M*. and just against the Degree and Minute desired in the Common Angle you have the *Sine* and *Tangent* correspondent, thus the Tangent of 58d. 9m is [10,206744] and the Sine of that Arch is [9,929129].

[*Note that if your Ark or Angle given exceed 90d. you are to seek the Complement thereof to 180d. for your Canon exceeds not 90d. (or a Quadrant.)*]

II. To find the deg. and min. answering to any *Sine* or *Tangent* given is but the contrary work; for find out your Number in the Table, (or the nearest) and in the top or bottom you shall have the Degree, and in the first right or left hand Column the Minute correspondent; this is obvious to the nearest Capacity, and therefore needs no more words.

III. The Sine of the *Complement*, or *Tangent Complement* of an Ark, or Angle, is what the given Arch wants of 90d. vulgarly, (and for brevity sake) call Co-sine, and Co-tangent. Thus the *Co-sine* of 21d. 36m. is the Sine of 68d. 24m. viz. [9968378] and the *Co-tangent* of the same Arch [10402384.]

IV. The *Arithmetical Complement* of an Artificial, or Logarithme *Sine*, or *Tangent* is the Remainder of any Logarithme subtracted out of the Logarithme of 10, viz. 10000000, as thus, suppose I would have the Arithmetical Complement of the *Sine* of 25d. 10m. viz. [9,628647] which substracted out of 1 with Cyphers, &c. leaves 0371353 for the Arithmetical Complement of the *Sine*, which is more readily performed thus. Begin at the first Figure to the left hand, and set down the Complement of them severally to 9, only the last towards the right hand unto 10 thus in the aforesaid *Sine* the Complement of 9 is 0, of 6 to 9 is 3, of 2 'tis 7, of 8, 1, of 6,3, of 4,5, and of 7 to 10, 3, which is the same as before.

V. The use that is made of this is briefly thus, in any proportion where three numbers of Sines, or Tangents, are given to find a fourth, 'tis useful to add the 2d. and 3d. together, and from their Sum substract the first Number, and the Remainder is the Logarithme of the 4*th*, required.

But if you take the Arithmetical Complement of the first number, you may add all three together, and their Sum (abating Radius) shall be the Logarithme of the 4*th*., as before.

Example I.

Operation			
	As the *Sine* of 8d.	9,143555	Substract
	to the *Tan.* of 8d.	9,147803	add
	So the *Tan.* 10d. 30m.	9,267969	
	Sum	18,415772	

The Sine of 10d. 48m. here 9272217 *remains. Here from the Sum of the 2d. and 3d. I substract the first Number, and there remains the fourth.*

Example II.

Operation			
	As S 8d. *Comp. Arith.*	C856445	add all
	to the *Tang.* of 8d.	9,147803	3 numbers
	So the *Tan.* 10d. 30m.	9,267969	together
The Sum is the Sine of 10d. 48m. fere		19,272217	*abating Radius.*

Thus you see by taking the Arith. Comp. there is a substraction saved, and the work the same, which is the easiest way, and most fit to be practiced in operation; for by this means you use only addition in all your work, &c.

[*Note that if you enter your Canon with above 90 degrees, you are to take the Complement to* 180d. *if it be less than* 180d. *if more, and less than* 270d. *deduct* 180d. *from your number given; but if more then* 270d. *take Complement thereof to* 360d. *and by this means you will always enter your Canon with a Number less than* 90d. *observe the same Method in the Arch that is produced in operation.*

SECT. II.

How to find the nearest Distance of a Star (or Planet) from the next Aequinoctial, or Solistical point.

It will be very necessary in Astronomical operations, that the Artist should have some Rule, readily to find the distance of a Star, or Planet from the neerest Aequinoctial, or Solstical points, which will be of frequent use in working by a Canon of Sines and Tangents, &c.

I. If you would account from the neerest Aequinoctial point ♈ or ♎ take this Rule.

That if the Star or Planet be in
- ♈ ♎ his longitude
- ♉ ♏ add 30d. to his longitude
- ♊ ♐ add 60d. to his longitude
- ♋ ♑ The *Comp.* of his *long.* to 90d.
- ♌ ♒ Subst. the *long.* 60d. (the residue)
- ♍ ♓ Subst. out of 30m.

is the stars dist. from the next aequinoctial point required.

II. If you would account from the next Solstitial point ♑ or ♋ observe,

That if the Star or Planet be in
- ♈ ♎ the *Comp.* of the *long.* to 90d.
- ♉ ♏ Subst. the *long.* 60d. (the residue)
- ♊ ♐ Subst. out of 30d. the
- ♋ ♑ his present *longitude,*
- ♌ ♒ add 30d. to his *longitude*
- ♍ ♓ add 60 to his *longitude*

is the stars dist from the next Solstitial point.

III. If your Planet be in ♈ ♉ ♊ | ♑ ♒ ♓ the distance found is accounted from ♈ | ♑

If your Planet be in ♎ ♏ ♐ | ♋ ♌ ♍ the distance found is accounted from ♎ | ♋

IV. But to make this the more plain, and easily understood, I have Inserted this following Table, which performs this work by Inspection, if the Premises be but well considered.

A Table shewing the distance of the Degrees of the Signs from the beginning of ♈ or ♎, ♑ or ♋.							
1	2	3	4	5	6	7	8
♈	0	♑	90	♎	0	♋	90
5	5	5	85	5	5	5	85
10	10	10	80	10	10	10	80
15	15	15	75	15	15	15	75
20	20	20	70	20	20	20	70
25	25	25	65	25	25	25	65
30	30	30	60	30	30	30	60
♉	0	♒	0	♏	0	♌	0
5	35	5	35	5	35	5	55
10	40	10	50	10	40	10	50
15	45	15	45	15	45	15	45
20	50	20	40	20	50	20	40
25	55	25	35	25	55	25	35
30	60	30	30	30	60	30	30
♊	0	♓	0	♐	0	♍	0
5	65	5	25	5	65	5	25
10	70	10	20	10	70	10	20
15	75	15	15	15	75	15	15
20	80	20	10	20	80	20	10
25	85	25	5	25	85	25	5
30	90	30	0	30	90	30	0
♋	0	♈	0	♑	0	♎	0

The use of this Table is briefly thus, and first for a Stars distance from the Aequinoctial points.

I. Suppose a Planet is 15d. of ♉ (as in the first Column) he is then 45d. from the beginning of ♈ (noted in the second Column:) so a Planet in 10d. of ♐ noted in the fifth Column is 70d. from the first point of ♎ noted in the sixth Column.

II. Let a Planet be 10d. in ♑ (noted in the third Column) he is 80d. from the first point of ♈ noted in the fourth Column, or a Planet in 20d. of ♋ (noted in the seventh Column) is 70d. from the first point of ♎ noted in the last Column.

III. But if you would know a Stars distance from the beginning of ♋, or ♑; suppose a Planet 10d. in ♒ (as in the third Column) he is 40d. from the first point of ♑ (as in the second Column,) so a Planet in 15d. of ♍ (as in the seventh Column) is 75d. from the beginning of ♋ (noted in the sixth Column.)

IV. Although their distances from the Aequinoctial points are set down but to every 5 degrees, yet you may from those numbers find a stars distance; let his Longitude be what it will, by a mental Addition, or Substraction of your overplus number, in the several Columns. As suppose a Planet in 18d. of ♉ for the which I add 3 to true 15d. (in the first Column) and I also substract 3 from the 45d. in the fourth Column, and his distance is 42d. from the beginning of ♑. *Et sic in aliis.*

[I should not have been so large upon these particulars, but for the sake of Tyro's, and would not willingly leave anything obscure.

In the next place I shall present the Reader with the whole Fabrick, neatly contracted long since into this Platform, by my loving Friend Mr. J. E. (a most excellent Mathematisian) which I have many particulars enlarged and explained to compleat the Work.

SECT. III

Exhibiting a brief Compendium of all the Propositions that are useful in the Doctrine of Directions to be wrought by a Canon of Sines and Tangents only, without reference to the Triangles themselves.

Prop. I. To Convert hours and minutes, &c. into degrees and minutes, &c.

Put a Cypher behind the hours to the right hand, and under them set half the said Sum, and under that one fourth of the minutes and seconds adhering, and the Sum will be the degrees desired.

Example.

Suppose 22h. 24m. 44s. are to be turned into degrees.

	d.	m.	s.
The hours with a Cypher	220	00	00
Half of which is	110	00	00
One fourth of 24m. is	006	00	00
One fourth of 44m. is	000	11	00
The Sum in degrees is	336	11	00

This is a ready way to carry in memory if you have no Table for this purpose at hand.

But because some may affect a Table to perform this, much better, I have also added one hereunto with its Converse Table which are so plain, that there needs no other directions then the bare Titles themselves.

A Table of converting Hours and Minutes of Time, into Degrees and Minutes of the Aequator.					
Hours	Degrees of the Aequator	Min.	Deg. and Min. of the Aequat. D M	Min.	Deg. and Min. of the Aequat. D M
1	15	1	0 15	31	7 45
2	30	2	0 30	32	8 0
3	45	3	0 45	33	8 15
4	60	4	1 0	34	8 30
5	75	5	1 15	35	8 45
6	90	6	1 30	36	9 0
7	105	7	1 45	37	9 15
8	120	8	2 00	38	9 30
9	135	9	2 15	39	9 45
10	150	10	2 30	40	10 0
11	165	11	2 45	41	10 15
12	180	12	3 0	42	10 30
13	195	13	3 15	43	10 45
14	210	14	3 30	44	11 0
15	225	15	3 45	45	11 15
16	240	16	4 0	46	11 30
17	255	17	4 15	47	11 45
18	270	18	4 30	48	12 0
19	285	19	4 45	49	12 15
20	300	20	5 0	50	12 30
21	315	21	5 15	51	12 45
22	330	22	5 30	52	13 0
23	345	23	5 45	53	13 15
24	360	24	6 0	54	13 30
		25	6 15	55	13 45
		26	6 30	56	14 0
		27	6 45	57	14 15
		28	7 0	58	14 30
		29	7 15	59	14 45
		30	7 30	60	15 0
		S	M S	S	M S

A Table of converting Aequinoctial Degrees into Hours and Minutes of Time, and the contrary.							
D	H M		D	H M		D	H M
1	0 4		31	2 4		70	4 40
2	0 8		32	2 8		80	5 20
3	0 12		33	2 12		90	6 0
4	0 16		34	2 16		10	6 40
5	0 20		35	2 20		11	7 20
6	0 24		36	2 24		12	8 0
7	0 28		37	2 28		13	8 40
8	0 32		38	2 32		14	9 20
9	0 36		39	2 36		15	10 0
10	0 40		40	2 40		16	10 40
11	0 44		41	2 44		17	11 20
12	0 48		42	2 48		18	12 0
13	0 52		43	2 52		19	12 40
14	0 56		44	2 56		20	13 20
15	0 60		45	3 0		21	14 0
16	1 4		46	3 4		22	14 40
17	1 8		47	3 8		23	15 20
18	1 12		48	3 12		24	16 0
19	1 16		49	3 16		25	16 40
20	1 20		50	3 20		26	17 20
21	1 24		51	3 24		27	18 0
22	1 28		52	3 28		28	18 40
23	1 32		53	3 32		29	19 20
24	1 36		54	3 36		30	20 0
25	1 40		55	3 40		31	20 40
26	1 44		56	3 44		32	21 20
27	1 48		57	3 48		33	22 0
28	1 52		58	3 52		34	22 40
29	1 56		59	3 56		35	23 20
30	2 0		60	4 0		36	24 0
M	M S		M	M S		M	M S

Prop. II. *To find the Declination and right Ascention of any Planet in the Ecliptique (his place being given.)*

To the Sine	of 23d. 30 m.	add the	Sine	of the distance from ♈ or ♎ & the Sum is the	Sine	of the	Declination
To the Cosine	of 23d. 30pm.	add the	Tang.	of the distance from ♈ to ♎ & the Sum is the	Tang.	of the	R. Ascen.

Prop. III. *Having the right Ascention, or Declination to find the Longitude correspondent.*

To the Comp. Arithmetical of the	Sine	of 23d.30' add the	Sine	of the Dec. the Sum is the	Sine	of the Plan. Long.
To the Comp. Arithmetical of the	Cosine	of 23d. 30'	Tang.	of the R.As. the Sum is the Tang.		of the Plan. Long.

Prop, IV. *To find the Declination and right Ascention of any Planet, or Star, having Latitude from the Ecliptique.*

To the Sine of the Longitude from ♈ or ♎ add the Co-tangent of the Latitude, and the Sum is the Tangent of the first Arch.

When the Long. is	♈ ♉ ♊ ♋ ♌ ♍	and Latit.	North subst. South add	23d. 30m. to, or from the first Arch, and the Sum, or Remainder is the second Arch.	
When the Long. is	♎ ♏ ♐ ♑ ♒ ♓	and Latit.	North add South subst.	23d. 30m. to, or from the first Arch, and the Sum, or Remainder is the second Arch.	

To the Comp. Arithmet. of the	Co-sine	of the first Arch and	Co-sine	of the second add the	Sine Lat.	the Sum is the	Sine Dec.
To the Comp. Arithmet. of the	Sine	of the first Arch and	Sine	of the second add the	Tan. Lon.	the Sum is the	Tan.R.Asc.

[*If you would know of what Denomination the Declination of a Star, or Planet is,* viz. *either North, or South, take this brief Rule; If the Longitude, and Latitude be both of one kind,* viz. *both North, or both South, the Declination is of the same Denomination also. But if the Longitude, and Latitude be of contrary Denominations, then consider whether the Latitude be greater, or lesser than the Declination found; if greater, then the Declination is of the same kind, or denomination with the Latitude; if less then of the same kind with the Sign wherein the Planet is placed, North, if in a Northern Sign, and South if in a Southern.*

Prop. V. *To find the distance of a Star (in Right Ascention) from the Meridian*

If the Star be between the	M.C. and	Horoscope West Ang.	Substract the Right Ascention of the	M.C. Star	from the R. Asc. of the	Star M.C.	and what remains is the dist. from the Meridian.
If the Star be between the	I.C. and	7th House Ascendant	Substract the Right Ascention of the	I.C. Star	from the R. Asc. of the	Star M.C.	and what remains is the dist. from the Meridian

Clavis Astrologiae Elimita, The Key to Astrology New Filed

Which is no more but this, if the significator shall be between the Ascendant and Meridian above the Earth, or between the West Angle and the Meridian above the Earth, then substract the R. Ascention of the Meridian, from the Right Ascension of the Significator.

But if the Significator be in the opposit part of Heaven, let your operation be just contrary.

Note that,

If the Long. or the R. Ascension sought be in	♈ ♉ ♊ Take the same Arch as comes forth ♋ ♌ ♍ Take the Comp. of the Arch found to 180d. ♎ ♏ ♐ Add 180 to the Arch found ♑ ♒ ♓ Substract the Arch found from 360 d.		and you have the true Right Ascen. of the point sought.

Prop. VI. *To find the Ascentional difference of a Planet under its proper Pole of Position, and by that the Poles Elevation above the Circle of Position of the said Star, or Planet.*

When the Significators declination shall be	North above or South under the earth South above or North under	As the Sine of the Sum of the Aequinoctial height and declination to the Sine of their diff. As the Sine of the diff. of the Aequinoctial height & the declination to the Sine of the Sum	So to the Tan. of the half distance from the Meridian, to the Tan. of an Arch, the diff. between which and the half dist. is the Ascent. diff. under the proper Pole of Position.

[*But the Sum of these Arches are the Arch of the Aequator Intersected by the Circle of Position.*]

Then for the Poles Elevation, add the Co-tangent of the Declination to the Sine of the difference of Ascension (abating Radius) their Sum is the Tangent of the Pole of Position required.

Prop. VII. To find the Oblique Ascension, or Descension of a Significator, or Promittor.

When the declin. is	North subst. South add North add South subst.	the difference of Ascension	from to to from	the Right Ascen. and you have the Oblique		Ascension. Descension.

Prop. VIII. To find the Oblique Ascension, or Descension of your Promittor; first obtain his Ascensional difference thus.

I. Add the Tangent of the Promittors Declination to the Tangent of the Poles Elevation above the Circle of Position of your Significator) and the Sum (abating Radius) is the Sine of the Ascensional Difference required.

II. Now having the R. A. Declination, and Ascensional difference you may easily find the Oblique Ascension, or Descension by the seventh Proposition, from which, substracting the Oblique Ascension, or Descension of your Significator, the remainder is the Ark of Direction.

If your Significator be posited in the tenth, eleventh, twelfth, first, second, or third Houses, he is to be directed by Oblique Ascension. But if in the fourth, fifth, sixth seventh, eighth, or ninth Houses by Oblique Descension: except you will Direct the opposite point of the Significator, which is the easiest way.

These 8 Propositions are sufficient for the whole business of Directing by Trigonometry *which shall be cleared by Examples in its proper place. However I shall here present the Reader with some other varieties of this kind, (which perhaps may be grateful to the Sons of Art.)*

Prop. IX. How to obtain a certain Arch of the Circle of Position, by which you may find the Oblique Ascension, or Descension both of Significator and Promitter, and so direct as before. Or by this Arch of the Circle of Position, the Elevation of the Pole, &c. with much ease and exactness, which differs not much, but in the manner of operation, from *Prop. VI.*

[*And note, that this Arch here mentioned, is only an Arch of the Aequator Intercepted between the Meridian and the Intersection of the Aequator by the Circle of Position imagined to pass by the Body a Star or Planet, after the same manner as the Circles of Position of the Celestial Houses cut the Aequinoctial in 30, 60, and 90 degrees, &c. from the Meridian.*]

I. First take half the distance of your Significator in Right Ascension from the tenth, or fourth House, according as he is posited above, or under the Earth.

	North	Declination	above	the Earth	take the Complement of the
If the	South		under		Declination to 90 deg.
Planet					
have	South	Declination	above	the Earth	Add the Declination and 90 d.
	North		under		and you have the Planets dist. from the Pole.

II. Unto which Sum so found, add and subduct the Latitude of the place of Birth; and thereby gain their Sum and difference.

III. Add the Arithmetical Complement of the Sine of the Sum (or Complement unto 180d. if it exceed 90 d.) and the Sine of their difference, to the Tangent of half the Significators dist. from the Meridian, and their Sum shall be the Tangent of an Arch, which added to the aforesaid half dist. from the Meridian, is an Arch of the Circle of Position required. But the difference of this last Tangent and the half distance from the Meridian shall be the Ascensional difference under the proper Pole of Position, as *Prop*. VI.

IV. If the	10, 11, 12,	Houses	add	the Circle	to	R. Asc	gives the	Ascen.	
Significator	7, 8, 9	Houses	subst.	of position	from	of MC	Oblique	Desc.	of the
be posited in	4, 5, 6	Houses	add	the Circle	to	of MC	gives the	Desc.	significat
	1, 2, 3	Houses	subst.	of position	from	R. Asc.	Oblique	Ascen.	

V. For the Ascensional Difference of your Promittor that you would Direct unto under this Circle, 'tis found thus, add the Arithmetical Complement of the Co-tangent of the Latitude of the place, the Tangent of the promittors Declination and the Sine of the Circle of Position together, abating Radius; and their Sum is the Sine of the Ascensional difference. By which you may obtain his Oblique Ascension, or Descension, as before directed. *Prop*.

VII. And thus you may direct (if you please) under this Circle only, and it shall be the same Ascen. Diff. as under the Pole; and consequently the same oblique Ascension, or Descension of the Promittor.

But now if you would know the Elevation of the Pole above the Circle of Position, from this Arch last found, and so prove the truth of your work, (*viz.*) See if your Ark of Direction will agree one way with the other, 'tis thus easily obtained.

VI. To the Sine of this Arch of the Circle of Position, add the Tangent of the Latitude of the place (always abating Radius) and their Sum is the Tangent of the Elevation of the Pole above the Pole of Position (vulgarly called the Circle of Position.)

N B *Or having this Pole of Position, and would know this Arch of the Circle. 'Tis but adding the Cotangent of the Latitude of Birth, to the Tangent of the Pole of Position; and their Sum is the Sine of the Circle required.*

Prop. X. How to set a Figure artificially the Rational way.

To the time afternoon in degrees (allowing 15d. to an hour by the Table at the beginning of this Section) add the Right Ascension of the *Sun*, and the Sum is the right Ascension of the tenth House, to which add 30 d. and you have the Oblique Ascension of the eleventh House, unto which again add 30 d. and you have the Oblique Ascension of the twelfth House: And so by a continual Addition of 30 d. I find the Oblique Ascension of all the Houses from the tenth to the fourth House, &c.

    Now for the resolving of the Triangle for the Cusps of the Houses there are two ways:
        one by the Cadence of a Perpendicular, and the other without.

I. For the Cusp of the tenth House add the Co-tangent of the Right Ascension of the M.C. to the Co-sine of 23d. 30m. their Sum (abating Radius) is the Co-tangent of the Cusp of the tenth House from the Aequinoctial point your R.A. was taken.

II. To the 30 deg. add the Tangent of the Latitude, and the 9, 11, 3, and 5. Houses

To the Sine of 60 deg. Sum is the Tangent of the Pole of the 8, 12, 2, and 6. Houses

III. To the Co-sine of the Oblique Ascension of the House from ♈, or ♎, add the Co-tangent of the Pole of the House; and the Sum is the Cotangent of the first Angle.

When the Oblique Ascen. is nearest ♈ add 23d. 50m. to the 1st. Angle, and you have the 2d. Angle.

When the Oblique Ascen. is nearest substract 23d. 50m. from the 1st Angle, and you have the 2d. Angle.

Note that if the Oblique Ascension of the House be less than 90 d. *or more than* 270 d. *'tis neerest to the first point of* ♈; *if otherwise, 'tis neerest the first point of* ♎; *and if Substraction cannot be made, take the Complement of the first Arch to a Quadrant.*

IV. To the Complement Arithrnetical of the Co-sine of the first Angle, and the Cosine of the second Angle add the Co-tangent of the Oblique Ascension of the House, and the Sum is the Co-tangent of an Arch.

Which when the second Angle is less then 90d. is the distance in the Ecliptique from the same Aequinoctial point you accounted the Ob. Asc. from.

Which when the second Angle is more than 90d. is the distance in the Ecliptique from the other Aequinoctial point you accounted the Ob. Asc. from.

Note that if the Ob. Asc. be neerest ♈, *viz.* (Under 90 deg.) and the second Angle above 90 deg. then you are to reckon the Arch that comes forth short of the contrary Aequinoctial point ♎; But if the Oblique Ascen. be above 270d. and the second Angle exceed 90d. then the last Arch falls beyond the contrary Aequinoctial point ♎; understand the same if the Oblique Ascen. of the House be nearest ♎ and the second Angle more than 90d. account the Arch that comes forth beyond the contrary Aequinoctial point as Reason will direct better than many Rules.

Secondly, The other way to find the Cusps of the Houses is this: Having the Right Ascension of the M. C. The Cusps of the 10*th* may be thus had, substract the *Co-sine* of 23d. 30m. from the Tangent of the Mid-heavens, Right Ascension, and Radius, and there will remain the Tangent of the Cusp of the 10*th* house as before. But for the Cusps of the other houses, having before found the Oblique Ascensions and the Poles of the Houses work thus, *viz.*

I. Take the Complement of the Poles of each of the Houses to 90d. and to this Number, both add and substract 23d. 30m. so shall you have the Sum and difference belonging to the Pole of each House, reserve half their Sum and half these differences, as also half the Oblique Ascensions of each House; and then proceed after this Method, by resolving the Oblique Triangle without a Perpendicular, by the fourth Case of Oblique spherical Triangles.

II. If your Oblique Ascension be under 180 deg. take the half of it, and say, as the Sine of the half difference Comp. Arith. is to the Sine of the half Sum, so is the Tangent of the Semi Oblique Ascension, to the Tangent of half the difference in the Ecliptique.

III. As the *Co-sine* of this half difference *Comp. Arith.* is to the Co-sine of the half Sum. So the *Tangent* of half the Oblique Ascension to the *Tangent* of another Arch: Which added to the former Arch, gives the Cusp of the House from the next *Aequinoctial point,* ♈ because the Oblique Ascension is under 180d. But when the Oblique Ascension is above 180d. then the Sum of the two Arches added, must be accounted beyond ♎ for the Cusp of the House desired.

IV. If the Oblique Ascension be above 180d. substract 180d. from it, and take half the remainder, and now say, as the Sine of the half Sum *Comp. Arith.* is to the Sine of the half difference, *&c.*

V. For the second Operation, say, as to the *Cosine* of the half Sum *Comp. Arith.* to the Cosine of the half difference, *&c.* In all respects as before; and from the work may be drawn a brief *Table of Houses* for that Latitude, which shall be made more plain and evident when I come to Examples.

Now that this frequent Operation in Directing might seem the easier, 'twill be necessary, first of all (before you use your Canon of Sines and Tangents) to set down such notes as these, in a Scheme, that so you may not be hindred with them in the work.

Suppose a Star or Planet in ♈ 8d. 0m. Lat. South 0d. 51m. in the latitude 52d. 25m.

I. ♈ Sine Longitude 8d. 0m.	9143555 add
Co-tangent Lat. South 89 d. 9 m.	11828672
Tang. I. Arch 83d. 55m.	10972227
Add 23 30 their sum	

Is the second Arch 107 25 (*vel* 72d. 35') *viz.* Comp. to 180d.

II. Sine of the Lat. 0d. 51m.	8171280
Cosine of the 1. Arch Comp. Arith. 6d.5m.	0974797 add
Cosine of the 2. Arch 72d. 35m.	9476133
Sine of the Declination N. 2d. 24m. 1)	8622210
Sum abating Rx	
III. Tang. Lat. 52d. 25m.	10113712 add
Tang. Declin. 2d. 24m.	8622343
Sine Asc. Diff. 3d. 6m.	1) 8734055
Sum R	
IV. Tangent Longitude ♈ 8d. 0m.	9147003
Sine 1*st* Arch. Comp. Arith. 83d. 55m.	0002453 add
Sine second Arch 72d. 35m.	9979618
The Sum less Rx is the	
Tangent Right Ascen. 7d. 40m.	1) 9129074
Diff. Ascen. Sub. 3 6	
Oblique Ascension 4 34 Remains	

And thus when the Canon is open at the Longitude, set down the Sine and Tangent thereof in his proper place, and so for the Latitude, and also for the first and second Arches without opening twice for one thing; and this will much facilitate the work, and by a little practice will be as readily performed, as to work by the ordinary Tables.

In the next place I shall present the Reader with a brief Synopsis of all the Rules of Directing a Nativity in the Aequator, both Direct, and Converse; which I doubt not but will be easily understood by the Industrious Student, if what has already been express'd in the aforesaid Propositions be but duly considered, and studied.

To find the Arch of the Aequator Intercepted between the Significator and Promittor,
vulgarly called the Ark of Direction.

I. According to the Succession of the Signes if the Significator shall be posited.

1. In angles, *viz.* the Ascendant Substract the Oblique Ascen. of the Significator with Lat. from the Ob. Asc. of the Promittor under the same Pole. And the Remainder is the Arch of Direction, which may be converted into years, *&c.* by Nabod's Measure of Time, *&c.*

In angles, *viz.* the West-Angle. Substract the Oblique Descen. of the Significatoar with Lat. from the Ob. Desc. of the Promittor under the same Pole. And the Remainder is the Arch of Direction, which may be converted into years, *&c.* by Nabod's Measure of Time, *&c.*

Clavis Astrologiae Elimita, The Key to Astrology New Filed

In angles, *viz.* the M C. Substract the Right Ascen. of the Significatoar with Lat. from the R. Ascen. of the Promittor under the same Pole. And the Remainder is the Arch of Direction, which may be converted into years, &c. by Nabod's Measure of Time, &c.

In angles, *viz.* the I C. Substract the Right Ascen. of the Significatoar with Lat. from the R. Ascen. of the Promittor under the same Pole. And the Remainder is the Arch of Direction, which may be converted into y ears, &c. by Nabod's Measure of Time, &c.

2. Out of Angles, then take the distance of the Significator in Right Ascen. from the MC when the Significator is posited above the Earth & thereby find the Poles Elevation above the Circle of Position of the Significator, which if posited in the Oriental Part of Heaven take the Obl. Asce. with Lat. if occasion be, & Substract the Obl. Desc. Of the Significator taken under his Pole of Position from the Ascen. or Descen. of the Promittor (under the same Pole the Rem. is the Arch Direction sought.

Out of Angles, then take the distance of the Significator in Right Ascen. from the IC when the Significator is posited under the Earth & thereby find the Poles Elevation above the Circle of Position of the Significator, which if posited in the Occidental Part of Heaven take the Obl. Desc. with Lat. if they have any occasion be, & Substract the Obl. Asc. Of the Significator taken under his Pole of Position from the Ascen. or Descen. of the Promittor (under the same Pole the Rem. is the Arch Direction sought.

2. Contrary to the Succession of the Signes if the Promittor shall be posited

1. In angles, *viz.* the Ascendant West Angle substract the Oblique Ascen. Of the Promittor with Lat. from the Ob. Asc. Of the Significator under the Pole of the Promittor, And the Remainder is the Ark of Direction, required which ought to be converted into years & days according to what Measure of Time you please to follow.

In angles, *viz.* the West Angle. Substract the Oblique Descen. of the Promittor with Lat. from the Ob. Desc. of the Significator under the Pole of the Promittor. And the Remainder is the Ark of Direction, required which ought to be converted into years & days according to what Measure of Time you please to follow.

In angles, *viz.* the MC. Substract the Right Ascen. of the Promittor with Lat. from the R. Ascen. of the Significator under the Pole of the Promittor. And the Remainder is the Ark of Direction, required which ought to be converted into years & days according to what Measure of Time you please to follow.

In angles, *viz.* the IC. Substract the Right Ascen. of the Promittor with Lat. from the R. Asc. of the Significator under the Pole of the Promittor. And the Remainder is the Ark of Direction, required which ought to be converted into years & days according to what Measure of Time you please to follow.

2. Out of Angles, then enquire first the Distance in Right Ascen. from the Angle of the M C when the Promittor shall be posited above the Earth. Afterwards seek the Poles Elevation above the Circle of Position of the Promittor which if posited in the Oriental Part of the Heavens take the Obl. Asce with Lat. if they have any, & Sub. the Obl. Asc. Of the Promittor (taken under his proper Pole) from the Obl. Ascen. of the Significator (taken under the same Pole) & the Rem. is the Ark of Direction required.

Out of Angles, then enquire first the Distance in Right Ascen. from the Angle of the I C when the Promittor shall be posited under the Earth. Afterwards seek the Poles Elevation above the Circle of Position of the Promittor which if posited in the Occidental Part of the Heavens take the Obl. Desc. with Lat. if they have any, & Sub. the Obl. Asc. Of the Promittor (taken under his proper Pole) from the Obl. Desc. of the Significator (taken under the same Pole) & the Rem. is the Ark of Direction required.

SECT. IV

How to Reduce an Ephemerides (or Astronomical Tables) to another Meridian, and thereby Aequate for the difference of Meridians.

All men that are any thing knowing in the Doctrine of the Sphere, are sensible that the ☉ Rises and Sets sooner, to such persons as live in the East, than to those that live more Westerly; and by consequence it must needs be Noon sooner to such as live more Easterly, than to those that inhabit West; for when it is Noon with those West, it is past Noon at the same moment with all such as inhabit Easterly: and so the ☉ appears above our Horizon that live Westward, when set in their Horizon that live East.

II. And upon this consideration 'tis thought the Meridian Circle was invented by the Astronomers of old, this Circle is one of the greatest in the Sphere, passing by the Poles of the world, and the Zenith or Vertical Points over our heads; and as soon as the ☉ touches this Circle in any City or Place in the World, it is then Noon, or Mid-day with them.

III. Hence then may be discovered, that all places in the world have different Zeniths; it consequently follows, that they may have different Meridians also; that is, one place differs from another in Longitude; and the Longitude of any place is only an Arch of the Aequinoctial, intercepted betwixt the first Meridian that passes through the *Canary* Islands, and the Meridian of the proposed place: And this difference of Meridians is an Arch of the Aequinoctial, comprehended by two Meridians; and being reduced into time by allowing 15 degrees to one hour, and four degrees for one minute of time (or by a Table for that purpose inserted in this Book) gives the difference of the Meridians of any two places in hours and minutes, or only minutes, &c.) for many places.

IV. Now the way of Reduction of an Ephemeris, from one Meridian to another is briefly thus; *viz.* if the two places proposed, lye both in the same longitude, and so are equally distant from the Grand Meridian; *viz.* of the *Canary* Islands there needs no Reduction: But if the Longitude of your place be either greater or lesser than the Longitude of that place for which your Ephemerides was calculated, then 'tis requisite there be an Aequation of time, made for the difference of Meridians.

V. To perform which, you must by some good Catalogue (or otherwise by observation) obtain the true Longitude of your place, (which to do exactly I conceive will be found a matter of difficulty) and compare it with the Longitude of that place for which your Ephemerides was made, if your Longitude exceed that, then your place lies more Eastward; but if it be less, more Westward; and by substracting the greater from the lesser, you have the difference of Meridians desired, which may be converted into Time, according to the usual manner, you will find Tables to this purpose in every Ephemerides, and what use you make thereof shall immediately follow.

VI. Having shewed what the difference of Meridians is, take this brief explanation of those Catologues of places, and difference of Meridians, &c. The knowledge of which is, absolutely neceaaary. Let it be supposed in a Catologue of places, with their difference of Meridians from *London*, I find against *Vraniburge 50m.* [*A.*] this letter [*A.*] denotes it lyes East of *London*, and therefore if I would Reduce the Planets motions or aspects from *London* to *Vraniburge*, I must observe this Rule.

	motion of the Planets	Sub.		from	the
In the	from *London*		50'		given
	Aspect to *Vraniburge*	Add		to	Time.

But now on the contrary, because *London* lyes West from *Vraniburge*, (as in those Catalogues noted with [*S.*]) if I would reduce the motions or aspects of the Planets from *Vraniburge* to *London*, I must in this case work contrary according to this Rule.

	motion of the Planets	Add		to	the
In the	from *Vranib*		50'		given
	Aspect to *London.*	Sub.		from	Time.

VII. Hence then in places Oriental of your Ephemerides (usually noted with *A.*) in the motions of the Planets you are to substract, and in places Occidental (usually noted with *S*) you are to add the difference of time, But in Eclipses, Aspects, Revolutions, and Ingresses the clean contrary. *viz.* In places East, add, in places West, Substract, &c.

[*Here note that a Conjunction of the* ☉ *or* ☽*, or other Aspects of the Planets happen at one certain Moment of time all over the world: But the Meridians, or Noontide of most places of the world differ; for when 'tis Noon at* one place in the world, 'tis either before or after Noon in another by the space of some hours or minutes; and therefore the knowledge of Reduction thereof is absolutely necessary to be known.]

SECT. V.

A perpetual Table of the Aequation of Time for the Inequality of Natural dayes, in Minutes and Seconds of an Hour, according to *Ticho*.

	♈ ♎	♉ ♏	♊ ♐	
	Add	Add	Add	
D.	M. S.	M. S.	M. S.	
0	0 0	8 25	8 47	30
1	0 20	8 36	8 37	29
2	0 40	8 45	8 26	28
3	0 59	8 55	8 15	27
4	1 19	9 04	8 03	26
5	1 30	9 12	7 50	25
6	1 59	9 19	7 36	24
7	2 18	9 26	7 22	23
8	2 38	9 32	7 07	22
9	2 57	9 37	6 52	21
10	3 16	9 42	6 36	20
11	3 35	9 46	6 20	19
12	3 57	9 50	6 03	18
13	4 12	9 52	5 46	17
14	4 30	9 54	5 28	16
15	4 47	9 56	5 10	15
16	5 05	9 56	4 51	14
17	5 22	9 56	4 32	13
18	5 38	9 55	4 12	12
19	5 55	9 53	3 53	11
20	6 11	9 51	3 33	10
21	6 26	9 48	3 12	9
22	6 41	9 44	2 51	8
23	6 56	9 40	2 31	7
24	7 10	9 34	2 09	6
25	7 24	9 28	1 48	5
26	7 37	9 21	1 27	4
27	7 50	9 14	1 05	3
28	8 02	9 06	0 43	2
29	8 14	8 57	0 22	1
30	8 25	8 47	0 00	0
	Subst	Subst	Subst	D.
	♓ ♍	♒ ♌	♑ ♋	

Enter this Table with the Signe and Degree of the ☉'s place, either in the uppermost, and left hand Column descending, or in the lowermost and right hand Column ascending, and in the common Angle is the Aequation (according to the Titles) to be added, or substracted to, or from the Equal time, that it may be made apparent.

But to Reduce the apparent to the Equal, take the contrary Title, viz. for Add, Subtract, and for Subtract, Add to or from the apparent time given to make it Aequal: As for Example,

Having the exact time of the Nativity Rectified, that you may reduce the Planets places to the true and apparent time unto which all Clocks and Dyals agree. You are in the next place (after the Reduction of Meridians) to make an Aequation by this Table of Inequality of natural dayes, and lastly to Reduce the Planets to that moment of time so Aequated: thus the ☉ is in 5 deg. of ♏ Octob. 18, just at Noon, I would know the Aequation of time, &c. by this Table, against 5 deg. in the first Column to the left hand, and right under ♏ at the top in the common Angle I find the Aequation 9' 12" to be added to the equal time to make it apparent: So that the ☉ is not apparently in 5 deg. of ♏ till 9' 12" P.M. But to Reduce the apparent time to the Equal for which the Ephemerides is Calculated, you are to use the contrary titles as before directed; *viz.* in this case Substract; *& sic de ceteris.*

Some admit not of any Aequation of time, others will have the Aequality proceed from these two Causes; the first from the Inequality of the Sun's *motion in the Zodiack, and the second from the Obliquity thereof: But Noble* Ticho Brahe (*that Famous Astronomer*) *makes the difference between the* Sun's *true Longitude, and his right Ascention to be the absolute Aequation of Natural dayes, which has been many years since demonstrated upon the* Copernican Systeme *by an Ingenious Astronomer of this Age, viz. Mr. T. S.*

The Agreement between Calculations by Trigonometry and the Vulgar Tables of Directions.

In the Tables of *Position* for the Lat. of *London*, entering with 10 deg. of North Declination above, or South under the Earth, the distance from the Meridian under the Pole of 20 deg. is 20d. 30m. which I prove by Trigonometry thus; according to *Prop.* VI.

As the Sine of the Sum of the Aequinoct. height)	
(*viz.* the Comp. of the Latitude of the place)	0125868
& the Declination 48d. 28m. Comp. Arith.)	
Is to the Sine of their Difference 28d. 28m.	9678197
So is the Ta. of ½ the dist. from the Mer. 10°. 15'.	9257269
To the Tangent of an Arch, *viz.* 6d. 34m.	9061224

The Difference between which, and the ½ distance from the Meridian is 3d. 41m. which is the Ascensional Diff. of that Planet or Star, so posited as aforesaid under his proper Pole; But their Sum is an Arch of the Aequinoctial intersected by the Circle of Position, which here call Circle of Position, *viz.* 16d. 49m. Now if I add this Circle of Position, and Ascen. Diff. (because the Declination is south under the Earth) that produces the Distance from the Meridian 20 d. 30 m. as by the Tables.

Lastly, to the Sine of the Circle 16d. 49m.	9461364
Add the Tangent of the Lat. 51d. 32m	0099913
Their Sum—Rx is the Tan. of the Pole of Pos. 20°	9561277
Or to the Sine of the Ascen. Diff. 3d. 41m.	8807819
Add the Co-tang. of the Declination 10d.	0753681
Their Sum—Rx is the Tang. of P. P. 20d. 2m.	9561500

If the Declination be South above the Earth, subtract the Ascen. Diff. from the Circle of Position, and there remains the Distance from the Meridian: *And note, that when the Declination is South above, or North under the Earth, you are always in this case to substract; but when South under the Earth, or North above, add the Ascen. Diff. &c. as in the Example.*

Number	Names	The deg. of the Zodiac.	The degrees in Time.	Degr. of the Aequino. that rise with the Signes.	The time that the Signes continue in the As. La. 51.32	Degr. of the Aeq. that pass through the Meridian	The time the Signes pass through the Meridian
Sig.	ch.	Gra.	Hor.	D. M.	H. M. S.	D. M.	H. M. S.
0	♈	0	0	13 4	00 52 16	27 54	1 51 36
1	♉	15 30	1 2	17 8	01 08 32	29 54	1 59 36
2	♊	45 60	3 4	26 36	01 46 24	32 12	2 8 48
3	♋	75 90	5 6	37 48	02 31 12	32 12	2 8 48
4	♌	105 120	7 8	42 39	02 50 36	29 54	1 59 36
5	♍	135 150	9 10	42 45	02 51 0	27 54	1 51 36
6	♎	165 180	11 12	42 45	02 51 0	27 54	1 51 36
7	♏	195 210	13 14	42 39	02 50 36	29 54	1 59 36
8	♐	235 240	15 16	37 48	02 31 12	32 12	2 8 48
9	♑	255 270	17 18	26 36	01 46 24	32 12	2 8 48
10	♒	285 300	19 20	17 8	01 08 32	29 54	1 59 36
11	♓	315 330	21 22	13 4	00 52 16	27 54	1 51 36
		345 360	23 24	360 0	24 00 00	360 0	24 0 0

This Table is so plain and easie that it needs no further Explanation than the bare Titles direct: 'tis adapted for the Latitude of London, the same may be performed for any Latitude from the common Tables of Ascention, and is of good use to shew the continuance of the Signes in the Ascendant or Mid-heaven, &c.

	\multicolumn{7}{c}{A Table of Logistical Logarithmes for the Investigation of}
'	0	1	2	3	4	5	6
"	0	60	120	180	240	300	360
0	—	17782	14771	13010	11761	10792	10000
1	35563	17710	14735	12986	11743	10777	9988
2	32553	17639	14699	12962	11725	10763	9976
3	30792	17570	14664	12639	11707	10749	9964
4	29542	17501	14629	12915	11689	10734	9952
5	28573	17434	14594	12891	11671	10720	9940
6	27782	17368	14559	12868	11654	10706	9928
7	27112	17302	14525	12845	11636	10692	9916
8	26532	17238	14491	12821	11619	10678	9905
9	26021	17175	14457	12798	11601	10663	9893
10	25563	17112	14424	12775	11584	10649	9881
11	25149	17050	14390	12753	11566	10635	9869
12	24771	16990	14357	12730	11549	10621	9858
13	24424	16930	14325	12707	11532	10608	9846
14	24102	16871	14292	12685	11515	10594	9834
15	23802	16812	14260	12663	11498	10580	9823
16	23522	16755	14228	12640	11481	10566	9811
17	23259	16698	14196	12618	11464	10552	9800
18	23010	16642	14165	12596	11447	10539	9788
19	22775	16587	14133	12574	11430	10525	9777
20	22553	16532	14102	12553	11413	10512	9765
21	22341	16478	14071	12531	11397	10498	9754
22	22139	16425	14040	12510	11380	10484	9742
23	21946	16372	14010	12488	11363	10471	9731
24	21761	16320	13979	12467	11347	10458	9720
25	21584	16269	13949	12445	11331	10444	9708
26	21413	16218	13919	12424	11314	10431	9697
27	21249	16168	13890	12403	11298	10418	9686
28	21091	16118	13860	12382	11282	10404	9675
29	20939	16069	13831	12362	11266	10391	9664
30	20792	16021	13802	12341	11249	10378	9652

the Part proportional both in Time and Motion, &c.							
'	0	1	2	3	4	5	6
"	0	60	120	180	240	300	360
30	20792	16021	13802	12341	11249	10378	9652
31	20649	15973	13773	12320	11233	10365	9641
32	20512	15925	13745	12300	11217	10352	9630
33	20378	15878	13716	12279	11201	10339	9619
34	20248	15832	13688	12259	11186	10326	9608
35	21022	15786	13660	12239	11170	10313	9597
36	20000	15740	13632	12218	11154	10300	9586
37	19881	15695	13604	12198	11138	10287	9575
38	19765	15651	13576	12178	11123	10274	9564
39	19652	15607	13549	12159	11107	10261	9553
40	19542	15563	13522	12139	11091	10248	9542
41	19435	15520	13495	12119	11076	10235	9532
42	19331	15477	13468	12099	11061	10223	9521
43	19228	15435	13441	12080	11045	10210	9510
44	19128	15393	13415	12061	11030	10197	9499
45	19031	15351	13388	12041	11015	10185	9488
46	18935	15310	13362	12022	10999	10172	9478
47	18842	15269	13336	12003	10984	10160	9467
48	18751	15229	13310	11984	10969	10147	9456
49	18661	15189	13284	11965	10954	10135	9446
50	18573	15149	13259	11946	10939	10122	9435
51	18487	15110	13233	11924	10924	10110	9425
52	18403	15071	13208	11908	10909	10098	9414
53	18320	15032	13183	11889	10894	10085	9404
54	18239	14994	13158	11871	10880	10073	9393
55	18159	14956	13133	11852	10865	10061	9383
56	18081	14918	13108	11834	10850	10049	9372
57	18004	14881	13083	11816	10835	10036	9362
58	17929	14844	13059	11797	10821	10024	9351
59	17855	14808	13034	11779	10806	10012	9341
60	17782	14771	13010	11761	10792	10000	9331

	A Table of Logistical Logarithmes for the Investigation of						
'	7	8	9	10	11	12	13
"	420	480	540	600	660	720	780
0	9331	8741	8239	7782	7368	6990	6642
1	9320	8742	8231	7774	7361	6984	6637
2	9310	8733	8223	7767	7354	6978	6631
3	9300	8724	8215	7760	7348	6972	6625
4	9289	9715	8207	7753	7341	6966	6620
5	9279	8706	8199	7745	7335	6960	6614
6	9269	8697	8191	7738	7328	6954	6609
7	9259	8688	8183	7731	7322	6948	6803
8	9149	8679	8175	7724	7315	6942	6598
9	9238	8670	8167	7717	7309	6936	6592
10	9228	8661	8159	7710	7302	6930	6587
11	9218	8652	8152	7703	7396	6924	6581
12	9208	8543	8144	7696	7289	6018	6576
13	9198	8635	8136	7688	7283	6912	6570
14	9188	8626	8128	7681	7276	6906	6565
15	9178	8617	8120	7674	7270	6900	6559
16	9168	8608	8112	7697	7264	6894	6554
17	9158	8599	8104	7660	7257	6888	6548
18	9148	8591	8097	7653	7251	6882	6543
19	9138	8582	8039	7646	7244	6877	6538
20	9128	8573	8031	7639	7238	6871	6532
21	9119	8566	8073	7632	7232	6865	6510
22	9109	8556	8066	7625	7225	6859	6521
23	9099	8547	8058	7618	7219	6853	6516
24	9089	8539	8050	7611	7212	6847	6510
25	9079	8530	8043	7604	7206	6841	6505
26	9070	8522	8035	7597	7200	6836	6500
27	9060	8513	8027	7590	7193	6830	6494
28	9050	8504	8020	7583	7187	6824	6489
29	9041	8496	8012	7577	7181	6818	6484
30	9031	8187	8004	7570	7175	6812	6478

Clavis Astrologiae Elimita, The Key to Astrology New Filed

	the Part Proportional, both in Time and Motion, &c.						
'	7	8	9	10	11	12	13
"	420	480	540	600	660	720	780
30	9031	8487	8004	7570	7175	6812	6478
31	9021	8479	7997	7563	7168	6807	6473
32	9012	8470	7989	7556	7162	6801	6467
33	9002	8462	7981	7549	7156	6695	6462
34	8992	8453	7974	7542	7149	6789	6457
35	8983	8445	7966	7535	7143	6784	6451
36	8973	8437	7959	7528	7137	6778	6446
37	8964	8428	7951	7522	7131	6772	6441
38	8954	8420	7944	7515	7124	6766	6435
39	8945	8411	7936	7508	7118	6761	6430
40	8935	8403	7929	7501	7112	6755	6425
41	9826	8395	7921	7494	7106	6749	6420
42	8917	8386	7914	7488	7100	6743	6414
43	8907	8378	7906	7481	7093	6738	6409
44	8898	8370	7899	7474	7087	6732	6404
45	8888	8361	7891	7467	7081	6726	6398
46	8879	8353	7884	7461	7075	6721	6393
47	8870	8345	7877	7454	7069	6715	6388
48	8861	8337	7869	7447	7063	6709	6383
49	8851	8328	7862	7441	7057	6604	6377
50	8842	8320	7855	7434	7050	6698	6372
51	8833	8312	7847	7427	7044	6692	6367
52	8824	8304	7840	7421	7038	6687	6362
53	8814	8296	7832	7414	7032	6681	6357
54	8805	8288	7825	7407	7026	6676	6251
55	8796	8279	7818	7401	7020	6670	6346
56	8787	8271	7811	7394	7014	6664	6341
57	8778	8263	7803	7387	7008	6659	6336
58	8769	8255	7796	7381	7002	6653	6331
59	8760	8247	7789	7374	6996	6648	6323
60	8751	8239	7782	7368	6990	6642	6320

	A Table of Logistical Logarithmes for the Investigation of						
'	14	15	16	17	18	19	20
"	840	900	960	1020	1080	1140	1200
0	6320	6021	5740	5477	5229	4994	4771
1	6315	6016	5736	5473	5225	4990	4768
2	6310	6011	5731	5469	5221	4986	4764
3	6305	6006	5727	5464	5217	4983	4760
4	6300	6001	5722	5460	5213	4979	4757
5	6294	5997	5718	5456	5209	4975	4753
6	6289	5992	5713	5452	5205	4971	4750
7	6284	5987	5709	5447	5201	4967	4746
8	6279	5982	5704	5443	5197	4964	4742
9	6274	5977	5700	5439	5193	4960	4739
10	6269	5973	5695	5435	5189	4956	4735
11	6264	5968	5691	5430	5185	4952	4732
12	6259	5963	5686	5426	5181	4949	4728
13	6254	5958	5682	5422	5177	4945	4724
14	6248	5954	5677	5418	5173	4941	4721
15	6243	5949	5673	5414	5169	4937	4717
16	6238	5944	5669	5409	5165	4933	4714
17	6233	5939	5664	5405	5161	4930	4710
18	6228	5935	5660	5401	5157	4926	4707
19	6223	5930	5655	5397	5153	4922	4703
20	6218	5925	5651	5393	5149	4918	4699
21	6213	5920	5646	5389	5145	4915	4696
22	6208	5916	5642	5385	5141	4911	4692
23	6203	5911	5637	5380	5137	4907	4689
24	6198	5906	5633	5376	5133	4903	5685
25	6193	5902	5629	5372	5129	4900	4682
26	6188	5897	5624	5368	5125	4896	4678
27	6183	5892	5620	5364	5122	4892	4675
28	6178	5888	5615	5359	5118	4889	4671
29	6173	5883	5611	5355	5114	4885	4668
30	6168	5878	5607	5351	5110	4881	4664

	\multicolumn{7}{c}{the Part Proportional, both in Time and Motion, &c.}
'	14	15	16	17	18	19	20
"	840	900	960	1020	1080	1140	1200
30	6168	5878	5607	5351	5110	4881	4664
31	6163	5874	5602	5347	5106	4877	4660
32	6158	5869	5598	5343	5102	4874	4657
33	6153	5864	5594	5339	5098	4870	4653
34	6148	5860	5589	5335	5064	4866	4650
35	6143	5855	5585	5331	5090	4863	4646
36	6138	5850	5580	5326	5086	4859	4643
37	6133	5846	5576	5322	5082	4855	4639
38	6128	5841	5572	5318	5079	4852	4636
39	6122	5836	5567	5314	5075	4848	4632
40	6118	5832	5563	5310	5071	4844	4629
41	6113	5827	5559	5306	5067	4841	4625
42	6108	5823	5554	5302	5063	4837	4622
43	6103	5818	5550	5298	5059	4833	4618
44	6099	5813	5546	5294	5055	4830	4615
45	6094	5809	5541	5290	5051	4826	4611
46	6089	5804	5537	5285	5048	4822	4608
47	6084	5800	5533	5281	5044	4819	4604
48	6079	5795	5528	5277	5040	4815	4601
49	6074	5790	5524	5273	5036	4811	4597
50	6069	5786	5520	5269	5032	4808	4594
51	6064	5781	5516	5265	5028	4804	4590
52	6059	5777	5511	5261	5025	4800	4587
53	6055	5772	5507	5257	5021	4797	4584
54	6050	5768	5503	5253	5017	4793	4580
55	6045	5763	5498	5249	5013	4789	4577
56	6040	5758	5494	5245	5009	4786	4573
57	6035	5754	4490	5241	5005	4782	4570
58	6030	5749	5486	5237	5002	4778	4566
59	6025	5745	5481	5233	4998	4775	4563
60	6021	5240	5477	5229	4994	4771	4559

	A Table of Logistical Logarithmes for the Investigation of						
'	21	22	23	24	25	26	27
"	1260	1320	1380	1440	1500	1560	1620
0	4559	4157	4164	3979	3802	3632	3468
1	4556	4354	4161	3976	3799	3629	3465
2	4552	4351	4158	3973	3796	3626	3463
3	4549	4347	4155	3970	3793	3623	3460
4	4546	4344	4152	3967	3791	3621	3457
5	4542	4341	4149	3964	3788	3618	3454
6	4539	4338	4145	3961	3785	3615	3452
7	4535	4334	4142	3958	3782	3612	3449
8	4532	4331	4139	3955	3779	3610	3446
9	4528	4328	4136	3952	3776	3607	3444
10	4525	4325	4133	3949	3773	3604	3441
11	4521	4321	4130	3946	3770	3601	3438
12	4518	4318	4227	3943	3768	3598	3436
13	4515	4315	4123	3940	3765	3596	3433
14	4511	4311	4120	3937	3762	3593	3431
15	4508	4308	4117	3934	3759	3590	3428
16	4505	4305	4114	3931	3756	3587	3425
17	4501	4302	4111	3928	3753	3585	3423
18	4598	4298	4108	3925	3750	3582	3320
19	4494	4295	4105	3922	3747	3579	3417
20	4491	4292	4102	3919	3745	3576	3415
21	4488	4289	4099	3917	3742	3574	3412
22	4484	4285	4006	3914	3739	3571	3409
23	4481	4282	4092	3911	3736	3568	3407
24	4677	4279	4089	3908	3733	3565	3404
25	4474	4276	4086	3905	3730	3563	3401
26	4471	4273	4083	3902	3727	3560	3399
27	4467	4269	4080	3899	3725	3557	3396
28	4464	4266	4077	3896	3722	3555	3303
29	4460	4263	4074	3893	3719	3552	3391
30	4457	4260	4071	3890	3716	3549	3388

	the Part Proportional, both in Time and Motion, &c.						
'	21	22	23	24	25	26	27
"	1260	1320	1380	1440	1500	1560	1620
30	4457	4260	4071	3890	3716	3549	3388
31	4454	4256	4068	3887	3713	3546	3380
32	4450	4253	4065	3884	3710	3544	3383
33	4447	4250	4062	3881	3708	3541	3380
34	4444	4247	4059	3878	3705	3538	3378
35	4440	4244	4055	3875	3702	3535	3375
36	4437	4240	4052	3872	3699	3533	3372
37	4434	4037	4049	3869	3696	3530	3370
38	4430	4234	4046	3866	3693	3527	3367
39	4427	4231	4043	3863	3691	3525	3365
40	4424	4228	4040	3860	3688	3522	3362
41	4420	4224	4037	3857	3685	3519	3359
42	4417	4221	4034	3855	3682	3516	3357
43	4414	4218	4031	3852	3679	3514	3354
44	4410	4215	4028	3849	3677	3511	3351
45	4407	4212	4025	3846	3674	3508	3349
46	4404	4209	4022	3843	3671	3506	3346
47	4400	4205	4019	3840	3668	3503	3344
48	4397	4202	4016	3837	3665	3500	3341
49	4394	4199	4013	3834	3663	3497	3338
50	4390	4196	4010	3831	3660	3495	3336
51	4387	4193	4007	3828	3657	3492	3333
52	4384	4189	4004	3825	3654	3489	3331
53	4380	4186	4001	3822	3651	3487	3328
54	4377	4183	3998	3820	3649	3484	3325
55	4374	4180	3995	3817	3646	3481	3323
56	4370	4177	3991	3814	3643	3479	3320
57	4367	4174	3988	3811	3640	3476	3318
58	4364	4171	3985	3808	3637	3473	3315
59	4361	4167	3982	3805	3635	3471	3313
60	4357	4164	3979	3802	3632	3468	3310

	A Table of Logistical Logarithmes for the Investigai						
'	28	29	30	31	32	33	34
"	1680	1740	1800	1860	1920	1980	2040
0	3310	3158	3010	2868	2730	2596	2467
1	3307	3155	3008	2866	2728	2594	2465
2	3305	3153	3005	2863	2725	2592	2462
3	3302	3150	3003	2861	2723	2590	2460
4	3300	3148	3003	2859	2721	2588	2458
5	3297	3145	2998	2856	2719	2585	2456
6	3294	3143	2996	2854	2716	2583	2454
7	3292	3140	2993	2852	2714	2581	2452
8	3289	3138	2991	2849	2712	2579	2450
9	3287	3135	2989	2847	2710	2577	2448
10	3284	3133	2986	2845	2707	2574	2445
11	3282	3130	2984	2842	2705	2572	2443
12	3279	3128	2981	2840	2703	2570	2441
13	3276	3125	2979	2838	2701	2568	2439
14	3274	3123	2977	2835	2698	2566	2437
15	3271	3120	2974	2833	2696	2564	2435
16	3269	3118	2972	2831	2694	2561	2433
17	3266	3115	2969	2828	2692	2559	2431
18	3264	3113	2967	2826	2689	2557	2429
19	3261	3110	2965	2824	2687	2555	2426
20	3259	3108	2962	2821	2685	2553	2424
21	3256	3105	2960	2819	2683	2551	2422
22	3253	3103	2958	2817	2681	2548	2420
23	3251	3101	2955	2815	2678	2546	2418
24	3248	3098	2953	2812	2676	2544	2416
25	3246	3096	2950	2810	2674	2542	2414
26	3243	3093	2948	2808	2672	2540	2412
27	3241	3091	2946	2805	2669	2538	2410
28	3238	3088	2943	2803	2667	2535	2408
29	3236	3086	2941	2801	2665	2533	2405
30	3233	3083	2939	2798	2663	2531	2403

Clavis Astrologiae Elimita, The Key to Astrology New Filed

	the Part Proportional, both in Time and Motion, &c.						
'	28	29	30	31	32	33	34
"	1680	1740	1800	1860	1920	1980	2040
30	3233	3083	2939	2798	2663	2531	2403
31	3231	3081	2936	2796	2660	2529	2401
32	3228	3078	2934	2794	2658	2527	2399
33	3225	3076	2931	2792	2656	2525	2397
34	3223	3073	2929	2789	2654	2522	2395
35	3220	3071	2927	2787	2652	2520	2393
36	3218	3069	2924	2785	2649	2311	2391
37	3215	3066	2922	2782	2647	2516	2389
38	3213	3064	2920	2780	2645	2514	2387
39	3210	3061	2917	2778	2643	2512	2384
40	3208	3059	2915	2775	2640	2510	2382
41	3205	3056	2912	2773	2638	2307	2380
42	3203	3054	2910	2771	2636	2505	2378
43	3200	3052	2908	2769	2634	2503	2376
44	3198	3049	2905	2766	2632	2501	2374
45	3195	3047	2903	2764	2629	2499	2372
46	3193	3044	2901	2762	2627	2497	2370
47	3190	3042	2898	2760	2625	2494	2368
48	3188	3039	2896	2757	2623	2492	2366
49	3185	3037	2894	2755	2621	2460	2364
50	3183	3034	2891	2753	2618	2488	2362
51	3180	3032	2889	2750	2616	2386	2359
52	3178	3030	2887	2748	2614	2484	2357
53	3175	3027	2884	2746	2612	2482	2355
54	3173	3025	2882	2744	2610	2480	2353
55	3170	3022	2880	2741	2607	2477	2351
56	3168	3020	2877	2739	2605	2475	2349
57	3165	3018	2875	2737	2603	2473	2347
58	3163	3015	2873	2735	2601	2471	2345
59	3160	3013	2870	2732	2599	2469	2343
60	3158	3010	2868	2730	2596	2467	2341

\	\	\	A Table of Logistical Logarithmes for the Investigation of				
'	35	36	37	38	39	40	41
"	2100	2160	2220	2280	2340	2400	2460
0	2341	2218	2099	1984	1871	1761	1654
1	2339	2216	2098	1982	1869	1759	1652
2	2337	2214	2096	1980	1867	1757	1650
3	2335	2212	2094	1978	1865	1755	1648
4	2333	2210	2092	1976	1863	1754	1647
5	2331	2208	2090	1974	1862	1752	1645
6	2328	2206	2088	1972	1860	1750	1743
7	2326	2204	2086	1970	1858	1748	1641
8	2324	2202	2084	1968	1856	1746	1640
9	2322	2200	2082	1967	1854	1745	1638
10	2320	2198	2080	1965	1852	1743	1636
11	2318	2196	2078	1963	1850	1741	1634
12	2316	2124	2076	1961	1849	1739	1633
13	2314	2192	2074	1959	1847	1737	1631
14	2312	2190	2072	1957	1845	1736	1629
15	2310	2188	2070	1955	1843	1734	1627
16	2308	2186	2068	1953	1841	1732	1626
17	2306	2184	2066	1951	1839	1730	1624
18	2304	2182	2064	1950	1838	1728	1622
19	2302	2180	2062	1948	1836	1727	1620
20	2300	2178	2061	1946	1834	1725	1619
21	2298	2176	2059	1944	1832	1723	1617
22	2296	2174	2057	1942	1839	1721	1615
23	2294	2172	2055	1940	1828	1719	1613
24	2291	2170	2053	1938	1827	1718	1612
25	2289	2169	2051	1936	1825	1716	1610
26	2287	2167	2049	1934	1823	1714	1608
27	2285	2165	2047	1933	1821	1712	1606
28	2283	2163	2045	1911	1819	1711	1605
29	2281	2161	2043	1929	1817	1709	1603
30	2279	2159	2041	1927	1816	1707	1601

	the Part proportional both in Time and Motion, &c.						
'	35	36	37	38	39	40	41
"	2100	2160	2220	2280	2340	2400	2460
30	2279	2159	2041	1927	1816	1707	1601
31	2277	2157	2039	1925	1814	1705	1599
32	2275	2155	2037	1923	1812	1703	1598
33	2273	2153	2035	1921	1810	1702	1596
34	2271	2151	2033	1919	1808	1700	1594
35	2269	2149	2032	1918	1806	1698	1592
36	2267	2147	2030	1916	1805	1696	1591
37	2265	2145	2028	1914	1803	1694	1589
38	2263	2143	2026	1912	1801	1693	1587
39	2261	2141	2024	1910	1799	1691	1585
40	2259	2139	2022	1908	1797	1689	1584
41	2257	2137	2020	1906	1795	1687	1582
42	2255	2135	2018	1904	1794	1686	1580
43	2253	2133	2016	1903	1792	1684	1578
44	2251	2131	2014	1901	1790	1682	1577
45	2249	2129	2012	1899	1788	1680	1575
46	2247	2127	2010	1897	1786	1678	1573
47	2245	2125	2009	1895	1785	1677	1571
48	2243	2123	2007	1893	1783	1675	1570
49	2241	2121	2005	1891	1781	1673	1568
50	2239	2119	2003	1889	1779	1671	1569
51	2237	2117	2001	1888	1777	1670	1565
52	2235	2115	1999	1886	1775	1668	1563
53	2233	2113	1997	1884	1774	1666	1561
54	2231	2111	1995	1882	1772	1664	1559
55	2229	2109	1993	1880	1770	1653	1558
56	2227	2107	1991	1878	1768	1661	1556
57	2225	2105	1989	1876	1766	1659	1554
58	2223	2103	1987	1875	1765	1657	1552
59	2220	2101	1986	1873	1763	1655	1551
60	2218	2199	1984	1871	1761	1654	1549

	A Table of Logistical Logarithmes for the Investigation of							
'	42	43	44	45	46	47	48	49
"	2520	2580	2640	2700	2760	2820	2880	2940
0	1549	1447	1347	1249	1154	1061	969	880
1	1547	1445	1345	1248	1152	1059	968	878
2	1546	1443	1344	1246	1151	1057	966	877
3	1544	1442	1342	1245	1149	1056	965	875
4	1542	1440	1340	1243	1148	1054	963	874
5	1540	1438	1339	1241	1146	1053	962	872
6	1539	1437	1337	1240	1145	1051	960	871
7	1537	1435	1335	1238	1143	1050	959	869
8	1535	1433	1334	1237	1141	1048	957	868
9	1533	1432	1332	1235	1140	1047	956	866
10	1532	1430	1331	1233	1138	1045	954	865
11	1530	1428	1329	1232	1137	1044	953	863
12	1538	1427	1327	1230	1135	1042	951	862
13	1527	1425	1326	1229	1134	1041	950	860
14	1525	1423	1324	1227	1132	1039	948	859
15	1523	1422	1322	1225	1130	1037	947	857
16	1522	1420	1321	1224	1129	1036	945	856
17	1520	1418	1319	1222	1127	1034	944	855
18	1518	1417	1317	1221	1126	1033	942	853
19	1516	1415	1316	1219	1124	1031	941	852
20	1515	1413	1314	1217	1123	1030	939	850
21	1513	1412	1313	1216	1121	1028	938	849
22	1511	1410	1311	1214	1119	1027	936	847
23	1510	1408	1309	1213	1118	1025	935	846
24	1508	1407	1308	1211	1116	1024	933	844
25	1506	1405	1306	1209	1115	1022	932	843
26	1504	1403	1304	1208	1113	1021	930	841
27	1503	1402	1303	1206	1112	1019	929	840
28	1501	1400	1301	1205	1110	1018	927	838
29	1499	1398	1300	1203	1109	1016	926	837
30	1498	1397	1298	1201	1107	1015	924	835

	the Part proportional, both in Time and Motion, &c.							
'	42	43	44	45	46	47	48	49
"	2520	2580	2640	2700	2760	2820	2880	2940
30	1498	1397	1298	1201	1107	1015	924	835
31	1496	1395	1296	1200	1105	1013	923	834
32	1494	1393	1295	1198	1104	1012	921	833
33	1493	1392	1293	1197	1102	1010	920	831
34	1491	1390	1291	1195	1101	1008	918	830
35	1489	1388	1290	1193	1099	1007	917	828
36	1487	1387	1288	1192	1098	1005	915	827
37	1486	1385	1287	1190	1096	1004	914	825
38	1484	1383	1285	1189	1095	1002	812	824
39	1482	1382	1283	1187	1093	1001	911	822
40	1481	1380	1282	1186	1091	999	909	821
41	1479	1378	1280	1184	1090	998	908	819
42	1477	1377	1278	1182	1088	996	906	818
43	1476	1375	1277	1181	1087	995	905	816
44	1474	1373	1275	1179	1085	993	903	815
45	1472	1372	1274	1178	1084	992	902	814
46	1470	1370	1272	1176	1082	990	990	812
47	1469	1368	1270	1174	1081	989	899	811
48	1467	1367	1269	1173	1079	987	897	809
49	1465	1365	1267	1171	1078	986	896	808
50	1464	1363	1266	1170	1076	984	894	806
51	1462	1362	1264	1168	1074	983	893	805
52	1460	1360	1262	1167	1073	981	891	803
53	1459	1359	1261	1165	1071	980	890	802
54	1457	1357	1259	1163	1070	978	888	801
55	1455	1355	1257	1162	1068	977	887	799
56	1454	1354	1256	1160	1067	975	885	798
57	1452	1352	1254	1159	1065	974	884	796
58	1450	1350	1253	1157	1064	972	883	795
59	1449	1349	1251	1156	1062	971	881	793
60	1447	1347	1249	1154	1061	969	880	792

	A Table of Logistical Logarithmes for the Investigation of									
'	50	51	52	53	54	55	56	57	58	59
"	3000	3060	3120	3180	3240	3300	3360	3420	3480	3540
0	792	706	621	539	458	378	300	223	147	73
1	790	704	620	537	456	377	298	221	146	72
2	789	703	619	536	455	375	297	220	145	71
3	787	702	617	535	454	374	296	219	143	69
4	486	700	616	533	452	373	294	218	142	68
5	785	699	615	532	451	371	293	216	141	67
6	783	607	613	531	450	370	292	215	140	66
7	782	696	612	529	448	369	291	214	139	64
8	780	695	610	528	447	367	289	213	137	63
9	779	693	609	526	446	366	288	211	136	62
10	777	692	608	525	444	365	287	210	135	61
11	776	690	606	524	443	363	285	209	134	60
12	774	689	605	522	442	362	284	208	132	58
13	773	687	603	521	440	361	283	206	131	57
14	772	686	602	520	439	359	282	205	130	56
15	770	685	601	518	438	358	280	204	129	55
16	769	683	599	517	436	357	279	202	127	53
17	767	682	598	516	435	356	278	201	126	52
18	766	680	596	514	434	354	276	200	125	51
19	764	679	595	513	432	353	275	199	124	50
20	763	678	594	512	431	352	274	197	122	49
21	762	676	592	510	430	350	273	196	121	47
22	760	675	591	509	428	349	271	195	120	46
23	759	673	590	507	427	348	270	194	119	45
24	757	672	588	506	426	346	269	192	117	44
25	756	670	587	505	424	345	267	191	116	42
26	754	669	585	503	423	344	266	190	115	41
27	753	668	584	502	422	342	265	189	114	40
28	751	666	583	501	420	341	264	187	112	39
29	750	665	581	499	419	340	262	186	111	38
30	749	663	580	498	418	339	261	185	110	36

Clavis Astrologiae Elimita, The Key to Astrology New Filed

	the Part proportional, both in Time and Motion, &c.									
'	50	51	52	53	54	55	56	57	58	59
"	3000	3060	3120	3180	3240	3300	3360	3420	3480	3540
30	749	663	580	498	418	339	261	185	110	36
31	747	662	579	497	416	337	260	184	109	35
32	746	661	577	495	415	336	258	182	107	34
33	744	659	576	494	414	335	257	181	106	33
34	743	658	574	493	412	333	256	180	105	31
35	741	656	573	491	411	332	255	179	104	30
36	740	655	572	490	410	331	253	177	103	29
37	739	654	570	489	408	329	252	176	101	28
38	737	652	569	487	407	328	251	175	100	27
39	736	651	568	486	406	327	250	174	92	25
40	734	649	566	484	404	326	248	172	98	24
41	733	648	565	483	403	324	247	171	96	23
42	731	647	563	482	402	323	246	170	95	22
43	730	645	562	480	400	322	244	169	94	21
44	729	644	561	479	399	320	243	167	93	19
45	727	642	559	478	398	319	242	166	91	18
46	726	641	558	476	396	318	241	165	90	17
47	724	640	557	475	395	316	239	163	89	16
48	723	638	555	474	394	315	238	162	88	15
49	721	637	554	472	392	314	237	161	87	13
50	720	635	552	471	391	313	235	160	85	12
51	719	634	551	470	390	311	234	158	84	11
52	717	633	550	468	388	310	233	157	83	10
53	716	631	548	467	387	309	232	156	82	8
54	714	630	547	466	386	307	230	155	80	7
55	713	628	546	464	384	306	229	153	79	6
56	711	627	544	463	383	305	228	152	78	5
57	710	620	543	462	382	304	227	151	77	4
58	709	324	541	460	381	302	225	150	75	2
59	707	623	540	459	379	301	224	148	74	1
60	706	621	539	458	378	300	223	147	73	0

SECT. VI.

How to Reduce the Planets places to any hour of the Day or Night, also to find the hour and minute, that a Planet comes to any particular point in the Ecliptique, by the Tables of Logistick Logarithmes.

I. For the more ready performance hereof, I thougIt it convenient to add this Table of Logistical Logarithmes, which are muoh easier then to work by vulgar Arithmetick, since all Operations are performed by Addition and Substraction; and if you please, Addition only.

II. The Diurnal motion of the Planets are easily obtained, if Direct, by substracting their places at Noon the day precedent, from their places at Noon the day subsequent; But if Retrograde, the contrary, *viz.* the day subsequent from day precedent.

III. The Table is figured at top with 1, 2, 3, 4, 5, 6, &c. and so from 1 to 59. And in the first Column of each Page is certain Seconds, *viz.* the left hand Page from 1" to 30", and the right hand Page from 30" to 60", so that in all it comprehends 60 parts at top and sides, which do not only represent min. and deg. of motion, but time also, as occasion requires; and their correspondent Logarithmes are found in the common Angles, as shall be illustrated by Examples.

IV. By the help of these *Logistical Logarithmes* you are inabled to make all necessary proportions sexaginary, where, Note that if your first Number be above 60m. you are to take half, and the proportion will be the same; unto which I add, that if your second Number be above 60m. you may say as 60 is to the excess of the second Number above 60, so is your third Number to a fourth proportional Number to be added to your third Number; as for Example. Suppose the proportion were as 60m. is to 87m. so 45m. to what?

	L. L.	
As 69 is to the excess above 69, *viz.* 27	3468	Add
So is 45m.	1249	
To 20m. 15"	4717	

Which added to 45m. your third Number gives 65m. 15' So that if 60m. gives 87m., 45m. gives 65m. 16", and so in any other of this kind.

V. By these Tables you may make proportion for Time and Motion also, and is briefly thus. First, if you would reduce the Planets motion to a certain hour of the day, 'tis but adding the Logist. Log. of the Planets Diurnal motion, to the Logist. Log. of time P. M. and from their Sum abate the Logist. Log. of 24 hours , *viz.* [3979] and you have the Logist. Log. of the deg. and min. or min. and seconds to be added. Secondly if you, desire to know at what hour and minute a Planet, or Star comes to such a point of the Ecliptique, substract the Logist. Log. of the Planets Diurnal motion, from the Logist. Log. of 24 hours (aforesaid) added to the Logist. Log. of the degrees and minutes the Planet wants of the desired point, and the remainder is the Logist. Log. of the hours and minutes P. M. desired.

Example, I.

If the ☉s Diuirnal motion be 58m. What doth he move in 2 hours? I work thus, *viz.*

As the Logist. Log. of 24 hours is the Logist. Log. of the ☉s Diurnal Motion 58m. so the Logist. Log. of 2 hours to the Logist. Log. of 4m. 5 seconds.

Operation.

The L.L. of	the ☉ D. m. 58'	147	
	2 hours	14771	added
		14918	Sum
The L.L. of	24 hours, substract	3979	
The L.L. of	4m. 50s.	10939	Rem.

Clavis Astrologiae Elimita, The Key to Astrology New Filed   211

Or if you take the *Arithmetical Complement* of the Log. of 24 which will be found [6021] and add to the other 2 Logar. and from their Sum abate a unite towards the left hand it produces the same Result.

Example, II.

Suppose the ☉ be 27d. 55m. in ♈ at Noon, and his Diurnal motion 58m. I would know by the Logistical Logarithmes what hour and minute the ☉ will be in 28d. 20m. of the same sign. Here the ☉ wants 25m. at Noon of the desired point.

Then say, as the Logist. Log of the ☉s Diurnal motion 58m. is to the Logist. Log. of 24 hours, so is the Logist. Log. of 25m. (that the ☉ wants if the point desired) to the Logist. Log of 10 hours 21m. fere.

Operation.

The Logist. Log of	24h.	3979
	25m.	3802 added
		7781 Sum.
The Logist. Log. of	58m	147 Subst.
	10h.21' sere	7634

Note, that if a Planets Diurnal motion be above 60m you are then to add to the Logist. Log of half the Diurnal motion of the Planet to the Logist. Log. of the time After-noon given, and from their Sum substract the Logist. Log. of 24h. and there remains half the minutes required, which must be doubled.

And here observe, that wherever Substraction is required by these Logar. you need only take the Arith. Comp. of the Log. to be Substracted [viz. Substract it from 1000] and then add all 3 Log. together, abating a Radius, and the work will be the same.

How to find the time of the Aspects by the Tables of *Logistical Logarithmes.*

The Rule.

I. Get the Planets Diurnal motion, whose Aspect you desire to the day whereon you find it will happen; and if the Planets be both Direct, or both Retrograde, let the lesser Diurnal motion be substracted from the greater; But in case the one happen to be Direct, and the other Retrograde, add both their Diurnal motions together, and their Sum, or Aggregate, is their Difference, or Diurnal Excess.

II. Take the Planets places (as you find them noted in the Ephemeris) for the Noon preceding the Aspect, and substract that Planets place which is swiftest in motion, from the place of the Planet which is slowest, and the remainder is their distance in Longitude.

III. Substract the *Logistical Logarithme* of the aforesaid Diurnal Excess, from the *Logist. Log.* of their difference (or distance) in Longitude, and the remainder is the Logarithme of the hours and minutes after Noon that the Aspect happens, which by Arithmetick is performed by this proportion, as the Diurnal Excess is to 24 hours, so the distance of the 2 Planets to the true time of the Aspect.

Example.

October the 15th. 1667. There happened a square Aspect between ♄ and ♀, and I desire to know the true time thereof; according to the foregoing Rules, I operate thus, *viz.*

			d. m.		d. m.
Oct. 15	♄	is in	26 1 ♈	Diurnal	♄ 0 3
at Noon	♀		24 54 ♎	motion of	♀ 1 15

Their difference in Longitude is 1d. 7m.

Diurnal Excess 1d. 12m.

Then say, if 1d. 12m. (*or* 72') *requires* 24h. *what* 1d. 7m. (*or* 67') *Answer* 22h. 20m. *By these* Logist. Log. *thus.*

		Operation.	
	1d. 7m.	17302	
	24h.	03979	add
		21281	Sum.
Logist. Log. of	1d. 12'	16990	subst.
	22h. 20'	4291	
		The thing required.	

Here if you add the *Complement Arith*. of the L. Log. of the first Number in the proportion abating Radius, Addition only performs the work.

Note that this is nothing different from that way of operation in finding the time when a Planet comes to a particular point of the Ecliptique; but only in this, instead of the Planets Diurnal motion there used, here is taken the Planets Diurnal excess: because both Planets have a motion, and so come to an Aspect; but in the other Case only one Planet moves to a point, the time thereof being required, &c.

I have been the larger upon this, because it is exceeding useful; and I would willingly make it as plain as may be, to the meanest apprehension. There be many Tables for this purpose, as Mr. Shakerly's, *Mr.* Newtons, *and others. But these Logist. Log are inferiour to none, and in my opinion (for general use) the best extant. Yet, let every Man use those he best affects, and before I conclude this Section take one useful Example more, viz.* [How to Aequate the Cusps of the Houses, found in any Table of Houses, &c.] *by the said Table of Logistical Logarithmes. In a certain Nativity.*

I. Let the ☉ be supposed in 5d. 20m. ♏ I turne to the Tables of Houses for the Latitude of the place (as suppose of *London*) under the Column of the tenth House in the Page ☉ in ♏, I find against 5d. 14m. 10m. 48" and under 6 deg. I find 14h. 14m. 40" in the first Column their difference is 3m. 52"; Now because I have 20m. more belonging to the ☉s place, I must Aequate for them thus, *viz.* If 1d. or 60m. gives 3m. 52", or 232", what will 20m or 1200" give?

The Logist. Log. of	3m. 52"	11908	
	20 0	4771	add
Logist. Log	1m. 18" fere	16679	

Here note because 60 is the first Number, I add the Logist. Log. together, and their Sum is the Logist. Log. of the fourth proportional Number; now I add this fourth Number 1m. 18" to the Number I find in the first Column under the Title *Time from Noon*, against 5. deg. of the tenth House, thus.

h.	m.	s.	
14	10	48	
00	1	18	add
14	12	06	The Sum.
2	14	32	T.P.M. add
16	26	38	R.A. of M.C.

And so I have the true Right Ascension in time belonging to the ☉s. place 5d. 20m. ♏, unto which I add my time from Noon, for which I would set my Figure agreeable to the ☉s. place, *viz.* 2h. 14m. 32" as in the Margin, and it amounts to 16h. 26m. 38" which is the true Right Ascension of the M.C. or tenth House unto which I would find the degrees and minutes of the Signs correspondent thus, *viz.*

The next	Greater	time from	16	29	8
	Lesser	Noon is	16	24	52
		1. Diff.	0	4	16
The true R. A. of time is			16	26	38
The next lesser substract			16	24	52
		2. Diff.	00	01	46

Clavis Astrologiae Elimita, The Key to Astrology New Filed

II. Then I say as the difference of the greater and lesser Ark 4m. 16" is to 60m. so is the difference between the next lesser Ark and thd true R. A. of time, *viz.* 1m. 46" to 24m. 51" which is the fourth proportional to be added to 8d. of ♐, which answers in the Tables of Houses to the Cusp of the tenth House, against 16h. 24m. 52" and so the true Cusp of the M.C. is ♐ 8d. 24m. 51".

The work is thus,

The Logist. Log. of		1m. 46"	15310	
	4	16	11481	Substract
Logist. Log. of	14	51	3829	

Here note because 60m. is the second Number I substract, &c. unless I take the Arith. Comp. of the Log. to be Substracted, then Addition performs it, as was intimated before.

III. To find the exact Cusp of the eleventh House, proceed thus, *viz.* The Cusp of the eleventh House agreeable to 8d. ♐ upon the tenth is 21d. 20m. ♐; which Substracted from the next greater, *viz.* 22d. 16m. ♐, leaves 56m. the difference.

Then reason thus, If 60m. or 1d. of the tenth gives 56m. difference, what shall 24m. 51" (that belongs to the Cusp of the tenth House before found) give. Answer 23m. 12" to be added to 21d. 20m. ♐, and so the true Cusp of the eleventh House is ♐ 21d. 43m. 12" as appears by the work.

The Logist. Log. of	56m. is	300
	24m. 51	3829 add
Logist. Log	23m. 12"	4129

After the same manner as you Aequate for the eleventh House, work for the twelfth, first, second, and third; and having the six Oriental Houses, the six Occidental Houses are the opposite Signs and Degrees, as hath been hinted before.

The Cusps of the Houses in the Tables of Houses, against 16h. 24m. 52" in the Column of Time from Noon are thus, *viz.*

House	d.	m.			d.	m.		Houses
X	8	0	♐	But being Ae-	8	25	♐	X
XI	21	20	♐	quated as before	21	41	♐	XI
XII	7	32	♑	directed, they pre-	7	58	♑	XII
I	9	52	♒	sent themselves	10	37	♒	I
II	12	48	♈	thus (omitting	13	42	♈	II
III	20	24	♉	Seconds.)	20	56	♉	III

By this Example, may the Cusps of the Houses be Aequated in any Figure, by the help of those Tables, with much ease, and no less exactness. And observe, that by the Example of the second Rule hereof you may, in like manner, Aequate for the finding the part proportional for the true Cusps of the Houses by the Tables of Right and Oblique Ascention of *Regiomontanus*, or *Argol*, much more exact then by the vulgar Sexaginary Tables, but not with so much speed.

SECT. VII.

How these Sexaginary Logistical Logarithmes *may be made, by the help of the* Logarithmetical *Tables of Absolute Numbers.*

[What the Arithmetical Complement is, and how to take it, is shewed Sect. I. of this Chapter,] also the use of a Canon of Sines and Tangents.]

I. Let the Arithmetical Complement of the abeoluteNumber of 3600 (which are the Seconds in an hour) be added to the Logarithme of every such Integer from 1 to the succedent Number, and it shall make the *Logistical Logarithmes* in *J. Keplar*, and those in Mr. *Newtons* help to calculation, as also those in *Shakerly's* Abreviation;

or the same (more compleat) in Mr. *Wings Astronomie Brittanica*. Sold at the *Bible* on *Ludgate-hill*.

Example, I.

The Log. of 3600" Comp. Arith.	64436975
The Log. of 1800" in 30m.	<u>32552725</u>
The Logist. Log. Correspondent	96989700

II. Let the *Arithmetical Complement* of the Logarithme 1440 (the minutes in 24 hours) be added to the Log. of every Integer from 1 to that Number, and the Sum will be the *Logist. Log.* for hours and minutes.

Example, II.

The log of 1440m. Comp. Arith.	68416375
The Log. of 720m. in 12 hours is	<u>28573325</u>
The *Logist. Log.* Correspondent	96989700

As you may see in *Shakerly's* Tables, &c.

III. These Logist. Logarithmes are the Arithmetical Complement of those in Mr. *Newton's Help to Calculation*, and may be made by Inverting the terms, thus.

Example, III.

The Log. of the absolute Number 3600" is	3,556303
The Log. of 240" in 4m. Comp. Arith. is	<u>7,610889</u>
The Logist. Log. Correspond. (abating Radius I)	1167192

Lastly, those in *Durrets Ephemerides* the proportion is Inverted by a second Operation, &c.

SECT. VIII.

Shewing the most Compendious way of Aequating the Cusps of the Coelestial Houses, in setting a Figure, with some uses of a Table of Houses, in the following Section.

I. Suppose I would erect a Scheme, exactly, by the Tables of Houses for the Latitude of 48d. North. The time given is *October* the *6th. Stilo novo* at six hours after Noon; and in a Catalogue of Places I find the Difference of Meridians from *Vraniburge* 40 min West; therefore, the time given now is 6 hours 40 min. P.M.

II. *October* 6m. S. N. the ☉ is found in ♎ 13d. 30m. 54s. to which agrees in *Ticho's* Aequation Table 4m. 21s. substract; then I say 40m. less by 4m. 21 seconds is equal to 35m. 39 seconds; and now the time is 6 hours 35m. 39s. P.M. and the ☉s. Diurnal motion is found to be 59m. 27s. Then I say if 24 hours gives 59m. 27s. what shall 6 hours, 35m, 39s. give facit 15m. which I add to the ☉s. place and the *6th* day at Noon; and so the ☉s. place is Aequated, and found, exactly to be in 13d. 45m. 54s. of *Libra*.

III. In the Table of Houses for the Lat. of 48d. 0m. against 14d. of *Libra* under the Colunm of the tenth House, I find the *Suns Right Ascension* in Time (in the first great Colunm, entituled *Time from Noon*) to be 12h. 51m. 29s. and against 13d. of *Libra* 12h. 47m. 47s. their Difference is 3m. 42s. and the odd min. and sec. adhering to the *Suns* place are 45m. 54s. Now I say as 60m. is to 3m. 42s. (the aforesaid Difference in R. A) so is 45m. 54s. to 2m. 46s. which added to the Right Ascension of Time against 13d. of *Libra*, amounts to 12h. 50m. 33s. for the true R. A. of the *Suns* place in 13d. 45m. 54s. of *Libra*.

IV. To this 12h. 50m. 33s. I add the Time from Noon given, *viz.* 6h. and the Sum is 18h. 50m. 33s. (which is the Right Ascension of the Mid.heaven in Time) and I desire the Cusps of the Houses exactly Correspondent thereunto in the aforesaid Lat. of 48d. And thus I proceed by the Tables of Houses.

Clavis Astrologiae Elimita, The Key to Astrology New Filed

Lat. 48d. h. m. s.	X ♑	XI ♑	XII ♒	I ♈	II ♊	III ♊
	d. m.	d. m.	d. m.	d. m.	d. m.	d. m.
18. 52. 12	12. 0	29. 0	29. 27	26. 38	7. 13	27. 14
18. 47. 52	11. 0	27. 49	27. 38	24. 33	5. 57	26. 13
0. 4. 20	11. 0.	1. 11	1. 49	2. 5	1. 16	1. 1

From 18h. 50m. 33s. my R. A. given I Substract the next lesser Ascen. in the Tables, *viz.* 18h. 47m. 52s. there remains 2m. 41s.

	Minutes.		Min.	
(Then I say as 4m. 20s.	60		30	(The
(the Diff. of the next grea-	76		36	several
ter and lesser R. A. in the	101	to	55	proportional
Table) is to 2m. 41s (the	129		63	parts) to
Diff. between the True	75		38	be Added
R.A. & the next letter) so is	61		31	as followeth.

Lat. 48	X ♑	XI ♑	XII ♒	I ♈	II ♊	III ♊
h. m. s.	d. m.	d. m.	d. m.	d. m.	d. m.	d. m.
18. 47. 52	11. 0	27. 49	7 38	24. 33	5. 57	26. 13
h. m. s.	add 30	add 36	add 55	1. 3	0. 38	add 31
18. 50. 33	11. 30	28. 25	28. 33	25. 36	6. 35	26. 44

Opposite	IV	V	VI	VII	VIII	IX
Houses Opposite d. & m.	♋ 11. 30	♋ 28. 25	♌ 28. 33	♎ 25. 36	♐ 6. 35	♐ 26. 44

[*And thus here is presented a plain Example of Aequating the Cusps of the Houses, which Method is General in all Latitudes, &c.*]

SECT. IX.

Containing several Propositions of the use of a Table of Houses.

Prop [I.] *To find when any Proposed degree (or degree and minute) of any Sign of the Zodiack shall rise above the Horizon.*

I. Having the true place of the *Sun* that day at Noon, enter the *Tables of Houses* for your Latitude under the Title of the tenth House, and seek there the *Suns* place; also the R. Asc. in Time Correspondent in the first Column, making proportion for the odd Minutes, if need be.

II. Find the degree, or degree and minute proposed under the Title of the Ascendant, and search the time in the first Column Correspondent thereunto; then substract the first Time before found from this last (adding 24h. if Substraction cannot be made) and you have the time (*prope verum*) that the degrees, (or the degrees and minutes) shall arise.

III. But if you would have the precize time, take the true place of the *Sun* for the time found, and go over again (or reiterate) the former Work, and you will have the exact time required; so in the former Example 16d. of ♌ will arise 13h. 9m. *post Meridiem*, &c.

Prop. [II.] *To find the time when any proposed degree of the Zodiack shall set.*

This is performed, in all respects, as the former; only instead of the degree proposed, observe when the opposite degree of the Ecliptique shall arise; and thus 'twill appear that 16 degrees of ♒, in the former Example, sets at 13h. 9m. *post Meridiem*. In the same manner you may find the hour that any proposed degree shall possess any of the other Cusps of the Houses; also what hour the *Sun* rises, or sets; and consequently is known the Quantity, both of Day or Night.

Prop. [III.] *To find the Quantity of an Arch of the Ecliptic that shall rise above the Horizon or set below the same, in any proposed time, from a point thereof given.*

I. First seek the point of the Ecliptic given in the Column of the Ascendant (in the Tables of Houses for your Latitude) as also the Time after Noon Correspondent in the first great Column of your Table, to which add your time proposed, and seek the Aggregate in the aforesaid Column of R. A. in Time; and right against that in the Colum of the Ascendant the degree of the Ecliptick sought: the Difference between which, and that point given is the Quantity of the Arch desired. *Exempligratia.*

II. So the proposed time being 2h. 41m. 44s. and the point of the Ecliptick given the beginning of ♎, then the Arch of the Ecliptick that shall arise, in that time, will be found 29d. 37m. of the same Sign in the Lat. of 48d. after the same manner proceed for any other Latitude; as also for the Quantity of the Arch that shall descend the *Horizon* in the same time, but then work by the opposite Sign.

Prop. [IV.] *To find in what time any Sign, or Arch of the Ectiptick shall rise, or set.*

I. Seek the beginnihg or the Sign propos'd in the Column of the Ascendant, and note the Time from Noon Correspondent; in like manner search for the end of the same Sign, in the aforesaid Column, and the time from Noon agreeable thereunto. Lastly substract the first Time from Noon (observed) from this last, and the Remainder is the time that the Arch, or Sign of the Zodiack is ascending, or rising.

II. And by this Rule you may discover the Quantity of Time any Sign of the Zodiack continues in the *Ascendant*: Now if you desire to know long a Sign is descending the *Horizon*, take the opposite Sign, and proceed in the same manner, and you have your desire; and thus you will find that the Sign *Aries* is ascending 59m. 21s. in the Lat. of 48d. *By the same Method you may obtain the Right, or Oblique Ascention (in an Oblique Sphere) of any point of the Ecliptick to any Circle of Position of the several Houses of a Coelestial Figure. Also by this Work may a* Significator *be directed to a* Promittor, *either* Direct, *or* Converse; Direct *is performed under the Circle of Position of the* Significator, *but* Converse Directions *under the Circle of the* Promittor: *and lastly, if a* Significator *be upon any of the* Cusps *of the Houses in Direct Direction, or Promissors in Converse the Quantity of a Direction is most easily found by the help of a Table of Houses only; together with a Table to Convert hours and minutes into degrees, and the contrary; which I have also inserted in this Third Part of this Book.*

I. *To make these things the more Intelligible to the Apprehensions of Young Students, I have here added some Examples, which are to be understood for the Latitude of 48d.*

The Rule.

Let the *Significator* be posited upon the Cusp of the eleventh House in 18d. 58m. of ♉, and the *Promissor* in 25d. 13m. of ♋; I search for 18d. 58m. in the Column of the eleventh House, and the Time Correspondent in the first great Column is 25m. 29s. which I reserve; in the same manner I seek for 25d. 13m. of ♋ in the Column of the eleventh House, and the time from Noon agreeable thereunto, *viz.* 4h. 50m. 10s. from which I deduct the aforesaid 0h. 25m. 29s. and there remains 4h. 33m. 31s. which Converted into degrees of the Aequator is 68d. 22h. 45s. The *Ark of Direction* required.

II. *To find what part of the Zodiack a Significator (posited upon the Cusp of any House) by Direct Direction shall come in any proposed Year.*

The Rule.

Substract the Year of the Radix, from the Year proposed, and Reduce the Remainder into Time, (*viz.* hours and minutes) which reserve: Then find the degrees of the Radical House in his proper Column, and the *Time from Noon* respondent in the first great Column of the Tables of Houses; to this Time, so found, add the aforesaid Time reserved, and the same shall be the Time from Noon; to which answers the beginning of each of the Houses agreeable to the *Progress*, or *place* of the *Significator* that year; But if you add 4 minutes to the beginning of the Houses which Respond, the Aggregate shall be Time from Noon for the Year following; and thus you may find the Quantity of any Ark of the Houses to any proposed Year, and the way and progress of the Direction you desire, which shall thus *Exemplifie*, viz. There was a certain person Born 1612. Whose Midheaven was 10 degrees 4m. of ♒, and the Ascendant 11 degrees 0 min.

II. In the Latitude of 48d. I desire to know to what degree of the Zodiack, or to what Cusp of the Houses a Direction shall come, in the Year, 1633. First I Substract 1612. from 1633. and the Difference is 21 Years; which Reduced into minutes of an hour, by multiplying by 4m. the product is 84 minutes, or 1 hour 24 minutes; which I reserve. In the next place I search for the degrees of the Mid-heaven, *viz.* 10d. 4m. under the Column of the tenth House, or the degrees of the Ascendant 11d. ♊ Under its proper Column, and in the Column of Time from Noon Respondent, I find 20h. 50m. 7s. to which I add 1 hour, 24 min. reserved, and the Sum is 22h. 14m. 7s. which sought in the first great Column of Time from Noon, the six Oriental Houses answering thereunto will present themselves as followeth.

10 ♓	11 ♈	12 ♉	1 ♋	2 ♋	3 ♌
o m.	d. m.	d. m.	d. m.	d. m.	d. m.
1. 30	5. 3	25. 23	2. 6	23. 46	11. 7

And these are the places of the Ecliptick, to which every House is come by Direction for the end of the twenty-first year of the Natives Age; but for the Year following, *viz.* the twenty-second Year, add 4m. in Time to the aforesaid 22h. 14m. 7s. the Sum is 22h. 18m. Search for this in the Colunn of Time from Noon, and you have the six Oriental Houses, to which the Directions are come at the end of twenty two Years, as followeth.

10 ♓	11 ♈	12 ♉	1 ♋	2 ♋	3 ♌
d. m.	d. m.	d. m.	d. m.	d. m.	d. m.
2. 33	6. 29	26. 43	3. 4	24. 34	11. 58

Lastly, if you Substract the Directions of the Houses for the end of the twenty-first Year, from those of the twenty-second Year, you have the Quantity of the Arches of the *Ecliptick* which every House makes by Direction in a proposed year, thus.

10	11	12	1	2	3
d. m.	d. m.	d. m.	d. m.	d. m.	d. m.
2. 33	6. 29	26. 43	3. 4	24. 13	11. 58
1. 30	5. 3	25. 23	2. 6	23. 46	11. 7
1. 3	1. 26	1. 20	0. 58	0. 48	0. 51

And this I have Illustrated the use of a Table of Houses of which the Young Artist ought not to be ignorant.

SECT. X.

Of the Several ways of Dividing the Heavens for the Erecting of a Scheme,

I. According to the Antient Astrologers, as *Ptolomy, Cardan, Schoner, Julius, Firmicus, &c.* Let the Ecliptick be divided into twelve equal parts, beginning at the Ascendant, as if the Ascendant be 10d. of ♈, the second is 10d. of ♉, the third 10d. of ♊, &c. To this relateth that Natural Astrology, published in *Arcandam*, or *John Indagine*; and thus the Ecliptick is divided into twelve equal parts by Circles meeting in the Poles of the Ecliptick, or Zodiack, to which *Ptolomy* Assents.

II. The second way is according to *Alcabitious*, which is thus; Take the Right Ascension of the 4 Angles, *viz.* the 10*th* House, Ascendant, 4*th*, and 7*th* let the difference of the Right Ascensions of these Angular points be divided into three equal parts, and the points in the Ecliptick Correspondent thereunto, are the Cusps of the intermediate Houses; and this is no more but dividing the Aequator into twelve equal parts by Circles meeting, or Intersecting in the Poles of the World.

III. According to *Porphyrius*, let the Angular distsnces of the tenth House, and Ascendant, &c. be divided into three equal parts in the Ecliptick. This Method differs very little from the second way used by the Antient Astrologers.

IV. But a fourth way is according to *Campanus* and *Gazulus*; Let the Circle of the East and West be divided into twelve equal parts, by Lines, or rather Circles meeting, or intersecting at the North and South points of the Horizon, as in the Rational way; and as this is the most difficult way, so perhaps may be most approved of by some, at least above the other three ways; and therefore I have inserted this Table following, for the more ready finding the Cusps this way.

Latit.	Ascend.	Houses II VIII	Houses XII VI	Houses III IX	Houses XI V
	Dist.	Polates	Dist.	Polars	Dist.
	d. m.	d. m.	d. m.	d. m.	d. m.
50	41 56	41 34	27 43	22 31	20 21
51	42 32	42 18	27 30	22 52	19 58
52	43 09	43 01	27 16	23 12	19 34
53	43 49	43 45	27 01	23 32	19 10
54	44 29	44 28	27 46	23 52	18 45
55	45 11	45 11	26 29	24 11	18 20

Note that in Calculating this Table, having obtained the distance from the tenth to the eleventh House; search also the distance from the eleventh to the twelfth House, by subducting the distance from the tenth to the eleventh, out of the distance from the tenth to the twelfth House: and note likewise that the distance from the Midheaven to the Ascendant is always 90 degrees, or a Quadrant. It is farther to be noted that the distance in the last Column of the Table is the distance from the tenth to the eleventh House, and in the fourth Column you have the distance from the eleventh to the twelfth House, and in the second Column you have the distance from the twelfth to the Ascendant in all 90 degrees in the Aequator.

The use of this Table.

Having the Right Ascension of the tenth House, to the same add the distance for the eleventh, and you have the Oblique Ascension of the eleventh House, to which again add the distance from the twelfth, and you have the Oblique Ascension of the twelfth, to which add the distance for the Ascendant, and you have its Oblique Ascention, as in the common way, only instead of 30d. you use these proper distances; and having the Oblique Ascention of the Houses against the said distances, you have also the Polar Elevations, under which these Oblique Ascensions will give the Cusps of the Houses desired.

Example.

In the Latitude 51d. let the Right Ascention of M. C. be 307d. 21m. the distance in the Table for the eleventh, fifth, ninth, and third Houses, is 19d. 58m. which being added, is 327d. 19m. the Oblique Ascention of the eleventh; and this in the Pole of 22d. 52m. will give the Cusp of the eleventh House 18d. 10m. ♒, to 327d. 19m. the Oblique Ascention of the eleventh add 27d. 30m. the distance of the twelfth, eighth, second, and sixth Houses, and you have 354d. 49m. the Oblique Ascention of the twelfth, which in the Pole 42d. 18m. will give the Cusp 20d. 40m. ♓, &. *sic in aliis.*

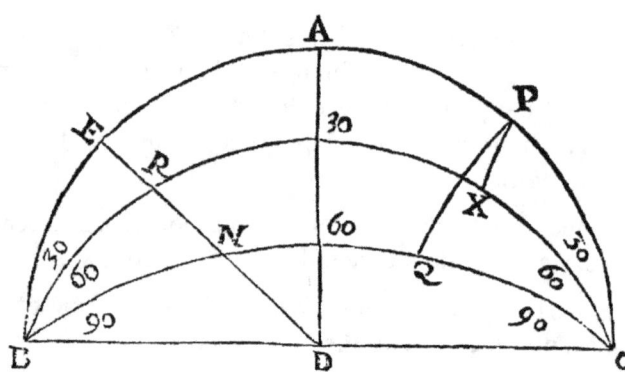

The Construction, and making of this Table is thus, viz.

I. In this Diagram Let B, E, A, P, C, represent half the grand Meridian Circle; and B, D, C, half the Horizon; B, 30 C, and B, 60 C, two Circles of Position, which divide a quarter of the Prime vertical Circle A, D, into three equal parts, (and consequently the whole into twelve.) Hence I desire to find the Polar Numbers in the Table, *viz.* the Poles Elevation above the Circles of Position, P, X, and P, Q; also at what distance these Circles Intersect the Aequinoxal, E, D, from the Meridian at E.

In the Rectangled Triangle, P, X, C, Right Angled at X, (for P, X, and P, Q. are Arches supposed to fall at Right Angles upon the Circles of Position) there is given the side, P, C, 52d. the Latitude of the place, and the Angle C, 30d. to find the Side opposlite, P, X; now in regard the Right Angle is supposed at X, X, P, will be the middle part because it lies remote from the rest, and separated from P, C, which here is the Hypotenusa by the Angle P, and from the Angle C, by the Side C, X; therefore by the fourth Case of Right Angled Triangles, I add the Sine of 30 degrees to the Sine of 52d.

Example.	Sine 30d.	969897
	Sine 52d.	989653
Their Sum—Rx is = to the Sine of 23d. 12m		959550

This 23d. 12m. is the Polar Number, as in the Table.

II. For the Aequinoctial Distance in the Rectangle, Spherical Triangle, R, E, B, (which is Right Angled at E, where the Aequator cuts the Meridian) there is given B, E, the Aequinoxial hight 38d. and the Angle at B, 30 to find E, R; here E, B, is the middle part, because the Right Angle E, separates nothlng; and therefore by the eleventh Case of Right Angled Spherical Triangle, I operate thus; and to bring Radius in the first place instead of Co-tangent, I use the Tangent, and abate, Radius.

Tangent 30d. B,	976144
+ Sine of 38d. B, E,	978934
Rx is = to Tan , E, R, 19d. 34m.	955078

Which is the Aequinoctial distance desired, as in the Table.

III. Now in setting a Figure this way, instead of adding 30d. 60d. &c. *viz.* the Aequinoctial distance used in *Regiomantanus* his Rational way. (*so called, because the Houses are distinguished by circles drawn in the same manner with those that Constitute the four Cardinal points of Heaven; but by others 'tis accounted Irrational, because this way of his will not hold Universally*) to the Right Ascention of the Mid-heaven, thereby to gain the Oblique Ascention of the Houses; in this way of Division of the Heavens, according to *Campanus*, add the distances found in the Table (under their respective Houses and Latitudes) to the Right Ascention of the Mid-heaven, as in the Latitude of 52d. for the eleventh and third Houses, add 19d. 34m. and for the twelfth and second 27d. 16m. and for the Ascendant, 43d. 9m. &c. as you find the Numbers in the Table, always abating 360d. if your Number exceed; and thus you will have the Ascentions of the six Oriental Houses: then find the Cusps under their respective Poles, as the Cusp of the eleventh House under 23d. 12m. the twelfth under the Pole of 43d. lm. and the Ascendant under the Pole of 52d. &c. Just after the same Method as in the Rational way, either by Tables of Oblique Ascention, or by the Doctrine of Triangles, as shall be exemplified at large.

Where note that the four Angles alter not in all the five Modes of dividing the Heavens, except in the first way.

These are the several ways of setting a Figure of Heaven, according to the Antients; but that way which is most approved of by all Modern Astrologers, and generally received, is called the Rational way of *Johannes Regiomontanus*, who divides the Aequator into twelve equal parts by six great Circles drawn through the Mutual Section of the Horizon, and Meridian, whose distances are accounted 30d. in the Aequator; the chiefest are the Meridian, and Horizon, which cut each other at Right Angles, and divide the Heavens into four Quarters, or Quadrantals, each Quarter being again sub divided into three equal parts more; and Consequently the whole Heavens into twelve Divisions, called *Houses*, the Cusps whereof cut the Zodiack into unequal parts, as by the setting of a figure doth appear.

My next business shall be to present the Reader with Examples, first how to Rectifie a Nativity several ways; and in the next Chapter, shew how to set a Scheme Artificially the Rational way, by a Canon of *Sines* and *Tangents*.

CHAP. III.

Of a Nativity, and the several ways of Rectification thereof.

SECT. I.

What a Nativity is.

By a Nativity we are to understand, that very moment of time that the Infant is delivered, or separated from the Mothers Womb, and receives the Impression of Air upon it's tender Body; and not that point of time wherein part of the Body appears, (as some are pleased to Cavil at) *Cardan* affirms that to be the moment, in which the Infant draws his first Breath, or moves the Lungs: in short, that very punctilio of time, wherein the Child is said to be compleatly Born into the World, is the moment of the Nativity, in which the Stars are said to have Influence upon the tender Body of the Native; and the Position of Heaven for that very instant is to be considered, as the Ground-work, and Foundation whereon to Build an Astrological Judgement of the Future Actions, or Fate of the Native in the World. But since the obtaining of this true moment of time is so exceeding difficult by reason of the uncertainty of Clocks, Dials, or Watches, or any other means, Astrologers have found out several ways for Rectification thereof, which I come in the next place to speak of.

SECT. II.

How to Rectifie a Nativity several ways.

Amongst those several ways, the Antients have given, to Correct a Nativity, and thereby bring the supposed time, to the true time: that of Accidents, is accounted the most Certain, and Infallible, which is thus, *viz.*

I. Having the Estimate time given, erect your Scheme, either by a Table of Houses for the Latitude of Birth, or otherwise; and let the Planets places be exactly reduced.

II. Draw this Scheme into a *Speculum* (or Table) according to the usual Form, which is done after this manner; take half, or a quarter of a Sheet of Paper, and divide the breadth thereof into thirteen Columns, and the length into thirty one: In the top of the uppermost Column, set the twelve Signs in order, &c. ♈, ♉, ♊, ♋, &c. and in the first left hand Column, place the degrees of the Signs beginning with 0, 1, 2, 3, &c. to 30.

III. Take the Planets out of your Figure, and place them in their respective Columns, *viz.* right against the degrees of their places in the first Column, and just under the Signs they are in, noted at top. Into this Speculum you are also accordingly to Insert the ☊ and ☋ the ⊗ the Antiscions, and Contra-antiscions of the Planets; as also their terms which you may take out of the Table of Essential Dignities, and some of the most eminent Fixed Stars of the first Magnitude that are near the Ecliptick.

IV. Having proceeded thus far, note down the several Aspects of the Planets, both Dexter, and Sinister: as suppose ♄ in ♉ his ✶ Sinister falls in the same degree of 4, and his F Dexter in ♓, his □ Sinister in ♌, □ Dexter in ♒, his △ Sinister in ♍, △ Dexter in ♑, and his ☍ in ♏, which you may easily do by a small Table of the Aspects of the Planets at the beginning of the first part of the Book, understand the like in all other Planets, &c. And lastly, in the Collaterate Column of the Sign and Degree of the Ascendant and Mid-heaven: note *Asc.* and *M. C.* and your *Speculum* is finished; I have been the larger upon this, because I would make it plain to Learners.

V. Collect as many Accidents from the Native (as are of note) that can be procured, and the Year, Month (and Day, if it be possible) they happened; as thus, Aged so many Years, Months, and Days, the Native was Invaded with a strong Feavour, Small Pox, or the like. Aged so many Years, and Months, to a place of preferment, or Marriage, &c. having Collected your Accidents that have happened, after this manner, repair to the *Speculum*; and if you would find a Direction for an Accident of the Body, as Sickness, &c. Begin at the Ascendant, and run down that Column, and see if the Ascendant meets with the Body, or Aspect of some Planet that may denote the Accident within such a space of time, or not; allowing about a degree of Oblique Ascention for a Year, if not remove our Ascendant backward, or forward, (provided you go not far beyond the estimate time) till you make the degree ascending correspondent, After the same manner for an Accident or Preferment, or Honour, examine the M. C. see what direction that met withal in such a space of time, this is performed by Right Ascension, as the Ascendant by Oblique, *viz.* Substract the Oblique Ascension of the Ascendant, or R. Ascension of the *M. C.* from the Oblique or Right Ascension of the Promittor, and the remainder are the degrees of the Direction, usually called the Ark of direction, and by Rectifying either of those Angles, the true time of Birth will be exactly found. The same Method you may use in the *Sun*, or *Moon*, if the Accidents agree with their Directions; but first their Circle of Position must be known.

SECT. III.

Here follows Examples, how to verifie the Ascendant by an Accident.

I. Let the Ascendant be supposed to be 18d. 28m. ♈ in the Latitude 52d. and ♄ in 2d. 31m. ♍, put the case I have an Accident of the nature of the Ascendant to the □ of ♄ which falls in 2d. 31m. ♊; suppose it some tedious Ague, &c. Aged 36 Years current (and the estimate time *March* the 11*th*. 6h. 30m. A. M.)

I find the Ob. Asc. of the □ of   d. m.
♄ in 2d. 31m. ♊, in Lat. 52d.   31 29

```
        The Ob. Ascention of the Ascendant
            18d. 28m. ♈ in that Latitude is        07   8 Subst.
        Remains the Ark of Direction              23  51
```

II. Here the Ark of Direction is but 23d. 51m. which allowing about a deg. for a Year is now 24 years, and the Accident happened at 35 years 115 dayes, now suppose a degree notes a year, 35 years gives 35d. and to 115 days (according to that measure) answers 19m. 10s. in all 35d. 19m. 10".

III. To the Oblique Ascension of the □ to ♄ add 360d. that so Substraction may be made, and it will amount unto

```
                                        391d.   29m.   00"
From which Substract                    035     19     10
And there remains the Oblique
    Ascension of the Horoscope          356     09     50
```

Unto which. answers 20d. 36m. ♓, for the true Ascendant Rectified.

```
From the Ob. Ascen.                     356     09     50
Substract the Quadrant 90d               90     00     00
Rests the R. Ascen. M. C.               266     09     50
```

Unto which answers ♐ 26d. 28m. omitting Seconds.

IV. Lastly, to find the hour and minute of the day corespondent, I proceed thus; I take the Oblique Ascension of the Ascendant of the estimate time agreeing with 18d. 28m. ♈, and thereunto add the Circle, that Substraction may be made; and the Aggregate is 367d. 38m. from which I Substract the true Corrected Oblique Ascension 356 deg. 9m. 50" and there remains 11d. 28m. 10s. which in time gives 45m. 52' 40" you may omit the seconds and thirds, and say 46m. which Substracted from the estimate time 6h. 30m. leaves, *March* 11. 5h. 44m. A.M. for the true time Corrected.

[*Here note that if you desire the hour of the day unknown for which any Scheme is set, 'tis but subducting the R. Asc. of the Sun from the R. Ascen. of the Midheaven (by adding 360d. where Substraction cannot be made) and the Remainder is the R. Ascen. of the Time from Noon, which Converted into Time by the Table for that purpose, shews the hour of the day, or night required.*]

Example, II.

Which shall be upon the exemplary Geniture.

I. The estimate time of Birth of a certain *Gentleman* was *March* the 11*th*. 1650 current at 18h. 30m. P. M. the Latitude of the Place was 52d. 18m. the true *R. Ascen.* of the *Sun* Correspondent to his place at that time, (*viz.* 1d. 49m. of ♈) is 1d. 40m. unto which I add the time given 18h. 30m. Converted into *Aequinoctial degrees*, viz. 277d. 30m. and the Sum thereof is 279d. 10m. for the R. Ascen. of the *Mid heaven* of the estimate *Figure*, unto which I add 90d. or a Quadrant; and the Sum is the Oblique Ascen. of the estimate Figure, *viz.* 369d. 10m. then the Cusp of the Mid-heaven will be about 7d. of *Capricorn*, and of the Ascendant about 19d. of *Aries* (agreeable to 9d. 10m. the Oblique Ascen. abating the Circle.)

II. Now to Correct the estimate Figure, by Accidents, I proceed thus, when the Native was 15. years, 142. days old, he was Invaded with a *Strong Feavour*, and other Distempers, which much afflicted the Body; *Mars* was in *Aries* in the Radix and therefore casts his *Quartile Aspect* to *Cancer*: Now considering this Direction might properly signifie such an Accident, I may adventure (other Testimonies concurring) to verifie, or Correct this supposed Time thereby.

III. The Time of the Accident Reduced into degrees and minutes, according to *Nabod's* Measure, is 15d. 18m. which I Substract from the *Oblique Ascen.* of the □ of ♂ in ♋, *viz.* 63d. 15m. *Sub. Lat.* 52d. 18m. and the Remainder is 47d. 57m. the true Oblique *Ascension* of the *Ascendant* of the Corrected, or *Rectified Figure*; unto which I first add the Circle 360d. that so I may abate 90d. (or if you please, add 270. which is the same thing) and so I have the true *Right Ascen.* of the Corrected *Mid-heaven* also, *viz.* 317d. 57m. from which I Substract the R. A. of the estimate M. C. *viz.* 279d. 10m. and there remains 38d. 47m. or if you please, Substract 9d. 10m. the *Oblique Ascen.* of the Estimate *Figure* from 47d. 57m. the *Oblique Ascen.* of the *Rectified Scheme*, and there remains 38d. 47. as before; which Converted into Time (by the Table for that purpose) gives 2 hours, 25 minutes, 8 seconds later than the Estimate, or supposed Time; and hence then the true Corrected Time of Birth appears to be the 11*th*. day of *March*, 1650. Current 21 hours 5 minutes, 8 seconds *Post Meridiem*, viz. the 12*th*. day at 9h. 5m. 8s. *mane.*

SECT. IV.

How to Rectifie a Nativity by the Sun, or Moon.

I. When you have an Accident of Note given, and cannot find it agree with any Direction of the M. C. or Ascendant. then consider the Position of the Luminaries, and see to which of them it may most Rationally Correspond; in the next place having pitch'd upon the most probable Significator, you may neerly estimate by his place in the Figure what Circle of Position he is upon, (*viz.* how much the Pole is elevated above it,) and having guessed at the Pole of Position either of the *Sun* or *Moon*) direct him, or her, to the most significant Promittor under that Pole, noting how much the Ark of Direction is wide, or comes short of the time of the Accident given.

II. Estimate (or guess) the second time at the Pole of Position, and accordingly work out the Direction as before; having done so, note the difference between these two Directions, and by the Rule of Proportion you may find the true Pole of Position, and consequently the exact Ascendant: Reasoning thus, if the difference of these two Arks of Direction gives so much in the Pole of Position, What shall the difference between the true Direction, and the neerest thereunto, give in the Pole of Position? &c. And thereby you will come to have the true Pole of Position; and from thence the true Oblique Ascention, or Descention of the Luminary, its distance from the Meridian, and by Operation the Figure Rectified, &c. as for Example.

Suppose a Man Aged 19 Years, 82 days, had a terrible fit of Sickness, (the time of which being thus exactly known,) and there be no Direction of the Ascendant to any Promittor that may aptly signifie so eminent an Accident; I proceed thus, and examine the progress of the *Moon* who, I perceive, meets with the *Quartile of Mars* in 21d. 12m. *Aries*; which I may adventure to pitch upon for an apt Direction: Now according to the Rule, I guess at the Pole of Position of the *Moon*, who is Significator, (as by her Position in any Figure a Man may easily do and not far wide from truth knowing the Poles Elevation above the several Circles of the Houses) let her Pole of Position be supposed 50d. then her Declination being 17d. 31m. (before known) her Ascen. Differ. under that Pole will be found 22d. 27m. and therefore her Ob. Ascen. 351d. 24m. then the Ob. Ascen. of the *Quartile* of *Mars* falling into *Aries*, aforesaid, will be found under that Pole of the *Moon* 9d. 33m. (and here note by the way you must always Direct a Promittor under the same Pole of the Significator) now I add to the Oblique Ascen. of *Mars* 360 that Substraction may be made; the Sum is 369d. 33m. from which Sub-duct the Ob. Ascen. of the *Moon, leaves* 18d. 9m. for the Ark of Direction, but the true Arch should be 19d. 14m. the Differ is 1d. 5m. too little.

Therefore I will suppose again, the Pole of the *Moon*, 49d. her Ob. Ascen. under that Pole is 350d. 35m. and the Ob. Ascen. (under that Pole) of the *Quartile* of *Mars* is 369d. 54m. and so the Ark of Direction is 19d. 19m. the Difference is 5m. too much, and the Difference between these two Arches (proceeding from these two Poles 49d. and 50m.) is 1d. 10m. Then I say if 1d. 10m. *viz.* 70m. (Arch Direct.) gives 1d. or 60m. of the Pole of Position, what shall 5m. give *facit* 4m. therefore I say the *Moons* true Pole of Position is 49d. 4m. having before her Declin. and R. A. find her Ascen. Diff. and so her Ob. Ascen. under that Pole *viz.* 350d. 39m. and now to find her Circle of Position, I say by Prop. IX. *ult.* N. B. As the Tangent of the Lat. of

Pole of the place 52d 30m	1011502
To the Tang. of the Pole of Posit. 49d. 4m	1006185
So is the Radius	1000000
To the Sine of the Cir. Posit. 62. 14.	994683

Which 62d. 14m. added to her Ob. Ascen. (under her true Pole) 360d. 39m. gives 412d. 53m. (by the Inverse of the fourth Rule, Prop. IX.) from which Deduce 360d. leaves 52d. 53m. the *Right Ascention* of the *Imun Coeli*; and Consequently the R.A. of the M.C. Rectified by this Method and the true Figure sought, unto which time you are again to Reduce the Planets places; and therefore 'tis necessary first of all to Compute their Motions for every 4 or 5 minutes, or thereabouts, &c.

[*Note that you ought to be exceeding careful in Rectifying the* Suns *place in any Nativity; for the mistake of one minute in his motion, begets 24m. in time* (*the reason is the* Sun *moves about one minute in 24 minutes of time according to his mean motion.*]

SECT. V.

How to Rectifie a Nativity by the Trutine, or Scale of Hermes, (that famous Person,) and allowed by Ptolomy *himself.*

Hermes, who is reputed by an Eminent Author, to have been the wisest of Men in his time, was of this Opinion; that the very degree of the same Sign wherein the *Moon* was at Conception of the Child, should be the true degree of the Ascendant at Birth. And *Ptolomy* saith, *look what Sign the* Moon *is in at the time of Birth, make that very Sign the Ascendant at Conception*; and what Sign you find the *Moon* in at Conception, make that, or its opposite, the Sign ascending at Birth: This way of Rectification comes short of that by Accidents, however, because some have much applauded it, I thought good to Insert it, lest the Book without it should be thought deficient. Here is also a Table added different from that vulgarly used, and much more ready to find the true Conception, by the Nativity, and the contrary.

Now having found the day of Conception by the Nativity to find the time of day when the *Moons* place in the Radix ascends, turn to the Schemes and find the neerest Ascendant, then note what hours and minutes stand over it, from which Substract the hours and minutes. of the R. A. of the *Sun* for the day of Conception, and you have the hour and minute desired agreeable to the Figure of Conception, to which reduce the Planets places; and so compleat the Scheme thereof, which will be necessary to be consulted, and some help also in the Judgment of the Scheme of the Natives Birth.

A Table for the ready finding the Conception by the Nativity & Contra.													
Nativity Concep.	J. A.	F. M	M J.	A. J.	M A.	J. S.	J. O.	A. N.	S. D	O. J.	N. F.	D M	Nativity Concep.
S D	A	A	S	A	S	S	S	S	A	S	S	A	S D
0 0	2	3	0	1	0	0	0	0	1	0	0	2	6 0
0 13	1	2	1	S	1	1	1	1	S	1	1	1	5 17
0 26	S	1	2	1	2	2	2	2	1	2	2	S	5 4
1 9	1	S	3	2	3	3	3	3	2	3	3	1	4 21
1 21	2	1	4	3	4	4	4	4	3	4	4	2	4 9
2 4	3	2	5	4	5	5	5	5	4	5	5	3	3 26
2 17	4	3	6	5	6	6	6	6	5	6	6	4	3 13
3 0	5	4	7	6	7	7	7	7	6	7	7	5	3 0
3 13	6	5	8	7	8	8	8	8	7	8	8	6	2 17
3 26	7	6	9	8	9	9	9	9	8	9	9	7	2 4
4 9	8	7	10	9	10	10	10	10	9	10	10	8	1 21
4 21	9	8	11	10	11	11	11	11	10	11	11	9	1 9
5 4	10	9	12	11	12	12	12	12	11	12	12	10	0 26
5 17	11	10	13	12	13	13	13	13	12	13	13	11	0 13
6 0	12	11	14	13	14	14	14	14	13	14	14	12	0 0
S D	A	A	A	A	A	A	A	A	A	A	A	A	S D
6 0	2	3	0	1	0	0	0	0	1	0	0	1	0 0
5 17	3	4	1	2	1	1	1	1	2	1	1	2	0 13
5 4	4	5	2	3	2	2	2	2	3	2	2	3	0 26
4 21	5	6	3	4	3	3	3	3	4	3	3	4	1 9
4 9	6	7	4	5	4	4	4	4	5	4	4	5	1 21
3 26	7	8	5	6	5	5	5	5	6	5	5	6	2 4
3 13	8	9	6	7	6	6	6	6	7	6	6	7	2 17
3 0	9	10	7	8	7	7	7	7	8	7	7	8	3 0
2 17	10	11	8	9	8	8	8	8	9	8	8	9	3 13
2 4	11	12	9	10	9	9	9	9	10	9	9	10	3 26
1 21	12	13	10	11	10	10	10	10	11	10	10	11	4 9
1 9	13	14	11	12	11	11	11	11	12	11	11	12	4 21
0 26	14	15	12	13	12	12	12	12	13	12	12	13	5 4
0 13	15	16	13	14	13	13	13	13	14	13	13	14	5 17
0 0	16	17	14	15	14	14	14	14	15	14	14	15	6 0

SECT. VI.

The use of the Table of Conception, &c.

I. This is very easily understood, for the two uppermost rows of Months, the one shews the Month for the Nativity, and the other the answering Month of Conception, *& Contra*. Seek the *Moons* Position from the Ascendant or seventh House, in the sides of the Table, either in the Nativity or Conception, and the Month at head, in the Angle of meeting you have the days to be added or substracted, to, or from the day of Birth, or Conception.

II. Note that if the *Moon* be above the Earth in your Figure estimate, *viz.* in the 12*th*. 11*th*. 10*th*. 9*th*. 8*th*. or 7*th* House, take her distance from the Cusp of the West Angle or 7*th* House; but if she be under the Earth, *viz.* in the 1*st*. 2*d*. 3*d*. 4*th*. 5*th*. or 6*th* House, take her distance from the Sign and Degree ascending, always substracting the Signs, Degrees, and Minutes of the Angles, from the Sign, Degree, and Minute of the *Moons place*, by adding 12 Signs where Substraction cannot be made; and with this distance enter the Table, as above directed.

III. Let the *Moon* in some Figure be above the Earth, and the day of Birth, suppose *April* 13. Let the *Moons* distance from the 7*th* be 1 Sign 21 Degrees. I look *April* at top, to which answers *July*, for the Month of Conception; then I repair to the first great Column on the left hand, against the *Moon, supra Terram, ab Occasu in Nativitatibus*, and I find 1 Sign 21 Degrees; (or if I had not found my just Number I should accept the neerest) and right under *April*, and against 1 S. 21 D. I find 11 days to be added, (as the Letters direct) to the 13*th* day, and that points out the 24*th*. of *July* for the day of Conception; after the same manner, having the *Moons* distance from the 1*st*. or 7*th*. in the Figure of Conception, I repair to the right hand Column, and proceed as before, and find the true day of Birth, from the Figure of Conception, &c. This shall be farther explained in the Exemplary Geniture. Note that if the Year of your Birth be Leap Year, you must add a day more.

Note that having found the Conception, and by that your desire to find the Birth-day, 'tis but the Invers to the former Operation, seeking the *Moons* Position on the right hand of the Table, and the Aequation of days, add, or substract contrary to the Letters, A, or S, &c.

IV. Lastly, there are some other ways as the Animodar of *Ptolomy*, the Transits of the Planets upon the principal Places of the Geniture, and the directions of Profectional Figures, (*viz.* the chief Angles thereof) to their several Promittors; but since there is but small certainty in any of these ways to Rectifie a Nativity by, I shall not here trouble my self to insert them; for undoubtedly, that by Accidents is the most Rational, and hath the most probability of truth in it, and the only way as yet known, to verifie the Genesis of any Person.

This is not only my Opinion, but of all the most Eminent Artists, this day living in *England*, who have sufficiently confirmed this Doctrine by Experience, which is the best Moderater.

[*Note that though Directions are approved of to be very efficatious in their Operations upon Humane Bodies, yet it must be understood with the Concurrence if suitable Transits of the Planets, especially the Superiours, as also Revolutions; and hence Accidents verified by Directions are thought no sufficient verification without the Revolutions and Transits agree.*

CHAP. IV.

An Example how to set a Scheme of the Heavens the Rational way, according to the Directions given in Proposition the tenth, which depends upon the fourth Case of Oblique Spherical Triangles, a Perpendicular being let fall, and the Oblique Triangles thereby Reduced into two Right Angled Triangles, &c.

I. Having before given the Proportions how this is to be performed, 'twill be necessary here to explain it by an *Example*, which shall be upon the Nativity of a loving Friend of mine, Born *March* the 11*th*, 1650. *Current* 21 hours 5 min. 8 seconds, P.M. in the Latitude of 52 deg. 18 min. North; being the Corrected time, and the *Suns* Place (with the rest of the seven *Planets*) Calculated some Years since, and exactly *Reduced* to the Meridian of Birth from the *Caroline Tables* present themselves thus, both in Longitude and Latitude, &c. as in the following Table.

Names of Plan.	Longit.	Latitude	Ants. & Contra.
	d. m.	d. m.	d. m.
Saturn	24 ♊ 24	0 S 51	♋ 5. 36 ♑
Jupiter	8 ♏ 16	1 S 28	♒ 21 44 ♌
Mars	6 ♈ 39	0 S 39	♍ 23 21. ♓
Sol	1 ♈ 55	0. 0	♍ 28 5. ♓
Venus	21 ♓ 56	1 S 26	♎ 8. 4 ♈
Mercury	4 ♈ 2Rx	3 N 10	♍ 25. 68 ♓
Luna	29 ♏ 52	1 S 00	♒ 0. 8 ♌
Part of Fort.	20 ♒ 29	Caudo	♏ 15. 30 ♒
Dragons H.	20 ♉ 1	20 ♏ 1	As. 22. 32 ♊

III. For the Right Ascention of the Sun, according to *Prop*. II.

I add the Co-sine of 23d. 30m. the ☉s. Dec. max   9962398
I add the the Tangent of ld. 55m. the ☉s. Dist. â ♈   8524586
Their Sum is the Tang. of R. A. ☉ ld. 45m.   8486984

IV. For the R. A. of Time after Noon, *viz*. 21 hours 5 min. 8 seconds, I repair to the Table Intituled *A Table of Converting Hours and Minutes of Time*, &c.

```
                              d.   m.
              21h.           315.  0
Against       5m.    I find  001. 15  add
              8s.            000.  2
              R.A. of Time   316  17  add
                    Sun      001. 45
```

	d.	m.
V. The R. A. of the M. C.	318	02
To which add	30	00
The Sum is the Ob. Ascen. of the 11*th*. House	348	02
Add	30	00
The Sum is the Ob. Ascen. of the 12*th*. House	378	02
abating the Circle, *viz*.	18	02
Add	30	00
The Sum is the Ob. Ascen. of the Ascendant	48	2
Add	30	0
You have the Ob. Ascen of the second House	78	2
To which again add	30	00
And the sum is the Ob. Ascen. of the third house	108	2

And thus you have the Oblique Ascentions of the six Oriental Houses, where Note that by this continual Addition of 30d. the Aequinoctial is divided into twelve equal parts from the Meridian, by six great Circles of Position, which are supposed to Intersect with the Horizon and Meridian, and to divide the Ecliptique unequally for the Cusps of the Houses, and make Oblique Angles with the Aequator, called Oblique Ascention; as shall be demonstrated, and may more easily be apprehended by the Coelestial Globe; which is the only Instrument to inform the Fancy in all such Speculations as these.

VI. Having proceeded thus far, the next thing is to find the Cusps of the several Houses, *viz.* in what parts of the *Ecliptique* these *Circles of Position* (cutting 30 degrees distant in the *Aequator*) shall Intersect therein; and first for the Cusp of the *Mid-heaven* or tenth House, 'tis but the Resolution of a Right Angled Spherical Triangle, wherein is given the *Suns* greatest Declination 23d. 30m. and the Right Ascension of the M. C. *viz.* an Angle and a Leg, or Side, to find the Hypotenusa by Case the tenth, and may be performed by Rule 1. Thus, Because I must enter my Canon with a Number less than 90, *according to the Note*. I first Substract the R.A. of the M.C. 318d. 2m. from 370. and the Remainder is 41d. 58m. for the R.A. short of the Aequinoctial point, *Aries*, then according to the Rule,

I add the Co-tang. of 41d. 58m. (*Sine Rad.*)	0046071
To the Cosine (or Sine Comp.) of 23d. 30m.	9962398
Their Sum is the Co-tangent of 44d. 27m.	10008469

That is 44d. 27m. short of the Aequinoctial point *Aries*, this being Substracted also from 360d. according to the aforesaid Note (as indeed Reason will direct) there remains 315d. 33m. from the first point of *Aries*, viz. *Aquarius* 15d. 33m. for the Cusp of the *tenth House* required, [*as may be seen by the third Column against* Aquarius *in the Table before the Logistick Logarithmes.*]

VII. Before the Cusps of the other Houses can be obtained, the Poles Elevation above their several Circles of Position must first be found, where in a Right Angled Spherical Triangle you have given the Hypotenusa, and one of the Acute Angles to find the other, *viz.* the Intersections of the Circles of Position and Latitude of the Place to find the Poles Elevation above each Circle; which is performed by the third Case of R. A. Spherical Triangles, or (which is all one) by the *second Rule, where note that in Case the third, 'tis said from the Co-sine of the Hypotenusa (viz. 30d. or 60d.) and Radius, Substract the Co-tangent of the Angle (viz. the Latitude of the Place) and the Remainder is the Co-tangent of the Angle required, (viz. the Poles Elevation &c.)* But because Addition is easier than Substraction, and to bring the Radius in the first place, I work by their Complements according to the aforesaid second Rule, which may be observed in all such cases.

I. *For the Poles Elevation above the Circle of Position of the eleventh, and third Houses, viz. 32d. 54m. appears by the Work.*

Add the Tangent of the Latitude 52d. 18m.	10111883
To the Sine of 30 degrees	9698970
The Sum less Radius is Tang. of 32d. 34m.	1)9810853

II. *For the Poles Elevation above the Circle of Position of the twelfth, and second Houses, viz. 48d. 15m. found after the same manner, thus.*

To the Tangent of the Latitude 52d. 18m.	10111883
Add the Sine of 60 degrees	9937531
The Sum less Radius is the Tang. of 48d. 15m.	10049314

VIII. The next work is to Calculate the Cusps of the Houses according to the third and fourth Rules of Proposition the tenth, in which you have an Oblique Spherical Triangle, and there is given the *Suns* greatest Declination, the Poles Elevation above the Cusps, and the Oblique Ascention of each House, *viz.* two Angles and the included Side to find another Side,) which may be performed by the fourth Case of Oblique Spherical Triangles without letting fall a Perpendicular, which I shall afterwards exemplifie; but first I shall perform the Work with a Perpendicular, reducing the Oblique Triangle into two Right Angled Triangles, which may be easier understood by some.

N. B. [*And note that for ease in Calculation, it will be necessary that you set down apart the Co tangent of the Poles of the House out of your Canon in some convenient place, because they are often used in Operation, and so likewise at once opening of your Canon you may take out the Co-sine and Co tangent of the Oblique Ascention of each House, &c. which will very much facilitate the Work.*]

IX. *For the Cusp of the eleventh House whose Pole was found* 32d. 54m. *and Oblique Ascention thereof* 11d. 58m. (viz. *the Comp. of* 348d. 2m. *to* 360 *degrees.*)

I. *Operation.*

Add the Co-sine of the Ob. Ascen. 11d. 58m.	9990458
To the Co-tang. of the Pole of the House 32d. 54'.	0189143
The Sum is the Co-tang. of the 1*st*. Ang. 33d. 28'	10179601
Unto this Ang. add	23d. 30m.
According to the Rule produces	56d. 58m. the 2*d*. Ang.

II. *Operation.*

Add the Co-sine of 33d. 28m. Comp. Arith.	0078726
To the Co-sine of the second Ang. 56d. 58m.	9736497
And the Co-tang. of the Ob. Ascen. 11d. 58m.	0673769
Their Sum is the Co-tang. of 17d. 59m.	10488992

This 17d. 59m. must be Substracted out of 360d. because the Oblique Ascension was less than 360d. and more than 270d. and the Remainder 342d. 1m. from the first point of *Aries, viz.* 12 deg. 1 min. of ♓ is the true Cusp of the eleventh House required.

And here you are to Note that, because the second Angle is less than 90d. the distance in the Ecliptick must be accounted from the same Aequinoctial point that the Oblique Ascension was reckoned from, according to the Rule before given in Prop. X.

X. *For the Cusp of the twelfth House, whose Oblique Ascension is* 18d. 2m. *and the Poles Elevation* 48d. 15m.

I. *Operation.*

Add the Co-sine of the Ob. Ascen. 18d. 2m.	9978124
To the Co-tang. of the Pole of the House 48d. 15'.	9950625
The Sum is the Co-tang of the first Ang. 49d. 41m.	9928749
To which add	23d. 30m.
The Sum is the second Angle	73d. 11m.

II. *Operation.*

Add the Co-sine of the 1*st* Ang. 49. 41. Comp. Ar.	0189188
And the Co-sine of 73d. 11m. the 2*d*. Ang.	0461364
To the Co-tang. of the Ob. Ascen. 18d. 2m. Rx	0487364
The Sum is the Co-tang. of 36d. 4m. from ♈	10137817
Therefore the Cusp of the twelfth House is	♉ 6d. 4m.

[*And Note that when you have found the Co-tangent of the first Angle, at the same time you may take out also the Arithmetical Complement of the Co-sine thereof ready for use in the second operation.*]

XI. *For the Cusp of the Ascendant, whose Oblique Ascension is* 48d. 2m. *and the Poles Elevation* (*or Latitude of Birth*) 52d. 18m.

I. Operation.

Add the cs. of the Ob. Ascen.	48d. 2m.	9825230
To the Co-tang. of the Pole of the Ascen.	52d. 18m.	9888116
The Sum is the Co-tang. of the first Arch	62. 40.	9713346
And still because the Ob. As. is next ♈ I add according to the Rule.	23. 30.	
The Sum is the second Arch, or Angle	86. 10.	

II. Operation.

Add the Co-sine of the first Ang. Comp. Ar.	62. 40.	0338030
And the Co-sine of the second Angle	86.10.	8825130
To the Co-tangent of the Ob. Ascen.	48. 2.	9953929
Their Sum is the Co-tangent of	82. 32.	9117089

Which because the second Angle is less than 90d. I account from *Aries*, and hence it appears the Cusp of the Ascendant is *Gemini* 22d. 32m.

XII. *For the Cusp of the second House, whose Oblique Ascention is* 78d. 2m. *and the Poles Elevation above the Circle thereof* 48d. 15m.

I. Operation.

To the Co-sine of the Ob. Ascen.	78d. 2m.	9316688
Add the Co-tang. of the Pole of the House	48. 15'.	9950625
And their Sum is the Co-tang. of the 1. Ang.	79. 31.	9267313
Unto which add	23. 30.	
The Sum is the second Angle	103. 1.	

whose Complement to 180d. is 79d. 59m.

II. Operation.

To the Co-sine of	79d. 31m. Comp. Arith.	0740049
Add the Co-sine of	76d. 59m. the second Ang.	9352635
And the Co-tang. of the Ob. Ascen	78d. 2m.	9326230
The Sum is the Co-tang. of	75d. 18m. short	9418914

of the first point of *Libra*.

Here, because the secomd Angle is above 90 *degrees, I substract the last Co-tangent* 75 deg. 18 min. *from* 180 deg. *and there remains* 104 deg. 42 min. *from the first point of Aries, viz.* 14 deg. 42 min. *of Cancer for the Cusp of the second House; because the Oblique Ascention was neerest to the Aequinoctial Point,* Aries.

XIII. *For the Cusp of the third House, whose Oblique Ascention is* 180d. 2m. *and the Poles Elevation* 32d. 54m.

I. Operation.

To the Cos. of the Co. of the Ob. As. to 180.	71. 51.	9490759
Add the Co-tang. of the Pole of the House	32.54	0189143
The Sum is the Co-tang. of	64d. 26m.	9679902

From which I substract 23d. 30m. because the Ob. Ascen. now is neerest the Aequinoctial point, *Libra*, there remains 40d. 56m. for the second Angle.

II. *Operation.*

To the Co-sine of the first. Ang. 64. 26. Com. Ar.	0364958
And the Co-sine of the second Ang. 40. 56.	9878219
Add the Co-tangent of the Ob. Ascen. 71. 58.	9512635
The Sum is the Co-tang. 60d. 19m. short of ♎	9755812

Which Subtracted from 180. leaves 119d. 41m. from the first point of ♈, *viz.* ♋ 29d. 41m. for the true Cusp of the third House required.

	Cusp of the 6 Orient. Hous. d. m.		Cusp of the 6 Occident. Hous. d. m.
And the Cusps of the six Oriental Houses present themselves thus (omitting the Seconds for ease in Calculation.	X ♒ 15. 33 XI ♓ 12. 1 XII ♉ 6. 4 I ♊ 22. 32 II ♋ 14. 42 III ♋ 29. 41	And their Opposits	IV ♌ 15. 33 V ♍ 12. 1 VI ♏ 6. 4 VII ♐ 22. 32 VIII ♑ 14. 42 IX ♑ 29. 41

Here is presented the Figure itself, being a Synopsis of the whole Calculation.

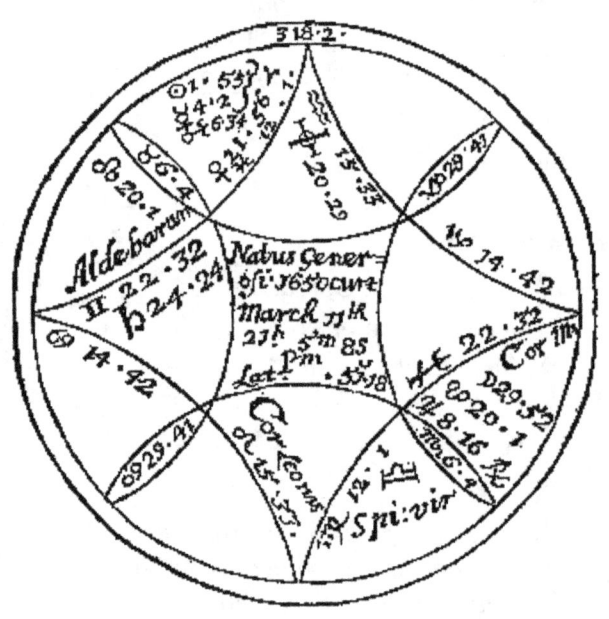

For the Place of the Part of Fortune.

	s. d. m.
The true place of the Moon	07. 29. 52
Sun Substract	00 01. 55
The distance of the *Sun* and *Moon*	07. 27. 57
Add the Ascendant	02. 22. 32
The Sum is the true place of *Sors* the Lot, or ⊕	♒ 10. 20. 29

CAAP. V.

How to set a Figure the Rational way, and Resolve the Triangle, without the Cadence of a Pendicular; according to the fourth Case of Oblique Spherical Triangles.

I. In the Diagram; E, ♈, ♎, N. represents the Aequinoctial A. the Centre is the North Pole; the Prickt Circle ♈, ♎, W, S, represents the Ecliptick, put in his due position, according to the Exemplary Scheme; the several Arches Intersecting at B, and cutting the Aequator in twelve equal parts, and the Ecliptick in twelve unequal parts are Circles of Position of the twelve Coelestial Houses, and where the Ecliptick Intersects the Aequinoctial as at ♈ and ♎, these are the Aequinoctial points; and these 2 Circles make an Angle of 23d. 30m. equal to the *Suns* greatest Declination. Now for the resolving the Oblique Spherical Triangles for the eleventh, twelfth, first, second, and third Houses, there is given two Angles and the Side included to find one of the other Sides, as may better be understood by the little Triangle apart P, R, Q, then by the Projection; the Angle P, is the *Suns* Declination, the Angle R, the Pole of the House, and the Side P, R, the Oblique Ascention of the House to find the Side P, Q, *viz.* where the Circle of Position Intersects the Ecliptick from the next Aequinoctial point.

Note that this Triangle apart represents the Triangle in the Projection, which is resolved in finding how far from the Aequinoctial points Aries *and* Libra *the Circles of Position cut, or intersect the Ecliptick as the Triangle* Gemini [E. Aries, *and the Triangle* Aries II, Pisces, &c.]

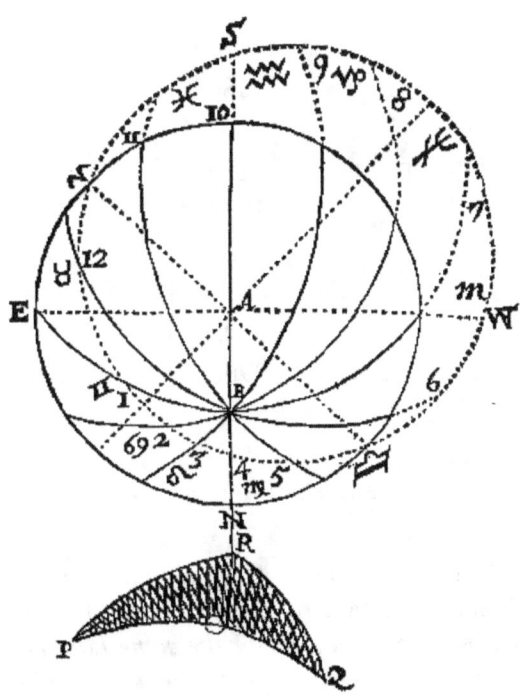

II. Consult the Rules given, and those will very much Illustrate and explain the fourth Case of Oblique Spherical Triangles in obtaining the Cusps of the Houses, as for Example: First make this easie preparation; suppose I would Calculate the Cusp of the eleventh House in the precedent Geniture, I proceed thus; the Oblique Ascention of the House is 348d. 2m. from which Substract 180d. there remains 168d. 2m. the half of which is 84d. 1m. which I reserve; the Pole of the House is 32d. 54m. whose Complement to a Quadrant 90d. is 57d. 6m. to which both add, and subduct 23d. 30m. (the greatest Obliquity of the Ecliptick) the Sum will be 80d. 36m. and the Difference 33d. 36m. *ergo* the half Sum 40d. 18m. and the half Difference 16d. 48m.

III. Being thus prepared, I proceed according to the Rule, when the Oblique Ascention falls beyond 180d. *viz.*

	I. *Operation.*
Add the S. of the half Sum Co-ar. 40d. 18m.	0189237
Add the Sine of the half Diff. 16d. 48m.	9460946
To the Tang. of ½ the remaining Ob. As. 84d. 1m.	0979597
Their Sum is the Tang. of 76d. 48m.	10629780

	II. *Operation.*
Add the c.s. of the half Sum 40d. 18m. Co-ar.	0117664
And the c.s. of the half Diff. 16d. 48m.	9981047
To the Tang. of half the remaining Ob. As. 84. 1.	0979597
their Sum is the Tang. of 85d. 13m. +	11078308
To which add the aforesaid Tang. 76d. 48	

For the Cusp of the eleventh 162d. 1m. beyond ♎, therefore if you add 180d. to this Sum, the last total will be 242d. 1m. from the beginning of ♈, that is 12d. 1m. of ♓ for the true Cusp of the eleventh House, as before.

IV. Again for the Cusp of the second House, whose Pole is 48d. 15m. the Complement thereof to a Quadrant, or 90d. is 41d. 45m. to which if I add, and Substract 23d. 30m. the Sum is 65d. 15m. the Difference 14d. 15m. the half Sum 32d. 37m. the half Differ. 9d. 7m. the Oblique Ascension 78d. 2m. the half thereof 39d. 1m. this being premised, I proceed according to the Rule when the Oblique Ascension is less than 180d.

	I. *Operation.*
Add the Sine of the half Diff. 9d. 7m. Co. Arith.	0800121
And the Sine of the half Sum 32d. 37m.	9731601
To the Tang. of half the Ob. Ascen. 39d. 1m.	9908627
Their Sum is the Tang. of 70d. 4m.	10440349

	II. *Operation.*
Add the Co-sine of the half Diff. 9d. 7m. Co. Arith	0005521
And the Co-sine of the half Sum 32d. 37m.	9925464
To the Tang. of the half Semi Oblique Ascen. 39. 1.	9908627
Their Sum is the Tang. of 34d. 38m.	9839612
To which add the aforesaid 70d. 04m.	

The Sum is   104d. 42m. for the Cusp of the second House from the first point of *Aries*, *viz.* 14d. 42m. of ♋, as before the other way.

After this manner may the Cusps of the other Houses be obtained, these two Examples being sufficient to Illuminate the understanding in the Manner and Method of Operation. [*And note that this way you do not only set a Scheme for the time proposed, but a Table of Houses for the same Latitude may be also made from the Work by an Addition of the two uppermost Sums in each Operation, to be used with the Addition of the Tangent of the Semi Oblique Ascension of each House twice, as in the aforesaid Operation.*]

V. Take an Example how the Tables are made, *viz.* by Addition of the aforesaid Sums.

I find the 12*th*. and	♈ = 0531722	♈ = 9930985
2*d*. Houses next,	♎ = 9468278	♎ = 0069015
And		
The 11*th*. and 3*d*.	♈ = 9901289	♈ = 0349817
Houses next.	♎ = 0098711	♎ = 9650183

VI. After the same manner operate for the Ascendant, having the Sum and Difference, as before is Illustrated. Where you may observe those Numbers you find against the Aequinoctial Sign, *Aries*, are Composed by adding the *Arithmetical Complement* of the *Sine* of the half Difference, to the *Sine* of the half Sum; and those Numbers against *Libra* are the *Arithmetical Complement* of those very Numbers against *Aries*, and may be made by adding the *Arithmetical Complement* of the *Sine* of the half Sum &c. And lastly, if the Tang. of the *Semi Oblique Ascention* of each Respective House be twice added to those proportional Numbers, (as if the Ob. Ascen. be less than 180d. to those against *Aries*; if above, to those against *Libra*) you have thereby two *Tangents*, the Sum of which gives the Distance of the Cusp from the same *Aequinoctial point*, as plainly appears by the precedent Examples. And note that in Operation by any such Tables you use your Canon of Tangents always to the same Radius. Tables of Houses, Calculated by the same Rules, to several Latitudes follow, to be used as already directed.

New Tables of *Houses* for several Latitudes, Calculated (mostly) to the Obliquity of the Ecliptick 23 deg. 31 min. 30 sec.

Lat [49d.] for the Ascend.		Lat. [52d.] for the Ascend.	
♈ 054503	♈ 993214	♈ 060762	♈ 993768
♎ 945597	♎ 006786	♎ 939238	♎ 006232
For the 12 and 2 Houses.		For the 12 and 2 Houses.	
♈ 047819	♈ 992480	♈ 052616	♈ 992991
♎ 952181	♎ 007520	♎ 947384	♎ 007009
For the 3 and 11 Houses.		For the 3 and 11 Houses.	
♈ 032690	♈ 989407	♈ 034754	♈ 990069
♎ 967310	♎ 010503	♎ 965246	♎ 990031

Lat [50d.] for the Ascend.		Lat. [52d. 17m.] for the As.	
♈ 056433	♈ 993411	♈ 061332	♈ 993811
♎ 943567	♎ 006589	♎ 938668	♎ 006189
For the 12 and 2 Houses.		For the 12 and 2 Houses.	
♈ 049322	♈ 992668	♈ 053085	♈ 993089
♎ 950678	♎ 007332	♎ 646915	♎ 096911
For the 3 and 11 Houses.		For the 11 and 3 Houses.	
♈ 032334	♈ 989685	♈ 024968	♈ 990129
♎ 967666	♎ 010315	♎ 965032	♎ 009871

Lat. [51d.] for the Ascend.		Lat. [52d. 21m.] for the As.	
♈ 058512	♈ 993591	♈ 061617	♈ 993830
♎ 941488	♎ 006409	♎ 938383	♎ 006170
For the 2 and 12 Houses.		For the 2 and 12 Houses.	
♈ 050914	♈ 992855	♈ 052381	♈ 993075
♎	949086	♎	007145
♎	947619	♎	006925
For the 3 and 11 Houses.		For the 3 and 11 Houses.	
♈	034021	♈	989775
♈	035084	♈	990168
♎	965979	♎	010225
♎	964916	♎	009832

New Tables of Houses for several Latitudes, Calculated (mostly) to the Obliquity of the Ecliptick 23 deg. 31 min. 30 sec.

Lat. [51d. 32m.] for the As.		Lat. [53d.] for the Ascend.	
♈	059712	♈	993685
♈	065818	♈	994120
♎	940288	♎	000315
♎	934182	♎	005880
For the 12 and 2 Houses.		For the 12 and 2 Houses.	
♈	051821	♈	992928
♈	056488	♈	993406
♎	948179	♎	007072
♎	943512	♎	006594
For the 3 and 11 Houses.		For the 3 and 11 Houses.	
♈	034419	♈	989978
♈	036346	♈	990464
♎	965581	♎	010022
♎	963654	♎	009536
Lat. [51d. 46m.] for the As.		Lat. [55d.] for the Ascend.	
♈	060220	♈	993727
♈	068816	♈	996295
♎	939780	♎	006273
♎	931184	♎	003705
For the 12 and 2 Houses.		For the 12 and 2 Houses.	
♈	052169	♈	993003
♈	058621	♈	993599
♎	947831	♎	006997
♎	941379	♎	006401
For the 3 and 11 Houses.		For the 11 and 3 Houses.	
♈	034582	♈	990024
♈	037227	♈	009666
♎	965418	♎	009976
♎	962773	♎	009334
Lat. [53d.] for the Ascend.		Lat. [56d.] for the Ascend.	
♈	063206	♈	993945
♈	072071	♈	994469
♎	936794	♎	006055
♎	927929	♎	005531
For the 2 and 12 Houses.		For the 2 and 12 Houses.	
♈	054472	♈	993229
♈	068957	♈	993783
♎	945528	♎	006771
♎	931043	♎	006217
For the 3 and 11 Houses.		For the 3 and 11 Houses.	
♈	035528	♈	990245
♈	038115	♈	990873
♎	964471	♎	009755
♎	961885	♎	009127

CHAP. V.

How to Aequate for the odd Minutes of .the Circle of Position, if you work by the ordinary Tables of Argol or Regiomontanus, *by which it will appear that the Operation (to that exactness) by Trigonometry is altogether as expeditious, and in some Cases more certain.*

I. Let the Moon be supposed in 10d. 55m. of *Libra*, and Latitude 0d. 21m. South, then her Declination will be found to be 4d. 37m. South, and her Right Ascention 189d. 50m. Let the R.A. of the M.C. be 238d. 38m. and her Distance from thence in R.A. 48d. 48m. above the Earth, and the Birth in the Latitude of 51d. 0m.

II. Turn to the Tables of Position, and find 4d. South Declination above the Earth in the first Column, and so direct your Eye along in the Line right against it till you find the nearest Number to your Distance given 48d. 48rn. which will be found 47d. 35m. and the Pole of Position Correspondent 44d. Now because you have 37m. more of Declination, and the next Number under 47d. 35m. is 46d. 36m. their Difference is 59m. I must make proportion, and say, if 60m. of Declination abate 59m. then 37m. shall abate 37m. *fere*, which subducted out of the aforesaid Distance 47d. 35m. leaves 46d. 58m. this is more too little.

III. I proceed to the next Column under the Pole of 45d. and right against 4d. of Declination I find 50d. 3m. and the next Distance underneath is 49d. 3m. Differ. 60m. so that if 60m. give, or rather abate 60m. 37m. will abate 37m. out of 53d. 3m. and the remainder is 49d. 26m. and this is more then the Distance from the Meridian required; and in the Head of the Table I find 44d. for the Pole of position.

IV. So that had the Declination been 4d. 37m. and the Distance from the Meridian just 46d. 58m. the Pole of Position must have been [44d.] and no more: also to the same Declination had the Distance been 49d. 26m. the Poles Elevation had been just [45d.] Now the Difference between 46d. 58rn. and 49d. 26m. is 2d. 28m. or 148m. and the Difference between 46d. 58m. (the lesser Distance) and 48d. 48m. the true Distance is 1d. 50m. or 110m. Then I say, if 148m. gives 60m. in the Pole of Position, what shall 110m. give *facit* 44m. and hence I conclude the true Circle, or Pole of Posit ion of the *Moon* to be 44d. 44m. and this is the true way of Aequation, which few Artists practice, but are content to Direct under the neerest whole degrees thereof; which sometimes cannot but make considerable errour in the Ark of Direction.

V. The manner of Operation is as followeth:

	d.		Pole 44	m. m. m. m.
I. Dec.	4	Dist.	47.35	Then as 60:59::37:37.fere
	5		46.36	47d. 35m. — 37 = 58m.
Difference abates			00.59	
			Pole 45	m. s. m.m.
2. Dec.	4	Dist.	50.3	Then as 60:60::37:37:
	5		49.3	50d. 3m. 37m. = 49. 26.
Difference — 01.0				
Pole	44	Dist. â	46.58	The true Dist. â Merid. 48.48.
	45	Merid.	49.26	from which Substract 46.58
		Differ.	2.28 or 148'. Diff. is 1°. 50' or 110'.	

Lastly, by the Logist. Log., say, as 148m. to 60m. the Diff. of the Poles Elevation, so is 110m. to 44m. which added to the 44d. of the Poles Elevation gives 44d. 44m. for the true Elevation of the Pole above the Circle of Position of the *Moon* in the Latitude of 51d. which would require much more work, had there been odd minutes adhering thereunto, and the whole work is more easier performed by Proportions in Trigonometry, as shall be exemplifed.

Clavis Astrologiae Elimita, The Key to Astrology New Filed

CHAP. VI.

How to find the Declination and Right Ascention of a Star or Planet with Latitude by the Common Tables for that purpose.

I. If your Difference in Longitude, and Latitude, both increase; take the Sum of your proportional parts, and add to the lesser Right Ascension given, and you have your desire.

On the contrary, if both the Difference in Longitude and Latitude decrease, take their Correspondent proportional parts, and add them together, and Substract their Sum from the next lesser R. Ascen. gives the Right Ascension, or Declination desired.

II. If the Difference increases in Longitude, and decreases in Latitude, or the contrary; take the Difference of your proportional parts adhering; and observe whether the greater, or lesser of them be noted with add, or substract: if the greater Number be noted add, then add the Difference of your parts proportional, to the Right Ascension, or Declination, under the lesser Latitude; but if the greater part proportional be noted substract, take their Difference, and Substract the Remainder from the Right Ascension, or Declination agreeable to the Longitude under the lesser Latitude, and the Work is done.

Observe the same Method, if the Differences increase in Latitude, and decrease in Longitude, as oft-times it doth in a Planets Declination. These Rules will appear more plain if Illustrated by Example, which take as followeth.

First, Let *Mars* be supposed to be in 17d, 54m. of *Libra* with 2d. 41m. North Latitude.

```
               d.              d.             d. m.      m.
1. Against   18 ♎  under 2. N. Lat. I find   197.21   Diff. 56
             17                              196.25
```
Then as 60':56'::54:50. add because the Diff. increases.
```
               d.                            d. m.
2. Against   17 ♎  under 3 N.L. I find R.A. 196.48   D.23
             17           2                  196.25
```

Then say, If 60'. of Lat. gives 23'. what 31' *facit* 16' *fere*. Unto which I add the aforesaid 50m. (because both Longitude and Latitude increase) their Sum is 66m. or 1d. 6m. this added to the leaser R.A. 166d. 25m. produces the true R.A. 197d. 31m.

Again I desire the Right Ascension of *Venus* in 20d. 7m. of *Virgo* with Lat. South 3d. 50m. Work thus as the most Compendius way.

```
            ♍ d.  m.                 d.
1. R.A. ♀ 21 170. 33      Sub. Lat. 3 South.
          20 169. 38
   Diff.     00. 55 Increasing.
```
Then say, as 60m:55m::7m:6m. add.
```
          Sub. d.  d.  m.
2. R.A. ♀      3 169. 38
          Lat. 4 169. 14
   Diff.      1  00. 24 Decreasing.
```

Then say, as 60 to 24m::50:20 substract.

And 20m. - 6m. = 14 which Substracted from the lesser R.A. 169d. 38m. remains the true R. A. of ♀ 169d. 24m.

[*Note here because the lesser proportional part is noted with Add, and the greater with Substract; I take their*

Difference 14m. and Substract from the lesser Right Ascension, gives the true R. A. but had the greater propprtional part been noted Add, and the lesser Substract, as I must have added their Difference, as Reason will better direct, then many Rules.]

Secondly, Suppose a Planet be in 12d. 15m. *Virgo* with Latitude North 3d. 24m. and his Declination be required by the Tables.

I. Seek 12d. of *Virgo* in the first Column, and 3d. of Lat. North at the Head of the Table; under which I cast mine Eye down that Column, till I come against 12d. of *Virgo*, which I find in the Common Angle to be 9d. 51m. and the Difference between this and the Declination next following (*viz*. against 13d. *Virgo*, 9d. 28m.) is [23m] decreasing.

Then say, as 60m:23m::15m:6m. *i.e.* if 60m. of Longitude decrease 23m. in Declination, what 15m. adhering to the Longitude, *facit* 6. which I note down with the Title Substract, because the Declination decreases.

II. I make search in the next Column under 4d. of Latitude, right against 12d. of *Virgo* in the first Column, where I find 10d. 46m. the Difference between which, and 9d. 51m. under 3d. of Lat. is 55m. increasing.

Then say, if 60m. of Lat. increase 55m. what shall 24m. (the odd min. of Lat. given) *facit* 22m. because the Latitude increases; and this I note down with the Title Substract.

III. Now because the one is Add, and the other Substract; I take their Difference, *viz*. 6m. from 22m. aforesaid, rests 16m. which I add to the lesser Declination on 9d. 51m. and that amounts to 10d. 7m. the true Declination of *Venus*, desired; [*Where note that the Difference of the proportional parts are added to the lesser Declination, because the greater of those parts were noted with add; but had that part been noted Substract, I must have taken the Difference, and Substracted the remainder from the Lesser Declination, or R. A., &c. and thus the business is made plain to the meanest Capacitie, or Learner, whom I have known to stumble very much at these things, which to an Artist, I must confess are superfluous: But these Rules are apt to slip out of the Memory of those who have been very ready in Operation after a dis-continuing of this Practice for a small time; and upon that consideration may be acceptable, both to the expert Teacher and the Learner also.*

IV. Having the Oblique Ascention of any of the six Northern Signs (which may be Computed by Prop. VII.) under any Elevation, you may from thence gain the Oblique Ascention of the six Southern Signs, and the contrary, thus *viz*. As suppose the Oblique Ascention of 10d. of *Sagittarius* under the Pole of 41d. is 268. 55. which Substracted from 360 leaves 91d. 5m. for the Oblique Ascention of 20d. of *Cancer*, according to the following Position of the Signs, and Degrees.

1	2	3	4	5	6	7	8	9	10	20	25	30
29	28	27	26	25	24	23	22	21	20	10	5	0

♈	♉	♊	♋	♌	♍
♎	♏	♐	♑	♒	♓

So the Oblique Ascention of 15d. of *Cancer* under the Pole of 41d. is 85d. 1m. this Substracted out of 360d. leaves the Oblique Ascention of 15d. of *Sagittarius*, *viz*. 274d. 59m. & *sic in aliis*.

Note that the six Northern Signs with North Latitude have the same R. Ascen. with Southern Signs, and South Latitude abating 180d. & contra; so North Signs, and North Latitude decrease the R. A. and increase in South Latitude, and North Latitude in Southern Signs increase their R. A. as much, and decrease in South Latitude, &c. as may be observed by the Tables themselves.

CHAP. VII.

SECT. I.

Necessary Considerations before Judgment upon a Nativity.

I. Consider the strength, or weakness of the Planets in general, and see how they behold each other; and in particular, whether they cast any benevolent Aspect to the Ascendant, Lord thereof, or the *Sun*, or *Moon*.

II. See whether the Luminaries behold the Ascendant friendly, also in what Houses and Quarter of Heaven they and the rest of the Planets with ⊕ are posited.

III. Take notice what Eminent fixed Stars of the first, or second Magnitude (that have but small Latitude from the Ecliptick) fall in any of the Angles, or near unto the chief Significators in the Figure; consider the nature of these fixed Stars, if so be they agree (in nature) with those Planets they are nearly joined with; this doth augment their signification, be it good or bad: But if those Stars happen to be of contrary natures, order your Judgment accordingly.

IV. Consider also in what Houses, or parts of the Heavens the Antiscions, or Contra-antiscions of all the Planets fall, whether upon the Cusps of the chief Houses thereof, or near the degrees of any of the Planets places, or fixed Stars therein; and accordingly moderate your Judgement.

V. From these (and such like) considerations you may be able Rationally to Judge and Determine (in a general way) what the Natives Fate may be; having also respect to the Directions that fall in the Nativity, both good and bad, for the effects of both, Persons of all degrees must (undoubtedly) be sure, more or less, to partake of, during the time of their Operations; although it so happens, that in some Nativities, the good Directions do much to surmount the bad, and in others the contrary.

For if we are content with the effects of good Directions, we must of necessity bear with the force of bad also, because Squares and Oppositions must have their Operations as well as Sextiles and Trines; for without the one, the other cannot be; and therefore some sower, as well as sweet, will attend all Persons. Hence then I may conclude, that the fore-knowledge of these events is very convenient; For thereby we may put our selves in a Capacity to receive all promised good, and if we cannot withstand approaching dangers, yet we may be able, in part, to mittigate their force; and thereby the more easily evade. Now the particular times when either of these things may happen is artificially pointed out by the Art of Directions.

VI. Lastly, in Judging any thing concerning the Native, whether Life, Estate, Marriage, Preferment, Travel, &c. The Artist ought rightly to understand (and be exceedingly perfect in) the nature and significations of the *Significators*, and *Promitters*; also their Fortitudes, and Debilities, and how they are beheld, either by good or bad Aspects of the other Planets, and thereby assisted or afflicted; I say, without such considerations an Artist cannot well Judge (or thereby inform the Native) of his future Fate, and what may, probably, happen unto him in the whole Course of his Life, according to Natural Causes.

SECT. II.

Of the general signification of the Lord of the Ascendant in a Nativity.

I. That Person which is born under *Saturn* shall more or less, in conditions, participate of his Nature, *viz.* He will be a close subtile Person, altogether aiming at his own Interest; high minded, self conceited, sufficiently churlish, and of a dogged disposition; Timerous, a contemner of Women, (as to Marriage) yet Luxurious, and many times addicted to swear, lye, and dissemble; and not altogether a stranger to Drunkenness. But if *Saturn* be well seated in the Nativity, those evil inclinations will be much abated and the Native proves a man of profound Judgment, few words, very studious, Grave and Severe, and one that heaps up the goods of this Life.

II. Such as are born under *Jupiter* prove Vertuous Persons in the general, they will be Just and Honest in all their dealings and actions, Wise and Prudent, Liberal to those that stand in need, having a desire to benefit all Persons and perfect haters of all unworthy Acts.

But if *Jupiter* be ill disposed in the Nativity, the Native then proves a very Extravagant Person, ignorant, careless; and in fine, but of a dull Capacity, a fawning, dissembling Companion, and not fit to be trusted.

III. Those that are Born when *Mars* bears Rule, will be inclinable to all manner of Rash Actions, and generally subject to any kind of Mischief; as Quarreling, Fighting, Swearing, Lying, Stealing, Killing, &c.

But if *Mars* be well seated in the Figure, the Natives Inclinations are not altogether so bad; yet, if Authors may be credited, bad is the best; for they usually prove Perjured, Turbulent, Treacherous Persons, &c. — Proud, Boasters, &c.

IV. Such as are Born when the *Sun* bears Rule, will aim at high things, having a desire of Sovereignty; generally Lofty Spirits, proud, and high, but of excellent sound Judgements; lovers of Honour, and all honourable Actions, searchers into many rare Secrets; and usually not without success.

But if the *Sun* be weak in the Nativity, or much afflicted, the Natives Inclinations are not at all so commendable, but much of this good signification is abated, as before hinted in the other Planets.

V. Those Persons that are Born under the Dominion of *Venus*, (and she well dignified in the Nativity) will be inclinable (for the most part) to mirth; and in general they are virtuous Persons, delighting much in taking their pleasure, and to go spruce and neat in their Apparel; often insnared in Love matters, constant in their Affections, free from Jealousie, &c.

But note that if *Venus* happen to be ill dignified in the Geniture, then the Native is usually inclinable to pleasures of the worser sort; as Drunkenness, Wenching, and such like sordid Actions, not fit to be (so much as) mentioned.

VI. Such as are Born under the Dominion of *Mercury* (and if *Mercury* in the Nativity be free from affliction, and strong) are usually great Searchers into many Curiosities; such Persons generally have most excellent Wits, sharp Fancies inclinable to all kind of Learning, Eloquent, good Orators; and in short, capable of understanding the most occult Misteries, belonging to any Science, without much instruction.

If *Mercury* be ill disposed, this good signification is much abated; and then the Native proves a meer verbal Person, a great Boaster, pretending to much knowledge, and guilty of very little, if any at all; and many times too much addicted to Lying, Cheating, Pilfering, and such like vitious and dishonest Actions.

VII. Lastly, Those Persons Born under the Dominion of the *Moon*, are usually unstedfast, and wavering, timerous, delighting to be wandring, and shifting, from place, to place; (but for the most part) they are ingenious, lovers of all kinds of Novelties, and such as are willing to live at peace.

But if the *Moon* be weak in the Nativity, and much debilitated, or afflicted, this argues the Native to be but a loose kind of Person, a mere sottish, idle, lazy Creature, having no spirit, but doth (as it were) delight to be careless of himself, and to live in a poor, low, mean, and beggerly condition.

Note that what is spoken here of the Lord of the Ascendant in a Nativity, may also be understood of the *Lord of the Geniture*, which is that Planet that hath most Essential, and Accidental Dignities in the Figure of the Geniture. But if any other Planet therein should happen to be neerly as strong as he, or if any other Planet (or Planets) should behold him, or the Lord of the Ascendant; in this case, the Artist is to mix his Judgement according to their several Significators, and from thence Judge the Qualities, and Conditions of the Native.

SECT. III.

Of the Faces of the Signs being Horoscopial in any Geniture.

The Faces of the Signs are accounted, by some, very necessary in Astrological Judgements; and have been verified in many Nativities. For which *John Angelus* hath described convenient Images that very well express their several significations, which are briefly thus, *viz.*

I. If the first Face of *Aries* ascend, the Native will be a Person of an undaunted Spirit, confident and bold, courageous and valiant; because 'tis a face of *Mars*.

The second Face signifies the Native will be preferred, and come to bear Rule, it being the Face of the *Sun*.

The third Face declares the Native to be accute, addicted to Musick, to Mirth, and to Pleasures in general; because 'tis a Face of *Venus*.

II. If the first Face of *Taurus* ascend, the Native will be skilful in Husbandry, and inclinable to study, several things Mathematical; as Geometry, Surveying, &c. for 'tis a Face of *Mercury*.

The second Face shews the Native shall have great power but be Instrumental in the Ruine of Places, and impoverishing the Inhabitants thereof; this is the Face of the *Moon*.

The third Face denotes the Native shall be much afflicted by hard Labour, Want, and Misery, as also suffer Bondage and Slavery, unless the Fortunes interpose their friendly Rayes; for 'tis a Face of *Saturn*.

III. The first Face of *Gemini* ascending, intimates the Native may prove a Scrivener, or an Accomptant; or one imployed about receiving, and paying Money; it also declares many other Imployments where in the Wit is much exercised, and small profit arising thereby; this is a Face of *Jupiter*.

The second Face declares much affliction to the Native, by Hard Labour, and Oppression, obtaining nothing without much study, and difficulty; and in fine, it denotes but a kind of knavish Wit, subtile, and cunning, but little bettered thereby; this is the Face of *Mars*.

The third Face signifies the Native will be subject to many foolish Pleasures of the worser sort, having a dull Wit, very forgetful, yet subject to jearing, and deriding of others, to his own shame, and disgrace; this is accounted the Face of the *Sun*.

IV. The first Face of *Cancer* arising, denotes the Native will be much concerned amongst the Female Sex, and take much delight in such kind of pleasures; it signifies Riches to the Native, and that he will prove a subtil Person, easily procuring the favour of such as he desires; this is said to be the Face of *Venus*.

The second Face signifies a pleasant Life, and that the Native shall enjoy the Riches of this World, yet much given to the Dalliance of Women. But if a Woman, she will be fruitful, and know no want; 'tis the face of *Mercury*.

The third Face declares the Native will delight in Hunting, and several Martial Exercises, and Actions, also subject to Quarrels, and Contentions, and to heap Riches thereby; 'tis a Face of the *Moon*, and the rest which follow as you find them in the Table of Essential Dignities, Part I.

V. If the first Face of *Leo* be Horoscopial, the Native will be bold, and cruel, lustful, and subject to Act many evil deeds, without other things happen to mittigate it; and in fine, the Native must of necessity run through many unavoidable hardships, and dangers.

The second Face signifies many unexpected Contentions, Miseries, and necessities; yet Victory over others, and much concerned in the occasioning of Quarrels, Fightings, and Discords; many times Blood shed.

The third Face is said to signifie a peaceable Person, and one that will endeavour to shun, and avoid all means of Strife, and Debate.

VI. The first Face of *Virgo* arising, signifies the Native shall be very fortunate in all things, relating to the Earth; as Plowing, Sowing, Planting, &c. and by such means gain much Wealth, and heap together the Goods of this Life.

The second Face shews the Native shall be exceeding covetous, and greedy after Riches; desiring the help and assistance of others, to advance himself.

The third Face of *Virgo* Intimates the Native may live to an old Age, and be full of Infirmitites, and Weaknesses, many times the Native loses a Member, and in his Life Roots, and Demolishes what others have Planted before him.

VII. The first Face of *Libra* ascending, Intimates the Native may come to be a Judge, or Magistrate that will do Justice, and help the Poor against their powerful Oppressors.

The second Face signifies the native shall live a peaceable Life, and enjoy much content and plenty.

The third Face denotes the Native to be a gluttonous, rioting Person, much addicted to bad Company, Lust, and Jollity.

VIII. The first Face of *Scorpio* Horoscopial, signifies the Native to be Contentious, Quarrelsome, Deceitful and Treacharous.

The second Face signifies a Sower of Sedition, a Person exceeding high Spirited; and one that generally delights in mischief.

The third Face denotes the Native will not only be Forward, Peevish, and Quarrelsome; but it signifies he shall prove a Drunkard, a Fornicator, and a Person sufficiently puffd up in Pride.

IX. The first Face of *Sagittarius* arising, signifies the Native shall be of a bold undaunted Spirit in all War-like Actions.

The second Face denotes the Native to be subject to many Scarrs, and that he will sustain many Bodily sorrows, and afflictions.

The third Face denotes the Native to be a Wilful, Obstinate, and Selfish Person; a ready Wit for Mischief, but very averse to good Actions, and delights to be threatening and crossing all he converseth withal.

X. If the first Face of *Capricorn* ascend, it denotes the Native shall Travel much, and both gain, and lose thereby; so that his Life shall not be very Fortunate, or Unfortunate, but intermix'd with both.

The second Face signifies the Native shall be very Inquisitive, and search after such things that (notwithstanding his great pains and study) he shall not find out or attain unto.

The third Face denotes the Native will be exceeding Covetous, and have an itching desire after Soveraignty, as well as the Wealth of this World.

XI. If the first Face of *Aquarius* arise in the Horoscope (or Ascendant) of a Nativity, the Native is extreamly concerned in heaping together the Wealth of the World, and in continual trouble of Spirit, by reason thereof; yet notwithstanding all his Pains and Toyl, he rarely attains to be Rich; but still as it comes it passeth away, to the great perplexity of the Natives mind.

The second Face signifies the Native to be of a covetous Disposition, but of a good Understanding; a Comly Person, and one that loves his Liberty.

The third Face denotes the Native to be of a forward Disposition, he will be subject to be hated without cause; many will be ready to affront, and abuse him, and he not much behind-hand with them (when Occasion is offered) but forward enough to Calumniate their good Names and Reputations.

XII. The first Face of *Pisces* ascending, denotes the Native to be mutable in his thoughts, often shifting from place, to place; useing much diligence to make himself known, and get himself a Name, and Estate; but rarely accomplishing his desires.

The second Face signifies the Native to be of an Aspiring Brain, and one that aims at very high things.

The third Face denotes the Native to be a great lover of (and a Person that delights much in) unlawful pleasures amongst Women, yet a peaceable quiet Person in the general.

These are general significations, and reputed, by some, to be very significant, and material in Judgement; however, 'twill be necessary that the Artist do also consider the Planet (or Planets) in the Ascendant (or beholding it) and the Sign they are in, and what other configurations he finds that may, in any kind, alter these general significations; and in so doing he will be the better able to Judge the natural Inclination, and general Fate of the Native.

CHAP. VIII.

Of the significations of the Planets, as they are Rulers of the Several Houses; from their Positions in any of the twelve Houses of a Genethliacal Scheme of the Heavens.

SECT. I.

Of the Lord of the Ascendant, his Position in any of the twelve Houses, &c.

I. If the Lord (or Ruler) of the Horoscope shall be Posited in the *Ascendant*, or *First House*, it signifies the Native should be not only long liv'd, but prosperous, and very industrious to acquire both Honour, and Profit; and to merit respect, both from Relations as well as others; this is to be understood if he be there free from affliction, and well beheld of the Fortunes, or the Luminaries; if otherwise, judge the contrary.

II. If the Lord of the first House be posited in the second, this shews the Native should gain Riches by his own endeavours, if he be well beheld there, and free from Impediment, there is the greater probability of considerable profit, and advantage; but if he be afflicted, and weak, it portends the contrary, *viz.* much Poverty, and Misery, and with many Calamities, and Afflictions.

III. If posited in the third House, the Native then is much afflicted to short, or In-land Journeys, or to Reside, or Sojourn amongst his Kindred, and Relations, as Brothers, Sisters, Kinsmen, *&c.* If he happen to be afflicted, or infortunate there, he is unkindly greeted from such Relations, or meets with many unhappy Accidents in his short Journeys.

IV. If in the fourth House, then the Native may very well expect a hopeful Patrimony, or enjoy the Houses, or Lands of his Father; he should be prosperous, and successful in Buildings, Plantations, or dealing in moovable Goods, *&c.*

But this is still to be understood if he be fortunate, and well placed therein: if unfortunate, the Native may make an ill end; and perhaps dye in Prison, or some deplorable Death.

V. If in the fifth House, and fortunately placed there; the Native lives happily, and sees many joyful days; delights in Mirth, and Recreations; loves his pleasure, and sometimes Gameing also, he should have hopeful Children, and much prosperity and comfort from, or by, them; and in fine, enjoy the happiness of many Friends. But if he be there in *Scorpio,* especially, or any other Watry Sign, Combust, or debilitated, Judge the contrary in all respects, *viz.* that the Native should be too much inclined to Good fellowship, and Delights of the worser sort; and many times receive much prejudice thereby; and not only so, but by Surfeiting, Drunkenness, and other Intemperances, he may, at length, end his days.

VI. In the sixth House, the Native is usually sickly, or subject to many Infirmities, or to live a servile Life (unless very strong in his own Dignities;) if weak, or much afflicted there the Native is then seldome well in health, but but afflicted often with tedious Distempers, by which he may at last expire, after much affliction and sorrow.

VII. In the seventh House, if hopefully posited therein, Judge the Native may be fortunate in Wives, Partners, Factors, *&c.* he then seldome fails to be much concern'd with divers sorts of Persons; and probably Women more than ordinary: he should delight in Contests, and Law Suits, upon small occasions; and often becomes

Victor in such undertakings: But on the other side, if you find the Lord of the Ascendant afflicted, or much debilitated, either by Combustion, or otherwise; then he is like a Person in the hands, or at the dispose of his profest Enemies; he meets then with an ill Wife, or Wives: sometimes they (in such a case) are the Instruments of his Ruine, and Destruction; the manner whereof must be considered from the Nature of the Sign upon the Cusp of the seventh (or rather the eighth) if *Scorpio* be there, let the Native beware of Poyson; if an Earthy Sign, he may receive much detriment, if not death, by a fall into some deep Pit; if an Airy Sign, by a fall from some high place: consider other concurring Testimonies, and accordingly frame a Judgement.

[And note that he that would become an expert Artist in the Judiciary Part of Astrology must not expect a Precept for all he Writes, but an apt Genius is also required; and he should always remember the first Aphorisme of Ptolomy, *&c.]*

VIII. The Lord of the Ascendant in the eighth House, Authors tell us, signifies a Person of a short Life, a fearful, sorrowful Person, subject to deceit, and indirect Actions; Covetous of other Mens Goods, and if unfortunate therein, this Judgment is much aggravated, to which may be added, that the Natives Mother should be in much danger of Death at his Birth, without the Interposition of the friendly Rayes of the fortunate, and adjuvant Planets.

IX. The Lord of the Ascendant in the ninth House, shews the Native should be strongly inclined to Travel; and if he be fortunate therein, he should very much advantage himself thereby, otherwise Judge, the contrary, that he will fall into the hands of Theeves and Robbers, and receive much damage by their means.

X. In the tenth House, it shews the Native arrives to some Preferment, Office, or Dignity; or gains Honour by some commendable undertaking: But if afflicted there, let him beware of the Sentence of a Judge, or the frown, and displeasure of some Prince, or great Person, probably Restraint; and at last Death, for some disloyal Action, or Actions committed.

XI. If the Lord of the Ascendant happen to be fortunately placed in the eleventh House, this argues the Native should be very fortunate, and successful in his hopes and desires; and that he should be happy in his Acquaintance, and Friends, yet not many Children; on the contrary if he be much afflicted there by Combustion (which is the greatest) or otherwise, then his Friends are meer pretenders, and he receives prejudice, and unkind Offices from them, and not only so, but all his hopes, and expectations, for the most part, have an ill end.

XII. If he be posited in the twelfth House, the Native rarely escapes Injuries secretly hatched, and contrived against him, by private Enemies, which he will not fail to be pester'd withal, and this to purpose, if afflicted in that House; to which I may add there is then great danger the Native may end his days in Prison, at least endure much sorrow thereby, and loss by the greater sort of Cattle if he happen to deal in such Creatures.

SECT. II.

Of the Lord of the second House in any of the twelve Coelestial Houses.

I. The Lord of the second House, posited in the first; shews that the Native, without much pains, should gain a considerable Estate, or Fortune (the Capacity of Birth being considered) and that most of his Actions should produce profit; and this the rather, if he be free from the Hostile Rayes of the Infortunes, or other afflictions.

II. If in the second House, the Native will be assuredly Rich, and gain an Estate; and this the more certain, provided he be not Combust therein; and if the Lord of the second House be also in friendly Aspect with the Lord of the Ascendant, 'tis then an assured Testimony the Native must prosper, unless miraculously prevented.

III. In the third House, this signifies profit by short, and In-land Journeys; and Consequently, by Brethren and such kind of Relations, unless much afflicted therein; if so, Judge the contrary, as reason will direct.

IV. If in the fourth House, it portends an Estate (or profit at least) from the Natives Parents, probably by Houses or Land, or such kind of immovable Goods, or things; which Judgment is augmented, if the Lord of the second be well beheld by fortunate Planets, if otherwise, the Artist ought to moderate his Judgement accordingly; and also to consider well the Quality of the Native.

V. If posited in the fifth House Fortunate, it denotes that the Native should be enriched, by his Children, or gain much by Play, or some other delightful Recreative means: he shall undertake much business for himself, and other Persons; by which he may Reap considerable profit, and advantage: but if he be Combust, or afflicted there, the profit will be the less; and sometimes the Native is much damnified from such Relations, or undertakings.

VI. If you find him posited in the sixth House, 'tis ten to one but the Natives Servants prove persidious, or neglect his Service; from whom as also from small Cattle, and by Sickness he sustains much loss, unless other Testimonies in the Figure demonstrate the contrary, or at least mittigate the evil portended.

VII. If the Lord of the second be posited in the seventh House, the Native will receive damage in Estate, by Law Suits, or other Controversies; he spends much amongst the Female Sex, or has a Wife that helps him away with his Substance; and this the more certain, unless the Ruling Planet of that House be in friendly Aspect to the Lord of the second, the Native should warily deal with Partners, and beware also how he falls into the hands of Theeves (which he should be more than ordinary subject to) but if the Lord of the Second House be free from Impediment, the danger is the less, and some good may be expected.

VIII. If in the eighth House, the Native is usually very extravagant in his Expences; and if he be also in good Aspect, or Reception with the Lord of the eighth House, the Natives Estate will be much deminished, either by engagements for others, or some other means equivolent; but if the Lord of the second be fortified, or assisted by the Lord of the eighth, and disposed of by him also; then the Native gains by others, either by the Wills and Legacies of the dead, or by the Portion of a Wife, *viz.* an Estate, Goods, or Possessions may be transferrd unto him.

IX. If the Lord of the second shall be posited in the ninth House, free from affliction; the Native then gains by all things signified thereby, as merchandizing, or adventuring to Sea, either in Person, or Estate; or by some secret thing, or new Invention; and (if inclined that way) by the Law, or Clergy: this must always be understood, if he be well posited there, if not, Judge the contrary; and if he be in friendly Aspect of other Planets, this doth much confirm the aforesaid Judgement.

X. In the tenth House well seated, it shews the Native should gain by his Profession, or Imployment he follows. whether it be a Trade, or Office; or else it may be by the means of some Noble Person.

XI. If in the eleventh House, the Native thrives by the assistance of his Friends and acquaintance; he is generally fortunate in his hopes and gathers Wealth accidentally; and sometimes by buying, and selling, or managing the Estate of some Eminent Person.

XII. If in the twelfth House, and in his own Dignities, the Native then improves his Estate, by dealing in great Cattle; and strangely gains by the means of such Persons that secretly indeavour to injure him: but if unfortunately placed there, then Judge the contrary; to which add he may be much damaged by Imprisonment, and other vexatious sorrows that may unhappily fall upon him.

SECT. III.

Of the various signification of the Lord, or Ruler of the Third House, being posited in any of the twelve Houses of Heaven.

I. If the Lord of the third House happen to be Located in the Ascendant, this imports the Native may take many short Journeys, and prove a good Friend to his Kindred and Relations, whether Brothers, Sisters, Kinsfolks, &c. it argues he should bear Rule over them, and friendly Exercise his authority amongst them, unless the Lord of the third House be afflicted in the Ascendant by the Lord thereof, or otherwise; if so, he proves too severe, and unnatural.

II. If in the second House, the Natives Brethren, &c. contend with him for Goods, or Money (unless in good Aspect to the Lord of the Ascendant) and sometimes it betokens that the Native should make many short Journeys in order to the procuring, Augmenting, or confirming of an Estate, &c.

III. But if the Lord of the third House be in the third and happily placed therein; this shews not only assistance from Relations, but that the Native will delight to Journey up and down from one place to another.

IV. If in the fourth House, the Natives Relations will endeavour to inrich themselves by his Fathers Estate (at least, get what they can from him, though but little bettered thereby) yet to the Detriment of the Native; and this the more certain, if the Lord of the third House be ill affected in the fourth.

V. By being Located in the fifth House (which is the third from the third) this Naturally signifies many short Journeys taken by the Natives Kindred, no way prejudicial to him; they should be kind, and respective to the Natives Children also, and he should much delight to entertain his Relations, and Neighbours with Sports, Pastimes, and other Recreations, by which he receives no detriment, unless the fifth House be much afflicted.

VI. If in the sixth House, the Native lives in enmity and hatred with his Relations; and there is sometimes much Controversie promoted amongst them, unless some other over-ruling Testimonies occurr.

VII. If in the seventh House, the Native may be put to the trouble of many Journeys, occasioned by Controversies, and other discontents; sometimes in point of Marriage, or for the sake of his Brothers Wife, with whom he may be too familiar, according to the Opinion of some Authors: the seventh House is the Ascendant of the Natives Wife, and the fifth from the third; and therefore this Judgement is not improper.

VIII. If in the eighth House, it shews the condition of the Natives Brethren to be very mean, and Indigent; and that he should take many Journeys (chiefly occasioned by the Wills of deceased Persons.)

IX. If in the ninth House, the Natives Brethren shall Travel into remote parts of the World far from their Native Country, and there Marry, and Inhabit with their Wives. *Note that the ninth House is the seventh from the third, whence arises this Judgement.*

X. If in the tenth House (which is the eighth from the third) the Natives Brethren, &c. shall dye before him (or live but a short time) and whilst living, great differences, and dissentions shall arise amongst them, so that they will live very uncomfortably thereby; and it also portends some short Travel to the Native to gain preferment.

XI. But if in the eleventh House, this shews great love and amity between the Native and his Relations; and not only so, but that he will be very prosperous, and successful in most of his affairs, (especially if he be free from Combustion, or other affliction,) he also takes many pleasant Journeys to visit particular Friends.

XII. If the Lord of the third be posited in the twelfth House, the Native and his Brethren (and other Relations) are perfect Enemies one against the other, and seek out many private ways to perplex each other; and this is not all, but it portends much affliction to the Native; and he is forced to fly to secure himself from Imprisonment and other dangers, which the Native will be too often subject unto.

SECT. IIII.

Of the Lord of the fourth House, his Position in any of the twelve Houses of Heaven.

I. If you find the Lord of the fourth House posited in the Ascendant, the Native should be much concerned in Husbandry, in Building of Houses, and dealing in Land, or immovable Goods; and he should be very successful in all such undertakings, provided the Significator be no way Impeded; and not only so, but oft-times the Native proves the top of his Relations, and Kindred; and excells them all, and gains Respect and Honour from Eminent Persons.

II. If in the second House, it portends the Parents of the Native to be very responsible Persons, and both able and willing to assist, and support the Native; by whose favour he lives credibly, and hath good success in Purchasing of Houses, and Lands, &c.

III. When in the third House (which is the twelfth from the fourth) well placed, and free from affliction, the Native gains by all such things that are signified by the fourth House, whether Houses, Land, or Hereditaments, &c. from, or by the means of Relations; as Brothers, Sisters, Kinsfolks, &c. who should in some kind damnifie their Parents, or the contrary.

[These Judgements ought to be warily pronounced, and not peremptorily without the Consideration of other Circumstances in the Figure.]

IV. By being posited in the fourth House, and well beheld of the fortunate Planets; also free from Combustion &c. you may predict much happiness, and good success to the Native from dealing in Houses and Land, and all immovable Goods; and no less respect from Antient Persons, whence his Name becomes famous, and he leaves a good report after his Death: but if unfortunate, or afflicted in the fourth, this good promised is much abated, and the Native then may not expect to enjoy such Prosperity, nor live in that Splendor.

V. But if he shall be posited in the fifth House, free, this intimates the Father of the Native shall be liberal, and kind in disposing his Substance to the Natives Children; and that they may in all probability be much bettered thereby: but if the Lord of the fourth be in any bad Aspect with the Lord of the fifth House, or if the fifth House be afflicted, then Judge the contrary, that they will not enjoy the benefit of their Grandfathers Estate, or else he will not leave any thing considerable for them to boast of.

VI. If in the sixth House, the Native may thrive by Physick, small Cattle, and good Servants, (if no other Testimonies contradict,) it sometimes shews also the mean condition of the Natives Parents; and that the Native may be too much addicted to fraudulent, treacherous Actions; except the fortunate Planets assist by their friendly Rayes.

VII. If you find the Lord of the fourth, posited in the seventh House, strong; this signifies profit to the Native by a Wife, or Wives; or from some Publique Imployment, or by dealing with divers People of different Qualities in the World; sometimes the Natives Father proves his Enemy, or strangely opposes the Person, or Interest of his Son.

VIII. If he happen to be Located in the eighth House, this portends, not only danger to the Natives Mother in Child-bed, but also a short Life to the Father; but if the Lord of the fourth be well posited in the eighth, the Native may be much bettered by the Wills, and Legacies of deceased Persons; and in the end perhaps lay his Bones in some Forreign Country.

IX. If you find the Lord of the fourth in the ninth House, well seated, and free from the Hostile Beams of infortunate Planets; then Judge the Native acquires profit, or advantage, from some thing properly signified by the ninth House, whether by Travail, or some Religious means, or otherwise by some secret Mistery which he may discover; but it also intimates the Natives Parents to live in a very servile, mean, and low condition (the Father more especially,) and this the more certain, if weak, and a.fflicted in the said House.

X. But if posited in the tenth House, the Native and his Father, are then much esteemed by Honourable Persons, he then lives happily by his Imployment; and is generally accounted a Person of good Credit in the World, (unless you find other Arguments in the Scheme, to contradict this Judgement.)

XI. If in the eleventh House (which is the eighth from the fourth) and therein ill affected; this threatens short Life to the Father, and many Disasters to attend him during Life; but if well posited therein, Judge the contrary; and that the Native for the most part shall be happy and fortunate, during Life.

XII. If you find the Lord of the fourth in the twelfth House; 'tis then very probable that the Natives Friends (I mean his Parents) may be much afflicted with Poverty, and other Crosses, which may occasion them to try their Fortunes, in some remote part of the World, far distant from the Land of their Nativity. It also portends no great good to the Native himself; and shews he may end his days in a strange Country. These general Judgements may be Contradicted, in part, from other Configurations of the Planets, which ought to be well considered, and reconciled by the Artist.

SECT. V.

Of the Lord of the fifth House, his position in any of the twelve Houses.

I. The Lord of the *fifth* in the *Ascendant*, signifies the Native should have many Children, and be respected by them; the Native should also delight in Sports, Games, and other Recreations, sometimes to his prejudice.

II. If in the second, and free from affliction, it denotes profit to the Native by the indeavours of his Children; it shews they should thrive, and get Estates, and assist the Native thereby.

III. If the Lord of the *fifth* House be posited in the third, (which is the eleventh from the fifth,) the Natives Children are happy in their Friends, and acquaintance; and he takes many delightful and profitable short Journeys.

IV. If posited in the fourth House, *Schoner* says, the Native will enjoy an Estate from his Parents; others say, it signifies many Children, which unless he be strong and free from affliction, they may sustain many troubles, and vexations; and probably Imprisonment.

V. If in the fifth House well seated, it denotes the happy and prosperous condition of the Natives Children; and that the Native will be very propense to delights, and pleasures.

VI. If in the sixth House, the Natives Children prove good, and profitable Servants to the Native; and are not much afflicted with Diseases, unless other Testimonies concur.

VII. If in the seventh House, the Natives Wife, and Children hold together to his prejudice; they sometimes prove his professed Enemies, unless there happen some benevolent Aspect between the Lord of the Ascendant, and the Lord of the fifth House.

VIII. If in the eighth House free from affliction, the Natives Children generally thrive, or gain by deceased Persons; and so doth the Native also.

IX. If in the ninth House, the Natives Children will delight to take their pleasure, and to Travel long Journeys; they should be ingenious, and apt to search after new Inventions; and probably to good purpose: they should be Religious also, or concerned in matters, or things relating to the Church.

X. If posited in the tenth House, the Natives Children may be advanced by the means of great and potent Persons, to the honour of the Native; and in regard 'tis the sixth House from the fifth, the Children of the Native may prove but sickly Persons, or at least be much afflicted thereby.

XI. By being posited in the eleventh House, it denotes ill to the Natives Children in the general; they will meet with many Adversaries, and strange Oppositions, if other Testimonies contradict not; but the Native should be very prosperous in his hopes, and delight in the Company of his Friends.

XII. When the Lord of the fifth House shall be posited in the twelfth House, this shews but few Children; and such as will be very unnatural, and bring sorrow and trouble to the Native; but they may thrive by dealing in great Cattle.

SECT. VI.

Of the Position of the Lord of the Sixth, in any of the twelve Houses.

I. The Lord of the sixth in the Ascendant unless strong and well posited therein; shews that the Native may suffer much by Diseases of the Nature of that Planet; and that his Servants, and small Cattle should prove unfortunate unto him in the general.

II. But if posited in the second House, this shews prejudice to the Natives Estate, chiefly occasioned from Sickness, and Servants; and notwithstanding all the Natives Indeavours, he will rarely acquire an Estate, unless other good Arguments of Riches appear in the Figure.

III. If in the third House, the Natives Brethren should be sickly, and he himself subject to Diseases; and many times in his short, or In-land Journeys.

IV. If in the fourth House, the Natives Father lives a poor Servile Life; and he himself, together with his Family, suffer much by Sickness; and this the more certain, if the Lord of the sixth be Combust, or much afflicted in the Scheme.

V. By being posited in the fifth House, the Native is then afflicted with Sickness, proceeding from great Intemperance, Surfeits, and Debauchery; or from troubles of Spirit, arising from the affliction of the Natives Children.

VI. If the Lord of the sixth House be posited in the sixth House, strong, and in good Aspect to the Lord of the Ascendant; then the Native is strong and healthful for the most part, otherwise Judge the contrary.

VII. If in the seventh House, the Native will be subject to prejudice from, or by the means of the Female-sex; he may be afflicted with Diseases taken from them, unless he be more than ordinary careful: it shews also that the Natives Wife should be sickly, and Infirm; and the Native guilty, or at least accused of many evil Actions.

VIII. If the Lord of the sixth be in the eighth House, my Author says, the Native shall be healthy, and survive his Enemies, and Servants; but if the Lord of the Ascendant apply to the Lord of the sixth in the eighth, or the contrary; the Native then must expect to undergo Sickness, and great danger of Death also.

IX. If posited in the ninth House, unless strong, and potent there, or in good Aspect to fortunate Planets; the Native will be afflicted by sickness in his Travels; and not only so, but addicted to deceitful, and vitious Actions.

X. When posited in the tenth House, and weak; the Native is afflicted by disturbance in Body, or Mind, proceeding from much Labour in his Profession, or striving to gain Honour, or the favour of great Men, and attains not his desire; but if he be strong in the tenth, or in reception, or good Aspect with the Lord of the Ascendant, or tenth House, Judge the contrary.

XI. If in the eleventh House, he confides too much in pretended Friends, or suffers prejudice from new acquaintance; except there be other Arguments to Ballance this Judgement.

XII. But being posited in the twelfth House, the Native suffers affliction by Diseases, which may Invade his Body in Prison, or proceed from much sorrow, or vexation of Spirit; he receives injuries, and affronts, from base, and unworthy Persons; or from private Enemies &c. and this Judgement is the more aggravated, if the Lord of the sixth House be unfortunate in the twelfth.

SECT. VII.

Of the Position of the Lord of the Seventh, in any of the twelve Houses.

The Lord of the seventh House, posited in the Ascendant, shews that the Native shall be well beloved by the Female sex, and gain by them; but he must not expect to live free from Controversies, and if the Lord of the seventh vitiate the Ascendant, the Judgement is the more certain, that discords will arise, as well between the Native and his Wife, as between him and others.

II. The Lord of the seventh, in the second House, no way afflicted; the Native is then enrich'd by a Wife, or Wives; but if unfortunate therein, Judge the contrary; yet he may survive her, and many of his profest Adversaries; and rarely escapes prejudice in Estate from Theeves, or other Enemies; or at least, much contention, and debate, concerning such matters.

III. If in the third House, well dignified; there is a good agreement between the Native and his Relations; and sometimes Marries one of his own Kindred: but if you find the Lord of the seventh ill affected in the third, the Native, and his Relations, do not affect each other, but live at variance.

IV. If posited in the fourth House, the Native may enjoy the Possessions of his Father; and Marry one of his own Relations, who should prove vertuous and honest; but if ill dignified in the fourth, he may meet with trouble, or contention about some Estate in Houses, or Lands, formerly appertaining to his Ancestors.

V. If in the fifth House, ill dignified; the Native will have vexation, both with Wife and Children; but if well posited, he Marries a young Person, which should be a Woman of a good deportment, and behaviour; and not only vertuous, but beautiful.

VI. If in the sixth House, and ill dignified therein; the Native Marries a Person of low, and mean esteem; and it shews the Native to be guilty of lying, and treachrous Acts, unless contradicted by other Aspects that are friendly, and benevolent.

VII. If the Lord of the seventh be posited in the seventh House, and well dignified therein; the Native Marries credibly, and doth not dishonour himself thereby; but if afflicted there, Judge the contrary: it also shews an ill agreement and much discord, and contention with Women, either Sweethearts, or others.

VIII. If Located in the eighth House, and free from Combustion, or other affliction; the Native may Marry a Rich Wife, and be much bettered by her Fortune; yet he must also expect some trouble, and vexation concerning the Wills, or Legacies of deceased Persons, unless other Testimonies of good concurr.

IX. If in the ninth House, ill affected; the Native meets with some Controversie with his Wifes Relations; and not only so, but danger in his long Journeys, and perhaps Marries in another Countrey; sometimes it signifies differences in point of Religion: but if well dignified there, the evil is much abated.

X. When posited in the tenth House, Authors affirm, the Native shall Marry a Wife, both Rich, and Noble; and thereby come into the favour of great, and honourable Persons; but if he be afflicted there, the Native is perplext in his Imployment and all things signified by the tenth House.

XI. When you find the Lord of the seventh in the eleventh (which is the fifth House from the seventh) the Native, in all probability, may Marry a Widdow with whom he may live happily, though she have Chiidren; yet if ill dignified in that House, the Wife proves none of the best, perhaps addieted too much to Good-fellowship; and the Friends of the Native unhappily prove unkind unto him also, which must needs aggravate his discontent.

XII. If in the twelfth House, ill placed; this signifies an unfortunate Marriage, he meets with a very unworthy Woman, which proves treacherous and hateful, (unless some other way contradicted) it also shews many secret Enemies, and much trouble, and contention by their means, which will render the Natives Life very uncomfortable; but if the Lord of the seventh be well affected in the twelfth House, this evil is very mtch mittigated, if not totally abated.

SECT. VIII.

Of the Position of the Lord of the eighth, in any of the twelve Houses.

I. If the Lord of the eighth House be posited in the Ascendant, the Native scarce lives many years, but is very subject to misfortunes, and infirm in Body; his Life is no way happy, unless it be a fortunate Planet, and he in good Aspect to the Lord of the Ascendant or the Luminaries.

II. If posited in the second House (especially there in his own Dignities,) then Judge the Native may receive much profit, lest by Persons deceased or by the Dowry or a Wife; but it unfortunately placed there, Judge the contrary.

III. If in the third House, Judge the Natives Brethren will be Indigent Persons, not likely to live long, being much afflicted with Diseases, and other Disasters which frequently fall upon them to their great Detriment and the more, if the Lord of the fifth be much afflicted there: it also shews danger or Death to the Native in some short or In-land Journey.

IV. If you find him posited in the fourth House, ill affected; this prenotes much ill to the Natives Parents, they should be strangely afflicted, sickly, or unfortunate, unless befriended by the Benevolent Aspects of fortunate Planets; and for the Native, he will end his dayes at home, or in his own Native Countrey: *Schoner* sayes, *& quod mors nati erit in propria domo.*

V. When posited in the fifth House, the Natives Chidren dye in their Infancy, or if they live, they become Eminent; and are much Noted, either tor their Famous Actions, or for their vitious humours, according as their proper Significator shall be affected in the Scheme.

VI. By being placed in the sixth House, this denotes prejudice from Servants, or small Cattle, or from some Relation signified by the sixth House; but these Aphorismes must be understood warily, and with consideration of other Circumstances in the Figure, notwithstanding what some Authors preemptorily affirm in their Writings.

VII. If posited In the seventh House, this signifies the Native shall Marry a Wealthy Person, in some remote Country from his, (or her) Native Place, and be the surviver; and lastly, end his dayes in some Foreign Countrey.

VIII. The Lord of the eighth in the eighth House afflicted, shews great danger of a violent Death; but if strong and potent there, the Native enjoys his health reasonably well for the most part; and lastly, expires by a Natural easie Death.

IX. If in the ninth House, the Native rarely lays his Bones in his own Countrey, but dyes in some strange Land; if he be unfortunately placed there, then the Native is very prone to evil Actions, which may be a means to shorten his dayes; If strong, and free from affliction, Judge the contrary.

X. If in the tenth House, unfortunate; the Native may be put to Death, by the Sentence of a Judge, for the breach of the Law; yet he will dye no Ignoble Death, but end his dayes honourably, and probably by the Command of his Prince (whether the planet be strong or weak in the mid-heaven of the Scheme.)

XI. If in the eleventh House, the Native may expect but few real, and true Friends in whom we may confide, but rather a continual jarring, and debate arising between them; and lastly, he dyes in the Prime of his Years, unless thls Judgement happen to be mittigated by other more prevelant Causes concurring.

XII. If the Lord of the eighth be posited in the twelfth House, there afflicted, or infortunate; the Native may dye in Prison, or receive much Injury from his Enemies, insomuch that his Life will be uncomfortable, and interwoven with aboundance of misfortunes; if strong in the twelfth, the danger is the less considerable, and the Native may evade.

SECT. IX.

Of the Position of the Lord of the ninth, in any of the twelve Coelestial Houses.

I. If the Lord of the ninth House be posited in the Ascendant, the Native will have a desire, or strong inclination to Travel, or see strange Countreys; he will be just in his Actions, and thereby gain the affections of knowing Men, who will be ready to guide, or intrust him in Curious Arts, to which he may be very propense, if other Configurations contradict not.

II. If in the second House, the Native gains by Travel, long Journeys, Merchandizing; or any thing signified by the ninth House: and this the more certain, if he be posited there in his Essential Dignities, and in good Aspect to the Lord of the second House; if otherwise, 'tis not Irrational to Judge the contrary.

III. If posited in the third House, the Native may Travel, and his Brethren, and Kindred may be advantaged thereby; and probably he may Marry a Wife of some Foreign Countrey, (for the third is the seventh from the ninth House:) always consider, in Judgement, the strength, or weakness of the Significator, &c. since there is no general *Aphorisme*, or *Rule*, but admits of exception, and must be moderated by the Judicious Artist.

IV. When in the fourth House, (which is the eighth from the ninth House,) the Native may end his dayes in another Countrey; and the Natives Parents should be very Infirm in Body, or afflicted with some Occult Distemper; and the occasion of the Natives Travel may be from his Parents Advice, or Promotion. *Significat peregrinationis in causis Parentum* saith *Schoner*.

V. If posited in the fifth House, the Native will have many pleasant Journeys, and probably Children in some remote Countrey, in whom he will be happy, and take much pleasure.

VI. But if in the sixth house, *Natus ducet Seruam, &c.* saith *Schoner*: To which *Argol* agrees in his *Ptol. Parv.* The Native Marries a Servant, and may gain much by Servants and small Cattle; and probably undergo some sickness in his Journeys, or other prejudice, either to himself, or Family, unless the Significators happen to be well assisted by fortunate Planets, or their propitious Rayes.

VII. If posited in the seventh House, the Native should then meet with a vertuous Wife, a Woman well bred, and of an excellent Deportment; and not only so, but very tractable, and obedient to the Native, for the most part;

yet the Native should be subject to many vexatious Journeys, or meet with great discontent with Persons in his Travel.

VIII. Being Located in the eighth House, This Imparts to the Native Travel, sometimes upon some dangerous score, and sometimes to gain the Portion of his Wife, as a Legacie left him by a deceased Friend: let this be understood with the aforesaid Cautions, often hinted in this Chapter.

IX. If posited in the ninth House, the Native Travels but few Journeys; be is a very just Person, a curious searcher into Divine Misteries, and secret things, and his Dreams prove, for the most part, true; in fine, he proves a Person generally respected by most, and may at some time of his Life, take a long Journey upon the account of Religion, or the Discovery or some Occult thing.

X. By being posited in the tenth House, the Native will then undertake some Journey to acquire honour, or advancement; or he Travels with honourable Persons, or probably to acquaint himself with some excellent Art, or to gain preferment, or a new Imployment; and the Natives Brethren usually, upon such a Position, gain Rich Wives, or match themselves into Credible Families.

XI. If in the eleventh House, the Native is a Person had (for the most part) in good esteem, and well respected by his Friends; and deserves no less, both in his Native Countrey, and in those places to which he may Travel, (though perhaps unwillingly,) to which may be added (according to the Opinion of some Authors) that the Native Brethren should Marry out or their own Countreys, I suppose, because the eleventh is the ninth from the third House.

XII. If the Lord of the ninth be posited in the twelfth House, ill dignified; it denotes the Native to be Irreligious and Athestical; also unnatural to his Brethren, and Kindred: but sometimes it falls out, the Natives Relations prove false, and treacherous to the Native, unless the Lord of the third, or ninth, be in good Aspect, or reception with the Lord of the Ascendant.

SECT. X.

Of the Lord of the tenth's Position, &c.

I. The Lord or the tenth in the Ascendant, denotes the Native shall bear Rule over Inferiour Persons; he gains honour in his Imployment, or the execution of his Office; and is much in esteem with Persons of Eminency; if he be weak, and unfortunate in the first House, it abates something of the excellent good prenoted.

II. If in the second House, strong, and well posited; this conferrs honour, and advantage upon the Native for his Riches, which he gains in some Eminent Imployment, or Office under a great Person, or Man in Power.

III. If posited in the third House, the Native gains honour, and esteem, by the performance of short Journeys; and though he will not have many Brethren, yet by their means he is advanced to some preferment, which wlll be profitable; and this the more considerable as the Significator shall be assisted by the Benevolent Rayes of the fortunate Planets, &c.

IV. If the Lord of the tenth House shall be posited in the fourth, it promises advantage to the Native, from Houses, Lands, Antient Buildings; and all things signified by the fourth House: and from the great Friendship he will receive from Noble Men, in the management of their affairs, honour, and preferment is thereby conferr'd upon the Native; and finally, he is prosperous in most kinds of Possessions, and innovable Goods; and this more, or less, according the strength, or weakness of the Significator, and the good, or evil Aspects which the other Planets cast unto him.

V. If posited in the fifth House, strong, and in good Aspect to the Lord of the fifth; this denotes honour to the Native by means of his Children; but they should be no healthful Persons, but rather sickly, and infirm: and consequently, but short-liv'd. *Note that the fifth House is the eighth from the tenth, &c.*

VI. If in the sixth House or a Nativity, this argues the Estate, or Fortune of the Native to be very mean, and indifferent; yet if he be well posited in that part of the Figure, it imports the Native will obtain a moderate good respect in general; and much kindness wlll be express'd unto him for his worth and deserts.

VII. If posited in the seventh House, the Native overcomes, in most Contentions he is concerned in; he also Marries honourably, and is much advanced thereby, and brought into great Reputation, according to the strength or the Significator; &c.

VIII. If placed in the eighth House, it signifies wealth to the Native, in his younger years, by Legacies, or the Inheritances of the dead; and Honour, and Dignity thereby: but my Author says, the Mother wlll be in danger of Death at the Natives Birth.

IX. If he happen to be posited in the ninth House, strong; the Native arrives to great preferment by his Learning, or from some notable Voyage, or new Invention; he should be a very just, and honest Person in all his Actions; and yet at last end his dayes in some remote Countrey, or Kingdom, from the Land of his Nativity.

X. It posited in the tenth House, strong; the Native acquires most excellent preferment, or attains some great Honour or Dignity, even beyond his Capacity of Birth; probably same good preferment under the King, or Prince, &c.

XI. If in the eleventh House, well seated; the Native hath not only many Famous Friends, by whom he reaps much profit, and honour; but is also very beneficial to those that are in his favour; he is no less fortunate, and happy in most of his Affairs in general; and leaves his Children possest with very considerable Estates; but if the Significator be ill affected, much of this good will be diminished.

XII. If the Lord of the tenth be posited in the twelfth House, this denotes much loss, and prejudice to the Native, from Persons in power; he will be in great danger of Imprisonment, and generally unfortunate; but in the end he gains respect, even from those which were his private Enemies.

SECT. XI.

Of the Position of the eleventh House, &c.

I. If the Lord or the eleventh be posited in the Ascendant, strong; the Native then cannot want for many good and faithful Friends, from whom he may be very happy in his hopes, and expectations, and be a Conqueror over all his Enemies; and by his upright dealing, and good merits, he will dayly augment the Number of his Friends, and acquire a good Estate, and live in Fame, and Credit in the World; and in fine, be generally fortunate in all his Actions: If he be weak, or afflicted in the Ascendant, it abates of this promised good; but doth not wholly obliterate this promising signification.

II. If in the second House, well seated; it also denotes Riches, or considerable advantage from Friends, and Aquaintance; and some good from the Natives Children also, in whom he should be very happy, and take much comfort.

III. If posited in the third House, the Native is then fortunate in his Brethren, and Kindred, who should be Persons of good Credit, and Estimation; they should also be more than ordinary Friendly to the Native: and all his short Journeys should prove exceeding prosperous. This Judgement is more certain if the Lord of the eleventh be well affected in the third House, or be in good Aspect, or reception with the Lord of the Ascendant, the Luminaries, or fortunate Planets.

IV. If placed in the fourth House, the Natives Parents will be very subject to Diseases; and consequently not live to any great Age: yet they should be fortunate, and the Native will be much bettered by them, and all Immovable Goods he shall happen to deal in, or be concerned withal.

V. If the Lord of the eleventh be posited in the fifth House; this signifies to the Native much content, and joy in his Children, who should be very prosperous and happy; yet if the significator be unfortunate, it imports that the Native may be inclined to let loose the Reins of his desires, and give himself an unlimited Liberty, as to pleasures, and Recreations, &c. if other Significators contradict not.

VI. If posited in the sixth House, and especially ill dignified there; then the Native lives not to an old Age, and is perplext with many miseries and vexations, so that his Life is no way comfortable; but if strong, the Native struggles through difficulties with much more ease; and becomes a moderate Conqueror over his troubles that occur in his Affairs in the World.

VII. If you find him Located in the seventh House, Authors affirm, it signifies Poverty in the Natives younger Years, but Riches toward the latter part of his Life; it also portends the Native shall Marry happily, to a Wife that will enrich him arid affect him well, with whom he shall live very prosperously, and with great content; and probably Marry more than once, and so enrich himself that way.

VIII. If he happen to be posited in the eighth House, the Native may not expect to be fortunate in Merchandizing; but in all probability, he may be advantaged very much by the Wills, and Legacies of the dead; and enjoy Possessions and a considerable Estate thereby; and this more certain if the Lord of the eleventh House be well dignified in the eighth, &c.

IX. Now if the Lord of the eleventh House be posited in the ninth House of the Scheme, and strong; then the Native may expect profit, and advantage by Merchandizing, and venturing into far Countreys; and if he happen to Travel himself, he will be fortunate, and happy in his Travels, and reap more profit abroad in the World, than in his Native Countrey: and not only so, but gain good Friends, and Acquaintances also, &c.

X. If in the tenth House, and free from affliction; the Native then wants for no Friends, and those Friends indeed by whom he is advanced, and promoted; and as the Proverb is, held up by the Chin, as it were; so that it is impossible for him to sink in the World, and what can a Native desire more? But if the Significator be weak, or much debilitated, the Native must then expect to fall short or such great kindnesses, which in these days are very rare.

XI. If posited in the eleventh House, this still presages to the Native much Wealth, and many Friends; and consequently, a notable Name, and Fame, according to his Degree, and Quality of Birth, he should be blessed in his Children also; and notwithstanding all this, the Natives Fortune will be subject to vary, unless special care be taken.

XII. If placed in the twelfth House, the Natives hopes will be often frustrated; he is very vain, and foolish, for the most part, in his Actions; he meets with few Friends to support him and many Enemies to afflict him; let him beware of Imprisonment, and other misfortunes: But if the Lord of the eleventh be in good Aspect, or Reception with the Lord of the Ascendant, or either of the Luminaries, the danger will be somewhat mittigated, and the Natives Fortune, in general, more kind and favourable.

SECT. XII.

Of the Position of the Lord of the twelfth, in any of the Houses of a Nativity.

I. The Lord of the twelfth in the Ascendant or a Nativity, shews the Native should be all along (more, or less) perplexed with Enemies, and encompassed about with many troubles, and vexations; also divers treacherous Acts, and unkind dealings from those of his own Family, especially in the former part or his Life, which afflicts both Body and Mind; but the latter part of his Life should Be more peaceable, and prosperous: then he may expect an emendation, and in all probability gather Substance, and live comfortably in the World.

II. If in the second House, the Native suffers much by Losses in his Estate and other Crosses from his Enemies, daily heaped upon him, to his great Detriment; strange Reports will be raised of him, and his happiness very much envied; also attempts made to impoverish the Native, if there be not other more prevalent Testimonies to Countermand the evil threatened.

III. If the Lord of the twelfth be posited in the third House, then the Brethren of the Native are his Enemies, and he meets with many Remarkable Treacheries, and Unkindnesses from them; and they themselves will not escape the same Fate rrom others: also the Native should be very unfortunate in his In-land, or short Journeys; and this Judgement is the more aggravated if the Lord of the twelfth be afflicted.

IV. If posited in the fourth House, weak, or unfortunate; this prenotes Contention between the Native, and his Parents, about Possessions, and Lands, &c. great Animosities are fomented between the Native and his Kindred, concerning Immovable Goods; insomuch that the Native may be dispossessed his House, and many Distractions follow, unless the fortunate Planets assist by their friendly Beams.

V. If placed in the fifth House (which properly signifies Children) and unfortunate therein; this presages that the Natives Chlldren should be disobedient, and he should have much vexation, and sorrow heaped upon him by their means; and if the Lord of the fifth House be in the twelfth, Authors affirm, the Native Shall Nurse the Children of others, but he will rarely be fortunate, or happy in any.

VI. If Located in the sixth House, (which signifies Servants, and small Cattle,) then the Native must expect to meet with great Infelicity, and Prejudice, by the means of treacherous deceitful Servants; as also loss by Cattle and all things properly signified by the sixth House.

VII. If you find the Lord of the twelfth in the seventh House, and unfortunate therein; it denotes prejudice to the Native from his Wife, or base Contemptible women; who will be very enemical unto him, and give him much trouble, and molestation; insomuch that his Life will be miserable, and he will end his dayes in sorrow.

VIII. By being posited in the eighth House, this portends a moderate good Fortune to the Native; he enjoys a Competent Estate and is pestered with very few Enemies, either publique or private; yet he meets with some troubles concerning the Estates of Persons deceased.

IX. If posited in the ninth House, the Native meets with troubles from Church-men in Ecclesiastical Affairs; and is not prosperous in his long Journeys, or Voyages to Sea; his Wifes Relations, and Kindred, are infortunate, (for the ninth is the third from the seventh) and suffer much oppression by their Enemies, unless there be some other Testimonies of good in the Scheme to alevlate the Evil.

X. In the tenth House, unfortunate; it denotes danger of Imprisonment from the displeasure of some great Person or Magistrate; the Natives Honour, and Reputation will be much abated, or Clouded; he loses his preferment, and all his affairs (for the most part) are strangely obstructed by continual Oppositions, to the Natives great Detriment, and Sorrow.

XI. If posited in the eleventh House and ill Dignified; the Native is strangely disappointed in his hopes, his Friends, and Acquaintance fall off, and prove unfaithful; he suffers much by the frowns of Fortune, in most of his Affairs, unless miraculously prevented.

XII. Lastly, the Lord of the twelfth in the twelfth House, denotes the Native may suffer prejudice by the means or his secret Enemies, as it were insensibly, and shall not know who hurts him; he should have but few real friends, and many Enemies that secretly exercise their Malice against him, but the injury they do the Native will not be considerable; yet let him be careful to avoid Imprisonment, or Restraint, which such a Position (unless Corrected by other Configurations) doth naturally import. *And thus much shall serve for the significations of the Planets (being Rulers of the several Houses) from their Positions in any of the Houses of a Nativity, where note that all the aforesaid Aphorismes are certain and true in themselves with those Cautions I have intimated all along, that is, when the Lord of the House is posited alone in another House of the Figure, and neither in Aspect with fortunate, or unfortunate Planets, nor peregrine or combust, &c. but if otherwise let the Artist consider it, and order his Judgement accordingly, and he cannot err.*

CHAP. IX.

Sheweth the general signification of the Aspects of the Planets in a Nativity.

SECT. I.

Of the Conjunction of the Planets one with another.

I. The Conjunction of *Saturn*, and *Jupiter*, signifies, to the Native, many good Possessions, and Inheritances; and many wayes of profit to the Native, if they are not evilly beheld by *Mars*.

II. The *Conjunction* of *Saturn*, and *Mars* in a Nativity, shews the Native may be intrusted, but shall not accomplish his desires, without great difficulty; he shall survive his Brethren, but end his dayes before his Parents.

III. The *Conjunction* of *Saturn*, and the *Sun*, shews loss of Patrimony and great trouble to gain Riches; but the most danger is in such Nativities which are Nocturnal.

IV. The *Conjunction* of *Saturn*, and *Venus*, signifies the Native may Marry a Widdow, or a Person much older than himself, by whom he shall have no Male Children; sometimes it denotes the Natives Wife to be a vile Contemptible Person, by whom he, and his Parents are much dishonoured.

V. The *Conjunction* of *Saturn*, and *Mercury*, shews the Native should have an Impediment in his Speech; and that he should be a mean, inconsiderable Person, and rarely capable or any Trade, or Profession.

VI. The *Conjunction* of *Saturn*, and the *Moon*, denotes an Indigent Person, weak in Body, and loss from his Parents.

VII. The *Conjunction* of *Jupiter*, and *Mars*, promises him Riches by Command in Warr; and renders the Native a Person of good Credit, and Renown, in all Martial Enterprizes.

VIII. The *Conjunction* of *Jupiter*, and *Sol*, shews poverty, or loss, if the *Sun* be not Oriental; if so, the Father will be Fortunate, and by him the Son, and his Children also.

IX. The *Conjunction* of *Jupiter*, and *Venus*, shews the Love, and Friendship of great Persons; and profit by their means.

X. The *Conjunction* of *Jupiter*, and *Mercury*, denotes the Native may prove a Lawyer, Secretary, or Chancellor, &c.

XI. The *Conjunction* or *Jupiter*, and *Luna*, prenotes great Riches, according to the Capacity of the Natives Birth.

XII. The *Conjunction* of *Mars*, and *Sol*, signifies loss of Patrimony and Goods; a short Life to the Father, and great danger the Native may be burnt, or perish by Fire.

XIII. The *Conjunction* of *Mars*, and *Venus*, shews that the Native may suffer many strifes, and Debates concerning Women; and sometimes shews the Native should be a great Adulterer, or Lover of Women of a most Infamous Name, or Reputation in the world.

XIV. The *Conjunction* of *Mars*, and *Mercury*, usually produces a Lyar, a Deceiver, a Babling, Prating Person; yet ingenious, and eloquent; and for his own Interest, very diligent.

XV. The *Conjunction* of *Mars*, and the *Moon*, prenotes a short Life to the Native; sometimes a violent Death by Fire, by Iron, or by the fall or some Ruinous Building; and sometimes by Blows, or Wounds from the hands of Men.

XVI. The *Conjunction* of the *Sun*, and *Venus*, shews the Native should be a Person of good Renown (the Birth considered) he shall do many praise-worthy Acts, and gain the favour of Women in general.

XVII. The *Conjunction* of the *Sun*, and *Mercury*, denotes Wisdom, Learning, Science, and great Estimation thereby; the Native is skilful in many things.

XVIII. The *Conjunction* of the *Sun*, and *Moon*, signifies a short Life; and that the Native shall bear Rule, and delight in honourable Company.

XIX. The *Conjunction* of *Venus*, and *Mercury*, inclines the Native to the love of Musick, and Dancing, *&c.* such a Position makes a pleasant merry Companion; yet if they are conjoyned under the *Sun* Beams, the Nattve is defective in the Parts of Generation, and receives prejudice from, or by the means or Women.

XX. The *Conjunction* of *Venus*, and the *Moon*, gives a pleasant jocular Person, fair spoken, yet proud; and if *Mars* dart his malignant Beams, the Native and his Wife should be extravagant, and wander in strange Pasture; unless Jupiter interpose his friendly Rayes.

XXI. The *Conjunction* of *Mercury*, and the *Moon*, shews a good Inclination to Science, and ingenious Arts, by which the Native gains Reputation; yet he should be very fickle, and unconstant.

SECT. II.

Of the Trine Aspects of the Planets in a Natvity, &c.

I. The *Trine* of *Saturn*, and *Jupiter*, denotes the Native should enjoy the Goods of this Life plentifully, whether in Houses, Lands, hid Treasure, or Inheritances, it matters not; this is the more certain if they are in good places of the Figure.

II. The *Trine* of *Saturn*, and *Mars*, promises great advantage to the Native by preferment, honour in bearing Rule, either in Towns or Countries; and he survives his Brethren.

III. The *Trine* of *Saturn*, and the *Sun*, presages honour, and preferment to the Native; some Place, or Office of Credit is conferr'd upon him, if the Nativity be Diurnal; if Nocturnal, the Native squanders away his Patrimony; but in the end, by some worthy Action, he retrieves all again, to his great Fame, and Reputation.

IV. The *Trine* of *Saturn*, and *Venus*, Indues the Native wlth a modest shamfac'tness; he is just in his Actions, a Person of good Conversation, and Repute; yet much envied by base sordid Persons, and Marries not till after thirty Years of Age.

V. The *Trine* of *Saturn*, and *Mercury*, renders the Native a very prudent Person, yet subtile in most of his Affairs; a Person of a pregnant Fancy, sometimes studious in the Mathematicks, or other Curious Arts; a fit Person to make a Chancellor, Secretary, General Register, or Publique Notary, *&c.*

VI. The Trine of *Saturn*, and the *Moon*, promises much favour from great Persons of both Sex; it shews the Native may have a popular applause, and be advanced to great Honour, and Dignity; and probably bear great Rule over others.

VII. The Trine of *Jupiter*, and *Mars*, denotes Boldness, Victory, Honour, the favour of great Persons, Government; and a very considerable Fame in the World, the Capacity of Birth considered.

VIII. The *Trine* of *Jupiter*, and the *Sun*, produces (in a Natural way) to the Native great Honour, and Estimation in the World; much Riches, and Noble Possessions, also many Children.

IX. The *Trine* of *Jupiter*, and *Venus*, presages a comly Person, vertuous and much obliging to all; the Native will be both faithful, and honest, and be enriched by Wives, or the means of Women; as also be preferr'd to Dignity, according to the Capacity of the Native.

X. The *Trine* of *Jupiter*, and *Mercury*, shews an ingenious Person, of a pregnant Fancy, and able to Administer good Counsel, or Advice; the Judgement should be sound, and not impaired; and consequently, the Native should be successful in most Enterprizes, and a fit Person, if his Education corresponds, to make a Judge, or Counsellor, or perform some Eminent Office of trust.

XI. The *Trine* of *Jupiter*, and the *Moon*, demonstrates the Native to be or a Noble Mind, and a Person or an Aspiring Brain, who may acquire much Honour, and Renown; a true lover, and promoter of Vertue, and all just Actions in general, *quo ad.*

XII. The *Trine* of *Mars*, and the *Sun*, presages advancement according to the Quality of the Native; he gains much Honour by War-like Actions, and Exployts; and from thence is promoted to great Dignity, and Government; and probably to be the General, or Conductor of an Army, or something equivolent.

XIII. The *Trine* of *Mars*, and *Venus*, prenotes to the Native in the first place, profit, and considerable gain from, or by the means of Women; and it renders the Native of a lofty Spirit, much puff'd up with Pride; and a great delighter in the Company of the Female-sex.

XIV. The *Trine* of *Mars*, and *Mercury*, denotes the Native to be prudent, and crafty; a Person of a searching Fancy, capable or any thing he desires to attain; it signifies a good Oratour, or Disputant; and no less knowing in Arithmetick, or the Nature of Numbers.

XV. The *Trine* of *Mars*, and the *Moon*, signifies happiness to the Native in most of his Affairs; a rising Person, capable of bearing Rule, and able to mannage Business with prudent Severity, by which he gains Honour and Renown.

XVI. The Benevotent Aspects of the *Sun*, and *Venus*, are not much different from what was said of the *Trine* of *Mars*, and *Venus*, *viz.* profit from, or by the means of Women, *&c.* it rather imports much more Honour, and Advantage than what was berore Intimated; but these are Rare.

XVII. The *Trine* of *Venus*, and the *Moon*, signifies the Native should be Beautiful; a comly Person, delighting to go neat in Apparreel, somewhat proud, and easily tempted, if a Woman; and as Amorous, if a Man.

XVIII. The *Trine* of *Mercury*, and the *Moon*, shews the Native to be an ingenious Person in his Imployment; and is had in great Estimation for the same, whether it be *Musick, Singing, Dancing, Painting*, or any such Airy Fancy, *&c.*

[*Note that the* Sextile *Aspects of the Planets have the same signification with those of the* Trines, *but not altogether so forcible; and therefore they need not be again repeated. The same I may say of the* Quartiles, *in respect of the* Oppositions; *therefore I shall only treat of the* Oppositions *of the Planets, and omit the* Squares *as superfluous.*]

SECT. III.

Of the Oppositions *of the Planets in a Nativity,* &c.

I. The *Oppositions* of *Saturn*, and *Jupiter*, in any Nativity; shews a contnued Series of troubles, and vexations; many Mischiefs, and Tribulations occur to the Native, to his great Detriment, also loss of Chlldren; and if *Saturn* be in the Ascendant, and *Jupiter* in the seventh, the Native suffers most of his Infortunances in the fore-part of his Life; and after thirty Years of Age, he lives reasonable happy, and quiet to the end or his dayes.

II. The *Opposition* of *Saturn*, and *Mars*, in any Nativity (except *Jupiter*, or *Venus* interpose their friendly Rayes) declares Superlative troubles to the Native; many Conspiracies are Hatched against him, and he is afflicted most intollerably with Diseases; and subject to prejudice by the fall of Ruinous Buildings, or by falls from high places, danger by Water, sometimes expires by the Plague, or some violent Death aforesaid; and the Native is most unhappy in a Father.

III. The *Opposition* of *Saturn*, and the *Sun*, without the friendly Aspects of the Fortunes, decyphers to the Native, danger or a violent Death; it produces many Tribulations, Sorrows, and Vexations, sometimes occasioned from the loss or Goods, or Estate, or other Disasters equivolent.

IV. The *Opposition* of *Saturn*, and *Venus*, destroyes the Beauty, and Vertue of the Native; and renders him, or her, vitious, and infamous; especially in all things relating to unlawful desires.

V. The *Opposition* of *Saturn*, and *Mercury*, afflicts the Native in his, (or her) Elocution; it produces a great Impediment in the Speech (as I have experimented in several Nativities) and not only so, but the Fancy is also stupified; and such a Person is unfit to make an *Orator*, or *Astrologer*. Authors tell us, such an Aspect disperses the Natives Brethren also.

VI. The *Opposition* of *Saturn*, and the *Moon*, shews troubles, and danger to the Natives Mother; and also to the Native of some violent Death by Water, (consideration being had to the Nature of the Sign wherein the *Moon* is posited.

VII. The *Opposition* of *Jupiter*, and *Mars*, in any Nativity, denotes the Native to be ungrateful to his Friends, from whom he has received great favours; it renders him a very rash, head-strong Person; a destroyer of his own Substance, and a Person of a very mutable Fortune.

VIII. The *Opposition* of *Jupiter*, and the *Sun*, declares the Native to be an Extravagant, and a Person that will squander away his Patrimony, (unless other Testimonies fall in) and not only so, but freely dispossess himself of his Imployment, and Honour.

IX. The *Opposition* of *Jupiter*, and *Venus*, in a Nativity, declares the Natives Friends to be very mutable, and unconstant in their Affections of the Native, who is too subject to be rewarded with ingratitude; otherwise he injoys a moderate Fortune, according to his Quality, or Degree.

X. The *Opposition* of *Jupiter*, and *Mercury*, demonstrates many Strifes, and Contentions, in which the Native should be Involved; oftentimes strange things are conspired against his Person, and Interest, difference with his Brethren, many Enmities against him; and probably, Law Suits, which may even weary out the Native to Death, unless there be other Arguments of Assistance in the Scheme.

XI. The *Opposition* of *Jupiter*, and the *Moon*, shews some petty difficulties which the Native will overcome, and afterward live reasonable happy.

XII. The *Opposition* of *Mars*, and the *Sun*, shews, in any Persons Nativity, danger to the Eyes, but more especially to the right Eye; and not only so, but as great danger of a violent Death, and a destruction of his Patrimony; let him beware of falls from some high place, and generally of all rash Actions; it also portends a short Life to the Father.

XIII. The *Opposition* of *Mars*, and *Venus*, renders the Native a Person too much addicted to his Pleasures, and Delights; oftentimes very vitious, generally mutable and unconstant, and a grief to both Wife, and Children: if it fall from Tropical Signs, the Native Marries Wives of ill Repute, or frequents too much the Company of scandalous Women.

XIV. The *Opposition* of *Mars*, and *Mercury*, and no friendly Aspect from *Jupiter*, presages the Native to be an unjust Person, and one of vitious Principles naturally; and consequently, guilty of many Crimes, for the which he may justly be exil'd, chiefly if *Mercury* be in the House of *Saturn*, nor may his Children be expected to be much better than their Father.

XV. The *Opposition* of *Mars*, and the *Moon*, alwayes shews prejudice, or blemishes to the Eyes, especially the left Eye; nor doth the Body escape Wounds, and Hurts, and other accidental Infirmities: the Native hath many Enemies, abhors Marriage; and rarely escapes a violent Death.

XVI. The *Opposition* of the *Sun*, and *Moon*, declares to the Native a very mutable Fortune; sometimes the Native lives and enjoys much happiness, and suddenly his condition is changed into misfortune; sometimes his Reputation is good, and splended, and in a short time he receives as much dishonour; one while he enjoys his health well, and afterwards he is much afflicted with sickness; so that his whole Life is very mutable, and various, continuing im no state long.

XVII. The *Opposition* of *Venus*, and the *Moon*, shews that the Native should be unfortunate in Marriage, and Women should prove injurious to him in the general; nor can be expect to be happy in his Children, except some other good Aspects of the Planets may alter this Judgement, which is almost infallibly true, as all Artists must needs confirm.

XVIII. Lastly, the *Opposition* of *Mercury*, and the *Moon*, in a Nativity, shews the Native shall meet with many Oppositions in the Course of his Life, and many treacherous Acts shall be contrived against him, of which he himself should be somewhat guilty, and therefore justly paid in his own Coyn; such an Aspect in a Nativity where *Mercury* is Lord of the Ascendant, shews the Native to be a very mutable, inconsiderable Person, conceited, and yet vold of reason, and good manners. [*And thus I have shewed something of the Planets significations in any Nativity, according as they shall behold each other; but the Artist ought also in his Judgement to consider what Houses they govern and from what Signs, and parts of the Figure they behold each other; and from thence (together with these general Rules) form his Judgement suitable to the quality, and condition of the Native; to perform which there can be no other general Rules given, but must be left to the ability, and discretion of the Artist, as in many places of this Book I have aleady hinted.*] And here I might have also shewed the significations of each Planet, being posited in any of the twelve Houses; but that I conceive to be needless, since be that well understands the Natural signification of each Planet, strong, or weak; as also the Judgements proper to each House, (which is already shewed in the first part) cannot be to seek how to Form and Compound an apt, and congruous Judgement from the Accidental Position of each Planet in any part of the Scheme or the Heavens.

CHAP. X.

How to give an Astrological Judgement upon the twelve Houses of a Nativity, with the resolution of the most necessary Questions appertaining thereunto.

SECT. I.

Judgements proper to the first House.

May the Life of the Native be long, or short?

Least an Artist take much pains to small purpose, 'twill be convenient, (before he proceed to Directions) to consider whether the Native be likely to live long, or not; therefore if it be possible to procure the Parents Nativities, consider therein the strength, or weakness of the Significators of Children, *viz.* See if the fifth House, or the Lord therof be not afflicted by the presence, or malevolent Aspect of *Saturn*, or *Mars*, or the *Dragons Tail* posited therein; if you find the Significators ill placed, or infortunate by the aforesaid Aspects, or Combust of the *Sun*, or Retrograde, &c. These are Arguments their Children are not long Liv'd, but subject to Diseases, and consequently short Life; Judge the contrary if you find the Significators strong, and potent; but if the Parents Nativities cannot be had (as for the most part they are very rarely obtained) then Judge from the Natives Geniture according to these following Rules, which are termed (almost) Infallible, and have been often proved in divers Nativities.

I. Consider whether the Degree Ascending, or the Lord thereof be afflicted or not, by the Presence, or Aspect of the Infortunes, or Lord of the eighth; or whether the Lord of the Ascendant be Combust, Peregrine, Retrograde, or Cadent.

II. Consider whether *Saturn*, or *Mars* be in *Conjunction* in the Ascendant, or in *Opposition* from the first, and seventh, or an Eclips happening in the Degree Ascending, or fixed Stars of an evil Nature Arising therewith; there are dangerous Arguments.

III. The Light of the time afflicted, or Eclipsed at the hour of Birth, is sometimes fatal to the Native.

IV. The *Moon* in *Quartile*, or *Opposition*, of *Saturn* or *Mars*, in the fourth, sixth, eighth, or twelfth Houses; or if she be Besieged of *Saturn*, and *Mars*, or of *Sol*, and *Mars*, and in no good Aspect of the Fortunes; these are dangerous Testimonies that the Native is not designed for a long Life (in a Natural sense) unless Divine Providence shall determine otherwise.

V. Lastly, Many Planets in the sixth, eighth, or twelfth, and the Lord of the Ascendant not beholding them; or the *Sun*, or *Moon*, or Ascendant with any good Aspect, shews danger.

These are the most Considerable Testimonies of a short Life; but if none of these take place in the *Geniture*, but the Fortunes, or Luminaries, friendly behold the Ascendant, or his Lord, the Native may then (in all probability) live until some powerful Direction of the Ascendant, or Luminaries to an evil Promittor, cut him (or her) off from the Land of the Living.

1.

Of the Significator (or giver) of Life, called Hylech, Hyleg, *or* Apheta.

There hath been some difference amongst Authors in this particular, *viz*. What Planet to take for the giver of Life; but waving all their Arguments, and several Opinions herein, I shall assent to those which affirm that the giver of Life ought to be Elected from the Luminaries, and the Ascendant; and the strongest of them ought to be chosen. [*This seems Rational, and therefore ought to be imbraced; and I suppose there are few (or none) of our Modern Astrologers but will acknowledge the same.*] Which take in these three following Rules.

I. If the Birth be Diurnal, and the *Sun* in the seventh, ninth, tenth, eleventh, or Ascendant, (or not far from the Degrees thereof) these being accounted the only *Aphetical* places proper unto him, he shall then be accounted for *Hyleg*, or giver of Life.

II. If the Birth be Nocturnal, and the *Moon* posited in the Ascendant, or any of the aforesaid Houses (or near the Degrees of the cusps thereof) she shall then be accepted for the giver of Life.

III. Lastly, If in a Diurnal, or Nocturnal Nativity, the Luminaries are not found in those *Aphetical* places, but Located in any of the other Houses; in this Case, the Ascendant must be taken for *Hyleg*, or giver of Life.

2.

Of the giver of Years, or Alchocoden, *(as the* Arabians *term it.)*

I. See what Planet hath most Essential Dignities in the place of the *Hyleg*, and that Planet (by the Antients) is termed *Alchocoden*, or giver of Years; and this the rather, if he be in Aspect to the place of the giver of Life.

II. If either of the Luminaries happen to be *Hyleg*, or giver of Life; and are also strong, and potent, as being in their own Houses, or Exaltations, &c. Then account that Luminary, so Dignified, both *Hyleg*, and *Alchocoden*; but being *Hyleg*, and void of the aforesaid qualifications, *viz*. Essentially strong, they cannot then be admitted giver of Years.

III. If many Planets happen to be neer equal in strength in the place of the giver of Life, so that the Artist may be at a stand which to take; then consider which of them behold the *Hyleg* by a friendly Aspect, and take him to be the true giver of Years. Always observing that an Oriental Planet, if the Birth be by day, is preferred before an Occidental.

IV. The use of the *Alchocoden* is briefly thus, if you find him strong, and Angular in his own Dignities, it intimates the Native may live the Old Years that Planet signifies; if in a Succedent House, his Mean Years; (here the eighth House is Excepted) if in a Cadent House, his Least Years; this is according to the Doctrine of the *Arabians. Here follows a Table of the Great, Mean, and Least Years the Planets give as they are set down by* Argol; *and with small variation from* Schoner, *and* Origanus.

Planets		Old Years	Mean Years	Least Years
Saturn	♄	57	43	30
Jupiter	♃	79	45	12
Mars	♂	66	40	15
Sol	☉	120	69	19
Venus	♀	82	45	8
Mercury	☿	76	48	20
Luna	☽	108	66	25

3.

Of the Lord of the Geniture, or Almuten *of the Nativity.*

I. Some Astrologers (in former Ages) took this way of finding the Lord of the Gen1ture, *viz.* Diligently to enquire what Planet had most Essential Dignities in the place of the *Moon*, and *Mercury*; and that very Planet they took to be Lord of the Geniture, because *Mercury* signifies the Spirit, and the *Moon* the Body.

II. But it is now generally received (amongst Modern Artists) to be that Planet which hath most Accidental, and Essential Dignities in the Scheme of Birth; and the Natives Dispositions, and Inclinations, (for the most part) concurs with the Nature of that very Planet which is strongest in the Figure. [*The Natures, and several significations of the Planets (well Dignified, or otherwise) you may Read in the first part hereof.*]

III. The manner of finding the Lord of the Geniture, is performed thus, *viz.* Collect, into a Table, all the Planets Essential, and Accidental Dignities, and Debilities, by the Tables for that purpose, of the first Part; and by Substraction of the lesser Number from the greater, you will easily see the strength, or weakness of each Planet; and lastly, discover the Planet that surmounts all the rest in Essential Fortitudes, and therefore Lord of the Geniture, with the provisor, that if two Planets have equal strength in your Figure, you are to accept him for the *Almuten*, who hath most Essential Dignities in the Horoscope; and the rather, if he friendly behold it, or the Lord thereof, or either of the Lights. (*See also an Example hereof in the following Chapter.*)

4.

Of the Complexion of the Nativve.

This is thought to be a matter of difficulty by several Authors, yet some Physicians account it very easie to Judge of the complexion of any Person; and indeed they should be best acquainted therewith: Their Method is briefly thus:

I. Consider what Sign possesseth the Horoscope (or Ascends at Birth) and Judge according to the Nature of that Sign, as if *Gemini* Ascend an Aireal Sign, the Native is Sanguine; if *Cancer* a Watry Sign, Phlegmatique; if *Leo* a Fiery Sign, Cholerique; if *Scorpio* an Earthy Sign, Melancholy, *&c*. If two signs are concerned in the Ascendant, mix their Significations.

II. You are also to consider the Lord of the Ascendant, the Planet, or Planets therein, or in Aspect (partly) thereunto.

III. The *Moon*, and those Planets she is in aspect with.

IV. The Lord of the Geniture, and Sign the *Sun* is in, (*viz.* the Quarter of the Year.)

V. Lastly, Consider the qualities or the several Significators, and collect their Testimonies, *viz.* Hot, Moist, Cold, Dry; and Judge according to the Major Testimonies. [*The qualities of the Signs, and Planets, you will find in the first part.*]

If Heat, and Moisture Predominate, the Native is Sanguine; if Cold, and Moisture, Phlegmatique; if Heat, and Dryness, Cholerique; if Cold, and Dryness, Melancholy. [*Note that if one Planet be* Almuten *of the Geniture, and Lord of the Horoscope, allow him a threefold Vertue in the Complexion of the Native, or the* Moon *in the Ascendant, you are to double her Testimonies.*]

This being premised 'twill be no hard matter to find the Temperament, or Complexion of the Native in any Geniture.

Note that the qualities of the Moon *in her quarters are thus. accounted*

From her	☌ to the first qu.	is	Hot & Moist	that is	Sanguine.
From her	first q. to the full	is	Hot and dry	that is	Choleric.
From her	full to the last q.	is	Cold & dry	that is	Melanch.
From her	last q. to the cha.	is	Cold & moist	that is	Phlegm.

5.

Of the Manners of the Native.

I. Any Planet in the Ascendant, whether Intercepted or upon the Cusp thereof, shall be the principal Significator of Manners [especially if he be Lord of the Ascendant, or Nativity, or have Dignities in the Sign Ascending, or be in any Partile Aspect of the *Moon,* or *Mercury.*]

II. Many Planets in the Ascendant, gives variety of Manners, *i. e.* [shews the qualities of the Mind are accordingly mutable, and various] but that Planet which is the most strong, and powerful, signifies the most Durability; and those that are less potent, intermix their Nature, and Influence in the discovery of the Natives Manners also.

III. If no Planet be in the Ascendant, Judge from the Lord of the Ascendant (if the Dispositer behold him) or rather the Lord of the Geniture, or that Planet that forcibly beholds *Mercury,* or *Luna,* as aforesaid, Consideration had to those fixed Stars neer the Ecliptick, that are Joyned to the Significator.

IV. When it shall so happen, that a good, or benevolent Planet is Significator of the Qualities of the Mind, it argues the Native to be or a most excellent, and commendable Deportment, and Behaviour: on the contrary, if a Malevolent Planet signifie the Manners of the Native, it declares him to be an ill Disposition, sufficiently Clownish, and Brutish. In fine, indued with Unsavory, and Corrupt Manners, or Behaviour;· and this according to the Nature of the significator, and his Position.

V. The Durabllity, or Continuance of the Natives Manners is known from the *Directions* of the Ascendant, and the *Moon.* And the several Changes, and Renovations are known from the Nature of the (several) Promittors they are directed unto; if to the good Aspects of the Fortunate, and good Planets, it imports (this much) that the Natives Manners, and Inclinations are then commendable; his Actions civil and honest &c. On the contrary, if under a bad Direction of those Significators to some evil Aspect of the Infortunes, then the Native is of a very unhandsome, uncivil Deportment and Behaviour; and his Manners noway Laudable, but Offensive, and Distastful, &c.

6.

Of the Wit, or Understanding of the Native.

I. The Wit, or Understanding of the Native is taken from *Mercury* chiefly, and his Configuration with the *Moon*; *Mercury* governs the Animal Spirits in the Brain, and the *Moon* the strength thereof; hence then if these Planets be well posited in any Geniture, it argues the Native to be of a most pregnant Wit, and excellent Understanding. Understand the same if they friendly behold each other, or there be mutual Reception between them; but if you find these Significators ill posited, weak, or afflicted, Judge the contrary.

II. The *Quartile* Aspect of *Mercury*, and the *Moon*, gives Plenty of Wit to the Native; but 'tis unpollish'd, and rugged: the *Opposition* of *Luna*, and *Mercury*, from Angles, gives a very stubborn, and turbulent Wit, *Mercury* in Reception of *Mars* from *Aries*, sharpens the Wit: *Mercury* swift in motion, shews the Native to have a very quick apprehension, but subject to mutability in his Opinion: if *Mercury* be under the Earth, the Native is very propense to Arts, and Sciences; if above the Earth, his Inclinations are more to Oratory, and strives to speak well; *Mercury* in an Angle, and free from the affliction of *Saturn*, or *Mars*; or if *Mercury* be posited in Aireal Signs, in Aspect with the Fortunes, this argues the Native hath a good Understanding, a sharp Wit; and in fine, a most excellent Genius, capable of any thing; a Person or admirable Conceptions.

III. Look upon the Position of *Mercury* in any Nativity, and consider, the stronger he is, the greater is the Understanding, and Ingenuity of the Native; take notice also what Planets he is in Aspect (or Opposition) with; and accordlngly moderate your Judgment. [*Thus according to the Position (strength, or weakness) of Mercury, you may most easily Judge of the Natives Wit, and Understanding. For if you find him Cadent, or in Detriment, Combust, Peregrine, or Retrograde, or otherwise afflicted, or slow in motion, &c. this argues but a very mean Wit, and raw Understanding; if strong, and potent, and in good Aspect of the Moon, or the Fortunes, Judge the contrary, as before intimated.*]

7.

Of the Stature, and Form of the Body.

In Judging of this, you are first to consider the Sign Ascending, the Lord thereof, and those Planets that are in the Ascendant; as also the Luminaries according to the Signs they are in, not omitting the consideration of the fixed Stars that arise at Birth; and by a judicious mixture, according to their several Descriptions, and Shapes, you cannot fail exactly (according to Art) to give a true Description of the Stature, Form, and Shape of the Body.

I. If you find the Planets in Aireal, or Firy Signs, they declare the Native to be of a full, and large Stature; but if in Watry, or Earthy Signs, it signifies the Body more short, and little, the Members thereof tendtng much to Brevity. If they have South Latitude, the Native is active, and nimble; if North Latitude, more heavy, and sluggish.

II. If you find the Lord of the Ascendant, or Planets therein, to be strong, and potent, the Body will be more Decent, and Comly, and well proportioned; if the Significators be weak, and much debilitated, Judge the contrary.

III. More especially, take notice of the Nature of the Sign Ascending, the Lord of the Ascendant, and his Position, also the place of the *Moon*, (in every Nativity,) for by these you may most Rationally Judge of the Proportion, and Stature of the Body, as to Descriptions: What the Signs, and Planets signifie alone, you are sufficiently directed in the first part; and by a due consideration thereof, and these brief directions, an Artist cannot be much at a loss in his Judgement in this particular. [*Much might be said upon this very Subject (of the Descriptions of Persons,) but I only touch at the principal heads, leaving the several Circumstances adhering, as useless, and too much burthensome to the Memory; for multiplicity of Rules concerning one thing, do rather confound, than inform the Judgement.*]

8.

Of the Fortune, or Misery of the Native in general.

All the Planets Essentially dignified, or many Receptions between them, argue the Natives general Fortune to be exceeding good; more particularly, if you find the Luminaries well posited, as also the *Part of Fortune*, this confirms the Judgement; consider also the Lord of the Ascendant, and *Almuten* of the Geniture if they are well seated in the Figure, and in good Aspect of the Fortunes, these are notable Arguments that the Native will live happily in the world; and this according to the Degree, or Quality of Birth, many times the Native is much advanced above his Original Capacity; but withal the *Directions* of the Nativity (in this Case) must be consulted, and see what good or ill is promised thereby; if these happen to concur, the Native will be more Famous, though whilst he continues under the force of bad Directions, he must expect to have his Felicity somewhat clouded.

II. If in the Figure you find the Planets weak, and debilitated, and posited in Abject places thereof, &c. then you may conclude the Native will be subject to many Miseries, and Misfortunes, divers Changes, and Mutations; and in fine, but a disconsolate, and dejected Life in the general, except upon the force of some good Directions the *Sun* may shine upon him (as I may say) and so between whiles, intermix some Comfort to the Native; but he rarely arrives to any height of Honour, for continuance in the World.

Of these things there hath been many eminent Examples of both kinds in the World, and may be discovered from the Nativity, by Rules of Art, grounded upon Experience.

Thus much for the Judgement of the first House. I have been the larger hereon, because it doth (in a manner) comprehend all the rest. I must be more brief in those which follow, otherwise I shall too much exceed my purposed Limits, and leave no room for other things intended of very good use.

SECT. II.

Judgement proper to the second House of a Nativity, viz. Concernng the Substance, Riches, or worldly wealth of the Native, &c.

1.

Of the several Significators which at the Birth (in an Astrological sence) design Riches, or Poverty, to the Native, &c.

I. You are to consider the Cusp of the second House, the Lord thereof; and any Planet, or planets posited therein.

II. The *Part of Fortune*, and his Disposiser, with those Planets that behold either of the aforesaid Significators, let their Aspect be good, or evil.

III. Having taken a serious view or these several Significators, and their strength, or weakness; you may from thence Judge of the Natives worldly Estate, and the Goods of Fortune; whether it will be considerable, or not; or whether the Stars threaten him with Poverty, Penury, and want, &c.

IV. If by a diligent Collection of Testimonies, you find the major part to be very strong, and Fortunate; this is an Argument that the Native shall enjoy a very competent Fortune, and live happily in the World. But if they are found Weak, and much Debilitated, Judge the contrary: If the Testimonies happen to be equally Ballanced on both sides, Judge a Mediocrity, that then the Native shall live in a mean way, seldome sensible of much want, and rarely at any time abound, but make a shift to struggle along in the World. [*Though upon the effects of some good Directions of the Significators of Substance, the Native may be sensible of an unwonted Revenue, but of no long continuance.*]

2.

Arguments of Wealth, and Poverty, &c.

I. If *Jupiter* be Essentially strong in the second House and in any good Aspect with the Luminaries; or Lord of the Ascendant; or if the *Moon* be in the Ascendant, or hath Dignities in the second; this shews the Native shall enjoy a considerable Fortune, and durable.

II. The Luminaries beholding each other by a Benevolent Aspect, from good places of the Figure, denotes the Native shall arrive to great Honour, and abound in Riches; and the rather if both (or either) of them be essentially strong: the same you may Judge if the *Part of Fortune* be Located in the second, and well Dignified, or friendly Irradiated by the Fortunes, especially *Jupiter*, who is a general Significator of Wealth.

III. If *Jupiter*, *Venus*, the *Part of Fortune*, or *Caput Draconis* be posited in the second House; or if the Fortunes behold the cusp thereof friendly; or if the Luminaries be near Benevolent fixed Stars; or lastly, many Planets strong, and potent in the second; these are all strong Arguments (in Art) that the Native shall be blessed with a most excellent Fortune, and sufficiently stored with Riches, even to his own hearts content.

IV. But on the contrary, if you find none or these Testimonies, Judge the condition of the Native will be but low and his Fortune very inconsiderable; especially if you find the Significators much afflicted, or the *Dragons Tayl* in the second, or many Planets ill Dignified therein; if so you may be confident the Native shall not be troubled much with worldly Wealth, but live in a very Poor, Mean way in the World; and consequently much dis-esteemed, and of no Repute therein.

V. The *Sun,* or *Mars* in the second, wastes the Natives Estate; the same you may Judge if you find *Saturn* in *Conjunction* with *Luna* in an Angle, or if *Saturn*, or *Mars* afflict in the second House, or Lord thereof, or *Part of Fortune*; or if *Part of Fortune* be near violent fixed Stars: these are Arguments of Poverty, and that the Native shall be reduced to Want, although once he (for a time) enjoyed an Estate; this hath been often verified, and many have found it too true, by woful experience.

VI. If you find Arguments of Riches in the Figure, and would know by what means the Native shall obtain it; then consider the Nature of the promising Planet, and what House he is Lord of; and accordingly moderate your Judgment, and you cannot fail of satisfaction in this particular: [*after the same Method you may Judge on the contrary part.*]

SECT. III.

Judgement upon the third House of a Nativity.

1.

Shall the Native have Brethren, Sisters, &c.

I. Observe the Sign of the third House, the Lord thereof, and the *Moon*; and (as Astrologers Direct) examine whether any (or all) of them be posited in fruitful Signs, or fruitful Planets posited in the third House; [*What those Signs be*, See the first part.] If you find the Significators posited in such Signs, it argues the Native either hath or may have Brothers, or Sisters; or if any of them are in good Aspect of fruitful Planets, *viz. Jupiter*, *Venus*, or the *Moon*, Judge the same.

II. But on the contrary, if you find the aforesaid Significators in Barren Signs, or in Aspect (or Configuration) with Barren Planets, (as *Saturn*, and *Mars*, which are accounted Steril) or the *Dragons Tayl* in the third, this argues the Native will have no Brethren, or Sisters: Judge the same in the third House, or Lord thereof be much afflicted.

III. If you find Testimonies that the Native may have Brothers, or Sisters; then consider whether the Significators be in Masculine or Feminine Signs, and Houses, or in Aspect with Masculine, or Feminine Planets; and accordingly Judge whether the Native will have most Brethren, or Sisters.

IV. It the Significators themselves are Masculine, and posited in such Signs, or in Aspect with Masculine Planets; this argues the Native may have most Brethren: But if in Feminine Signs, *&c.* Most Sisters.

V. If you find their Significators strong, and potent, and well Located in the Figure; Judge their Condition to be Fortunate, and happy; but if weak, or much afflicted, Judge the contrary: if some Significators are weak, and others strong, moderate your Judgement accordingly, as Reason will direct you.

2.

Will the Native, and his Brethren, and Kindred, accord, and agree together?

I. If you find a friendly Aspect, or Reception between the Lord of the Ascendant, and Lord of the third House, from good places of the Figure; and the *Moon* separate and apply well, from, and to the Significators; this argues a good agreement, and much unity, between the Native, and his Kindred: but if there be no Aspect between their Significators, this prenotes very little familiarity between them, but rather an unnatural kind or strangeness and no mutual Love, and Affection the one towards the other.

II. If the Significators behold each other by some Malevolent Aspect, or if the Infortunes happen to be posited in the third House; this signifies much hatred, and discord, between the Native, and his Kindred; and oft-times he is much injured by them.

[*By what hath been said 'twill be very easie to Judge of the Natives short (or In-land) Journeys whether they will prove Fortunate, and Prosperous, or the contrary.*]

SECT. IV.

Judgement proper to the fourth House.

I.

Of the Natives Patrimony, or Estate left by the Father, &c.

I. Consider whether the Birth be Diurnal or Nocturnal. In a Diurnal Geniture, if the *Sun* be in any good Configuration of the Fortunes from the second, and fourth Houses; it signifies the Native may have a considerable Patrimony, and shall much improve the same: This is the more certain, if they have any Dignities in the fourth House. Understand the same if the Birth were Nocturnal, and the *Moon*, and *Saturn* well Configurated with *Jupiter*, or *Venus*, as aforesaid; on the contrary, if you find either in a Diurnal or Nocturnal Geniture, the Significators afflicted, and no interposition of the friendly Rayes of the Fortunes; this declares a Consuumption of the Natives Patrimony and that he shall be little bettered thereby.

II. The Fortunes posited in the fourth House, and free from malignant Rayes of *Saturn*, or *Mars*, denotes good success to the Native in all things, relating, or signified by the fourth House; as Husbandry, Purchasing of Land, hidden Treasure, Mines &c.

This is the more confirmed if the *Part of Fortune*, or the *Dragons Head* happen to be there also, and well beheld by their Dispositer; it also signifies much Riches to accrue to the Native towards the latter part or his Life (or when he grows Antient.)

III. The condition of the Father is known by the strength, or weakness, of the Lord of the fourth, or the *Sun* in a Diurnal Geniture; and the *Moon*, and *Saturn* in a Nocturnal.

The *Sun, Saturn, Mars*, or *Mercury*, in the fourth, signifies the short Life of the Father; the same if they cast bad Aspects thereunto.

But if the Fortunes are posited therein, or friendly Irradiate the same; Judge the contrary.

2.

Of the mutual Love, and Agreement, of the Native, and his Father.

I. If you find Reception between the Lord of the fourth, and the Lord of the Ascendant; or if they behold each other by *Sextile*, or *Trine* Aspects; this argues much Love and Amity, between the Native, and his Father; the same you may Judge if the *Moon* do well behold the Significators, or translate the Benevolent Rayes of Light of the one to the other; or if she, or the Lord of the Ascendant do friendly behold *Saturn* or *Sol*.

II. But if you find the aforesaid Significators evilly beholding each other from bad places of the Figure, or from Angles without Reception, you may Judge the contrary; and positively conclude but an ill Agreement, and a low ebb of mutual Love between the Native, and his Father.

[*Pro statu patris Dominus quarte domus Planeta beneficus in angulis vel succedentibus orientalis in suis dignitatibus absque maleficis, honores, exaltationem, atque statum optimum patris discernit post Nativitatem filij quod semper Intelligitur.* Argol *in* Ptol. parv.]

SECT. V.

Judgment upon the sixth House of a Nativity.

1.

Of the Diseases (or Bodily Infirmities) the Native may be most subject unto.

I. The health of the Body is discovered from the strength of these several Significators. As *First* the Sign Ascending, and the Lord thereof. *Secondly*, The Luminaries. *Thirdly*, From the sixth House, and the Lord thereof, or Planets posited therein. *Fourthly*, From the seventh House, and Lord thereof, because 'tis opposit to the Ascendant, which signifies the Life, and Temperament of the Native; the *Sun* rules the Vital Spirits, and the *MOOn* the humours of the Body.

II. If in any Geniture you find these several Significators (or the major part of them) strong, and potent, and favourably beheld by the Fortunes, being free from the malitious Aspects (or Bodies of *Saturn* and *Mars*,) these are arguments that the Native is of a very healthful Constitution, and will not be subject to Diseases; but, for the most part, enjoy health, and be a Person of a sound able Body.

But if you find the Significators weak, or much afflicted, either by the Infortunes, or the presence of Malevolent fixed Stars; Judge the contrary. [What Diseases the Planets, and Signs do signifie, you may read in the first part.]

[*Defects of the Eyes.*]

III. If you find the Luminaries afflicted by the Infortunes, especially from Angles; it threatens great danger to the eyes, and many times absolute Blindness; Judge the same if the *Sun*, and *Moon* are in *Opposition*; and the more certain if the *Opposition* happens from Angles. *Note that if Saturn be in the Ascendant in any Sign, except Capricorn or Aquarius, he greatly affects the Teeth.*

[*Defects in Hearing.*]

IV. If *Mercury* happen to be much afflicted by the Malevolent Aspects of *Saturn*, it signifies some defect in the Hearing; and threatens the Native with Deafness. If *Mercury* be Lord of the sixth House, or have great Dignities therein, or in the twelfth, Judge the same.

[*Defects in the Speech.*]

V. Take this for a general Rule, that wherever you find *Mercury* Lord of the sixth much afflicted, or in *Conjunction* of the Sun, or evilly beheld the *Moon, Saturn*, or *Mars*, especially from Angles, the Native then is sure to have some defect in his Speech; and is either subject to Stammering, or (at least) has a very ill Delivery, or Elocution.

2.

Of Servants, or small Cattle.

[Arguments of honest Servants.]

I. It you find the fortunate Planets posited in the sixth House, and free from affliction; it declares the Natives Servants to be just and honest; or that he shall gain by them or any small Cattle he shall happen to deal in; and this the rather, if they behold the Ascendant, or Lord thereof, with any Benevolent Aspect; Judge the same if you find the *Moon*, or Lord of the sixth, and *Mercury* fortunate in an Angle; or if there be any good Aspect, or Reception between the Lord of the sixth, and the Lord of the Ascendant: For these are strong Testimonies of Diligent, and Faithful Servants; and consequently such as the Native may receive much profit by. [*The same is (in all respects) to be understood of all sorts of Cattle of the smaller sort, as Sheep, Hogs, &c.*

II. If you find the Infortunes in the sixth but weak, and in an ill Aspect to the Ascendant, or Lord thereof; or if the Lord of the sixth be in *Quartile*, or *Opposition* to the Lord of the Ascendant, or Mercury much afflicted (which is a general Significator of Servants) you may then Judge the Natives Servants to be very knavish and careless Persons, such as he will receive much damage by, *Ergo* no way to be trusted unto, or confided in; neither can expect to be fortunate in dealing in small Cattle of any sort, under which is Included all kind of tame Fowl, Birds, and poultry, *&c.*

[*Note that all Cholerique Diseases proceed from Fiery Signs, all Melancholy from Earthy, Phlegmatick from Watry, and Distempers of the Blood from Airy Signs.*]

See more of Diseases, of the first part Chap. 7, and so on; where you may read what Disease every Planet signifies througout the twelve Signs at large: Consult Chap. 6, part the second also, and no more need be said of that Subject in this place.

SECT. VI.

Judgement proper to the seventh House of a Nativity.

3.

Shall the Native Marry, &c.

The Significators of Marriage are, first, the Cusp of the seventh House, and Lord thereof, the Planet, or Planets posited therein. Secondly, the *Moon*, and *Venus*, are general Significators in Mens Nativities; and the *Sun*, and *Mars* in Womens Genitures. Now by a due Consideration of the positions of these Significators, and their several Configurations with the Lord of the Ascendant; as also how they behold the Degrees Ascending, you may draw your Judgement concerning the Marriage of any Native, whether ever they will Marry, or if more than once, *&c.*

Arguments of Marriage.

I. If you find the Lord of the first apply by any good Aspect to the Lord of the seventh, or if they be in Reception; or if *Venus*, or the *Moon* be in any good Aspect, or Reception with him, the *Sun*, or *Mars*, the Native will have a propensity to Marriage; Judge the same if you find the Significators in fruitful Signs.

II. *Sol*, *Jupiter*, or *Venus*, friendly Irradiating the Cusp of the seventh House, signifies the Native will assuredly Marry.

[Not Marry.]

III. When you find the Significators weak in sterrill (or Barren) Signs, or *Saturn* strong posited in the first, fifth, seventh, or eleventh Houses in Barren Signs; or if *Venus*, and the *Moon*, are in *Quartile*, or *Opposition* of *Sat-*

urn; this shews an Indisposition in the Native to Marriage, and presages a single Life; Judge the same if *Venus* be unfortunate in *Leo*.

[*If Marry more than once.*]

IV. If you find the Significators in fruitful Signs, or the *Moon*, and *Venus* posited strong in the seventh House, in a double-bodied Sign, being free from the Malevolent Rayes of the Infortunes; this declares the Native will Marry more than once.

V. If the *Moon*, or *Venus* apply to many Planets, and posited in any double bodied Signs, or if you find many Planets in the seventh, although they behold not *Venus*, or the *Moon*, especially if the Lord of the Ascendant be there; or if the Lord or the Ascendant be in any friendly Aspect with the Lord of the seventh from Bi-corporeal Signs: these are Arguments of plurality of Wives. Judge the same if the Significators of Marriage behold each other well, and are at Unity amongst themselves from good Houses of the Figure.

VI. If the Significators are afflicted by the Infortunes, and posited in Signs representing one Form; then you may be confident the Native shall Marry but once, if at all.

[*Aphorismes.*]

VII. *Venus* Oriental, and strong, being essentially dignified in any Geniture, most aptly denotes the Wife will predominate and near the Breeches,

VIII. If *Venus* in any Nativity, be posited in the tenth House, shews the Native shall Marry into a Credible Family, and gain much profit (as well as honour and preferment) thereby. But if she be posited in the second House in any Geniture of either Sex, the Native Marries more for Money than Love.

IX. *Venus* in *Aquarius*, or *Cancer* in *Quartile*, or *Opposition* to the Moon and posited in the North Angle, signifies such Natives will be very subject to wander beyond their own Limits to satisfie their Lusts. If *Venus* happen to be in *Conjunction*, *Quartile*, or *Opposition* of *Mars*; Judge the same that such Natives will not only be of very high Spirits, but frequently change their Pasture, and make use or more than lawfully belongs unto unto them, *i. e.* Much guilty of Adultery, *&c.*

X. *Venus* afflicted by *Saturn* in the seventh, denotes the Person the Native Marries to be deficient, and weak in Venereal Sports. Or if she be with *Saturn*, or *Mars* in the sixth, the Native Marries a very dishonest Person. If in *Capricorn*, or *Cancer* there, assure your self the Person the Native Marries, either Man, or Woman, will prove such as we term *RIGHT*.

XI. But if *Venus* be in Configuration with *Saturn*, *Jupiter*, and *Mercury* all together; this signifies the Native to Marry a very Careful, Industrious, and Laborious Person.

2.

What manner of Person shall the Native Marry? Whether Fair, or Deformed, and how qualified, &c.

I. Having carefully observed the Sign of the seventh, and Lord thereof; also any Planet posited in the seventh House by a Judicious Commixture of their several Descriptions, you may artificially make a Description of her Person; which if you find them posited in *Gemini*, *Virgo*, *Libra*, or *Sagitary*, they signifie a Neat, Handsome, and Comely Creature; and this the rather, provided the Significators be strong, and essentially dignified; if you find them in *Aries*, *Taurus*, *Capricorn*, or *Leo*, this declares a Person much Deformed, and no way Beautiful, or Lovely: and so much the worse if the Significators be weak, or afflicted.

If in *Cancer*, *Scorpio*, *Aquarius*, or *Pisces*, it intimates the Person the Native shall Marry should be indifferent handsome, not much Commendable, nor very Contemptible. But if *Saturn* should affect the Significators, or they happen to be but weak, it signifies the Person to be Incomposed in Body, and perhaps Conditions Unsavory enough, unless other Testimonies contradict.

But the *Moon* in good Aspect of *Jupiter*, or *Venus*, or friendly beholding the Cusp of the seventh; denotes a well Composed, Compleat, Proportioned Body.

Thus much for the proportion of the Body, as for the Description of the Face, Colour of the Hair, Complexion, &c. it may be performed by the first part, where you have the Description of the Signs, and Planets at large, &c.

[*Conditions.*]

II. If you would Judge the Quality, and Condition of the Person, consider the strength, or weakness of the Lord of the seventh, or Planet posited therein, as also the *Moon*; and accordingly order your Judgement with Discretion, by the Rules given in the second part.

Something to this purpose is already shewed at the latter end of hte last *Sub-section*; therefore I proceed to consider their,

[*Agreement.*]

III. If you desire to know what Agreement there will be, consider the Significators of both Parties, and see how they behold each other; if it be by good Aspect, and there be Reception between them, it argues a good Agreement; if they behold each other by *Quartile*, or *Opposition*, the contrary: if they are in no Aspect, it declares little, or no Respect they bear unto each other, &c.

[*Disagreement.*]

IV. The Lord of the Ascendant, or the *Moon*, in *Quartile*, or *Opposition* of the Lord of the seventh from Angles in movable Signs, presages much Contention, and Discord; so doth the *Dragons Tail* in the seventh. But their Love, and Hatred might be best discovered by considering the *Simpathy*, or *Antipathy* that is between their Genitures, (if they may be procured.)

[*Time of Marriage.*]

V. The Time of Marriage is best discovered by Directions, *viz.* when the Ascendant comes to the *Sextile*, or *Trine* of the Lord of the Seventh, the *Moon*, or *Venus*, or the Degree of the Cusp of the seventh, to the aforesaid Significators, &c. or rather the *M. C.* directed to any Aspect of *Venus* if she were strong in the *Radix*, or the *Moon*, or Lord of the seventh, Directed to the aforesaid Promittors, Direct, and Converse.

VI. If all the Significators of Marriage be Oriental of the ☉ Swift and Direct, declares Marriage in youth, but if Occiddntal of the ☉ and slow in motion, or Retrograde, and more especially if ♄ be in the seventh, he then either Marries being pretty well ln years, or else an ancient Maid or Widdow in his youth.

VII. Lastly, If you consider the strength of the Lord of the eighth, and how he Aspects the Lord of the second, you may judge of the Portion of the Wife, whether it be considerable or not. If the Lord of the eighth behold, the Lord of the second by ✶ or △, or if there be Reception between them, or if ♃, ♀, or the ☊ be in the eighth, you may conclude she hath a Portion considerable, and you shall be bettered thereby; but if the Significators of her Substance be weak, Afflicted, or any wayes Debilitated, or ♄, ♂, or ☋ in the eighth, judge the contrary.

VIII. Again, if you find the Lord of the Ascend. stronger, or more potent than the Lord of the seventh, you may conclude the Native may probably survive the person he Marries; But if the Lord of the seventh be strongest, or the Lord of the Ascendant goes first to Combustion of the ☉, judge the contrary.

Note that what hath been said of Mens Marriages, the same may be understood of Womens also; Consideration had to the general Significators mentioned at the beginning of this Section; and for a person to know whether he or she shall marry one of the same Country or not, I hold it not worth inserting; for it signifies little, neither are the Rules laid down by the Antients in that particular to be deemed infallible.

3.

Of the Natives Pablick Enemies.

I. If the Lord or the Ascendant be more strong and potent than the Lord or the seventh, the Native needs not fear the malice of any or his publick Adversaries. Or if the Lord of the seventh be in any good Aspect or Reception with the Lord of the Ascendant or the ☽, the Native will have few or none that shall oppose or molest him.

The same you may understand if the Fortunes be well placed in the seventh House.

II. On the contrary, if you find the Infortunes posited there, or the Lord of the seventh in □ or ☍ of the Lord of the Ascendant, then the Native shall be perplexed and troubled by the means of his publick Enemies more or less continually, to his great vexation and discontent.

[*Causas inimicitiarum extrahit hoc sehola ex domo in qua fuerint Constituti Domini duodecima & septima, & ex domo cui Dominabitur Planeta existens In septima ant duodecima.* Ptol. Parv.]

SECT. VII.

Judgment appertaining to the Fifth House of a Nativity.

1.

May the Native have Children or not?

I. Here you are to observe the Cusps of the first, fifth, and eleventh Houses, (*viz.* the Wives fifth House, or House of Issue) together with their Lords: See If there be fruitful Signes possess the Cusps of those Houses; or if their Lords are Fruitful Planets, or ♃ or ♀ posited in Prolifical Signes; if so, these are assured Testimonies the Native shall have Issue.

II. If the Lords of the aforementioned Houses, or the ☽ be in fruitful Signes, either in ☌ or good Aspect from such Signes, it Presages the Native shall have many Chilldren. Judge the contrary if you find the Significators in barren Signes, or otherwise much afflicted of the Infortunes, &c.

III. Lastly, Having seriously considered the Testimonies of fruitfulness and barrenness, judge by the Major Testimonies; if they fall equal, help your self from Revolutions and Directions; but more especially have regard to the stock from whence the Native sprung; and if there be no powerful Arguments in the Radix, that will much inform your Judgment. *Circa filiorum numerum difficilis conjectatio*, &c. Ptol. Par.

It's the greatest Argument of having no Children, when the Lord or the fifth is Retrograde or Combust, espetially when the Significator is an Infortune.

2.

Of the Life and Condition of the Natives Children, as also their Sex, &c.

I. As to the Life or the Natives Children you are to consider the strength of the Significators; if you find them essentially Dignified, and friendly assisted by the beams of the Fortunes, you may conclude they will live to a considerable age, and their lives will be sufficiently Fortunate, and conveniently happy.

II. But if you find the Significators weak, and much Afflicted or Debilitated, or ♄, ♂, or ☋ posited in the fifth or eleventh Houses, Judge the contrary.

III. The Lord of the fifth in the eigth, or ☿ in ☍ to ♄, from the first and seventh; or ♂ or ♄ in ☍ of ♃ or ♀, there are strong Arguments the Natives Children are but short liv'd, and live to no Maturity.

IV. The condition of the Natives Children is also known from the strength or weakness of the Significators; which if they happen to be strong and fortunate, it declares their condition to be more prosperous; but if you find them ill posited, and much debilitated, Judge the contrary.

V. The Sex is easily discovered by Collecting the Testimonies of the several Significators, if most Masculine judge most Males, if most Feminine, say most Females; if they fall equal, conclude as many of the one Sex as of the other, *&c.*

[*In Nativitate viri si Mars fuerit separatus a Venere, & Saturno, & aliqna junctus familiaritate Jovi pradicit Natum Purum in oitu, verecundum naturalem que modum, & usum servmem cum Modestia & Temporantia.* Ptol. Par.]

SECT. VIII.

Judgment belonging to Ninth House.

1.

Shall the Native Travel or not.

I. Here you are to consider the ninth House, the Lord thereof, and Planets posited therein, together with the ☽ and ☿, (and some say ♂) from the consideration of these Significators, *&c.* Judgment may be drawn whether the Native shall Travel out of his own Native Land yea or no?

II. The Signe of the ninth moveable, and the Lord thereof posited in a moveable Signe, or if there be any Reception between the ☽ and ☿, or ♂ or Aspect from moveable Signes, this argues the Native may have a propensity to Travel, and a strong inclination to see far Countreys: judge the same if you find ☿, the ☽, or the Lord of the Ascendant in the ninth; or ☿ & the ☽ in the third; or the Lord of the third, or the ninth in the Ascendant. Farther observe whether the Lord of the Ascendant or the ☉ be posited in the Houses of the ☽ & ☿, or in ☌, Aspect or Reception, with either of them or the Lord of the ninth, these are strong arguments the Native will Travel. Lastly, if you find none of the Significators posited as aforesaid, but the ninth House and his Lord in fixed Signs, *&c.* Judge the contrary, that the Native will rarely Travel; but if Travel,

Consider towards what part of the world, &c.

III. If you would know towards what part or Quarter of the world the Native shall Travel, then warily observe the Signs and Houses the Significators are posited in, and accordingly order your Judgment; if you find them in the Fiery Triplicity judge Eastward, (and the rather if they are posited in the Eastern quarter of the Figure) if in the Watry Triplicity, Northwards. But if in the Earthy Triplicity, Southwards, *&c.* see the quarters signified by the Signes and Houses of the *first part.* As also the several Countreys under the twelve Signes, and by a Collection of Testimonies judge from the major part, *&c.* In the next place you are to consider,

Whether the Native shall Profit or not by Travel.

IV. If the Lord of the ninth and the several Significators of Travel be in good Aspect with the Lord of the Ascendant and second House, or otherwise strong and fortunate, judge the Native will advantage himself by Travel; but finding them weak and infortunate, or in any bad Aspect of the Significators of the Native or his Substance, judge the contrary.

If you would know what places may be most profitable to Travel unto, consider the Signs of the first, second, tenth, and, eleventh Houses, as also the Signs wherein they are placed, the Lord of the second, ♃, ♀, ☊, or ⊕, and see what Countreys are under those Signes, and to those places let the Native chuse to Travel.

The occasion of Travel is easily discerned by a due consideration of the Significators, viz. *the Houses they are posited in, and the Planets they are in Aspect withal, and from thence order your Judgment according to the Rules of Art.*

[Argol *sayes, Tempora Itinerum habentur ex Directionibus Ascendentes, vet etiam medij Coeli ad Corpora, vel Radios Solis, Lunis, Martis, & multoties Mercurij, & Partem Fortuna,* &c. Ptol. Parv.]

2.

Of the Natives Religion; viz. Will he prove Religious? &c.

I. The Stars do signifte the inclinations of Persons in this particular also, but the operation of their effects are chiefly upon those that continue in their Natural state and condition. It is the grace of God implanted in the heart, that makes persons persue after (and delight in) Godliness; and only the operations of the Spirit of God which causes them to be Religious, *&c.* The Stars only shew the natural propensity of the Native to good or ill, and the durability thereof.

II. He that hath ♃, ♀, or ☊ in the ninth or third Houses, in good Aspect or Reception with ♃, or of the ☉, ♀, ☿, or the ☽, these are notable Arguments the Native will be a great lover of Religion, having a strong inclination to Godliness; and in fine, a Virtuous, Religious, Godly person. *Judge the same if Saturn be in his Essential Dignities in the ninth.*

III. But if ♄, ♂, or ☊ be posited in the ninth House, weak, or otherwise afflicting the Lord thereof, or the Lord of the Ascendant, or the ☽, or if ♃ be afflicted of the Infortunes, these denote the Native to be a person of no Religion, but a meer Atheist, having no inclination to any thing of Godliness, or whatsoever is termed Religious.

[*Dreams.*]

IV. By what hath been spoken as to the Natives Religion, viz. the position of good Planets in the ninth, &c. It may also inform the Student concerning the truth or falsity of the Natives Dreams; for if the ninth House be fixed, and fortunate as aforesaid, the Natives Dreams are generally pleasant, and the effects thereof correspondent: so that whatsoever his Dreams be, they usually prove very true, or rarely fail.

But on the contrary, if you find the ninth House afflicted by the presence of the Infortunes, or the Lord thereof with ♄, ♂, or ☋, in bad Houses of the Figure, why then you may conclude the Natives Dreams to be terrible, and so hideous, that he is (often times) much afrighted thereby, and whatsoever they be, shall come to nothing, but prove altogether false, and insignificant. This is the more certain if the Signe of the ninth House be moveable.

SECT. IX.

Judgment proper to the Tenth House of a Nativity.

1.

Shall the Native arrive to any considerable degree of Honour or Preferment in the World, &c.

I. The Significators of Preferment, Honour, or Profession of any Native is taken from the Cusp of the Tenth House, the Lord thereof, the Planet, or Planets, and fixed Stars posited therein, having well observed the strength or the Significators, and how they behold the Ascendant or his Lord, you may from thence be able to judge of the forementioned particulars appertaining to this House, *&c.*

Preferment.

II. If you find the Significators aforesaid well placed in the Figure essentially strong in any good Configuration of the Fortunes, this argues the Native shall attain to a very considerable degree of Fortune and Advancement in the World, and this according to his capacity and quality, or degree of Birth, (for this must (*in such cases*) alwayes be understood.)

III. But if the Significators be partly strong, and partly weak, judge a medium, that the Native shall neither come to any great advancement, or become much contemptible in the World, but live in a handsome mean way, never expecting to soar very high, or be greatly dejected.

I say, if you find the Significators thus qualified, it plainly signifies a mediocrity in things of this nature, and accordingly order your judgment as reason will prompt you.

No Preferment.

IV. If you find the Significators debilitated, or afflicted, and located in abject places of the Figure, this intimates the Native shall live in low esteem, and never come to Honour, (except upon the effects of some good Direction of the *M. C.* that may a little support more than ordinary for a time) but in general the Natives Credit and Reputation in the world remains obscure, and generally continues at a very low ebb.

V. *Sol,* or *Jupiter* posited in the *M. C.* and well beholding the Ascendant, or Lord thereof, or the *Moon,* denotes much Credit in the World; and that Honour shall be conferred upon the Native considerably. Yet if *Saturn,* and *Mars,* or either or them behold them, or cast a Malevolent Aspect unto the tenth House; it denotes a *Catastrophe* of the Natives Dignity, and Honour; and that he shall never Ascend so high, but he shall be brought down again with much Disgrace, and Contempt.

[*Note that the Dignity of the Native will be durable, and of long continuance when the Significators thereof are Angular, and in their own Essential Dignities, strong, and potent, free from the Malevolent Aspects of* Saturn *or* Mars, *or any way supported by the Benevolent Rayes of* Jupiter, *or* Venus.]

Lastly, The Persons, or Means by whom Preferment shall come, is Discovered from the Nature, and Significations of the Significations themselves; as also those Planets they are in Configuration withal.

2.

Of the Natives Trade, Magistery, or Profession he may be most Inclinable unto, or propense to follow.

I. The general Significators of Magistery are accounted, by the Antients, to be *Mars, Venus,* and *Mercury*: *Mars* declares the strength, and ability of Body; *Venus* signifies the pleasure and delight any Man hath in his Profession; and *Mercury* denotes the Capacity, and Understanding of the Native. Now if either or these happen to be Located in the tenth House, or in any good Aspect to the Lord thereof, these may with more Reason be accepted as Co-significators of the Natives Trade, otherwise they cannot have much to do therein. Therefore (as in all the other Houses) take the Lord of the tenth, or any Planet posited therin, to be Significator of Trade; and according to his signification Judge. [*What Professions the Planets signife you may Read in the Introductory Part thereof.*]

3.

Brief Rules which design the kind of Trade.

I. Consider the Lord of the tenth, and Planets therein, observe also the Signs they are posited in, and the Trades appropriated to those Planets (concerned or) being Rulers of the House of Trade; and accordingly Moderate your Judgement, what kind of Profession the Native may be propense unto.

II. If in movable Signs, they intimate Witty, Ingenious Professions; if in humane Signs, such Trades as are more Noble, &c.

III. If the Significators be in Fiery Signs, Judge such Trades as are much conversant therein; and this the rather, if the Planet that is Lord of the tenth simpathize therewith, *viz.* Smiths, Bakers, &c. And all kind of *Martial* and *Solar* Professions.

IV. If in Watry Signs, the Native will be inclinable to such kind of Professions, as Water-men, Saylors, Brewers, Vintners, &c. and all kind of *Lunar* Professions.

V. If in Airy Signs, it portends all kind of pleasant delightful Professions, as Milliners, Musitioners, Painters, &c. and all *Venerial*, and *Mercurial* Imployments.

VI. If in Earthy Signs, it denotes such Professions that relate only to the Earth, *viz.* all kind of Husbandry, Digging, Sowing, Planting, &c. and all *Saturnine* vulgar Professions.

Lastly, These things being seriously inspected into, will abundantly help to enlighten the Judgement as to the Natives Natural Inclination, in point of Magistery, Trade, or Profession.

Aphorismes of Soveraignty, & contera.

I. The *Sun* is the chief Significator of Honour, and Soveraignty; and being posited in the *M. C.* in a Fiery Sign, with *Jupiter*, *Venus*, or *Mars* in his own House, declares that the Native shall undoubtedly attain to great Dignity, and Honour, and come to bear Rule in the World. The same if the three superiours are strong and potent, the one having great Dignities in the tenth House, the other in the Ascendant.

II. That Person born at Noon the same Day the *Sun* enters *Aries*, or *Leo*, shall assuredly mount to great Soveraignty, and Dominion; or if *Jupiter* in a Diurnal Geniture happen to be posited in the tenth House in *Trine* to *Sol*, Judge the same.

III. The *Moon* denotes Soveraignty by being placed in her Exaltation in *Conjunction* with *Venus*, or in her own House in *Conjunction* with *Jupiter*; and this more especially if placed in the tenth House: the same if she behold *Sol*, or *Jupiter* by a *Trine* Aspect, and be with Kingly fixed Stars.

IV. The *Sun*, *Jupiter*, and *Mars* in *Trine* from Fiery Signs, or *Sol*, *Jupiter*, and *Venus* joyned to regal fixed Stars of the first Magnitude, do declare the Native shall be preferred to a very considerable Degree of Honour, and Soveraignty in the World. *Quoad Capax.*

V. *Saturn* in the tenth, or in *Opposition* thereunto, and the Lord of the tenth in a Fiery Sign, conjoyned with *Mars*, this denotes that Native, though arrived to a very high pitch of Honour, shall be brought to a fatal end.

VI. If *Saturn*, or *Luna* shall be in *Quartile*, or *Opposition* to the Lord of the tenth, or the *Sun*, it signifies that Person then Born shall be strangely Ruined, and come to nothing, by vulgar Rusticks, and such as were abundantly beneath him, Comparatively as much as the Dignity of a King transcends that of a Beggar.

SECT. X.

Judgement upon the eleventh House of any Nativity.

1.

Shall the Native have Friends? (viz. unrelated, &c.)

I. If you find the Cusp of the eleventh House, or Lord thereof, well Fortified, or Benevolent Planets posited therein, or friendly beholding it; this argues the Native shall meet with faithful Friends, and such as he may confidently impose trust in. The contrary is easily discovered by what hath been said before, *&c.*

II. If good, and bad Planets are posited in the eleventh House, or are in Aspect unto it, or the Lord thereof; Judge the Native shall have Friends of two sorts, some real, others pretenders; and if so be they behold the Lord of the eleventh by *Quartile*, or *Opposition*, it intimates a scarcity of Friends, and those few that are, to be very mutable Persons, Unconstant, False, Perfideous, and by no means to be trusted unto, as having no real Love for the Native.

III. If by any means the Genitures of both Persons can be procured, you may easily discover their Friendship whether it be real, or the contrary, by comparing them together thus, *viz.*

If in your Friends Nativity you find the *Sun*, or *Moon*, or Ascendant in *Sextile*, or *Trine*, to their places in the

Natives Geniture; or if the eleventh House in the one, be in the Ascendant in the other, or the contrary: These are Arguments of Friendship. The same Judge if the Lord of the Ascendant and the eleventh House in each others Geniture be in *Sextile* or *Trine*, or Planets that are Naturally Friends, if none or these things be; but instead of *Sextiles*, and *Trines*, you find *Quartiles*, and *Oppositions*, &c. You may conclude the contrary, because you find a disagreement, &c. This is according to *Ptolomy's* Rule *Centilop. Aphr. 33.*

2.

Aphorismes to be observed relating to Friendship, &c.

I. Contrary to the mind of some Authors, if *Cancer* be Horoscopial the Native rarely procures Friends; and this the rather if the *Moon* be weak, or afflicted; or if she be in *Conjunction* of *Jupiter* in *Capricorn* (or *Venus* in *Scorpio*) Judge the same.

II. All the Planets above the Earth, and the Lord of the Ascendant in good Aspect with the superiours, they being strong and potent, or the Light of the Time above the Earth, and in any good Aspect of *Saturn*, *Jupiter*, or *Mars*, being Essentially dignified, are Eminent Testimonies of Friendship, &c. The same if many Planets are in Reception, or friendly beholding the Ascendant.

III. The *Moon,* or Lord of the Ascendant in Aspect with many Planets, or many Planets Located in the first, or eleventh Houses, signifies the Native shall meet with diversity of Friends.

IV. If *Jupiter,* or *Venus* do both behold the Ascendant, or his Lord, or the eleventh House, &c. It presages many Faithful, Honest Friends; or if *Jupiter*, and *Venus* be Located in the eleventh House, or in the fifth, tenth, seventh, or ninth Houses; this denotes the Native shall enjoy many Eminent, and Worthy Friends, and such as will assist him in his greatest extremity.

SECT. XI.

Judgement upon the twelfth House.

1.

Of the Natives Private Enemies, &c.

I. Observe the Lord of the twelfth House, and Ascendant, also the Planet, or Planets posited in the twelfth House, and their Configuuration with the Lord of the Ascendant; and thence Judge the Qualities, and Conditions of the private Enemies of the Native.

II. Many Planets ill disposed in the twelfth House, Intimates many Treacherous Enemies, unknown to the Native. But if they are Essentially Dignified there, they denote private Enemies, but of more Noble Spirits, and such Persons as as are more able to vend their Malice against the Native.

III. The Lord of the Ascendant in the twelfth, or Lord of the twelfth in the Ascendant, signifies that the Native shall have divers secret Adversaries, of whom he ought to be exceeding careful; for he shall receive much prejudice by their means: But if no Planet be posited in the twelfth House, or there be a Benevolent Aspect between the Lord of the twelfth, and the Lord of the Ascendant; this argues the Native shall have none, or at least so few that he will be sensible of no Injury from them.

IV. If the Lord of the twelfth be in *Conjunction* of *Mercury* and the *Moon* in the seventh House, it argues the Native shall be perplexed continually with a company of Inveterate, Malitious Adversaries; and this the more certain if they behold the Lord of the Ascendant by an ill Aspect: What Relation, or what kind of Persons these shall be, are most easily known by considering the nature of their Significators and the Houses they govern.

V. Lastly, if you find the Lord of the twelfth stronger and better Fortified than the Lord of the Ascendant, the Natives Enemies will overcome; But on the contrary if the Lord of the Ascendant be strongest the Native will prevail over his private Enemies.

2.

Of the Imprisonment, or Restraint of the Native.

I. If you find the Infortunes in *Quartile*, or *Opposition* to the *Sun*, or *Moon*, in Signs of a violent Nature, and posited in the seventh, or twelfth Houses; this signifies that the Native will be very subject to suffer by Imprisonment, and Captivity: Judge the same if the *Sun*, or *Moon*, are posited in the twelfth House, or in *Opposition* to the Lord or the Ascendant in the sixth House; or if you find the Infortunes or the *Moon* in the fourth, it declares the same; and so doth *Mars*, and *Venus* in the eighth in *Quartile*, or *Opposition* of the Infortunate Planet, *Saturn*.

II. *Mercury*, and *Luna*, posited in the twelfth House, signifies the Native shall be well acquainted with Imprisonment. And if *Saturn* be in *Opposition* to the *Sun*, or *Moon*, and posited in the seventh House; this denotes the Native shall end his dayes in Prison.

III. *Sol*, *Saturn*, and *Mercury*, posited in the tenth House and in an evil Aspect of *Mars*, argues the Native will be guilty of Robbery, and sometimes Murther; and consequently Imprisonment, and in the end, Death by the Law.

IV. Lastly, When the Significators of Imprisonment are located in fixed Signs, this presages long, and tedious Captivity and Restraint; But if the Benevolent Planets Interpose their Friendly Rayes, and behold well the several Significators, it intimates the Native will gain his liberty by the means of such Persons signified by them.

The Premisas being well considered, 'tis no matter of difficulty to Judge concerning the Natives success in great Cattle, as Horses, Cows, Oxen, &c. or the contrary.

SECT. XII.

Judgement proper to the eighth House, &c.

1.

Shall the Natives Death be Natural, or Violent.?

I. If the Lord of the Ascendant, or the *Moon* be in good Aspect, *viz*. *Sextile*, or *Trine* with the Lord of the fourth, or eighth Houses; this (according to the Rules of Astrology) indicates a Natural Death. Judge the same if the Fortunes be Located in the eighth House, or if they are weak there, provided they are in *Sextile*, or *Trine* to the Lord of the Ascendant, or the *Moon*, it prenotes no less.

If neither the Lord of the Horoscope, or the *Moon*, or Lord of the eighth House be posited in violent Signs, or near violent fixed Stars, the Native need not fear a violent Death.

II. If the Lord of the eighth, or Planets in the eighth House be strong, and Fortified Essentially, it argues he shall dye a very easie Death, and drop away insencibly.

III. The *Sun*, or *Mars* Lord of the eighth, and posited therein in *Cancer*, *Scorpio*, or *Pisces*; it signifies the Native shall expire by a Disease occasioned from a superabounding of Hot, and Moist Humours; so Mercury Lord of the eighth in *Quartile*, or *Opposition* of *Saturn*, shews the Native shall dye of a very potent Melancholy; But *Mars* being the afflicting Planet, threatens Death by a *Vertigo*, or *Megrim* in the Brain, &c.

IV. If *Venus* be Lady of the eighth House, and afflicted by *Mars*, it advises the Native to beware of Death, occasioned from a Venereal Distemper, *viz*. *Gonorrhea*, or *Morbus Gallicus*, &c. But if *Saturn* afflict *Venus* it threatens a *Leprosie*, *Illiack Passion*, *Black-Jaundies*, &c.

Violent Death,

I. The *Sun*, or *Moon* evilly beholding from Angles, or otherwise afflicted by the Infortunes, this signifies a Violent Death; and this the rather, if *Saturn*, or *Mars* bear Rule in the House or Death: The same if the *Sun*, or *Moon* are posited near Violent Fixed Stars, or in Violent Signs, and in no Aspect together.

II. The Infortunes Conjoyned in the *M. C.* or in *Opposition* from Angles, and posited in Violent Signs, presages a Violent Death: The same if the Lord of the Ascendant be posited in the eighth in a violent Sign, or with Violent Fixed Stars; or otherwise afflicted by *Saturn*, or *Mars*, or if the Lord of the eighth be weak in the Ascendant in such Signs, or with such Stars; These are strong Testimonies (in Art) the Native shall dye a Death unnatural.

III. The kinds of Violent Death that a Man may dye are somewhat scrupulous and nice points absolutely to determine, but Astrologers have given divers Rules for the knowledge of the same; as, *Guido, Bonatus, Origanus, Albubatur, Schoner*, and others; unto which I refer those that desire to be farther satisfied in this point, and all the other also; or to Mr. *Lilliy's* Works, who is very copious in this matter.

But an Artist may nearly guess at the kind of Violent Death by a due consideration of the nature of the afflicting Planet, and Signs they are in; and so Judge whether the Native may expire by Drowning, Hanging, Killing, Beheading, or by Falls from High places.

Anareta what?

IV. In the first House you are shewed how to find the giver of Life, and here it will be necessary how to find the Interficient, or Killing Planet, vulgarly called *Anareta*, and that is the Lord of the eighth, or a Planet posited therein, or that hath great Dignities in the eighth House.

Now when the Giver of Life is Directed to the *Conjunction, Quartile*, or *Opposition* of the *Anareta*, this is accounted Mortal; and the rather, if it happen to be *Saturn*, or *Mars*, and contrary in nature to the *Hyleg*; the same may be understood if either of the Luminaries be so Directed, notwithstanding they neither of them be propagator of Life.

V. Or when the Ascendant, or either of the Lights be Directed to any of the Malevolent Aspects of *Saturn*, or *Mars*, especially having Dignities in the House of Death, and contrary in Nature to the Sign Ascending or place where the Direction falls, being much debilitated there; this hath been often experienced to cut assunder the Thread of Life. And it rarely fails to prove fatal to the Native, unless there happen another Direction at the same time to mitigate it, or the Revolution, and Transits contradict it, to which I may add if the Fortunes beheld the place of the Direction Radically, or at that present time by Transit; these may indeed mittigate the force of a Killing Direction, and so the Native may possibly escape at that time.

Note that it is dangerous for the Ascendant to be directed to the Opposition of the Sun, or Moon, or the Luminaries to the Quartile, or Opposition of each other, having respect how the Direction falls, as before Intimated.

[Here I have briefly (yet fully enough) shewed the ways and manner of Judging a Nativity according to the Canons of Astrology; the Antients indeed have largely Written upon this Subject, and from them (in a more succinct method) our Modern Authors; but my endeavoar hath been only to contract the most significant Judgements proper thereunto, and as it were Epitomize, and digest it into so brief, plain, and familiar a method, that any Person, though but meanly read in things of this Nature, may from thence be enabled to give a Rational Judgement upon any Nativity whatsoever.]

And now to Illustrate these Rules, and Aphorismes, I shall Present the Reader with an Astrological Judgement deduced from the Exemplary Figure; by which Example, with small study, and pains he may be able to perform the like upon any other, having an apt Genius to prompt him thereunto; 'tis Practice that Compleats an Artist in this Particular, and some are far more excellent in this Knack of Judgement than others, although they all Judge from the same Foundation; and so 'tis with the Students of other Arts, as all Men know.

CHAP. XI.

Contains only a Speculum of the Nativity, and the Dignities and Debilities of the Planets, &c.

A *Speculum* of the Geniture, or Table of the Radiations of the Planets.													
Planets places, &c.		♈	♉	♊	♋	♌	♍	♎	♏	♐	♑	♒	♓
☉. 1. 55. ♈.	1.	☉		✶	□	△		☍		△	□	✶	
☿ 4. 2. ♈.	4	☿		✶	□	△		☍		△	□	✶	
Dom. XII. ♉	6		DXII						DVI				
♂. 6. 39. ♈.	6	♂		✶	□	△		☍		△	□	✶	
♃. 8. 16. ♏.	8		☍		△	□	✶		♃		✶	□	△
Dom. XI. ♓.	12						DV						DXI
Don. II. ♋.	14				DH						DVIII		
M.C. ♒. 15.	15					IC						MC	
☊. ⊗. ♒.	20		☊						☋			⊕	
♀. 21. 56. ♓. Ascen. 22. 32.	21 22		✶	□ Asc.	△		☍		△	□ D7	✶		♀
♄. 24. 24. ♊.	24	✶		♄		✶	□	△		☍		△	□
Dom. III. ♋.	29												
☽. 29. 51. ♏.	29		☍		△	□	✶		☽		✶	□	△

A Table of the Fortitudes and Debilities of the Planets in the Geniture, both Essential and Accidental.

Dignities.	Debilities.		Dignities.	Debilities.
Of *Saturn*.	Of *Saturn*.		Of *Venus*.	Of *Venus*.
In his Termes 2 Triplicity 3 Ascendant 5 Not Combust 5 Direct 4	Occidental 2		Exaltation 4 In the 11*th* H. 4 Not Combust 5 Direct 4	Slow 2 Oriental 2
♄'s Dignities 19	Debilities 2		♀'s Dignities 17	Debilities 4
Of *Jupiter*.	Of *Jupiter*.		Of *Mercury*.	Of *Mercury*.
Not Combust 5 In his Terms 2	Retrograde 5 Slow 2 In the 6*th* H. 2 Occidental 2		In the 11*th* H. 4 Occidental 2	Combust 5 Retrograde 5 Peregrine 5 PL ☌ with ♂
♃'s Dignities 7	Debilities 11		☿'s Dignities 6	Debilities 8
Of *Mars*.	Of *Mars*.		Of the *Moon*.	Of the *Moon*
In the 11th H. 4 In his House 5 Face 1 Swift 2 Oriental 2 Direct 4	Combust 5		Not Combust 5 Swift 2	In the 6*th* H. 2 In her fall. 4 Decreasing. 2
♂'s Dignities 18	Debilities 5		☽'s Dignities 7	Debilities 8
Of the *Sun*.	The *Sun*.		Of *Part of Fort*.	*Part of Fortune*.
Exaltation 4 In the 11*th* H. 4 Triplicity 3 Swift 2	Inplatick 2 ☌ of ♂		In the 10*th* H. 5 Not Combust 5 Terms Jupiter 2	*Part of Fortune* is strong by 12 Testimonies.
☉'s Dignities 13	Debilities 2		⊕'s Dignit. 12	Debilities 0

Saturn is Almuten, or Lord of the Geniture; and *Mars*, *Sol*, and *Venus* are Co-partners.	Hence it appears that, *Testimonies*. *Saturn* is strong by 17 *Jupiter* weak by 4 *Mars* strong by 13 The *Sun* strong by 11 *Venus* strong by 13 *Mercury* weak by 12 The *Moon* weak by 1

CHAP. XII.

Judgment Astrological upon the first House.

In the Judgment of this House I shall consider these following (Particular) Sections; *viz.*

1. *Whether the Life of the Native may be long or short, (in a Natural way.)*

2. *Who is Significator or giver of Life? viz.* Hyleg, *or* Hylech.

3. *Who is* Alchocoden, *or giver of Years*?

SECT. 4. *The Lord of the Geniture, viz.* Almuten?

5. *The Temperature, or Complexion of the Native, his Stature, Form,* &c.

6. *The Wit or Ingenuity, Understanding or Manners of the Native.*

Lastly, *The Fortune or Misery of the Native in General.*

SECT. I.

May the Natives Life be long or short?

I. In Answer hereunto, according to the Directions given in the tenth Chapter, I am to examine, (1.) Whether the Degree Ascending, or Lord thereof be afflicted or not, either by the Bodies or Aspects of the Infortunes or Lord of the eighth House, &c. (2.) The Strength or Weakness of the *Lord* of the Ascendant. (3.) Whether either of the Infortunes do vitiate the Degree *Ascending*. (4.) Whether the light of the time be Eclipsed, or otherwise afflicted, with some other Considerations equivolent to the Former.

II. In this *Geniture* I find the *Twenty third* Degree of the Coelestial Twins *Horoscopical*, and *Saturn*, Lord of the eighth House posited neer the very Degree Arising, there in *Quadrat* Aspect to the *Sun*, (within Orbs) who is *Lux temporis*; and of *Mercury*, Lord of the *Ascendant*, who is *Retrograde* and *Combust*, &c. These are strong Arguments in Art, that a long life (according to secondary Causes) is not designed for the Native.

III. Upon that Consideration I presume (had not the Fortunes Favoured) the Native might have expired in his Infancy, upon the Direction of the *Horoscope* to the Body of *Saturn*; *viz.* in the year 1653. But at the same time the *Moon*, (who beholds the *Sun*, *Mars*, *Venus*, and *Mercury*, in the eleventh House by a Friendly *Trine* Aspect) was Directed to a *Trine Sinister* of the *Sun*, the giver of life, and *Jupiter* that year was in *Aquary*, or beheld the place of the Direction by a *Trine* Aspect also: Moreover, the *Part of Fortune* (that some Authors conceive to be a helper of Nature, which

Clavis Astrologiae Elimita, The Key to Astrology New Filed

I question) was then Directed to a *Trine Dexter* of *Saturn*, and Venus, to a *Trine Sinister* of the *Moon*; all which considered, might in reason abate of the force of the aforesaid Direction to the Body of *Saturn*, and of the *Sun* to the Body of M*ars*, then operating.

IV. There was some Assistance added from the Figure of the *Suns* Revolution for that year, and other Directions operating, which did much aleviate the danger portended, and he remains yet in the Land of the Living, now 26 years of Age current: But he confesses that all his younger years he was very sickly and crasie in Body, scarce ever in good health for many years successively: Nor doth this Figure demonstrate the *Native* to be of a strong and healthful Constitution, but rather (for the most part) very subject to Diseases and Infirmities of Body, through the whole course or his life. *Of which, I may write more in the Judgment of the sixth House.*

SECT. II.

Who is Hyleg, *or Giver of Life?*

I. Here, according to the given Rules, I am to consider (1.) Whether the Birth be *Diurnal* or *Nocturnal*. (2.) The Position of the *Luminaries*, whether either of them are posited in such places of the Figure which are accounted *Aphetical*; viz. the seventh, ninth, tenth, eleventh, or *Ascendant*, &c.

II. The Nativity being Diurnal, and the *Sun* being the Light of the Time, so strong in the eleventh House, a fit *Aphetical* place in the Figure, and there in the Dignities of Exaltation, I may therefore accept him for *Hyleg*, or *Giver* of *Life*.

III. Had not the *Sun* been found posited as aforesaid, I must then have accepted the *Ascendant* for *Hyleg*: The *Moon* in this case is not to be taken notice of; for had the Birth been *Nocturnal*, she being posited in the sixth House, the Ascendant must therefore have been taken according to the Rule given *Sect. 2. Chap. 10.*

SECT. III.

Who is Alchocoden, *or Giver of Years?*

I. Here I am to consider what Planet hath most Essential Dignities in the Signe *Aries*, wherein the *Sun*, giver of Life, is posited, *Mars* hath *Aries* for his *Day-House*, and a *Terme* and *Face* in that Signe also; But the *Sun* having *Exaltation, Triplicity*, and *Face* in the same Signe, should rather be accepted for *Giver* of *Years*; but in regard they are both so well dignified in that Signe, and both posited therein, upon that consideration I may elect the *Sun* not only *Hyleg*, but *Alchocoden*, and M*ars* Co-partner, who hath no less than *Eighteen* Testimonies of Fortitude Essential and Accidental in the *Scheme*, and the *Sun* only *Thirteen*, as may be seen in the Table.

II. The Native has already passed the *least years* of M*ars* and the *Sun*, and may in all probability live to the *mean years* of the *Sun*, who is, in *Quartile* of *Saturn*, and *Conjunction* of M*ars*, and have both great Dignities in the eighth House; but the great strength of the *Sun* and *Mars* in a good place of the Figure, befriended (together with *Mercury* and *Venus*) by the *Trine* of the *Moon*, may (in a Natural way) protract the life of the Native beyond the expectation of many persons that may view the *Scheme. And so I proceed to the fourth Particular*, viz.

SECT. IV.

What Planet is Almuten, *or Lord of the Geniture?*

I. Some of the Antients (as before I hinted in *chap*. 10) were of Opinion, That we ought to examine what *Planet* hath most Essential Dignities in the place of the *Moon* and M*ercury*, and accept of him to be Lord of the Figure; if so, I find the *Sun* to have most Essential Dignities in the place of M*ercury*, and M*ars* in the place of the *Moon*, and by that Rule they should be chief Rulers of the Nativity, as indeed they will be found in part, by reason of their great strength in the Figure.

II. But our Modern Astrologers do rather accept of that *Planet* which surmounts all the rest in Essential and Accidental Fortitudes; (which is most rational) if so, *Saturn* will be found *Almuten*, as appears by the Table; but the *Sun*, *Mars* and *Venus* must also be admitted as Co-partners, by reason of their strength as aforesaid: And hence the Actions, Inclinations and Conditions of the Native should be according to the Nature of these Planets, and his Complection, Humours, and Manners much Regulated, according to the Properties and Signification Assigned them.

SECT. V.

Of the Temperature, Complexion, Stature, and form of the Native, &c.

I. This must be Discovered (as has been already shewed) by considering the Sign Ascending, and the Lord thereof; the *Planets* posited in the *Ascendant*, or beholding the same; also the position of the Lunminaries, &c. But first for the *Temperature* of the Native, I proceed thus, and Consider:

	Hot	Moist	Cold	Dry
II. The Sign Ascending is ♊	hot	moist	oo	oo
The Lord thereof ☿	oo	oo	cold	dry
who is posited in ♈ a Sign	hot	oo	oo	dry
♄ in part *Almuten*	oo	oo	cold	dry
In ♊ an Aireal Sign	hot	moist	oo	oo
♄ neer the Degree Ascending	oo	oo	cold	dry
Season of the Year *March*	hot	moist	oo	oo
The ☽ in her last Quarter	oo	oo	cold	dry
☿ Lord of the Ascend. in ☌ with ♂	hot	oo	oo	dry
The ☽ in the end of ♏ very neer ♐	hot	moist	oo	oo
the ☽ in △ of the ☉ from ♈	hot	oo	oo	dry
	7	4	4	7

III. Hence it appears the Native should be Cholerique, and Phlegmatique, *viz.* Hot, and Moist; But in regard *Saturn* is posited so neer the Degree Ascending, strong, and in good Aspect to *Mercury* his Disposi234er, 'tis a strong Argument the Native should not withstanding be very subject to *Melancholy*.

IV. *Of the Natives Stature, and Form of Body*, which is also taken from the Sign Ascending, and Lord thereof, &c. In the Nativity the last Decade of *Gemini* Ascends, and *Saturn* posited therein, *Mercury* Lord of the *Ascendant* is in *Conjunction* with the *Sun*, and *Mars* in *Aries*. *Gemini* personates an upright, strait, and tall Body, well set, a decent Composure, a good Colour (though not veneclear) bright Eyes, and good sight, long, Arms, brown Hair, an accute Wit; in fine, an ingenious Person, and an active Body, &c. as you may Read. The position of *Saturn* in the Ascendant, and *Mercury* in *Aries*, in *Conjunction* with the *Sun* and *Mars*, doth not much alter this Discription, but rather the Natives Inclination, and Manners, which shall be considered in the next Section.

SECT. VI.

Of the Ingenuity, Understanding, and Manners of the Native.

I. The Manners, or Natural Humour, Disposition, or Temper of the Native (according to the Rule given) is usually considered (Astrologically) from that Planet which is posited in the Ascendant; and more especially if he happen to be Ruler thereof, or in Aspect to the *Moon*, or *Mercury*: if many Planets be found in the Ascendant, it Presages variety of Manners; if no Planet be in the Ascendant, then Judgement must be taken from the Lord of the Ascendant, and those Stars that are neer the Significator, &c.

II. In this Figure I find *Saturn* just arising neer the very Degree of the Horoscope, and therein *Quartile* to *Mercury* Lord thereof, therefore I may Rationally accept of him to be the only Significator of the Qualities of the Mind;

now considering he is partly Lord of the Geniture, and Angulur, &c. this shews the Native to be a serious, solid Person, and very Grave in his Behaviour, and Deportment, and no less prudent in the management of his general Affairs; and not only so but very affable, obliging, and courteous to all Persons he converses with in general.

III. Sometimes 'tis true he hath his share of *Melancholy*, but that continues not long, *Mercury* being in a Fiery Sign Besieged by the *Sun* and *Mars*; but in *Trine* to the *Moon*, doth very much abate his Inclination to Melancholy, and sometimes inclines the Native to various resolutions, but rarely to rash Actions which he would be very subject unto, did not *Saturn* bear so much sway in the *Ascendant*.

IV. *The Ingenuity of the Native*, which should be principally considered from the position of *Mercury*, who in the Scheme I find in *Trine* to the *Moon*, but neerly in *Quartile* to *Saturn*, Retrograde, and Combust of the *Sun*, and in *Conjunction* of M*ars*. *Mercury* being in *Trine* to the *Moon*, gives a most excellent Understanding, a pregnant Wit, a large Capacity, &c. But considering *Mercury* is thus afflicted by both the Infortunes, as also by the Light of the Time; this doth much abate the aforesaid good signification, but yet doth not greatly stupifie, or dull the Natives active Fancy in regard he is posited in *Aries*, a Fiery Sign, and a Sign of Activity so neer the Body of *Mars*; and hence I conclude the Native to be of a moderate sharp Fancy, which I can confirm by my own experience; for I know him to be a Person of admirable Conceptions, and able to Argue with great Judgement in most Subjects, whether Divinity, Phylosophy, Physick, &c.

SECT. VII.

Of the Natives general Fate, &c.

I. In this case there ought to be considered the several positions, and strength of the *Planets*; as also how they behold each other, whether by Benevolent, or Malevolent Aspects.

II. The *Directions* should not be neglected in this particular, the Artist should warily consider whether they (or the major part of them) promise much Felicity, and Advantage, or Danger, Damage, and Affliction to the Native, either in Body, or Estate, or both, &c. which being premised.

III. In the next place I return to the *Nativity*, wherein I find four *Planets* above the Earth, and posited in the eleventh House (which Astrologers note to be the Mansion of Friendship) they are also beheld by a friendly *Trine Aspect* of the M*oon*, who Rules that part or the Heavens, which denotes the Natives Estate, or Substance: The *Part of Fortune* is posited in the Angle of Honour, there disposed of by *Saturn*, who casts a benevolent *Trine* thereunto.

IV. Most of the *Planets* are Essentially strong (as appears by the Table of Dignities before Collected) the *Sun* is in *Aries*, wherein he hath the Dignity or Exaltation, and Triplicity; *Mars* is posited in his own House, and face *Saturn* in his Triplicity, and Terms, and *Venus* in her Exaltation, to which may be added that the Number of good *Directions* exceed the bad; all these are promising Arguments or advantage to the *Native*.

V. Hence it Naturally follows that the Natives Fate should be exceeding good, consideration had to his Quality of Birth, and Education, which was very credible and propitious: and it is no irrational Judgement to conclude that (according to Natural, and secondary Causes) his *general Fate* should be favourable, and happy; since I presume he will very rarely want Friends that will assist, and support him upon all occasions, and probably indeavour his promotion.

VI. The Native is advised, notwithstanding, to beware of Rash Actions, because M*ercury* is in a Fiery Signe, and so neer the S*un* and M*ars*, whence he may prejudice his own Honour and Reputation, in regard *Saturn*, Lord of the tenth House, is in the Ascendant, and within the Orbs of a *Quadrat* of *Mercury*, Lord of the Ascendant.

VII. Let him not put too much confidence in pretended Friends, neither (such I mean of the Female Sex) because though *Venus* be strong in the eleventh House (having great Dignities therein) yet she is in *Square* to *Saturn*, Lord of the Angle of Honour, posited in the *Horoscope*. And thus having considered all Circumstances, I conclude the Native will enjoy more years of plenty and splendour, than of trouble and misfortune; notwithstanding *the position of* Saturn *in the East Angle, which by vertue of his Influence did much afflict the Native with weakness in hsi Child-hood, which now he hath most happily out-grown and overcome. And thus much may serve by way of Example for the Judgement of the first House.*

CHAP. XIII.

Judgment proper to the Second House.

In which I shall Consider only two Particuiars, *viz.*

1. *I shall examine whether the Native shall enjoy a considerable Fortune or Estate in the World?*
2. *If so, By what means, or from what kind of Persons?*

SECT. I.

Shall the Native Enjoy or Acquire any Considerable Estate, &c.

I. This Judgment is usually deduced from the Consideration of the second House, the Cusp thereof, the Planets (if any be) posited therein; the Ruler of the second House, the *Part of Fortune*, and their Dispositors: also any Planets that are in good Aspects to the aforesaid Significators.

II. In the nativity I find the Coelestial Crab (*viz.* the Signe *Cancer*) upon the Cusp of the second House, and the M*oon*, Lady thereof, just entering the Signe *Sagitary*, and there in *Trine* to no less than four Planets (within Orbs) in the eleventh House.

III. The *Part of Fortune* is posited in the Mid-heaven, and beheld by a *Trine* of its Disposiier, to which I may add *Jupiter* (who is exalted in the second House) casts a Friendly *Trine* to the Cusp thereof. These are Arguments that the *N*ative should enjoy no mean or inconsiderable Fortune in the World; but they shew the *N*ative will be made happy in the enjoyment of an Estate; and that he should be industrious in Acquiring or Augmenting the same, is not meanly seconded by the position of *Saturn* in the Angle of life, there disposing and Friendly beholding *Fortune* in the tenth House. This Judgment is real, and I can confirm it by my own Experience; for I have known the *N*ative some years, to live most happily, and is still in a Rising Condition. And so *I* come to consider the second Particular, *viz.*

SECT. II.

By what means, or from whom shall the Natives Estate or Fortune proceed?

I. In this Case consideration ought to be had to those Planets that do friendly behold the Significators of Substance, *&c.* And here I find the M*oon* (which signifies the Natives Estate in particular) is not only in *Trine* to M*ars* and M*ercury*, the Natives Significator, but to the S*un* also, who is Lord of the fourth House, and posited in the eleventh, which Demonstrates in an Astrological sense that much of the *N*atives Estate should be settled upon him by his Father; which he has already lived to see performed, and it is a Confirmation of the verity of the Rules of Art.

II. The Friendly *Trine* of *Jupiter*, Lord of the seventh, who has Dignities in the Mansion of Substance, as also in the eleventh House, as before intimated, shews the *N*ative may Advantage himself in Estate by the Marriage of a Wife; as also Merchandizing, or dealing with such persons as are signified by *Jupiter* in *Scorpio*; whether intimate Friends and Acquaintance, or others.

III. S*aturn* is Lord of the eighth House, and (as I said before) friendly beholds and disposes of Fortune, and he is posited in the Ascendant, which is the eighth House from the Place of *Jupiter* and the M*oo*n: Hence I conclude the Native may be Enriched by the Wills or Legacies of the Dead, (as well as by a Portion or Dowry of a Wife,) and in respect S*aturn* properly signifies Land and Houses; therefore part of the Natives Estate should be therein, though the Premises being well considered, declare also considerable Sums of Money which cannot be denyed.

IV. And thus 'tis clear from the Rules of Astrology, that this *N*ative should be blessed with a considerable Estate in the world; and the persons from whom it may be expected are (1.) The *N*atives Father. (2.) From or by the means of his Friends and Relations; and (3.) By the Portion of a Wife: to which I may add, by Vulgar persons also, with whom the *N*ative may have Trade and Commerce; in regard the M*oo*n being a general *Signifficatrix*, is not only Lady of the second House, but in friendly *Trine* to M*ercury*, Lord of the Ascendant, and to the S*un* and M*ars* also, as before remembred, who are proper Significators of the *N*atives Humour and Disposition, and (though S*aturn* be in the Ascendant) render him sufficiently Free and Noble, and very rarely guilty of a covetious Action.

V. Something as to the time when the *N*ative should expect an increase (or loss) of Estate should be hinted, but that is best discovered from a due Consideration of the Directions; their Effects being considerable, and worth Observation in these matters——. Therefore such as delight in those Speculations, should carefully observe when the Significators of Substance meet the hopeful and promising Beams of Promittors, which are the most probable times that Riches may drop in; and on the contrary, when the Significators are Directed to bad Promittors then loss and damage usually follows, unless Miraculously prevented by other Causes. *And thus much shall serve (by way of Example) for the Judgment of the second House of this Nativity.*

CHAP. XIV.

Astrological Judgment deduced from the Third House of the Exemplary Scheme: which (only for Example sake) I shall divide into these three following Sections.

SECT. I.

Shall the Native have Brothers, Sisters, or both, &c.

I. I find the last degree of *Cancer* upon the *Cusp* of the third House, and the M*oo*n, Lady thereof, in *Partile Trine* thereunto; but in regard that Signe is so neerly off, the *Sun* must be accounted a Co-significator of such Relations, he is in *Trine* to the M*oo*n; *Jupiter* is in *Scorpio*, and *Venus* in *Pisces*, both fruitful Signes, she also casts a *Trine* Aspect to the Cusp or the third House: now for as much as the Significators are both Masculine and Feminine, and posited in such Signes, I conclude the Native should have both Brothers and Sisters, according to the Rules given.

II. Now their Condition can be no wayes mean or bad, because the S*un* is in his Exaltation, and in *Trine* to the M*oo*n, as aforesaid, yet they should be persons of no healthful Constitutions, or strong able Bodies, (no more than the *N*ative himself) because S*aturn*, being Lord of the sixth House from the third House, is in *Quartile* to the S*un*, their principal Significator. Moreover, M*ars* is Lord or the sixth House in the Scheme (which is the eighth from the eleventh, the place of the S*un*; also the fourth from the third House, and exalted in the eighth, the sixth from the third) now his position in the Figure so neer the S*un* (as well as to *Mercury*, the *N*atives Significator) doth not improperly import that the *N*atives Brothers and Sisters should be no long livers, but much subject to Diseases, and Crasiness of Body; and consequently persons whose lives (in a natural sense) cannot be or any long date or continuance: But these things I confess are best discovered from their own Genitures, *I only touch at these Particulars by the way.*

SECT. II.

Of their Concordance and Agreement together, &c.

I. The *N*ative and his Brothers and Sisters should agree reasonable well together, and live in Amity for the most part, because the *Luminaries* are in *Trine*, and the Lord of the third is posited in the eleventh House, (which is accounted the House of Friendship) But S*aturn* in the Horoscope (and therefore partly the Natives Significator) in *Quartile* to the *Sun* and *Mercury* Combust, shews also sometimes a disagreement between the Native and his Brother in particular, or Brethren in general; or that there should not be so real an Unity between the Brethren themselves, as between the Brothers and Sisters: And this I rather Judge, because, *Mars* (being accounted a General Significator of Brethren) doth afflict *Mercury* as well as the *Sun*; and not only so, but dispose of him also.

II. Hence I conclude but an indifferent Agreement as aforesaid; but I question not but *Mercury* in *Aries*, the House of *Mars*, (notwithstanding his affliction) may influence the Native so much Activity Joyned wtth something of Subtilty, that he may thereby be enabled in some reasonable measure to defend himself from the power of the *Sun* and *Mars*, whose presence so neer *Mercury*, I presume add Courage to the Significator of the Native, and not only Courage, but an elevated Spirit also: by vertue of which he will by no means suffer himself to be over-powered by his Relations.

SECT. III.

Of the Natives Inland or short Journeys, &c.

I. The *Sun*, being Lord of the third chiefly, and posited in his Exaltation in the eleventh House (which is in *Sextile* to the Ascendant) declares the Native will take many pleasant and Fortunate short Journeys; which Judgment is also confirmed by the *Trine* of the Luminaries.

II. Yet the former Reasons also considered, (*viz.* the *Quadrat* of the *Sun* and *Saturn*, and the Combustion of *Mercury*) these are Arguments the Native must expect to meet with some Toyl and Trouble, and probably (at sometimes) Danger also in his short Journeys.

III. The Premises being considered, I may conclude, That the Natives Journeys will be pleasant and successful in the general; but at sometimes (unless more than ordinary care be taken) they may prove neither Profitable nor Delightful, but rather Disadvantagious and Prejudicial either to the Natives Body or Estate; and perhaps undertaken when the Native hath but small inclination thereunto. But I pretermit all farther enquiry into any thing relating to this House, and proceed to the Consideration of other Circumstances more material.

CHAP. XV.

Examples of Judgment Astrological upon the Fourth House of the Nativity, to Illustrate the former Rules, Divided into two Sections only; viz.

SECT. I.

Shall the Native and his Father Agree together?

I. The Natives Father is Signified by the *Sun* (which is a General Significator of Fathers) also *Sol* is very potent in his own Dignities in the eleventh House or Mansion of Friendship and Hope, which intimates he may prove a sure Friend to the Native; That Benevolent Fixed Star of the first Magnitude, called the *Virgins Spike*, is posited in the fifth House, the Fathers second, and *Jupiter* in *Sextile* to the Cusp thereof, which shews the Natives Father to be a person of Ability, as well as of a Noble Spirit, and large Heart, somewhat inclined to Choller or Passion, as the *Sun,* in *Aries* in *Conjunction* of *Mars*, and *Cor Leonis* in the fourth, very naturally portends. But now to the Question.

II. What was said of the Agreement between the Native and his Brethren may in part be understood in this Case, in regard the S*un* bears Rule both in the third and fourth Houses; *i. e.* That is a Reasonable Agreement between the Native and his Father is portended, I say, a Reasonable or moderate Concordency may be expected, and sometimes (though perhaps rarely) there will arise Jarring and Difference, which the Native in Prudence will easily bear with, and pass by, as in Duty bound, &c.

III. This small difference that may casually arise or happen between them will no way abate the natural Affection of the Father, for the S*un* doth receive *Mercury* in his Exaltation, neither is it any great affliction for *Mercury* to be Combust, since he is never far Elongated from the Body of the S*un*, but constantly attends upon him.

SECT. II.

Shall the Natives Patrimony be Considerable?

I. The Nativity being Diurnal, the S*un* is not only Significator of the Natives Father, but of his Patrimony also; according to the Judgment of the Antients. *Now* the S*un* being strong Essentially in the Figure, (*viz.* in his Exaltation and Triplicity) I therefore Judge the Natives Patrimony to be considerable; and the more, in respect that the S*un* darts a favourable *Trine* Aspect to the *Moon*, Lady of the Natives House of Substance.

II. It may be objected, that *Saturn* is in *Square* of the *Sun*; but that is the less material, by reason of the great strength of *Sol*, if it be also considered that *Saturn* is not Ascended above the Horizon at Birth, which was Diurnal; and in case the Natives Patrimony should be deminished, it will be occasioned partly by his own means: But this shall suffice for the Judgment of the fourth House, which might I confess be branched out into divers other Particulars, that I shall leave to the practise of the Student, my design being rather to Illustrate the General Rules already laid down, than to touch upon all the Circumstances, and Curiosities that may be Naturally deduced, or otherwise extracted from each House or the Coelestial Scheme.

CHAP. XVI.

Examples of Judgment Astrological deduced from the Sixth House; for the Illustration of the General Rules and Aphorisms already laid down.

SECT I.

Shall the Native be afflicted with Diseases, &c.

I. This Question is already answered in effect in the Judgment of the first House; but more particularly thus: Finding the first Decade of that *Stigmatized* Signe *Scorpio* descending upon the Cusp of the sixth, and *Mars*, Lord thereof, in *Conjunction* with *Sol*, Light of the time, or giver of Life, (or *Hylech*) and afflicting *Mercury*; Also *Jupiter*, Lord of the seventh, Retrograde in the sixth House, and the *Moon* posited therein neer *Cauda Draconis*: These are Arguments in Art, that the *Native* should be often afflicted in Body by the malignancy of Diseases, the presence of *Saturn* in the Ascendant in *Quartile* to the *Sun* and *Mercury* (within Orbs) confirm the same, which is the more aggravated in that he hath Dignities in the eighth House.

II. But on the other side, *Jupiter* being a Benevolent Planet (though posited in that Turbulent Signe *Scorpio*) is still a friend to nature, and disposes of *Venus*, Lady of the twelfth) and neerly of the *Moon* also, who friendly beholds several Planets in the eleventh House from the sixth, or House of Diseases: This doth something aleviate the aforesaid evil, so that although I cannot, upon good grounds, pronounce the *N*ative to be a Person of a sound and healthful Constitution; yet it doth meliorate and (in a natural sense) not a little befriend nature against such Diseases that may unhappily invade the *N*ative, and in part be procured by his own means.

III. *Of the Nature and kind of Diseases*, &c. And those I judge may proceed from moist humours abounding in the Body, or from the corruption of the Blood, whence Surfeits, or the Dropsie may be feared (as is aptly denoted by *Jupiter* in *Scorpio* in the sixth House) also obstruction of the Liver and Stomach, *&c*. *Saturn* in the Ascendant in an Airy Signe sometimes afflicts the *N*ative with the Gout, and advises him to be careful of all Chronique Distempers arising from the Putrifaction of the Blood; and *Mars* in *Aries* afflicting of *Mercury* naturally portends the same; whence breakings out and swellings in several parts of the body may ensue, with violent pains in the Head and Feavours of dangerous consequence, if not carefully prevented in time—(But those Diseases of *Mars*, Lord of the sixth, are sometimes mitigated by the friendly *Trine* of the *Moon*) And hence the *N*ative is cautioned to keep his body in as equal a temper as may be, since the *N*ativity so plainly demonstrates he is obnoxious to such dangerous assaults. *In the next place I shall consider whether the Natives Servants may prove faithful or perfidious*, &c. which I examine thus; *viz*.

IV. *M*ars, Lord of the sixth House, afflicting *M*ercury in the eleventh, shews the *N*ative will have such Servants that, notwithstanding their fair pretences, may not really affect him; and consequently not discharge their trust with that fidelity as they ought to do; which is confirmed by the *Quadrate* of *M*ars to the Cusp of the second House, and the position of the *Dragons Tayl* in the sixth; the *N*ative ought therefore to be careful of such Servants as are signified by *M*ars in *Aries*, which will not want for boldness and confidence, as also such dissembling fellows signified by *Jupiter* in *Scorpio*; but those by the *M*oon in *Trine* to *M*ercury and the *Sun*, the *N*ative may justly impose confidence in, as being the likeliest persons to perform faithful service to the *N*ative; and such I describe thus; *viz*. persons of a moderate, large stature of Body, pale Complexioned, round fac'd, grey ey'd, much hair of a sad colour, and the whole body somewhat corpulent, plump, or fleshy; and from the premises 'tis easie for the *N*ative to judge what success he may have if he should happen to deal in small Cattle, as Sheep, Hoggs, Doggs, Birds. *&c*.

CHAP. XVII.

Judgment Deduced from the seventh House—in these four following Sections, by way of Example.

SECT. I.

Shall the Native Marry,

I. As it has been shewed, I am to consider the cusp of the seventh House, the Lord thereof, or any Planet posited therein, also the position of the *M*oon and *Venus*, and how they behold the Lord of the Ascendant, or the Cusp thereof.

II. In the Geniture there is 23 degrees of *Sagitary* descending upon the Cusp of the seventh House, and *Jupiter*, Lord thereof, in *Scorpio*, a fruitful Signe; (2.) the *Moon* is just leaving *Scorpio*, and hasting to the Cusp of the seventh House in *Trine* to *M*ercury and *Venus*, who is also in *Pisces* a fruitful Signe, and disposed of by *Jupiter*, Lord of the seventh House (though in her own Dignities) besides *Venus* is in *Conjunction* with the part of Marriage (if any thing may be found from thence) all which are Testimonies that the Native will have an inclination to Marriage, and therefore in all probability may live to unite himself to a Wife; which Judgment is confirmed by the *Trine* of the M*oon* and M*ercury*, Lord of the Ascendant. Thus I conclude the Native may Marry, but rarely above once, because S*aturn* is in the Ascendant, and in exact *Square* to *Venus* (a generl Significatrix of Marriage) and she in S*quare* to the Cusp of the seventh House, which may retard the business till thirty years at least, but may be effected probably upon the Direction of the Ascendant to the *Trine* of *Venus*, which will not be till 33 years at soonest.

SECT. II.

What manner of Person may the Native Marry, and how qualified, &c.

I. The Description of her Person is taken in particular from the Sign *Sagitary* descending upon the cusp of the seventh House, and her qualities from *Jupiter* Rx in *Scorpio* having no Aspect to any of the other Planets in the *Scheme*. *Sagitary* usually gives a Person of a strait well proportioned Body, rather tall than otherwise; or a Person above a middle Stature, of a Cheerful Countenance, Oval Visage, Brown Hair, and in fine, every way well Composed with a handsome Conformity of all the Members.

II. *As to Conditions, Jupiter* generally signifies a Person of a most excellent Conversation, Just, Noble, Prudent, and a real Friend where he, or she do fix their Affections, yet perfect haters of all base, and unworthy Actions; but this must be understood where *Jupiter* is essentially Dignified: Now in this Nativity finding *Jupiter* posited in the very worst Sign in the Heavens (as it is accounted by all Astrologers) *viz. Scorpio* Retrograde in the sixth House, and in no Aspect with the *Lumiinaries*; I therefore conclude the Person the Native shall Marry will not be altogether so well qualified as aforesaid, yet ingenious, active, and moderately well tempered; and therefore her Qualities, and Disposition not much to be disliked.

III. *Their Agreement* should be reasonable good (yet no extraordinary fondness on either side, because *Saturn* is in the Ascendant and in *Quartile* to *Venus*) I say a reasonable good Agreement in respect I find the *Moon* did separate from a *Conjunction* of *Jupiter*, and applies to a *Trine* of *Mercury*, Lord of the Ascendant, and thereby transfers the Vertue of *Jupiter*, not only to *Mercury*, but to *Mars*, and the *Sun* also.

IV. *The portion of the Wife*, I judge, should not be inconsiderable, because *Saturn*, the Significator thereof, is in *Trine* to the *Part of Fortune*, and disposes thereof in the Mid-Heaven. There is an Aphorisme in *Astrology, that the Person that hath not* Venus *in some good Aspect of* Mars *in his Nativity will assuredly suffer many Inconveniencies in his Love, or Affections*, here *Venus* is in no Aspect of M*ars*; but the *Moon* being in *Trine* to *Venus* takes off all danger in that particular.

V. *As to the Quarter of Heaven*, from whence she may come, finding the M*oon*, and *Jupiter* posited in the Western part of the Heavens; intimates she should come from that Quarter, or rather West, North-west from the place of the Natives Birth. — And this is all shall be Written concerning the Person the Native shall Marry; although I could easily enlarge, which I presume is not much material in this place.

SECT. III.

Shall the Native have Publique Enemies?

I. In order to the Resolution of this Question, I am still to consider the position of *Jupiter*, who is Lord of the seventh (there being no Planet Located therein) and finding him Retrograde in *Scorpio* in the sixth House in no Aspect to M*ercury*, or the M*oon*, nor to S*aturn*, who is in the Ascendant; hence I conclude the Native need not fear prejudice from publique Enemies, nor is there any danger that he should be afflicted with any; and those which may accidentally shew themselves, will be Persons very inconsiderable, and scarce worth the Natives notice: now what kind of Persons are signified by *Jupiter* in *Scorpio* is already shewed.

II. To confirm this Judgement, I find the principal Significator of the Native much stronger, and better placed than the Lord of the seventh House, who is in *Trine* to the Cusp of the second, and the Moon separates from the *Conjunction* of *Jupiter*, and applies to the *Trine* of *Mercury*, &c.

SECT. IV.

Of the Natives Law Suits, and Partnership.

I. The Lord of the Ascendant, and Lord of the seventh are both very meanly dignified, and Retrograde; which argues if the Native should Casually happen to have any Suit in Law, as there is no danger of losing much thereby; so there is but small hopes on the other side that he should profit much by such Contests.

II. But considering the Native is not signified by *Mercury*, but by *Saturn* also (who is *Almuten* of the *Geniture*) I may hence rationally conclude that he shall contend very rarely with any Person but he will come off Victor; yet let not the Native voluntarily attempt such Controversies, unless justly provoked thereunto; because *Jupiter* is in a treacherous Sign.

III. Lastly, As to *Parhership*, by what has been said, it Naturally follows that if the Native happen to engage therein, he should rather advantage himself thereby, than suffer loss, or prejudice; for *Saturn* Lord of the eighth is in the Ascendant in *Trine*, (and Disposiler) of the *Part of Fortune*, and *Jupiter* is also in *Trine* to the Cusp of the second House, and exalted therein.

CHAP. XVII.

Judgement Astrological, deduced from the fifth House of the exemplary Geniture.

I. *If it be enquired whether the Native may have Children*, &c. Here I consider the Sign of the fifth House, as also the eleventh House (which is the Wives fifth) and the Ascendant, together with the Lord of those Houses, and the Planets that are posited therein.

II. Finding *Virgo*, a Barren Sign, upon the Cusp of the fifth, and *Gemini* another Barren Sign Ascending upon the Cusp of the *Horoscope*, also *Mercury* Lord of both Houses in *Aries* in *Conjunction* of the *Sun* and *Mars*; these Testimonies barely considered, denyes Issue: But to Ballance this Judgement, on the other side, I find a benevolent fixed Star (*viz. spica virginis*) Intercepted in the fifth in *Libra*, and therefore disposed of by *Venus*, who is posited in her Exaltation in the eleventh House, and there in *Trine* to the *Moon*; these are Arguments the Native may have Issue.

III. But considering the Lord of the Ascendant, and fifth Houses, are so much afflicted in the eleventh, by the *Sun* and *Mars*; and *Venus*, who is also Lady of the twelfth House (the eighth from the fifth) in *Quartile* to *Saturn* (Lord of the fourth, fifth, and sixth Houses from the fifth) I hence conclude the Native will have very few Children (if any) and those sickly and weak, and consequently not long Vitall; and in all probility they should be of the Male-kind, because *Mercury* is posited in *Aries*, a Masculine Sign, and in *Conjunction* with the *Sun*, and *Mars*, two Masculine Planets; which is confirmed the more by the *Trine* of the *Moon*, who is just entering a Masculine Sign, and the Aspect which is between *Venus*, and *Saturn*, another Masculine Planet from the Ascendant and eleventh Houses.

IV. *Concerning the Natives Recreation, Gaming, Sports, Pastimes, Mirth*, &c. Finding the Lord of the Ascendant, and fifth House one Planet, and afflicted by the presence of the *Sun*, and *Mars* in an Opposite House to the fifth: also *Saturn* in the *Ascendant* in S*quare* to *Venus*, shews that the Native should have small inclination, or delight in any such Exercizes (in which is also included Musick, and Dancing) and this I know to be true, the Native will rather be reserved, and Contemplative in misterious matters, and yet sometimes mounts upon the Wings of an Active Fancy, &c.—The Native delights not at all in Musick, or any Airy Divertisement, but is generally Melancholy, unless more than ordinary moved, or prompt by a fit Object beyond his Natural Temper, and Humour; the premises being considered here's no great incouragement for the Native to hope for gain by Gaming, had he an inclination thereto; but since he is altogether averse to such kind of Diversion: no more need be Written of this Subject; in fine, our Native is a sociable generous Spirited Person, and so I conclude this Chapter.

CHAP. XVIII.

Judgment Astrological deduced from the Ninth House of the Geniture, to illustrate the former Rules.

1. If the Enquiry be made whether the Native may Travel or not at some time of his life? I consider that part of *Capricorn* is descending upon the Cusp of the ninth House, but just passing off, and therefore *Aquary* should rather be accepted; however, *Saturn* is still Ruler of the said House, and disposed of by *Mercury* in the Ascendant; *Mercury* is in a moveable Sign in *Trine* of the *Moon*, the *Sun* and *Mars*, these are strong testimonies in Art, that the *N*ative should have a strong inclination to Travel, to see remote Countreys of the world; or at least to undertake some long Voyage to Sea, and probably South-Eastward, because the Significators are located in that Quarter.

II. Now *Saturn* being Lord of the ninth House in the *Horoscope*, and well dignified, argues the Native should not only be propense to Travel, but advantage himself thereby; which is seconded by the M*oons Sextile* to the Cusp of the ninth House, (she being Lady of the second) but in regard the Lord of the Ascendant is afflicted, and *Saturn*, Lord of the ninth is in *Quartile* to *Venus*, not beheld by *Jupiter* or the M*oon*, I shall not encourage the Native to adventure himself or expose his Body to that affliction which he may totally evade if he continue in his own native Countrey.

III. The motive that may induce the Native at any time to see far Countreys (and I know he was once strongly inclined and fully resolved some few years since upon such an undertaking had not Friends and Relations otherwise prevailed with him) must be chiefly out of Curiosity to see strange Countreys rather than hope to enrich or advance himself to Dignity or Honour thereby, and yet something of that nature would please the Native; (though I know him to be free from Covetousness, Pride, or Ambition.) S*aturn* Lord of the eighth, ninth, and tenth Houses in the Ascendant in *Gemini*, the House of M*ercury*, and M*ercury* with M*ars* and the S*un* in the eleventh in *Aries* doth not improperly afford such a judgment according to the Canons of Astrology — the time when is best discovered by *Directions*.

IV. *As to the Natives Dreams*, finding S*aturn* Lord of the ninth House in the Ascendant strong and Angular, denotes the Natives Dreams should for the most part prove true; and probably, at sometimes somewhat terrible or frightful to the Native; for 'tis the opinion of Astrologers that if *Saturn* be Lord of the ninth House, (and more especially being located in the Ascendant and no Planets in the ninth) that then the Natives Dreams should be of Persons, or things S*aturnine*, and therefore many times produces fear and horrour, or affords Dreams of occult and hidden things, Visions, Apparitions, &c.

V. Lastly, the premises being considered, and also the S*un*, the Disposiler of M*ercury*, both in *Trine* to the M*oon*, this argues that the Native should be of solid and sound Principles as to Faith and Religion in the General, though the Position of S*aturn*, Ruler of the ninth House in the Ascendant in *Gemini*, doth naturally signifie the *N*ative should also know how to be Critical in some matters where he sees occasion, and have also an inclination to Science, &c. yet he deviates not much from those Princlples he has been educated in. *This much is sufficient to be hinted upon this Subject, and shall conclude the Judgment of the ninth House.*

CHAP. XIX.

Judgment deduced from the Tenth House, or Angle of Honour.

I. *If Enquiry be made whether the Native may arrive to any considerable degree of Honor,* &c. I consider that Saturn is Lord of the tenth, Angular and strong, S*ol* a general Significator of Honour and Dignity, is posited in *Aries* his Exaltation in the eleventh House, and there in exact *Trine* to the M*oon*; moreover the *Part of Fortune* is posited in the Mid-heaven, and the M*oon* in S*extile* thereunto: these are Arguments that the Native (according to his capacity, and condition of Birth) should arrive to a considerable degree of Honour and Estimation in the world, and consequently live most splendid and happily therein.

II. But it cannot be expected that this Judgment should take place to the height thereof, in regard *Saturn*, Lord of the tenth, is within the Orbs of a *Quadrate* of the *Sun* from the Ascendant and eleventh Houses; howbeit the major Testimonies demonstrate Honour, and a good Reputation in the general, although perhaps some occurrences of difficulty may interpose and (only seemingly) for a time frustrate the hopes of the Native in that particular; and this in all probability from or by the means or indeavours of persons *Solar* and *Saturnine*.

III. In fine, what Honour is conferred upon the Native should be for the most part acquired by his own industry or deserts, because of the position of *Saturn* in the Horoscope; and therefore let not seeming difficulties discourage the Native in his hopeful Attempts: and in regard a fixed Signe (viz. *Aquary*) possesses the Cusp of the tenth House, it imports the Natives Honour and Renown should remain fixed and durable.

IV. *As to the Natives Magestery and Profession*; The Determination thereof is not easily performed; but in this Nativity, finding an Aiery Sign both upon the Mid heaven and Horoscope, and S*aturn* therein, and in particular in *Gemini*, the House of *Mercury*, this aptly denotes some kind of Merchandizing, and that the Native should delight to deal in such matters, or things that are both *Venereal*, and *Mercurial*; he was bred to a Gentile Profession, sutable to his Birth and Education, and is indeed capable of excellent things, being a person qualified both with an apt and pregnant Genius, and a notable worklng active Fancy, well signified by S*aturn* in *Gemini* in the Ascendant and Mercury his Disposiler in *Conjunction* with the S*un*, and *Mars* in the Aequinoctial sign *Aries*.

CHAP. XX.

Judgment upon the Eleventh House of the Exemplary Nativity.

I. *As to the Friends of the Native, such as are unrelated unto him, also their Qualities and Conditions,* &c. Considering the Constitution of the Scheme, and finding so many planets in the House of Friendship, I conclude the Native should have many Friends and Acquaintance; and in regard the *Moon* doth behold those Planets by a *Trine* Aspect, 'tis an Argument they should (for the most part) be real; yet I conjecture the Native will be sensible of some that may prove meer Pretenders, only for their own particular ends, and to serve themselves, because M*ercury* is afflicted by M*ars* and the S*un*, and *Venus* is in *Quartile* to *Saturn*.

II. Hence the Native may expect to find many Friends, some that are really so, others the contrary, which he will quickly discover, and respect them accordingly; but for such Friends which he finds real, he is so ingenious as to oblige them so to continue; and in short, the Native will notwithstanding be so happy as to enjoy divers Friends which may prove assistant upon occasion, beyond all prejudice or injury that can be designed against him by subtle pretenders; the several humours or qualities of both kinds are discovered from the Nature of those Planets that are posited in the eleventh House, *&c.*

III. *As to the Natives Hopes.* From a due consideration or the position of the Significators aforesaid, the Native should be sometimes crossed or thwarted therein, though not much to his prejudice, but generally reasonable Fortunate in most affairs he Hopes or Desires to accomplish; because the M*oon*, Lady of the second House, doth so friendly behold M*ercury*, and those other Planets in the eleventh House.

IV. Let the Native, if it be possible, gain the Nativities or those persons he has much Conversation withal, and compare his own therewith; and if he finds a convenient Harmony between them, it is a confirmation of true Friendship; if not, he ought to be the more wary how he trusts them; See *Ptolomy's Centiloquium,* Aphor. 33. together with some Aphorisms relating thereunto in the general Judgment of the eleventh House, and you may be the better able to judge of the real love or hatred or two persons.

CHAP. XXI.

Judgment upon the Twelfth House.

I. *If it be demanded whether the Native shall have private Enemies, or receive prejudice from such*? I find in the Nativity that *Venus* is Lady of the Twelfth House, and in *Quartile* to the Ascendant and to S*aturn* therein, which denotes the Native may have secret Enemies, such as are signified by *Venus* and the M*oon* also (who is in Platique *Trine* to *Venus*) possibly they may be of the Female Sex, and such as would be accounted, or at least pretend themselves to be real Friends, because of the position of *Venus* in her own Dignities in the eleventh House.

II. Yet *Saturn* being a Superiour Planet, and in the Ascendant, and in *Quartile* to *Venus*, shews the Native cannot be much injured by any such persons; it rather intimates he may by unpleasont carriage, or strangeness, give distaste or offence to some or his Female Friends, and in Revenge thereof they may become his private Enemies, but not sufficiently able to prejudice the Native thereby; for *Saturn* is the Afflicting Planet, and *Venus* was Passive, and suffer'd by the beams of *Saturn* darted upon her at Birth.

III. *As to Captivity or Restraint.* I conclude from the Premises that the Native will never suffer thereby, yet he may I confess be sometimes oppressed with Melancholy, and discontented thoughts; and I tear too oft be subject thereunto, by reason of the presence of S*aturn* in the Ascendant in *Quartile* to *Venus*, Lady of the Twelfth, (which ts the House of sorrow, &c.) Lastly, from these Considerations it doth also follow, that the Native should be but reasonably Fortunate in Dealing in great Cattle, (properly signified by this House;) but in regard the Native hath no inclination that way, (*viz.* to deal in such Creatures) this shall conclude the Judgment of the twelfth House, which is sufficient to illustrate the Rules before laid down. *Here I might confess have been much much more Copious in Judgment upon this and the other Houses, but I forbear purposely, that the young Student may have occasion hereby to what his Active Fancy in the Amplification of what remains.*

CHAP. XXII.

Judgement proper to the eighth House of the Exemplary Scheme.

I. From this part of the Heavens Judgement is taken concerning the Death of the Native, as has already been shewed; and herein I shall only consider two things (1.) who is *Anareta*, or the *interficient*, or *Killing Planet*; (2.) by what kind of Death the Native may expire, whether Natural, or violent?

II. Now the Planet that in this Scheme appears to be the *Abcissor*, or Destroyer of Life, is S*aturn* in the Horoscope, Lord of the eighth House; and when the giver of Life, or *Hylech* meets with the Body of the Killing

Planet in this Figure, is the most dangerous time. The *Sun* is *Hylech*, and about the sixtieth Year of the Natives Age meets with the Body of *Saturn* by Direction according to *Naibods* measure of Time (being Directed in the Aequator according to the usual Method,) yet the Native may labour some Years under the effects thereof before he change this Life for a better; thus much I intimate from the consideration or Natural Causes, no Man can, or dare be positive in this particular, since the Lives of all Persons are only at the Dispose of the great Creator of Heaven and Earth.

III. The Native has already passed the Direction of the Ascendant to the Body of *Saturn*, as also the *Moon* to the *Opposition* of *Saturn*; both which Directions have had their effects sufficiently upon the Natives Body, as he will readily acknowledge for the Confirmation, and Verification of Art to any Ingenious Person that may doubt of the secret Operations of the Coelestial Bodies upon Mortals.

IV. *As to the kind of Death by which the Native may expire*, whether *Natural* or *Violent*, &c. I answer thus, That considering the *Sun* is *Hylech*, and Lord of the fourth, and in *Conjunction* with *Mercury* Lord of the Ascendant in *Aries* a violent Sign, within the Orbs of a *Square* of *Saturn* in the Ascendant; and *Capricorn*, another violent Sign, descends upon the cusp of the eighth: I say, these are Arguments that the Native may be in great danger of violent Death, which cautions him to be the more careful to forbear all violent Actions. But on the other side (although the *Moon* be in a violent sign) she beholds *Mercury*, the *Sun* and *Mars* (as bas been hinted) by a *Trine* Aspect; also *Venus*, and *Jupiter* (both the Fortunes) are in *Sextile* to the Cusp of the eighth House, and no violent fixed Star posited therein; and therefore I conclude the Native may expire rather by some Disease proceeding either trom Melancholy, or from Phlegm, and moyst humours too much abounding; but at a considerable Age, as before Intimated; and thus I conclude the Judgement of this House, and or the whole Exemplary Scheme.

Before I come to treat of Directions, I thought convenient here to Insert these Proposals therein, which I had long since from a loving Friend, and singular Mathematician; and so leave them to the consideration, and scanning of theSons of Art.

I.'Tis probable that the Antient Astrologers, by what they termed Directions upon Nativities, intended thereby some Position, or Configuration of the Heavens, happening within some certain dayes after the same, to signifie Accidents, good, or evil to the Native at the end of so many Years.

II. And probably the Directions or the S*un* and *Moon* only their applications to the Bodies, and Aspects of the other Planets, and Fixed Stars, every dayes distance in Time, from the Birth to the said Aspects giving one Year, and every two hours, one Month.

III. The Direction of the *M.C.* being the days elapsed from the Radix till the Bodies, or Aspects of some of the Planets do culminate at the same hour of the day, or point of time with the Nativity.

IV. And consequently, the Direction of the Ascendant, the dayes elapsed from the Nativity till some Promittor Ascendeth the Horizon at the same time of the day agreeable with the Radix. These Propositions seem to agree with *Keplar*'s way or Direction, as any Person may try if he please.

Thus, suppose the *Sun* in some Nativity should Culminate in 0 d. of *Aries*, and *Venus* should be posited in 0 d. of *Taurus*; now the common Arch of Direction would be near 28 deg. but the *Sun* wlll not come to that point till more than 30 dayes, shewing the Accident to happen at the end of 30 years.

[*There is a measure of Time mentioned in this Book, which agrees to this method of Direction; unto which* J. Keplar*'s is equivolent.*

CHAP. XXIII.

Of Directions of Significators to their several Promittors in any Nativity.

SECT. I.

Shewing what a Direction is, and how it is defined; as also, which is called the Significator, and which the Promittor, &c.

A *Direction* (or rather a *Deduction*) is defined by *Argol* to be the Arch of the Aequator, intercepted between two places in the Heavms, *viz.* The Artificial measure of its Progress, which the Promissor doth absolve by the Motion of the *Primum Mobile*; or to Direct, is to find what Degrees of the Aequator pass through the Meridian, while the Promissor (or place inferiour) by the aforesaid Motion comes to the point of the Significator, (or place superiour) *i.e.* Until the Promissor comes to the very Semicircle of Position of the Significator, which is vulgarly said to be Directed; this Motion in Directions is real, and no way feigned. Hence then that Motion of rising, wheeling, or turning about of the Promissor to the place of the Significator, by the swift Motion of the *Primum Mobile*, which is from the East to the West, is really absolute, and produces its effects according to the distance of the Degrees of the Aequator, between the Significator, and Promissor, giving for every Degree, or space of Time the Sun makes his Diurnal mean Motion, a certain Determinate Measure of TIme, allowed by Experience, *viz.* about a Year, *&c.* of which more in its proper place.

II. Others (and in particular one very Learned in Astronomy) defines Directions to be the Harmony of the Earth's Annual, and Diurnal Revolutions about the Sun; and Protections (if any thing) are destined to be the Harmony of the M*oon*'s Mensural, and Diurnal Revolutions about the Earth; from this ground, *Keplar*'s Method of Direction is termed a most Demonstrative way, which in some place of this Book I shall endeavour to make plain, and easie, Yet *Argol*'s Method is now generally received, and practiced by all Astrologers of *Europe*, and is the same with *Regiomontanus*, the which hath been followed by many Learned Astronomers, and Mathematitians, as *Johannes Keplerus, Tycho*, the *Danian School, Johannes, Antonius, Maginus*, and others, as atested by that great Master of Astronomy, *viz. Andreas Argol* himself, who hath taken much pains in this kind, being a Professor, as he saith, for above fifty Years, and never found the least Scruple whereby he might be enforc'd to alter his Judgement, being well satisfied that this Subject is Built upon a true, and sure Foundation; and grounded upon Mathematical Reasons, and Demonstrations.

III. By a *Significator* you are to understand any Planet or place of the Ecliptick, that may signifie any matter, or thing in the Heavens, about the affection of the Body of the Native; as Life, Manners of the Mind, Preferment, Fortune, and any other thing, inwardly, or outwardly happening thereunto; for which *Ptolomy* assigned the Ascendant, Mid-heaven, *Sol, Luna*, and *Part of Fortune*: These five are termed *Hylegiacals*, and *Significators*, by whose Directions all Accidents, as well prosperous, as unfortunate, are pointed out, according as their Significators meet with the Bodies, or Aspects of Benevolent, or Malevolent Stars, or Planets. This Opinion is generally followed, others have added the rest of the Planets, *Saturn, Jupiter, Mars, Venus*, and *Mercury* for Significators also, and may discern good or evil in those things that are signified by them; as also the Cusps of the Coelestial Houses, according to their several Signiftications; as the second House for Riches, the seventh for Marriage, *&c.* and so of the rest.

IV. The *Promissor* (or *Promittor*) is that point of the Ecliptick wherein the Body, or Aspect of any Star, or Planet that is said to be Directed unto, (or rather brought to the place of the Significator, as before noted) which may discry, or promise anything to the Native, either good, or evil, denoted or signified by the *Significator*.

V. There is another sort or Direction, which by Astrologers is termed *Converse*, or Retrograde, that is to bring the Significator to the Promissor, which is contrary to the Motion of the *Primum Mobile*, and by *Argol* utterly abolish'd as feigned, and without a Foundation. Put *Converse Direction* taken in the right sense, is nothing discrepant from direct Direction, as is testified by *Carol, Antonius, Manginus* in his *Nova Dirigendi Ars,* Printed 1626. But only in taking the Poles Elevation above the Circle of Position. For as in direct Directions you are to take the Circle of Position, (as it is vulgarly termed) of the Significator; and so direct the Promissor under that Pole. So here in Converse Directions you are to take the Circle of Position of the Promissor only, and not the Significator; and under that Pole find the Ascention, or Descention of the Significator, and Subtract the Oblique Ascention, or Descention of the Promissor from the Oblique Ascention, or Descention of the Significator, &c. and the difference is the Ark of Direction required.

Example.

Suppose the Ascendant or some Nativity were 2 deg. *Libra*, and the *Trine* of *Jupiter* fell in 5 deg. 10 m. of *Virgo* in the twelfth (this is contrary to the succession of the Signs) and I would know when the Ascendant or Horoscope came to the said Aspect of *Jupiter*. Now I find the Pole of Position of the *Trine* of *Jupiter* to be 46 d. 2m. I take the Oblique Ascenttion of the Horoscope under that Pole, which is 183d. 24m. from which I deduce the Oblique Ascention of the *Trine* of *Jupiter*, 147d. 21m. and there remains the Arke of Direction required, 36d. 3m. so that here you may observe that the Ascendant, which is the Significator, is brought to the Promissor still according to the Motion of the *Primum Mobile*, and the Pole of Position taken at every Direction, which in the direct way is taken but once; and hence the difference between Direct, and Converse is plainly laid open, and discovered, I suppose, if it were practised, (which indeed is very laborious) it would be found as significant as the former, since 'tis in effect but the same thing. But this I leave to the consideration of the more able Artists, who are Competent Judges in such Cases. 'Tis too laborious I confess, and few Clyents will be willing to pay an Artist for such serious Work, I presume, because they are not sensible of the great Pains that must be taken therein.

SECT. II.

Of the Latitude of the Planets to be considered in Directions.

I. There hath been much Dispute amongst Authors concening this very point, occasioned (as is supposed) by the false Interpretations of *Ptolomy*'s Writings; but all that are skillful in Mathematical Demonstrations, do unanimously agree that the Latitude of the Planets in Directions ought every where to be observed. For every Man that is but meanly versed in these matters may easily apprehend that the Stars do unequally arise with, and without Latitude; so in these Northern Countreys that have Oblique Horizons where the North Pole is elevated, 'tis apparent that a Star with North Latitude riseth sooner, and sets later than the place of the Ecliptick; and contrarily, those Stars having South Latitude, rise later, and set sooner than the place of the Ecliptick they are in; this is very easily discovered by the Globe, or Sphere, or by any Tables of Oblique Ascention with Latitude.

II. As in the Latitude of *London*, the Oblique Ascension of 10 degrees of *Aries Sine Lat*. is 4 degrees, 12 minutes, but with 1 degree of North Latitude 'tis 2 degrees, 36 minutes, and agrees to about 6 degrees or *Aries*; but with 1 degree of South Latitude, the Oblique Ascention is 5 degrees, 43 minutes, which agrees to almost 14 degrees of *Aries*; by which it is plain that a Planet with South Latitude ariseth farther in the Sign than the place of the Ecliptick he is in, and having North Latitude, the contrary; and by consequence the Ark of Direction is either increased, or diminished, by reason of the Planets Latitude North, or South; this needs no more words to explain it, being a business so obvious.

III. Note this by the way, that notwithstanding North Latitude diminisheth the Oblique Ascension, and South Latitude augmenteth it; yet you are to understand the contrary in their Oblique Descentions: for as much as North Latitude makes the Oblique Ascention lesser than the Descention of the Ecliptick, so much the Oblique Descention will be greater; and so much as South Latitude increaseth the Oblique Ascension, so much it decreaseth the Oblique Descention less than the degrees of the Ecliptick [*I have said the more in this particular to explain the business to Tyro's.*]

IV. The Premises considered, then the Latitude ought undoubtedly to be observed in Directions; *Origanus* contends for an Aequation of the Stars Latitude in their Aspects to be made in the Longitude. But *Blanchinus*, and *Argol* will have their Latitude Aequated in the Aspects only. Others would have the Stars Latitude Aequated, both in their Longitude, and Aspects too; but if you Direct only to the Aspects of the Planets (which never have much Latitude, neglecting the Aspects of the Fixed Stars, as all Modern Astrologers do, except *Hartgil*) there needs no Aequation in the Longitude for the *Sextile*, or *Trine* Aspect, at eight degrees of Latitude (which is the most the Planets have) alters but 14 minutes in the Longitude, which is inconsiderable, considering the uncertainty of the Planets places in some Ephemerides; therefore to Aequate the Aspects only according to *Argol* is altogether sufficient, neglecting the Longitude Aequatlon, unless you Direct to the Aspects of Fixed Stars that have great Latitude, then indeed the Longitude will be altered considerably, as will appear by the following proportions.

Now the Reason why *Argol* gives that short Rule in his *Primum Mobile*, (the premises considered) is because that in so small Angles, *viz.* 30 degrees from the acute Angle (*i.e.* the *Sextile*, or *Trine* Aspect from the *Quartile*) the Perpendicular is near half the said Angle; and because the sides including so small Angles are almost the same, therefore *Argol* and others take half the Latitude in the *Sextile*, and *Trine*, and the side 60 degrees in the Ecliptick, although not exactly so, yet the difference is inconsiderable, as appears by this following Example, *viz.*

First for the Aequation of the *Longitude.*

As the Radius to the Tangent of the Aspects distance from the □, *viz.* 30 degrees	976144
So the Co-sine of the Latitude in the ☌ which is never above 8 deg. in the Planets.	999575
To the Tangent of the Aspects Long. from the Square 29 deg. 46 min.	975710

Secondly for the Latitude.

As the Radius to the Sine of the Aspect from the □ 30 deg.	969897
So the Sine of the Lat. at the ☌ 8d. 0m	914356
So the Sine of the Lat. at the Aspects 3d. 59m.	884253

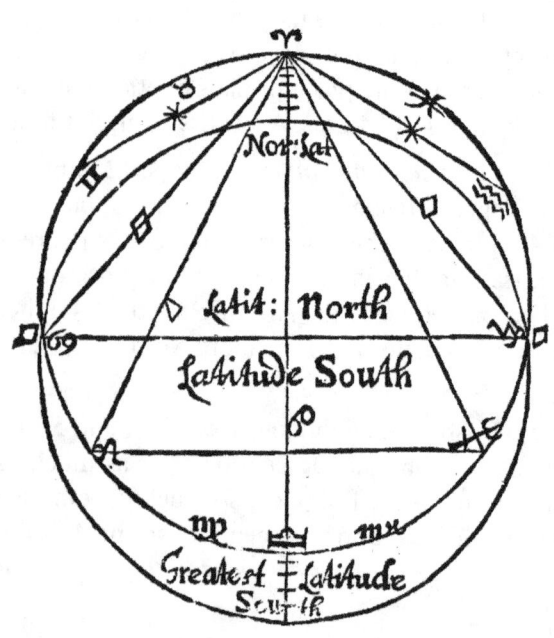

Here follows Blanchinus*'s and* Argol*'s Demonstration of the Latitude of the Planets in their Aspects; by which, what is Asserted in the following Paragraph is confirmed by Oculer Demonstration, and therefore may be some satisfaction to the Curious Searcher into the verity of this kind of Learning, which to some Readers may be accounted no less than Riddles, Misteries, or very Occult Secrets, if not worse.*

V. Thus 'tis apparent that if a Planet hath 8 degrees of Latitude, in the conjunction he hath but 14 min. difference in the *Sextile*, or *Trine*, which is not considerable for the reasons before hinted; and a Planet that hath the same Latitude in the *Conjunction*, the *Sextile*, or *Trine*, will be but half, within less than one minute. Therefore we may use *Argol*'s method in the Aequation of the Planets Aspects, *viz.* the *Quartile* terminates in the Ecliptick, and therefore hath no Latitude, the *Opposition* the same Latitude, but of the contrary denomination, to that of the *Conjunction*; But in a *Trine*, or *Sextile*, take half the

Latitude (as before proved) the *Sextile* is of the same, and the *Trine* of the contrary denomination, of the Latitude in the *Conjunction*. To this Aequation *Argol* subscribes as agreeing with Observations in above 1000 Genitures (as he saith) and with him many more Astrologers, and so lays aside the Aequation of *Regiomontanus*, and others, as void of Mathematical Demonstrations: Those that have a rnlnd to Aequate the Longitude of the Planets also, as well as their Aspects, may make use of this short Table following.

A Table of the Aequation of the Longitude, and Latitude of the Planets Aspects according to Blanchinus *and* Argol.

Pla.	Lat.	I	II	III	IV	V	VI	VII	VIII
S.S.	Lat.	0 52	1 42	2 36	3 28	4 10	5 22	6 3	6 56
QC	Aeq.	0 0	0 1	0 2	0 4	0 6	0 8	0 11	0 14
✶	Lat.	0 30	1 0	1 30	2 0	2 30	3 0	3 30	4 0
△	Aeq.	0 30	0 1	0 2	0 4	0 6	0 8	0 11	0 14

Note that the second, and fourth Lines in the Table are the Aequation of Latitude; and the third and last the Aequation of Longitude.

VI. The Aequation of the *Semi-Sextile*, and the *Quin Cunx* are the same, because they are both equally distant, (*viz.* 60 deg.) from the *Quartile*; so likewise is the Aequation of the *Sextile*, and *Trine*, they being equally distant 30d. from the *Quartile*; and this is to be understood, both in Longitude and Latitude: The Aequation of the Aspects are to be used as before directed; but for the Aequation of the Longitude of the Planets, take this Rule.

In the
- ✶ Sinister, & △ Dexter.   add the aequation to the given Longitude.
- ✶ Dexter & △ Sinister.   sub. the aequation from the Given Longitude.

Understand the same in the *Semi-Sextile*, and *Quincunx* (if you have a desire to Direct to those Aspects.)

VII. This Method is now generally received, and approved of by most modern Astrologers; yet there are some particular Persons, and those very able Artists, and skilful Mathematicians that are not well satisfied herein. Amongst whom, the Learned *Morine* in his *Astrologia Gallica* doth largely discourse, and thinks it absurd to account a Planets Aspects that hath Latitude in two Circles. But my ingenious Friend, Mr. *John Eyres* [*a Person well versed in Astronomy, as also in most parts of the Nathematicks*] hath made a large progress, and diligent search into this Subject, being put upon it chiefly, because that in Rectification and after Directions, in divers Genitures the Accidents and Directions did not so nearly agree together as was expected; and this (many times) when neither contrary Directions, Revolutions, or Profections did either hasten, or retard the same.

VIII. A second Motive was, he considered that most other wayes had been tryed before, and did not answer expectation as he supposed, neitber was this way of his ever assayed by any (as he could understand) before; for *Morine* (whose Method doubtless had its first Conception from the same Foundation) was not then extant.

IX. A third Motive that put him on scrutiny in this case, was this consideration, that the reason of the difference of the *Dexter*, and *Sinister* Aspect, is, because a Planets in the one doth dart, and direct his Beams forward; and in the other relinquish, and draw them after him: and therefore he concluded the Rayes were principally in the Orbit (or way wherein the Planets continually make their Revolution.)

X. Here follows his way of Operation in five Propositions (with their Mathematical Demonstrations) how to take the Planets Latitudes in their Aspects, performed by the *Caroline Tables*, which I thought convenient to Communicate to the true Sons of *Urania*.

Prop. 1. Substract the place or the Aspect from the place or the *Sun*, and the remainer call the Elongation.

Prop. 2. Substract the praecession of the Aequinoctial at the time of the Nativity, from the place of the Aspect, so have you the place of the Syderial Longitude thereof; with which in the Tables take out the Correspondent Logarithme Distance from the *Sun*, viz. the Geocentrick, Long. or Longitude from the first Star of *Aries*.

Prop. 3. To the Complement Arithmetical, of which Logarithme add the Logarithme Distance of the Earth from the *Sun* at Birth, and the Sine of the Elongation, taken by the first Proposition; and the Sum will be the Sine of the Prostapharesis. Which,

When the Elongation is more then 6 Signs add.
                       less   subtract.

to, or from the Sydereal Longitude of the Aspects; and with the Sum, or Remainer, enter the Table again, and thereby take out the Correct Logar. distance from the *Sun*, wherewith Iterate your third Operation again, and the Result will be the Correct *Prostapharesis*; which again add, or subtract to, or from the mean Sydereal Longitude of the Aspect according to the former Rule; and the Sum, or difference will be the Excentrique Distance, wherewith in the Tables take out, and reserve the inclination of the Orb.

Prop. 4. Add, or Substract this Correct Prostapharesis, to, or from the Elongation, contrary to the former Rule, *viz.* If more than 6 Signs, substract; if less, add, and you will have the Anomaly Orb.

Prop. 5. Then reason thus, *viz.* As the Sine of the Anamoly Orb, is to the Sine of the Elongation; so the Tangent of the Inclination, to the Tangent of the Latitude sought.

Illustration by Example.

In a certain Nativity *Mars* was in *Scorpio* 13 deg. 20 m. his *Quartile* Aspect falls in 13d. 20m. *Aquarius*; and at that time the precession of the Aequinoctial was 27d. 52 m. and the *Sun* in 26d. *Cancer*.

(1.) Reserve the Log. dist. 5006962
☉ from the ⊕ at Birth.
Long. ☉   15s. 26d. 56m.
Long. Asp. 10. 13. 20. subst.
Elongation 05. 13. 36.

(2.)   s. d. m.
Long Asp.   10. 13. 20
Preces. sub. 0. 27. 52
Syde. Long.   9. 15. 28.

Logar. dist. of ♂ from the ☉ correspondent, 5141867 which you will find in Tab. Loc. Heliocent. *Martis* the neerest Number, 9s. 15d. 30m. 43s

(3.) As the distance of ♂ from the ☉   4858133
     in that Longit. Comp. Arith.
To the distance of the Earth   5006962   add
     from the ☉ at Birth.
So the Sine of the mean Elongation   9450775
     5s. 13d. 36m.
To the Sine of the mean Prost. 11d. 57m. 9315870

Which substracted according to the third Proposition, there will remain 9s. 3d. 31m. the Syderial Longitude first Corrected, and the distance from the ☉   5144727.

The Logar. 5144727. Comp. Arith. is   4855273
The Logar distance from the ☉   5006962   add
Sine of 5s. 13d. 36m. is   9450775
Sine of the Cor. Prost. 11d. 52m. is   9313010
which is equal to the Paralax of the Orb.

This again substracted, there will remain 9s. 3d. 36m. the Syderel Longitude Correct; and the Inclination against the same is 1d. 48m.

[*The Sydereal Long. is the Dist. from the first ✶ of ♈.*]

(4.) But contrariwise, if you add this Correct Prostaphaeresis to the Elong. then you will have the Anomaly Orb 5s. 25d. 28m. or Comutation. Having now gotten the Comutation, Elongation, and Inclination, the Lat. is easily had according to the Common Rule given in the Table.

(5.) The sine thereof Comp. Arith.   110216
Elongation Sine thereof   945077   add
Tangent of Inclinations, 1d. 48m.   849729
Tangent of Latitude South 6d. 24m.   905022

[*This is but the Converse to that of Computing the Planets Longitude; for in finding their Heliocentrick Longitude, you thereby gain their Geocentrick places; but here the Geocentrick place is taken first, and the Heliocentrick Longitude and Latitude that the Planet will have in the place where the Aspect falls, found from thence.*]

XI. Let this way be made use of in such Genitures that the Births are certainly known, (or very nearly) and Directions will not agree the old way; this Operation may be thought tedious by some. But note, that the second Work for the correct Prostaphaeresis may be omitted in *Saturn* and *Jupiter*; for in those Planets the difference is but small, and there needs no proportion to be made for the Logar. Distance from the *Sun*, nor the Inclination; but take it at the nearest whole Degrees, as is done in the aroresaid Example.

XII. But for the Inferiour Planets, *Venus*, and *Mercury*, take the Latitude the same in quantity, and the same denonination as in the *Conjunction* paralel to the Ecliptick in all their Aspects (for there will be an extraordinary disparity in conferring their Directions, and the Accidents any other way) because their Orbs (especially *Mercury*'s) are small, and far within the Orbit of the Earth, and make their Revolution (about their Centre the *Sun*) in a far shorter time; and should Aspects be taken in their Orbits, it would be absurd. Therefore their Rayes, or Aspects are chiefly directed, or remitted by the motion of the Earth, or *Sun*, being always upon the Eclicktick Line. Now the Reason why the Planets have Rayes allowed, and not the Fixed Stars, is, because they have Motion and the Stars none.

XIII. For the *Moon*, Substract the *Dragons Head* from the Aspect; and accordingly find the Latitude, as in the *Conjunction*, &c. Or more easily by the Ephemeris you may most readily find the exact Latitude of the *Moon* in all her Aspects, both Dexter, and Sinister, (as well as in the *Conjunction*) which you are to observe in Directing unto any or them, as for Example.

XIV. If you would Direct to the *Sextile*, or *Trine* of the *Moon*, search in the Ephemeris what Latitude the *Moon* had when she came to those places where the Aspects fell; and find her Right, or Oblique Ascention, with that Latitude under the Pole of the Significator, and so work out the Directions; thus, in the *Moon*'s Aspects it is plain, and easie to be performed, although in the three Superiours there is a little more trouble; and whatever may be said in contradiction of this way in the other Planets, yet nothing can be objected concerning this of the *Moon*, because she is a secondary Planet, always moving about the Earth, and respecting that for her common Node, or Centre, as the Primary Planets do the *Sun*.

XV. This demonstrative Figure wlll sufficiently inform the Fancy. For that Circle where the Characters of the Aspects are set, is the Orblt of the Planet, wherein the Centre of his Body (and according to Computation, the very Apex of all his Aspects) are in one part, or other to be found; The prickt Circle is parallel to the Ecliptick tnough not Con-centrick with it: The Intersection of those two Circles are the Nodes of the Planet; and their distance, the Planets Inclination, or Latitude at the *Sun*. The innermost Circle is the Orbite of the Earth, and her place at •, from whence the Planets place, and Aspects are formed; the Center thereof is the *Sun*. Thus you have, in as brief a Method as could be, the manner of Computation, as also the Demonstration.

XVI. Now that the former Rule for the three Superiours, *Saturn*, *Jupiter*, and *Mars*, is Rational, and Universal, may be seen in this; for having the same things known, *viz.* the *Sun*'s Longitude, and Distance, the Precession, and Longitude of a Planet; you may thereby find the Planets Latitude (as by tryal wlll appear.)

Morine in his Thesis seemeth to speak the same thing about the Latitude of the Aspects, although in practice he cometh short thereof, I suppose not having a facil way to perform it by; For indeed before Mr. *Sreet*'s Tables were made publique it was difficult, and exceeding troublesome by any Tables now extant. From this brief Method may particular Tables be made for each Planet. Thus having this opportunity, I thought good to make publique these new Proposals, which (if rightly understood) cannot but be very acceptable to all lovers or Art. And so I proceed. Unto,

SECT. III.

Observations to be noted in Directing.

What a Significator, or Promittor is, I have already shewed; but in what order you are to direct them shall in the next place be plainly discovered, and thus laid down, *viz.*

I. In Directing the Ascendant, or Horoscope, you are to perform your Operations by Oblique Ascentions only, taken under the Latitude of the place of Birth, *viz.* having the Oblique Ascention of the Ascendant, find also the Oblique Ascention of your Promittor (with Latitude, if he have any) under the same Elevation of the Pole aforesaid: and lastly, Substract the Obllque Ascention of your Significator (*viz.* Ascendant) from the Oblique Ascention of your Promittor (*viz.* the Body, or Aspect of a Planet) and the remainer is the Ark or Direction required. See.the 25*th* Aph. of *Ptol.* Centiloq.

II. In Directing of the Meridian Circle, *(viz.* the *M.C.* or *I.C.* or Cusps of the tenth, or fourth Houses) that is alwayes performed by Right Ascentions. Thus, substract the *R.A.* of the *M.C.* or *I.C.* from the *R.A.* of your Promittor, (alwayes regarding his Latitude, if he be not in the Ecliptick) and the remainer is the Ark (or Arch) of Direction sought, which you are to measure out into Time; as shall be shewed in its proper place.

Note, As the Ascendant is Directed, the same Method must be used in Directing the West Angle, or seventh House, which is opposit to the Ascendant; and as the Angles, so any Planet Posited upon the Cusps of any of the four Angles, &c.

III. To Direct the *Sun, Moon,* and *Part of Fortune,* you are to observe another Method (*viz.*) The Elevation of the Pole above the Circles of Position they are upon, must first be obtained, provided they are not posited upon the very Cusp of some of the Houses; for then you have it given without farther trouble, but this seldom happens. The Rule is as followeth.

First, having the Planets Longitude, and Latitude; (exactly reduced, as hath been shewed.) *Secondly,* Find his Declination North, or South, above or under the Earth. *Thirdly,* His Right Ascention. *Fourthly,* By that his distance from the Meridian, *(viz.* The tenth, or fourth House, according as he is plac'd under, or above the Earth.) *Fifthly,* By that the Poles Elevation above the Circle of Position. *Sixthly,* His Oblique Ascention under that Pole, if posited in the tenth, eleventh, twelfth, first, second, or third Houses; or Oblique Descention, if posited in the fourth, fifth, sixth, seventh, eighth, or ninth Houses; except you will work by the Planets opposit place in the Figure, for then you are always to make use of the Oblique Ascention only: having thus gained the Oblique Ascention of your Significator, you are also to find the Promittors Oblique Ascention under the same Pole of Position; and lastly, Substract the Signif icators Oblique Ascentton, from the Promittors; and the remainer is the Ark of Direction required. After the same manner are all the rest of the Planets to be Directed, if you would Direct them as Significators.

These things, if rightly understood, will be exceeding easie by practice; and shall be farther cleared by familiar Examples, from the precdent Exemplary Geniture.

A Synopsis of the whole Work of Directions, both Direct, and Converse, previously in this Book, which with Examples will be sufficient, I hope, to instruct the Ingenious Tyro.

SECT. IV.

Of the effects of Directions in General.

I. Let the Artist be well acquainted with the Nature, and the significations of the Planets, what they signifie of themselves, and what by Accident in any Nativity. Let them also consider their strength, and weakness therein; as also what Houses they are Lords of.

II. In the next place he ought to look upon the Directions, and consider whether they be good or bad; which is most easily discovered by considering whether they may be Benevolent or Malevolent; and especially take notice of the condition of the Promissor, and how he was Fortified, or Debilitated in the Radix; and accordingly order your Judgment concerning the signification of the Direction.

III. If the Significator, and Promissor were both strong in the Radix, and the Direction falls in a good place of the Figure, or in their Dignities, and it be also a good Direction, (*viz.*) To the *Conjunction*, *Sextile*, or *Trine* of some Benevolent Planet, &c. Then you may conclude the Effects thereof will be very Famous to the Native; and he shall receive much good from thence. But on the other side, if the Significator, and Promittor, were both weak in the Radix, and the Direction fall in their Debilities, Judge the contrary; or if a Significator, and Promittor were but meanly Fortified in the Radix, and the Direction happen to be good, and fall well; the Native may not expect that the Accidents signified thereby should take place so effectually, as otherwise they might have done, had they been also potent in the Geniture.

IV. Note farther, that a good Direction brings much Prosperity, and Happiness, along with it, to the Native; and it will be of the same kind that the Significator doth properly denote of himself, consideration had to the House he governs in the Radix, or is constituted in: and hence it will not be hard for the Artist to inform himself from what kind of Persons, or things; or of what Nature the good, promised by such a Direction, will be.

V. The Promissors signification is also to be consulted, which intimates the cause of the happiness that is promised; thus as you Judge of the Significator, in the same manner order your Judgement for the Promissor, or that Planet that promises Felicity to the Native. So if the Direction be bad, and threatens Mischief, and cross adverse Fortune to the Native; consider the Nature thereof by the signification or the Significator, as before directed; and the cause from whence the evil may arise is known from the signification of the Promissor in the Radix, not neglecting to take notice of the place wherein the Direction falls, *viz.* Both the Sign, and House of Heaven; and likewise the strength, or weakness of Significator and Promissor at the time that the Direction happens; as also what Planets then do behold them, or the Place of the Direction by Transit, &c.

[*In all Directions, consider the Age of the Native; for Events: should be accommodated to the diffeences of times.*]

VI. The Ascendant, or Horoscope, which signifies the Life of any Person in his Nativity; as also his Body, Complexion, Manners, and Affection of the Mind, is therefore Directed to his several Promittors; which if it meets with good Directions, and the Aspects, or Bodies of fortunate Planets, it denotes health, prosperity, and happiness to the Native; and much Earthly Felicity, and peace of Mind. But on the contrary, if the Ascendant meete with bad Directions, *viz.* the Bodies, or Beams of the Malevolent Planets (or Stars) which accidentally govern evil Houses in the Radix; then this Direction portends much Mischief, Sickness, or other Infirmities, or Crosses, to happen to the Native; and in fine much affliction to the Body of the same nature, or kind that those Planets denote, who are Promissors in this Direction.

VII. The *M.C.* or Mid-Heaven is directed for Preferment, Honour, Offices, Friendship from Great Persons, Trade, or Profession, also for Accidents to the Mother of the Native; with divers other things of this Nature (principally signified by this House) that may happen accidentally to the Native.

But (oftentimes) it is Directed by some Persons for Accidents relating to the Body also, as Sickness, &c. (as well as the Angle of the Horoscope) which in my Judgment is improper, unless for some Honourable Death, as Beheading, &c.

VIII. The *Sun* is directed for Honour, and Preferment, be it publique, or private; for Friendship, and Favour from Persons in power, *&c.* But more particularly it is Directed for Accidents relating to the Body, as the Health, or Sickness of the Native. The Direction of the *Sun* points out many things relating to the Estate, and Condition of the Natives Father also; and many times brings afflictions to the Body, as well as changes, and alterations, both good and bad, in his publique Concerns in the World, *&c.*

IX. The *Moon* Is Directed as a Signtricator, because she hath a large signification in the Geniture of any Person, (as well as the *Sun)* she signifies the Constitution, and Complexion; as also the Inclination and Intentions of the Native, the Natives Journeys, long, or short, Marriage; and in particular, the Estate, and Condition of the Wife; Women in general, and all near Relations, as Kinsfolks, and such like, as well Male, as Female.

X. The *Part of Fortune* is Directed for Profit, and Increase, or loss of Estate, according as it meets with the Aspects, or Conjunctions of good, or bad Planets (or Stars;) if the *Part of Fortune* meets with a good and fortunate Promissor, and the Direction falls in a good place of Heaven, where they are either, or both or them well dignified; this promises an augmentation of Riches to the Native; but if he meets with the evil Aspects of the Infortunes, Judge the contrary.

XI. These five *Hylegiacals* are only Directed (usually) in any Geniture, but many times those those that affect Curiosity will also Direct the other Planets. Their significations (being Directed as Significators) are generally thus, as Authors Write.

First *Saturn* is Directed, to signifie the Fruits of the Earth, Inheritances, Possessions, Buildings, *&c.* Fears, and Jealousies, *&c.* And this according to the strength, or weakness of *Saturn* in the Nativity.

Jupiter is Directed for Wealth, Prosperity, Advancement, *&c.* Children in general, Wisdom, Prudence, Temperance, *&c.*

Mars is Directed for Courage and boldness of Spirit, *viz.* Animosity, Victory, War, Contentions, and Lawsuits, as also the Estate and condition of Brethren and such like.

Venus is Directed for all kind of Pleasures, and Delights, Love, Matrimony, Costly Ornaments, *&c.*, and for the Female Sex in general.

Mercury is Directed for Learning, Ingenuity, the Understanding; as also for Merchandizing, and Trade, Industry, Journeys, *&c.* Lastly, for younger Brethren and such like.

XII. These are but general significations which the Planets properly declare of themselves, barely considered. But you are to moderate your Judgement, according to the Houses they are accidentally Posited in, in any Gentture; as also to consider what Houses they chiefly govern, as is before intimated: Thus, the Premises being but well considered, you cannot fail to give a most significant, and rationat Judgement upon any Direction whatever; as also perfectly understand the true intent, and meaning of whatsoever is signified by Directions in general.

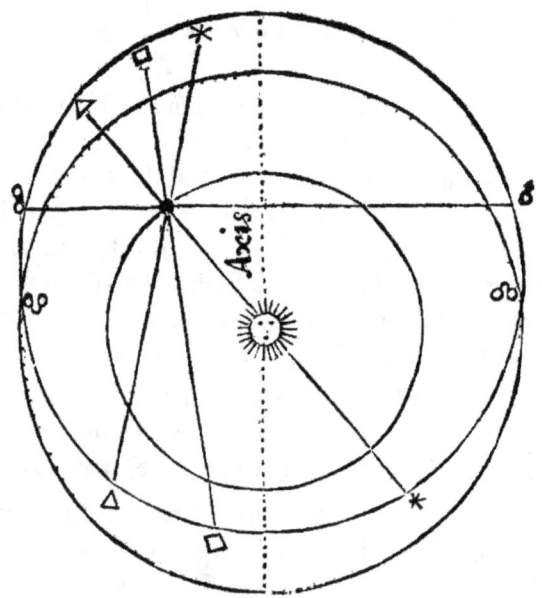

XIII. If you would know how long the force of a Direction shall continue, you are to consider the strength, or weakness, both of Significator, and Promittor in the Geniture, if they are both strong, or essentially dignified therein, the effects of the Direction shall powerrully manifest it self; and whatever is promised thereby, shall take place effectually, and continue durable, until such time as the Significator meets with another Promittor.

XIV. But if they are but weak in the Radix, the effects of this Direction will be inconsiderable, and leave but a small shew of its force upon the Native; if the Significator were strongest, the Direction operates and with much ease the Native attains to that good thereby signified; if the Promissor were strongest, although the Direction may take place, yet it shall not be so forcible as is promised, neither will it be answerable to the pains, and industry that the Native uses, in attaining the good thereby signified.

XV. Observe also that if the Infortunate Planets happen to be Promissors in any Direction, and therein threaten some eminent danger unto the Native; this evil will not afflict the Native, and take place to the height, if so be they were strong, and potent in the Radix. But if they were debilitated therein, you may expect the greater infelicity to happen; 'tis also to be observed that *Jupiter*, and *Venus* may accidentally happen to be Infortunes; and *Saturn*, and *Mars*, Fortunes in some Mens Genitures, according to the Houses they govern, or their Position in the Figure.

XVI. If two Directions happen to be in force together, and operate at one, and the same time, the one being good, the other exceeding bad; consider which of them is the strongest and to which the Revolution of the Year doth best agree, and Judge that Direction will operate most forcibly; which if it be the good Direction, it will much mittigate (if not quite extinguish) the effects of the bad; or if the bad Direction, 'twill overpower the force of the good one, so that the shadow thereof will only appear, and the effects will not be considerable. [*Here I intended to have Inserted the effects of Directions, but the Book being already swelled beyond my expectation, I must forbear, and refer my Reader to the perusal of my Honoured Friend Mr.* Lilly's *Introduction (which I presume most Artists have already by them) where they will find the general signification of Directions to the Bodies, and Aspects of the Planets very Copiously handled, and more full than in any Author, either in* English, *or* Latine.]

CHAP. XXIV

Of Directions in Nativities, and their effects, according to Morinus.

Since 'tis certain that the Term of Directions, *i.e.* the places of the Significators, and Promittors are fixed in the *Primum Mobile*, as appeareth by the Planets, Transits by the same; and that the effect of a Direction is neither from the Significator, or Promator alone, but from both concurring, and that such concourse cannot be of Terms immovable; hence arises no small difficulty, to apprehend how the effects come to be produced, and break forth into Act, after they have so long lain hid in power.

First, for the untying which Knot we say,

I. The several Cusps of the Houses, the Planets, and their Aspects at the Moment of Birth, are actually determined to some particular thing in respect of the Native, but potentially to divers other things; so *Saturn* in the first house is actually determined to the Natives temperament, health, manners, ingenuity, &c. But potentially to all Accidents represented by the other Houses respectively, as to cause Diseases by Direction or the *Sun* in the twelfth, &c. And *Jupiter* in the eleventh is actually determined concerning the Natives Friends, but potentially concerning the Natives Honours, which he is found to cause by Direction to the Mid-heaven, and so of the rest.

Secondly, That the Influx of the Coelestial Figure at the Moment of Birth is impressed on the sensible part of the Native, not confusedly, but distinctly; that is as the parts of Heaven, and the Planets are determined in the Figure, so is the Influential Character of that Figure in the Native, observing vertually the same scituation, order, and distances of Significator, and Promittor, as are found in the Figure it self, erected for the Longitude, and Latitude of the place of Birth: so that the Coelestial Figure is not only the external Principle of Life to the Native, but likewise the efficient Cause of a like internal Principle in the Native; whence arises that manifest, yet admirable consent between Heaven and the Native, in doing, and suffering.

Thirdly, That every Significator in the Figure of Heaven, whether Planet, or Cusp, Ruling by its Vertue, as well essential, as accidental in the Native, by imprinting his Character, is some Principle of Life, Action, Marriage, or Passion; to which, by a potential Determination, the other parts of the Figure, whether Planets, or Aspects, are referred; so that such things will happen concerning that Principle, as the said places are naturally, or accidentally determined unto, and in the same order of time, as is the distance of those places from such Principles, so as the nearest will soon be brought out of Power into Act, *i.e.* will first produce its effect; As if there follow the *Horoscope*, first *Mercury* being Lord thereof, then the Quadrat of *Mars* Lord of the eighth House, then the *Trine* of *Jupiter* Lord of the ninth; From the first Direction the Native will be inclinable to Learning, or some other Discipline, afterwards; by the second he will be lyable to a dangerous Sickness, which if he escape, the third Direction will render him much addicted to Religion, and of a very devotional temper, *&c.*

Fourthly, That since the Coelesetial Figure at Birth is a thing stable, and permanent, wherein casually and implicitely is contained the whole Life of the Native, with his Accidents; and that such Accidents admit of succession, and order, there must be some cause in Heaven thereof, which can be no other than the succession, and order of the Promittors potentially determined, in respect of the Anticedent Significators; for all determination potential, tends of it self to an actual, *i.e.* the Planets, and their Aspects are to be reduced from this potential Determination into Act, which is done by the first Revolution of the first Heaven that begins at the Moment of Birth; for which by such Natural Revolution every Promittor is brought to the Circle of Position, which each Significator possessed at that Moment of Birth, the same is actually determined to produce an effect at some time, according to the Significators nature and scituation, whereby according to the several natural Directions of the Promittor to the several Antecedent Significators, there is a Vertue successively impressed on the Native as a suppliment of the Universal impression at Birth, and which doth explain its particular Fate; and efficatiously combines, and orders the same, according to the series of time.

Fifthly, Now the effects of a Direction cannot be produced at the very Moment of the Nativity, because then the Promittor is not actually in the place of the Significator, but only potentially; and therefore its effects afterwards brought into Act by successive Motion, about so many Years from the Genesis, as the Promittor is distant in Degrees of the Aequator from the Circle of Position of the Significator; the reason whereof is thus, *viz.*

I. The determinative Vertue of the Houses to divers kinds of effects is known by Experience, now the Cusps of the Houses are Circles of Position; and that Circle of Position, on which a Planet, or other Significator falls at Moment or Birth, receives from such a Planet, or Significator, a peculiar Vertue in respect of the Native, concerning things belonging to that House, according to the nature, and state of such a Planet, and this Vertue is impressed in the Native at the Moment of Birth; and therefore when the Promittor by the first Revolution of the first Heaven, is brought to the same Circle, it is determined for the producing an effect at some certain time, as aforesaid; and the Vertue of such determination being made by successive Motion, is likewise impressed on the Native; and there being both in Heaven, and the Native such a Concourse, and Union of the Promittors, and Significators Vertues, as they are successilvely in the same Circle of Position; it thence come to pass, that in the time mark'd out by the Ark of that Motion something happens to the Native, of the nature of the Significator, and Promittor in things essentially signified by that House, wherein such a Circle of Position is found, from all which it is evident.

Sixthly, That though the Terms of Directions remain fix'd, and unmovable in the Heavens, yet their effects may be produced on Earth, *viz.* in Man, because by the Radical Influx of the Coelestial Figure at the Moment of Birth, and the first Revolution of Heaven afterwards, there is made, and impressed on the Native a Concourse of these Terms, efficacious for the producing effects at a certain designed, and limited time, *viz.* after so many annual Revolutions of the *Sun*, as the Ark of Direction contains of his Diurnal ones, or thereabouts. Thus it appears that the effects of a Direction is not produced solely by the impression made at the Moment of Birth, nor from Heaven alone, but from both conspiring; and that too not without the actual Concourse of annual (and monthly) *Revolutions*, and *Transits* which are required; and again produces the Vertue of the Directions Imprinted at the Nativity into Act; and thence it comes to pass that the effects not always happen precizely at the time signified by the Ark of Direction, but are sometimes hastened, or retarded, and fall out before, or after it.

Seventhly, A *Significator* is nothing but a Coelestial substance, *i.e.* a part of Heaven, or a Planet signifying of it self, by reason of its Determination, concerning some kind of Accidents of a Native; whence it is also said to be the Significator of such a kind or Accident, so far as the same is to be effected by the Direction. Hence it appears there are so many Significators for *Directions,* as there are Planets and Houses; to which if we add the *Part of Fortune*, there will be twenty in all.

Eightlty, But note by Planets we mean not the Bodies of the Planets, but their fixed places in *Prime Mobile*, or those parts or the *Primum Mobile*, determined to the nature of the said Planets at Moment of Birth; note farther, that each Planet may have as many significations as it hath wayes to be determined concerning the Native, as being in one House, and Lord of another; it will signifie the different Accidents belonging to each of those Houses, and therefore shall be Directed for them both; so also every kind of Accident hath several Significators, as Life by the *Horoscope* and its Lord, or a Planet in the first, or its disposter, *&c.*

Ninthly, A *Promissor* is a part or the *Primum Mobile*, determined concerning some certain kind of those Accidents happening to a Native, or the second Term of a Direction, as it by it self presages something to come concerning any thing represented by the Significator, or to the Native in respect of such a Subject; as *Mars* concerning Life represented by the *Horoscope*, portends danger to the Natives Life (or to the Native in respect or his Life) by some Disease, Wound, or Death, *&c.*

CHAP. XXV.

Of the Measure of Time in Directions.

I. *Ptolomy*'s Measure is for every degree of the Aequator, to allow one year, and for every minute 6 dayes, 2 hours 6 minutes. And so 365 dayes, 6 hours contain one whole degree, or 60 minutes, as appears by this following Table. [*Ed. Shown on the facing page.*]

This Opinion of *Ptolomy*'s, (as to the Measure of Time in Directions) continued without contradiction, until the last Age.

II. Then *Antonius Maginus*, a Learned *Italian*, and Mathematician, began to question it (as Mr. *Lilly* relates) and affirms that the Measure of Time ought to be taken from the true, and apparent Motion of the *Sun*, and not from his simple Motion; as you may read in *Maginus* his *Primum Mobile*, Fol. 51. So then he concludes that the difference between the *Sun*'s Right Ascension at the Birth, and the same hour, and minute the next day following, shall be the Measure of Time for a Year. By which Method a Table may be fitted to any particular Geniture, or you may see a general Table thereof, page, 711, of *Christian Astrology*; this Measure hath been in great esteem with some able Artists of this Nation.

III. But a third Measure of Time (and now generally approved as best) is that of *Valentine Naibod*, a singular Mathematician; which is grounded upon the *Sun*'s mean Motion, to be the Measure of Time for a Year. And by that Rule one whole degree gives one year, 5 dayes, 8 hours, and 59 minutes, 8 seconds gives one compleat Year; and so every minute gives 6 dayes, and about 4 hours. A Table whereof you may see in the followlng pages.

IV. This last Measure by all Modern Authors approved as the best, and *Maginus* highly esteems of it, and looks upon it as the most certain Measure of Time hitherto made use of in general, and so do I. Now there is no considerable difference in any of those Measures of Time, and either of them may be indifferently used; for in some Nativities the one (it may be) wlll agree better than another, and therefore every Man may use the Measure which pleases him best.

\multicolumn{4}{c}{A Table of the Measure of Time in Directions, according to *Ptolomy*.}			
M.	D. H. M.	M.	D. H. M.
1	6 2 6	31	188 17 6
2	12 4 12	32	194 19 12
3	18 6 18	33	200 21 18
4	24 8 24	34	206 23 24
5	30 10 30	35	213 01 30
6	36 12 36	36	219 03 36
7	42 14 42	37	225 05 42
8	48 16 48	38	231 07 48
9	54 18 54	39	237 09 54
10	60 21 0	40	243 12 00
11	66 23 6	41	249 14 06
12	73 1 12	42	255 16 12
13	79 3 18	43	261 18 18
14	85 5 24	44	267 20 24
15	91 7 30	45	273 22 30
16	97 9 36	46	280 00 36
17	103 11 42	47	286 02 42
18	109 13 48	48	292 04 48
19	115 15 54	59	298 06 54
20	121 18 00	50	304 09 00
21	127 20 6	51	310 11 06
22	133 22 12	52	316 13 12
23	140 0 18	53	222 15 18
24	146 2 24	54	328 17 24
25	152 4 30	55	334 19 30
26	158 6 36	56	340 21 36
27	164 8 42	57	346 23 42
28	170 10 40	58	353 01 48
29	176 12 54	59	359 03 54
30	182 15 0	60	365 06 00

A Table of the Measure of Time in Degrees, and Mintues, for finding the Years, and Dayes of a Direction, according to Naibod.

Min	D H	Deg	Y. D. H.	Deg	Y. D. H.	Deg	Y. D. H.
1	6. 4	1	1. 5. 8.	31	31.165.23	61	61.326.13
2	12. 8	2	2. 10.17	32	32.171. 7	62	62.331.21
3	18.13	3	3. 16. 1	33	33.176.16	63	63.337. 6
4	24.17	4	4. 21.10	34	34.182. 0	64	64.342.14
5	30.21	5	5. 26.18	35	35.187. 8	65	65.347.23
6	37. 1	6	6. 32. 3	36	36.192.17	66	66.353. 7
7	43. 6	7	7. 37.11	37	37.198. 1	67	67.358.16
8	49.10	8	8. 42.20	38	38.203. 9	68	68.364. 0
9	55.14	9	9. 48. 4	39	39.208.18	69	70. 4. 3
10	61.18	10	10. 53.13	40	40.214. 3	70	71. 9.11
11	67.23	11	11. 58.21	41	41.219.11	71	72. 14.20
12	74. 3	12	12. 64. 6	42	42.224.20	72	73. 20. 4
13	80. 7	13	13. 69.14	43	43.230. 4	73	74. 25.13
14	86.11	14	14. 74.23	44	44.235.13	74	75. 30.21
15	92.16	15	15. 80. 7	45	45.240.21	75	76. 36. 5
16	98.20	16	16. 85.16	46	46.246. 6	76	77. 41.14
17	105. 0	17	17. 91. 0	47	47.251.14	77	78. 48.22
18	111. 4	18	18. 96. 8	48	48.256.23	78	79. 52. 7
19	117. 9	19	19.101.17	49	49.262. 7	79	80. 57.15
20	123.13	20	20.107. 1	50	50.267.16	80	81. 62.24
21	129.17	21	21.112.10	51	51.273. 0	81	82. 68. 8
22	135.21	22	22.117.18	52	52.278. 8	82	83. 73.17
23	142. 1	23	23.123. 3	53	53.283.17	83	84. 79. 1
24	148. 6	24	24.128.11	54	21.289. 1	84	85. 84.10
25	154.10	25	25.133.20	55	55.294.10	85	86. 89.18
26	160.14	26	26.139. 4	56	56.199.18	86	87. 95. 3
30	185. 7	27	27.144.13	57	57.305. 3	87	88.100.11
40	247. 2	28	28.149.21	58	58.310.11	88	89.105.20
50	308.20	29	29.155. 6	59	59.315.20	89	90.111. 4
60	365.14	30	30.160.14	60	60.321. 4	90	91.116.13

The Years and Dayes of the Ark of Direction *may be found according to* Naibod's *Measure without this Table, thus; let the Ark of* Direction *be 26d. 18m. the* Logist. Logar. *thereof is* [3582] *from whence Substract the Lo-gist. Logar. of 59m. 8s. (the Sun's Mean Diurnal Motion) viz.* [6s.] *and the remainder is* [3519] *the Logist Log. of 26d. 41m. This 26d. is 26 Years, and 41 min. in Ptolomy's Table gives 249 dayes, 14h. 6m. & sic in aljis.*

Clavis Astrologiae Elimita, The Key to Astrology New Filed

A Table for the Converting the Years, and Dayes of an Accident into Time, according to Valentine Naibod's *Measure.*							
D.	M. S.	Y.	D. M. S.	Y.	D. M. S.	Y.	D. M. S.
1	00.10	1	0.59. 8	31	30.33.18	61	60. 7.28
2	00.19	2	1.58.12	32	31.32.26	62	61. 6.36
3	00.29	3	2.57.25	33	32.31.35	63	62. 5.45
4	00.39	4	3.56.33	34	33.30.43	64	63. 4.53
5	00.48	5	4.55.42	35	34.29.51	65	64. 4. 1
6	00.58	6	5.54.50	36	35.29. 0	66	65. 3.10
7	01.08	7	6.53.58	37	36.28. 8	67	66. 2.18
8	01.18	8	7.53.07	38	37.27.16	68	67. 1.26
9	01.27	9	8.52.15	39	38.26.25	69	68. 0.35
10	01.37	10	9.51.23	40	39.25.33	70	68.59.43
20	03.14	11	10.50.31	41	40.24.42	71	69.58.51
30	04.51	12	11.49.40	42	41.23.50	72	70.58. 0
40	06.29	13	12.48.48	43	42.22.58	73	71.57. 8
50	08.06	14	13.47.57	44	43.22. 6	74	72.56.16
60	09.43	15	14.47. 5	45	44.21.15	75	73.55.24
70	11.20	16	15.46.13	46	45.20.23	76	74.54.32
80	12.57	17	16.45.22	47	46.19.31	77	75.53.42
90	14.34	18	17.44.30	48	47.18.40	78	76.52.50
100	16.11	19	18.43.38	49	48.17.48	79	77.51.58
120	19.25	20	19.42.47	50	49.16.56	80	78.51.07
140	22.39	21	20.41.55	51	50.16. 5	81	79.50.15
160	25.53	22	21.41.03	52	51.15.13	82	80.49.23
180	29.08	23	22.40.12	53	52.14.22	83	81.48.31
200	32.33	24	23.39.20	54	53.13.30	84	82.47.40
230	37.13	25	24.38.28	55	54.12.38	85	83.46.48
260	42. 4	26	25.37.37	56	55.11.46	86	84.45.57
290	46.56	27	26.36.45	57	56.10.55	87	85.45. 5
320	51.48	28	27.35.53	58	57.10. 3	88	86.44.15
350	56.39	29	28.35. 1	59	58. 9.11	89	87.43.22
365	59. 8	30	29.34.10	60	59. 8.20	90	88.42.30

This, and the foregoing Table needs no farther explanation than the Titles direct, being plain and obvious to a mean apprehension.

A General Aequation Table to be added to the Ark of Direction, aocording to Naibod's *Measure of Time.*						
	Min.			Min.		Min.
Ar.Dir.	Aeq.add		Ar.Dir.	Aeq.add	Ar.Dir.	Aeq.add
1	1		31	27	61	53
2	2		32	28	62	54
3	3		33	29	63	55
4	3		34	30	64	56
5	4		35	31	65	57
6	5		36	32	66	58
7	6		37	32	67	59
8	7		38	33	68	60
9	8		39	34	69	60
10	9		40	35	70	61
11	10		41	36	71	62
12	11		42	37	72	63
13	11		43	38	73	64
14	12		44	39	74	65
15	13		45	40	75	65
16	14		46	40	76	66
17	15		47	41	77	67
18	16		48	42	78	68
19	17		49	43	79	69
20	17		50	44	80	69
21	18		51	45	81	70
22	19		52	45	82	71
23	20		53	46	83	72
24	21		54	47	84	73
25	22		55	48	85	74
26	23		56	49	86	75
27	24		57	50	87	75
28	25		58	51	88	76
29	25		59	52	89	77
30	26		60	53	90	78

The use of this Table is plain, and easie, thus, viz.

I. Let the Ark of Direction be supposed 29d. 30m. seek 29 under the TItle, Ark of Direction, and against it I find 25m. which is always to be added to the Ark of Direction given; and it makes the former Number 29d. 55m. the Aequated Arch. So then I conclude that at 29 years, 11 months the Direction wIll hit. And Here it is to be noted, that if an Accident happen within the compass of a Month, either before, or after the Direction, you may, notwithstanding, conclude the Nativity is exactly Rectified; for indeed it is as near as an Artist will presume to go, though many times it may fall out nearer, but very rarely.

Another Example for Practice.

II. Suppose the Ark of Direction be 32d. 12m. I enter the Table always against the whole degrees of Direction in the lesser Column, Intituled *Arch Direct.* and there I seek the Number 32d. against which I find 28m. to be added, and it makes the aforesaid Arch 32d. 40m. then I repair to the Table of *Ptolomy*'s Measure, allowing for every degree, one year; and entering the Table wtth 40m. I find against it 243 days, 12 hours. So that the Direction should take place at 32 years, 243 days, &c. Thus having aequated your Arch of Direction, you have the years, and days thereof by inspection, according to *Naibod's* Measure.

III. And hence a Table may be fitted Particular to any Geniture by the help of *Ptolomy's* Table, as for Example in the proposed Geniture, The Native was Born *March* the 12*th*. in the aforesaid Table against 1m. in the first Column, I find 6 days, &c. Therefore in my prepared Table following I set against 1m. *March* 18. against 2m. *March* the 24*th*, and so on as the first Table directs; and is easily understood by this following Example.

A fitted Table to the Exemplary Geniture for the more ready finding the Day of a Direction agreeable to the odd Minutes of the Aequated Arch.							A Table of the Years of our Lord Correspondent to the Years of the Natives Age, &c.			
M	Months	D	M	Months	M		Aet	Anno D	Aet	AnnoD
1	March	18	31	Septem.	16		0	1650	31	1681
2		24	32		22		1	1651	32	1682
3		30	33		28		2	1652	33	1683
4	April	5	34	Octob.	5		3	1653	34	1684
5		11	35		11		4	1654	35	1685
6		17	36		17		5	1655	36	1686
7		23	37		23		6	1656	37	1687
8		29	38		29		7	1657	38	1688
9	May	5	39	Nov.	4		8	1658	39	1689
10		11	40		10		9	1659	40	1690
11		18	41		16		10	1660	41	1691
12		24	42		22		11	1661	42	1692
13		30	43		28		12	1662	43	1693
14	June	5	44	Decem.	5		13	1663	44	1694
15		11	45		11		14	1664	45	1695
16		17	46		17		15	1665	46	1696
17		23	47		23		16	1666	47	1697
18		29	48		29		17	1667	48	1698
19	July	5	49	January	4		18	1668	49	1699
20		11	50		10		19	1569	50	1700
21		17	51		16		20	1670	51	1701
22		24	52		22		21	1671	52	1702
23		30	53		28		22	1672	53	1703
24	August	5	54	Febru.	3		23	1673	54	1704
25		11	55		10		24	1674	55	1705
26		17	56		16		25	1675	56	1706
27		23	57		22		26	1676	57	1707
28		29	58		28		27	1677	58	1708
29	Septem.	4	59	March	6		28	1678	59	1709
30		10	60		12		29	1679	60	1710
		Tt 2					30	1680		

The use of the Table is thus.

I. In the Exemplary Nativity I find the *M. C.* is Directed to the *Conjunction* of *Venus*, and the *Ark of Direction* is 35d. 7m. the *Aequation* for 35d. is 31m. to be added to the 7m. of the *Ark of Direction;* and the sum is 35d. 38m. the Aequated Arch of Direction, here 35d. gives 35 years; and 38m. In *Ptolomy's* Table gives 231 days, and near 8 hours from the day of Birth, for the time of Initiation of the Direction; and in the fitted Table if you enter with 38m. it points out October the 29th. and in the other Table of Years adjoyning against 35 years of the

Natives Age you will find 1685. & sic in alijs.

II. By this Method the *Artist* ts freed from the trouble of Collecting the dayes of the Year from the Birth into a Table, according to the old Method; and afterward make two, or three Operations from *Naibod*'s Table of Measure to find the years, and dayes that a *Direction* begins to operate here 'tis done by Inspection, and altogether as exact, seldome differing above two, or three dayes, a thing inconsiderable in this matter.

III. *There is another Measure of Time which seems very Rational*, and here I commend it to the Practice of all Curious Artists as the most excellent *Measure of Time* this day in use; for it has been much practised by some Curious Searchers into the verity of *Directions*, and verified to admiration; here let the Student observe that by this Method every *Nativity* wlll have something a different Measure of Time, which depends wholly upon the Motion of the *Sun*, as shall be shewed at large.

IV. The Rule to Form a Table, is thus; Take the apnarent *Right Ascension* of the *Sun* from the day of the Nativity (be it more or less than equal degrees) day by day, forward on; as thus, let the difference of *R.A.* of the *Sun* from the day of Birth to ten dayes after compleat, be the Measure of Time for ten Years, &c. This may be brought into practice, and fitted to any particular Geniture by this following Method, viz. Take the *R. A.* of the *Sun* at Noon for the day of Birth, and the like the next day after, and so on *tor* 70 or 80 dayes; and then take the Complement of the daily difference from the *R. A.* to equal degrees, and put them into a Table; and so you have an Aequation Table to be used as before directed. Now to make the business more plain, and because this Method is Noval, and known but to very few, I have inserted two Tables thereof the better to Illustrate this new Measure, which take as followeth.

V. *Examples of making Aequation Tabtes to be used with the Ark of Direction, viz. sometimes Substracted from, and sometimes Added thereunto, according as the Difference of the daily Right Ascension of the* Sun *increases, or decreases more, or less than 60 minutes. This first Example is for* Novemb. 9. 1645. *and the* Suns *place from* Durets Ephemerides.

Dayes	☉s.place	☉s R.A.	Dif.R.A.	Aeq.Sub.	Ar.Dir.
Nov.	d. m.	d. m.	d. m.	d. m.	Years
9	27 ♏ 21	235. 13	00. 00	00. 00	0
10	28. 32	236. 15	01. 02	00. 02	1
11	29. 33	237. 18	02. 05	00. 05	2
12	00 ♐ 34	238. 22	03. 09	00. 09	3
13	01. 35	239. 27	04. 14	00. 14	4
14	02. 36	240. 31	05. 18	00. 18	5
17	05. 39	243. 44	08. 31	00. 31	8
21	09. 43	248. 2	12. 49	00. 49	12
25	13. 47	252. 24	17. 11	01. 11	16
22	17. 52	256. 48	21. 35	01. 35	20
Decé 3	21. 57	261. 14	26. 01	02. 01	24
7	26. 2	265. 40	30. 27	02. 27	28
11	00 ♑ 7	270. 8	34. 55	02. 55	32
15	04. 12	274. 35	39. 22	03. 22	36
19	08. 18	279. 3	43. 50	03. 50	40
A	B	C	D	E	F

The Titles explain the several Columns, and note that this Aequation is to be Substracted from the *Ark of Direction*, because the difference of *R. A.* for 24 hours is more than 60 min. or l deg. and here you see that Column *D* - Col. *F*. is = to Col. *E*. which is the Aequation to be Substracted, as for Example. Suppose the Ark of Direction be 24d. 29m. against 24d. (sought in the last Col.) I find 2d 1m. in Col. *E*. to be Substracted from the aforesaid 24d. 29m. ergo the Ark Direct, is 22 Years, and almost 6 months, allowing 60 min. to a Year.

Here follows another Exemplary Table where the Aequation must be added (to the Ark of Direction to bring it into years and sixtieth parts) because the Difference of the Diurnai R. A. is less than one degree, or sixty Minutes.

Dayes	☉s.place	☉s R.A.	Dif.R.A.	Aeq.add	Ar.Dir
July	d. m.	d. m.	d. m.	d. m.	Years
9	26 ♋ 23	118. 25	00. 00	00. 00	0
13	00 ♌ 12	122. 24	03. 59	00. 01	4
17	04. 02	126. 22	07. 57	00. 03	8
21	07. 52	130. 17	11. 52	00. 08	12
25	11. 42	134. 10	15. 45	00. 15	16
29	15. 32	138. 1	19. 36	00. 24	20
Aug. 2	19. 23	141. 50	23. 25	00. 35	24
6	23. 14	145. 36	27. 11	00. 49	28
10	27. 5	149. 19	30. 54	01. 06	32
14	00 ♍ 57	153. 01	34. 36	01. 24	36
18	04. 39	156. 41	38. 16	01. 44	40
22	08. 41	160. 19	41. 54	02. 06	44
26	12. 34	163. 56	45. 31	02. 29	48
A	B	C	D	E	F

By this Table you may see that 3d. 59m. in Column *D* answers to 4 years In Column *F*; so that if the Ark of Direction be 4d. 20m. I must add 1 min. Aequation, as in Column *E*; and so the true Ark of Direction is 4 years 21 parts of 60 of another year, *viz.* 128 dayes feré: and thus this new Method of Measuring Time, (*viz.* the daily Difference or the *Sun's R.A.* for one Year,) is brought into Practice. And the like may be performed for any Geniture whatsoever, if the Artist thinks it not too much pains.

Note that both these Tables ought to be continued to 60 or 70 dayes, gradually, day by day, which I have omitted for brevity sake, those being sufficient to explain the manner of Operation.

Note that in the former Table the Difference between the Columns F and D is the Column E Substract. But here their Sum is Column F Add.

This measure of time is supposed (by some) to be that which *Maginus* hinted at many years since, and hath been much used and well approved by my loving Friend Mr. *J. E.*, who hath found (as he saith) abundance of verity therein above all other wayes; neither is it different (I suppose) from the learned *Keplers* measure, who takes the ☉s dayly motion in the Ecliptique, but this for more conveniency is the ☉s Diurnal R. A. &c. which measure of time exactly agrees with that method of Directing proposed before the beginning of this Chapter.

VII. And I have the more willingly inserted it, because Artists might experiment the truth thereof in their daily practice. But in this present work I shall wholly adhere to *Naibod*'s measure of time, and *Argol*'s method of Direction in the Aspects, by reason they have been hitherto generally received and well approved or by diverse Learned Authors, who have sufficiently verified the truth thereof in many Genitures; therefore I have chosen to Rectifie the exemplary Nativity according to *Naibod*'s measure: Where Note that it is the opinion of *Morine* who was a great Astrologer, that Converse Directions may be best made use of in Rectification, &c. [*This Converse Direction I have explained in Chapter* 23.] to conclude, observe this as a general Rule, that whatsoever measure of time you Rectifie a Nativity by, you are to use the same measure in all the Directions, but to Rectifie by one kind of measure and Direct by another is absurd.

CHAP. XXVI.

How to obtain the Declinations and Right Ascentions of all the Planets by proportions in Trigonometry according to Proposition the Fourth.

I. In order thereunto, the true Longitude of each Planet from the neerest Aequinoctial point must first be procured, (as is shewed *Sect.* 2. of *Chap.* 2.) as for Example;

Saturn is posited in 24d. 24m. of *Gemini*, therefore unto his Longitude I add 60d. according to the Rule, and the Sum is 84d. 24m. distant from the next Aequinoctial point *Aries*.

II. *Jupiter* is posited in 8d. 16m. of *Scorpio*, therefore I add 30d. to his place, and the Sum is 38d. 16m. the true distance of *Jupiter* from the neerest Aequinoctial point *Libra*.

III. And thus, according to the aforesaid Rules, I find *Mars* is 6d. 39m. distant from the next Aequinoctial point *Aries*, the *Sun* is distant from the same point 1d. 55m. *Venus* is distant from the first point of *Aries* 8d. 4m. *Mercury* 4d. 2m. Lastly the *Moon* will be found distant from the Aequinoctial point Libra 59d. 52m.

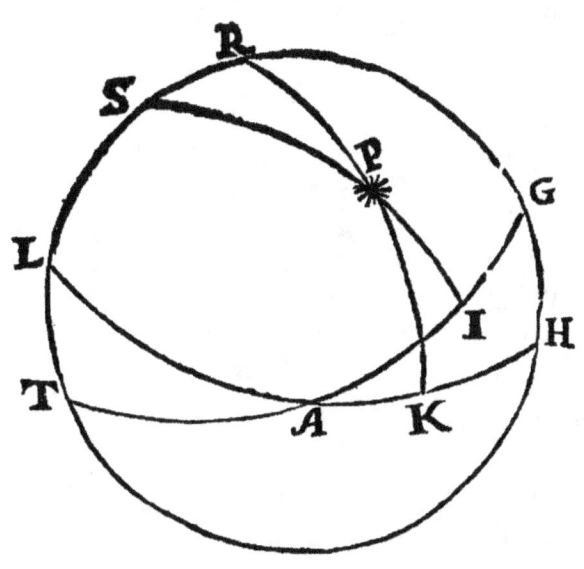

IV. Having the Longitude or distances of the Planets from the neerest Aequinoctial points in the next place proceed according to the Rules given to find their *Declinations* and *Right Ascentions*, which will appear very plain by these following Examples and Demonstrations; and first for the Declination of a Planet with Latitude.

V. The *Sphere* may be projected in Plano into any great Circle thereof, as into the *Horizon, Aequator, Meridian,* &c. I have chosen this *Meridianal Projection*; it also represents one of the *Colures* as occasion serves.

VI. In the Adjunct Diagram, for Demonstration sake, let R, S, L, T, H, G. represent the Solstitial Colure, L, A, H. the Aequator, T, A, G. the Ecliptick, S, P, I. a Circle of Latitude, R, P, K. a Circle of Declination; then in the *Oblique Spherical Triangle* S, R, P. there is given or limited, (1.) The side sR. 23d. 30m. *viz.* the distance of the Poles of the Aequator and Ecliptick. (= to the *Suns* greatest declination.) (2.) The side sP. the Complement of the Latitude. (3.) P, S, R. the Complement of the Longitude, to find the side R, P. the Complement of the Planets or Stars Declination Required: Here it appears that in the aforesaid Triangle there is two Sides and an Angle included known to find the third Side, which may be performed by the *ninth* Case of *Oblique* Spherical Triangles, but more readily by *Proposition* the 4th, as for Example;

First for *the Declination and Right Ascention of* Saturn *in the Exemplary Geniture*.

I. By *Pr.* 4, I add the Sine of the Long. 84d. 24m. 9997921
   To the Tang. Comp. of the Pl. Lat. 0d. 51m. <u>1828672</u>
And the Sum will be the Tangent of the 11826593
   first Arch 89d. 9m.

Now because *Saturn* is in *Gemini* a Northern Signe, and his Latitude South, a contrary Denomination therefore, according to the Rule given to this first Arch 89d. 9m. I add 23d. 30m. the *Suns* greatest Declination, and their Sum wlll be the second Arch, *viz.* 112d. 39m. whose Complement to 180d. is 67d. 21m. (this must be so taken because you enter the Canon always with a number under 90d. or a *Quadrant*.)

Clavis Astrologiae Elimita, The Key to Astrology New Filed

II. To the Comp. Arith. of the first Arch 89d. 9m.   1828720
I add the Co-sine of the second Arch 67d. 21m.   9585574
Add the Sine of *Saturns* Latitude 0d. 5m.   8171280
Their Sum is the Sine of his Declination   9585574
   Nor. *sub terram* 22d. 39m.

III. For the Right Ascention of *Saturn*, in the same Triangle all the sides are given and one Angle, to find the Angle R. this may be performed by Case the third of *Oblique Angled Spherical Triangles*, but more easily by the aforesaid *Proposition*, (being thus prepared) as for Example.

To the *Sine* of the first Arch 89d. 9m. C. Arith.   0000048
I add the *Sine* of the second Arch 67d. 21m.   9965143
And the *Tang.* of *Saturns* Long. 84d. 24m.   1008549
The sum is the *Tangent* of 83d. 56m. his   10973740
   Right Ascention from *Aries*.

Secondly for the Declination and Right Ascension of Jupiter.

I. Add the *Sine* of the Long. 38d. 16m. from ♎   9791917
To the Co-tangent of *Jupiters* Latitude 1d. 28m.   1591696
The Sum is the *Tan.* of the first Arch 87d. 38m.   1383613
From which, according to the Rule subst. 23d. 30m.
There remains the second Arch   64d. 08m.

II. To the *Co-sine* of the first Arch 87d. 38m. C.A.   1384109
Add to the Co-sine of the second Arch, *viz.* 64d. 8m.   9639764
And the *Sine* of the Lat. of *Jupiter* 1d. 28m.   8408161
The Sum is the *Sine* of his Declination   9432034
   South *sub terram* 15d. 42m.

Thirdly for the Right Ascension.

Add the *Sine* of the first Arch 87d. 38m. C. Arith.   0000371
To the *Sine* of the second Arch 64d. 8m.   9954152
And the *Tang.* of ♃'s Long, from ♎ 38d. 16m.   9896971
The Sum is the *Ta.* of 35d. 23m. the R.A. from ♎   9851494

To which add a Semi-circle 180d. and the true R.A. of *Jupiter* from *Aries* is 215d. 23m.

Thirdly for the Decliination and Right Ascension of Mars.

I. Add the *Sine* of the Lon. of *Mars*, 6d. 39m. â ♈   9063724
To the *Co tangent* of his Latitude 0d. 39m.   1945180
The Sum is the *Tan.* of the first Arch 48d. 24m.   11008904

Now because the Long. and Lat. is of contrary Denomination I add 23d. 30m. unto 84d. 24m. and the Sum is the second Arch 107d. 54m. whose Complement to 180d. is 72d. 6m.

II. To the *Co-sine* of the first Arch C.A. 84d.24m.   1010626
Add the *Co-sine* of the second Arch 72d. 6m.   9487642
And the *Sine* of the Latitude 0d. 39m.   8054781
The sum is the Sine of the Declination of   8553049
   Mars, 2d. 3m. North *supra terram*,

Thirdly for the Right Ascention of Mars.

Add the *Sine* of the first Arch 84d. 24m. C. Arith.	0002079
To the *Sine* of the second Arch 27d. 6m.	9978452
And the *Tang.* of Mars his Longitude 6d. 39m.	9066655
The Sum is the *Tangent* of the Right Ascention of *Mars* from *Aries* 6d. 22m.	9047186

Fourthly for the Declination and Right Ascension of the Sun *by Proposition the* 2d.

To the *Sine* of the Suns Longitude 1d. 55m.	8524343
Add the *Sine* of the Suns greatest Dec. 23d. 30m.	9600700
The sum is the *Sine* fr the *Suns* Dec. 0d. 46m.	8125043

The R.A. of the *Sun* was before found to be 1d. 45m., and therefore need not to be exemplified here.

Fifthly for the Declination and Right Ascension of Venus.

I. Add the *Sine* of the Long. from ♈ 8d. 4m.	9147136
To the *Co-tangent* or her Latit. 1d. 26m. South	1601685
And the sum is the *Ta.* of the first Arch 79d. 53m.	10748821

From which substract 23d. 30m. because she is in a Southern Signe ♓, and South Latitude, and there remains the second Arch 56d. 23m.

II. To the *Co-sine* of the first Arch 79d. 53m. C.A.	0755344
Add the *Co-sine* of the seond Arch 56d. 23m.	9743223
And the *Sine* of the Latitude 1d. 26m.	8398179
The Sum is the *Sine* of the Declnation 4d. 31m.	8896746

Thirdly for Venus her Right Ascension.

To the *Sine* of the first Arch 79d. 53m. C. Arith.	0005805
Add the *Sine* of the second Arch 56d. 23m.	9920520
And the *Tang.* of ♀ her Long. 8d. 4m. from ♈	9151454
The Sum is the *Tangent* of 6d. 50m.	9078779

The R.A. of *Venus* short of the Aequinoctial point *Aries*, therefore I substract this 6d. 50m. out of the whole Circle 360d. because *Venus* is in *Pisces*, and the remainder 353d. 10m. is the true Right Ascension of *Venus* from the first point of *Aries* desired.

Sixthly for the Declination and Right Ascension of Mercury.

I. To the *Sine* of his D. from the first p. of ♈ 4d. 2m.	8847183
Add the *Co-tangent* of his latitude 3d. 10m.	1257078
The Sum is the *Tang.* of the first Arch 51d. 49m.	10104261

Now because *Mercury* is in *Aries* with North Latitude I subduct 23d. 30m. according to the Rule, and there remains 28d. 19m. for the second Arch.

II. I add the *SineCo.* of the first Arch C.A. 51d. 49m.	0208885
To the *Sine Comp.* of the second Arch 28d. 19m.	9944650
And the *Sine* of *Mercury's* Lat. 3d. 10m. North	8742259
The sum is the *Sine* of his Declination	8895774

    North *supra terram* 4d. 30m.

Thirdly for Mercury's *Right Ascension.*

Add the *Sine* of the first Arch 51d. 49m. C.A.	0104557
To the *Sine* of the second Arch 28d. 19m.	9676094
And the *Tang.* of ☿'s Long. from ♈ 4d. 2m.	<u>8848240</u>
The Sum is the *Tan.* of his R.A. from ♈ 2d. 26m.	8628791

Seventhly for the Declination and Right Ascension of the Moon, *I proceed in the same Method.*

I. Add the *Sine* of the *Moon*'s Distance from the first Point of ♎ 59d. 52m.	9936945
To the *Co-tangent* for her Latitude 1d. 0m South	<u>1758078</u>
The Sum is the *Tan.* of the first Arch 88d. 51m.	11695023

From whence deduce 23d. 30m. there remains 65d. 21m. for the second Arch.

II. Add the *Co-sine* of the first Arch 88d. 51m. C.A.	1697454
To the *Co-sine* of the second Arch 65d. 21m.	9620213
And the *Sine* Of the Lat. Of the *Moon* 1d. South	<u>8241855</u>
The Sum is the *Sine* of the *Moons* Declination South *sub terram* 21d. 16m.	9559522

Thirdly for *her Right Ascension*, as in the rest, I Add

The *Sine* of the first Arch 88d. 51m. Comp. Ar.	0000058
To the *Sine* of the second Arch 65d. 21m.	9958503
And the *Tan.* of *Luna*'s Lon. 59d. 52m. from ♎	<u>236230</u>
The sum is the *Tan.* of 57d. 26m. the R.A. from ♎	10194821

To which add 180d. because the *Moon* is beyond *Libra* in *Scorpio*, and the Sum 237d. 26m. is the true Right Ascension of the *Moon* from the first point of Aries.

Lastly for the Declination and Right Ascension of the Part of Fortune, *by Prop.* 2.

I. To the *Sine* or Long. of ⊕ 39d. 32m. from ♈	9803664
I add the *Sine* of 23d. 23m. the ☉'s greatest Decl.	<u>9600700</u>
And the Sum is the *Sine* of the Dec. of ⊕ 14d. 42m.	9404364

Secondly for the Right Ascension by the same Proposition.

I add the *Tan.* of the Lon. of P 39d. 3lm. from ♈	9916362
To the *Co sine* of 23d. 30m.	<u>9962398</u>
And the Sum is the *Tang.* of 37d. 6m. short of ♈	9878765

Which Substracted from 360d. because ⊗ is in the last Quadrant, *viz.* in ♒ (as the Rule directs) there remains 322d. 54m. the true Right Ascension required from the first point of *Aries*.

CHAP. XXVII.

Examples of taking the Distane of each Planet from the Meridian in Right Ascention, according to the Direction of Prop. V.

First for Saturn, *who is posited between the Ascendant and Meridian under the Earth.*

	d. m.
From the R. Ascen. of the Cusp of the 4*th* House	138. 02.
subst. the R. Ascen. of ♄ (according to the Rule)	83. 56.
And there remains his D. from the *Immun Coeli* in R.A.	44. 6.

The half thereof being 22d. 3m. I reserve.

Secondly for the Distance of the Opposite place of Jupiter *from the M.C. to be Directed by oblique Ascention (though in the Descending part of Heaven.)*

	d. m.
From the R.A. of the oppo. place of ♃ *cum circuio*	395. 23.
I substract the Right Ascension of the M.C.	318. 02.
There remains the Dist. of ♃'s oppo. place in R.A.	77. 21.

The half thereof is 38d. 40m. 30s.

Thirdly for *the Distance of* Mars *in R. A. from the M.C.*

	d. m.
From the R.A. of *Mars cum circulo*	366. 22.
I deduct the Right Ascension of the M.C.	318. 02.
Remains the Distance of *Mars* in Right Ascen.	48. 20.

Whose half is 24d. 10m.

Fourthly for the Distance of the Sun *from the M.C. in R.A.*

	d. m.
From the Right Ascension of the *Sun cum circulo*	361. 45.
I substract the Right Ascension of the Mid-heaven	318. 02.
And there remains the Dist. from the Meridian	43. 43.

The half thereof is 21d. 51m. 30s.

Fifthly the Distance of Venus *is obtained in the same manner.*

	d. m.
The Right Ascension of *Venus* in *Pisces* was found	353. 10.
Right Ascension of the M.C. substract	318. 02.
Remains the Dist. in Right Ascen. from the M.C.	35. 08.

Whose half is 17d. 34m.

Sixthly for the Distance of Mercury &c.

	d. m.
The R.Ascen. of Mercury in *Aries cum circulo*	362. 26.
The R.Ascen. of the M. C. substract	318. 02.
Remains the Distance of *Mercury*	44. 24.

The half is 49d. 42m.

Seventhly for the Distance of the Moons *Opposite place to be Directed by Oblique Ascention, &c.*

	d. m.
The R. A. of the *Moons* oppo. place in ♉. *cum circ.*	417. 26.
The R.A. of the Midheaven substract	318. 02.
The Distance of the opposite place of ☽ in R.A.	99. 24.
The half is 49d. 42m.	

Lastly for the Part of Fortune, *&c.*

	d. m.
The R.A. of the *Part of Fortune* in *Aquary* is	322. 54.
The R.A. of the Mid-heaven substract	318. 02.
Distance from the M. C. in Right Ascension	4. 52.
The half thereof is 2d. 26m.	

CHAP. XXVIII.

Examples of finding the Poles Elevation above the Circles of Position of the Planets, in the Examplary Nativity, as also (by the help of the Ascentional Differences) their oblique Ascentions, by Prop. VI. *with its Demonstration, as followeth:*

Before I come to the Examples themselves, I shall add this necessary Demonstration from the Sphere it self, the better to inform the Fancy of the Industrious Student.

I. Let the outward great Circle represent the *Meridian*, H.O. the *Horizon*, AE.A. the *Aequinoctial*, D.S. a Parallel of Declination, X. the place of a *Star* or *Planet*, H, X, Y, O. a Circle of Position, X, R, the Planets or Stars Declination, X, P. the Complement thereof to a Quadrant, P, Y. the Poles Elevation above the Circle of Position, P, O. the Latitude of the Place, AE, H. the Complement of the Latitude, or the Aequinoctial Hight, AE, R. the Distance or Arch of the *Aequator* the Star is from the *Meridian*, AE, ♃ half thereof, and N, AE. the Arch of the *Aequator*, Cut by the Circle of Position, N, R. the Ascentional Difference under the Stars proper Pole, P, which is not only the Poles Elevation above the Circle as aforesaid, but it is

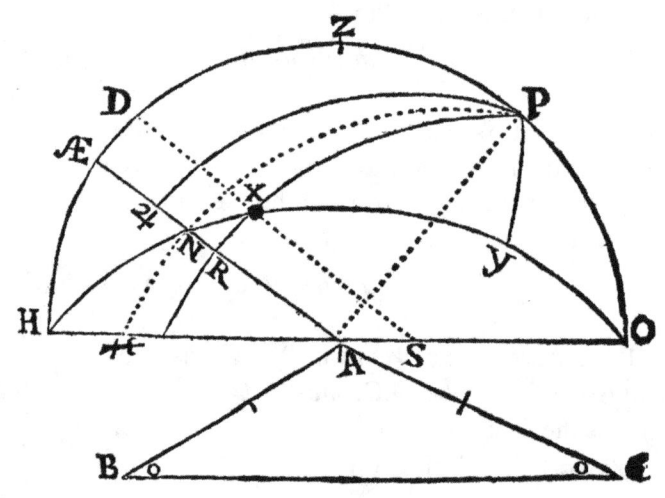

also the Measure of the Angle, P, N, Y. (being a Quadrantal Triangle) So that having the Sides AE, H. and AE, N. there may be found the Angle AE, N, H. (by the 13th case of Right Angled Spherical Triangles) which Angle is the Complement to P, N, Y. equal to H, N, ♐: Or having N, R. the *Difference of Ascention* (viz. the Difference between the Right and Oblique Ascention of the Star) and R, X. the Declination, you may find the Angle X, N, R. by the same Case of Right Angle Spherical Triangles, equal to the Angle AE, N, H. whose Complement P, N, Y. equal to H, N, ♐ is the Poles Elevation above the Circle of Position of the Star: Or having the Angle P, O, Y. equal to AE, P, N. and the Side P, O. the side P, Y. may be found (by the sixth Case of the Right Angle Spherical Triangles.)

Now to shew the Similitude that there is between a Spherical and Plain Triangle.

II. Note that the Angle AE, P, R, in the Quadrantal Spherical Triangle is supposed to be equal to the Acute Angles B, and C, in the Plain Triangle, A, B, C, being the Complement of the obtuse Angle X, P, O, as the Angles B, and C, are of the obtuse Angle A in the plain Triangle, to 180 deg. or a Semi Circle. Now in the Oblique Angled plain Triangle A, B, C, there is given the Sides, A B, A C, and the Angle A, to find either of the Angles B, or C. Now for as much as the three Angles of a plain Right Lined Triangle are equal to 180 degrees, therefore having the Angle A, the Sum of the Angles B, and C, are also known, and the proportion is *as the Sum of the Sides, is to their Difference,* so *is the Tangent of half the the Sum of the Angles sought to the Tangent of a fourth Arch,* (viz. half of the Difference of the Angles) which added to the aforesaid half sum, gives the greatest Angle, or substracted from the half sum gives the lesser Angle.

II. By the same Reason it the Oblique Spherical Triangle X, P, O, obtuse Angled, at P may be found the several parts of the Quadrantal Triangle AE, P, R, (which is the complement of X, P, O, to a Semi circle) as the Angle A, is to the Angles of B, and C, in the Right Lined Triangle aforesaid.

Therefore I may say as the Sine of the Sum of the Sides, P O, and X P, is to the Sine of their Difference; so is the Tangent of half the Angle AE P R. viz. AE P ♃, to the Tangent of a fourth Arch or Angle ♃ P N; which added to the Halfe Angle AE P ♃ gives the Angie AE P N desired.

> [*Note that the Sine of the Sum of the Sides is here taken, because the Angles of a Spherical Triangle are measured by Arches of Circles, being continued out to Quadrants, &c. and are all calculated only by Sines and Tangents; But plain Triangles by Sines and Tangents for the Angles, and the Logarithms of whole Numbers or equal measures foe the Sides, &c.*]

I have made this Digression that I might the better explain the Reason of the Proportion which is given in the sixth Proposition, I proceed now to Examples, that no doubt may remain to puzzle the Learner.

First for Saturn, *&c.*

	d. m.
The Aequi. hight or Comp. of the Lat. of Birth is	37. 42.
The Declinat. of Saturn North under the Earth	22. 39.

The Sum is 60d. 21m. and the *Difference* 15d. 3m.

Then according to the Rule I say,

As the Sine of the *Diff.* Comp. Arith 15d. 13m.	0585592
Is to the Sine of the Sum 60d. 21m.	9939051
So is the Tang. of ½ ♄'s dist. from the Mer. 22°3'	9607500
To the Tangent of 53d. 35m.	10132143

From which substract 22d. 3m. the half distance.

Remains ——— 31d. 32m. the Ascential *Differerice* of *Saturn* under his proper Pole as yet unknown, then the second operation is thus;

Add the Co-tang. of ♄'s Declination 22d. 39m.	0379568
To the Sine of his Ascen. *Differ.* 31d. 32m.	9718497
And the Sum is the Tan. of the Poles Ele. 51°25'.	10098065

Lastly, I substract the Ascen. Diff. of ♄ 31°. 32m. from his Right Ascen. 83d. 56m. because his Declination is North, (according to the Rule) and there Remains 52d. 24m. for ♄'s oblique Ascention under that Pole.

Secondly for the Poles Elevation above the Circle of Position of Jupiters *opposite place, &c.*

	d. m.
I. The Sum of the Compt. of the Lat. and Declinat.	53.24
The Difference thereof is	22.00

Clavis Astrologiae Elimita, The Key to Astrology New Filed

Now becasue the Declination is North above the Earth,

I say, as the *Sine* of the Sum Co.Ar. 53d. 24m.	0095383
Is to the Sine of the Difference 22d. 0m.	9573575
So the Tang. of ½ ♃s. opposite place Dist in R. A. â M. C. 38d. 41m.	9903455
To the *Tangent* of an Arch of 20d. 29m.	9572413

This 20d. 29m subducted from the aforesaid ½ Dist. 38°. 41 Leaves 18d. 12m. the Ascen Differ of ♃ under his proper Pole unknown.

II. I add the *Co tang*. of the Declin. 15d. 42m.	0551159
To the *Sine* of 18d. 12m. the Ascen. Differ.	9494620
The Sum is the *Tang*. of the Pole of Posit. 48°. 1'.	10045779

	d. m.
R.A. of *Jupiters* opposite place is	35.23
From which Substract the Ascen. Diff.	18.12
Remains the Ob.Asc. of ♃ under that Pole,	17.11

Thirdly for the Poles Elevation above the Circle of Position of Mars, *&c.*

	d. m.	
I. The Sum of the Comp. of the Lat. and Dec. of ♂ is,	39.45	
The Difference between them will be found	35.39	
The *Sine* of the Sum 39d. 45m. Co. Ar.		0194201
Difference 35d. 39m.		9765544
The *Tang*. of Tang. of ½ ♂ his dist. â merid. 24d. 10m.		9651974
An Arch 22d. 15m		9611719

The Differ. between this last Arch, and the aforesaid ½ distance of *Mars, &c.* is 1d. 55m. *viz.* the Ascentional Differ. of this Planet under his true (but unknown) Pole of Position.

	d. m.	
II. Add the *Co tang*. of ♂ his Declinat.	2. 3.	1446183
And the *Sine* of his Asc. Diff.	1.55	8524343
The Sum is the *Tang*. of the Poles Elevat. 43. 3.		9970526

	d. m.
The R.A. of ♂ before found, was	6 22
From which Substract the Ascen Diff.	1 55
There reamins the true Oblique Ascention of *Mars* under that Pole.	4 27

Fourthly for the Pole of Position of the Sun, &c. I proceed as in the rest, viz.

	d. m.
I. The Sum of the Co. of the Lat. and Dec. is	38 28
The Difference of these are	36 56

The *Sine* of the Sum Co.Ar. 38d. 28m.	0206168
Differ. 36d. 56m.	9778792
The *Tangent* of The Suns ½ Dist 21d. 52m.	9603493
An Arch 21d. 12m.	9588453

Whose difference from the ½ distance of the *Sun* from the Meridian in R.A.. is 0d. 40m. the *Suns* true Ascent. Differ. under the true Pole unknown.

II. Add the *Co tang.* of the Dec. of the ☉ 0d. 46m.	1873409
And the *Sine* or the Asc. Diff. 0d. 46m.	8065776
The Sum is the *Tang.* of the Pole or Position 41° 0'.	9939185
The *Suns* R. A. was round to be	1d. 45m.
From which Sub. the Ascen. Diff.	0d. 40m.

And there remains the true Ob. Ascen. of the *Sun* under that Pole, 1d. 5m.

Fifthly for the Poles Elevation above the Circle of Position of Venus, &c.

	d. m.
The Sum of the Comp. of the Lat. and Dec. is	42 13
The Difference is	33 11

Now because the Declination is South above the Earth, according to the Proposition, I operate thus *viz*.

The *Sine* of the Differ. 33d. 11m. Co. Ar.	0261759
The *Sine* of the Sum 42d. 13m.	9827328
The *Tang.* of Venus her ½ Dist. 17d. 34m.	9500481
The *Tang.* of an Arch 21d. 41m.	9589568

From this last Arch Substract 17d. 34m. the half Dist. aforesaid, there remnins the Ascen. Diff. of *Venus* 3d. 40m. as in the rest of the Planets.

II. Add the *Co-tang.* of the Declinat. 4d. 31m.	1102404
And the *Sine* of the Asc. Diff. 3d. 40.	8805852
The Sum is the *Tang.* of the Pole of Posit. 39d. 0m.	9908256
The R.A. of Venus (before found) is	253 10
In this case, add the Ascen. Differ.	3 40
And the Sum is the true Ob. Ascen. of ♀	256 50
Under the Pole of	39 0

Sixthly, for the P. P. of Mercury, &c.

	Com. Ar.
I. The Sine of the Sum. of the Co. of the Lat.	
& Declina. 42d. 12m.	1202404
Differ. 33d. 12m.	9738434
The ½ Dist. â Merid. 22d. 12m.	9610758
Tang. of An Arch 18d. 12m.	9522003

Whose Difference from the half Dist. is 3d. 37m. the Ascen. Dffer. of ☿, &c.

II. Add the *Co tang.* Declinat. 4d. 30m.	1104016
And the *Sine* of the Asc. Diff 3d. 47m.	8819436
The Sum is the *Tang.* of the *P.P.* 39d. 59m.	9923452

And *Mercury*'s oblique Ascen. under that Pole, found by the Rule, is 358d. 39m.

Seventhly, for the P. P. of the Moon, &c. her opposite place.

	d. m.	Co.Ar.
I. The Sine of the Sum of the Lat. & Dec.	58.58.	0067086
Difference	16.26.	9451623
The Tang of. The ½ Dist. â Merid.	49.42.	0071572
A fourth Arch	21.17.	9590290

Clavis Astrologiae Elimita, The Key to Astrology New Filed

The Difference between which Arch, and the half Dist. is 28d. 5m. the *Moons* Ascen. *Diff.* under her proper Pole of Position.

    II. Add the *Cotang.* of the ☽s Dec. 21d. 16m.   0409812
    To the *Sine* of the Asc. Diff 28d 5m.   9672795
    The sum is the *Tang.* of the ☽s *P.P.* 50d. 25m.   10082607

    R.A. of the *Moons* opposite place   57d. 26m.
    Substract the Ascen. Differ.   28d. 5m.
    There remains the Ob. Ascen of Luna   29d. 21m.

    Lastly, for the P.P. *of the* Part of Fortune, &c.

        d. m.
The Sum of the Comp. of the Lat. and Dec. is   52 23
The Difference thereof is   23 00

The Declination being South above the Earth, I operate as followeth, accoridng to the Rule given.
    I. The *Sine* of the Differ. 23d. Comp. Arith   0408122
    The Sum 52d. 24m.   9898844
    The *Tang.* of The half Dist. 2d. 26m.   8628340
    The *Tang.* of A fourth Arch 4d. 55m.   8935346

The Differ. of the fourth Arch from the half Dist. (as in all the other Examples) is the Ascen. Diff. of ⊕ 2d. 29m.

    II. Add the *Co tang.* of the Declinat. 14d. 42m.   0581127
    And the *Sine* of the Asc. Diff. 2d. 29m.   8636776
    The Sum is the *Tang.* of the *P. P.* 10d. 46m.   9217903

        d. m.
R.A. of the *Part of Fortune*   322 54
Ascen. Differ. Add   2 29
The Sum is   325 23

The Ob. Ascen. of ⊕ under its proper Pole 10d. 46m.

And thus are the Rules exemplified sufficiently for the Instruction of any Ingenious Student that desires the knowledge of this kind of Calculation.

Now follows a Synoposis of the whole Work, in one Page, that the Reader may behold, at one view, all the Operations Reduced into a brief Table for his more easie Inspection &c. and may seve, for an Example, to perform the like in any Persons Nativity whatsoever.

	A Brief Synopsis of all the foregoing Calculation presented at one view.							
Names of the Plan.	Longit.	Latitude	Declinat.	R. Ascen.	Dist. â mer	Pole of P.	Asc. Diff.	Ob. Asc.
Saturn	d. m. 24 ♊ 24	d. m. 00 S. 51	22 N. 39 Sub.Ter.	d. m. 83 56	d. m. 44 6	d. m. 51 25	d. m. 31 32	d. m. 52 24
Jupiter	d. m. 8 ♏ 16	d. m. 1. S. 28	15 S. 42 Sub. Ter.	35 23 in oppos.	77 21	48 1	18 12	in oppos. 17 11
Mars	d. m. 6 ♈ 39	d. m. 0 S. 39	2 N. 3 Sup.Ter.	d. m. 06 22	48 20	43 3	1 55	4 27
Sol	d. m. 01 ♈ 55	00 00	0 N. 46 Sup.Ter.	d. m. 1 45	43 43	41 0	0 40	1 5
Venus	d. m. 21 ♓ 56	d. m. 1 S. 26	4. S. 31 Sup.Ter.	353 10	35 8	39 0	3 40	356 50
Mercury	d. m. 4 ♈ 2 Rx	d. m. 3 N. 10	4 N. 30 Sup.Ter.	02 26	44 24	39 59	3 47	358 39
Luna	d. m. 29 ♏ 52	d. m. 1 S. 0	21 N. 16 Sub.Ter.	57 26 in oppos.	99 24	50 25	28 5	in oppos. 19 21
Part.Fort	d. m. 20 ♒ 29	0 0	14 S. 42 Sup.Ter.	322 54	4 52	10 46	2 29	325 23
Mid-hea.	d. m. 13 ♒ 53	0 0	0 0	318 2	0 0	0 0	0 0	0 0
Ascendant	d. m. 22 ♊ 32	0 0	0 0	0 0	0 0	0 0	0 0	48 2

CHAP. XXIX.

Examples of Directing the Five Hylegiacals in the Exemplary Geniture; and Consequently any of the other Planets by the same Method to their several Promittors, by the help only of a Canon of Artificial Sines *and* Tangents, *(according to the Propositions for that purpose.) also the Demonstration of the Arke of Directions, &c.*

Let H Z O represent the Meridian, AE C Q the Aequator, H O the Horizon, P the North Pole. X the South Pole, H F D E O a Circle of Position above the Earth, S D K, and A E G Y two Parallels of Declination, ✶ ☽ a *Significator*, AE R the Arch of the *Aequator*, (correspondent, (*viz.* his Right Ascension or rather *Distance* from the Meridian in Right Ascention,) D R his Declination North above the Earth G F a Promittor, AE B the Arch of the *Aequator* Correspondent, *viz.* his Right Ascension, G B the *Promittors* Declination. Now by the motion of the *Globe* or *Sphere* when the *Promittor* at G, comes to the place of E, in the same Circle of position with *Significator* D, the Circle of the *Declination* of the *Promittor* is then P E N, and so the Arch of the *Aequator* A E N, is the Right Ascension of the *Promittor* at E, (or distance from the Meridian in Right Ascension) and hence the Arch of the Aequator N B is the *Ark* of *Direction* required; and P M is the Poles Elevation above the Circle of Position 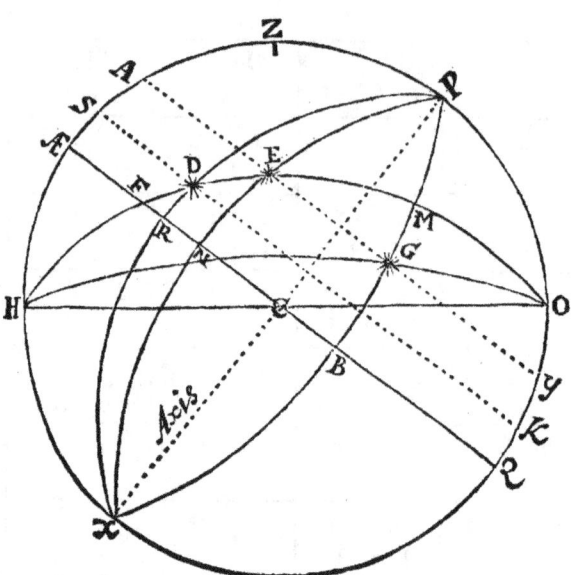 of the Star or Planet which is *Signijicator*, and thus the Business of *Directing* is only to find the quantity of the aforesaid Arch of the *Aequator* N B, interjacent between the Significator and Promittor.

II. Observe also that the Arch of the *Aequator* F R is the Ascen. Difference of the Significator at D, and the point R the Right Ascension, because it cuts the Meridian at AE at Right Angles; but it cuts the Circle of Position H F D E O (which here is a certain Horizon) with an oblique Angle at F. Again F N is the Ascen. Difference of the *Promittor* at E under the same Pole of the *Significator*, being also upon the same Imaginary *Circle* of *Position*; Now the *Difference* between F R the Ascen. Difference of the *Significator* at *D*, and F N the Ascen. Difference of the *Promittor* at F is R N, *viz.* a Certain Arch of the *Aequator* which may be called the Aequation of the Ascentional Difference; now add this Aequation R N, to AE R, (R being the point of Right Ascen. of the Significator) and you have AE N, this subducted out of AE B, which is accounted the R.A. of the Promit. leaves N B [*according to the first of the five Rules given after the Examples of Directions*] the Ark of Direction because the Declination of the *Significator* and *Promittor* are both North, &c. if otherwise consult the aforesaid five Rules, this being sufficient to shew upon what Foundation a *Direction* hath its dependence. Having premised these things, I shall now proceed to Examples, that the Rules may thereby be the better understood and apprehended by the Industrious Student.

[*Note that the Point R. is the Right Asc. of the Significator at D from the Center C, (which represents* Aries *and* Libra) *and that the outward Circle in this* Projection *may represent the Meridian, and the Solstitial Colure also, and then the Points* Aries *and* Libra *must be in the Centre, supposing one point upon the one side of the Sphere, and the other opposite thereunto on the other side thereof.*]

First, *An Example of Directing the Ascendant to the* Trine Dexter *of* Venus *which falls in* 21d. 56m. *of* Cancer, *with half Latitude of Contrary Denomination., viz.* 43m. *North, the Pole of the Ascendant or Latitude of the Place of Birth being* 51d. 18m.

For the Declination and Right Ascension of the Trine Dexter *of* Venus.

I. To the *Sine* of the Longitude of the Aspect from *Libra* 68d. 4m.	9967370
Add the Co-tang. of the aforesaid ½ Lat. 0d. 43m.	1902783
The sum is the Tan. of the first Arch 89d.14m.	11870153

Now because the Longitude and Latitude is of one Denomination I substract 23d. 30m. the greatest Obliquity of the *Ecliptick* from 89d. 14m. and the Remainder is 65d. 44m. for the second Arch.

II. Add the C. *Arith.* of the *Co-sine* of 89°. 14'.	1873529
Add the *Co-sine* of 65°. 44'. the second Arch	9613825
Add the *Sine* of the Latitude or 0°. 43'.	8097183
The Sum abating R. is the *Sine* of the Decl. 22°25'	9584537

III. Add the *Arith. C.* of the Sine of 89°. 14'.	0000030
Add the *Sine* of the second Arch 65°. 44'	9959768
Add the *Tangent* of the Long. 68°. 4'.	0395047
The sum is the Tang. of the R.A. 66°. 10' â ♎	10354854

Which in this case must be substracted from 180d. leaves the true R.A. of the △ Dexter of ♀ in 21d. 56m. of ♋, *viz.* 156d. 10m. which may also be found by the Tables or R.A. and Declination making proportion according to the *Directions* given in *Chap.* 6.

IV. Add the *Tang.* of 52°. 18'. the Lat. of Birth	0111883
Add the *Tang.* of the Aspects Decl. 22°. 35'.	9619008
The Sum is the *Sine* of the Ascen. Diff. 32°. 33'.	9730891

This *Ascen. Differ.* substracted from the R.A. because the Declinat. is *North,* leaves the *Oblique Ascen.* of the *Trine* of *Venus* 81d. 27m. under the Pole of the *Ascendant* from which substract the *Oblique Ascention* of the Ascendant 48d. 2m. there remains 33d. 25m. for the *Ark of Direction,* then against 33d. in the *General Aequation Table,* you have 29m. to be added, which makes the *Ark* of *Direction* 33 years and 54 parts of 60 of another, which in the fitted Table to the *Geniture* points out *February* the 3d, 1681.

Secondly, *An Example of Directing the Mid-heaven, which shall be to the* Conjunction *of* Venus *in* 21d. 56m. *of* Pisces *with South Latitude* 1d. 26m. *This must be performed by Right Ascention.*

For the Right Ascension of Venus *cum. Lat.*

I. Add the Sine or her D. from the 1 p. of ♈ 8°. 4'.	0147136
Add the Co-tangent Latit. 1d. 26m. South	1601685
The sum is the *Tan.* of the first Arch 79d. 53m.	10748821
Subduct 23d. 36m.	
Remains the second Arch 56d. 23m.	

	Com. Arith.
II. Add the *C. Arith* of the *Sine of* 79d. 53m.	0006805
Add the *Sine* of the second Arch 56d. 23m.	9920520
Add the *Tang.* of ♀ her Long. â ♈ 8d. 4m.	9151454
The Sum is the Tang. of the R.A. of *Venus* 6d. 50.	9076779

That is short of the *Aequinoctial* point *Aries;* therefore because *Venus* was in the last Quadrant of the *Ecliptick* I substract this 6d. 50m. out of 360d. and there remains 353d. 10m. for the true R.A. of the *Conjunction* of *Venus cum Lat.* from the first point of *Aries* from which I substract 318d. 2m. the R. A. of the *Mid-heaven* there Remains 35d. 8m. the *Ark of Direction:* Now against 35 deg. in the *General Aequation Table* answers 31m. which added to 35d. 8m. the Sum is 35 years and 39 parts, and against 39m. in the *particular Table* answers *November* the *4th*, and 35 years from the Birth points out 1685. and then will the *Direction* begin to operate according to *Naibods* Measure of Time; *& sic de cateris.*

Thirdly, *An Example of Directing the* Sun *which shall be to the Opposition of the* Moon *which falls in* 29d. 52m. of Taurus, *with Opposite Latitude,* viz. 1d. *North.*

I. To the *Sine* of the Long. of the *Moons* Oppos. place from *Aries* 59d. 52m.	9936945
Add the Co-tangent or her Latitude 1d. 0m.	1758078
The Sum is the Tan. of the first Arch 88d 51m.	11695023
Now because 'tis a Northern Signe and the 23d. 30m. same Lat. I substract the Obliquity, *&c.* Reamains the second Arch 65d. 21m.	
II. Add the *Co-sine* of 88d. 51m. Comp. Arith.	1697454
Add the *Co-sine* of 65d. 21m. the 2d Arch	9620213
Add the *Sine* of the latitude North 1d. 0m.	8241855
The Sum is the *Sine* of the Declination of her Opposite place 21d. 16m.	9559522
III. Add the *Sine* of 88d. 51m. Comp. Arith.	0000083
Add the *Sine* of 65d. 21m. the 2 â Arch	9958503
Add the *Tang.* of her Long. â ♈ 59d. 52m.	0236230
The Sum is the Tangent or 57d. 26m. her Right Ascention from *Aries*	10194821
IV. Add the Poles Eleva. above the ☉ 41°.0'.	9939163
Tan. of the *Moon*'s Declination 21d. 16m.	9590188
The Sum is the Sine of the ☽'s As. Diff. 19d. 46m.	9529351

This Ascen. Differ. substracted from the R. A. of the *Moons* opposite place 57d. 26m. there remains the Oblique Ascen of the *Moons* opposite place, from which deduct the *Oblique Ascen.* of the *Sun* under his proper Pole of Position 41d. viz. 1d. 5m. and there remains 36d. 35m. for the Ark of Direction sought, them against 36d. in the *Aequation Table* answers 32m. add, which makes the *Ark* of Direction 37d. 7 parts; now against 37 I find in the Particular Table 1687, and against 7 parts *April* the 23*d*, so that *April* the 23*d* 1687, the *Sun* by Direction met with the Opposition of the *Moon*, according to *Naibods* Measure.

After the same Method may be *Directed* the *Moon*, the *Part of Fortune*, and the rest of the Planets, if the Artist will be so curious.

Fourthly, *Having the Right Ascension and Ascentional Difference of both Significator and Promissor you may find the Ark of Direction without forming the Oblique Ascention or Descention thus*; viz.

I. Take the *Difference* of the Ascentional *Differences* of the Significator and Promittor, (by substracting the lesser from the greater) call that for distinction sake, the Aequation, *&c.*

II. If the Declination of Significator and Promissor be both North, add this Aequation to the *R. A.* of the Significator, or substract it from the *R. A.* of the Promittor, and then deduct the *R. A.* of the Significator from the *R. A.* of the Promittor, and the Remainder is the true Arch of *Direction* desired.

III. If the *D*eclination of Significator and Promittor be both South, substract the Aequation from the *R. A.* of the Significator, or add to it the Promittors *R. A.* and proceed as before.

IV. If the Declination of the Significator be North and Promittor South, then instead of taking the Difference between the Ascentional Differences, take the sum, and reserve for the Aequation, and add it to the *R.A.* or the Promittor, *&c.*

V. But if the *D*eclination of the Significator be South, and the Promittor North, take the Aequation according to the fourth Rule, and add it to the *R.A.* of the Significator, and so proceed, *&c.*

[*A Caution.*]

All these five Rules you may observe if the Significator be in the Asceending part of Heaven, and you Direct by Ob. Ascention. But should the Significator be poised in the descending part of Heaven, & you Direct by Oblique Descention, then you are to operate just contrary to this method laid down, *that is*, If a Significator and Promittor have both North *D*eclination, instead of adding the Aequation to the *R. A.* of the Significator, *&c.* add it to the *R. A.* of the Promittor, *&c.* and so understand in the other varieties.

This, I confess will save no labour in the work; for having the Ascen. Differ. and the *R. A.* and the Ark of Direction is soon obtained by Oblique Ascention or Descention; yet I thought convenient to insert it as a variety, and those that like it not may make use of the Common way; however the one may serve to prove the truth of the other, *&c.* The Reason thereof is clearly demonstrated by the Coelestial Globe, and the Diagram before inserted.

Note that if you desire to know how far the Direction of any Significator is come at any certain point of time, turn those years and days into degrees and minutes, according to the usual manner in Directions, which add to the Oblique Ascension or Descension of your Significator. And lastly, Find what degrees and minutes of the Eclip-tick corresponds thereunto; and thus you may easily know the progress of any Significator in any propounded year, &c. which is but the Converse to the Method of Rectificqtion of a Nativity by Accidents.

Thus I have shewed in as plain a manner as 'tis possible how to direct by *Trigonometry*, which is the most curious, and exact, and to be preferred before the Tabular way; for doubtless had the Antients been acquainted with such easie wayes as have in our dayes been found out (especially in Logarithmetical Calculations) they would never have taken that pains to make the Tables of Directions, as those of *Regiomontanus* and *Argol*, (*viz.*) of Oblique Ascentions with, and without Latitude of Positions, aud Ascentional Differences, *&c.* Which considering the trouble of making proportions, and of Parallel and Lateral Entrances, are altogether as laborious as to Direct by the Canon, which is abundantly more Artificial, Portable and Convenient, and gives you the Declination and Right Ascension with Latitude at three Operations (as hath been shewed) the Ascen. Differ. at one facile Operation, and consequently the Oblique Ascension or Descension under any Elevation, with much facility.

Here follows an Example of the Form and Method of Direction in a Table, as also a Speculum *of the Directions of the Hylegiacal Points of the Nativity, that the young Student may thereby the better understand how to perform the Work in any other.*

An Example of Directing the Mid-heaven to Promittors in the Exemplary Geniture, the same Method ought to be observed in Directing the other four Hyligiacals, which is omitted here for brevity sake.					
MC. Directed to Promittors R. A. 318d. 2m.	Longit of Promit. d. m.	Right Asc. of Promittors.	Ark of Direction.	The Arch red. into Y. & 60 pts.	Years, months, and dayes, according to *Naibod*.
Cusp of M. C.	15 ♒ 33	318.02	Deg. Min.	Y.& 60 p.	Measure of Time.
Ad △ D of ♄	24. 24	326.15	08.13	08.20	July 11. 1658.
Ad □ S of ☽	29. 52	331.58	13.56	14. 7	April 23. 1664.
Ad ☌ ♀ cum Lat.	21 ♓ 56	353.09	35.07	35 38	October 29. 1685.
Ad □ S of ♄	24. 24	354.52	36.50	37.22	July 24 1687.
Ad △ S of ☽	29. 52	359.34	41.32	42. 7	April 23. 1692.
Ad ☌ of the ☉	01 ♈ 55	361.45	43.43	44.21	July 17. 1694.
Ad ☌ ☿ cum Lat.	04. 02	362.25	44.23	45. 2	March 24 1695. curt.
Ad ☌ ♂ cum Lat.	06. 39	366.15	48.13	48.55	Feb. 10. 1699. curt.
Ad cont An ♀	08. 4	367.23	49.21	50.04	April 5. 1700.
Ad ✶ D of ♄	24. 24	382.45	64.43	65.39	November 4. 1715.
Ad Ter. of ♄	27. 00	385.02	67.00	67.59	March 6. 1718. curt.
Ad Dom. XII.	6. ♉ 4	393.42	75.40	76.47	December 23. 1726.

A Speculum of the Directions belonging to the Exemplary Nativity.						
Aeta.	An Dó.	Ascend	Mid H.	Sun	Moon	Part F.
20	1670			Dó XII 48 parts	□ D ♀ 23 parts	
21	1671			☍ ♃ 57 T ☿ 6 p.	Dó VII 58 p.	
22	1672		T ♃ 54 parts		☍ ♄ 21 p.	T ☿ 16 p.
23	1673					
24	1674					
25	1675	T ☿ 3 p.	Dó XI 41 parts		T ♂ 33	
26	1676	Dom 2. 57 parts				
27	1677			Ter ♃ 45 parts		T ♂ 27 p.
28	1678		T ☿ 35 parts			
29	1679				T ♀ 51 p.	☌ ♀ 5p. C.A. ♂
30	1680			☌ ☊ 43 parts		
31	1681				□ D ☉ 59 p.	□ ♄ 31p C.A. ☿
32	1682			✶ D ♀ 4 parts		
33	1683	△ D ♀ 42 parts		T ♄ 0		C.A. ☉ 29 p.

		A Speculum of Directiosn belonging to the Exemplary Nativity.				
Age	An.Dó	Ascend.	Mid H.	Sun	Mon	Part F.
34	1684		T ♂ 11p.		□ ☽ ☿ 25 p.	△ ☽ 36 p.
35	1685		☌ ♀ 38p.			
36	1686		C.A. ♂ 24 p.	T ♂ 36 p.	C.A. ♄ 16 p.	☌ ☿ 43 ☌ ☉ 45
37	1687		□ ♄ 22 p.	☍ ☽ 7 p.	T ☿ 23 p.	
38	1688		C.A. ♀ 55 p.			
39	1689	T ♄ 47		✶ S ☿ 11 p.		
40	1690		C.A. ☉ 46p.	☉ 13 p.	✶ S ♃ 35 p.	
41	1691					☌ ♂ o p.
42	1692		△ ☽ 42 p.			C.A. ♀ 58 p.
43	1693					
44	1694		☌ ☉ 44 p.	✶ S ♂ 1		
45	1695	△ D ☽ 50p.	☌ ☿ 2	T ♃ 34 p.	Ter. ♃ 16 p.	
46	1696	D III 17 p.				
47	1697	Ant. ☽ 15	☌ ♂ 48y. 55p.	☌ Ald. 49y. 17	Dó VIII 22 p.	T ☿ 54 p.

CHAP. XXX.

How to Rectifie and Direct a Nativity according to the new and Natural way of that famous Mathematician, and Astronomer, John Kepler, *sent by him to the Students in the Art of Nativities, [And Intituled in his* Rudoiphine Tables, *Sportula Genethliacis Missa.]*

SECT. I.

A new and demonstrative way of Direction, according to the Method of J.K.

That Laborious Artist, Mr. *T. S.* (Author and Composer of the *Caroline Tables*), in his Ephemeris 1655 did most ingeniously, and very Concisely explain this manner of Direction, but many young Students complained they understood it not, by reason of its brevity, &c. For which cause I have here endeavoured to explain it to the meanest Capacity, and this I hope without the least prejudice to any person now professing the same.

I. The *Chaldeans* Rationally considered to deduct, or bring *Promittors* to their *Significators*, by equal degrees of the Ecliptick, some by the mean Diurnal Motion of the ☉, others by the true Diurnal Motion, and a third sort by Right Ascention.

II. *Ptolomy* Rationally concluded to bring the Promittor to the like place or the Significator, by the Arch of every one or the *Diurnal Motions*, having weighed the like equal parts, with the Arch or the *Aequator*, which will concur or agree with any of them.

III. *Regiomontanus* did rationally determine as aforesaid to deduce the Promittor to the same Circle of Position in which the Significator was, although he would not always drive or constrain it to the same part of the Circle which it kept.

IV. *Lastly,* The learned *Kepler* saith, he would willingly have Experience Judge in the Case, to determine between these ways, and farther affirms, that it is the part of Revilers, or the weak judgment of the Credulous if they despise the admonisher, since he declares it impossible by trial to come so neer as minutes, although we may suppose the neerest Knot or juncture or time.

There is a course of all causes or humane affairs by Directions alone, if so be you will grant some other causes to intervene. Therefore *Kepler* guarding himself with the Examples of his Predecessors, (not by experience attained) thinks it a thing Rational to bring the Significators in order of the Signes, to their Promittors by the proportion of a natural day to one year. Namely, if for every one year the place of the ☉ be added, &c.

And so *Kepler* goes on to Examples from an Illustrious persons Geniture, and performs his operations by the *Rudolphine Tables*, working out the Directions by the ☉'s *Anonaly* and *Apogaeon* Co-aequated, &c. making the ☉ the ground and foundation of all his work. What he performs by *Anomaly* and *Apogaeon* of the ☉ may much easier be effected by an Ephemeris, and no less exact, as I shall (in the next place) immediately shew, by plain Rules and Examples as followeth in the following Sections.

SECT. II.

How to Rectifie a Nativity by Accidents, and make them Correspond with Directions.

First, collect a Table of the ☉'s Diurnal Motion for 60 or 70 dayes after the Birth, and this shall be the Arches of Direction for so many years, &c.

To Rectifie the Ascendant.

[*The RULE*] I. Having the years and dayes of an Accident, for the years account so many dayes from the Nativity in the aforesaid Table (making proportion for the odd dayes) and note what Signe, degree and minute the ☉ is then posited in.

II. Take the Right Ascention of the ☉ in that place, (your figure being before set to estimate time) and also the Oblique Ascension of your elected Promissor with Latitude (as is usual if he have any) under the Pole of the Place of Birth.

III. *Lastly,* Substract the aforesaid R.A. of the ☉ from the Obl. Ascen. of your Promittor (which is most agreeable to the Nature of the Accident) and 270d. added thereunto, and the residue shall be the R.A. of time from noon in the Radix Rectified.

I. Example from a certain Persons Nativity, a Friend of Mine.

Married, aged 24. years 162 dayes the Ascen. Directed to the Body of ♀, &c.

		d. m.
♀ in ♍ 6d. 32m.	Obl. Asc. under	
Lat. Sept.0.30.	pole 51.27	146.25
Unto which add 3 quarters of the Circle		270.00
And you have the R.A. of the		
Dir. of the M.C. with the Circle		416.25

Then account forward in your prepared Table in the Margent 24 years (in the last Column) & there I find the ☉'s place in [15d. 19m. ♏,] Now because the fourth day at noon the ☉ exceeds his Radical place [26 m.] deduct 26 m. from 15d. 19m. and there remains [14d. 53m. ♏] the ☉'s true Direction for 24 years.

Again for the 162 dayes, I repair to the Proportional Table at the end of this Chapter, and there I seek the ☉'s

Diurnal Motion at 24 dayes from the Birth, *viz.* 61m. at top in the last Column, in which I seek for 162 dayes, which I find not exactly at one entrance, but at two entrances find the given dayes against 25m. and 2m. in the first Column, so that 27m. answers to 162 dayes, add this 27m. to the aforesaid [14d. 32m. ♏] and it produces [15d. 20m ♏] whose Right Ascension is 222d. 51m. which substracted out of the above mentioned [416d. 25m.] there remains [193d. 34m.] the Right Ascension of time from Noon in the Radix Rectified, which converted into time (by the Table for that purpose) gives 12 hor, 54'. 16". *P. M.*, which is but 2'.4". of time different from the Rectification the old way.

    II. *If you would Rectifie a Nativity by an Accident compared with the* M.C. *Directed, &c.*

[*The RULE*] I. Find the Promissors R.A., (as is usual.)

II. Substract the R.A. of the ☉ agreeable to the year and day of the Accident (as before shewed) from the R.A. of your Promissor (by adding the whole Circle if substraction cannot be made) and the remainder is the R.A. of the time from Noon in the Radix rectified as before.

Example 2.

Aged 17 years 144 dayes an Accident happened compared with the M.C. ad □ ☽ *cum Lat.*

R.A. of the □ of the ☽ in 21d. 31m. ♉ with 1d. 17m. South Lat. is 49d. 26m.

Then for 17 years I account forward in the prepared Table, and against 17 years I find [8d. 17m. ♏] from which I substract the aforesaid 26m. (for the Excess of the ☉'s place in the Radix and there reamins [7d. 51m. ♏] Again from the odd 144 dayes under Diurnal Motion ☉ 61m. (which the ☉ had at that time) in the proportional Table, I find 24m. to answer, which added to [7d. 51m. ♏] makes [8d. 15m. ♏] whose R.A. is 215d. 52m. which substracted from the R.A. of the □ of the ☽ and 360d. *viz.* [409d. 26m.] there remains [193d. 34m.] the R. A. of the time from Noon, in the Radix Rectified and agrees with the Vulgar way.

[Note that the *Directing* of the M. C. and the Ascendant, according to this Method, is not far different from the usual old beaten way, *&c.*

But the Direction of the ☉, ☽, ⊕, ♄, ♃, ♂, ♀, and ☿, will be found sometimes considerably different, which makes many persons apt to suspect the truth hereof. But the reason is, these last are Directed in the Ecliptick, the other, (*viz.* M. C. and Ascendant) to Promittors in the Aequator, as shall be shewed.]

    III. *If you would Rectifie a Nativity by the* ⊗, *(which is only the Distance of the* ☉ *from the* ☽ *projected from the Ascendant.*

[*The RULE*] I. Substract the *Suns* place from the *Moons*, as is usual, &c.

II. Substract the distance of the Luminaries from the Signe, deg. and min. where the Promittors Body or Aspect falls, the Remainder is called the Ascendants *Direction.*

III. Take the Oblique Ascention of this Remainder under the Lat. or Pole of the place, and unto it add 270d. (which is called the *Direction* of the M. C. with the Circle.)

IV. *Lastly*, Substract the R. A. of the *Sun* agreeable to the time of the Accident (found as before directed) out of this last found number, and the Remainder is the R.A. of the time, *P. M.* in the Radix rectified, as in the other.

Example 3.

Suppose in the Exemplary Nativity the Native being aged 27 years, 323

From Octob. 4 1641. *at noon.*		
da	☉'s place	ye
4	21 ♎ 19	0
8	25 18	4
12	29 17	8
16	3 ♏ 17	12
20	7 17	16
21	8 17	17
22	9 18	18
23	10 18	19
24	11 18	20
25	12 18	21
26	13 19	22
27	14 19	23
28	15 19	24
29	16 20	25
30	17 20	26
31	18 21	27
Novemb.		
1	19 22	28
2	20 22	29
3	21 23	30
4	22 22	31
5	23 24	32
and so on.		

dayes, should have an Accident happen agreeable to the ⊕ ad □ ♂, &c.

	s.	d.	m.
The □ of ♂ in ♑, viz.	9.	9.	30
The Luminaries Distance substract	4.	0.	38
Remains the Direct. of the Ascen. ♍	5.	8.	52
The Oblique Ascen. of 8d. 52rn. ♍ Sub. Lat.		51.	17
Will be found to be		150.	2
Add		270.	0
Gives R. A. Dir. *Cum Circulo*		420.	2

In the prepared Table against 27 years answers [18d. 21m. ♏] substract 26m. the aforesaid Excess, rests [17d. 55m. ♏] then the ☉'s Diurnal Motion being 61m. I find by the proportional Table that 54m. answers to 323 dayes, this 54m. add to [17d.55m. ♏] makes [18d. 49m.] whose R. A. is [226d. 28m.] which substracted from [420d. 2m.] before found, leaves 193d. 34m., the R.A. of the Time, *P. M.* in the Radix, as in the rest. *Et sic de cateris.*

These things being premised, *D*irecting will be very easie, being no more but the converse work; as will appear by the Examples following.

SECT. III.

How to Direct the five Hylegiacals (and the other Planets) to their several Promittors in any Geniture, According to Johan Kepler.

To Direct the Ascendant is to find how many dayes after Birth, the Bodies or Aspects of Promittors do Ascend the Horizon at the same point of Time with the Nativity.

The RULE.

I. Take the Oblique Ascention of your Promittor after the usual manner, with Latitude (if he have any) under the Elevation of the place of Birth.

II. Add to this Oblique Ascention found, 270d. and from their sum substract the R. A. of Time from Noon in the Radix, and the remainder is the R.A. of the Direction of the *Sun*.

III. Find the Signe deg. and min. that answers to this R. A. of the *Sun*.

IV. Search for the ☉ in this place in your prepared Table, or the neerest less, and from every day from the Birth account one year, (making proportion for the old min.) and you have the year and day desired.

Or thus, Havtng the Obl. Ascen. of the Promisser, substract from thence the R. A, of the Time from Noon in the Radix, increased by a Quadrant, or 90d. (adding the Circle to the aforesaid Oblique Ascention if need require, and the remainder will be the R. A. of the Direction of the ☉, then proceed as before. *The like may be observed in the* ⊕.

	Example 4.
Ascend. ad ☌ of ♀, &c.	
The Oblique Ascention of ♀ *cum Lat.*	d. m.
and 270d. added was	416. 25
Right Ascention of time from Noon substract	193. 34
Rests R.A. Direct ☉	222. 51
	Or Thus.
The Oblique Ascention of ☌ ♀, and 360d. is	506. 25
R. A. of Time *P. M.* and 900d. substract	283. 34

Remains the R.A. of the Direction of the ☉ as before	222 51	

Unto which answers [15d. 20m. ♏] (as is most readily found by a Table of Houses, whose Cusps of the 10*th* House is answerable in the Ecliptick to every deg. of *R. A.* such a one you may find in Mr. *Wings* Ephemerides, by which the work may be performed oftentimes by a mental proportion,) Unto which I must now add 26m. for the excess of the ☉'s place in the *Radix*, and that produces [15d. 46m. ♏] which I seek in the fitted Table, and find the next less against 24 years [15d. 19m. ♏,] and the Diurnal Motion of the ☉ in that place is 61m. the difference between [15d. 19m. and 15d. 46m.] is 27m. the dayes answering thereunto in the last Column of the Proportion Table under 61m. Diurnal Motion will be found 162, so that the Ascendant met with the ☌ of ♀ at 24 years 162 dayes as aforesaid: [*For if 60m. gives one year 6 hours, 27m. will point out 162 dayes, as in that Table.*]

[*Note that if the* Suns *place at noon the day of Birth, exceeds the Suns true Radical place, (as in this our Example) add that overpluss in Directions. But if it wants, [substract. But in Rectification observe the contrary, as you will better understand by the precedent, and subsequent Examples.*]

II. *How to Direct the M. C.* &c. Is to find by the Suns *place how many dayes after the Nativity the Bodies or Aspects of Promittors do Culminate at the same hour of the day that the Birth was.*

[*The RULE*] I. Find the R. A. of your Promittor (as is usual.)

II. Substract the *R. A.* or time from noon in the Radix, from the *R. A.* of the Promissor, and the Remainder is the R. A of the ☉'s Direction.

III. See what Signe, d. and m. agrees thereunto.

IV. Find the *Sun* in that place, either in the Ephemeris or prepared Table, and work in all respects as before in the Ascendant.

Example 5, M. C. ad □ ☾ *cum Lat.*

	d. m.
R.A. of the □ of the ☾ in 21d. 31m. ♉	
Lat. 1d. 17m. South	49. 26
Add the Circle that substraction may be made	360. 00
Their Sum is	409. 26
R. A. of time from noon substract	103. 34
Remains the R.A. Dir. ☉	215. 52

To which answers 8d. 15m. ♏. Unto this add the excess 26m. in the Radix, and that produces [8d. 41m. ♏] the next less in the fitted Table is [8d. 17m. ♏] to which answers 17 years. The difference between [8d. 41m. and 8d. 17m. ♏] is 24m. and the Diurnal Motion of the ☉ 61m. which in the Proportional Table in the last Column thereof points out 144 dayes, so the M.C. came to the □ of the ☾ at 17 years 144 dayes, &c.

III. How the Part of Fortune *is Directed.*

[*The RULE.*] I. Take the true Longitude of the Promittor, (and neither Right nor Oblique Ascention as in the two former.)

II. Substract the *Suns* place from the *Moons* place in the Radix, and thereby you have their distance, &c.

III. Substract this distance in [*S. Deg., and Min.*] from the Longitude of the Promissor (by adding 30d. or one whole Signe, if Substraction cannot be made.)

IV. Note their difference (which is called the Direction of the Ascendant) and always take the Oblique Ascention of this difference under the Lat. of the place of Birth, (notwithstanding the ⊗ be posited in the descending part of Heaven) and add 270d. thereunto, which produces the R.A. of the Direction of the M. C. with the Circle.

V. As in Directing of the Ascendant, so here substract the R.A. of time from noon in the Radix from this last found number, (abating the Circle here and every where else if need require) and the Remainder is the R.A. of the Direction of the *Sun* desired, by which you may find the Arch of Direction as before Directed, &c.

Example 6.

The ⊕ Directed to the □ of ♂ in 9d. 30m. ♑.

The Luminaries distance substracted from the place of the Promissor, leaves (as before shewed) 5S. 8d. 52m. *viz.* in ♍ the Direction of the Ascendant, the Oblique Ascention of that point was before found 150d. 2m. which added to 270d. produces 420d. 2m. for the Direction of the M.C. with the Circle, &c. from which substract the time from noon in the Radix 193d. 34m. the remainder is 226d. 28m. (*viz.* the R.A. of the *Direction* of the ☉) unto which agrees 18d. 49m. ♏ in the Ecliptick, add the ☉'s excess 26m. produces [19d. 15m. ♏] the next less in the fitted Table is [18d. 21m. ♏] which wants 54m.: and the *Suns* Diurnal motion 61m. [18d. 21m.] points out 27 years and 54m. 323 dayes: So the ⊗ meets with the □ of ♂ at 27 years, 323 dayes, according to this manner of Calculation, &c.

IV. How to Direct the Sun to Promittors.

[The RULE.] I. Having the exact Longitude of your Promittors Body or Aspect, find the *Sun* in that place forward in the Ephemeris (or prepared Table) account the dayes from the Birth (making also proportion for the odd minutes) and you have with much ease the Ark of Direction desired.

Example 7.

The *Sun* Directed to the □ of ♃ in 3d. 26m. ♏, &c.

Add 26m. the excess, the sum is 3d. 52m. ♏, I find the next less in the fitted Table [3d. 17m. 8] against 12 years, take 3d. 17m. from 3d. 52m. ♏ there remains 35m. and the Diurnal Motion of the *Sun* 60m., this 35m. gives in the Proportional Table under D.M. 60m. Column 5,213 dayes, and so the *Sun* met with the □ of ♃ at 12 years 213 dayes, &c.

V. *The* Moon *is thus Directed; and after the same manner all the rest of the Planets*, viz. Saturn, Jupiter, Mars, Venus *and* Mercury *to their severed Promittors. Therefore observe this brief Rule following for all.*

[*The RULE.*] I. Substract the *Moons* place, or any of the aforesaid Planets in S.*D.* and M. from the place of the Promissor, the remainder is called the Ark of *Direction*, &c.

II. To which add the Radical place of the *Sun*, and the Sum is the true place in Signe, deg. and min. of the Direction of the *Sun*.

III. As in all the former, find how many dayes from the Birth, the *Sun* touches that point of the Ecliptick, by making proportion as before directed for the odd min. and you have the years and dayes or the *Direction* desired.

Example 8.

Of the *Moon* add ☍ of ♀ in 6d. 32m. ♓.

	S.	d.	m.
The *Opposition* of *Venus* falls in *Pisces*	11.	6.	32
Substract the Radical place of the *Moon*	10.	21.	30
Remains the Ark of Direction of the *Moon*	0.	15.	01
Add the Radical place of the *Sun*	6.	20.	53
True place of the *Suns* Direction *viz.* ♏	7.	5.	54
Add the Excess of the *Sun*'s Place, &c.	0.	0.	26
Produces *Scorpio* 6 degrees 20 minutes	7.	6.	20

The *Suns* place next less in the Ephemeris (from which the fitted Table was taken) is [♏ 6d. 17m.] against the 19th day, to which agrees 15 dayes (or rather years) from the Birth, the difference of [6d. 17m. and 6d. 20m.] is

0d. 3m., the *Suns* Diurnal Motion 60m., which in the proportional Table points out 18 dayes, odd hours (which unless they are neer 24 alwayes omit.) So the ☽ came to the ☌ of ♀ in the Ecliptick, according to this method of Direction at 15 years 18 dayes, &c.

I have been the larger in these Examples because I would make it easie to be understood by the meanest Artists.

Lastly, *if you would know the Direction of the* Hylegiacals *for any propounded year, as suppose for the Natives 27th year Compleat, work thus;*

I. For the *Sun*, (which all along is the Basis of the work) account 27 dayes from the Birth in the fitted Table of the *Sun's* place, at which time the *Sun* was 18d. 21m. in ♏, from which substract the 26m. of Excess in the *Sun's* place in the Radix, and you have the true Direction of the *Sun* in ♏ 17d. 55m. for 27 years compleat.

For the *Moon*.	S. d. m.
The Direction of the Sun is Scorpio or,	7. 17. 55
From which substract his Radical place	6. 20. 53
Remains the Ark of Direction	0. 27. 2
Unto which add the Radical place of the *Moon*, or any other Planet	11. 21. 13
The Sun is the true Direction of the *Moon* which falls in *Aries* 18d. 33m.	12. 18. 33

III. For the Direction of the M.C. Ascendant, and ⊕, operate thus by the Tables of R. and Ob. Ascen. as before in the Examples you are directed.

	d. m.
The *Sun's* Direction is in *Scorpio* 17d. 55m. the Right Ascention of that point is	235. 26
Add the Right Ascention of time P. M. in the Radix agreeable to 12h. 54m. 16".	193. 34
The Sum rejecting 360d. is	69. 00

Which is the R. A. of the Direction of M.C. to which answers *Gemini* 10d. 37m., and so far the M.C. is Directed the 27th year compleat. Add 90d. to 69d. 0m. you have the Oblique Ascention of the Direction of the Horoscope or Ascendant, *Viz.* 159d. 0m. to which answers about 15d. 5m. of *Virgo* for the Direction of the Ascendant, unto which add the distance of tne Luminaries in the Radix, *viz.* 4 Signes, 0d. 38m. their sum is 9S. 15d. 43m. for the *Direction* or the ⊗, *viz.* ♑, &c.

To Conclude this Chapter.

Let those that would *Direct* a Nativity this way, draw their work into this following Method, *viz.*

I. For the Ascendant, Rule a Quarto or Folio page into six Columns, and in the first place the Aspects of the Promissors, in the second Column the Longitude in the Signes wherein those Aspects fall, in the third Column the Oblique Ascention of the Promissors, in the fourth Column the R. A. of the *Direction* of the *Sun* (produced by substracting the R.A. of the *Direction* of the *Sun* (produced by substracting the R. A. of time from Noon in the Radix, from the Oblique Ascention of the Promissor, and 270d. &c.) in the fifth Column place the Signe, deg. and min. correspondent to the R. A. of the Direction of the *Sun*, which is termed the true Direction of the *Sun*, and in the 6th and last the years and dayes correspondent, pointing out the time of the Accident.

II. For the M. C. there should six Columns also; and in all respects ordered as the Ascendant, except the third Column, which must contain the *R. A.* of the Promissor, as the other did the Oblique.

III. The ⊕ wlll require seven Columns, (1.) the Aspects, (2.) the Longitudes, (3.) the *Directions* of the Ascendant, (4.) the Oblique Ascen. (5.) the *R. A.* of the *Direction* of the *Sun*, (6.) the point of the Ecliptick correspondent, (*viz. Direction of the Sun*) (7.) *Lastly,* the years and dayes of the Accident.

IV. The *Sun* needs but three Columns, *viz* (1.) Aspects, (2.) Longitude, (3.) years and dayes, &c.

V. The *Moon* and the rest of the Planets must have five Columns, (1.) the Aspects of the Promittors. 2. their Longitude in S. d. and m. (3.) the Ark of Direction, (4.) the Direction of the *Sun* in S. d , and m. (5.) the time of the Accident.

And thus the work will be disposed into a neat handsome form, and the more fit for use.

But for ordering the work in Directing the old way, that large Example of a Speculum of *Directions* in Mr. *Lylly*'s *Introduction* is as Methodical, and Artificial as may be; yet that Form of a Speculum of *Directions* that is inserted in this Book is more freqwently used by public Professors.

A Table of the dayes proportional (in Direction) to each min. of the ☉'s Diurnal Motion.					
Min.	D.M.☉ 58m.	D.M.☉ 58m.	D.M.☉ 59m.	D.M.☉ 60m.	D.M.☉ 61m.
	Da. Ho.	Da. Ho.	Da. Ho.	Da. Ho.	Da. Ho.
1	6. 10	6. 7	6. 5	6. 2	6. 0
2	12. 20	12. 14	12. 9	12. 4	11. 23
3	19. 5	18. 21	18. 14	18. 6	17. 23
4	25. 25	25. 5	24. 18	24. 8	23. 23
5	32. 1	31. 12	30. 23	30. 11	29. 23
6	38. 11	37. 19	37. 3	36. 13	35. 22
7	44. 21	44. 2	43. 8	42. 15	41. 22
8	51. 6	50. 9	49. 13	48. 17	47. 22
9	57. 16	56. 16	55. 17	54 19	53. 21
10	64. 2	62. 23	61. 22	60. 21	59. 21
15	96. 3	94. 11	92. 21	91. 8	89. 20
20	128. 4	125. 23	123. 20	121. 18	119. 18
25	160. 5	157. 11	154. 18	152. 5	149. 17
30	192. 6	188. 22	185. 17	182. 15	179. 15
35	224. 6	220. 10	216. 10	213. 2	209. 14
40	256. 7	251. 22	247. 15	241. 12	239. 12
45	288. 9	283. 9	278. 14	273. 22	269. 11
50	320. 9	314. 21	309. 13	304. 9	299. 9
55	352. 10	346. 9	340. 11	334. 19	320. 8
57	365. 6	358. 23	352. 20	346. 23	330. 7
58		365. 6	359. 1	353. 1	336. 7
59			365. 6	359. 4	342. 6
60				365. 6	359. 6
61					365. 6

This Table was thus made, viz. (*by the Golden Rule*) *as the* Sun's *Diurnal Motion is to* 365 *dayes* 6 *hours, or* 8766 *hours, So is* 1m. *to the dayes and hours desired,* &c.

CHAP. XXXI.

Of the Revolution of the Sun to his Radical place in any Persons Nativity, and how to find the exact time thereof, &c.

I. A *Revoiutional Figure* is no more but the *Suns* Annual Conversion, or the true position of the *Heavens* for that very moment or point of *Time* that the *Sun*, (or *Moon* or any other *Planet*) returns to his Radical place, *viz.* to the Sign, deg. and min. of the Ecliptick precizely that it was posited in at the moment or Birth.

II. Now the most certain way to gain the true time of the *Suns* return to his *Radical* place, is first to compute the *Suns* true place in the *Radix* from some good *Astronomical Tables*, (such as these as are annexed to this Book, *viz.* the *Rudolphine Tables*, or what other the *Artist* is pleased to make use of;) then for the *Annual Revolution* of the *Sun,* Calculate his place again and from the same Tables for the *Noontide* of the day before and after the day of Birth, and thereby you may produce the *Suns Diurnal* Motion, and then consult *Example 2.* where by the help of the *Logistical Logarithms* the true hour and minute of the *Suns* return to any point of the Ecliptick may be most easily obtained.

III. Or you may Aequate for the true time from the *Suns Diurnal Motion* taken out of some exact *Ephemerides*, provided his Radical place were taken from the same foundation, (*i.e.* Calculated from the same Tables that the Ephemerides were extracted from) otherwise 'tis irrational so to do; and without the *Artist* observes this Caution he runs himself into an Errour, and rarely (if ever) produces an Exact *Revolutional Figure*.

But if either of these wayes be thought too troublesome in the setting of many *Revolutions* together, then let the *Student* make use of this following *Revolutional Table* which performs the Work with much ease and exactness, and the more exactly it corresponds to Truth, provided the *Artist* Calculate the *Suns* Radical place from the *Rudolphine Tables*, from whence this *Table* was Calculated, and is perpetual for the *Suns Revolution*, Accommodated to the Motion of his *Apogaeon* in years Compleat.

This Table *may be of good use also in finding the true time when the* Sun *makes his Ingress into* Aries, *or any of the other Cardinal Points, whence a Judgment is usual drawn concerning General Accidents of the World, &c.*

	Tabula Revolutionis Solis perpetua;				
	Anni completi.				
Anomsalia veraS.	1.	2.	3.	4.	5.
	H.M.S.	H.M.S.	H.M.S.	H.M.S.	H.M.S
0	5.48. 2	11.36. 5	17.14. 7	23.12.10	5.0.12
10	5.48. 4	11.36. 7	17.24.11	23.12.14	5.0.18
20	5.48. 6	11.36.12	17.24.18	23.13.24	5.0.30
30	5.48.10	11.36.20	17.24.30	23.12.40	5.0.50
40	5.48.15	11.36.30	17.24.45	23.13. 1	5.1.16
50	5.48.22	11.36.45	17.25. 7	23.13.29	5.1.52
60	5.48.31	11.37. 1	17.25.32	23.14. 3	5.2.34
70	5.48.39	11.37.18	18.25.57	23.14.36	5.3.15
80	5.48.49	11.37.37	17.26.26	23.15.14	5.4. 3
90	5.48.58	11.37.55	17.26.53	23.15.51	5.4.48
100	5.49. 7	11.38.13	17.27.20	23.16.26	5.5.33
110	5.49.16	11.38.32	17.27.48	23.17. 4	5.6.20
120	5.49.31	11.39. 49	17.18.14	23.18.38	5.7. 3
130	5.49.31	11.39. 3	17.28.34	23.18. 6	5.7.37
140	5.49.38	11.39.16	17.28.54	23.18.32	5.8.10
150	5.49.43	11.39.26	17.29. 9	23.18.52	5.8.35
160	5.49.47	11.39.34	17.29.21	23.19. 8	5.8.54
170	5.49.49	11.39.39	17.29.28	23.19.18	5.9. 7
180	5.49.51	11.39.41	17.29.32	23.19.23	5.9.13
190	5.49.50	11.39.39	17.29.29	23.19.19	5.9. 9
200	5.49.48	11.39.35	17.29.23	23.19.10	5.8.58
210	5.49.44	11.39.28	17.29.12	23.18.56	5.8.40
220	5.49.39	11.39.18	17.28.57	23.18.36	5.8.15
230	5.49.33	11.39. 6	17.28.39	23.18.12	5.7.44
240	5.49.26	11.38.52	17.28.17	23.17.43	5.7. 9
250	5.49.18	11.38.35	17.27.53	23.17.11	5.6.28
260	5.49. 9	11.38.17	17.27.26	23.16.34	5.5.43
270	5.48.59	11.37.59	17.26.58	23.15.57	5.4.57
280	5.48.50	11.37.41	17.26.31	23.15.22	5.4.12
290	5.48.41	11.37.21	17.26. 2	23.14.43	5.3.23
300	5.48.32	11.37. 3	17.25.35	23.14. 7	5.2.38
310	5.48.24	11.36.47	17.25.11	23.13.35	5.1.59
320	5.48.17	11.36.34	17.24.50	23.13. 7	5.1.24
330	5.48.11	11.36.22	17.24.32	23.12.43	5.0.54
340	5.48. 7	11.36.13	17.24.20	23.12.26	5.0.33
350	5.48. 4	11.36. 8	17.24.11	23.12.15	5.0.19
360	5.48. 2	11.36. 5	17.24. 7	23.12.10	5.0.12

	Accommodata Apogaeo mobili.				
	Anni. completi.				
Anomalia veraS.	6.	7.	8.	9.	10.
	H.M.S.	H.M.S.	H.M.S.	H.M.S.	H.M.S.
0	10.48.15	16.36.17	22.24.20	4.12.22	10. 0.24
10	10.48.22.	16.36.25	22.24.29	4.12.23	10. 0.36
20	10.48.36	16.36.43	22.24.49	4.12.55	10. 1. 1
30	10.49. 0	16.37.10	22.25.20	4.13.30	10. 1.40
40	10.49.31	16.37.46	22.26. 1	1.14.16	10. 2.31
50	10.50.14	16.38.36	22.26.59	4.15.21	10. 3.43
60	10.51. 4	16.39.35	22.28. 6	4.16.37	10. 5. 7
70	10.51.54	16.40.33	22.29.13	4.17.52	10. 6.30
80	10.52.52	16.41.40	22.30.29	4.19.17	10. 8. 6
90	10.53.46	16.42.43	22.31.41	4.20.39	10. 9. 3
100	10.54.40	16.43.46	22.32.53	4.22. 0	10.11. 6
110	10.55.36	16.44.53	22.34. 9	4.23.25	10.12.41
120	10.56.27	16.45.52	22.35.16	4.24.41	10.14. 5
130	10.57. 9	16.46.40	22.36.12	4.25.43	10.15.15
140	10.57.49	16.47.27	22.37.15	4.26.45	10.16.11
150	10.58.18	16.48. 2	22.37.45	4.27.28	10.17.11
160	10.58.41	16.48.28	22.38.15	4.28. 2	10.17.49
170	10.58.57	16.48.46	22.38.36	4.28.25	10.18.15
180	10.59. 4	16.48.55	22.38.45	4.28.36	10.18.26
190	10.58.58	16.48.48	22.38.38	4.28.27	10.18.17
200	10.58.45	16.48.33	22.38.20	4.28. 8	10.17.55
210	10.58.24	16.48. 8	22.37.52	4.27.36	10.17.20
220	10.57.55	16.47.34	22.37.13	4.26.52	10.16.31
230	10.57.17	16.46.50	22.36.23	4.25.56	10.15.29
240	10.56.35	16.46. 0	22.35.26	4.24.52	10.14.18
250	10.55.46	16.45. 3	22.34.21	4.23.39	10.12.56
260	10.54.52	16.44. 0	22.33. 9	4.22.17	10.11.26
270	10.53.56	16.42.56	22.31.55	4.20.54	10. 9.54
280	10.53. 2	16.41.53	22.30.43	4.19.34	10. 8.24
290	10.52. 4	16.40.45	22.29.25	4.18. 6	10. 6.47
300	10.51.10	16.39.42	22.28.13	4.16.45	10. 5.17
310	10.50.22	16.38.46	22.27.10	4.15.33	10. 3.57
320	10.49.41	16.37.58	22.26.14	4.14.31	10. 2.48
330	10.49. 5	16.37.15	22.25.26	4.13.37	10. 1.48
340	10.48.39	16.36.46	22.24.52	4.12.59	10. 1. 6
350	10.48.23	16.36.26	22.24.30	4.12.34	10. 0.38
360	10.48.15	16.36.17	22.24.20	4.12.22	10. 0.24

	Tabula Revolutionis Solis perpetua;				
	Anni completi				
Anomalis vera S.	20.	30.	40.	50.	60
	H.M.S.	H.M.S.	H.M.S.	H.M.S.	H.M.S.
0	20. 0.49	6. 1.13	16. 1.38	2. 2. 2	12. 2.27
10	20. 1.12	6. 1.49	16. 2.25	2. 3. 1	12. 3.37
20	20. 2. 2	6. 3. 2	16. 4. 3	2. 5. 4	12. 6. 5
30	20. 3.21	6. 5. 1	16. 6.41	2. 8.21	12.10. 2
40	20. 5. 3	6. 7.34	16.10. 5	2.12.36	12.15. 8
50	20. 7.27	6.11.10	16.14.54	2.18.37	12.22.21
60	20.10.15	6.15.22	16.20.30	2.25.37	12.30.45
70	20.13. 1	6.19.31	16.26. 1	2.32.32	12.39. 2
80	20.16.12	6.24.18	16.32.23	2.40.29	12.48.35
90	20.19.13	6.28.49	16.38.25	2.48. 1	12.57.38
100	20.22.12	6.33.18	16.44.25	2.55.31	13. 6.37
110	20.25.22	6.38. 2	16.50.43	3. 3.24	13.16. 9
120	20.28.10	6.42.15	16.56.20	3.10.25	13.24.30
130	20.30.30	6.45.44	17. 0.59	3.16.14	13.31.29
140	20.32.42	6.49. 3	17. 5.24	3.21.45	13.38. 6
150	20.34.21	6.51.32	17. 8.43	3.25.54	13.43. 4
160	20.35.38	6.53.27	17.11.16	3.29. 5	13.46.54
170	20.36.30	6.54.44	17.12.59	3.31.14	13.49.29
180	20.36.03	6.55.19	17.13.46	3.32.12	13.50.39
190	20.36.34	6.54.52	17.13. 9	3.31.26	13.49.43
200	20.35.51	6.53.46	17.11.42	3.29.37	13.47.33
210	20.34.40	6.51.59	17. 9.19	3.26.39	13.43.59
220	20.33. 2	6.49.33	17. 6. 4	3.22.35	13.39. 5
230	20.30.58	6.46.27	17. 1.56	3.17.24	13.32.53
240	20.28.35	6.42.53	16.57.11	3.11.28	13.25.46
250	20.25.53	6.38.49	16.51.45	3. 4.42	13.17.38
260	20.22.52	6.34.18	16.45.44	2.57.10	13. 8.36
270	20.19.47	6.29.41	16.39.35	2.49.28	12.59.22
280	20.16.48	6.25.12	16.33.36	2.42. 0	12.50.24
290	20.13.33	6.20.10	16.27. 7	2.33.53	12.40.40
300	20.10.33	6.15.50	16.21. 6	2.26.23	12.31.39
310	20. 7.54	6.11.51	16.15.48	2.19.45	12.23.42
320	20. 5.36	6. 8.24	16.11.11	2.13.59	12.16.47
330	20. 3.35	6. 5.23	16. 7.10	2. 8.58	12.10.46
340	20. 2.11	6. 3.17	16. 4.22	2. 5.18	12. 6.33
350	20. 1.16	6. 1.53	16. 2.31	2. 3. 9	12. 3.47
360	20. 0.49	6. 1.13	16. 1.38	2. 2. 2	12. 2.27

Anomalia vera S.	Accommodata Apogaeo Mobili. Anni completi.			
	70.	80.	90.	100.
	H.M.S.	H.M.S.	H.M.S.	H.M.S.
0	22. 2.51	8. 3.15	18. 3.40	4. 4. 4
10	22. 4.13	8. 4.49	18. 5.26	4. 6. 2
20	22. 7. 5	8. 8. 6	18. 9. 7	4.10. 8
30	22.11.42	8.13.22	18.15. 3	4.16.43
40	22.17.39	8.20.10	18.22.42	4.25.13
50	22.26. 4	8.29.48	18.33.31	4.37.15
60	22.35.52	8.41. 0	18.46. 7	4.51.15
70	22.45.32	8.52. 3	18.58.33	5. 5. 3
80	22.56.41	9. 4.47	19.12.53	5.20.59
90	23. 7.14	9.16.50	19.26.27	5.36. 3
100	23.17.43	9.28.49	16.39.55	5.51. 1
110	23.28.46	9.41.27	19.54. 7	6. 6.48
120	23.38.36	9.52.41	20. 6.46	6.20.51
130	23.46.44	10. 1.58	20.17.13	6.32.28
140	23.54.26	10.10.47	20.27. 8	6.43.29
150	0. 0.15	10.17.26	20.34.37	6.51.47
160	0. 4.43	10.22.32	20.40.21	6.58.10
170	0. 7.43	10.25.58	20.44.13	7. 2.28
180	0. 9. 5	10.27.32	20.45.58	7. 4.24
190	0. 8. 0	10.26.17	20.44.35	7. 2.52
200	0. 5.28	10.23.24	20.41.19	5.59.15
210	0. 1.19	10.18.38	20.35.58	6.53.18
220	23.55.36	10.12. 7	20.28.38	6.45. 9
230	23.48.22	10. 3.51	20.19.20	6.34.49
240	23.40. 4	9.54.21	20. 8.39	6.22.56
250	23.30.34	9.43.30	19.56.27	6. 9.23
260	23.20. 2	9.31.29	19.42.55	5.54.21
270	23. 9.16	9.19. 9	19.29. 3	5.38.57
280	22.58.48	9. 7.12	19.15.36	5.24. 0
290	22.47.26	8.54.13	19. 0. 0	5. 7.46
300	22.36.56	8.42.12	18.47.29	4.52.46
310	22.27.40	8.31.37	18.35.34	4.39.31
320	22.19.35	8.22.23	18.25.11	4.27.59
330	22.12.33	8.14.21	18.16. 8	4.17.56
340	22. 7.39	8. 8.44	18. 9.50	4.10.55
350	22. 4.24	8. 5. 2	18. 5.40	4. 6. 2
360	22. 2.51	8. 3.15	18. 3.40	4. 4. 4

The Use of the Table in Setting a Revolutional Figure of the Sun
appertaining to any Persons Geniture.

I. From the Tables of the *Planets* Motion Compare the *Suns Apogaeon* for the Year and Month of Birth, (which you will have in Calculating the *Sun's* Radical place.)

II. Substract this *Apogaeon* from the Sun's true place before found (by adding the Circle where Substraction cannot be made) and the Remainder is the *Sun's Anomaly* which you may convert into degrees and minutes, &c.

III. With this *Anomaly* (in degrees) enter the first Column of the Revolutional Table (which is set down to every 10d.) and take the neerest Number, or make proportion (which exactness is here needless as you may perceive by the inconsiderable difference the Table affords) and under the years compleat at head of the Table in the Common Angle of meeting you have certain hours, min. and seconds, to be added to the time after Noon in the Radix (calling away 24 hours if it exceed) and the Sum gives the true time of the *Sun's* Return to his Radical place, for which you are to set your *Figure* by a *Table* of *Houses* or otherwise, not forgetting to make Reduction for the *Difference* of *Meridians*, if the place of abode be far remote from that of Birth.

[*Note that by reason of the Leap-year, the Revolution may not alwayes happen upon the same day of the Moneth the Radix was on, but by the* Sun's *place in your* Ephemeris *you may easily discern the truth.*]

IV. To explain the aforesaid Precept, observe this Example: Suppose I would set a Revolutional Figure to the Exemplary Geniture. For the Natives 29th year Current Commencing *March* 11. 15h. 57m. p.m. 1678. Current, as appears by this following Examination.

The *Suns* Apogaeon to the year and month of Birth will be found by the Tables to be 3 Signes, 6d. 35m. ferè, which substracted from the *Sun's Radical* place 12 Signes, 1d. 55m. there remains 8 Signes, 25d. 20m. for the Anomaly, which converted into degrees, amounts to 265d. 20m. the minutes are here inconsiderable, I enter the Table with 265d. of *Anomaly*, and accept of 270d. (without Aequation) against which I have a Revolutonal Table proper to this Geniture, as in the Margent. Now for the Time of the Revolution, agsint 20 years compleat in the Table I find 20h. 19m. 47s. and agsint 8 years compleat 22h. 31m. 55s. which added to the former, makes 42h. 15m. 42s. to which last Sum I also add the time from Noon at Birth, *viz.* 21h. 5m. 8s.

	h.	m.	s.
And the last Total is	63.	56.	50
From whence sub. twice 24h. viz.	48.	00.	00
And there Remains	15.	56.	50

ye	H. M. S.
1	5.48. 5
2	11.37. 5
3	17.26.58
4	23.15.57
5	05.04.57
6	10.53.56
7	16.42.56
8	22.31.55
9	04.20.54
10	10.09.54
20	20.19.47
30	06.29.41
40	16.39.35
50	02.49.28
60	12.59.22
70	23. 9.16

So that the *Sun* returns to his Radical place at athe 28th year compleat of the Natives Age, *viz. March* 11. 1678. current, 15h. 56m. 50s. *P. M.* for which time I set the Scheme for the Latitude of *London*, the place of the Native's preent Habitation. *The Figure follows.* [Ed. See following page.]

How to Judge of a Revolutional Figure.

I. Having obtained the true position of the Heavens at the time of the *Suns* Return to his *Radical* Place, &c. then consider what agreement there is between the *Radical and Revolutional Figures*, if you find them in *Sextiie* or *Trine* to each other, and the *Planets* in the *Revolution* beholding their *Radical* places friendly, these are good Arguments of a fortunate and happy year, which will be much Augmented if at the same time there be some propitious *Direction* of either of the *Hylegiacals* in force; the *Directions* opperating must be considered in the Judgment of the Revolution; for in that both *Directions* and *Revolution* must be conjoyned together.

II. But if the *Radix* or *Revolution* happen to be in *Square* or *Opposition* (in respect of the Eclipticks) to each other and the *Planets* in the same *Aspects* to their Radical places,

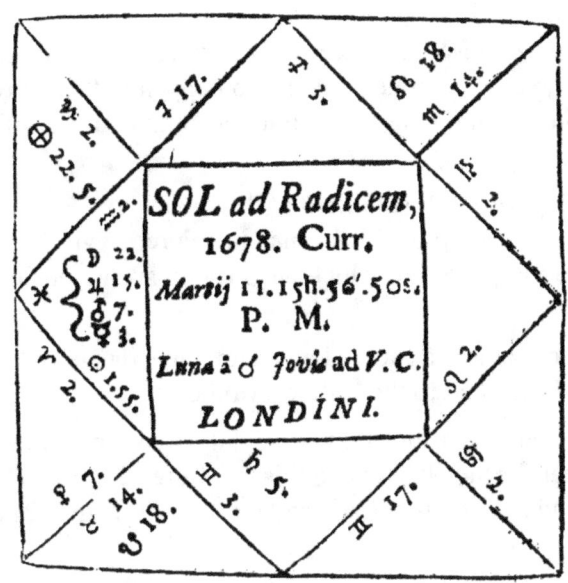

then you may rationally judge that the years Actions will prove very unfortunate to the Native; and consequently all his Indeavours insuccessful for the most part, unless mitigated by hopeful *Transits* of the superiours, which ought not to be forgotten for they are very prevalent.

III. Finally the greater the Harmony is between the *Scheme* of the *Nativity* and that of the *Revolution* the more Fortunate and Successful will the Actions and Affairs of the Native be that year; and the greater their disagreement is, the more unhappiness may be expected, which must be left to the Judgment of the *Artist* to point out or discover the Nature of the evil impending that year to the Native.

And here 'tis worth the Students Observation, that notwithstanding the *Revolution Figure* of the *Sun* be never so promising and hopeful, yet if the *Natiuity* be unfortunate, or promise little, (the Planets being weake and ill disposed therein) then the Native will find very slender and mean effects from the influence of the *Planets* at the *Suns* Return, unless he can live above their *Energy*, or the common Principles of mankind; the Reason is that an essential and ill-grounded evil cannot be removed or abated by an accidental good: a cruel and unhappy *Fate* will be found too difficult to root out, though favorable Influences may intervene, and probably mittigate the danger Originally threatened; yet I would not be understood here by to affirm a Fatal necessity: *But I proceed to shew some select and choice* Aphorismes *to inform the Student more particularly how to Judge a Revolution Figure*; which take as followeth.

General Aphorismes to be Observed in the Judgment of a Revolution, &c.

I. When the *Lord* of the *Ascendant* of the *Revolution* shall be in good Aspect with the *Lord* of the *second House* in the *Radix;* or if the *Lord* of the *Ascendant* in the *Radix*, be in the same Aspect with the *Lord* of the second in the *Revolution*, this denotes profit to the Native that year by his own proper industry and labour.

II. If the Revolutional Ascendant be vitiated by an infortunate Planet, either by Body or Aspect, this signifies much detriment and affliction to happen to the Native that year, of the nature of the afflicting Planet, consideration had to the Signe and House he is posited in.

III. The Lord of the Ascendant or the Radix being strong and well located in the Revolution, and in friendly Aspect with the Fortunes, promises health of Body to the Native, and much good to attend his affairs that year, and this the rather if the aforesaid Significators are posited in good places of the Figure.

IV. The Lord of the second in the Revolution in the Ascendant, or the ⊗ posited in a good place of the Figure, and well beheld, or in the place of Fortunate Planets in the Radix; this declares much profit to the Native that year, and this without any great matter of toyl to obtain it.

V. When in a Revolution you find the Lord or the Ascendant thereof much afflicted, or in Combustion of the *Sun*, this portends much afflliction to the Native that year, and that he shall unavoidably suffer much loss and detriment in one kind or other, unless the Lord of the Ascendant happen to be in his own Essential Dignities; if so, he will be able to struggle in the midst of dangers, and receive the less Prejudice; but if he be posited in his debility, and affected as aforesaid, then you may positively conclude his Troubles will that year preve exceeding great.

VI. The Luminaries both, or either of them ill posited in a Revolution, and much afflicted therein, threaten detriment in Body or Estate, or both, to the Natives Father and Mother; if the *Sun* be concerned judge the Father, and

Moon the Mother of the Native, &c.

VII. See whether either of the Luminaries happen to suffer an Eclipse in, or neer their own Radical places, or in any of the Angles of the Geniture, this is an argument of great and eminent danger to happen to the Natives Body, especially if it fall in the Radical Ascendant; for oftentimes it threatens death to the Native, unless other good Configurations strongly interpose, &c.

VIII. The *Sun* in the Revolution being posited in *Quartile* or *Opposition* to the Lord of the Radical Ascendant, is a certain note of many troubles to incur to the Native the ensuing year; probably he may be injured by his Father, or suffer by the frowns of some great person, or men, or man in power, of which he is (upon such a position) Cautioned to beware.

IX. The Infortunes in *Conjunction* in the M. C. in a Revolution, bids the Native beware of some dangerous fall from a high place, loss of Honour and Repute, Damage and Detriment to the Natives Mother, &c.

X. If the Lord of the Ascendent in the Revolution happen to be much afflicted in the eighth House, and no way afflicted by the Fortunes, it intimates danger of death that year for the Native; and this the more certain if a bad Direction happen at the same time. Judge the same if you find the *Moon* in *Conjunction* of *Saturn*, and *Saturn* behold the Ascendant, or Lord thereof by *Quartile* or *Opposition*.

Lastly, If you find all the Planets well posited strong and potent in the Revolution, this denotes much good to succeed to the Native in that years actions; but if they are found weak, and posited in bad places of the Figure, judge the contrary, consideration (all along) being had to the Concordancy or Discordancy that is between the Radix and Revolutional Figures, as was noted before.

Here I might have added many more Aphorismes *as to the judging a Revolution, but these are the most significant, and sufficient to enable an ingenious Lover of Art how to extract a Judgment from any such Figure. Those that would read more, may satisfie themselves from such Authors (both Antient and Modern) that have written Copiously hereof, and so I proceed to give a brief Judgment upon the precedent Revolutional Figure, according to the Rules before exprest.*

Judgment upon the Figure of the Sun's Return from the 29th Year Current of the Natives Age.

The Directions that are Operating this year are only these; (1.) ♀ *ad* Terms of ☿, 28. 3. (2.) ♂ *ad* Terms of ♄ 28. 18. (3.) ♂ ad ✶ *Dext*. of ♀ 28. 27. (4.) M. C. *ad* Terms of ☿ 28. 35. All which do naturally promise felicity to the Native, except the second; that may a little discompose his Body, but 'twill be of no continuance, the other three *Directions* are more prevalent, and portend not only vigilency in the Native, but moderate success and pleasure in the management of his affairs; also health of Body, and a Convenient Profit arising from or by the means of many New Friends and Acquaintance that he may this year meet withal. In the *Revolution* finding so many *Planets* Posited in the *Ascendant* and *Jupiter* and the *Moon* (neerly in *Trine* to their Radical places, this argues it will prove a very busie year and produce much Imployment ot the Native of one kind or other: and the *Sun* so neer the Cusp of the second House in his own Dignities may aptly denote profit; but withal liberal and Noble Expence; this is not a little aggravated by the *Quadrat* of *Saturn* and *Mars* Lord of the Second; it also advises the Native to be careful to keep up his Honour and Reputation; for *Saturn* is not only in *Quartile* to *Mars*, but in *Opposition* to the Angle of Honour: but the greatest danger should be towards the close of the Revolution; Yet conisdering also that *Jupiter* Lord of the tenth House is potent in the Ascendant, there in *Conjunction* with the *Moon*, and *Mars* Lord of the second House of the *Revolution*, who is also in *Sextile* to *Venus* in her Dignities in the Second, these are more prevalent Arguments, and portend success and advantage to the Native in most of his affairs, notwithstanding some casual (but inconsiderable) dangers may fall in, which will be such as cannot much prejudice the Native either in his Honour, Person, or Estate: much more might be written upon this Revolutional Figure; but this is sufficient for an Example, to informe the young Student how he may judge any other Revolutional Figure, &c.

CHAP. XXXII.

How to Direct a Revolutional Figure.

I. Some have taught to Direct the five *Hylegiacals* in a Revolutional Figure quite round the 12 Signes every year, and allow 59m. (the *Suns* Diurnal Motion) for the measure of time for a day, *&c.* But by this means the Revolutional Directions will happen to be the same every year (in one part or other thereof) which seems to be vary absurd.

II. But the most rational way is this, (which hath been much Experienced by able Artists) to Direct the chief Angles of the Revolution, *viz.* the M. C. and Ascendant to their several Promittors till you come to the Cusp of the M. C. and Ascendant for the next years Revolution, making the difference of time between those two Revolutions the measure of Time for one year, *&c.* as shall be cleared by Example, and in the Revolutional Directions wholly to neglect the Latitude of the Planets in their Aspects, by reason the Revolution serves but for a year, and all the Directions thereof terminate in the same space of time; neither is it much material whether you take notice of odd minutes in Right or Oblique Ascention, but Direct by whole degrees, or by the Tables of Houses, which in this case is much more ready and easie, and sufficiently exact.

III. Before I come to Examples, 'twill be convenient for ease and method sake to insert a necessary Table or two, which will be of great use in Directing Revolutions, as also a Speculum of the Revolution aforesaid, contracted as followeth.

A Speculum of the Revolution Figure.

deg. Pla.	♈	♉	♊	♋	♌	♍	♎	♏	♐	♑	♒	♓
1 ☉ 55. 2. Asen.	☉		✳	□	△		☍		△ As.	□	✳ As.	
3. M.C. 3. ☿		✳	□	△		☍		△	mc □	✳		☿
5. ♄ 7. ♂	✳	✳	♄ □	△	✳	□ ☍	△	△	☍	✳ □	△	□ ♂
7. ♀ 18. ☊		♀		✳	□	△		☍ ☊		△	□	✳
12. ☽		✳	□	△		☍		△	□	✳		☽

A general Revolutional Table to Degrees and Minutes			
de	da hor	M	hor. mi.
1	4 5	1	1 41
2	8 10	2	3 22
3	12 14	3	5 3
4	16 18	4	6 44
5	20 23	5	8 25
6	25 4	6	10 6
7	29 9	7	11 47
8	33 13	8	13 28
9	37 18	9	15 9
10	41 23	10	16 50
20	83 22	20	33 40
30	125 20	30	50 30
40	167 19	40	67 20
50	209 18	50	84 10
60	251 16	60	101 0
70	293 14		
80	335 12		
87	365 6		

A Table of the dayes of the year Numbred from the day of Birth		
March	31	19
April	30	39
May	31	80
June	30	110
July	31	141
August	31	172
September	30	202
October	31	233
November	30	263
December	31	294
January	31	325
February	28	353
March	12	365
In Leap year add a day more in February.		

[*Note that these, and the following Tables are Calculated to the Suns Mean Motion, and are of General Use in* Revolutional Directions; *the one to be used if you Direct by Tables of Right and Oblique Ascention, inferred at the end of this Book; and the other of Use if you Direct by the Tables of Houses; Examples of both, follow after the Tables from the Exemplary Geniture.*]

	A General Table for Revolutional Directions in Time.					
H.	0 Hour.	1 Hour.	2 Hour.	3 Hour.	4 Hour	5 Hour.
M.	*Da.hour*	*Da.hour*	*Da.hour*	*Da.hour*	*Da.hour*	*Da.hour*
0	0 0	62 22	125 20	188 11	251 16	314 14
2	2 2	65 0	127 22	190 20	253 18	316 16
4	4 5	67 3	130 0	192 24	255 20	318 18
6	6 7	69 5	132 2	195 1	257 23	320 21
8	8 9	71 7	134 5	197 3	260 1	322 23
10	10 12	73 10	136 7	199 6	262 3	325 1
12	12 14	75 12	138 10	201 8	264 6	327 4
14	14 16	77 14	140 12	203 20	266 8	329 6
16	16 19	79 37	142 14	205 12	268 10	331 8
18	18 21	81 19	144 17	207 15	270 13	333 11
20	20 23	83 21	146 19	209 17	272 15	335 13
22	23 2	86 10	148 21	211 19	274 17	337 15
24	25 4	88 2	151 0	213 22	276 20	339 17
26	27 6	90 4	153 2	216 0	278 23	341 20
28	29 9	92 7	155 4	218 2	281 0	343 22
30	31 11	94 9	157 7	220 5	283 3	346 1
32	33 13	96 11	159 9	222 7	285 5	348 3
34	35 16	98 14	161 11	224 9	287 7	350 5
36	37 18	100 16	163 14	226 12	289 10	352 8
38	39 20	102 18	165 16	228 14	291 12	354 10
40	41 23	104 21	166 18	230 16	293 14	356 12
42	44 1	106 23	169 21	232 19	295 17	358 15
44	46 3	109 1	171 23	234 21	297 19	360 17
46	48 6	111 4	174 1	236 23	299 21	362 19
48	50 8	113 6	176 4	239 2	302 0	364 21
50	52 10	115 8	178 6	241 4	304 1	367 0
52	54 13	117 10	180 8	243 6	306 4	
54	56 15	119 13	182 11	245 9	308 7	
56	58 17	121 15	184 13	247 11	310 9	
58	60 20	123 17	186 15	249 13	312 11	
60	62 22	125 20	188 18	251 14	314 14	

\multicolumn{7}{	c	}{*A Particular Revolution Table fitted from the General Table to the proposed Geniture, which points out the day of the Direction sought only by Inspection.*}
H.	0 Hour.	1 Hour.	2 Hour.	3 Hour.	4 Hour.	5 Hour.
M	Mon.da	Mon.da	Mon.da	Mon.da	Mon.da	Mon.da
0	Mar. 12	May 13	July 15	Sept. 16	Nov. 20	Jan. 21
2	14	16	18	18	22	23
4	16	18	20	20	24	35
6	18	20	22	23	26	27
8	20	22	24	25	28	30
10	22	24	26	27	Dec. 1	Feb. 1
12	24	26	28	29	2	3
14	26	28	30	Octo. 2	4	3
16	28	30	Aug. 1	4	6	7
18	30	June 1	3	6	8	9
20	April 1	3	5	8	10	11
22	4	6	8	10	12	13
24	6	8	10	13	14	15
26	8	10	12	15	17	17
28	10	12	14	17	19	19
30	12	14	16	19	21	21
32	14	16	18	21	23	23
34	16	18	20	24	25	25
36	18	20	22	25	27	28
38	20	22	24	27	30	Marc. 2
40	22	24	26	29	Jan. 1	4
42	25	27	29	Nov. 1	3	6
44	27	29	31	3	5	8
46	29	July 1	Sept. 2	6	7	10
48	May 1	3	4	8	9	12
50	3	5	6	10	11	
52	5	7	8	12	13	
54	7	9	10	14	15	
56	9	11	12	16	17	
58	11	13	14	18	19	
60	13	15	16	20	21	

Brief Examples of Directing a Revolutional Figure, both by Tables of Ascention, and by Tables of Houses.

I. As in the *Nativity* Form the Figure of the *Revolution* into a *Speculum* (as the Exemplary *Revolution Figure* is contracted) and thereby you may most readily see what Directions will occur; Having so done, direct your eye in the Column of the *Ascendant*, and you will find in our Example the Ascendant first meets the △ of Saturn in 5d. of ♒, then the □ of ♀ in 7d. of that Signe, next the ☌ of ☿ in 3d. of ♓, then the □ of ♄, and the rest as you find them in the *Speculum*.

II. Now suppose I would know when the Ascendant meets the Body of Mars, who is in 7d. of ♓, by the Tables of Oblique Ascention for the Latitude of *London*, I find the Oblique Ascention of 7d. of ♓ is 350d. 12m. from which I substract the Oblique Ascention of the Ascendant, *viz.* 2d. of ♒ 331d. 13m. and there remains the Ark of

Direction 18d. 59m. Then turn to the Revolution Table to deg. and min. and at several entrances I find that 18d. 59m. gives 81 dayes 0 hours, which by the little Table of the dayes of the year collected from the Birth, points out *June* the first, and then the Ascendant meets the ☌ of ♂ by *Direction*.

III. Or by a Table of Houses more easily, thus; against 2d. of ♒ under the Ascendant in the first great Column stands 16h. 4m. which substracted from 17 hours 21m. which stands against 7d. of ♓ in the Column of the *Ascendant*, there remains 1h. 17m. which sought in the *Particular Revolution Table* to the *Exemplary Geniture* made from the General Table, *viz.* 1 hour at top, and 17 in the first Column to the left hand, in the Common Angle of Meeting, answers *May* 31, an inconsiderable difference Occasioned for want of proportional work in the Operation, and farther exactness is needless in this Case.

After the same Method the *Mid heaven* is Directed by Tables of Right Ascention, or from the first great Column in the Tables of Houses correspondent to the *Significator* and *Promittors* places found under the Column of the tenth House: as for Example; Suppose I would Direct the M. C. to the *Quartile* of the *Moon* in the Revolution, the M.C. is ♐ 3d. whose Right Ascention is 240d. 57m. and the Right Asention of the □ of the ☽ in 22d. of that Signe is 261d. 17m. their difference 20d. 20m. is the Ark of Direction, this 20d. 20m. in the Table for that purpose points out 85 dayes from the Birth, *viz. June* the fifth, by the little Table of the dayes of the year collected from the Birth, and then the Direction did initiate; but by the Tables of Houses for *London*, if I substract 16h. 4m. the Right Ascention in time answering to 3d. of ♐, upon the M. C. from 17 hours 25 min. the Right Ascention of Time Correspondent to 22 degrees of *Sagitary*, their difference is 1h. 21m. which by the General *Revolution Table* points out neer 85 dayes, and by the Particular Revolutional Table *June* the 4th; so there will not be above a day difference (and rarely that) if you use either of these wayes, wich is sufficiently exact in this Case, and needs no farther preciseness.

V. To clear all doubts, I shall insert an Example which shall be upon the *Sun's* Return for the year 1671 current, which was *March* 12. 11h. 14m. *mane*, and the Planets places were as in the next page is exprest, *&c.*

1671.

The Revolutional M.C. and Ascend. Directed as followeth.

M.C. *ad*	Ascendant *ad*	P. d. S.
☌ ☉ May 1	△ ☉ May 23	♄ 13. ♓
☌ ☊ May 7	☌ ♃ June 28	♃ 8. ♌
△ ♃ May 22	△ ♀ July 21	♂ 16. ♉
☌ ♀ June 8	□ ♂ Aug. 14	☉ 1.55 ♈
△ ☽ July 8	☌ ☽ Oct. 27	♀ 12. ♈
⚹ ☿ Sept. 2	☍ ☿ Dec. 1	☿ 5. ♓
□ ♃ Sept. 18	☍ ♄ Jan. 26	☽ 28. ♌
⚹ ♄ Octob. 10	△ ♂ Feb. 13	☊ 4. ♈
☌ ♂ Octob. 23		M.C. 19 ♓
□ ☽ Decem. 13		Asc. 19 ♋
⚹ ☉ March 4		

[*Lastly*, These Tables are made by the *Golden Rule*, and by this proportion; If 87d. or 5h. 48m. gives 365 dayes 6h. what shall one day give ♐ *&c.* Or, if 348m. (the minutes in 5h. 48m.) give 8766h. the hours in 365 dayes and a quarter, what shall 1m. 2m. 10m. *&c.* give?]

Note that the Column intituled *Time from Noon* in the Tables of Houses, is nothing else but the R.A. in Time agreeable to the several deg. of the 12 Signes in the Column of the tenth House; as for Example, the R.A. of 1d. of ♈ is 55m. which converted into Time gives 3'.40". and so of the rest. Again, if you would have the Oblique Ascention of any point of the Ecliptick for the Latitude of the place, seek the degree desired under the Ascendant, and right against it in the Column of *Time from Noon* you have the Oblique Ascention desired in Time, alwayes adding 6 hours to that R.A. found; if under the Pole of the eleventh House add 2 hours, if under the Pole of the twelfth add 4 hours to the R. A. of Time from Noon correspondent, and you have the Oblique Ascention in Time under those several Elevations; this being known, you may Direct any other Significator by the Tables of Houses exact enough for a Revolutional Figure, as also find the Rising and Setting of the *Sun*, or any Planet without Latitude, &c. as I have already shewed in this Book.

This foregoing method of Directing the Ascendant and M. C. in a Revolution is the same with that by Tables of Ascention; for here you find the degrees of the Aequator in Time intercepted between the Significator and Promittor, which if you convert into degrees, &c. the thing is the same as before shewed.

CHAP. XXXIII.

Of Projections, &c.

I. Projections (or Progressions) are three fold, *viz.* Annual, Monthly, and Diurnal; but I shall only insist upon Annual Profections, and shew the method of their Directions, because I know some able Artists now living have a good esteem of them, and I shall leave the other two as superfluous, and scarce worth mentioning, being but a Nicity of the Antients.

II. Annual *Progression* is no more but a Regular change of the Signes and Degrees successively upon the Cusps of the Houses every year, but the Planets are to remain fixed in the same parts, or Houses of the Heavens that they were posited in in the *Radix*; as if *Gemini* were *Ascending* at Birth, the next year *Cancer* shall be the *Ascendant*; the third year *Leo,* and so on, &c. so that once in *twelve years* the *Profectional Figure* will be the same, as you may better conceive by Inspection of the following Table fitted to the Exemplary Nativity.

A Particular Profection Table to the Geniture, according to the years Current.

M.C.	Anno Do.	Anno Do.	Anno Do.	Anno Do.	Anno Do.	Anno Do.	Asce.
♒	1650	1662	1674	1686	1698	1710	♊
♓	1651	1663	1675	1687	1699	1711	♋
♈	1652	1664	1676	1688	1700	1712	♌
♉	1653	1665	1677	1689	1701	1713	♍
♊	1654	1666	1678	1690	1702	1714	♎
♋	1655	1607	1679	1691	1703	1715	♏
♌	1656	1668	1680	1692	1704	1716	♐
♍	1657	1669	1681	1693	1705	1717	♑
♎	1658	1670	1682	1694	1706	1718	♒
♏	1659	1671	1683	1695	1707	1719	♓
♐	1660	1672	1684	1696	1708	1720	♈
♑	1661	1673	1685	1697	1709	1721	♉

III. By a Profectional Figure you may neerly discover the Time when a *Direction* begins to operate, and is therefore accounted by some a lesser way of *Direction*; if so, they must needs be of good use, and they have been approved of by Curious Observers, although some Astrologers are pleased to reject them.

IV. My worthy Friend, Mr. *Lilly,* who has had greater Experience and Practice in the Art of Astrology than any man this day living in England, in his *Introduction,* affirms that "*Profections* do manifest what years are like to be "most prosperous and happy, and the contrary by the "Progression of the Principal Cusps of the Houses, *viz.* the

Ascendant and *Mid-heaven*; For it is generally observed, that those years that fall in ✶ or △ to the *Horoscope* or *M. C.* (especially when those Houses or Signes were *Radically* well fortified and Fortunate) shall prove very prosperous years to the Native; but those that fall in □ or ☍ to the Angles aforesaid are generally bad years, and very unhappy. Note also that Profections of themselves without the Concurrence of Directions and Revolutions are not so prevalent.

V. Judge of the effects of *Projections,* as before of *Directions*, always considering what the *Significator* signifies of himself, and what by his Accidental Position; so take notice of the *Promittor* also, which plainly declares the cause of the good or evil approaching, *&c.*

The *Profection* of the *Ascendant* is to be look'd unto for the Affection of the Life and Body of the Native, *&c.* the M. C. for Honour and Preferment; and so order your Judgment for the *Sun,* the *Moon,* and *Part of Fortune's Directions* to their several *Promittors*, as hath been before sufficiently exprest, always considering the *Directions* in force, and how the Revolution agrees, *&c.*

VI. The Manner of *Profectional Directions* is briefly thus; *viz.* To substract the place of the *Significator* in the *Ecliptick* whose *Profection* you desire from the place of the *Promissor,* by adding 30 deg. if otherwise substraction cannot be made, what remains shall be their distance, and for every degree allow 12 dayes 4 hours 12m. For if 30 deg, (*viz.* one Signe) gives 365 dayes, 1 degree gives 12 dayes 4 hours 12 min. *&c.* (or 4 hours) [as in the following Table.]

Or thus, (which by some is look'd upon as the truest measure, although the difference is not great, as I have often proved,) Substract the Significator from the Promittor, and multiply their difference by 12, and add this product in Signes and degrees to the *Sun's* place in the Radix, and when, the *Sun* approacheth to this very point so added, is the true time of the Directions *&c.*

This being plain and easie, I presume wlll be sufficiently understood by most, and therefore an Example is needless here.

In the next place I shall present the Reader with a General Table of the Measure of Time in *Profections*, as also a Particular Table fitted to the Exemplary *Nativity*, with its Construction and Use; which will, I doubt not, appear as pleasant as *Noval* to the Ingenious Student: for whose sake I have omitted nothing which lay within the *Peremiter* of my Understanding, that I thought might be serviceable to the Sons of Art; and the better to incourage them, I have, I hope, presented them with sufficient variety, to allure them to the more serious Contemplation and Study in this Sublime Subject; *viz.* the *Syderal Science.*

VII. A Table for the Measure of Time in Profections.					
A Table to convert deg. into d. &h.			A Table of Converting Minutes into Dayes, and Hours.		
Deg.	D. H.		M.	D. H.	
1	12 4		1	0 5	
2	24 9		2	0 10	
3	36 13		3	0 15	
4	48 17		4	0 20	
5	60 21		5	1 0	
6	73 1		6	1 5	
7	85 5		7	1 10	
8	97 10		8	1 15	
9	109 14		9	1 20	
10	121 18		10	2 1	
11	133 22		11	2 6	
12	146 2		12	2 10	
13	158 7		13	2 15	
14	170 11		14	2 20	
15	182 15		15	3 1	
16	194 19		16	3 6	
17	206 23		17	3 11	
18	219 3		18	3 16	
19	321 8		19	3 21	
20	243 12		20	4 1	
21	255 16		21	4 6	
22	267 10		22	4 11	
23	280 0		23	4 16	
24	292 5		24	4 21	
25	304 9		25	5 2	
26	316 13		26	5 7	
27	328 17		27	5 12	
28	340 21		28	5 16	
29	353 1		29	5 21	
30	365 6		30	6 2	

M	D. H.
31	6 7
32	6 12
33	6 17
34	6 22
25	7 3
36	7 8
37	7 13
38	7 18
39	7 22
40	8 3
41	8 8
42	8 13
43	8 17
44	8 22
45	9 3
46	9 8
47	9 13
48	9 18
49	9 23
50	10 4
51	10 8
52	10 13
53	10 18
54	10 23
55	11 4
56	11 9
57	11 14
58	11 18
59	11 23
60	12 4

VIII. A Table fitted to the Exemplary Nativity which, by Inspection, only points out the Day of a Profectional Direction for any Year of the Natives Age.									
Promittor	Mid H.	Promittor	Ascend	Promittor	TheSun	Promittor	The ☽	Promittor	P.Fort
☊ ♄ ☋	May 4	♄	April 3	☿	April 6	☉	April 5	♀	Mar. 26
⊕	May 10	D.III.IX.	June 6	D.XII.VI	Apr. 30	☿	May 1	Asc. VII	April 5
♀	May 28	☽	June 8	♂	May 8	D.XII.VI	May 26	♄	Apr. 28
Asc. VII	June 4	☉	July 3	♃	May 27	♂	June 2	D.III.IX.	July 1
♄	June 27	☿	July 29	D.XI.V.	July 12	♃	June 21	☽	July 3
D.III.IX	Aug. 18	D.XII.VI.	Aug. 23	D.II.VIII.	Aug. 5	D.XI.V.	Aug. 6	☉	July 28
☽	Sept. 1	♂	Aug. 30	M.C.IV.	Aug. 24	D.II.VIII	Sept. 8	☿	Aug. 23
☉	Sep. 26	♃	Sep. 19	☊ & ☋	Oct. 17	M.C.IV	Sep. 18	D.VI.XII.	Sep. 18
☿	Oct. 22	D.XI.V.	Nov. 3	⊕	Oct. 23	☊ & ☋	Nov. 12	♂	Sep. 24
D.XII.VI	Nov. 17	D. VIII.II	Dec. 6	♀	Nov. 10	⊕	Nov. 17	♃	Oct. 13
♂	Nov. 23	M.C.IV.	Dec.16	Asc.VII.	Nov. 18	♀	Dec. 5	D.V.XI.	Nov. 28
♃	Dec. 12	☊ ☋	Feb. 9	♄	Dec. 9	Asc. VII	Dec. 10	D.II.VIII	Dec. 31
D.XI.V	Jan. 27	⊕	Feb. 14	D.III.IX.	Feb. 12	♄	Jan. 4	M.C.IV.	Jan. 10
D.II.VIII	Feb. 28	♀	Mar. 4	☽	Feb. 14	D.III.IX	Mar. 9	☊ & ☋	Mar. 5

The Use of the Tables in Directing the Hylegiacal Points of a Profectional Figure.

I. In the proposed *Geniture* suppose the *Profectional Figure* for the year 1678. (being the 29th year current) were to be Directed; in the first Table in the fourth Column I find 1678 and *Gemini* under the M. C. in the first Column, and *Libra* under the *Ascendant* in the last Column of that Table, which accordingly are to be set upon the *M. C.* and *Ascendant* in the *Profectional Scheme*, also the degrees and minutes correspondent as they were in the Radix, with the rest of the Cusps of the Houses in order, as the *Radical Figure* will better direct than many words, alwayes remembering that the Position of the Planets are to remain in the same Houses as they were at Birth, the Progression being only in the *Signes*, &c. and thus you may easily gain the *Profectional Scheme* either in this or any other Geniture for any year desired.

II. The *Ascendant*, *M. C.* the *Sun*, *Moon*, and *Part of Fortune* may by help of the last Table, be *Directed* to these several *Promittors* with much ease after this manner, which I shall explain by a familiar Example.

Suppose I would Direct the *Ascendant* or *M. C.* of the aforesaid *Profectional Figure* for the year 1678. the *Ascendant* is Devolved to *Libra* 22d. 32m. and the *M. C.* to *Gemini* 15d. 33m. I enter the *Speculum* of the *Nativity*. I Direct my eye to 22d. of *Libra*, where I begin, and the first Aspect in that Column is the *Trine* of *Saturn*: then under *Scorpio* in the next Column I find Dom. VI. then the Body of ♃, then ☋, then the △ of ♀, *&c.* (as for the Antiscions of the Planets, those I reject here.) Now to know when any of these Directions fall (or any other under either of the five Hylegiacals) I enter the last Table (made purposely for this use) and in the second Column belonging to the Ascendant against ♄ I find *April* the 3d. and agsint D.VI. I find *August* 23, and so against ♃ *Sep.* 19. against ☋ *Feb.* 9. and lastly, against ♀ *March* 4. And thus I have the true time when the aforesaid *Profectional* Directions Initiate, only by Inspection without farther Trouble.

III. The *M. C.* in the *Profectional Figure* is Divolved to ♊ 15d. 33. in the *Speculum* of the Nativity: If I guide my eye down that Column I find the first *Direction* of the M. C. is to the □ of ♀, the second to the Ascendant, the third to the Body of ♄, the fourth to the □ of the ☉ under the Column of ♋, the fifth Direction is to the □ of ☿, the sixth to the □ of ♂, and the next to the △ of ♃, and so on: Now in the prepared Table under the Column of the M. C. against ♀ I find *May* 28, against the Ascendant *June* 4. against ♄ *June* 27. agaisnt the ☉ *September* 26. against ☿ *October* 22. against ♂ *November* 23. and against ♃ *December* 12. The same Method is to be understood and used in Directing the ☉, ☽, and ⊕, which when the prepared Table is made, is performed after this manner with abundance of ease: But otherwise, it would be found somewhat tedious and laborious, especially to Learners, or such persons as are not well grounded in this kind of Operation.

How to make such a Useful Table to any Persons Nativity, which (with the help of the Radical Speculum) points out the day of a Profectional Direction by Inspection, as hath been shewed.

I. Having drawn the Nativity into a *Speculum*, Begin at top thereof, and take out upon a loose paper the degrees and minutes appertaining to all the *Planets*, *Cusps* of the *Houses*, *Dragons Head and Tayl*, *Part of Fortune*, &c. as I have done in the Margent out of the aforesaid *Speculum*.

II. Substract the degrees and minutes appertaining to the five *Hylegiacal* points successively from the degrees and min. of the other *Planets*, *Cusps* of *Houses*, &c. 'till you come to the same point where you began, by adding 30d. where substraction cannot be made: As suppose the Ascendant 22d. 32m. subducted from 24d. 24m. (appertaining to ♄) there remains 1d. 52m. this 1d. 52m. I convert into *Time* by the Table of the measure of *Time* in *Profections*, and that gives 22 dayes 17 hours, for which I may take 23 dayes; then accounting 23 dayes from the day of Birth inclusive (by the Table for that purpose or otherwise) it points out *April* 3. After the same Method I work for all the other *Promittors* in Order, from the *Ascendant* till I come to the *Ascendant* again, and put the several operations into a Table, as you may see in the Exemplary Table, where 'tis apparent also, That the *Ascendant* Directed to the third or ninth House will fall *June* 6. So the *Ascendant* Directed to the Body or any Aspects of the *Moon* will fall *June* 8. &c. And thus as I make the Column of Moneths and Dayes appertaining to the *Promittors* Directed under the *Ascendant*, by the same Method I proceed with the rest of the *Hylegiacals*, viz. the M. C. ☉, ☽, and ⊕, and put them into a Table for use, as you may most easily understand by the Example it self.

How to Judge of the Profectional Figures.

Consider the Signe of the Ascendants and M.C. and look whether they were the places of Fortunate Planets, or good Houses in the Radix, as also what Planets are essentially dignified therein, or what Planets beheld those degrees with any amicable Aspect in theRadix, if you find the Signes of the Profectional, as also the Radical Figures no way vitiated, and their Lords well dignified, *&c*. It argues the year shall prove successful and very Fortunate; and this the rather, if the Revolutional Figure concur, for then you may conclude the Native shall proceed in his affairs with content, and enjoy health of Body, increase of Estate; and in fine, go on with much cheerfulness and delight in all his actions in general: and thus if you consider what hath been said before of Nativities, you cannot fail to judge of the Profectional Figure thereon depending.

[*Much more might be said as to the Judgment of* Profections*; But in regard the Rules given to Judge a Nativity may be also applyed to the Judgment of these Figures, I shall therefore forbear, and proceed to what remains, viz.* Transits, *&c.*

CHAP. XXXIV.

Of Transits

I. The *Transit* of a *Planet* is no more but his passing by the place or *Aspect* of any other *Planet*, or by the Cusps of the Houses, *&c*. in any *Nativity*, which is easily discovered by an *Ephemeris*, thus: Suppose any person hath ♄ in 20d. of ♋ in their Nativity, now in the *Ephemeris*, when I find ♄ in 20d. of ♑, he then Transits his opposite place; and if at the same time I find ♂ in 20d. of ♈ or ♎, he is said to *Transit* the Radical place of ♄ by a *Quartile* Aspect, *&c*.

II. When ♃ or ♀ both pass by, or *Transit* their own places, or the Radical places of the ☉ or ☽, or if they are in any benevolent Aspect of their places at Birth; this is an argument of good to the Native. But if they behold the

Luminaries, or their own places by □ or ☍, this signifies ill to the Native; neither doth the good Aspects of ♃ and ♀ always promise much good to any person, although they are termed Fortunes, except they were fortunate at Birth, and Lords of good Houses, &c. And so in some Nativities ♄ and ♂ may be the greater Fortunes.

III. If ♄ and ♂ were unfortunate in the Radix, and bearing no Signification of good to the Native there. I say if these *Planets* shall *Transit* the places of the Luminaries, or ♃ or ♀, or the chief Angles of the Figure, or their own Radical places, it portends no good to the Native, but Crosses and Vexation, and his business upon such kind of bad Transits, generally goes on very unfortunately, and untowardly (as we usually term it.)

d.	m.
1.	55. ☉
4.	02. ☿
6.	4. D XII. & VI.
8.	16. ♃
12.	1. D XIV.
14.	42. D. VIII. II
15.	33. M.C. IV.
20.	01. ☊ and ☋
20.	29. ⊕
21.	56. ♀
22.	32. Ascen. VII.
24.	24. ♄
29.	41 D IX. III.
29.	51. ☽

IV. ♃ and ♀ (not unfortunate) and Transiting the degree Horoscopial at Birth, declares the Native at that time to be cheerful, inclining to mirth, healthful, and his business to go on very successfully, &c.

V. If they pass by the degree of the second House, or any good Aspect of the Lord thereof, this is accounted a very fit time to get into Moneys, or to lay it out to advantage. Accordingly order your Judgment, if they Transit the Cusps of the other Houses, or their Lords, and judge according to their several Significations.

VI. Mr. *Lilly* affirms, if ♂ do Transit the degree ascending in any Nativity, he stirs up the Native to Choler for two or three dayes, or gives occasion whereby he is stirred up to wrath and passion, &c. So if ♄ Transits the Cusp of the Ascendant, the Native is grave and Sober, inclineable to Melancholy, &c. And for the most part those days are accounted very Fortunate and successful, when either the Fortunes, or the Luminaries behold the degree ascending with any benevolent Aspect, or the Cusp of the tenth, or their own Radical Places: But those days are generally found to be unfortunate, when the Infortunes ♄ or ♂ Transit the aforesaid places, or the places of the Luminaries, or of ♃ or ♀. Judge the same if they happen to be in any bad aspect of the Radical places of the aforesaid Significators.

But to compleat this Chapter of Transits, I shall add this following Discourse thereof from the Learned Morinus.

Of the Transits of the Planets, &c.

I. The Doctrine of *Transits* is the last, but not the least Part of *Astrology*; for since of every particular Effect, as such, proceeding from Coelestial Causes, there must be a particular Actual Coelestial cause, which cannot be the Scheme of Birth, nor its Directions; since all these, at least in respect of future Accidents, are Potential Causes subordinate each to other, and some or them Superiour, and more Universal than others, tending in order to some particular cause which is wholly Actual, and by which, that which in them is Potential, may be brought forth into Act; and such is the *Transit* of Planets by apt places of the Radical and Revolutional Figures.

II. In a Planets *Transit* three things are especially to be observed.

1. Its proper Nature, not only whether Benevolent or Malevolent, but also whether it be *Jupiter* or *Venus*, *Saturn* or *Mars*, each of which have their respective proper Natures, though the first two be Benevolents, as the last are Malevolents.

2. Its Radical Detemination; for according to that chiefly it operates in its *Transit*; and therefore the *Transit* of ♂, who was in the Radix, determined concerning Death or Diseases, as being posited in, or Lord of the eighth or twelfth Houses, is very dangerous to the Natives Life or Health, &c.

3. Its State and Condition at the time of the *Transit*, whether agreeable with, or contrary to its Radical Signification, and its Combination with the Signification of the place it *Transits*; as also whether it be strong or weak: For when it shall be found agreeable and strong, either for good or evil it will act strongly; but when incongruous or weak, little or nothing at all. Nor are these things to be heeded only in the Planet *Transiting*, but also in the Planet or Cusp by whose place the *Transit* it made: For as the Signes determined at the beginning of the World to the

Natures of the Planet's act in dependance to the state of their Lords; so the places of Heaven in the Radix peculiarly determined by the Planets, action the Natlve durtng his Life in dependance to the state of such Planets so determining: and therefore the *Transit* of *Jupiter* by the *Horoscope* of the Radix at a time when *Venus*, Lady thereof, is Peregrine, Retrograde, or Afflicted by the Malignant Ray of *Saturn* and *Mars* will be of little or no advantage to the Native.

III. But since the chief foundation of this Learning concerning *Transits*, is to apprehend how a Planet passing by that place which was one of the Cusps, (especially if a Cardinal one) of the Genethliacal Figure, or which another Planet at the hour of Birth did possess, should come to act according to the particular Signification in the Radix of such place or Planet, though now at the tlme of the *Transit* the Planet which so occupied that place be absent. *This very Consideration hath tortur'd the Wits of divers Students*; and therefore we deem it necessary first to explain, and to that purpose offer thus; *viz.* Natural effects proceed not from the first Heaven (or *Primum Mobile*) alone; for that being an universal cause, is of it self determined to no particular Species of effects, nor from the Planets alone; for we see ♂ does one thing in, or rather with *Aries*, and another in or with *Taurus*, &c. but from a mutual Concurrence of both; wherein yet the Heaven claims Principality, without which, though the *Sun* and all the other Planets should remain, yet Nature would Droop and Languish for want of its formal Virtue, which like a soul or Spirit enlivens and conserves the whole Corporeal World. Now although this first Heaven be ever the same to all things in its Nature and formal Virtue, which is immutable, yet doth it not continue so in respect of the Continuation of its parts, which are continually varied by its motion; the cause therefore as from the *Primim Mobile* of the different Effects in men is its divers situation in respect of several men at the moment of their Birth respectively, of whom one perhaps hath *Aries* in the Ascendant, another *Taurus*, &c.

IV. The same may be said of every Planet, which at the same time is the same to all Sublunary Subjects in its Nature, and universal Virtue, but divers in site or position, whereby its universal Nature being diversly determined in respect of the several Natives, produces in every one of them at the same instant divers Effects; and doth also determine that part of the first Heaven under which he is beheld from the Earth, to his own Nature and Virtue, both as well essential from its proper Nature, as accidental, which it acquires by its present position in respect of the Native; and this is done so powerfully, that such a part of Heaven, wherein for Example, the *Sun* is so beheld, becomes to the Native during his whole Life, as it were another *Sun*, and is in the same manner determined by the House of the Figure, as the *Sun* its self was in the *Genesis*, where it may not undeservedly be said, that in the Impression of the Coelestial Constitution which the Native receiveth at Birth, a Planet is a certain proportional medium between Heaven and the Native, which connects and Conjoynes them both together, whereby the Native contracts such a Sympathy and Antipathy with Heaven; that, as his Production, so his Conservation depends on, and consists in such Situation of the Coelestial Bodies in respect of him; and consequently his Alteration and Corruption must proceed from some contrary Constitution, or repugnant Situation. For look what Planet and Signe by Body, Dominion or Aspect possest each House at Birth, such both Active and Passive Power doth the Native receive as to the Accidents signified by that House, and such a sympathy with that Coelestial Constitution, that as often as any change happens therein, so oft there will happen to the Native some mutation in the thing or kind of Accident signified by that House, if at at least such Change were agreeable to the Directions and Revolutions then Operating.

V. The Planet then *Transiting* moving and exciting the Causes of such Effects, both Active and Passive, whether intrinsick to the Native, or extrinsick in universal Nature; so that some things happen to the Native of that kind of Signification, belonging to the place by which the *Transit* is made; where we are to observe that a planet *Transiting*, and place *Transitted*, do mutually determine each other concerning the Native: As first for Example, *Mars* Lord of the Eighth passing by the place of the Ascendant, and its Lord Determined them not only simply to Martial Nature, but also to death or danger of Life, because *Mars* by his Radical Determination contracted the Power of Death against the Native, which he cannot more efficatiously exercise than by passing, by Body or Inimical Ray, the places of the Radical Figure determined to Life; *viz.* That or the Horoscope and its Lord: For when Radical places by a *Transit* are determined to contrary Signification, then hath the Native reason to fear a great Change in the things Radically signified.

VI. Therefore Whilst he *Transits* the Significators by Body or ill Aspect, he is by them severally Determined as to the manner or kind, whereby the *Death* or *Danger* of life by him signified shall happen; and therefore when he *Transits* the *Horoscope*, he is Determined to exercise his *Killing* or *Morbisick Faculty*, by means of the *Temperament, Manners,* or *Ingenuity*; when the Mid heaven then by means of *Actions, Undertaking,* or *Dignities*, as it happens to Captains when they lead on their Souldiers to Battel, &c. This being premised, observe the following Aphorismes.

Excellent Aphorismes of the Transits *of the Planets in any Natives Geniture.*

I. The *Transit* of *Saturn, Jupiter,* or *Mars*, are of more force than those of the other Planets, because they stay longer in the places they pass by, especially if they be stationary.

II. The effects of each *Transit* is from the Actual Combination of the Radical Significators of the Planet *Transiting*, and the place by which the *Transit* is made.

III. *Transits* of the Planets out of the places of the Geniture; *viz.* The Cusps of the Houses the seven Planets places, their Aspects and Antiscions, are or no efficacy towards the Native.

IV. Observe the Corporeal place of tte Planet *Transiting*; for *Mars Transiting* the Cusp of the seventh House there in *Opposition* to the Horoscope, doth portend Strifes and Controversies more certainly, by reason of his local position, than Diseases by reason of his *Opposition* to the Horoscope.

V. During an effect of a Direction, observe diligently the motion of the *Moon*, and other Planets (which are thought to be the cause of such effects) their *Transiting* in the Radical Figure, and mutual application and Aspects; for thereby you may discover the success and end of such Effects.

VI. The *Moon* Transiting by the places of a Figure erected at the beginning of the Disease by *Quartile* or *Opposition* are found by experience to have great virtue; why not then in a Figure erected at the beginning of any other thing?

VII. All Planets both in Directions and Transits act according to their Radical Determination and proper Nature but in Genitures they are determined to some particular thing, as life, or its contrary, as diseases or death; or to neither of them, but some other thing, as dignities, or the like. Therefore in Directions and Transits a Promittor Planet Radically determined, to signifie concerning life, naturally benevolent and well affected, comeing to the Significators of Life, especially the Horoscope, strengthens life and all its faculties: and determined to the contrary shall prejudice life or destroy: But if determined in the Radix to neither of these, then it neither helps nor hinders, and operates nothing at all (at least that is notable) concerning life. In like manner a Planet adapted for Honour by its Nature, and Radical determination, Transiting the Mid heaven (or angle of Honour) confers Honour; but determined to the contrary, as Imprisonment, Banishment, Death, &c. especially if it be of a malifick nature, ill affected, or inimical to the Mid heaven, will destroy the Natives Dignities, or prejudice the same, or cause them not to happen; but if determined to neither of them, it will effect nothing (or at least eminently) concerning Honours, Actions, or Undertakings in general.

VIII. In Transits as well as in Directions, observe a Planet Transiting the Mid-heaven; the more wayes it is determined to Honours, and the stronger it is both in the Radix and at the time of the Direction or Transit, so much the more efficatiously will it assist the Native in his affairs and attempts: as thus; If the *Sun* or *Jupiter* be Lord of the Mid-heaven at Birth, and (at an age meet for Dignity) be Directed to the Mid-heaven as a Promissor, in that day of the compleat Direction wherein either of the said Planets well affected by Body or Aspect shall Transit the Angle of Honour, especially where the Revolution is agreeable) the same will cause a very signal illustrious happiness in undertakings, or raise the Native to some unexpected pitch of Preferment, as being so many wayes determined to honour; *viz.* by nature or Analogy, Dominion, Directlon, fit Transit, and fortunate Position: so on the contrary, *Saturn* in the twelfth House of a Native at Birth, and enemy to the Mid-heaven (which suppose hath *Leo* on its Cusp) coming by Direction, and Transitting, will cause some very grand disaster, defeating all the Natives designes, and blasting the most blooming of his hopes.

IX. If the Planets of the same, or neer related Signification either Analogical as the *Sun* and *Jupiter* for honor, *Saturn* and *Mars* for Diseases, or only by signification from the Radical determination, or both, shall at the same time Transit by Body or Aspect, the same place of the same, or like Significators too, then their signification and virtue, as to effect, will be doubled: But the *Conjunction* of a Planet Transitting in such a very place, is more powerful than their Aspects, especially if it be a *Conjunction* of the Luminaries, or of either of them with any other Planet; and therefore mark diligently the *Conjunction* of the *Sun* and *Moon* in the degrees of malefick Planets of the Radical Figure, or in those degrees opposite (especially when both or either of the Luminaries rule the Horoscope) for the malevolent Planet in whose degrees such a *Conjunction* happens may be accounted a Significator of death, or diseases, and inimical to the Horoscope, and rarely doth such a *Conjunction* happen upon a congruous Direction unattended with death or diseases, as hath often been experienced.

X. The Transit of two Planets or the like signification as aforesaid at the same time by divers places, of affinity between themselves, by nature or Radical determination (as the places of the Lords of the Mid-heaven and 2d House, or of the 12*th* and 8*th* Houses) do mutually strengthen each other to the producing of great effects.

XI. If there be many Planets in a House, a Planet Transitting the same shall act according to his own, and the nature and determination of every of these Planets, as he passes their respective places, and by the succession of the Transit the order of the accidents to be produced is discovered.

XII. The Luminaries joyned by Body or Aspect to a Planet Transiting, though they be wholly strangers to the Analogical or Radical signification of the Transit, do yet augment its virtue much more than when they are related in Signification.

XIII. Of those places by which Transits happen, we should note the state and condition in Revolutions; for if ♄ be in the 8th House of the Radix, and the 12d. of the Revolution, & weak or in bad configuration with his Radical place, then the same day when the Lord of the Horoscope shall Transit (or pass by) such a Radical place, there will happen some disease or danger of life, especlally if ♂ or either of the Luminaries shall then also cast an ill Aspect to such a place. Nor ought we to mind the place only passed by, but likewise of the Planet Transiting; for if ♂ Transitting the Horoscope shall have been in the eighth or twelfth House of the Revolution, and ill affected, it renders the Transit so much the worse.

XIV. The Transit of Planets in *Conjunction* over the degrees of some Direction in the Radix, though that place be empty, that is, be not the Radical place of any Planet, or Cusp of a House, wanteth not its effects: Nay the effect will be very eminent, if it be a Transit of the Luminaries conjoyned, especially with an Eclipse too.

XV. The actual virtue of the *Moons* Transits continues six hours before and after, the partile Transit, and in other Planets for a whole day before and after, by common consent of most Astrologers; yet as long as a Planet covers by his Orbe of virtue the place by which the Transit is said to be made, it hath an efficacy to produce the Transits effects, which sometimes happens swifter or slower than the aforesaid limits, because it requires a necessary concourse of other causes to its production: and here note, that the future effects depends on the Transit, not only as to its actual time, but also as to its nature, manner, and Circumstances, which are all actuated thereby, and consequently may thence be foreseen. Note also, when one bad Transit in small time succeeds another by the same place, during Manageable Direction, and Revolution; as if the Transit of ♄ Lord of the twelfth House, over the Horoscope, be followed by that of ♂, Lord of the eighth House, and these Transits be by Body □ or ☍ the same will prove mortal to the Native, or of very dangerous consequence. *Lastly*, If a benevolent Planet be in the Radical, Mid-heaven, or be Lord thereof, and during a congruous Direction or Revolution shall Transit the Horoscope, of the Radix, or the place of its Lord (especially when strong and in good configuration with the Lord of the Ascendant) the same shall produce great success to the Native in his Dignities and Undertakings.

According to these Aphorismes, if the Student be but so ingenious as to know by a penny how a shilling is Coyned, he may from the same parity of Reason rationally judge of the effects of all Transits whatsoever.

Here Ends the *Genethliacal* Part of Astrology.

A Catologue of the Eminent Cities and Towns in *England*, *Ireland*, *Scotland* and *Wales*, with their difference in time from the Honourable City of *London*, and the height of the Pole in each place.			
Names of Cities and Towns	Temporary Distan. H M		Hieght of the Pole. D M
Aberdeen Scot.	0 7	S	58 4
St. Albans	0 1	S	51 55
Amersham	0 1	S	51 42
Bedford	0 2	S	52 12
Bristol	0 12	S	51 28
Barwick	0 6	S	55 50
Boston	0 0	0	53 2
Buckingham	0 3	S	51 4
Cambridge	0 2	A	52 20
Canterbury	0 4	A	51 25
Carlisle	0 12	S	54 59
Chester	0 12	S	53 16
Coventry	0 6	S	52 30
Colchester	0 5	A	52 4
Carmarthen	0 17	S	52 2
Chichester	0 3	S	50 56
Darby	0 6	S	53 3
Datmouth	0 15	S	50 32
Dorchester	0 10	S	52 31
Dublin	0 27	S	53 11
Durham	0 6	S	54 47
Edenborough	0 10	S	57 6
Ely	0 1	A	52 20
Exeter	0 14	S	50 43
Gloucester	0 9	S	52 20
Grantham	0 2	S	52 58
Hertford	0 0	S	51 50
Hereford	0 11	S	52 14
Hull	0 1	S	53 50
Huntington	0 1	S	52 24
Lancaster	0 14	S	54 10
Leicester	0 4	S	52 41
Leverpool	0 11	S	53 22
Lincoln	0 1	S	53 15

Names of Cities and Towns	Temporary Distan.		Height of the Pole.
	H M		D M
Isle of Man	0 17	S	54 22
Manchester	0 9	S	53 24
Monmouth	0 11	S	52 2
Nottingham	0 4	S	53 3
Newark	0 3	S	55 2
Newcastle	0 1	S	53 3
Norwich	0 5	A	52 46
Northampthn	0 4	S	52 18
North Luffenha	0 2	S	52 45
Oxford	0 5	S	51 45
Peterborough	0 2	S	52 35
Penbrooke	0 19	S	51 54
Quinborough	0 4	A	51 35
Richmond	0 7	S	54 26
Rochester	0 2	A	51 30
S. Mich.	0 23	S	50 28
Mount Shrewsbury	0 11	S	52 49
Salisbury	0 7	S	51 12
Stafford	0 9	S	52 54
Stamford	0 2	S	52 41
Tredagh	0 27	S	53 38
Wakingham	0 5	A	52 54
Warwick	0 6	S	52 25
Waterford	0 27	S	52 22
Winchester	0 5	S	51 13
Worceller	0 9	S	52 18
Yarmouth	0 6	A	52 45
York	0 4	S	54 00
London, the Metropolir of Great Britain is under the Latitude of			51 32

A Catalogue of Fixed Stars exactly Rectified to the year 1680 By Ricciolus *in his* Astronomia Reformata.				
Mag.	Names of Stars.	Longitude.	Latitude.	
3	Bright * betwixt ♓	♈ 24. 13. 5	9. 4. 0 N	
4	1. In the Home of ♈	♈ 28. 42. 33	7. 8. 0 N	
4	2. In the Home of ♈	♈ 29. 28. 33	8. 28. 30 N	
3	Bright * in ♈	♉ 3. 11. 3	9. 56. 30 N	♂ ☽
3	Brightest of the seven *'s	♉ 25. 37. 43	3. 59. 0 N	
3	The lowest of Hyads	♊ 1. 7. 8	5. 46. 20 S	
2	North Eye of the Bull	♊ 3. 49. 36	2. 36. 0 S	♂
1	South Eye of the Bull	♊ 5. 18. 36	5. 30. 50 S	
3	The * in the S. Hor. of ♊	♊ 19. 58. 33	2. 13. 30 S	
2	In ♊'s bright foot	♋ 4. 34. 53	6. 48. 0 S	
2	♊'s Head of Pollux	♋ 18. 47. 59	6. 38. 30 N	♂ ☽
N	Preesepe	♌ 2. 51. 29	1. 14. 30 N	
4	North Assellus	♌ 3. 12. 59	3. 8. 0 S	
4	South Assellus	♌ 4. 12. 59	3. 0. 30 N	
3	In the Lyons Neck	♌ 23. 22. 23	4. 50. 4 N	
2	A bright * in his Crest	♌ 25. 1. 25	8. 45. 4 N	♂ ♃
1	Lyons Heart	♌ 25. 21. 28	0. 26. 10 N	
1	Lyons Tayl	♍ 17. 9. 53	12. 16. 20 N	
3	Vindiamatrix	♎ 5. 28. 27	10. 15. 0 N	
3	Bright * in Virg. Girdle	♎ 7. 1. 52	8. 40. 30 N	♃ ♀
1	Virgins Spike	♎ 19. 22. 53	1. 59. 30 S	
2	South Ballance	♏ 10. 39. 33	0. 25. 10 N	
2	North Ballance	♏ 14. 55. 2	8. 33. 30 N	
3	In the left Head of Ophin	♏ 27. 54. 53	7. 18. 20 N	
3	Middle * in ♏'s fore-h.	♏ 28. 3. 13	1. 52. 40 S	
3	South * in his fore-head	♏ 28. 28. 53	5. 0. 40 S	
3	North * in his fore-head	♏ 28. 40. 3	1. 6. 55 N	
2	Scorpions Heart	♐ 5. 18. 33	4. 26. 30 S	☿ ♂
1	In Ophincus right Knee	♐ 13. 34. 13	7. 17. 20 N	♄ ♀
3	In the Head of ♐	♑ 9. 5. 33	1. 45. 10 N	
4	The fore Home of ♑	♑ 9. 7. 3	7. 3. 11 N	
3	The lower Home	♑ 29. 40. 33	4. 42. 10 N	
3	In his left Hand	♒ 11. 56. 53	4. 50. 15 N	
5	Former in his Tayl	♒ 17. 23. 33	2. 24. 50 S	
4	In the left Shoulder of ♒	♒ 18. 56. 33	8. 42. 15 N	
3	Latter in his Tayl	♒ 19. 09. 33	2. 17. 50 S	
3	In his left Shoulder	♒ 28. 15. 3	10. 42. 15 N	
3	Southern Fish Occipus	♓ 16. 56. 5	7. 17. 0 N	
4	Nor. in the Tail of the Wh.	♓ 26. 29. 53	9. 58. 14 S	

A Table of Oblique Ascention for the Lat. 15°. 32'.

	Aries	Taurus	Gemini	Cancer	Leo	Virgo
	g ' "	g ' "	g ' "	g ' "	g ' "	g ' "
0	0. 0. 0	13. 2.28	30.10.40	56.46.27	91.34.26	137.15. 2
1	0.24.52	13.31.11	30.52.51	57.51.19	95.57.37	137.48. 1
2	0.49.45	14. 0.11	31.35.43	58.58.58	97.21. 8	140. 6.58
3	1.14.39	14.29.29	32.19.13	60. 6.25	98.44.44	141.32.54
4	1.39.34	14.59. 2	33. 2.28	61.14.40	100. 8.55	142.58.49
5	2. 4.31	15.28.55	33.48.23	62.23.40	101.33. 8	144.24.39
6	2.29.31	15.59. 5	34.34. 1	63.33.30	102.57.36	145.50.29
7	2.54.32	16.29.36	35.20.16	64.44. 2	104.22.14	147.16.16
8	3.19.39	17. 1.29	36. 7.30	65.55.19	105.47. 5	148.42. 1
9	3.44.48	17.31.41	36.55.21	67. 7.18	107.12. 6	150. 7.44
10	4.10. 1	18. 3.15	37.43.56	68.20. 0	108.37.16	151.33.22
11	4.35.18	18.35.11	38.33.19	69.33.24	110. 2.34	152.59. 2
12	5. 0.41	19. 7.32	39.23.27	70.47.27	111.28. 0	154.24.37
13	5.26.10	19.40.16	40.14.23	72. 2.12	112. 3.32	155.50.10
14	5.51.44	20.13.25	41. 6. 7	73.17.34	114.19. 9	157.15.40
15	6.17.26	20.46.59	41.58.39	74.33.33	115.44.53	158.41. 8
16	6.43.16	21.20.59	42.52. 0	75.50. 9	117.10.41	160. 6.34
17	7. 9.14	21.55.28	43.46.10	77. 7.19	118.36.32	161.31.58
18	7.35.19	22.30.22	44.41. 9	78.25. 3	120. 2.28	162.57.19
19	8. 1.34	23. 5.46	45.36.58	79.43.21	121.28.27	164.22.37
20	8:27:57	23.41.40	46.33.36	81. 2. 8	122.54.59	165.47.57
21	8.54.32	24.18. 4	47.31. 6	82.21.27	124.20.31	167.13.13
22	9.21.15	24.58.59	48.29.27	83.41.14	125.46.35	168.38.29
23	9.48.10	25.32.26	49.28.38	85.01.21	127.12. 8	170. 3.42
24	10.15.17	26.10.26	50.28.40	86.22.11	128.38.43	171.38.57
25	10.42.35	26.48.58	51.29.30	87.43.19	130. 4.49	172.54. 9
26	11.10. 7	27.28. 7	52.31.16	89. 4.50	131.30.52	174.19.20
27	11.37.50	28. 7.50	53.33.49	90.26.41	132.56.57	175.44.31
28	12. 5.48	28.48.10	54.37.12	91.48.57	134.22.59	177. 9.41
29	12.34. 1	29.29. 5	55.41.24	93.11.31	135.49. 0	178.34.59
30	13. 2.28	30.10.40	56.46.27	94.34.26	137.15. 2	180. 0. 0

The use of this Table is plain, and easie; for, enter with the Sign at the head of the Table, and the Degree in the first Column, to the left-hand; and in the Angle of meeting you have your desire.

A Table of Oblique Ascention for the Lat. 15°. 32'.

	Libra	Scorpio	Sagitary	Capricorn	Aquarius	Pisces
	g ' "	g ' "	g ' "	g ' "	g ' "	g ' "
0	180. 0. 0	222.44.58	265.25.34	303.13.33	329.49.20	346.57.32
1	181.25.10	224.10.59	266.48.29	304.18.36	330.30.55	347.25.59
2	182.50.19	225.37. 1	268.11. 3	305.22.48	331.11.50	347.54.12
3	184.15.29	227. 3. 3	269.33.19	306.26.11	331.52.10	348.22.10
4	185.40.40	228.29. 8	270.55.10	307.28.44	332.31.53	348.49.53
5	187. 5.51	229.55.12	272.16.41	308.30.30	333.11. 2	349.17.25
6	188.31. 3	231.21.16	273.37.49	309.31.20	333.49.34	349.44.43
7	189.56.18	232.47.21	274.58.39	310.31.22	334.27.34	350.11.50
8	191.21.31	234.13.25	176.18.46	311.30.33	335. 5. 1	350.38.45
9	192.46.47	335.39.29	277.38.33	312.28.54	335.41.56	351. 5.28
10	194.12 3	237 5.31	278.57.52	313.26.24	336.18.20	351.32. 3
11	195.37.23	238.31.33	280.16.39	314.23. 2	336.54.14	351.58.26
12	197. 2.41	239.57.52	281.34.57	315.18.51	337.29.38	352.24.41
13	198.28. 2	241.23.28	282.52.41	316.13.50	338. 4.32	352.50.46
14	199.53.26	242.49.19	284. 9.51	317.18. 0	338.39. 1	353.16.44
15	201.18.52	244.15. 7	285.26.27	318. 1.21	339.13. 1	353.42.34
16	202.44.20	245.40.51	286.42.26	318.53.53	339.46.35	354. 8.16
17	204. 9.50	247. 6.18	287.57.48	319.45.37	340.19.44	354.33.50
18	205.35.23	248.32. 0	289.12.33	320.36.33	340.52.28	354.59.19
19	207. 0.58	249.57.26	290.26.36	321.26.41	341.24.49	355.24.42
20	208.26.38	251.22.54	291.40. 0	322.16. 4	341.56.45	355.49.59
21	209.52.16	252.47.54	292.52.42	323. 4.39	342.28.19	356.15.12
22	211.17.59	354.12.55	294. 4.41	323.52.30	342.59.31	356.40.21
23	212.43.44	255.37.46	295.15.58	324.39.44	343.30.24	357. 5.28
24	214. 9.31	257. 2.24	296.26.30	325.25.59	344. 0.55	357.30.29
25	215.35.21	258.26.52	297.36.20	326.11.37	344.31. 5	357.55.29
26	217. 1.11	259.51. 5	298.45.20	326.46.32	345. 0.58	358.20.26
27	218.27. 6	261.15.16.	299.53.35	327.40.47	345.30.31	358.45.21
28	219.53. 2	262.38.52	301. 1. 2	328.24.17	345.59.49	359.10.15
29	221.18.59	264. 2.23	302. 8.41	329. 7. 9	346.28.49	359.34. 8
30	222.44.58	265.25.34	303.13.33	329.49.20	346.57.32	360. 0. 0

As for Example; Suppose I would have the Oblique Ascention of 10 deg. of *Sagitary*, I find *Sagitary* at top, and 10d. in the left-side of the Table, and the Oblique Ascen. Correspondent is 278d. 57m. 52s. If minutes be also given with the degrees, you must make Proportion as is usual in such Cases.

	\multicolumn{8}{c}{*Tables of Declination to six Degrees of Latitude.*}
	♈ North Latitude.						♎ South Latitude.	
♈	0	1	2	3	4	5	6	♎
0	0 0	0 55	1 50	2 45	3 40	4 35	6 00	30
1	0 24	1 19	2 38	3 33	4 52	5 47	6 42	29
2	0 48	1 43	2 38	3 33	4 28	5 23	6 18	28
3	1 12	2 07	3 05	3 57	4 52	5 47	6 42	27
4	1 36	2 31	3 26	4 21	5 16	6 11	7 06	26
5	2 00	2 55	3 50	4 45	5 50	6 35	7 30	25
6	2 24	3 19	4 14	5 09	6 04	6 59	7 53	24
7	2 47	3 47	4 38	5 33	6 28	7 13	8 17	23
8	3 11	4 07	5 02	5 57	6 52	7 47	8 41	22
9	3 35	4 30	5 25	6 20	7 15	8 10	9 05	21
10	3 58	4 54	5 48	6 44	7 39	8 34	9 29	20
11	4 22	5 18	6 12	7 08	8 03	8 58	9 53	19
12	4 46	5 42	6 36	7 32	8 27	9 22	10 16	18
13	5 09	6 05	7 00	7 55	8 50	9 46	10 40	17
14	5 33	6 29	7 24	8 19	9 14	10 10	11 04	16
15	5 56	6 52	7 47	8 42	9 37	10 33	11 27	15
16	6 19	7 14	8 09	9 05	10 00	10 56	11 51	14
17	6 42	7 37	8 32	9 28	10 23	11 19	12 14	13
18	7 05	8 00	8 56	9 51	10 46	11 42	12 37	12
19	7 28	8 23	9 18	10 14	11 09	12 05	13 00	11
20	7 51	8 46	9 42	10 38	11 33	12 28	13 23	10
21	8 13	9 05	10 09	11 01	11 56	12 51	13 46	9
22	8 36	9 32	10 28	11 23	12 19	13 14	14 09	8
23	8 58	9 55	10 51	11 46	12 42	13 37	14 32	7
24	9 21	10 17	11 13	12 08	13 04	14 00	14 54	6
25	9 43	10 39	11 35	12 30	13 26	14 22	15 17	5
26	10 05	11 01	11 57	12 52	13 48	14 44	15 39	4
27	10 26	11 23	12 19	13 14	14 10	15 06	16 01	3
28	10 48	11 45	12 41	13 36	14 32	15 28	16 23	2
29	11 09	12 05	13 02	13 57	14 53	15 49	16 05	1
30	11 31	12 27	13 23	14 19	15 15	16 11	17 06	0
	♓ South Latitude.						♍ North Latitude.	

| Tables of Declination to six Degrees of Latitude. ||||||||||
| ♈ South Latitude. |||||||| ♎ North Latitude. ||
♈	0	1	2	3	4	5	6	♎
0		0 55	1 50	2 45	3 40	4 35	5 30	30
1		0 31	1 27	2 21	3 16	4 11	5 06	29
2		0 07	1 03	1 57	2 52	3 47	4 42	28
3		0 17	0 39	1 34	2 29	3 24	4 19	27
4		0 41	0 15	1 10	2 05	3 00	3 55	26
5		1 05	0 09	0 46	1 41	2 36	3 31	25
6		1 28	0 33	0 22	1 17	2 02	3 07	24
7		1 52	0 57	0 02	0 53	1 48	2 43	23
8		2 16	1 21	0 26	0 29	1 25	2 20	22
9		2 29	1 44	0 49	0 06	1 02	1 57	21
10		3 03	2 08	1 13	0 18	0 38	1 33	20
11		3 27	2 32	1 37	0 41	0 14	1 09	19
12		3 51	2 56	2 01	1 04	0 10	0 46	18
13		4 14	3 19	2 24	1 28	0 37	0 23	17
14		4 37	3 41	2 57	1 52	0 56	0 00	16
15		5 00	4 05	3 10	2 15	1 19	0 23	15
16		5 23	4 28	3 32	2 38	1 41	0 40	14
17		5 46	4 51	3 55	3 00	2 04	1 09	13
18		6 09	5 14	4 18	3 23	2 27	1 32	12
19		6 32	5 37	4 41	3 46	2 50	1 55	11
20		6 55	5 59	5 04	4 08	3 12	2 17	10
21		7 17	6 21	5 27	4 30	3 34	2 39	9
22		7 40	6 44	5 50	4 53	3 57	3 01	8
23		8 03	7 07	6 12	5 15	4 10	3 23	7
24		8 25	7 30	6 34	5 38	4 42	3 35	6
25		8 47	7 52	6 56	6 00	5 04	4 07	5
26		9 09	8 14	7 18	6 22	5 26	4 29	4
27		9 31	8 35	7 50	6 43	5 47	4 50	3
28		9 53	8 57	8 01	7 04	6 08	5 11	2
29		10 14	9 18	8 22	7 25	6 29	5 32	1
30		10 35	9 38	8 43	7 46	6 50	5 53	0
♓ North Latitude.								♍ South Latitude.	

Clavis Astrologiae Elimita, The Key to Astrology New Filed

			Tables of Declination to six Degrees of Latitude.					
♉ North Latitude							♏ South Latitude.	
♉	0	1	2	3	4	5	6	♏
0	11 31	12 27	13 23	14 19	15 15	16 11	17 06	30
1	11 52	12 48	13 44	14 40	15 36	16 33	17 28	29
2	12 13	13 09	14 05	15 01	15 57	16 54	17 49	28
3	12 33	13 20	14 25	15 21	16 18	17 14	18 10	27
4	12 54	13 50	14 47	15 42	16 39	17 35	18 32	26
5	13 14	14 11	15 37	16 03	17 00	17 56	18 52	25
6	13 34	14 31	15 27	16 24	17 20	18 17	19 12	24
7	13 54	14 51	15 47	16 44	17 40	18 35	19 32	23
8	14 14	15 11	16 07	17 04	18 00	18 57	19 52	22
9	14 33	15 30	16 26	17 23	18 20	19 17	20 12	21
10	14 52	15 49	16 45	17 42	18 39	19 35	20 32	20
11	15 11	16 08	17 04	18 01	18 58	19 55	20 51	19
12	15 29	16 26	17 23	18 20	19 17	20 14	21 10	18
13	15 48	16 45	17 42	18 39	19 36	20 33	21 29	17
14	16 06	17 03	18 00	18 57	19 54	20 52	21 48	16
15	16 24	17 21	18 18	19 15	20 12	21 10	22 06	15
16	16 41	17 38	18 36	19 33	20 30	21 38	22 24	14
17	16 58	17 55	18 53	19 51	20 48	21 46	22 42	13
18	17 15	18 12	19 10	20 08	21 05	22 03	22 59	12
19	17 32	18 29	19 27	20 25	21 22	22 20	23 16	11
20	17 48	18 46	19 44	20 41	21 39	22 37	23 33	10
21	18 04	19 02	20 00	20 57	21 55	22 53	23 50	9
22	18 20	19 18	20 16	21 13	22 11	23 09	24 06	8
23	18 35	19 34	20 32	21 29	22 27	23 25	24 22	7
24	18 50	19 49	20 47	21 45	22 43	23 41	24 38	6
25	19 05	20 03	21 02	22 00	22 58	23 56	24 53	5
26	19 19	20 17	21 16	22 14	23 12	24 11	25 08	4
27	19 33	20 31	21 30	22 28	23 26	24 25	25 22	3
28	19 47	20 45	21 44	22 42	23 40	24 39	25 36	2
29	20 09	20 59	21 57	22 56	23 54	24 53	25 50	1
30	20 13	21 12	22 10	23 09	24 07	25 06	26 05	0
♌ North Latitude							♒ South Latitude.	

	Tables of Declination to six Degrees of Latinude.							
♉ South Latitude.							♏ North Latitude.	
♉	0	1	2	3	4	5	6	♏
0		10 35	9 39	8 43	7 46	6 50	5 53	30
1		10 56	10 00	9 04	8 07	7 11	6 14	29
2		11 17	10 20	9 24	8 28	7 31	6 34	28
3		11 37	10 40	9 44	8 48	7 51	6 54	27
4		11 58	11 01	10 04	9 08	8 11	7 14	26
5		12 18	11 21	10 24	9 28	8 31	7 34	25
6		12 38	11 41	10 44	9 48	8 51	7 53	24
7		12 58	12 01	11 04	10 07	9 10	8 12	23
8		13 17	12 20	11 23	10 26	9 29	8 31	22
9		13 36	12 39	11 42	10 45	9 48	8 50	21
10		13 55	12 58	12 01	11 04	10 07	9 09	20
11		14 14	13 17	12 20	11 23	10 29	9 27	19
12		14 32	13 35	12 38	11 41	10 43	9 45	18
13		14 50	13 53	12 56	11 59	11 01	10 03	17
14		15 08	14 11	13 14	12 17	11 19	10 21	16
15		15 26	14 29	13 31	12 34	11 36	10 38	15
16		15 43	14 46	13 48	12 51	11 53	10 55	14
17		16 00	15 03	14 05	13 08	12 10	11 12	13
18		16 17	15 20	14 22	13 24	12 26	11 28	12
19		16 34	15 36	14 38	13 40	12 42	11 44	11
20		16 50	15 52	14 54	13 56	12 58	12 00	10
21		17 06	16 08	15 10	14 12	13 14	12 15	9
22		17 22	16 24	15 26	14 28	13 29	12 30	8
23		17 37	16 39	15 41	14 43	13 44	12 45	7
24		17 52	16 54	15 56	14 58	13 59	13 00	6
25		18 07	17 09	16 10	15 12	14 13	13 14	5
26		18 21	17 23	16 25	15 26	14 27	13 28	4
27		18 35	17 36	16 38	15 39	14 41	13 41	3
28		18 48	17 50	16 51	15 52	14 54	13 54	2
29		19 01	18 03	17 04	16 05	15 07	14 07	1
30		19 14	18 16	17 17	16 18	15 20	14 21	0
♌ South Latitude.							♒ North Latitude.	

Tables of Declination to six Degrees of Latitude.								
♊ North Latitude.							♐ South Latitude.	
♊	0	1	2	3	4	5	6	♐
0	20 13	21 12	22 10	23 09	24 07	25 06	26 03	30
1	20 26	21 25	22 23	23 22	24 20	25 19	26 16	29
2	20 38	21 37	22 36	23 35	24 33	25 32	26 29	28
3	20 50	21 49	22 18	23 47	24 45	25 44	26 42	27
4	21 01	22 00	22 59	23 58	24 57	25 55	26 54	26
5	21 13	22 11	23 10	24 09	25 08	26 07	27 05	25
6	21 23	22 22	23 21	24 21	25 19	26 18	27 21	24
7	21 33	22 32	23 31	24 31	25 30	26 29	27 27	23
8	21 43	22 42	23 41	24 41	25 40	26 39	27 37	22
9	21 53	22 52	23 51	24 51	25 50	26 49	27 47	21
10	22 02	23 01	24 00	25 00	25 59	26 58	27 56	20
11	22 10	23 10	24 09	25 09	26 08	27 07	28 05	19
12	22 19	23 19	24 18	25 18	26 17	27 16	28 14	18
13	22 27	23 27	24 26	25 26	26 25	27 24	28 22	17
14	22 34	23 34	24 33	25 33	26 32	27 31	28 30	16
15	22 41	23 41	24 40	25 39	26 39	27 38	28 37	15
16	22 47	23 43	24 46	25 45	26 45	27 45	28 43	14
17	22 53	23 53	24 53	25 52	26 52	27 52	28 49	13
18	22 59	23 59	24 59	25 58	26 58	27 58	28 55	12
19	23 04	24 04	25 04	26 03	27 03	28 03	29 02	11
20	23 09	24 09	25 09	26 08	27 08	28 08	29 07	10
21	23 13	24 13	25 13	26 13	27 12	28 12	29 12	9
22	23 17	24 17	25 17	26 17	27 16	28 16	29 15	8
23	23 20	24 20	25 20	26 20	27 19	28 19	29 18	7
24	23 23	24 23	25 23	26 23	27 22	28 22	29 22	6
25	23 26	24 26	25 26	26 26	27 25	28 25	29 25	5
26	23 28	24 28	25 28	26 28	27 28	28 28	29 28	4
27	23 30	24 30	25 30	26 30	27 30	28 30	29 30	3
28	23 30	24 31	25 31	26 31	27 31	28 31	29 31	2
29	23 31	24 31	25 51	26 31	27 31	28 31	29 31	1
30	23 31	24 31	25 31	26 31	27 31	28 31	29 31	0
♑ North Latitude.							♋ South Latitude.	

	Tables of Declination to six Degrees of Latitude.							
♊ South Latitude.							♐ North Latitude.	
♊	0	1	2	3	4	5	6	♐
0		19 14	18 16	17 17	16 18	15 20	14 21	30
1		19 27	18 28	17 29	16 30	15 32	14 33	29
2		19 31	18 40	17 41	16 42	15 44	14 45	28
3		19 51	18 52	17 53	16 54	15 55	14 57	27
4		20 02	19 03	18 08	17 06	16 07	15 08	26
5		20 13	19 15	18 16	17 17	16 18	15 18	25
6		20 24	19 25	18 26	17 27	16 28	15 28	24
7		20 34	19 35	18 36	17 39	16 38	15 38	23
8		20 44	19 45	18 46	17 47	16 47	15 48	22
9		20 54	19 55	18 56	17 56	16 56	15 57	21
10		21 03	20 04	19 05	18 05	17 06	16 05	20
11		21 11	20 12	19 13	18 13	17 14	16 13	19
12		21 19	20 20	19 21	18 21	17 22	16 21	18
13		21 27	20 28	19 28	18 29	17 29	16 28	17
14		21 35	20 35	19 35	18 36	17 36	16 35	16
15		21 41	20 41	19 41	18 42	17 42	16 42	15
16		21 47	20 47	19 47	18 48	17 48	16 48	14
17		21 53	20 53	19 53	18 54	17 54	16 54	13
18		21 59	20 59	19 59	19 00	18 00	16 59	12
19		22 04	21 04	20 04	19 05	18 04	17 04	11
20		22 09	21 09	20 09	19 10	18 10	17 09	10
21		22 13	21 13	20 13	19 14	18 14	17 14	9
22		22 17	21 17	20 17	19 17	18 17	17 17	8
23		22 20	21 20	20 20	19 20	18 20	17 20	7
24		22 23	21 23	20 23	19 23	18 23	17 23	6
25		22 26	21 26	20 26	19 26	18 26	17 26	5
26		22 28	21 28	20 28	19 28	18 28	17 28	4
27		22 30	21 30	20 30	19 30	18 30	17 30	3
28		22 31	21 31	20 31	19 31	18 31	17 31	2
29		22 31	21 31	20 31	19 31	18 31	17 31	1
30		22 33	21 31	20 31	19 31	18 31	17 31	0
♑ North Latitude.							♋ South Latitude.	

Clavis Astrologiae Elimita, The Key to Astrology New Filed

	Tables of Right Ascension to six Degrees of Latitude.						
♈ North Latitude.						♎ South Latitude.	
	0	1	2	3	4	5	6
0	0 00	35937	35913	35849	35825	35801	35737
1	0 55	0 32	0 08	35944	45920	35856	35832
2	1 50	1 27	1 03	0 39	0 15	35951	35927
3	2 45	2 22	1 58	1 34	1 10	0 46	0 22
4	3 40	3 17	2 53	2 29	2 05	1 41	1 17
5	4 35	4 12	3 48	3 24	3 00	2 36	2 12
6	5 30	5 07	4 43	4 19	4 55	3 31	3 07
7	6 25	6 02	5 38	5 14	5 50	4 26	4 02
8	7 21	6 57	6 33	6 09	5 45	5 21	4 57
9	8 16	7 52	7 28	7 04	6 40	6 16	5 52
10	9 11	8 47	8 23	7 59	7 35	7 11	6 47
11	10 06	9 42	9 18	8 55	8 31	8 07	7 43
12	11 02	10 38	10 14	9 51	9 27	9 03	8 39
13	11 57	11 33	11 09	10 46	10 22	9 58	9 34
14	12 53	12 29	12 05	11 42	11 18	10 54	10 30
15	13 48	13 25	13 01	12 38	12 14	11 50	11 26
16	14 44	14 20	13 57	13 34	13 10	12 46	12 22
17	15 40	15 16	14 53	14 30	14 06	13 42	13 18
18	16 35	16 12	15 49	15 26	15 02	14 39	14 15
19	17 31	17 08	16 45	16 22	15 58	15 35	15 11
20	18 27	18 04	17 41	17 18	16 54	16 31	16 07
21	19 23	19 00	18 37	18 14	17 51	17 28	17 04
22	20 20	19 56	19 33	19 11	18 48	18 25	18 01
23	21 16	20 53	20 30	20 08	19 45	19 22	18 58
24	22 12	21 50	21 27	21 05	20 42	20 19	19 55
25	23 09	22 47	22 24	22 02	21 39	21 16	20 52
26	24 06	23 44	23 21	22 59	22 36	22 13	21 50
27	25 02	24 41	24 19	23 57	23 34	23 11	22 48
28	25 59	25 38	25 16	24 54	24 31	24 09	23 46
29	26 57	26 35	26 13	25 51	25 29	25 07	24 44
30	27 54	27 33	27 11	26 49	26 27	26 05	25 42
In Southern Signs add 180 degrees.							

| Tables of Right Ascention to six Degrees of Latitude. ||||||||
| ♈ South Latitude. |||| | | | ♎ North Latitude. |
	0	1	2	3	4	5	6
0		0 23	0 47	1 11	1 35	1 59	2 23
1		1 18	1 42	2 06	2 30	2 54	3 18
2		2 13	2 37	3 01	3 25	3 49	4 13
3		3 08	3 32	3 56	4 20	4 44	5 08
4		4 03	4 27	4 51	5 15	5 39	6 03
5		4 58	5 22	5 46	6 10	6 34	6 58
6		5 54	6 18	6 42	7 06	7 30	7 53
7		6 49	7 13	7 37	8 01	8 25	8 48
8		7 44	8 08	8 32	8 56	9 20	9 43
9		8 40	9 04	9 28	9 51	10 15	10 38
10		9 35	9 59	10 23	10 46	11 10	11 33
11		10 30	10 54	11 18	11 41	12 05	12 28
12		11 25	11 49	12 13	12 36	13 00	13 23
13		12 20	12 44	13 08	13 31	13 55	14 18
14		13 16	13 39	14 03	14 26	14 50	15 13
15		14 12	14 35	14 58	15 21	15 45	16 08
16		15 07	15 30	15 53	16 16	16 40	17 03
17		16 02	16 25	16 48	17 11	17 35	17 58
18		16 58	17 21	17 44	18 07	18 30	18 53
19		17 54	18 17	18 40	19 02	19 25	19 48
20		18 50	19 13	19 36	19 58	20 21	20 43
21		19 46	20 09	20 33	20 54	21 17	21 39
22		20 42	21 05	21 28	21 50	22 12	22 34
23		21 38	22 01	22 24	22 46	23 08	23 30
24		22 35	22 57	23 20	23 42	24 04	24 26
25		23 31	23 53	24 16	24 38	25 00	25 21
26		24 28	24 50	25 12	25 34	25 56	26 17
27		25 25	25 47	26 09	26 30	26 52	27 13
28		26 22	26 43	27 06	27 26	27 48	28 09
29		27 19	27 40	28 05	28 22	28 44	29 05
30		28 16	28 38	28 58	29 19	29 40	30 01
Except those As. in ♈, whose Lat. makes them more than 180.							

	Tables of Right Ascention to six Degrees of Latitude.						
♉ North Latitude.					♏ South Latitude.		
	0	1	2	3	4	5	6
0	27 54	27 33	27 11	26 49	26 27	26 05	25 42
1	28 51	28 30	28 08	27 47	27 25	27 03	26 40
2	29 49	29 27	29 06	28 45	28 23	28 01	27 38
3	30 46	30 25	30 04	29 43	29 21	28 29	28 37
4	31 43	31 23	31 02	31 39	31 18	30 57	30 35
5	32 42	32 22	32 00	32 38	32 17	31 56	31 34
6	33 40	33 20	32 58	33 37	33 16	32 55	32 33
7	34 38	34 18	33 58	34 36	34 15	33 54	33 33
8	35 36	35 17	34 56	35 36	35 15	34 54	34 33
9	36 34	36 16	25 56	35 36	35 15	34 54	34 33
10	37 33	37 15	36 55	36 35	36 15	36 54	35 33
11	38 33	38 14	37 54	37 35	37 15	36 54	36 33
12	39 32	39 14	38 54	38 35	38 15	37 55	37 34
13	40 31	40 13	39 54	39 35	39 15	38 56	38 35
14	41 31	41 13	40 54	40 35	40 16	39 57	39 36
15	42 31	42 13	41 54	41 36	41 17	40 58	40 38
16	43 31	43 13	42 54	42 36	42 18	41 59	41 39
17	44 31	44 13	43 55	43 37	43 19	43 00	42 40
18	45 31	45 14	44 56	44 38	44 20	44 01	43 42
19	46 32	46 14	45 57	45 39	45 21	45 03	44 44
20	47 32	47 15	46 58	46 40	46 23	46 05	45 46
21	48 33	48 16	47 59	47 42	47 25	47 07	46 49
22	49 34	49 17	49 00	48 44	48 27	48 09	47 52
23	50 35	50 18	50 02	49 46	49 29	49 12	48 55
24	51 36	51 20	51 04	50 48	50 32	50 15	49 58
25	52 38	52 22	52 06	51 51	51 35	51 18	51 02
26	53 40	53 24	53 09	52 54	52 38	52 22	52 06
27	54 42	54 27	54 12	53 57	53 42	53 26	53 10
28	55 44	55 15	55 15	55 00	54 45	54 30	54 14
29	56 46	56 18	56 18	56 03	55 49	55 34	55 18
30	57 48	57 21	57 21	57 07	56 53	56 38	56 23
In Southern Signs add 180 degrees.							

	\textit{Tables of Right Ascention to six Degrees of Latitude.}						
♉ South Latitude.					♏ North Latitude.		
	0	1	2	3	4	5	6
0		28 16	28 37	28 58	29 19	29 40	30 01
1		29 13	29 34	29 55	30 16	30 37	30 57
2		30 10	30 31	30 52	31 13	31 34	31 54
3		31 07	31 28	31 49	32 10	32 31	32 51
4		32 05	32 25	32 46	33 07	33 27	33 47
5		33 03	33 23	33 43	34 04	34 24	34 44
6		34 01	34 21	34 41	35 01	35 21	35 41
7		34 59	35 19	35 39	35 58	36 18	36 38
8		35 57	36 17	36 37	36 56	37 15	37 35
9		36 56	37 15	37 35	37 54	38 13	38 32
10		37 54	38 13	38 33	38 52	39 11	39 22
11		38 53	39 12	39 31	39 50	40 09	40 27
12		39 52	40 11	40 30	40 48	41 09	41 25
13		40 51	41 10	41 28	41 46	42 05	42 23
14		41 50	42 09	42 27	42 45	43 03	43 21
15		42 49	43 08	43 26	43 44	44 02	44 19
16		43 49	44 07	44 25	44 43	45 00	45 27
17		44 49	45 06	45 24	45 42	45 59	46 15
18		45 49	46 06	46 23	46 41	46 58	47 14
19		46 49	47 06	47 23	47 40	47 57	48 13
20		47 49	48 06	48 23	48 39	48 56	40 12
21		48 50	49 06	49 23	49 39	49 55	50 11
22		49 50	50 06	50 23	50 38	50 54	51 10
23		50 51	51 06	51 23	51 38	51 53	52 09
24		51 52	52 07	52 23	53 38	52 53	53 08
25		52 53	53 08	53 23	52 38	53 53	54 08
26		53 55	54 09	54 24	54 38	54 53	55 07
27		54 56	55 11	55 25	55 39	55 53	56 07
28		55 58	56 12	56 26	56 40	56 54	57 07
29		57 00	57 13	57 27	57 41	57 54	58 07
30		58 03	58 15	58 29	58 42	58 55	59 07
In Southern Signs add 180 degrees.							

Tables of Right Ascension to six Degrees of Latitude.							
♊ North Latitude.					♐ South Latitude.		
	0	1	2	3	4	5	6
0	57 48	57 35	57 21	57 07	56 53	56 38	56 24
1	58 51	58 38	58 24	58 10	57 57	57 42	57 38
2	59 53	59 41	59 27	59 14	59 01	58 47	58 33
3	60 56	60 44	60 31	60 18	60 05	59 52	59 38
4	61 59	61 47	61 35	61 22	61 10	60 57	60 44
5	63 03	62 51	62 39	62 27	62 15	62 02	61 50
6	64 06	63 55	63 43	63 32	63 20	63 08	52 56
7	65 09	64 59	64 47	64 37	64 25	64 13	64 02
8	66 13	66 03	65 52	65 42	65 30	65 19	65 01
9	67 17	67 07	66 57	66 47	66 36	66 25	66 14
10	68 21	68 11	68 02	67 52	67 42	67 31	67 21
11	69 25	69 16	69 07	68 57	68 48	68 38	68 28
12	70 29	70 21	70 12	70 03	69 54	69 45	69 35
13	71 34	71 26	71 16	71 09	71 00	70 51	70 42
14	72 38	72 31	72 22	72 15	72 06	71 58	71 49
15	73 42	73 36	73 28	73 21	73 13	73 05	72 57
16	74 47	74 41	74 33	74 27	74 19	74 12	74 04
17	75 52	75 46	75 39	75 33	75 26	75 18	75 12
18	76 57	76 57	76 45	76 39	76 43	76 27	76 20
19	78 02	77 56	77 51	77 45	77 40	77 34	77 28
20	79 07	79 02	78 57	78 52	78 47	78 41	78 36
21	80 12	80 08	80 03	79 59	79 54	79 49	79 44
22	81 17	81 13	81 09	81 05	81 01	80 56	80 52
23	82 22	82 18	82 15	82 11	82 08	82 04	82 00
24	83 27	83 24	83 21	83 18	83 15	83 12	83 09
25	84 33	84 30	84 24	84 25	84 22	84 20	84 17
26	85 38	85 46	85 33	85 32	85 29	85 28	85 23
27	86 44	86 42	86 40	86 39	86 37	86 26	86 34
28	87 49	87 48	87 46	87 46	87 44	87 44	87 42
29	88 55	88 54	88 53	88 53	88 52	88 52	88 51
30	90 00	90 00	90 00	90 00	90 00	90 00	90 00
In Southern Signs add 180 degrees, with the aforesaid Caut.							

| Tables of Right Ascention to six Degrees of Latitude. ||||||||
| ♊ South Latitude. |||||| ♐ North Latitude. ||
	0	1	2	3	4	5	6
0		58 02	58 15	58 29	58 42	58 55	59 07
1		59 04	59 17	59 30	59 43	59 55	60 07
2		60 06	60 19	60 31	60 44	60 56	61 08
3		61 09	61 21	61 33	61 46	61 57	62 09
4		62 11	62 23	62 35	62 48	62 58	63 09
5		63 14	63 25	63 37	63 50	63 59	64 10
6		64 17	64 28	64 39	64 52	65 01	65 11
7		65 20	65 31	65 41	65 54	66 02	66 12
8		66 23	66 34	66 44	66 56	67 04	67 13
9		67 27	67 37	67 46	67 58	68 06	68 15
10		68 30	68 40	68 49	68 59	69 07	69 16
11		69 34	69 43	69 52	70 01	70 09	70 17
12		70 38	70 46	70 55	71 03	71 11	71 19
13		71 42	71 49	71 58	72 05	72 13	72 21
14		72 46	72 53	72 01	73 08	73 15	73 23
15		73 50	73 57	73 04	74 11	74 18	74 25
16		74 54	75 01	75 07	75 14	75 20	75 27
17		75 58	76 05	76 11	76 17	76 23	76 29
18		77 03	77 09	77 15	77 20	77 26	77 31
19		78 07	78 13	78 18	78 23	78 28	78 33
20		79 12	79 17	79 21	79 26	79 31	79 35
21		80 17	80 21	80 25	80 29	80 34	80 38
22		81 21	81 25	81 28	81 32	81 39	81 40
23		82 25	82 29	82 32	82 35	82 39	82 42
24		83 30	83 31	83 36	83 39	83 42	83 45
25		84 35	84 37	84 40	84 42	84 45	84 47
26		85 40	85 41	85 44	85 45	85 48	85 49
27		86 45	86 46	86 48	86 49	86 51	86 52
28		87 50	87 50	87 52	87 52	87 54	87 54
29		88 55	88 55	88 56	88 56	88 57	88 57
30		90 00	90 00	90 00	90 00	90 00	90 00

Clavis Astrologiae Elimita, The Key to Astrology New Filed

	Tables of Right Ascenuon to six Degrees of Latitude.						
♋ North Latitude.					♑ South Latitude.		
	0	1	2	3	4	5	6
0	90 00	90 00	90 00	90 00	90 00	90 00	90 00
1	91 05	91 06	91 07	91 07	91 07	91 08	91 09
2	92 11	92 12	92 14	92 14	92 15	92 16	92 18
3	93 16	93 18	93 20	93 21	93 23	93 24	93 26
4	94 22	94 24	94 27	94 28	94 30	94 32	94 37
5	95 27	95 30	95 33	95 35	95 38	95 40	95 43
6	96 32	96 36	96 39	96 42	96 45	96 48	96 51
7	97 38	97 42	97 45	97 49	97 52	97 56	98 00
8	98 43	98 47	98 51	98 55	98 00	99 04	99 08
9	99 48	99 52	99 57	100 01	100 07	100 12	100 16
10	100 53	100 58	101 03	101 08	101 14	101 19	101 24
11	101 58	102 04	102 09	102 15	102 21	102 16	102 32
12	103 03	104 09	103 15	103 21	103 27	103 33	103 40
13	104 08	104 14	104 21	104 27	104 34	104 41	104 48
14	105 13	105 19	105 27	105 33	105 40	105 48	105 56
15	106 17	106 24	106 33	106 39	106 47	106 55	107 03
16	107 22	107 29	107 38	107 45	107 53	108 02	108 11
17	108 26	108 34	108 42	108 51	108 59	109 09	109 18
18	109 31	109 39	109 48	109 57	110 05	110 15	110 25
19	110 35	110 44	110 53	111 03	111 12	111 22	111 32
20	111 39	111 49	111 58	112 08	112 18	112 29	112 39
21	112 43	112 53	113 03	113 13	113 24	113 35	113 46
22	113 47	113 57	114 08	114 18	114 30	114 41	114 53
23	114 51	115 01	115 13	115 23	115 35	115 47	115 58
24	115 54	116 05	116 17	116 28	116 41	116 52	117 04
25	116 57	117 09	117 21	117 33	117 46	117 58	118 10
26	118 01	118 13	118 25	118 38	118 51	119 03	119 16
27	119 04	119 16	119 29	119 42	119 55	120 08	120 22
28	120 07	120 19	120 33	120 46	120 59	121 13	121 27
29	121 09	121 22	121 36	121 50	122 03	122 18	122 32
30	122 12	122 25	122 39	122 53	123 07	123 22	123 37
In Southern Signs add 180 Degrees							

	Tables of Right Ascension to six Degrees of Latitude.						
♋ South Latitude.					♑ North Latitude.		
	0	1	2	3	4	5	6
0		90 00	90 00	90 00	90 00	90 00	90 00
1		91 05	91 05	91 04	91 04	91 03	91 04
2		92 10	92 13	92 08	92 08	92 06	92 07
3		93 15	93 14	93 12	93 11	93 9	93 08
4		94 20	94 19	94 16	94 15	94 12	94 11
5		95 25	95 23	95 20	95 18	95 15	95 13
6		96 30	96 27	96 24	96 21	96 18	96 15
7		97 35	97 31	97 21	97 25	97 21	97 18
8		98 39	98 35	98 32	98 28	98 24	98 20
9		99 44	99 39	99 36	99 31	99 26	99 22
10		100 48	100 43	100 39	100 34	100 29	100 25
11		101 53	101 47	101 42	101 37	101 32	101 27
12		102 57	102 51	102 45	102 40	102 34	102 29
13		104 02	103 55	103 49	103 43	103 37	103 31
14		105 06	104 59	104 52	104 46	104 40	104 33
15		106 10	106 03	105 56	105 49	105 42	105 35
16		107 14	107 07	106 59	106 52	100 45	106 37
17		108 17	108 11	108 02	107 55	107 47	107 49
18		109 22	109 14	109 05	108 57	108 49	108 41
19		110 26	110 17	110 08	110 00	109 51	109 43
20		111 33	111 20	111 11	111 02	110 53	110 44
21		112 33	112 23	112 14	112 04	111 54	111 45
22		113 37	113 26	113 16	113 06	112 56	112 47
23		114 40	114 29	114 19	114 08	113 58	113 48
24		115 43	115 32	115 21	115 10	114 59	114 49
25		116 46	116 35	116 23	116 12	116 01	115 50
26		117 49	117 37	117 25	117 14	117 02	116 51
27		118 51	118 39	118 27	118 15	118 03	117 51
28		119 54	119 54	119 29	119 16	119 04	118 52
29		120 56	120 43	120 30	120 17	120 05	119 53
30		121 58	121 45	121 31	121 18	121 05	120 53
In Southern Signs, add 180 Degrees.							

Clavis Astrologiae Elimita, The Key to Astrology New Filed

	Tables of Right Ascention to six Degrees of Latitude.						
♌ North Latitude.					♒ South Latitude.		
	0	1	2	3	4	5	6
0	122 12	122 25	122 39	122 53	123 07	123 22	123 37
1	123 14	123 28	123 42	122 57	124 11	124 26	124 42
2	124 16	124 31	124 45	125 00	125 15	125 30	125 46
3	125 11	125 33	125 48	126 03	126 18	126 34	126 50
4	126 20	126 36	126 51	127 06	127 22	127 38	127 54
5	127 22	127 38	127 54	128 28	128 25	128 42	128 58
6	128 24	128 30	128 56	129 12	129 28	129 45	130 02
7	129 25	129 42	129 58	130 14	130 31	130 48	131 05
8	130 26	130 43	131 00	131 16	131 33	132 51	132 08
9	131 27	131 44	132 01	132 18	132 35	133 53	133 11
10	132 28	132 45	133 02	133 20	133 37	133 55	134 14
11	133 28	133 46	134 03	134 21	134 39	134 57	135 16
12	134 29	134 47	135 04	135 22	135 40	135 59	136 18
13	135 29	135 47	136 05	136 23	136 41	137 00	137 20
14	136 29	136 47	137 06	137 24	137 42	138 01	138 21
15	137 29	137 47	138 07	138 24	138 43	139 02	139 22
16	138 29	138 47	139 06	139 25	139 44	140 03	140 24
17	139 28	139 47	140 06	140 25	140 45	141 04	141 25
18	140 28	140 46	141 06	141 25	141 45	142 05	142 26
19	141 27	141 46	142 06	142 25	142 45	143 06	143 27
20	142 26	142 45	143 05	143 25	143 45	144 06	144 27
21	143 25	143 44	144 04	144 24	144 45	145 06	145 27
22	144 23	144 43	145 03	145 24	145 45	146 06	146 27
23	145 22	145 42	146 02	146 23	146 44	147 05	147 27
24	146 20	146 40	147 01	147 22	147 43	148 04	148 26
25	147 18	147 39	148 00	148 21	148 42	149 03	149 25
26	148 16	148 37	148 58	149 19	149 41	150 02	150 24
27	149 14	149 35	149 56	150 17	150 39	151 01	151 23
28	150 11	150 33	150 54	151 15	151 37	151 59	152 22
29	151 00	151 33	151 52	152 13	152 35	152 57	153 20
30	152 06	152 27	152 49	153 11	153 33	153 55	154 18
In Southern Signs, remember to add 180 deg.							

Tables of Right Ascention to six Degrees of Latitude.							
♌ South Latitude.						♒ North Latitude.	
	0	1	2	3	4	5	6
0		121 58	121 45	121 31	121 18	121 05	120 53
1		123 00	122 47	122 33	122 19	122 06	121 53
2		124 02	123 48	123 34	123 20	123 06	122 53
3		125 03	124 49	124 35	124 21	124 07	123 53
4		126 05	125 52	125 36	125 22	125 07	124 53
5		127 07	126 52	126 37	126 22	126 07	125 52
6		128 08	127 53	127 37	127 22	127 07	126 52
7		129 09	128 54	128 37	128 22	128 07	127 51
8		130 10	129 54	129 37	129 22	129 06	128 50
9		131 13	130 54	130 37	130 21	130 05	129 49
10		132 11	131 54	131 37	131 22	131 04	130 48
11		133 11	132 54	132 37	132 20	132 03	131 47
12		134 11	133 54	133 37	133 19	133 02	132 16
13		135 11	134 54	134 36	134 18	134 01	133 45
14		136 11	135 53	135 35	135 17	135 00	134 43
15		137 10	136 52	136 34	136 16	135 58	135 41
16		138 10	137 51	137 33	137 15	136 57	136 39
17		139 09	138 50	138 32	138 14	137 55	137 37
18		140 08	139 49	139 30	139 13	138 53	138 35
19		141 07	140 48	140 29	140 10	139 51	139 33
20		142 06	141 47	141 27	141 08	140 49	140 31
21		143 04	142 45	142 25	142 06	141 47	141 28
22		144 03	143 43	143 23	143 04	142 45	142 25
23		145 01	144 41	144 21	144 02	143 42	143 22
24		145 59	145 39	145 19	144 59	144 39	144 19
25		146 57	146 37	146 17	145 56	145 36	145 16
26		147 55	147 35	147 14	146 53	146 33	146 13
27		148 53	148 32	148 11	147 50	147 29	147 09
28		149 50	149 29	149 08	148 47	148 26	148 06
29		150 47	150 26	150 05	149 44	149 23	149 03
30		151 44	151 23	151 02	150 41	150 20	149 59
Add 180d. in South Signs, but with the aforesaid Caution.							

	Tables of Right Ascentzon to six Degrees of Latitude.						
♍ North Latitude.					♓ South Latitude.		
	0	1	2	3	4	5	6
0	152 06	152 27	152 49	153 11	153 33	153 55	154 18
1	153 04	153 29	153 47	153 09	154 31	154 53	155 16
2	154 01	154 22	154 44	155 06	155 29	155 51	156 14
3	154 58	155 19	155 41	156 03	156 26	156 49	157 12
4	155 54	156 16	156 39	157 01	157 24	157 47	158 10
5	156 51	157 13	157 36	157 58	158 21	158 44	159 08
6	157 47	158 10	158 33	158 55	159 18	159 41	160 05
7	158 44	159 07	159 30	159 52	160 15	160 38	161 02
8	159 40	160 04	160 27	160 49	161 12	161 35	161 56
9	160 37	161 00	161 23	161 46	162 09	162 32	162 56
10	161 33	161 56	162 19	162 42	163 06	163 29	163 53
11	162 29	162 52	163 15	163 38	164 02	164 25	164 49
12	163 25	163 48	164 11	164 34	164 58	165 21	165 45
13	164 20	164 44	165 07	165 30	165 54	166 18	166 42
14	165 26	165 40	166 06	166 26	166 50	167 14	167 38
15	166 12	166 35	166 59	167 20	167 46	168 10	168 34
16	167 07	167 31	167 55	168 18	168 42	169 06	169 30
17	168 03	168 27	168 51	169 14	169 38	170 02	170 26
18	168 58	169 23	169 46	170 09	170 33	170 57	171 21
19	169 54	170 18	170 42	171 05	171 29	171 53	172 17
20	170 49	171 13	171 37	172 01	172 25	172 39	173 13
21	171 44	172 08	172 32	172 56	173 20	173 44	174 08
22	172 39	173 03	173 27	173 51	174 15	174 30	175 53
23	173 35	173 58	174 22	174 46	175 10	175 34	175 58
24	174 30	174 53	175 17	175 41	176 05	176 29	176 44
25	175 25	175 48	176 12	176 36	177 00	177 24	177 48
26	176 20	176 43	177 07	177 31	177 55	178 19	178 43
27	177 15	177 38	178 02	178 26	178 50	179 14	179 38
28	178 10	178 33	178 57	179 21	179 45	180 09	180 33
29	179 05	179 28	179 52	180 16	180 40	181 04	181 28
30	180 00	180 23	180 47	181 11	181 35	181 59	182 23
In Southern Signs, add 180 Degrees.							

	Tables of Right Ascension to six Degrees of Latitude.						
♍ South Latitude.						♓ North Latitude.	
	0	1	2	3	4	5	6
0		151 44	151 23	151 02	150 41	150 20	149 59
1		152 41	152 20	151 59	151 38	151 16	150 55
2		153 38	153 17	152 55	152 34	152 12	151 50
3		154 35	154 13	153 51	153 30	153 08	152 47
4		155 32	155 10	154 48	154 26	154 04	153 43
5		156 29	156 07	155 44	155 22	155 00	154 39
6		157 25	157 03	156 40	156 18	155 56	155 34
7		158 22	157 59	157 36	157 14	156 52	156 30
8		159 18	158 55	158 32	158 10	157 48	157 26
9		160 14	159 51	159 28	159 06	158 43	158 21
10		161 10	160 47	160 24	160 02	159 39	159 17
11		162 06	160 43	161 20	160 58	160 35	160 21
12		163 02	162 39	162 16	161 53	161 30	161 07
13		163 58	163 35	163 12	162 49	162 25	162 02
14		164 53	164 30	164 07	163 44	163 20	162 57
15		165 48	165 25	165 02	164 39	164 15	163 52
16		166 44	166 21	165 57	165 34	165 10	164 47
17		167 40	167 17	166 52	166 29	166 05	165 42
18		168 35	168 12	167 47	167 24	167 00	166 37
19		169 31	169 07	168 43	168 19	168 55	167 32
20		170 26	170 02	169 38	169 14	168 50	168 27
21		171 21	170 57	170 33	170 39	169 45	169 22
22		172 16	171 52	171 28	171 04	170 40	170 17
23		173 11	172 47	172 23	171 59	171 35	171 12
24		174 06	173 42	173 18	172 54	172 30	172 07
25		175 02	174 38	174 14	173 50	173 26	173 02
26		175 57	175 33	175 09	174 45	174 21	173 57
27		176 52	176 28	176 04	175 40	175 16	174 52
28		177 47	177 23	176 59	176 35	176 11	175 47
29		178 42	178 18	177 54	177 30	177 16	176 42
30		179 27	179 13	178 49	178 25	178 01	177 37
If the Sum exceed 360d. abate the Circle.							

www.ingramcontent.com/pod-product-compliance
Lightning Source LLC
Chambersburg PA
CBHW080935020526
44116CB00034B/2612